To my wife Celia, who has been putting up with a house full of racing books, magazines, printouts and paraphernalia for over 36 years.

To all men and women whose participation in the sport is directly or indirectly mentioned or celebrated in this book.

Acknowledgments

I would like to give special thanks to Jose Santos, who was the first to generously allow me to use several photos taken during the 1971, 1972 and 1973 Macau Grand Prix, which are used to illustrate several areas of this book and Rogerio da Luz, who was also very liberal with the use of his outstanding photographic work. Rob Neuzel also provided dozens of exceptional portraits of drivers and pictures of rare cars. Gerald Swan provided a number of pictures from British racing. Colin Lourie provided excellent photos from Scottish racing, many of which are used in the manufacturers section. Paul Kooyman provided some pictures from Belgium and Le Mans. Paul-Henri Cahier provided a great cover picture taken by his late father Bernard. Many other photograpers, journalists, former drivers and enthusiasts from all over the world also deserve mention, having provided, or at least attempted to provide photos, results, clippings, information, leads or just plain support: Alejandro de Brito, Richard Woods, Kurt Oblinger, Vicky Chandhok, Carlos Nunez, Jim Llewellyn, Stephen Lawrenson, Martin Fokkens, Jan Borsboom, Pieter Kamp, Paul Maes, Ricardo Cunha, Wagner Gonzalez, Fritz Jordan, Eshan Pieris, Danielle Plomteux, Teddy Pilette, Bruce Allison, Jurgen Barth, Pete Austin, Rob Petersen, Russell Whitworth, Douglas Noordhoorn, Tony Trimmer, Bjorn Lahus, Enrique Soto, Michael Lochmann, Paul Rutten, Jari Debner, Harry Hammaren, Hans Hugenholz, Mike White, Glenn Moulds, Joey Anastasi, Therry Van Vreden, Ben Osten. Upon request of some photographers, such as Santos and Kooyman, the copyright watermark was maintained in some photographs, although this is not normative practice.

Best efforts have been made to trace copyright holders of photographs marked "author unknown" or unmarked that have been used in this book. Some of these photos have been published in blogs that do not answer emails or comments and may be dormant. Others have been provided by drivers, who might have mistakenly assumed to be the copyright owner. Any omission is not intentional and I will be glad to include a proper acknowledgment immediately. The platform allows me to edit books in a couple of days. Removal requests will also be honored immediately.

I would like to thank all my thousands of blog readers who encouraged me for years to put down on paper my passion and knowledge of this sport and go beyond the blogosphere. My blogs have enjoyed millions of page views since 2003, which allowed me to meet and befriend many wonderful people across the world, who at times, corrected me, for which I am grateful.

Instagram: carlosdepaula_official
Facebook groups:
Formula 1 Curiosities: facebook.com/groups/5929535860408635
24 Hours of Le Mans Curiosities:
facebook.com/groups/2084980351719834

FOREWORD

This is an updated and revised edition of the book originally released in 2018. I have in the course of the years made corrections, removed and added sections, added information and photos and did not change the tone or style of the book. I have learned one cannot please everybody and found some people do not fancy it.

This is, above all, the celebration of an era. A celebration of the feats of thousands of men and women that toiled half way around the world, under very difficult and dangerous circumstances, at extreme cost and little reward, to practice a sport which was not universally popular at the time, sometimes even loathed and mighty dangerous. In the process, I show the transition from romantic to organized that occurred during the decade.

My idea was to walk you through the several changes that took place in car racing during the course of the decade, providing applicable highlights and information not easily found, highlighted or discussed anywhere else. Thus, you will not find hundreds, upon hundreds of pages of race results or championship tables in this book, for these are readily available on the internet a click away. Read the bibliography and you will find good sources for this type of information. More specific statistics have been compiled to give you an overall picture of the racing scenes in different countries, categories and years and information placed in perspective.

Unlike the 2018 original edition, which had no photos, I saw it fit to include photographs in this version. Many of the pictures you will find here are not the best quality you have seen but understand that I focus mostly on the obscure. Some of the photographs were taken by amateurs, with substandard equipment and the negatives have probably gone to photographic cemetery a long time ago. As I still want as many people as possible to own a copy of this work for reference purposes, which means selling it for about US$ 35, I have have avoided the most obvious path, which is spending a ton of money on photographs from top photographers, which might look better but likely have been published in hundreds of Instagram accounts for free and myriad coffee table books.

This reference book comprises several sections, with as comprehensive as possible lists of significant drivers, racetracks and venues, car manufacturers, categories and assorted commentaries on money, sponsors, important personalities, female drivers, standalone races and more, contextualizing the focus of the work with much obscure information. In here you will find the most comprehensive list of 1970s racing champions from dozens of countries, venues and race car manufacturers. A new feature is the identification of countries where specific car brands were raced. The list of specific purpose marques now encompass over 2200 makes and identifies the nationality of the builder.

I am including in the scope of this book only contemporary automobile circuit, road racing and hill climbs. Thus, drag racing, karting, off-road, rallies, sprints, historic, motorcycle racing are excluded. Do not read any qualitative assessment in my part: all of these modalities are worthy but not only would it complicate research, it would also make the outcome less relevant, for information is even scarcer for these modalities than for car racing.

I have literally reviewed thousands of race results for these compilations, hundreds of books, publications and websites and where possible, cross checked references. Some of the rarer pieces of information come from unique sources, so I deemed them reputable at my discretion. In some areas of the book I actually discuss blunders committed even by well-known and best selling motoring authors and publications. As I am far from perfect, I do not expect this book to be error free and welcome any factual corrections.

I have conducted research in multiple languages besides English: Spanish, French, Portuguese, German, Dutch, Swedish, Norwegian, Danish, Finnish, Romanian, Russian, Turkish, Japanese, Greek, Malay, Indonesian, Thai, Latvian.

I hope this will be an ongoing project, with further editions expanding on the information and correcting mistakes in future editions, perhaps even including more and better photographs, which will depend on market conditions and cooperation, which is not always easy to find.

If you have any corrections, comments or input, write me at carlosdepaula@mindspring.com

Explaining bold text

Names of drivers, venues, manufacturers and years are mostly written in bold letters, to make this information stand out. Some readers did like this but I find this makes the book easier to navigate for most folks.

Why no index?

You may find it odd that there is no index, just a table of contents. The reason is very simple: the book mentions literally tens of thousands of drivers, racing people, sponsors, car makers, events, tracks, geographic locations and venues, etc., so a comprehensive index page would involve dozens upon dozens of pages, making the book much more expensive.

Nationality abbreviations. In certain instances, I have used nationality abbreviations. These are:

A – Austria	E – Spain	NZ – New Zealand
AND – Andorra	EC – Ecuador	P – Portugal
ANG – Angola	F – France	PE – Peru
ANT - Antigua	FL – Liechtenstein	PR – Puerto Rico
AUS – Australia	GB – Great Britain	RA – Argentina
B - Belgium	GR – Greece	RSR – Rhodesia
BR - Brazil	H – Hungary	RU – Russia
C – Cuba	I – Italy	S – Sweden
CDN – Canada	IRL – Ireland	SF – Finland
CH – Switzerland	J – Japan	SG – Singapore
CO – Colombia	L – Luxembourg	USA – U.S.A.
D – Germany	MEX – Mexico	YV – Venezuela
DK – Denmark	MOZ – Mozambique	ZA – South Africa
DZ - Algeria	N – Norway	
	NL – Netherlands	

CONTENTS

1. Acknowledgments, 4

2. Foreword, 5

3. Historicity, 9

4. Pivoting from Romantic to Organized, 11

5. Highlights, 35

   1970, 35

   1971, 41

   1972, 47

   1973, 53

   1974, 59

   1975, 65

   1976, 70

   1977, 76

   1978, 82

   1979, 87

5. Drivers, 95

   Significant drivers of the decade, 116

6. Venues and Local Racing Scenes, 151

7. Manufacturers, 211

   Carmakers, 211

   Racing car constructors, 249

   Engines, 278

8. Categories, 281

   Formula 1, 281
   Formula 2, 292

World Championship for Makes, 299
24 Hours of Le Mans, 314
European Two Liter Championship, 319
Can-Am, 323
Interserie, 329
European GT Championship, 334
IMSA Camel GT, 336
Formula Indy, 342
American Formula 5000, 348
European Formula 5000, 351
Shellsport Group 8/Aurora F1 Championship, 356
Tasman Cup, 359
Formula 3, 362
Formula Atlantic, 367
Formula Ford, 368
Formula Vee and Super Vee, 370
Other Single Seater Series, 372
Touring Cars, 373
NASCAR, 375
European Touring Car Championship, 380
Trophee de l'Avenir, 388
Trans-Am, 389
DRM and Other German Touring Car Championships, 390
IROC, 393
BMW Procar, 378
SCCA Amateur Racing, 394
British Club Scene, 396
European Hillclimb Championship, 398

9. Money, 401

10. Sponsors, 415

11. Press and Annuals, 421

12. Miscellaneous, 427

    Female drivers, 427

    Movers and Shakers, 431

13. Stand-alone Races, 451

14. Short International Series, 464

15. Bibliography, 482

HISTORICITY

Before embarking on this experience, which I hope, will be pleasurable, I believe a few words on historicity of the subject are necessary.

To make a story short, 1970 was over fifty years ago, over half a century ago. A different time, indeed. Man had gone to the moon the year before but remember, there were no personal computers, telecopiers were rare and expensive and no cell phones existed. Even regular land lines were very poor in many countries, a large portion of the world had no TV service yet and the first studies for establishment of the Internet would begin only in 1972, the network becoming commercially available in the 90s. History telling is only as good as its sources. And there are substantial gaps of information as it pertains to a lot of motor racing 50 years ago, in fact, dare I say that a lot of the information that I set out to cover has been lost, forever.

Information for a book of this type has to come from books, magazines, newspaper clippings, websites, racing programs, official results, film, blogs, TV recordings, occasional radio recordings and personal accounts. Rather unfortunately, a lot of the folks who participated in racing in the 70s have passed - some of them had been racing since the 50s, a few since the 1930s! Some participants who are still alive are quite elderly and details of their personal accounts are often patently incorrect, unreliable and generally optimistic.

As for magazine and newspaper reports, they often contained errors, for a number of reasons. A lot of reports were dictated over poor phone lines, telex being used here as well as airline couriers. Typesetters in many magazines and newspaper were obviously not racing aficionados, so a lot of what ended up going to print had mistakes. Even official race results, in America of all places, had omissions or blunderous mistakes that cannot be undone. Many cars, teams, drivers and even venues have more than one name in the literature. The identification of race cars is often insufficient. Let me give you an example. Several models of Opel were raced in the 70s but many a race result identified cars simply as Opel, so one will never be able to tell if it was a GT, Commodore, Ascona, Rekord, Manta...The same goes for Ford, Chevrolet, FIAT and even purpose made race cars such as Lotus and Brabhams. One entry list from a race in Chile provides three names of Austin car models that have never existed anywhere.

In a nutshell, the very thing that makes that era of racing interesting, the large number of manufacturers, car models, racing venues and engines, often makes the information questionable.

I have literally poured over thousands of books, articles, race results, forums, reports, facebook pages, conversations to prepare this book and can say that at least 25% of the information in such results can be questioned, one way, or another. Sure, Formula 1 information is all excellent and detailed (except for the 1973 Canadian Grand Prix) but there are huge question marks even about major races. In certain cases, online results list only the 3rd placed driver and then the

8th, I guess in the hopes that the gaps will be filled eventually, which does not happen most of the time.

Forums can be useful but sometimes, useless. Most forum and Facebook group posts comprise of unidentified photographs and press clippings. Members then take a crack at unveiling the mystery and often they are way off, even in obvious and widely known cases, so you can only imagine under obscure conditions. By and large, I consider trustworthy forum and Facebook posts that are backed by dated newspaper and magazine clippings. Even first hand witnesses often misquote dates, venues, car manufacturer and drivers' names.

Different cultures deal with information differently. Thus, while information from some countries is based on highly detailed data, other cultures prioritize anecdotal information that omits dates, locations and car identification, while over emphasizing the exploits of a given driver. These are often exaggerated. A Venezuelan source, for example, mentions one of the country's drivers was the European Formula 2 champion in 1976, while an African source claims races with formula 1 cars were held in Kenya during the 70s!

This means that a lot of the information on this book may be found to be incorrect, as new information is unveiled, mainly in the form of personal collections that are sometimes made available to researchers. All sources used for this book are deemed to be trustworthy but I have changed a few things from the original version, finding the initial information to be untrue or utterly unreliable.

As for the photographs, you will note that some of the pictures in this book are not top quality. Sure, I could probably spend thousands of dollars and buy publishing rights to magnificent pictures of top Formula 1 drivers but in all likelihood, you might have seen such excellent pictures somewhere else many times over. I chose most pictures based on their rarity: I see no point publishing tons of pictures of Porsche 917s and Jackie Stewart, when thousands of such pictures, taken by professional photographers with the best equipment and processing available, can be found all over the place, in the literature and internet. Yet, seeing racing cars in action in Ecuador and early Macau races seems to be more interesting for the historical record. Unfortunately, some of the pictures I have chosen are in pretty poor shape and no amount of photoshopping can restore them.

I find that now is the time to put this information out, for a lot of racing websites have been going off the air, as their owners die or stop paying hosting fees. It is possible that free blogs might not exist in twenty years. What guarantee do you have that google will keep thousands of space hungry blogspots on the air for free much longer? Or even that google will exist in 20 years? A lot of what is online might be gone forever in 20 years, so I tried to squeeze as much information as I can in this book.

This is a work in progress, so future revisions will incorporate more information and corrections as they become available.

THE 70S – THE END OF THE ROMANTIC ERA, PIVOTING TO ORGANIZATION

Ask yourself why is it that you love the 70s era in motor racing - and I assume that you do, after all you have spent good money buying this book - and a large number of reasons might pop up in your head. Those of us who lived through the era will nostalgically remember a number of pleasant things, including sights, sounds and aromas and will spend hours reminiscing, perhaps inventing or exaggerating a few things along the way but who is perfect? Allow me to start with what was not to be loved in 70s motor racing and from there, I will work the positive angles. I will demonstrate the several pivoting points that changed the sport from the so-called romantic era to a more organized and professional sport. My aim is to explore this without boring you, not only in this chapter but the rest of the book as well.

In the 70s, motor racing was still a very dangerous sport. I vividly remember **1973**, one of the first seasons I followed seriously. There were two deaths in Formula 1, one of them involving a leading driver in the last race, **Francois Cevert**; the other, displayed on TV worldwide the inefficacy of marshals in Holland (**Roger Williamson**). There were two deaths of prominent drivers in the Indy 500, resulting in the interruption of the race, plus a very bad practice accident involving a third driver. There were deaths in the World Championship of Makes, three dead drivers in the **24 hours of Spa**, death at NASCAR, Formula 2, local racing series all over. In fact death was all over the place. It was a bad year but the sad fact is, the whole early part of the decade was rather bloody, although there were efforts in many corners to reduce mortality at racetracks. From **1970** to **1972** death had already claimed the lives of **Rindt, McLaren, Courage, Siffert, Rodriguez, Bonnier**, to name a few. By the end of the decade, motor racing did not kill as much and today, considering the speeds attained, racing is a relatively safe endeavor, largely due to actions taken in the 70s. So here is one of the pivoting points.

On the subject of death in racing, observe that in the chapter **Highlights** there is a list of major deaths that occurred in circuit racing and hill climbs during each year of the decade. One notices two things: the overall number of deaths is not as outrageously high in **1979** as one might suspect. In other words racing had an unwarranted reputation, considering the thousands upon thousands of races held worldwide every year. I do not expect my list to be complete but the source is very reputable, the *motorsportmemorial.org* web site and the most important countries in terms of racing volume are well covered. Upon analysis of this list, one sees that most drivers were American short track racers, where the standard of safety was very poor and pile-ups, frequent. The second thing one notices is that the number of deaths of well-known drivers, not only Formula 1 but other major disciplines, drops substantially from **1970** to **1979**. Rather unfortunately, while the general press in most countries covered racing events sparingly, whenever there were major deaths these were covered in gory detail, specially in the United States.

A welcome addition to the big time was Interlagos. Pictured here is Pace's Surtees in the first edition of the Brazilian Grand Prix valid for the world championship. Photo by Rogerio da Luz.

As the decade went on, old styled venues were being phased out. Use of places like **Tulln-Langelebarn airfield, Vila Real** and **Chimay** was discontinued and long tracks like the **Nürburgring Nordschleife, old Spa** and **Clermont-Ferrand** were booted out of the Formula 1 calendar. There is a funny story about the Nordschleife's demise as a Formula 1 venue. **Denis Jenkinson**, who wrote Grand Prix reports for *Motor Sport*, was unashamedly old-style. He believed danger was inherent to motor racing and people (in other words, drivers) should live with it. This led to a very nasty exchange in the British press between **Jenkinson** and **Jackie Stewart**, one of the first safety activists in Formula 1, in the very beginning of the decade. When the **Nürburgring**'s Nordschleife was permanently dropped as a Grand Prix venue in the wake of **Lauda's** accident in **1976**, Jenks wrote two **1977** German GP race reports in the same issue of the magazine. One, pertaining to the actual race held at **Hockenheim**, was called "Der Kleine Preis von Deutschland" ("The Small Prix of Germany"). The other was a hilarious and fictional piece about a F1 race at the Nordschleife that never took place, called "Der Grosser Preis von Deutschland", which brought back to F1 the likes of **Derek Bell, Chris Amon** and **Tim Schenken**. In this fictitious piece Jenks speaks his mind and surely pokes some criticism into safety conscious drivers. The **Lauda** accident at the Nürburgring was indeed a major turning point and track safety was taken more seriously after that, with greater efforts to create a less accident prone environment not only in Formula 1 but racing in general. I comment further on this piece in my book **Formula 1 Curiosities Volume 1**.

Additionally, the last major European open road race, the **Targa Florio**, was off the international calendar for good, although it survived a few more years as an all Italian event. Pictures from the early 70s Targa are scary: fans sitting on rocks close to the "track", fast prototypes, essentially Formula 1 cars with sports car bodies zooming through sleepy Sicilian towns with no guardrails for protection and things of the sort. It should be noted that Argentines, Ecuadorians, Peruvians and Bolivians continued their open road races with gusto but although Turismo de Carretera cars were by no means slow, they were not 3-liter **Ferrari** barchettas. In neighboring Brazil, however, street racing was banned after **1972** for the rest of the decade. Indonesians also held road races during the decade.

A sample of pit practices in 70s endurance races. Le Mans, 1974 (Jurgen Barth collection)

Greece also banned street racing after a major accident in **1971**. Driver awareness, advocacy, activism and militancy were increased, in fact, there were pivotal incidents in **Zolder, 1973** and **Montjuich, 1975**, that would serve as the template for future action. In the latter mentioned incident, drivers criticized the state of the guard rails around the track, actually, a park, even helping to install some. Although there seemed to be some consensus the race should not go on, only the **Fittipaldi** brothers and **Arturo Merzario** did the promised slow first lap (**Emerson** with his hand raised) and the rest of the field took off in a crash fest that resulted in death of spectators and workers, caused by a nasty shunt that sidelined **Rolf Stommelen**, who was leading a F1 race for the first (and last) time. In **Zolder**, the asphalt was considered improper and the Grote Prijs van Belgie almost did not take place. **Lauda**'s accident at the **Nürburgring, 1976** and the mentioned **Williamson** crash in **Zandvoort, 1973,** clearly showed a few things that should be changed in terms of track emergency services and also that marshals were few and sometimes utterly inept, albeit well-meaning: more professional and trained accident response should be devised. In the first case, **David Purley** desperately tried to flip his friend`s fiery overturned car to take him out, while marshals looked on cluelessly. In the second, drivers **Arturo Merzario, Brett Lunger, Guy Edwards, Harald Ertl** took matters into their own hands and heroically saved **Niki Lauda** from the burning wreck. Making the strongest point of all, **Lauda** made the world know that risking his life again in the downpour at **Fuji 1976** was not worth it – he basically handed the championship to **James Hunt**, retiring in the early part of the race and leaving others to fight under very dangerous conditions. The Commendatore definitely did not approve.

Facilities at racetracks worldwide were generally very poor safety wise; a place like the 70s **Watkins Glen** would not be considered at all as a possible Formula 1 venue even in the late 90s. Many other venues – **Rouen** and to a certain extent, **Kyalami**, come to mind - had more deaths than should be expected.

Rouen's case is textbook. A very narrow circuit, which got a bad reputation when **Jo Schlesser** was killed in it in the **1968** French Grand Prix, **Rouen** was the site of one of those dark racing days, in **1970**. In a single Formula 3 race, **Bob Wollek** flew out of the racetrack at 200 km/h and was left hanging at a tree for a while. The former skier was lucky to have only broken an arm. A little later, **Denis Dayan** had a tire puncture and crashed badly. He was hospitalized, had a leg amputated and died three days later. Then **Jean-Luc Salomon**, who was poised to drive a Formula 1 **Lotus** in the French GP, was dicing for the lead on the last lap. Drivers were certainly being reckless, driving four abreast on a very narrow track, then, in a last desperate lunge for the lead, Jean-Luc lost control and was hit by four cars, dying on the spot. **Rouen** was supposed to be the site of the **1973** French Grand Prix but given its track record of recent years, the race was moved to **Paul Ricard**. That turned out to be a wise choice, for during qualifying for the Formula 2 race of **1973, Gerry Birrell** had an accident at Six Freres, dying from injuries. Drivers, led by standing Formula 1 champion **Emerson Fittipaldi**, threatened to boycott that very race and a compromise was made in the form of a polystyrene chicane which did not last the race. As a result of **Birrell**'s death, **Rouen** was removed from the European F2 championship in **1974**, returning in **1975**. The track would kill once more during the decade, claiming the life of **Francois Burdet** in qualifying for Formula Renault in **1977**. In addition to a narrow track and dangerous corners, **Rouen**'s organizers were also notoriously disorganized, which certainly contributed to the number of accidents and deaths.

Outside the major centers things were just as bad. Three years after opening, the **Tarumã** racetrack in Brazil had three deaths on the books, one of them a fiery crash involving two touring cars in a regional race that could be even more destructive, the other killing Italian **Giovanni Salvati** in the international Formula 2 event in **1971**. A race in Chile's **Las Vizcachas**, in **1975** turned deadly when **Eduardo Kovacs** and **Roberto Gomez Barrios** touched, and their cars were diverted to the unprotected pit area, in the process killing seven spectators and officials, plus several injured. As a result, a wall was built for **1976**, at the expense of several deaths.

The already mentioned excellent website motorsportmemorial.org contains story after story of needless death that took place during the 70s, as motor racing was expanding quantitatively. One will note a steep reduction of driver fatalities in the course of the last four decades, in major events, despite growing speed.

There is another side to this story. As racing was slowly becoming a TV darling during the decade, specially Formula 1, it was soon discovered that the reputation for death and danger actually turned people off the sport. This is a great change of thinking, because the prevailing attitude until then was that folks in general were attracted by accidents, rather than put off by them!!! Powers that be decided it was nigh time to make the "show" safer, so the "product" could be sold to a wider public and sponsors. It is a bit sad that commercial interest had more to do with the improvement of safety than consideration for the lives of all people at tracks (drivers, team members, marshals, responders, the press and spectators). However, the important thing is that it was done and this obvious pivoting took place in the 70s.

TV was not as ubiquitous as today. In fact, even in the so-called rich world, TV channels were a handful and many people did not have TV sets in the early part of the decade. Many countries did not even have TV service at all for much of the decade, including South Africa, which began broadcasts only in **1976**. Curiously, that was the same year when the South African Formula 1 championship was replaced by Formula Atlantic, no cause and effect suggested. Attending motor races suddenly lost some of its allure in this particular country, a permanent condition, I am afraid.

Finding a race on TV generally required patience, research and hope. Even NASCAR, which came to epitomize the standard for Motor Racing TV coverage, was not widely present on TV screens during most of the decade. NASCAR would only get a full TV deal in **1978** and up until then, you might get a highlights segment on a Saturday after an important race in the Wide World of Sports or Sports Spectacular. Formula 1, widely reckoned to be the top racing category in the world, did not enjoy the coverage it deserved in the early part of the decade, even in Europe. You actually had to go to the racetrack to watch a race, or read it in the papers the next day and use your imagination.

Bernie Ecclestone is widely considered the main driving force behind widespread TV broadcasting of Formula 1 races, which totally changed the metrics of the sport. While commercial sponsorship suddenly brought an influx of cash into the sport, the only numbers team owners had to sell to possible sponsors was racetrack attendance. Even in Formula 1 attendance was spotty. Take the French Grand Prix of **1967**, held at the Bugatti circuit. Depending on the source, anywhere from 8,000 to 20,000 people attended the race. Considering the likes of **Clark, Brabham, Hulme, Gurney, Amon, McLaren, Hill** were all on the track, this is a clear indication how badly some races were promoted. **Anderstorp** during the 70s also had some very low attendance figures. However, with TV, suddenly a team owner could talk about sponsor exposure to the tune of millions of people worldwide, in dozens of countries. Thus team budgets and earnings skyrocketed, as did driver retainers.

The book "No Angel", by Tom Bower, sheds some light and at the same time, question marks on this issue. On page 58, the author mentions that **Brabham**'s costs in **1971** totaled £80,000. A mere seven years later, in **1978**, **Ecclestone** managed to extract £10 million from sponsor Parmalat, "to cover costs" (page 92). As anybody with any business experience knows, costs include a host of things: rent, taxes, payroll, supplies, professional fees, travel and many other items. My thinking is that the £80,000 in **1971** appears extremely low, while £10 million extremely high for **1978**, even considering **Niki Lauda**'s hefty US$ 2 million retainer. It should be remembered that back in **1971 Brabham** was not only a Formula 1 team: it produced a reasonable number of customer chassis for Formula 2, Formula 3, Atlantic and occasionally, Indycar and Formula 1 customer cars, for drivers in Europe, North America and even the Far East. How could a company that produced a number of race car chassis have such a low annual cost figure? Additionally, although **Graham Hill** was no longer a top driver, he was a twice world champion, having won a GP as late as **1969;** he would not drive for peanuts or only start money and **Brabham** had no sizable sponsors. On the other hand, by **1978 Brabham** had not been producing race cars for others for a very long time (in fact, since **1973**), so all its manufacturing was restricted to a few Formula 1 cars. A typical Formula 1 team in the 70s did not employ all that many people, as they do today. Engines, electronics and gearboxes were not proprietary, they were bought from outside providers. In **Brabham**'s case, most design work was done

15

by **Gordon Murray**, there were no computer or electronics experts, aerodynamics was often a trial and error exercise, therefore, **Brabham** did not employ dozens of engineers. So I would take the actual figures from this book with a heavy pinch of salt; however, it does show that the amounts one could get from a sponsor based on TV figures was much higher than, say, the £100,000 allegedly paid by Marlboro to sponsor a large number of **BRMs** in **1972** when TV coverage was still very spotty.

Formula 1 team owners were no dummies, however, most of them were former drivers or engineers, passionate about racing, somewhat aloof but not very savvy in terms of business. **Bernie** changed all that, first getting more money from Formula 1 race organizers, representing team owners as a group, then negotiating TV rights. He turned Formula 1 into a bona fide business, whether one likes it or not. Plus his model was studied and more or less repeated to different extents in other categories worldwide. This did not come without some fighting. The political climate in the 70s was heavy, for where there is money and power involved, there is nasty fighting. I decided to leave the political details off this book and perhaps will cover it in a latter edition. Therefore, **Ecclestone** had an effect on the entire world of racing and this might be the biggest pivoting of all.

Things were a bit disorganized during most the decade, almost everywhere. The way a pace-car was used for the first time in the Canadian Grand Prix of **1973** and the ensuing timing confusion could be avoided. Races were cancelled on the spot, like the momentous Formula 2 Israeli Grand Prix of **1970**. The German club rounded up **Brabhams** for **Ernesto Brambilla, Vittorio Brambilla, Derek Bell, Peter Westbury, Tommy Reid, Brian Cullen, Mike Goth**, **Tecnos** for **Bruno Frey** and **Patrick Depailler**, a **March** for **Xavier Perrot** and **Patrick dal Bo**'s **Pygmee**. Two **Jean-Pierres**, **Beltoise** and **Jabouille** were on the entry list but their cars never came. The **Ashqelon** circuit, near Barnea, would host the race in November 22. **Brambilla** grabbed pole, followed by **Depailler** and Bell. There was a Formula Vee support race but the top billing was cancelled. The Orthodox party protested the event being held during Shabbat, the Jewish holy day and it was claimed there were bombs in several parts of the circuit, which was surrounded by barbed wire. Apparently, the Israeli public was very excited about the whole affair, Notwithstanding religions objections, there was no crowd control, so bye-bye race! End of story. Another curiosity about this "non-event" was the fact that the New York Times, never known to give too many inches to auto racing coverage, actually ran a little piece on this fiasco. Wonder why…

Even in major centers, like England, an event like the Race of Champions of **1978**, a F1 race after all, was simply cancelled a fortnight before, truly because of snow but teams had already condemned the race to failure by entering obsolete cars and number 2 drivers, so that a rain(snow) date in April was not used. A local race in Brazil was stopped by placing a Jeep across the track! Such unsafe handling of races by the very people who should oversee safety popped up all over the place. The picture on the following page shows a van sharing the track with a number of sprint cars. Consider the last non-championship Formula 2 held in Europe, at **Misano, 1976**. In the second heat, **Gaudenzio Mantova**, who was starting on the front row, raised his arm to indicate a gearbox problem. Some marshals began pushing the car off the track, however, the director still started the race. The marshals and **Mantova**'s car were very nearly hit and **Giancarlo Martini** and **Maurizio Flammini** could not avoid each other. There was no red flag. The race went on and **Mantova** even managed to get third gear going and join the proceedings.

Just what exactly is this van doing in the race course during a sprint car race is a mystery. Photo by Rob Neuzel.

One of the most tragic accidents of the decade was the one involving **Jean-Pierre Beltoise** and **Ignazio Giunti**, in **Buenos Aires, 1971**. Although it is easy to place all the blame on **Beltoise**, who was after all pushing his out of fuel car through the racetrack when hit by **Giunti**, marshals had a lot to do with mishandling the situation. They should have stopped **Jean-Pierre** and averted the accident. Similarly, the death of **Tom Pryce** and a marshal in **Kyalami**, in **1977**, also seemed avoidable, a clear evidence of poor marshal training.

Another example of poor management, not in the area of safety, also involves **Misano**. The Italian track was one of the few located out of Britain to be included in the **1973** European Formula 5000 championship calendar. Twelve drivers made the trek to Italy, all of them coming from England, quite a long trip one might add. They practiced, then they were told by local officials that a 2-liter limit had been imposed on the track, so the event was cancelled! Bye-bye, Brits. Note that an Interserie event, for even larger and more powerful sports cars, was held at the same track later in the season.

The truth is that early on the decade, agreements with drivers, teams, manufacturers, tracks, sponsors were often not enforced – the whole scene was a bit like the Wild West and even Formula 1 race purses were often paid in cash, sometimes mounds of it. One should recall that credit cards were very rare during most of the decade, so that people paid for their tickets with cash. Thus prizes were mostly in the local currency, there was no Euro at the time. Teams were left scrambling for foreign exchange brokers, often facing the risk of taking substantial amounts of cash out of the host country.

Good promotional ideas sometimes took a bad turn. In May of **1976**, promoters of a race meeting at **Mallory Park**, England, decided to mix pop music with racing.

Teenybopper group Bay City Rollers, the rage of the moment, was supposed to make an appearance and no less than 60,000 people showed up, many of whom teenage girls who had no interest in cars, racing or drivers. The crowd, the largest ever at the track, started to get rowdy. They wanted the Rollers, who were not performing, by the way, just appearing. To protect the band, they were taken to the island in the middle of the lake, where a helicopter rescued them. Hundreds of people were injured in the ensuing mayhem and racing had to be stopped so that a large number of trampled young girls could be taken to the hospital. Perhaps better planning would have saved the day.

As things became more organized, in other words, teams' revenue stream coming more from high sponsorship than race prizes, it follows that financial figures became more trustworthy and official, where early on the decade informality ruled. One would not expect Parmalat to pay **Brabham** £ 10 million in cash, after all…

So money was the big pivoting and more on that will be provided in the chapter appropriately called **Money**.

Racing was supposed to have glamour but real glamour only showed its face in **Monaco**. In most tracks, parking spaces were badly kept and even basic facilities, like grandstands and working bathrooms, amiss. The pits at **Le Mans**, widely responsible for the **1955** accident, were slightly better than 20 years before. The list can go on. A lot of what we perceive as romantic is, in fact, lack of organization which struck our interest. This aura of romantic flavor partly arose from unexpected happenings from race to race.

You definitely never knew what was going to happen from one race to the other: races were full of surprises even before they started. Is driver "X" going to race? Is team "Y" showing up? Did driver "Z" change teams? Quite the opposite happens today. Take, for example, current F1. At the time of writing, twenty drivers, are expected to make the show, race in, race out. Except if a driver is hurt or gets sick, the entry list is going to be the same the entire season. No change. Now, take the 70s DRM. I bothered to look, there were never two identical entry lists in all DRM races from **1972**, the first year of the series, until **1979** the last year of the decade, in both divisions. Sure, some rather unknown and perhaps not very talented local drivers in slow cars would be added and subtracted, on the other hand, some top international drivers like **Ronnie Peterson, Jacky Ickx, Niki Lauda** and **Clay Regazzoni** would mix with German stars **Ludwig, Mass, Stommelen, Heyer, Stuck, Glemser**. Only **Ford, BMW** and **Porsche** won races, however, cars such as **Ferrari, Toyota, Lotus, Alpine, Alfa Romeo, Opel, Chevy, Datsun, VW, NSU** were entered as well, bringing some "romantic flavor" to events: the surprise factor. There is little to no surprise anymore.

The same happened in Formula 2, which was then, as it is now, the stepping stone to Formula 1. Some races had better entries than others, depending on location and purses and early on the decade, it was usual finding a large number of graded FIA drivers on the grid, who often won the races, such as **Jochen Rindt, Emerson Fittipaldi, Graham Hill, John Surtees, Jo Siffert, Jackie Stewart** who could not score points towards the championship. Some of the F-2 races in the decade had more than 40 cars fighting for a position on the grid, while a **1973** B race, **Kinnekulle** in Sweden had a mere nine participants, giving you an idea of variation of scenarios.

As far as the European Touring Car Championship goes, a large number of local drivers and cars would participate in their country rounds. So it follows that **SEATS** would be found galore in the **Jarama** grid, **Skodas** were plentiful in **Brno**, **FIAT-Abarths** in Italy, **DAFs** in Holland and a number of **Mini** and **Imp** variations in England. In Germany, even **VW Beetles** made a few starts but would not venture in other ETCC rounds. As the sport as a whole ran into problems in the middle of the decade, caused by the global economy, some of the ETCC races had as few as 13 cars on the grid, while the **Nürburgring** race was usually over-subscribed even in the worst of times, with huge numbers of **Fords, BMWs, Opels, NSUs**, etc, which did not race elsewhere but at the 'Ring. Nowadays, the WTCC is a much more stable affair, with very little variation from race to race – thus, no surprises. This stability of entry lists was a process but that did not start in the 70s, for sure.

The World Sportscars (Makes) Championship was another place where local talent (or lack thereof) was displayed in full bloom. In the **Targa Florio**, many entrants were local Sicilians who were unknown even in Italy. By the same token, the **Nürburgring 1000 km** race had a large number of local drivers entered in the early part of the decade, although the enthusiasm diminished during the Group 5 age. In **1972** FISA quickly realized that the myriad race car constructors it believed would be enthralled to build F1-engined prototypes would not materialize, so prototypes of even 1.3-liter engine cars were allowed in races, plus GTs (mostly **Porsche** 911) and even touring cars, to boost up the fields. Some of the tracks used in the championship were short, like **Dijon** and **Oesterreichring** and the number of entries limited and even in the most competitive year of the 3-liter formula, **1973,** the races at these two venues had in the neighborhood of 20 entries. It must be remembered that organizers had a fair degree of discretion accepting or rejecting entries. In the US races, specially the 24 Hours of **Daytona**, there were many cars such as tuned **Volvos** driven by amateurs which made life difficult for the faster drivers, specially at night. There is nothing new about this, it has been a problem in endurance racing then, as it is now. The point is that the entry lists changed from race to race, this made races individually interesting and memorable. Sometimes there wasn't too much stability even within teams: for instance, top teams **Alfa Romeo** and **Ferrari** did a fair amount of seat shuffling in **1972**.

Sponsorship deals, team contracts and structures got more sophisticated during the 70s and one-off deals became less frequent by the time Group C was adopted in 1982. However, it must be said that the World Championship of Makes (Manufacturers) was in a major state of disrepair by **1979**, which only got worse in **1980** and **1981**. Prototypes, which had been ruled out of the Group 5 races in **1976**, were allowed back, because Group 5 was not embraced by manufacturers and races needed participants, badly.

As more money poured into the sport, exclusivity deals became the norm. Whereas until early on the decade a driver could jump from a **Ford** powered formula 1 to a **Ferrari** engined prototype and then race a **BMW** touring car the week after, this became harder, as contracts came with exclusivity clauses. Here is an example how lax the contractual situation was, a story involving **Teodoro Zeccoli**. A long standing **Alfa Romeo** tester and race driver, Teodoro was slated to drive one of the **Alfa Romeos** in the 1000 km of **Monza** of **1971**, when he was told there were orders from upper management to give his seat to someone else. Then, **Herbert Muller** came to ask him to share one of his **Ferraris** with **Gianpiero Moretti**, which he readily accepted. That is one version. The other version is that a fourth **Alfa** was entered for **Zeccoli** and **Gianluigi Picchi** but two prototypes had accidents by more senior drivers, so the entry was withdrawn. Autodelta gladly let **Teodoro** be borrowed by **Muller**. In spite of the different accounts, in this day and age it would be impossible to imagine a driver be shared by teams in such different camps. (**Alfa** and **Ferrari** were extreme rivals back in **1971**, one must remember, now they are more than buddies, they are brothers). This camaraderie at the driver and team level has been long gone.

Even Formula 1, by far the most organized and professional racing category, local drivers could find rides for their home GPs and realize a long standing dream of becoming a Formula 1 driver. This allowed drivers from France, Holland, Sweden, South Africa, Brazil, Britain, Germany, Belgium, Spain, Italy, etc., to get this off their bucket list.

Just for fun: a race for commercial vehicles in South Africa, 1972. Some of the participants were actually Formula 1 drivers. Photo by Russell Whitworth.

It seems to me that the stable entry lists of this age make racing less interesting and at one point, even the most fervorous follower of the sport fails to differentiate one race from the other, because everything "looks" or "feels" the same. There are few "markers" that allow us to remember individual races properly, even though a large number of them can be watched and recorded on TV or seen on Youtube. You consume the race visually on Sunday, forget about it Monday and are ready for the next one.

This brings me to the next "pivoting" topic, manufacturer involvement. As I repeat often in this book, the world was much poorer in the 70s and I am not even talking about correcting for inflation. Early in the decade many street going cars cost less than US$2,000.00, so that reaching US$ 1 million in sales took some doing. Some popular cars, like **British Leyland's Mini**, was sold by the tons but actually contributed heavily to corporate loss. The margin was so little on such a low price automobile that a little strike here and there – and there were many in the 70s British auto industry – turned the little profit into a little loss per car, which multiplied by a few hundred thousand was not so little anymore. So you get the idea: most car makers were not awash in cash, specially popular car makers.

So that **Renault**'s decision to go Formula 1 racing was a very pivotal point, for it was the first popular, high volume carmaker to go Grand Prix racing as a full works team in the modern era. Let me qualify my statement. **Alfa Romeo** has always been mid-size in terms of volume, more upscale pricewise. Alfas were expensive then, as they continue to be and never a high volume maker. **Mercedes** was exclusively a luxury car manufacturer back in the 50s (plus trucks and buses, of course). **Ford** was never involved in F-1 as a works team and one can argue that the Cosworth engine that carried the Dearborn badge had no **Ford** DNA, as much as there was no **Simca** DNA in **Matra**, or **FIAT** DNA in **Ferrari**. As for **Honda**, when it began its involvement in Formula 1 back in **1964**, it was the top motorcycle manufacturer of the world but had just began making cars, mostly tiny sports cars. By the time it closed the works team, in **1968**, **Honda** was still a low volume carmaker. So the Regie's decision to start a works team and use turbo technology for the first time was indeed a game changer. It is also noteworthy that **Renault** was not a private company back then.

Renault stayed as a works team for the first time for quite a few years, in fact, until **1985**, continuing as engine provider, then leaving for a very short while. It returned as an engine provider in **1989** and it has come back as a works team twice. It has more or less been present in Formula 1 since **1977**, with a few gaps and it has won two titles as a works team and several others as engine supplier. That set the footprint that would not only attract other manufacturers into Formula 1 but change the level of commitment to longer term. It also helped kill the Cosworth kit car model for a while, dragging the weaker Formula 1 teams that had no perspective of turbo engines into the mud. Very Darwinian, indeed.

There were many works teams of all shapes and forms elsewhere during the 70s. **Ford** might not have been a works Formula 1 team but **Ford** Germany was a major supporter of racing early in the decade and **Ford** supported Trans-Am and race teams in several other countries. **BMW, Alfa Romeo, Jaguar, Triumph** all had works teams, the former in a number of settings such as Le Mans, Formula 2, IMSA and ETCC. In the USA, **AMC** and Penske had a cozy tie-up for a while, **Plymouth** supported Petty, **Mercury** supported Pearson. **Porsche** was in for the long-term, since the beginning of the decade, while **Lancia** came in late in the 70s. **Mercedes-Benz** refused to call the AMG entries a works endeavor but it sure looked that way. Even Czech **Skoda**, in spite of the Iron Curtain that prevented much exchange, ran a works team in the ETCC, while **Mazda** spearheaded Japanese participation in European endurance and touring cars. However, most of these efforts were short-lived. Take **Renault**'s Le Mans assault, for example. The actual full-fledged, turbo assault lasted a mere three years, from **1976** to **1978** and once victory was achieved, the **Alpines** were gone. Compare that to **Audi**'s long Le Mans participation of latter years, incidentally, while supporting DTM and even GT programs and we get the full picture.

So when **Renault** came into Formula 1 with a new technology in tow, then fabulously won its first GP less than two years after its debut, other manufacturers began looking into ways of working their way into Formula 1. The **Renault** exercise did not just happen overnight. Alpine's **Andre de Cortanze** had built an unraced Formula 1 in the late 60s, which management did not approve of. Be that as it may, **Renault** was fully intent on getting a racing image, certainly enthused with **Matra**'s success but it did so methodically. First, there was Coupe Gordini, a one-make sedan series that began in **1966**, even before **Matra**'s success, followed by Formula Renault. Then the 2-liter **Alpine** prototypes of **1973-74**, plus Formula 3 engines, with a still timid attack on the World Championship of Makes in **1975**, which yielded a win. Then, the manufacturer joined Formula 2, providing engines that won two straight championships, **1976** and **1977**, concurrently with the early Le Mans program and a World Championship of Makes fight against **Porsche** in

1976. The obvious target, Formula 1, was achieved in **1977**. **Honda,** by then a mass producer with a more global presence was the first to follow suit, with a Formula 2 program in the 80s, then Formula 1. Not all manufacturers emulated **Renault**'s example but the French company showed it could be done and **Mercedes**, specifically, followed this pattern and has been around for more than 30 years now. So here is another important 70s pivoting point.

Some manufacturers, like **VW**, decided to sponsor categories, in this case Formula Super Vee, where **VW** product always won…Eventually, one-make championships became rather popular in many countries for the same reason, involving manufacturers such as **VW, FIAT, Renault, Alfa Romeo, Ford, Chevrolet, BMW, Volvo**, **Simca**, **British Leyland,** all over the world. That in itself is another pivoting point.

One-make races and championships had been happening for a while. A few races in the 20s and 30s were full **Bugatti** benefits but they were not series, even though the factory ran single make races for customers. In the 40s **Piero Dusio**, with the help of Swiss financiers, intended to start a one-make **Cisitalia** series, of all places, in Egypt. The undertaking was perhaps a bit too ambitious for the young marque and a single race took place, in **1947**, won by Italian **Franco Cortese**. The Italian drivers, which included **Alberto Ascari** and **Piero Taruffi,** plus **Louis Chiron**, had a blast and enjoyed their holiday but the folks putting up the money were very disappointed when only 6,000 scared Egyptians, plus the King, showed up. Then in Brazil, in **1951**, there was an all **Mercedes-Benz** 24 hour race in which **Emerson Fittipaldi**'s father and mother took part! Here and there, promotional one-make races were held, with **Minis, Fords, Dauphines, VWs**. In fact, there were **VW Beetle** races in the Bahamas in the 60s, where guys like **Dan Gurney** and **A.J. Foyt** could be watched muscling the little beasts about at the height of their fame.

An all **Opel** race was held yearly at the **Nürburgring** in the beginning of the decade, open to all types of **Opel** types, from GT to Manta to Commodore. As mentioned, **Renault** began Coupe Gordini in **1966**, which among others, provided a platform for **Jean-Pierre Jarier** to begin his career. Then there were the single seater categories, such as Formula Ford, Formula Vee, Super Vee and Formula Renault. As these categories were opened to different chassis manufacturers, one did not feel they were one-make and thus exclusive but that is what they were.

Eventually, marketing departments at a number of manufacturers discovered the obvious: against no competition, a manufacturer in a one-make championship always came out the winner, regardless of the fact the car was a rather sleepy **VW** Rabbit in the USA, a **FIAT** 147 in Brazil or **Alfasud** in Italy. There were upscale one make series, too, like **BMW**'s Procar (it began its two-year run in **1979**), which allowed Grand Prix drivers to drive something other than their Formula 1`s on race weekend and IROC, which in the first edition (**1973**) used **Porsche** Carreras, then shifting to **Camaros** for many years. One-make series proliferated to a great extent towards the end of the 70s and the practice has remained to this day. In fact there have been dozens upon dozens of one-make series worldwide since then, some very successful, others not so much. On the good side, cars and parts were often provided at a subsidized cost by the manufacturer, allowing many folks to practice the sport at an entry level with little cost. In some cases, the prize money was not bad, definitely better than in other entry level categories or club racing and even former Formula 1 drivers drove in the **Renault** R5 Cup in Europe for many years, such as **Boy Hayje** and **Michael Bleekemolen**. Manufacturers got the promotion they wanted, judging the money better spent than the embarrassment of fighting for 9th place at races against direct competitors or retiring often, like the **Jaguars** often did in the **1976** and **1977** ETCC. This reduced even further the variety that prevailed at racetracks early on the decade, leading to today's standardization. One-make series or races certainly did not emerge in the 70s but the practice definitely got traction during the decade.

There were some changes during the course of the 70s, that show racing became more organized and, in some cases, less dangerous. The old style **Le Mans** start, which many reckoned was an accident waiting to happen, was dropped at Le Mans, although still emulated in a few places around the world. The 3-2-3 grid formation used in some tracks in Formula 1 was eliminated after the **1973** season and I personally believe that a 2-2 staggered grid at **Silverstone** might have averted the huge crash that decimated 1/3 of the field in the early part of the **1973** race.

As far as organization, starting in **1973** GP cars had their own fixed assigned numbers, which helped identify cars, making things more tidy and more "marketing" and merchandising friendly. The practice would be followed little by little by many categories all over the world, as entry lists became more stable in many categories.

Although several new major championships appeared in **1969** to **1972**, the vast majority of races outside the United States were standalone events, sometimes with races for several categories, not connected to any championship. This meant a lot of car variety on the racetracks, where elderly **Maseratis** fitted with **BMW** engines shared real estate with prototypes of questionable pedigree or identity and could be mixed with more modern machinery, sometimes **Porsche** 917's and spanking new **Lolas**. Add to this **VW Beetles, DAFs, DKWs** and **Minis**. As the decade went on, the standalone events were quickly dying off. Even non-championship Formula 1 and Formula 2 races, which were common in the early part of the decade, mostly disappeared. The last non-championship Formula 2 race in Europe took place in **Misano**, in **1976** (previously mentioned) and there were some attempts to revive Argentina's Formula 2 Temporada races in **1978**, which was supposed to include races in Brazil, forbidden by the government's petroleum board. As for the last non-championship Formula 1 race, it took place in **1983**, which is not within the time frame of this book but you get the idea. Non-championship Formula 1 races were a dying breed for a number reasons, foremost, Formula 1 calendars had expanded to 15, 16 races, so the non-championship races basically became a nuisance. This is another pivot.

I noticed that no less than seventeen former or future Formula 1 champions raced during the decade, whose activities spanned from the 50s to the mid 90s. Check it out: **Jack Brabham, Phil Hill, Graham Hill, John Surtees, Denis Hulme, Jackie Stewart, Jochen Rindt, Emerson Fittipaldi, Niki Lauda, James Hunt, Mario Andretti, Jody Scheckter, Alan Jones, Nelson Piquet, Keke Rosberg, Alain Prost** and **Nigel Mansell**. This meant that here and there, you could expect to see a world champion at the racetrack, outside of a formula 1 race: in Formula 2, Le Mans, prototype races, Can-Am, touring car races, USAC, hill climbs, IROC, sprint car racing, even minor events. Now we make a real big deal when a F1 driver races some place other than GPs.

A.J. Foyt was one of the several greats that raced in the 70s. he won his fourth and final Indy 500 during the decade. Photo by Rob Neuzel.

Let us not restrict ourselves to Grand Prix greats: some of the best ever endurance drivers graced the tracks during the 70s: **Jacky Ickx, Jo Siffert, Pedro Rodriguez, Henri Pescarolo, Peter Gregg, Hurley Haywood, Jochen Mass, Rolf Stommelen, Arturo Merzario, Jo Bonnier, Derek Bell, Hans Stuck, Brian Redman, Gerard Larrousse, Klaus Ludwig, Bob Wollek, Vic Elford.** USAC greats **A.J. Foyt, Johnny Rutherford, Gordon Johncock, Al Unser, Bobby Unser, Wally Dallenbach, Mario Andretti** raced together the entire decade. In NASCAR, **Richard Petty, Cale Yarborough, Bobby and Donnie Allison, David Pearson, Darrel Waltrip, Buddy Baker, Benny Parsons, Bobby Isaac and Dale Earnhardt** were 70s mainstays. Some NASCAR drivers raced in USAC, some USAC drivers raced in NASCAR. Great drivers from different eras still raced in the beginning of the decade, **Hans Hermann, Umberto Maglioli, Masten Gregory, Chico Landi, Dan Gurney, Lloyd Ruby, LeeRoy Yarbrough, Fred Lorenzen, Charlie Glotzbach.** Even **Stirling Moss** made occasional appearances. Other major drivers in their respective categories and countries, such as **Dieter Quester, Hans Heyer, Al Holbert, Kazuyoshi Hoshino, Luis di Palma, Luiz Pereira Bueno, Masahiro Hasemi, Mark Donohue, David Hobbs, John Fitzpatrick, Frank Gardner, Graham McRae, Mauro Nesti**, were abundant. Fast lady drivers were hitting the tracks in droves, **Lella Lombardi, Janet Guthrie, Desire Wilson, Divina Galica, Waltraud Odenthal, Christine Beckers, Hannelore Werner, Yvette Fontaine, Anne Wong, Lianne Engemann, Lyn St. James, Michele Mouton**... Rally and motorcycle drivers also raced cars: **Rauno Aaltonen, Walter Rohrl, Simo Lampinen, Sobieslaw Zasada, Bjorn Waldegaard, Giacomo Agostini, Shektar Mehta, Barry Sheene.** Besides that, fast, outstanding famous drivers like **Chris Amon, Jean-Pierre Jarier, Jacques Laffite, Tim Schenken, Toine Hezemans, Gilles Villeneuve, Rene Arnoux, Jean Pierre Jaussaud,**

Peter Gethin, Mike Hailwood raced in a bewildering variety of venues and categories, all over the world. All of this happened during the same decade.

It is hard to get very excited about a current Formula 2 field, for we know that the vast majority of the category's drivers will not make it to Formula 1, in fact, many will give up on racing altogether because ultimately they failed to make the big time, after a few seasons of broken dreams and a few millions spent in the process. The same goes for Indy Lights and to a great extent, Formula 3. While GT racing is a bit more lively now than in the 70s but do you really know, or care, about many current GT drivers? Is there any **John Fitzpatrick, Claude Ballot-Lena, Clemens Schickentanz, Al Holbert, Peter Gregg, Hurley Haywood** in the whole bunch?

Then there were the cars. There was variety not only in terms of constructors but shapes as well. As some of my friends say, race cars had character back then. You can easily recognize a 70s **Tyrrell** from a **Lotus** from a **BRM** but if you take the livery off a current Formula 1 car, you will have difficulty differentiating one from the other. There were wedge shaped, round shaped, full width bubble noses of different shapes, triangular looking chassis, radiators in front or side, even in the back, tiny tires, wing cars, no frontal airfoil, side pods, 6-wheelers, large air boxes, small air boxes, ugly, pretty, scary looking, cars with fans in the back, 2-stroke and 4-cycle engines, two-engined cars, even a four-engined Can Am contraption! **Jim Hurtubise** continued trying to qualify a front-engined car at Indy into the late 70s, against all odds.

And now we are left to ponder at a 33-car Indy 500 field full of **Dallaras**. Nothing against **Dallara**. The company that had its roots in the 70s managed to remain solid in a very hard business, for making race cars commercially, on the long-term, is not an easy thing to do – just ask **March, Ralt, Reynard** and **Lola**, among the most successful. Yet, although 19 **Eagles** made the **1973** Indy field, there were still four other chassis constructors on the field, in addition to a whole bunch of other constructors which did not qualify but raced elsewhere during the season. There was a Dr. Ehrlich who insisted on fielding his eponymous all steel racer in British formula 3 for years, unphazed by the lack of success of his enterprise. There was the mysterious British **Scorpion** prototype, which for some reason appeared in the 1000 km of Oesterreichring, Portugal and Angola but not Britain! There was a plaster bodied **DKW** prototype made in Brasilia, Brazil, which had no name and apparently came apart before the race ended! You can probably add a few anecdotes of your own.

This book's section on race car constructors is a very large one. Sure, not everybody in the list is a **McLaren** but at least one Swiss constructor who humbly began his activities in his native country's hill climbs in the 70s remains as a Formula 1 constructor today. You guessed it, **Peter Sauber**, whose marque debuted in **1970**. It is possible that many of these race cars were nothing more than a sedan with the roof taken out, which was a popular way of creating "prototypes" early in the decade but I imagine very few people, if any, can now provide reliable information about early decade obscure Czech hill-climbs, Indian races or British club racing with any degree of certainty. But one notes, as the decade went on, a notable decrease of the number of race car manufacturers. Another pivotal point.

We tend to believe that racing is much more international today than in the 70s, because drivers of more exotic nationalities, such as Israel and Romania, seem able to get closer to Formula 1, or other top level series today. That is true up to a certain extent.

As one digs deeper, one finds out that racing in the 70s was by and large a regional endeavor. There was racing going on in most unusual places. As most of the influential press and annuals were written in English, access to racing information outside of Europe, America and to a certain extent, South Africa and Australia was very limited. Even though South Africa had a Formula 1 championship by the 70s the F1s were few in the field, boosted by Formula 2s and Formula 5000s, one of the reasons why the country adopted the slower and les glamorous Formula Atlantic for **1976**. Additionally, the relevance of racing in the Antipodes vanished during the decade, as the Tasman Cup disappeared from the map. It should be considered that a part of South Africa's and Australia's reputation as racing hotspots came from the early season Tasman Cup and Springbok series of the 60s, both of which did not survive the 70s.

However, it is interesting noting that both South Africa and Australia (including New Zealand) were regional hubs in their own, with influence on other nearby countries. The South African championship and the Springbok series included, after all, races in Mozambique (the Lourenco Marques racetrack had opened in 1962) and Rhodesia (currently known as Zimbabwe). In the Southern cone of Africa, Angola had a very lively racing scene, with multiple races in several venues, participation of foreign drivers (including South Africans) and reasonably well-kept **Alfa Romeo P33, Ford GT40, GRDs, Porsches** and **Lolas**, with various touring cars making up the numbers. Many of these came from neighboring South Africa.

The Australian/New Zealand racing scene was quite varied and interesting. Additionally, cars such as this Matich Formula 5000 were built down under. Photo by Glenn Moulds

As for Australia and New Zealand, drivers from those countries took part in many races in **Singapore, Philippines, Malaysia, Japan and Macau**, driving against local talent, Japanese drivers, a Pilipino and Indonesian participant here and there. In fact, Australian made **Elfins** were used by some Asian drivers, so there was regional interaction between these nations and Formula 2, then Formula Atlantic (called Pacific there for obvious reasons) was the connecting link between all these countries, for by the end of the decade only Australia had a Formula 5000 category anywhere in the globe. Pilipino motorsports got a boost when the Philippines Grand Prix was created in **1973**, at the **Greenhills** track, which was eventually toured by no other than **Jackie Stewart**. However, the Philippines did ban motorsport in the latter part of the decade, because of the second oil shock. For some time there was a Pacific championship with races in Indonesia, Malaysia, Macau and Brunei, the latter won by **Peter Marshall** in a **Ralt (1979)**. Brunei, awash in oil had no problems with the oil shock.

I wish I could include Cambodia in the list of venues, for it would make a good story, except I do not have documentation whether racing actually took place there in the 60s or 70s. It would be the only instance where a head of State raced! The rather exotic Prince **Norodon Sihanouk** claimed in an interview with Italian **Oriana Fallaci** that he fancied racing cars, in addition to making movies and directing a jazz band. I remember reading in a car magazine, sometime during the 90s, that racing actually took place in the country and Sihanouk's mount, if my memory serves me right, was an Alfa Romeo that had been located by a collector. As I recall, the note mentions that the other "drivers" were the Prince's cronies, who let him win (not an unusual thing in some corners, you will learn reading further). The one missing piece of the puzzle was the timeline. At any rate, **Norodon** was born in 1922, so he was a bit old for car racing in 1970, but, who knows, the man was full of surprises even though by 1971 he was out of Cambodia. The story is so interesting it is worth including in this book, which is, after all, full of oddities.

Remember that the world was much poorer in the 70s. There were no billionaires to speak of, air transport was extremely expensive and relatively rare, international tourism incipient in most places and currency exchange regulations very tough in many countries. Thus, these regional hubs emerged naturally – it was much easier to travel closer to home, in some cases, driving, than set up shop in England or America to hit the big time and find yourself on the pages of *Autosport* and *Auto Week*.

Even the most knowledgeable enthusiast might be surprised with the degree of exchange in the racing communities of countries in the Northern part of South America, to wit, Venezuela, Colombia, Ecuador and Peru. Peru already had its 6 hours back then, won in the 60s by a pair of Ecuadorian drivers who made it to Le Mans eventually and even drove in European Formula 2: **Fausto Merello** and **Guillermo Ortega**. Colombians raced in Venezuela and vice-versa and Ecuadorians and Venezuelans often raced in Colombia. Ecuador had a 12-hour race, the **1971** *12 Horas Marlboro* which first edition of it was won by no less than **Tony Adamowicz**, partnered by another American, **Gregg Young**, driving a **Ferrari** 512. Drivers from the rest of northern South America often raced in this endurance event.

Colombia was a rather peculiar place. The country's topography is very mountainous, to the extent that Colombia was one of the first countries to develop commercial aviation in the world due to the need to connect different areas of the country. As a result, racing developed regionally. In the South, there was quite a bit of exchange with Ecuadorian drivers, while in the East, Venezuelans were often joining the party. A large number of venues held races in the decade, including **Bogota, Tocancipa, Palmira, Cali, Pasto, Buga, Las Palmas, Santa Elena**. The topography favored hill climbing, which was relatively popular in the country. There were two attempts to include Colombia in the international calendar, a couple of

International Formula 2 events in **1971**, then a Formula B event in **1972**. Mostly, the events involved a number of categories, small to large sized touring cars and Fuerza Liebre, which included a very pretty **DKW** prototype built in **1971**. In fact, the country was peculiar in that DKWs were still racing by the middle of the decade and for other odd race car choices for a South American country, **Wartburg, Zastava and Skoda**. Add to that some **Mustangs, Porsches** and **BMWs** also participated in the races and a **Renault** 4 one-make series began in the middle of the decade.

Venezuela was a relatively rich country, because of oil, that had hosted a World Championship event in the 50s. Attempts were made to bring international racing back to the country, at La Chinita: a Formula B event won by **Andrea de Adamich** in **1973**, then a Formula Atlantic event won by local **Bobby Dennet** in **1974**. There were long distance races for touring cars with a variety of cars such as **AMC** Hornet, **Opel, Ford Cortina, Renaults, FIATs** and also two single seater categories, Formula Ford and Formula Vee, run with imported equipment. Some Venezuelans ventured out of the country, such as **Oscar Notz, Juan Cochesa, Bobby Dennet, Ernesto Soto** but the major exponent was yet to come in the 80s – **Johnny Cecotto**, who still raced bikes during the decade but raced a car here and there. There was some degree of interaction mostly in races in Eastern Colombia.

Bolivia had some racing of its own, mostly road racing that resembled rallies to a large extent, with little interaction with neighboring countries. **Oscar Crespo, Dieter Hubner, Rene Rocha** and **Helmut Seng** were exponents. In fact, the country's **Circuito Oscar Crespo-Ciudad del Sucre** was held for the first time in **1970** and it remains the most important race in the country.

Even an Alfa Romeo Montreal raced in Ecuador during the 70s (unknown author)

It should be remembered that the first South American driver to achieve success in Europe was Chilean **Juan Zanelli**, in the 30s and the country had a long, albeit obscure, motor racing history. Chilean racing mostly borrowed from Argentine tradition. There were races for Formula 4 single seaters and Carreteras, which looked like a cross between Argentine TCs and prototypes, some of them locally built, others Argentine. Among the exponents of the era were **Claudio Ibarra, Jaime Vergara, Luis Gimeno, Eduardo Kovacs, Boris Garafulic** and **Juan Gac**. There were also long distance races, such as the 6 Horas Chilenas, held at **Las Vizcachas**, contested by cars such as **Mustang, Falcon, Mini Coopers, Volvos, NSUs, Torinos** and **Fiat Abarths**. The 1970 edition was an international event, with the participation of Argentines **Joaquin Perrota** and **Manfredo Suiter**, among several others, which was won by **Garafulic/Ibarra**. There were few truly international races but in **1971** there was an Argentine Formula 2 regulation international tournament at **Las Vizcachas**, with participation of Argentine and Uruguayan drivers.

Brazil and Argentina, the two largest countries in the continent, basically did their own thing. There are, however, some surprises. Uruguayans often raced in Argentina, in fact Uruguayan **Pedro Passadore** was an Argentine Formula 1 champion. In the border between Brazil, Paraguay and Argentina, there was great exchange, since the early days of the decade: drivers from Brazil and Argentina raced in the **Aratiri** racetrack, in Paraguay, while Brazilian **Valdir Favarin**, having no place to race his **Manta-Chrysler** prototype in his own country in **1978**, raced it in neighboring small city Argentine tracks, such as **Posadas, Aristobolo del Valle e Eldorado**, which cultivated a Formula Libre mentality. In an event held at **Aratiri** in June of **1971**, several Brazilian drivers from the neighboring State of Parana were featured in a number of races for touring cars and prototypes, including **Paulo Nascimento, Pedro Muffato, Altair Barranco, Luiz Moura Brito** and **Zilmar Beux**. While Argentines and Paraguayans won in touring cars, the Brazilians excelled in prototypes, **Moura Brito** winning in the VW-engined **Manta**.

A Ford engined Bino prototype, a VW engined Puma and a BMW waiting for the start in Interlagos, Brazil, 1970. Photo by Rogerio da Luz.

Brazil and Argentina did try to set up a Sulam (also called Sudam) prototype championship back in **1971**, something that had already been tried in the 50s and early 60s. Argentina had a very strong prototype category, with locally made cars, while the strongest Brazilian contenders raced European cars and some locally made 2-liter prototypes. The experiment did not take off. The Argentines won at first but when a Brazilian driven **Porsche** 908-2 won a "round" of the championship, they cried foul. A last attempt at a South American prototype series was made in **1972**, by which time a stronger Brazilian prototype, a Chevrolet-engined **Avallone** showed up, plus an Alfa T33 driven by **Marivaldo Fernandes**. However, eventually national prototype racing ended first in Argentina (**1973**) and then in Brazil (**1975**), so the whole exercise was doomed to failure from the start.

A **Ford** Maverick 4-cylinder tournament was held in Brazil, in **1975**, to promote the launch of the car, with representatives from several South American countries, as well as **Vittorio Brambilla**! This was not an isolated event: in **1972**, FIAT promoted the Desafio de los Valientes in **Buenos Aires**, with a road race and a circuit race for their model 125. The circuit race had drivers from Brazil (**Luiz Pereira Bueno** and **Tite Catapani**), Chile (**Santiago Bengolea**), Paraguay (**Alfredo Jaegel**), Uruguay (**Diego Fernandez**), while the road race had Finland's **Simo Lampinen**, Italy's **Andres Cavallari** and **Luciano Smania**, plus Sweden's **Harry Karlstrom**, plus several Argentines, of course.

In **1971** Argentines brought 25 Formula 4 cars (equipped with 850 cc **Renault** engines) for a demonstration race in Brazil's **Tarumã**. Six cars were assigned to Brazilian drivers, such as **Fernando Sbroglio** and **Claudio Mueller** but Argentine **Carlos Andreeta** won both heats. The thinking, I suppose, was to make this a continental, or at least a regional category, for Brazil had no single seater category at that point in time. However, later in the year Formula Ford began, so there was no need for Formula 4.

As for Uruguay, it mingled with Brazilian and Argentine racing in the course of the decade. The **Rivera** racetrack was a stone's throw from Brazil's Santana do Livramento and Southern Brazilians often raced there. Other racetracks used were **Punta Fria, El Pinar, San Jose, Tamarinas, Paysandu** and **Salto. El Pinar** was reinaugurated in **1975** with a race contested by Brazilian Division 3 cars (highly tuned touring cars). 14 Brazilian cars came from Brazil's Rio Grande do Sul, mostly **VW** Beetles driven by the likes of **Voltaire Moog, Claudio Mattos** and **Fernando Moser**. The single car from Uruguay was a **Morris** Mini, driven by **Pedro Kent**. The winner turned out to be **Carlos Piegas**, born in Uruguay, naturalized Brazilian, who lived in Uruguaiana (Brazil) and was doing his 12th race, having already driven in Brazil, Uruguay and Argentina. Despite the large number of tracks for such a small country and enthusiastic races with cars from a number of categories, such as Touring cars, Formula Vee, Fuerza Libre, Fuerza Limitada, Argentine Formula 1, 2 and 4, only **Pedro Passador** achieved notoriety, having raced in British and Italian Formula 3 and winning the Argentine Formula 1 championship twice during the decade. **El Pinar** did host some Argentine Formula 1 races, between 1975 and 1977, as well as Argentine Formula 2 but no truly international events, like its two neighbors. The attitude was definitely enthusiastic but laid-back, without much ambition. They were happy doing what they were doing.

As the most technologically advanced racing country in the Southern cone, Argentina provided cars, engines, tires and components to drivers in several countries, such as Chile, Paraguay, Uruguay and even Brazil. Argentina's supremacy in this area could be felt as far as in the continent's Northern countries, running into latter decades.

El Salvador's claim to fame was a 6-hour race valid for the World Championship of Endurance Drivers (not the Makes championship), held in El Jabali racetrack in **1979**. However, drivers from that country, Guatemala, Panama and Costa Rica often raced each other in a Central American championship and even before El Jabali, other tracks were built in the area. Costa Rica's La Guacima was opened in **1974**, at which point the Rio Hato track in Panama was already in business. There were several long distance events in the area, such as 3 Hours of Costa Rica, Four Hours of Panama and 500 kms Viceroy, where the likes of **Kikos Fonseca** and **Jorge Valverde** (Costa Rica), **Pedro Cofino** (Guatemala), **Henry Schwartz** and **Rodrigo Teran** (Panama) and Salvadorans **"Jamsal"**, **"Fomfor"**, **Eduardo Melendez** and **Carlos Cromeyer** would fight for regional supremacy. The Central Americans were, in fact, the first to seriously race pickup trucks in circuit racing, against regular cars, by the way. The practice began in **1970** and the likes of **Kikos Fonseca** raced small engined **Datsuns** and **Toyotas**. Races for pickup trucks and delivery vans, of fairly large size, were held in a host of Latin American countries since the 50s and South Africans also dabbled in the modality for fun. Central America was and it still is a hub and some of the region's drivers actually competed in the IMSA series in the USA, while **Teran** made it all the way to Le Mans. The foundation for today's Central American racing scene was all laid out in the 70s, it must be said.

As for Mexico, one might add that in the wake of **Pedro Rodriguez**'s death, coming two years after **Moises Solana's**, the country's motor racing scene lost its two main heros. Adding insult to injury, the Mexican Grand Prix was cancelled, never returning to the F1 calendar during the 70s, due to the misbehaving crowds of **1970**. Without idols and without major international races, some drivers, like **Hector Rebaque, Fred Van Beuren Jr., Johnny Gerber**, decided to make a career outside the country, in categories such as Formula Atlantic, Formula B (US) and Formula 2, while quite a few took part in the IMSA series, such as **Juan Carlos Bolanos**. Out of the whole lot, only **Rebaque** made it to Formula 1 and even built his own car, the **Rebaque** briefly raced in the last year of the decade. **Josele Garza** also debuted during the 70s but would make his name in the 80s. Most racing comprised of races for small touring cars (called ponies) that included **VW Beetles**, plus races for larger displacement cars such as **BMWs** and **Porsches**. There were long-distance races as well, such as the 1000 km of Mexico, which was included as an IMSA Camel GT round in **1974**. One might say with a degree of certainty that the big name in the local scene was veteran **Memo Rojas Sr.**, who won championships in Touring Cars, GTs and Formula Ford during the decade. During the 80s, racing took a new vigor in the country but of course, this is not the subject of this book. Although a Central American country, Mexican drivers and cars barely ever took part in the Central American races, mostly because the Southern part of Mexico was (and still is), the poorest area of the country, so most racing teams were based farther up North, making the trip costly and dangerous.

In the Caribbean, gone were the days of the Bahamas Speed Week of the 60s and the Cuban races of the 50s. However, **Bushy Park (Barbados)** was inaugurated in **1971** and drivers from the islands, such as **Mike Tyrrell** (Antigua), **Richard Melville** (Jamaica) and **Diego Febles** (Puerto Rico) raced abroad, the latter being very effective in IMSA racing, in fact posting category wins in important races. **Tyrrell** won a British Formula 3 race in **1974**. Some drivers even raced in the Daytona 24 Hours and other IMSA races under Cuban nationality but I believe they were trying to make a political statement and were American by then. But there was racing elsewhere in the Caribbean. Jamaica had a track, **Vernamfield**, where local drivers would race competitors from other islands, like Puerto Rico and the Dominican Republic. Races where held in Puerto Rico in at least three locations, **Caguas, Anasco** and **Salinas**. The **1978** 3 Hours of Caguas had teams from the US, Venezuela, Haiti, Trinidad, Panama, Costa Rica, Colombia and the Dominican Republic. The Dominican Republic had races at **San Isidro** air base, in which drivers from other islands competed. Guyana, not an island but more in tune with the islands than the rest of South America for linguistic, geographic, cultural and social reasons, had reopened its **South Dakota** track in **1970**, in which British, Antiguan, Trinidadian and Barbadian drivers competed, in addition to Guyanese. Trinidad's **Wallerfield** track had hosted races since **1958** and all of these hosted a short-lived Caribbean Championship during the decade. In other words, there was quite a bit of exchange in the Caribbean region as well.

Then there was Eastern Europe. Teams, drivers and races from Russia and other formerly Eastern block countries such as Poland, Czech Republic, Slovakia, Azerbaijan, Hungary et al, seem very common these days. However, in the 70s the Iron Curtain was pretty much in existence, this was the height of the Cold War. Except for a Budapest round of the ETCC in **1970** and the Czech events at **Brno**(ETCC), a **Most** Interserie race and the **Ecco Homo** hillclimb, Eastern Europe was pretty much off the radar of European and international racing. They had their own regional racing scene, which inclued Pan-Eastern European categories, Formula 1, 2, 3 and 4 and then Formulas Easter and Junior, mostly Estonia single seaters equipped with **Moskvich** engines but some other variations as well. Additionally, there were prototype, touring car races and hill climbs where drivers from Russia, Ukraine, Estonia, Latvia, Czechoslovakia, Poland, Bulgaria, Yugoslavia, Lithuania, Georgia, etc. competed for honors. Soviet Formula 1 existed early in the decade, which was obviously not at all similar to international Formula 1. But the fact is that car racing happened behind the curtain, including Romania. The book lists a significant number drivers listed in the countries in the drivers section.

In Western Europe, there was great regional exchange in Scandinavia and Benelux (Belgium, Netherlands and Luxembourg), with regional races and championships throughout the decade. The picture on the next page shows the degree of such exchange. Taken at Keimola in 1974, it shows action in a Volvo 142 single-make series. Although held in Finnish soil, there was a single driver from that country on the field. The vast majority were Swedish, with a few Danish interlopers adding for diversity.

Other countries, such as Greece, had racing in circuits and hill climbs, such as **Pititsa**, first held in **1973**, with little to no international exchange. Its most famous driver, **George Mouschous**, used an **Alfa** T33 prototype to win **Pititsa** and many other Greek events in **1975** and **1976**. Races were held in many venues and even Greek race cars were built.

Except for the Southern cone of Africa and Morocco, circuit racing in Africa was pretty rare then, as it is today. However, the 6 Hours of Dakar, in the former colony of Senegal, managed to attract some European drivers, such as **Raymond Tourol** and **Carlo Facetti** and even Formula 1 star **Jean-Pierre Jarier**, who won the race in **1977**. As for Morocco, the intensive international motoring activity of the 50s had been long gone, although there was a Morocco Formula 3 championship in **1970**, won by **Jacky Berenger**, with races in several venues and Moroccan **Max Cohen-Olivar** became a well-known fixture in European racing for many years, while the Corniche race remained an international event for part of the decade. Kenya also had a proper racetrack by the name of **Nakuru** (also known as **Langalanga**) and a source refers to a race akin to a Formula 1 race being held there until the mid-70s. It was probably a race for some type of single seater (likely old 500cc Formula 3 cars or Formula Vees), which shared the track with touring cars in these mysterious **Nakuru** events.

Volvo Cup, Keimola, 1974 Photo by Harry Hammaren/Jari Debner

There were some isolated spots, such as India, where as many as 70,000 people would gather to watch races at the **Sholavaram** airfield, to witness the likes of mythical **Dr. Rossi** and his **Ferrari**, the **Maharkumar of Gondal**, competitors from Sri Lanka or perhaps an international driver practice their craft. Who would dream that local driver **Vijay Mallya** would one day become a factor in Formula 1 as a team owner and **Vicky Chandhok** would be considered for the post of FIA president? Again, the popularity of motor racing events in such places is partly explained by the lack of entertainment alternatives at the time, such as TV. I have seen pictures of esthetically challenged and unidentified Indian prototypes, **Premier** and even **Hindustan Ambassador** racers, the embryo of future Indian motor racing categories but little information was found to discuss the matter further.

During the course of the decade, there was a notable change in the way top drivers got into the business. Whereas a large number of European drivers in the late 60s to early 70s had began racing in motorcycles and hill climbs, by the latter part of the decade they were almost exclusively beginning in karting. This also applied to the USA, where most early USAC drivers began their careers driving sprint, stocks and midget cars in short tracks – by the late 70s, most were coming from Formula Super Vee and Formula Atlantic, while beginning in karts at an early age as well. Last, but not least, the sport became less informal. For instance, drivers stopped racing under pseudonyms, a quite common practice in Italy but use in several other countries like Belgium, Brazil, Greece, El Salvador, etc.

David Pieris winning the 1975 Sri Lankan Grand Prix on three wheels. Photo Pieris collection.

Thus we see that a lot of **pivoting** took place during the 70s, turning racing into a more organized and structured, less romantic and some would say, more boring activity. These were:

- Greater safety in racetracks, car design, race management, better trained and equipped first response.
- Sounder management, with greater legal, accounting and press relations presence.
- Commercial sponsorship became essential in almost every category worldwide.
- Contracts became more trustworthy.
- Television became an essential part of the equation.
- Drivers and team owners calling the shots, rather than race organizers.
- Firmer, long-term manufacturer involvement.
- Proliferation of one-make series worldwide.
- Substantial decrease of the number of standalone races – almost all races became connected to a championship.
- Change of way drivers progressed in their careers, in Europe and the U.S..
- A notable decrease of number of race car manufacturers, as cars became more complex and safety requirements more stringent.
- Exclusivity contracts slowly become the rule in the top echelons of the sport.
- A more serious, formal and professional stance.

This gives an overall picture of the 70s and I hope, the rest of the book will help you connect all the dots and clearly see this pivoting.

Highlights

This section provides some of the highlights of the decade, which will help you contextualize the changes that took place in motor racing from **1970** to **1979**. Broken down by years, there is a list of champions in dozens of categories and countries, including some rather obscure information, followed by a list of driver deaths during the year, then highlights for Formula 1, followed by other categories. The Formula 1 highlights include drivers who attempted to race in Formula 1 for the first-time, first-time winners, winners for the last time, debuting makes and makes winning for the first time. Some readers might find the criteria for highlight inclusion confusing: how can the inauguration of a racetrack in a small Central American country or a race in Brunei be more important than even the smallest thing that happened in Formula 1? One of the main points of this book is providing a global view of racing: books with greater detail of every nook and cranny of Formula 1 are numbered in the hundreds, while works that mention racing in India and Costa Rica even in passing are very few, if any. So emphasis is placed on interesting, rather than so-called important information. Additionally, a lot of information is included in other sections. This book does not analyze the highly charged political climate of the decade.

1970

NSUs were a rare sight in racing in the 70s but this Ro80 driven by Paul Maes took place in the Marathon de La Route. (Photo by Paul Maes)

Champions
Formula 1 (Drivers): Jochen Rindt
Formula 1 (Manufacturers): Lotus
European Formula 2: Clay Regazzoni (Tecno)

British Formula 3: Carlos Pace (Forward Trust), Dave Walker (Lombank), Tony Trimmer (Shell)
French Formula 3: Jean-Pierre Jaussaud
Italian Formula 3: Giovanni Salvati
Swedish Formula 3: Torsten Palm
World Manufacturers Championship: Porsche
Can-Am: Denis Hulme
Interserie: Jurgen Neuhaus
European 2 Liter Championship: Chevron/Joakin Bonnier
USAC Indy Car: Al Unser
European Formula 5000: Peter Gethin
American Formula 5000: John Cannon
Tasman Cup: Graeme Lawrence
South African Formula 1: Dave Charlton
NASCAR: Bobby Isaac
European Touring Car Championship: Toine Hezemans
DARM: Dieter Hegels
British Saloon Car Championship: Bill McGovern, Sunbeam Imp
Australian Touring Car Championship: Norm Beechey
Australian Gold Star Championship: Leo Geoghegan
Australian Formula 2: Max Stewart
New Zealand Gold Star Championship: Graham McRae
New Zealand Saloon Car Championship: R. Dawson/R. Coppins
New Zealand National Formula NZ: Ken Smith
Argentinian Formula 1: Emilio Bertolini
Argentinian Formula 2: Osvaldo Bessia
Argentinian Formula 4: Juan Laskac
Argentinian Turismo de Carretera: Luis di Palma (A), Eduardo Copello (B)
Argentinian Prototypes: Nestor Garcia-Veiga
Trans-Am: Parnelli Jones
Canadian Formula A/B: Eppie Wietzes
Mexican Modified Touring Cars: Memo Rojas, Sr.
European Hill Climb Championship: Johannes Ortner
Spanish Championship: Jorge Babler
Swedish Touring Cars: Bengt Ekberg
Danish Touring Cars: Arne Hojgaard/Jens Ingvorsen
Belgian Championship: Alain Dex
Dutch Touring Car Championship: Han Akersloot
Dutch Formula Ford: Huub Vermeulen
Austrian Championship: Karl Wendlinger
French Formula Renault: Francois Lacarrau
European Formula Ford: Claude Bourgoignie
European Formula Vee: Erich Breinberg
Portuguese Formula Ford: Ernesto Neves
Portuguese Formula Vee: Ernesto Neves
Portuguese GT and Sports: Carlos Teixeira dos Santos
Portuguese Touring Cars: "Dino"
Portuguese Special Touring Cars: Ernesto Neves
Formule Bleue (Citroen): Alain Couderc
Coupe Gordini: Bernard Mange
Porsche Cup: Gijs Van Lennep
SCCA Formula A – Dave Heinz, Lola-Chevrolet
SCCA Formula B – Skip Barber, Tecno
SCCA Formula C – Michael Rand, Brabham

SCCA Formula Super Vee – Tom Davey, Zeitler
SCCA Formula Vee – Harry Ingle, Zink
SCCA Formula Ford – Skip Barber, Tecno
SCCA A Sports Racing – Jerry Hansen, Mclaren
SCCA B Sports Racing – Milt Minter, Porsche
SCCA C Sports Racing – Dan Carmichael, Lotus-Ford
SCCA D Sports Racing – Marvin Thompson, Bobsy-Imp
SCCA A Production – John Greenwood, Chevrolet Corvette
SCCA B Production – Alan Barker, Chevrolet Corvette
SCCA C Production – John Morton, Datsun
SCCA D Production – Jim Fitzgerald, Datsun
SCCA E Production – Don Devendorf, Triumph
SCCA F Production – John Kelly, Triumph
SCCA G Production - William Koch, MG
SCCA H Production – Dennis Daly, Austin Healey
SCCA A Sedan – Ron Woods, AMC Javelin
SCCA B Sedan – Vic Provenzano, Alfa Romeo
SCCA C Sedan – Ed Spreen, Mini Cooper
SCCA D Sedan – Craig Fisher, Fiat Abarth
USAC Sprint Cars – Larry Dickson
USAC Midgets – Jimmy Caruthers
Australian Formula Ford – Richard Knight
Swiss Hill Climbing Championship – Xavier Perrot
German Hill Climbing Championship – Walter Struckmann
East German Formula 3 – Klaus Peter Krause
British Formula Vee - Mike Hayselden
Moroccan Sports Cars – Albert Benchaya
Moroccan Formula 3 – Jacques Berenger
Morocccan Touring Cars – Robert Sibony
ARCA – Ramo Stott
Nascar Modifieds - Fred de Sarro
Rhodesian Formula Vee – Isaac Codron
Rhodesian Saloons – Ron Lubon
IMCA Sprint Car – Jerry Blundy
French Hillclimbing: Herve Bayard
British Hillclimbing: Sir Nicholas Williamson
South African Saloon Car – G. Mortimer
South African Formula Vee – S. Taylor
Formula F100 – Ray Allen
Scottish Supertox – Alan Nelson
Russian Formula Libre – Yuri Andreev
Italian Formula Ford – Biagio Cammarone

Driver fatalities during the year in racing incidents: Bruce McLaren, Jochen Rindt, Piers Courage, Hans Laine, Jerry Titus, Marcelo Campos, Tab Prince, Carlos Blanco, Andrade Villar, George Farmer, Herminio Cuesta, Tom Sulman, Billy Jack Casper, Hans Dieter Frohle, Glenys Freeman, Johnny Huskey, Klaus Klein, Gene Crittendon, Werner Baldrian, Stuart MacQuarrie, Sigi Lang, Jay Opperman, Rene-Pierre Fouquet, Martin Brain, Ingert Molin, Dick Brown, Andre Willem, Steve Backenkeller, Jim O'Rourke, Lorenzo Zini, Jean-Luc Salomon, Derrick Williams, Denis Dayan, Gene Lovelace, Gill Hess, Herbert Schultze, Alejandro Calafio, Robert Henn, James Hardmann, Donato Silveri, Glyn Scott, Dieter Hausmann, John Watts, Wayne Rohn, Chet Moody, John Hubbard, Alejandro Couto, Kiyoshi Akiyama, Minoru Kawai, Jackie Evans, Chris Summers, John Delbridge, Terry

Doiel, Miroslav Hruby, Russ Laursen, Jimmy Smith, Jimmy Whitson Jr., Ernie Purssel, Dale Prochazka, Jim Powell, Hector Roberto Manzotti

Formula 1:
- Drivers participating for the first time: **Emerson Fittipaldi, Clay Regazzoni, Ignazio Giunti, Ronnie Peterson, Francois Cevert(*), Reine Wisell, Gus Hutchinson, Peter Gethin, Tim Schenken, Rolf Stommelen(*), Peter Westbury(*), Alex Soler Roig, Hubert Hahne (*)**
- Drivers who won for the first time: **Emerson Fittipaldi, Clay Regazzoni**
- First win, manufacturers: **March**
- Drivers who won for the last time: **Jack Brabham, Jochen Rindt, Pedro Rodriguez**
- New manufacturers: **Tyrrell, March, Bellasi, Surtees**
- **March's** Formula 1 debut could not be sweeter. During qualifying in the South African Grand Prix, the top two on the grid were products of the debuting marque, **Stewart** getting pole, followed by **Chris Amon**. Unfortunately, during the race (and most of the season, except for **Stewart**'s win in Spain) **March**'s performance was mostly disappointing. Even so, **Stewart**'s and **Amon**'s scores allowed **March** to finish third in its initial championship.
- **Jochen Rindt** becomes the first and so far, only, posthumous Formula 1 champion. He only took part in 9 of the 13 events, winning 5. All his points came from winning.
- **Alfa Romeo** returns officially as an engine provider, equipping **McLaren**s for **Andrea de Adamich** and **Nanni Galli**.
- **Johnny Servoz-Gavin** unexpectedly quits F1, claiming eyesight issues
- After many years off, **De Tomaso** returns as a constructor. The company's car is run by **Williams**, to no great effect.
- **Hockenheim** is used for the first time as the venue of the German Grand Prix.
- **Oesterreichring** is used for the first time as the venue for the Austrian Grand Prix.
- Bad crowd control: the reported 200,000 fans that flocked to the **Mexico City** track are to blame for the event being removed from the calendar. The police was insufficient to keep matters in order and in spite of pleas from drivers like **Pedro Rodriguez** and **Jackie Stewart**, they remained unruly during the proceedings, too close to the track. Luckily, no one got hurt.
- **Jack Brabham** wins the first race of the season but remains competitive throughout the year. He loses both the Monaco and British GPs under freak conditions. He crashes on the last lap of the Monaco GP, after leading 52 laps. Then in England, with a 14-second gap to **Rindt**, he runs of fuel and is passed by the Austrian. **Jack** lost two races to **Rindt** in a single year, on the last lap! But he was almost handed the British GP win when the **Lotus** was temporarily disqualified for wing issues.
- The South African GP was the day of veterans. While **Brabham** won his last race, **Surtees** scored his last fastest lap.
- A German is back on the podium, after many years. **Rolf Stommelen**, driving a **Brabham** finishes third in Austria. That is his first – and last – podium.
- **Chris Amon** finally wins his first Formula 1 race, the 2-heat non-championship Daily Express race.

Other categories:
- Discussions by USA and FIA authorities to standardize racing's top categories (4-liter engines for F1, Indy Cars and Prototypes) collapse and categories do business as usual. The matter would be discussed a few other times during the decade.

- For the first time, a Finn driver reaches the top echelons of motor racing: **Leo Kinnunen** wins four World Manufacturers Championship rounds, partnering **Pedro Rodriguez** in the J&W Engineering **Porsches**.
- However, a Finn driver dies at Le Mans, **Hans Laine**.
- **Porsche** wins Le Mans for the first time (**Richard Attwood/Hans Hermann**) under atrocious weather. The German driver retires with immediate effect after the win.
- Argentina holds two early season long distance prototype races, in preparation for a possible return as a World Championship venue. The races are won by **De Adamich/Courage** (**Alfa Romeo**) (Buenos Aires 200 km) and **Beltoise/Pescarolo** (**Matra**) (Buenos Aires 1000 km).
- In the end of the year **Matra** also wins the 1000 km of Paris, with **Jack Brabham** (his last win) and **Jean-Pierre Beltoise**.
- First edition of the 24 Hours of **Nürburgring**, which becomes a classic. The winner, the young **Hans Joachin Stuck**, driving a **BMW** with **Clemens Schickentanz**.
- Several new cars are fielded in Can Am: **BRM, March, Ti-22** and **Shadow**. A **Chaparral** fan car impresses but is quickly outlawed. Additionally, a four-engined racer unsuccessfully attempts to race in the series, the Mac Special, in the hands of **Hiroshi Fushida**.
- The Interserie, which was supposed to be the European Can-Am, was run for the first time. The first champion was **Jurgen Neuhaus**.
- The European 2-Liter Prototype championship is held for the first time. It quickly becomes a **Lola, Chevron** and **Abarth** benefit.
- **Brian Redman** clinches the crown for **Chevron** by pulling a last lap move on **Lola's Jo Bonnier**.
- Dirt tracks are used for the last time in the USAC National Championship.
- Actor **Steve McQueen** finishes 2nd in the 12 Hours of Sebring, partnering **Peter Revson** in a Porsche. The winners are **Andretti/Vacarella/Giunti**, in a works **Ferrari** 512. This ends up being the sole 512 win in a world championship event, the expected 917/512 fight soon fizzling.
- A Grand Prix of Israel for F2 cars was scheduled late in the year and actually several European drivers were convinced to show up. It was cancelled in the last minute, as crowds could not be contained. A Formula Vee support race did take place, won by Swede **Bertil Roos**.
- The Israeli GP was not the only F2 race to bite the dust. Races in **Zandvoort, Magny-Cours, Reims** and **Helsinki** were also cancelled.
- **Jean-Pierre Beltoise** wins a race for a **Matra** engined **Matra** Formula 1 car for the first time, at the **Mont Dore** Hill Climb.
- **Al Unser** wins not only his first Indy 500 but also, his first USAC (Indy) championship. He wins on asphalt and dirt.
- Veteran **Lloyd Ruby** wins his last Indy race.
- **Jochen Rindt**, the Formula 2 king, wins the first European Formula 2 Championship race of the decade, at **Thruxton**. It turns out to be his last win in the championship but as compensation, he wins the Formula 1 title.
- **Dieter Quester** wins the **Macau** Grand Prix, in a Formula 2 **BMW**, the last race for the F-2 **BMW** works car. The race was far from the more organized affairs of latter years: mixed with the works Formula 2 car were sports cars (**Teddy Yip**'s **Porsche 906**), a GT **Chevrolet Corvette** and even a Formula Vee car.
- As for **Quester, March** announces at one point he would partner **Peterson** in F1 for **1971** but instead, there is a tie-up with **Alfa Romeo**, plus paying driver **Alex Soler-Roig**.

- Lady driver **Anne Wong**, from Singapore, wins the Touring car race in Macau, leaving many a male driver wondering what hit them. It was just the beginning of a great decade for female drivers in many areas of the world.
- The first racetrack is opened in Ecuador, **Yahuarcocha**. A car that came third in the first race, a **Reliant Scimitar**, was not well known for its competitive accomplishments elsewhere. It finished behind a **Ferrari** and a **Porsche**.
- British female driver **Patsy Burt** wins both the British Sprint and British Hill Climb championships.
- Argentine driver **Carlos Pairetti** fails to qualify for the Indy 500.
- A 4-3-4 grid configuration is used at the **Tulln Langenlebarn** Formula 2 race. Probably not the last time it is used, certainly so at the FIA Championship level. A 4-3-4 grid was used in the Silverstone Daily Express Mail trophy, for example, a non-championship Formula 1 event.
- **Jack Brabham** takes part in the same event, driving a **Brabham**, of course and finishes 13th. He is the only foreign driver in the race.
- No less than 16 chassis manufacturers have cars on the Indy 500 field: they are **Colt, Lola, Eagle, McNamara, Hawk, McLaren, Coyote, Brabham, Vollstedt, Cecil, Watson, Hayhoe, Scorpion, Gerhardt, Mongoose** and **King**.
- A special tribute event is held in honor of **Jack Brabham**'s retirement in **Brands Hatch**. Also included in the program is an all-**Brabham** car race, won by **Allistair Walker**.
- **David Piper** is injured in the shooting of the Le Mans movie, losing part of his right leg.
- Drivers in Central America begin seriously using small engine pickup trucks, such as **Toyotas** and **Datsuns**, in circuit racing. Thus we debunk the Wikipedia myth that NASCAR introduced pickup circuit racing in **1983**.
- An injunction that was brought upon the **Crystal Palace** circuit in **1953**, limiting substantially the number of meetings the track could hold a year, lapsed in **1970**. As a result, the circuit that normally held 3, 4 events a year, had a total of 17 meetings between **1970** and **1972**.
- Always seeking ways to increase attendance, organizers at **Crystal Palace** contact **Paul Newman** for an appearance at the track, tied to the release of the movie Winning. **Newman**, however, asks a whopping £25,000 to simply show up at the track. That was a huge amount of money way back when. Leads me to think how much these Hollywood types charge to show up in current Formula 1 races.
- **Colin Vandervell**, son of **Vanwall**'s former owner, wins 29 Formula Ford races driving the ex-**Emerson Fittipaldi's Merlyn**.
- The **South Dakota** track in Guyana is reopened in November **1970**. An international event is held, with drivers from Britain and many South American and Caribbean countries.
- **Jackie Stewart** wins the JAF Grand Prix in Japan, in a **Brabham** Formula 2 car. Among other foreign drivers competing are **Max Stewart, Graeme Lawrence, Leo Geoghegan**. **Kunimoi Nagamatsu** was the best placed Japanese, in 3rd.
- New Zealand's **Graeme Lawrence** wins the **1970** Tasman Cup, driving a 2.5 **Ferrari** Dino. For the first time, Formula 5000 cars race in the series.
- **VW-Porsches** 914/6 finished 1-2-3 in the 86-hour Marathon de la Route held at the **Nürburgring**. The winners were **Gerard Larrousse/Helmut Marko/Claude Haldi**. This race was known for appearances by unusual cars. Among the **1970** entry were a works **Rover** 3500, plus **Citroen** DS 21, **NSU** RO 80s and even a **Peugeot**, a make barely used in top European circuit events during the decade, although widely and successfully used in Argentina.

1971

Champions
Formula 1 (Drivers): Jackie Stewart
Formula 1 (Manufacturers): Tyrrell
European Formula 2: Ronnie Peterson
British Formula 3: Roger Williamson (Lombank), Dave Walker (ShellMotor)
French Formula 3: Patrick Depailler
Italian Formula 3: Giancarlo Naddeo
Swedish Formula 3: Torsten Palm
World Manufacturers Championship: Porsche
Can-Am: Peter Revson
Interserie: Leo Kinnunen
European 2 Liter Championship: Lola/Helmut Marko
USAC Indy Car: Joe Leonard
European Formula 5000: Frank Gardner

Jackie Stewart brightened up the Can Am driving this Lola. Photo by Rob Neuzel.

American Formula 5000: David Hobbs
Tasman Cup: Graham McRae
South African Formula 1: Dave Charlton
NASCAR: Richard Petty
European Touring Car Championship: Dieter Glemser
DARM: Jochen Mass
British Saloon Car Championship: Bill McGovern, Sunbeam Imp
Australian Touring Car Championship: Bob Jane
Australian Gold Star Championship: Max Stewart
Australian Formula 2: Henk Woelders
Fuji Grand Champion: Masa Sakai
New Zealand Gold Star Championship: Graeme Lawrence

New Zealand Saloon Car Championship: P. Fahey
Brazilian Formula Ford: Francisco Lameirao
Brazilian Touring Cars: Pedro Victor de Lamare
Brazilian Sports Cars: Lian Duarte
Argentinian Formula 1: Jorge Cupeiro
Argentinian Formula 2: Osvaldo Bessia
Argentinian Formula 4: Juan Laskac
Argentinian Turismo de Carretera: Luis di Palma
Argentinian Prototype: Luis di Palma
Trans-Am: Mark Donohue
IMSA Camel GTO: Dave Heinz GTU: Peter Gregg/Hurley Haywood
British Formula Atlantic: Vern Schuppan
Canadian Formula B: Jacques Couture
Mexican Modified Touring Cars: Memo Rojas, Sr.
European Formula Super-Vee: Erich Bramberg
US Formula Super-Vee: Bill Scott
European Hill Climb Championship: Johannes Ortner
Spanish Championship: Alex Soler-Roig
Formula 1430: Paco Josa
Swedish Touring Cars: Ake Andersson
Belgian Championship: Jean Claude Frank
Dutch Touring Car Championship: Han Akersloot/Fred Frankenhout
Austrian Championship: Karl Wendlinger
French Formula Renault: Michel Leclere
Estonian Formula 1: Madis Laiw
British Oxygen Formula Ford: Bernard Vermilio
Euro Trophy Formula Ford: Mo Harness
Danish Formula Ford: Jorgen Herlevsen
Danish Touring Cars: Jac Nelleman
Dutch Formula Ford: Huub Vermeulen
European Formula Vee: Bertil Roos
Portuguese Formula Ford: Ernesto Neves
Portuguese Formula Vee: Antonio Portela Morais
Portuguese GT and Sports: Carlos Teixeira dos Santos
Portuguese Touring cars: Jose Lampreia
Portuguese Special Touring: Francisco Santos
Greek Speed Championship: Johnny Pesmazoglu
Formule Bleue (Citroen): Herve Labedan
Coupe Gordini: Marc Sourd
Porsche Cup: Erwin Kremer
SCCA Formula A – Jerry Hansen, Lola
SCCA Formula B – Bob Lazier, March
SCCA Formula C – Harry Reynolds, Brabham
SCCA Formula Super Vee – Tom Davey, Lola
SCCA Formula Vee – Garrett van Camp, Lynk
SCCA Formula Ford – Jim Harrell, Titan
SCCA A Sports Racing - Jerry Hansen, Lola
SCCA B Sports Racing – Pete Harrison, Lola
SCCA C Sports Racing – Tom Evans, Alfa
SCCA D Sports Racing – Harry Stephenson, Maru Honda
SCCA A Production – John Greenwood, Chevrolet Corvette
SCCA B Production – Allan Barker, Chevrolet Corvette
SCCA C Production – John Morton, Datsun
SCCA D Production – Robert McQueen, Datsun

SCCA E Production – Logan Blackburn, MGB
SCCA F Production – Larry Campbell, Austin Healey
SCCA G Production – Marshall Meyer, Triumph
SCCA H Production – Randy Canfield, Austin Healey
SCCA A Sedan – Warren Tope, Mustang
SCCA B Sedan – Bob Sharp, Datsun
SCCA C Sedan – Dick Davenport, Alfa Romeo GTA
SCCA D Sedan – Chris Gross, Mini Cooper
USAC Sprint Cars – Gary Bettenhausen
USAC Midgets – Danny Caruthers
USAC Silver Crown – George Snider
Euro Formula Vee – Bertil Roos
Australian Formula Ford – Larry Perkins
Swiss Hill Climbing Championship – Xavier Perrot
German Hill Climbing Championship – Dieter Kern
Danish Formula Ford 1600 – Jorgen Herlevsen
British Formula Vee - Brian Henton
Chilean Turismo de Carretera – Eduardo Kovacs and Boris Garifulic
Costa Rican Championship – Jacinto Xirinachs
ARCA – Ramo Stott
NASCAR Modifieds – Jerry Cook
Moroccan Formula 3 – Jacques Berenger
Moroccan Championship – Albert Benchaya
Rhodesian Formula Vee – Chris Wray Forshan
IMCA Sprint Car – Jerry Blundy
French Hillclimbing: Jimmy Mieusset
British Hillclimbing: David Hepworth
South African Formula Vee – G. Van Straaten
South African Formula Ford – R. Sterne
Formula F100 – Tom Pryce
Scottish Supertox – Malcom Paterson
Russian Formula Libre – Madis Laiv
Canadian Formula Ford – David Loring.

Driver fatalities during the year in racing incidents: Ignazio Giunti, Jo Siffert, Pedro Rodriguez, Giovanni Salvati, Antonio Verna, "Sneaky Pete" Robinson, Herb Spivey, James McDowell, John Wratten, Luis Montelparo, Mel Andrus, Harold Fryar, Fulvio Tandoi, Heber Pond, Bill Tennill, Leigh Gaydos, Ken Holden, Brian Tarrant, Ants Vaino, Clay Hayward, Kauko Eriksson, Jerry May, Fred Hadley, Jack Thomas, Stephen Wooley, Joe Messner, Stan Burnett, Alvin Gatlin, Raymond Mathay, Krzysztof Krajewski, Jack Belk, Link Toland, David Pearl, Drexel White, Jim Humphries, Duane Bonini, Gary Witter, Larry Dolphin, Klaus Reich, Dickie Harrell, Peter Hawtin, Wayne Kelly, Humberto Mataresse, Graham Coaker, Nolan Johncock, Mavros, Pablo Horyaans, Jim Cox, Gene Thomas, Ron Sheldon, Danny Caruthers, Willy Bendeck, David Ma, Geno Redd

FORMULA 1
- Drivers participating for the first time: **Niki Lauda, Helmut Marko, Gijs Van Lennep, Jean Max, Jean Pierre Jarier, Howden Ganley, Mark Donohue, Skip Barber, Sam Posey, Mike Beutler, John Cannon, Chris Craft, Francois Mazet, Dave Walker**
- Drivers who won for the first time: **Mario Andretti, Peter Gethin, Francois Cevert**
- First win, manufacturers: **Tyrrell**

- Drivers who won for the last time: **Francois Cevert, Joseph Siffert**
- New manufacturers: None
- A turbine car (**Lotus 56B**) takes part in the Formula 1 championship for the first time. It does not impress. The car also races in the **Hockenheim** Formula 5000 race, finishing second (**Emerson Fittipaldi**).
- **Bernie Ecclestone** buys the **Brabham** team from **Ron Tauranac,** allegedly for £100,000.
- **Paul Ricard** is used for the first time as a F1 venue (French GP). Purists loathe the place.
- **Spa-Francorchamps** is ordered to make some renovations or else. The track, a driver favorite, had some safety issues, so the powers that be demanded an overhaul. As there were some questions about the use of **Zolder** in **1972**, for some time **Oulton Park** was being considered as a venue for the Belgian Grand Prix! In the end, **Nivelles** was used in **1972**, so there was no need to relocate thousands of Belgians for a weekend…
- **Goodyear** introduces the slick racing tire in the category.
- The gap between first and fifth (**Howden Ganley**) in the Italian Grand Prix was only 0.89 sec. The winner, **Peter Gethin**, who started 11th, led merely 3 laps but the right ones. This was the fastest F1 race until the 2003 Italian GP and the last Monza epic slipstreaming battle. The fastest lap earner was also unique: **Henri Pescarolo,** in a Frank Williams **March,** 1m23.8sec.
- BRM loses its top two drivers in the course of the year: **Pedro Rodriguez** dies in an Interserie race at **Norisring**, while **Jo Siffert** dies some twenty minutes into the season ending Victory Race at **Brands Hatch**.
- **Mark Donohue** takes a **Penske** entered **McLaren** to third place in his first Formula 1 race in Canada. He does not start the US GP, choosing instead to race at a USAC event in **Trenton**.
- **Jean Max** or **Max Jean**? Known by both names, the right name was actually **Jean Max**. Having previously driven a **Matra-Simca** in private tests, **Jean Max** gets a shot at F-1 in the French Grand Prix, driving **Jo Siffert**'s **March** 701. Another Frenchman, **Francois Mazet**, also gets his shot in the same race, also driving a **March** 701 (Williams). Both cars were red and the two Gallic drivers started in the last row. Neither had a future in Formula 1.
- **Ronnie Peterson** is runner-up in Formula 1 without winning a single Grand Prix.
- **Chris Amon** wins his second Formula 1 race, also a 2-heat race, in Argentina.

Other Categories
- **Emerson Fittipaldi** was slated to drive an **Alfa Romeo** in the **Buenos Aires** round of the World Manufacturers Championship, with **Toine Hezemans**. The car had an accident in practice and **Emerson** ended up racing with **Carlos Reutemann** in a second-string **Porsche** 917. This was Emerson's only appearance in the championship.
- **Pedro Rodriguez** wins in his very last appearance in the World Manufacturers Championship, arguably his best performance. Having lost 3 laps in the pits, **Pedro** drove at Grand Prix speeds until getting very close to leader **Regazzon**i in a **Ferrari**. The Maranello car retires and **Rodriguez/Attwood** win, the last 917 victory in World Championship racing. **Pedro** drove 157 of 170 laps.
- No less than 33 of the 49 cars that raced at the 24 Hours of **Le Mans** were **Porsche**s. Although 25 model 917s had been manufactured, only 7 of the 33 were 917s in this race. A large number of 911s raced (18), plus four 908s, two 914/6, one 907 and one 910. On the downside, the last eight rows of the grid were all **Porsche**.
- As for finishing cars, all but one – **Ligier/Depailler**'s **Ligier** prototype, was neither **Porsche** or **Ferrari**.

- A **Ferrari** 365/GTB (Daytona) finished 5th and should have won the GT class, except that insufficient numbers had been built yet for homologation purposes. The model would win the GT class in the next three editions, though.
- There were more **Ferrari**s 512 (nine) than **Porsche** 917 (seven) in the race.
- USAC held two early season races in the **Rafaela** oval, in Argentina, both won by **Al Unser**. USAC (or CART) never returned to Argentina.
- **Al Unser** wins the Indy 500 again and also the most Indy races. However, **Joe Leonard** takes the championship, winning a single race.
- Last traditional NASCAR season, comprising a number of events in low-key tracks, including grassroots, dirt tracks, numbering as many as 50. NASCAR would change to a slicker profile in **1972**, at first, 30 races a year.
- **Brian Redman** retires from racing early on the year, moving to South Africa to take a salesman job, then returns. An accident at the **Targa Florio** sidelines him for part of the season. However, he leaves retirement for latter years.
- A **Mercedes-Benz** prepared by AMG finishes second in the 24 Hours of **Spa** (**Schickentanz/Heyer**). The car also races at **Paul Ricard**.
- For the last time a current Formula 1 driver wins an European Hill Climb championship round, **Francois Cevert** at **Ollon Villars**.
- **Peter Revson** becomes the first American to win the Can-Am title.
- A team of 4 Belgians drive Russian **Moskvich**s in the 24 Hours of **Spa**. The best finishes 16th.
- Foreigners in NASCAR: **Vic Elford, Jackie Oliver** and **Rolf Stommelen** tried the big-banger category in this season. **Stommelen** was up to 6th in **Talladega**. Oliver would do another 7 races in **1972**.
- The Greek government prohibits street racing, in the wake of death of driver **Mavros**, in **Rhodes**.
- American drivers **Tony Adamowicz** and **Gregg Young** win the 12 Hours Marlboro race in Ecuador, in a **Ferrari** 512. A mixed batch of local, regional drivers and a few others from Australia and the USA race in the event, which became a classic in Ecuador, also known as 12 Hours **Yahuarcocha**.
- Perhaps motivated by Argentina and Brazil, who were increasingly inserting themselves in the International calendar, two Formula 2 races are run in Colombia. One was won by **Jo Siffert**, in a **Chevron**, called Colombian Grand Prix. The other was called Bogota Grand Prix and it was won by **Allan Rollinson**, in a **Brabham**. Although well supported, the concept did not take hold and no further editions took place. These races were held at an altitude of 2440 meters (or 8,000 feet), the highest at the time for a single-seater race event.
- Some people never learn. The failed Grand Prix of Israel for Formula 2 was on the calendar a second time. This time, it was only on the calendar...
- **Derek Bell** wins his first World Sports car race, at **Buenos Aires**, partnering **Jo Siffert**. Although he would still try odd single-seater rides, from this point on it is clear his future lies in sports cars.
- Spain debuts its own entry level category, Formula 1430, also known as Formula **SEAT**.
- **Volkswagen**-supported Formula Super Vee debuts in Europe and it soon spreads to other areas of the world. The category was notable in grooming two future world champions, **Keke Rosberg** and **Nelson Piquet**.
- Formula Atlantic debuts in **Brands Hatch**. The winner of the first race is **Vern Schuppan**, driving a **Palliser**.
- **Vic Elford** writes a letter to a British motoring publication (which publishes it) venting-off his frustration for being unable to find a steady Formula 1 ride. He claims that all teams he spoke to demanded he bring sponsorship do get the ride. Sounds familiar?

- On the same subject, **Niki Lauda** famously gets a US$100,000 loan to get a place in the **March** Formula 1 team for **1972**.
- After a two-year hiatus, the Six Hours of Peru is held again. A **Lotus Elan** wins the race, driven by **Francisco Schettini-Kike Perez**. During the decade, the race is run in five different venues, **Collique, Agua Dulce, Santa Rose, Campo de Marte** and **Pasamayo**.
- **Bushy Park** track is inaugurated in Barbados.
- A number of star drivers are lured by excellent prize money to take part in the ETCC round in Paul Ricard: **John Surtees, Jacky Ickx** and **Graham Hill**.
- One-make **Ford** Escort Mexico series begins in England. In addition to the race for Escorts, races are held for "all-comers" (cars of different brands). A **Rolls-Royce** Silver Shadow takes part in one such race.
- **Enzo Osella** buys out **Abarth**'s race car operations.
- **Dave Walker** wins 25 heats and finals in Formula 3. His Formula 1 debut is disastrous, however.
- **Mo Nunn's Ensign** debuts as a constructor. The 2-person firm offers an innovative Formula 3 design, with side radiators and a chassis partly monocoque, partly space frame.
- **March**, on the other hand, offers both a monocoque and a space frame version of its cars.
- A 2-liter **Chevrolet** Vega engine prepared by Cosworth is offered for the first time. It is not successful.
- **Shadow** uses lead free fuel in racing for the first time, at the Can Am race in **St. Jovite**.
- A year of ends: the end of the 5-liter regulations in the World Manufacturers Championship and the end of 1.6-liter regulations in Formula 2. The former was to adopt a 3-liter maximum engine size as of **1972**, the latter, 2-liter.
- The last two rounds of the European Formula 2 championship were run at the same track, **Vallelunga**, one week apart. Many of the top drivers, including champion **Peterson** and **Cevert**, skipped the last round.
- **Cevert** actually looked the early season favorite for the F2 title in his **Tecno**. By the 5th round he had amassed 22 points. However, from then on, he did not score again and ended up fifth in the championship.
- The last edition of the Marathon de la Route, by then a 96-hour race, was held at the **Nürburgring**. There were only 39 starters this time around and the winners were **Jacques Henry/Jean-Luc Therier** and **Maurice Nusbaumer**, in an **Alpine-Renault**.
- The French had a great fascination with the **Chrysler Hemicudas**. In fact, one sees many of these cars featured in hill climbs and any other events they could fit in. **Chrysler** France went as far as maintaining a works team of drivers for these cars. Unfortunately the Automobile Club D'Ouest did not share such enthusiasm and attempts to enter these cars at Le Mans were always rejected.
- Just how professional were drivers in the 70s? **Bill McGovern**, winner of the British Saloon Car Championship in a **Sunbeam** Imp, was actually a used furniture salesman.

1972

Mark Donohue won the Indy 500. Most important, this was Penske's first win in the American classic. Photo by Rob Neuzel.

Champions
Formula 1 (Drivers): Emerson Fittipaldi
Formula 1 (Manufacturers): Lotus
European Formula 2: Mike Hailwood
British F2: Niki Lauda
British Formula 3: Roger Williamson (Forward Trust), Rikky Von Opel (Lombard), Roger Williamson (ShellSport)
French Formula 3: Michel Leclere
Italian Formula 3: Vittorio Brambilla
Swedish Formula 3: Conny Andersson
World Manufacturers Championship: Ferrari
Can-Am: George Follmer
Interserie: Leo Kinnunen
European 2 Liter Championship: Abarth/Arturo Merzario
USAC Indy Car: Joe Leonard
European Formula 5000: Gijs Van Lennep
American Formula 5000: Graham McRae
Tasman Cup: Graham McRae
South African Formula 1: Dave Charlton
NASCAR: Richard Petty
European Touring Car Championship: Jochen Mass

British Saloon Car Championship: Bill McGovern, Sunbeam Imp
DRM: Hans J. Stuck
DARM: Helmut Rosser
European GT Championship: John Fitzpatrick
Australian Touring Car Championship: Bob Jane
Australian Gold Star Championship: Frank Matich
Australian Formula 2: Larry Perkins
Fuji Grand Champion: Hiroshi Fushida
New Zealand Gold Star Championship: David Oxton
New Zealand Saloon Car Championship: R. Collingwood
Brazilian Formula Ford: Clovis de Moraes
Brazilian Sports Cars: Luiz Pereira Bueno
Brazilian Touring Cars: Pedro Victor de Lamare (C), J.Pedro Chateaubriand (B), Leonel Friedrich (A)
Argentinian Formula 1: Angel Monguzzi
Argentinian Prototypes: Luis di Palma
Argentinian Formula 2: Osvaldo Lopez
Argentinian Formula 4: Carlos Jarque
Argentinian Turismo de Carretera: Hector Gradassi
Trans-Am: George Follmer
IMSA Camel GTO: Peter Gregg GTU: Hurley Haywood
British Formula Atlantic: Bill Gubelmann
Canadian Formula B: Bill Robertson
Mexican GT Championship: Memo Rojas, Sr.
European Formula Super-Vee: Manfred Schurti
US Formula Super-Vee: Bill Scott
European Hill Climb Championship: Xavier Perrot
French Formula Renault: Jacques Laffite
Spanish Championship: Alex Soler-Roig
Formula 1430: Salvador Canellas
Swedish Touring Cars: Bengt Ekberg
Belgian Championship: Claude Bourgoignie
Dutch Touring Car Championship: Han Akersloot/Huub Vermeulen
Austrian Championship: Karl Wendlinger
European Formula Renault: Alain Cudini
Dutch Formula Ford: Roelof Wunderink
European Formula Vee: Tommy Brorsson
BARC Formula Ford: Syd Fox
BRSCC Formula Ford: Ian Taylor
Formula Italia: Giorgio Francia
BARC Saloon Car Championship: Tony Lanfranchi
BRSCC/BRDC/MCD Saloon Car Championship: Tony Lanfranchi
Portuguese Formula Ford: Ernesto Neves
Portuguese Formula Vee: Miguel de Lacerda
Portuguese GT and Sports: Americo Nunes
Portuguese Touring: Ernesto Neves
Portuguese Special touring: Mario Goncalves
Formule Bleue (Citroen): Philipe Bochet
Coupe Gordini: Rene Metge
Porsche Cup: John Fitzpatrick
SCCA Formula A - Jerry Hansen, Lola
SCCA Formula B – Chuck Sarich, March
SCCA Formula C – Harry Reynolds, Brabham
SCCA Formula Super Vee – Bob Wheelock, Lola

SCCA Formula Vee – Dave Weitzenhof, Autodynamics
SCCA Formula Ford – Eddie Miller, Hawke
SCCA A Sports Racing - Jerry Hansen, Lola
SCCA B Sports Racing – Pete Harrison, Lola
SCCA C Sports Racing - Bill Holbrook, Royale
SCCA D Sports Racing – Harry Stephenson, Maru Honda
SCCA A Production – Jerry Hansen, Chevrolet Corvette
SCCA B Production – Allan Barker, Chevrolet Corvette
SCCA C Production – Bob Sharp, Datsun
SCCA D Production – Robert McQueen, Datsun
SCCA E Production – Logan Blackburn, MG
SCCA F Production – Jon Woodner, MG
SCCA G Production – Rick Cline, Triumph
SCCA H Production - Randy Canfield, Austin Healey
SCCA A Sedan – Warren Agor, Chevrolet Camaro
SCCA B Sedan – Bob Sharp, Datsun
SCCA C Sedan – William Fox, Mini Cooper
USAC Sprint Cars – Sam Sessions
USAC Midgets – Pancho Carter
USAC Silver Crown – A.J. Foyt
Australian Formula Ford – Bob Skelton
Swiss Hill Climbing Championship – Xavier Perrot
German Formula Vee – Thomas Morstein-Marx
German Formula Super Vee – Helmut Bross
German Hill Climbing Championship – Karl Ludwig-Weiss
Danish Formula Ford 1600 – Dan Schilling
British Formula Vee - Graham Meek
Yugoslavian Championship – Sead Ali Hodzic
Chilean Formula 4 – Jose Manuel Salinas
Chilean Turismo de Carretera – Eduardo Kovacs and Luis Gimeno
Ecuadoran Champion – Fernando Madera
ARCA – Ron Hutcherson
Nascar Modifieds – Jerry Cook
Rhodesian Formula Vee – Chris Higson-Smith
Rhodesian Sports Car – John Aum
IMCA Sprint Car – Ray Lee Goodwin
French Hillclimbing: Jimmy Mieusset
British Hillclimbing: Sir Nicholas Williamson
South African Formula Vee – P. Haller
South African Formula Ford – R. Sterne
Scottish Supertox – Malcom Paterson
Uruguayan Formula Vee – Giulio Bertini
Luxembourg Championship – Nicholas Koob
Russian Formula Libre – Yuri Terenetski

Driver fatalities during the year in racing incidents: Joakin Bonnier, Jim Malloy, Ivo Grauls, "Noris", Kostas Pateras, Bryan Faloon, Friday Hassler, Bruce Helfert, Speedy Thompson, Lionel Chan, A. de Jong, Jon Giardina, Bert Hawthorne, Hengkie Iriawan, Bobby Hunley, Bill Hedley-Mathews, Rich Knepler, Rodolfo Mariani, Bobby Brown, Luigi Rinaldi, Michael Tucker, Clark Reefer, Hector Justiniano, Jack Smith, Kenny Dierking, Mike Hill, Don Jackson, Sonny Kirkland, Kelly Layne, John Stout, Manny Xuereb, David Chitwood, John Gott, Ralph A. Miller, Joe Allocco, Dave Stockslager, Louis Wusterhausen, Roger Clark, Brian Ferreira, Shui Fat Chan

This is what remained of Shui Fat Chan's Mini Cooper at Macau, resulting in the driver's death. Photo by Jose Santos

FORMULA 1
- Drivers participating for first time: **Jody Scheckter, Carlos Reutemann, Arturo Merzario, Jose Carlos Pace, Wilson Fittipaldi Jr., Francois Migault, Vern Schuppan, Patrick Depailler**
- Drivers who win for the first time: **Jean-Pierre Beltoise**
- First win, manufacturers: (none)
- Drivers who won for the last time: **Jean-Pierre Beltoise, Jacky Ickx**
- New manufacturers: **Connew, Politoys, Tecno, Eifelland (March)**
- Last **BRM** win in a world championship race (**Monaco**)
- **Matra-Simca** decides to leave Formula 1 on the same day it almost wins the French Grand Prix. The firm reckons it has a better chance of success with its prototype program and cannot afford both at the same time.
- First black car in Formula 1 (**JPS Lotus**)
- The world champion's regular teammate (**Dave Walker**) fails to score a single point for the first time.
- Lotus actually called back **Reine Wisell** for the Canadian Grand Prix who raced instead of the underperforming **Walker**. Then the team runs both **Wisell** and **Walker** in the US. However, the last two races of the **1972** season were disastrous for the champion team: not a single point earned from five entries.
- The **McLarens** qualify one-two in Canada but **Ronnie Peterson** leads away in the **March**, the car's only truly competitive race of **1972**. However, it ends up being disqualified and the race is won by **Stewart**.
- **Carlos Reutemann** scores pole in his World Championship debut.
- GP of Argentina back on the calendar for the first time since **1960**.
- **Clermont-Ferrand** is used for the last time as a F1 venue. Rocks around the track cause many punctures, including on leading driver **Chris Amon's** car, the driver and marque leading a F1 race for the last time. A rock hits **Helmut Marko** in the eye, blinding him – **Marko** was doing by far his best F1 race.
- **Nivelles** is used for the first time as a F1 venue. It was considered a very bland and boring track and would not survive the decade.
- For the second year running, **Lotus** is entered under a different name in Italy, where **Emerson Fittipaldi** clinched the title. World Wide Racing entered the single **Lotus** entry for fear of repercussions of the Italian investigation on **Jochen Rindt**'s death in **1970**.

- **Tecno** driver **Nanni Galli** gets a rare chance at **Ferrari**, deputizing for **Regazzoni** in France but does not do well. Then **Merzario** gets a chance in England and scores a point from 6th.
- **Tecno** actually got a podium in **1972**…in the 7-car Formula 1 race at **Vallelunga**, where **Nanni Galli** came in third. Only four cars finished.
- **Jackie Stewart** does not race at Belgium because of an ulcer and **Tyrrell** runs a single car for **Cevert**, who finishes second.
- **Surtees** does a **BRM** number and enters four cars in the Italian Grand Prix, including one for **John** himself, his last Grand Prix. Amazingly, the event turns out well and **Hailwood** scores **Surtees**' best result ever, second a little over 13 seconds behind winner **Fittipaldi**.
- Usually teams used previous year's models until getting the upgraded one ready. In **1972**, some teams used multiple models and specifications during the course of the year. **BRM** used the P160, P160B and P160C, in addition to previous model P153 and newer model P180. The **March** works team used the 721, 721X and 721G, plus customers Williams and Barber used the 711. **Brabham**, on the other hand, used the BT33, BT34 and BT37 during the season.
- The last two **Emerson Fittipaldi** wins in **1972** were earned in the spare car, the R5. In Austria the race car, R7, was reported undriveable. Then the truck bringing the race car to Italy had an accident and the R7 chassis destroyed. **Lotus** had no option but to race the R5.
- **David Charlton** brings his Lucky Strike **Lotus** to race in Europe but finds it much tougher than the more sedate pace of South African Formula 1

Other categories:
- **Graham Hill** wins the 24 Hours of Le Mans and thus becomes the first and thus far only driver to win the F1 Championship, the Indy 500 and Le Mans.
- **Matra-Simca** wins its first of three **Le Mans**, with **Pescarolo/Hill** finishing ahead of **Cevert/Ganley**.
- A **Mercedes-Benz** car is entered under the name of the works at Le Mans for **Schickentanz/Heyer**. It never shows up.
- A rare Polish driver almost makes the Le Mans race that year. **J. D. Jakubowski's** car, a **Taydec** Ford, actually qualified but did not start.
- This was **Alfa Romeo**'s last official participation at Le Mans. One of the Milanese cars finishes fourth, driven by **Andrea de Adamich** and **Nino Vacarella**.
- In the Targa Florio, a single **Ferrari** driven by **Arturo Merzario** and rallyman **Sandro Munari** beats 4 **Alfa Romeos**. **Arturo** drove 8 of 11 grueling laps.
- **Ferrari** wins all races of the World Manufacturers Championship, except **Le Mans**. **Jacky Ickx** and **Mario Andretti** are the main winners.
- Rather than a 24-hour race, **Daytona** runs a 6-hour race this year.
- **Jim Hurtubise** manages to qualify a front-engined Indycar for a race for the last time, in **Michigan**, ending 22nd. He tried to qualify front-engined **Mallards** at the Indy 500 a few more times, as late as **1981**, without any success.
- **Mark Donohue** wins the Indy 500, the first **Penske** team win in the famous race. Another Penske driver, **Gary Bettenhausen**, led the most laps. **Penske** would eventually become the winningest Indy Car (and Indy 500 team), often building its own cars. In **1972** they raced a **McLaren**, also the first time this British manufacturer won at Indy.
- The last 1000 km of Paris is held for many a year and far from Paris, at **Rouen-les-Essarts**. The winners are Frenchmen **Jean-Pierre Beltoise** and **Gerard Larrousse** driving an Ecurie Bonnier **Lola-Cosworth**.
- The **Chimay** race in Belgium is run for the last time. A F3 event in the latest guise, it is won by **David Purley**.
- A rare appearance in the ETCC: an **AMC Javelin** races at the **Silverstone** round.

- New Zealander **Graham McRae** wins a large number of F5000 races in Europe, US and Tasman Cup. He wins the latter two titles and finishes 3rd in the European Championship.
- With a £50,000 purse, the 50,000 Rothmans in **Brands Hatch** is called the richest racing event ever in Europe. In the end, it did not turn out too well. Expected specials, Indy and Can-Am cars never show up, so the top cars are a few Formula 1s. It is not a success with the public as well, only 21,000 people showed up. **Emerson Fittipaldi** wins it.
- **Maurice Philippe** designs win both the Formula Championship (**Lotus**) and USAC Championship Trail (**Parnelli**)
- Pilipino **Dante Silverio** beats highly rated **Allan Moffat** in the Greenhills Grand Prix in the Philippines. About 10,000 people watched the touring car race. **Silverio** was driving a Toyota.
- The final race Formula 2 race is held at **Crystal Palace**, a track located within London's city limits. A popular venue, about £250,000 would be required to bring the track up to more modern safety standards, money the management did not have. The winner was **Jody Scheckter**, in a **McLaren**.
- The king of impossible wins, **Peter Gethin**, wins the Pau Formula 2 race with a gap of 0.9 seconds, after one hour and a half. This time, **Patrick Depailler** was his victim.
- Inauguration of the **Estoril** racetrack in Portugal, the country's actual first track. **Carlos Gaspar** wins the inaugural race, driving a **Lola**.
- **Tony Lanfranchi** wins lots of races in his class and both BARC and BRSCC Saloon Car Championships, in a Russian **Moskvich** 412 in England's BARC Production Car Championship and continues to win in **1973**. He car ran in Class D, for cars costing up to £ 600. The first Russian car conquests outside of the Iron Curtain.
- Drivers from the Dominican Republic compete in their own cars out of the country for the first time. Drivers **Horacio Alvarez** (**Toyota**) and **Rafael Aguayo (Super Deserter**) were invited to race in Jamaica's **Vernan Field**. They win their respective races, too.
- A **Rolls-Royce**-engined single seater??? Not quite, the **Kitchiner** K8 was supposed to have a **Rolls-Royce** engine for the season but the unusual arrangement never came to fruition. The driver was to be **Gordon Spice**.
- **Hans Heyer** takes part in the 24 Hours of **Nürburgring** driving a **Mercedes** 300 SEL 6.8. He retired.

1973

Champions
Formula 1 (Drivers): Jackie Stewart
Formula 1 (Manufacturers): Lotus
European Formula 2: Jean-Pierre Jarier
British Formula 3: Ian Taylor (Forward Trust), Tony Brise (Lombard), Tony Brise (John Player)
French Formula 3: Jacques Laffite
Italian Formula 3: Carlo Giorgio
Swedish Formula 3: Hakan Dahlqvist
World Manufacturers Championship: Matra-Simca
Can-Am: Mark Donohue
Interserie: Leo Kinnunen
European 2 Liter Championship: Lola/Chris Craft

USAC Indy Car: Roger McCluskey
European Formula 5000: Teddy Pilette
American Formula 5000: Jody Scheckter
Tasman Cup: Graham McRae
South African Formula 1: Dave Charlton
NASCAR: Bennie Parsons
European Touring Car Championship: Toine Hezemans
British Saloon Car Championship: Frank Gardner, Camaro
DRM: Dieter Glemser
DARM: Peter Brand
Australian Touring Car Championship: Alan Moffat

Shadow's racing debut in Formula 1, South Africa. Follmer's car finished 6th. Photo by Russell Whitworth.

Australian Gold Star Championship: John McCormack
Australian Formula 2: Leo Geoghegan
New Zealand Gold Star Championship: David Oxton
New Zealand Saloon Car Championship: R. Coppins
European GT Championship: Clemens Schickentanz, Claude Ballot-Lena
Brazilian Formula Ford: Alex Ribeiro
Brazilian Touring Cars: Pedro Victor de Lamare (C), Ingo Hoffmann (A)
Brazilian Prototypes: Antonio Carlos Avallone (B), Mauricio Chulam (A)
Argentinian Formula 1: Nestor Garcia Veiga
Argentinian Formula 2: Carlos Jarque
Argentinian Formula 4: Jorge de Amorrortu
Argentinian Turismo de Carretera: Nasif Estefano
Trans-Am: Peter Gregg
IMSA Camel GTO: Peter Gregg GTU: Bob Bergstrom
Japanese Formula 2: Motoharu Kurosawa
Fuji Grand Champion: Noritake Takahara
British Formula Atlantic: Colin Vandervell (Yellow Pages), John Nicholson (BP)
Canadian Formula B: Bill Brack
European Formula Super-Vee: Helmut Koinigg
US Formula Super-Vee: Bertil Roos
US Formula Ford 1600: Bob Earl
European Hill Climb Championship: Robert Jimmy Mieusset
Spanish Championship: Jorge de Bagration
Formula 1430: Juan Villacieros

Coupe Simca-Shell: Max Mamers
Swedish Touring Cars: Boo Brasta
Belgian Championship: Rene Tricot
Dutch Touring Car Championship: Han Akersloot/Fred Frankenhout
Dutch Formula Ford: Roelof Wunderink
Austrian Championship: Sepp Manhalter
German Formula Ford: Tibor Meray
Danish Volvo 142 Cup: Poul Erik Jensen
European Formula Renault: Rene Arnoux
Polish Championship: Aleksander Oczkowski
Estonian Championship Formula 2: Peep Laansoo
Finnish Formula Vee Championship: Keke Rosberg
Scandinavian Formula Vee Championship: Keke Rosberg
European Formula Vee Championship: Keke Rosberg
BARC Formula Ford: Ted Wentz
BRSCC Formula Ford: Donald McLeod
Formula Italia: Giancarlo Martini
BARC Saloon Car Championship: Ivan Dutton
BRSCC/BRDC/MCD Saloon Car Championship: Ivan Dutton
Portuguese Hill Climb Touring: Bernardo Sa Nogueira
Portuguese Hill Climb Special Touring: Francisco Manuel Baptista Filho
Portuguese GT and Sports: Carlos Gaspar
Portuguese Touring: Bernardo Sa Nogueira
Portuguese Special Touring: Bernardo Sa Nogueira
Formule Bleue (Citroen): Jean-Pierre Maillard
Coupe Gordini: Jean-Pierre Gabreau
Porsche Cup: Clemens Schickentanz
SCCA Formula A - Jerry Hansen, Lola
SCCA Formula B – Ken Dusclos, Brabham
SCCA Formula C – Nichael Gilbert, Brabham
SCCA Formula Super Vee – Harry Ingle, Zink
SCCA Formula Vee – Rollin Butler, Zink
SCCA Formula Ford – Bob Earl, ADF
SCCA A Sports Racing – Bob Nagel, Lola
SCCA B Sports Racing - Jerry Hansen, Lola
SCCA C Sports Racing – Erick Keerman, Arachnid
SCCA D Sports Racing – Ronald Dennis, Ocelot Suzuki
SCCA A Production – Sam Feinstein, Shelby Cobra
SCCA B Production – Bill Jobe, Chevrolet Corvette
SCCA C Production – Bob Sharp, Datsun
SCCA D Production – Lee Mueller, Jensen Healey
SCCA E Production – Brian Fuerstenau, Triumph
SCCA F Production – John Kelly, Triumph
SCCA G Production – Rick Cline, Triumph
SCCA H Production – Mike Dale, Austin Healey
SCCA A Sedan – Carl Shafer, Chevrolet Camaro
SCCA B Sedan – Dave Frellsen, Datsun
SCCA C Sedan – Don Devendorf, Datsun
USAC Sprint Cars – Rollie Beale
USAC Midgets – Larry Rice
USAC Silver Crown – Al Unser Sr.
USAC Stock Cars – Butch Hartman
Australian Formula Ford – John Leffler
Swiss Hill Climbing Championship – Fred Amweg

German Formula Vee – Walter Loffelsender
German Formula Super Vee – Manfred Trint
German Hill Climbing Championship – Wilfried Vogt
East German Touring Cars, 1300 cc – M. Gunther
Danish Formula Ford 1600 – Jac Nelleman
British Formula Vee - Bruce Venn
Yugoslavian Championship – Regvart Drago
Salvadoran Championship – "Jamsal"
Chilean Formula 4 – Juan Carlos Silva
Chilean Turismo de Carretera – Eduardo Kovacs
Bolivian Championship – Oscar Crespo Meurice
Venezuelan Formula Ford – Bobby Dennett
ARCA – Ron Hutcherson
NASCAR Modified – Richie Evans
IMCA Sprint Car – Thad Dosher
French Hillclimbing: Jimmy Mieusset
British Hillclimbing: Mike MacDowell
South African Formula Vee – Miss.J. Wilter
South African Formula Ford – K. Gray
Scottish Supertox – Malcom Paterson
Scottish Saloon Stocks – George Marshall
Russian Formula Libre – Nikolai Kazakov
Mexican Formula Vee – Guillermo Sponda
Mexican Formula 3 – Fernando Flores

Driver fatalities during the year in racing incidents: Francois Cevert, Roger Williamson, Gerry Birrell, Swede Savage, Art Pollard, Roger Dubos, Hans-Pieter Joisten, Pedro Carneiro Pereira, Nasif Estefano, Ivan Iglesias, Nano Correa, Bob Criss, Jose Almeida Santos, Manfred Grau, Joe Huber, Dick Losenbeck, Charles Blyth, Giancarlo Biagiotti, Luis Alberto Stachiola, Massimo Larini, Kirk O'Connor, Lyle Nabberfeldt, Richard Antracolli, Rich Sennecker, Ray Abney, Oscar Zarzoso, Ed Pellegrini, Jack Clevenger, Randy Thompson, Ronald Troxell, Daniel Rouveyran, Ian Cook, Juan Carlos Grassi, Larry Derr, Sam Erwin, Jim Shinn, James Sears, Larry Smith, Lou Harton, Arnold Golding, Pollo Gonzalez, Dennis Shelton, Whitney Gerken, Cliff Johns, Humberto Pasciulli Carl Bergkvist, Brian Hough, Derek Huntley, Masaharu Nakano, Anselmo Perez,

Formula 1:
- Drivers participating for the first time: **James Hunt, David Purley, Roger Williamson, Tom Belso, George Follmer, Rikki Von Opel, John Watson, Jochen Mass, Luis Bueno, Eddie Keizan, Graham McRae**
- Drivers who won for the first time: **Ronnie Peterson, Peter Revson**
- Drivers who won for the last time: **Peter Revson, Jackie Stewart**
- Last time a **BRM** leads a GP (**Beltoise**, Canada) and scores a pole (**Regazzoni**, Argentina). **Lauda** also led at Canada.
- New manufacturers: **Shadow, Ensign, Iso-Marlboro**
- First GPs held in Brazil and Sweden
- Pace-car (safety car) used for the first time, in Canada. It goes in front of **Howden Ganley**, who some insist was indeed leading, others say was a back marker. To this day, there are doubts as to who in fact won the race. **Peter Revson** was declared the winner.

- **Andrea de Adamich**'s F1 career comes to an abrupt end in the British GP, in the wake of massive accident caused by **Jody Scheckter**. Coincidentally, this was the second disruption to **Andrea**'s F1 career in Britain: in **1968**, he suffered an accident in the Race of Champions which jeopardized any future plans **Ferrari** had for the Italian.
- Although near the end of his career, **Denis Hulme** scores his first ever pole in the **McLaren** M23's debut in South Africa. It would remain his only pole.
- For the second and last time all championship races are won by **Ford Cosworth** powered cars
- First 15-race Formula 1 season
- For the first time two races are held in South America
- For the last time grid formation 3-2-3 used in a championship race (German GP).
- Fixed car numbers used for the first time.
- For the first time, a Formula 5000 car beats a F1 field in a non-championship event. The winner is the ever lucky **Peter Gethin**, in a **Chevron**, at the non-championship Race of Champions in **Brands Hatch**.
- **Zolder, Interlagos** and **Anderstorp** are used for the first time as F1 venues.
- **Wilson Fittipaldi Junior** has his best F1 race ever at Monaco, racing in 3rd place in the latter stages of the race. The car retires, however.
- The top six on the Monaco GP finish in the same order they finished the championship: **Stewart-Fittipaldi-Peterson-Cevert-Revson-Hulme**.

Other categories:
- The duo **Gijs Van Lennep/Herbert Muller** won in a **Porsche Carrera** at the **Targa Florio**. In second, a rare **Lancia Stratos**, driven by **Sandro Munari/Jean Claude Andruet**. This is the last edition of the **Targa Florio** valid as world championship round is run. The race would continue for three additional years, as a non-championship event.
- The World Manufacturers Championship has a highly competitive season, with **Matra-Simca** and **Ferrari** fighting to the end, with **Porsche** never very far. In all, four manufacturers win races (**Matra-Simca, Ferrari, Porsche** and **Gulf-Mirage**)
- An **Alfa Romeo** car races at Le Mans for the last time. The car, entered privately by Scuderia Brescia Corse, finishes 15th, driven by **Carlo Facetti, Pam** and **Teodoro Zecolli**. Alfas are entered in **1974** by the works but entries are withdrawn due to cost considerations and the scant possibility the cars would last 24 hours.
- **BMW** x **Ford** ETCC battle comes to Le Mans. **Ford** fielded three Capris for **Glemser/Fitzpatrick, Birrel/Heyer** and **Birrel/Vinatier/Koinigg**. **BMW** had **Quester/Hezemans** and **Amon/Stuck**. **BMW** came out the winner, with **Hezemans/Quester**'s 11th place.
- The last race of the World Manufacturers Championship, at **Buenos Aires**, is cancelled.
- Bye, **Lotus** and **Brabham**. The two venerable British constructors build new Formula 2 contenders for the last time. The **Lotus** 63, also known as Texaco Star, fails to impress, although drivers are **Ronnie Peterson** and **Emerson Fittipaldi**. The **Brabham** BT40 manages to win a non-championship race at **Misano**, driver **Wilson Fittipaldi Junior**.
- **BMW** returns to Formula 2 as an engine supplier and wins the championship in commanding style, with **Jean-Pierre Jarier**. The Championship has a confusing system, with A and B races and a total of 17 dates. B races are generally poorly supported, its results have secondary importance and the system is never repeated.
- A Japanese car is fielded at **Le Mans** for the first time. The car is a **Sigma Mazda**, driven by **Patrick Dal Bo, Hiroshi Fushida** and **Tetsu Ikuzawa**. It retires.

- **Ford** manages to convince F1 champions **Jackie Stewart** and **Emerson Fittipaldi** to share a **Ford** Capri in the ETCC's **Nürburgring** round. The two highly rated drivers fail to improve **Ford**'s fortunes in the championship. **Stewart** would also race at **Paul Ricard** and **Monza**.
- Japanese driver **Hiroshi Kazato** briefly leads a Formula 2 race in **Hockenheim**.
- **Renault** tries the waters in the European 2 Liter championship, fielding an **Alpine** for **Jean Pierre Jabouille**.
- **March** builds a 2-liter challenger, which is fast but still lags behind the **Lola, Chevron** and **Abarth**. The British race car maker produces 80 cars in 1973.
- **Jan Lammers** begins racing at the ripe young age of 16 in his native Holland, a very unusual state of affairs at the time. He wins races right away – and competed until a few years ago.
- The first IROC is run in the USA. A nice concept that never quite took off, it was supposed to place European (F1) drivers up against American Indycar, NASCAR and Sports Cars racers and decide who was best. Europeans/F1 drivers rarely featured well and the tracks seemed to fit American driving style. The first edition used **Porsche Carreras**, soon replaced by Camaros. **Mark Donohue** won three races, **George Follmer** one. Representing F1 were **Denis Hulme** and **Emerson Fittipaldi**. The races were run in **Riverside** and **Daytona**. As the final took place in **1974**, it is listed under that year.
- Easy does it – **Benny Parsons** and **Roger McCluskey** win the two most important series in the USA, NASCAR and USAC although they won one race apiece. In NASCAR's case, **Yarborough, Petty, Baker, B. Allison** and **Pearson** all won more races than **Parsons. Pearson**, who raced only in large speedways, thus had only 18 starts, won a whopping 11 times.
- The single race win by **Benny Parsons** in NASCAR came under atrocious heat in **Bristol**. In fact, unknown local driver **John Utsman** drove 170 laps relieving **Parsons** but never got official recognition for this accomplishment.
- In USAC's case, **Dallenbach, Rutherford, Johncock** and **Foyt** all won more races than **McCluskey**, who scored more points anyway. These were the only times either driver won the championship.
- On the other hand, **Mark Donohue** simply destroyed the opposition, winning six of eight Can-Am races, including six straight races, a record.
- No less than 19 cars in the Indy 500 were **Eagles**, including the winner and runner-up. Now we complain there is a single chassis… At least there were **McLarens, Coyotes, King** and **Parnellis** on the field. However, it was already getting very tough for smaller builders to qualify for the big race.
- **Herbert Muller** decides to dust off his **Ferrari** 512 and wins several rounds of the Swiss Championship. As racing is prohibited in the country until recently, except for hill climbs, the Swiss championship was held in tracks in Germany, France, Austria, Italy and even Liechtenstein. An elderly **Lola** T70 also takes part in some races.
- An unusual 25 Hour race debuts in Brazil, the 25 Hours of **Interlagos**, for Division 1 (Group 1) touring cars. It is **Ford** Maverick's first major victory in the country. It is also **Chico Landi**'s last race and he finishes third in a **Ford** driven by son **Luis Landi** and **Antonio Castro Prado**. Landi had been racing since the mid 30s and was the first Brazilian to win a Grand Prix, at **Bari, 1948**.
- **Jody Scheckter** had a very busy season. Besides wreaking havoc in a Formula 1 **McLaren, Jody** won the US Formula 5000 Championship, raced in a few European F5000 rounds, was a regular in the Can-Am, drove a **Ford** in the ETCC, a **Motul** in Formula 2 and in the World Sportscar Championship.
- **Wendell Scott** races in his last NASCAR Grand National event. **Wendell** was the only African-American to race in the category in the 60s and 70s, winning one race.

- **Vic Elford** comes out of retirement to manage and drive in a team of **Marches** in the European 2 Liter Championship, **Alain Peltier** being the other driver. DART runs **GRD**s for **Dave Walker** and **John Miles**, both **Lotus** team rejects. Both efforts are fraught with failure.
- **Adrian Reynard** builds his first car. Eventually, **Reynard** became a very prominent race car manufacturer but like most top builders, it failed as a business.
- Sorry, my bad! FIA decides to name both **Clemens Schickentanz** and **Claude Ballot-Lena** European GT champions, because a mid-year bulletin provided the wrong scoring positions.
- The latest war between Israel and Arab countries had tremendous effects on the racing world in the next three years. The rise in oil prices mandated by OPEP resulted in worldwide economic slowdown, which in turn, resulted in corporate promotional cutbacks. Hundreds of races and a few championships were cancelled (European 2 Liters, European Formula 5000, Euro GT, Can-Am). In certain countries, such as Portugal and Brazil, racing was prohibited for a short while. Many felt that racing was a waste of precious fuel, indeed everybody was looking for a scapegoat. Cancellation of any type of public event was also seen as a way to save fuel, especially in Europe.
- **George Follmer** takes USAC to Court for suspending him because he took part in an SCCA event instead of a USAC one. USAC reverses the suspension.
- **Brands Hatch** buys a fleet of 25 **Ford Escort Mexicos**, which are prepared and used in celebrities events during the course of the next two years. The events are popular with the public. As some of the cars are written off during the year, replacements are bought for **1974**.
- **Peter Gregg** announces his retirement from racing after winning the 24 Hours of **Daytona**, then retracts.
- The **Cascavel** paved racetrack is inaugurated in Brazil. The ugly face of politics surfaces: Brazilian press wrongly reports that the city's current mayor, **Pedro Muffato**, who was also a driver, was the driving behind the paving of the track, when in fact businessman **Zilmar Beux** led the enterprise. The country would see several track openings during this decade. Besides **Cascavel, Taruma (1970), Goiania (1974), Brasilia (1974), Guapore (1976)** and the revised **Rio de Janeiro** track (**1978**) were all inaugurated during the decade. **Cascavel** is important because it was the first track inaugurated in a non-capital city.
- In a non-championship prototype race held in that track, an unusual car appears: a **Ford Maverick** engined **Alfa Romeo** T33, driven to 2nd place by **Angi Munhoz**. That was the car's single race.
- The Philippines Grand Pix is held for the first time, in **Greenhills,** like **Macau**, a street track. Participants raced Formula Atlantic cars and the winner was **John McDonald,** in a **Brabham.**
- The Malaysian GP is won by Singaporean/Malaysian driver **Sonny Rajah**, in a **March**. That is quite an accomplishment because usually these Asian races were won by Australians, New Zealanders or **John McDonald** (from Hong Kong).
- **Rajah** actually tried to break into European racing during the season, driving in the British Formula Atlantic championship. He did not set the world on fire, although the local media covered the novel attempt broadly.
- **Hector Rebaque** wins the 1000 km of Mexico at only 16 years of age. Another Mexican race prodigy but it did not work out as it did with the **Rodriguez** brothers. Hector shared the car, a **Porsche** 914/6, with **Guillermo "Memo" Rojas, Sr.**
- **Keke Rosberg** wins 15 Formula Vee races and three championships in Europe.
- In the wake of his win at the Tourist trophy, Austrian **Harald Ertl** shaves off his substantial beard – which is grown back fast.
- **Nasif Estefano** wins the Turismo de Carretera title in Argentina in advance but loses his life in the last race of the season.

- **Niki Lauda** wins his only 24 hour race. It happened at **Nürburgring**, sharing a **BMW** with **Hans-Pieter Joisten,** who died at the 24 Hours of Spa.
- France outlaws motor racing in the wake of the wake of the oil crisis. The sport would only resume in the country in March of 1974.

1974

Champions
Formula 1 (Drivers): Emerson Fittipaldi
Formula 1 (Manufacturers): McLaren
European Formula 2: Patrick Depailler
British Formula 3: Brian Henton (Forward Trust), Brian Henton (Lombard)
Italian Formula 3: Alberto Colombo
Polifac F3: Giorgio Francia
Swedish Formula 3: Conny Andersson
World Manufacturers Championship: Matra-Simca

Nice shot of the two Lolas, back in F-1. Photo by Lola Heritage.

Can-Am: Jackie Oliver
Interserie: Herbert Muller
European 2 Liter Championship: Alain Serpaggi
USAC Indy Car: Bobby Unser
European Formula 5000: Bob Evans
American Formula 5000: Brian Redman
Tasman Cup: Peter Gethin
South African Formula 1: Dave Charlton
IROC: Mark Donohue
NASCAR: Richard Petty
European Touring Car Championship: Hans Heyer
British Saloon Car Championship: Bernard Unett, Hillman Avenger
DRM: Dieter Glemser

DARM: Dieter Meyer
European GT Championship: John Fitzpatrick
Australian Touring Car Championship: Peter Brock
Australian Gold Star Championship: Max Stewart
Australian Formula 2: Leo Geoghegan
New Zealand Gold Star Championship: David Oxton
New Zealand Saloon Car Championship: J. Richards
Brazilian Formula Ford: Clovis de Moraes
Brazilian Formula Super-Vee: Marcos Troncon
Brazilian Touring Cars: Edgard Mello Filho (C), Ingo Hoffmann (A)
Brazilian Prototypes: Pedro Muffato (B), Mauricio Chulam (A)
Argentinian Formula 1: Luis Di Palma
Argentinian Formula 2: Jorge de Amorrortu
Argentinian Formula 4: Miguel Angel Guerra
Argentinian Turismo de Carretera: Hector Gradassi
Trans-Am: Peter Gregg
IMSA Camel GTO: Peter Gregg GTU: Walt Maas
Japanese Formula 2: Noritake Takahara
Fuji Grand Champion: Masahiro Hasemi
British Formula Atlantic: John Nicholson (Yellow Pages), Jim Crawford (Southern Organs)
Canadian Formula Atlantic: Bill Brack
Irish Formula Atlantic: Patsy McGarrity
European Formula Super-Vee: Freddy Kottulinsky
US Formula Super-Vee: Elliott Forbes-Robinson
Central American Championship: Kikos Fonseca
European Hill Climb Championship: Robert Jimmy Mieusset
Spanish Championship: Francisco Torredemer
Formula 1430: Federico van der Hoeven
Swedish Touring Cars: Bengt Ekberg
Coupe Simca-Shell: Patrick Perrier
Belgian Championship: Alain Peltier
Dutch Touring Car Championship: Rob Slotemaker/ Cees Siewertsen
Dutch Formula Ford: Boy Hayje
Austrian Championship: Joseph Schnabl
Danish Volvo 142 Cup: Poul Erik Jensen
European Formula Renault: Didier Pironi
Czech Championship: Jaroslav Bobek
Soviet Formula F1: Henri Saarm
Estonian Formula 2: Peep Laansoo
Yugoslav Champion: Milutin Gravilovic
Polish Championship: Otto Bartkowiak
Peace and Friendship Cup (Formula Easter): Karel Jilek
Peace and Friendship Cup (Touring cars): Jaroslav Bobek
Norwegian Formula Vee: Stener Svartrud
German Formula Ford: Bill Dawson
European Formula Vee: Kalle Jonsson
BARC Formula Ford: Richard Morgan
BRSCC Formula Ford: Syd Fox
Formula Italia: Gianfranco Brancatelli
BARC Saloon Car Championship: Bill Sydenham
BRSCC/BRDC/MCD Saloon Car Championship: Alan Minshaw
Formule Bleue (Citroen): Patrick Piget
Coupe Gordini: Gerard Delpalanque

French GT Championship: Claude Ballot-Lena
Porsche Cup: John Fitzpatrick
SCCA Formula A - Jerry Hansen, Lola
SCCA Formula B – Ken Duclos, Brabham
SCCA Formula C – Bill Anspach, Laminaire Special
SCCA Formula Super Vee – Fred Phillips, Elden
SCCA Formula Vee – Harry MacDonald, Lynx
SCCA Formula Ford – Eddie Miller, Lola
SCCA A Sports Racing – Warren Tope, Mclaren Chevy
SCCA B Sports Racing – Jerry Hansen, Lola
SCCA C Sports Racing – Sam Gilliand, Arachnid
SCCA D Sports Racing – Bob Marshall, Quasar
SCCA A Production – J. Marshall Robbins, Chevrolet Corvette
SCCA B Production – Bill Jobe, Chevrolet Corvette
SCCA C Production – Walt Mass, Datsun
SCCA D Production – Lee Mueller, Jensen Healey
SCCA E Production – Bill Schmid, Porsche
SCCA F Production – Rick Cline, Triumph
SCCA G Production – Joe Hauser, Austin Healey
SCCA H Production – John McClue, Austin Healey
SCCA A Sedan – Joe Chamberlain, Chevrolet Camaro
SCCA B Sedan – Dave Frellsen, Datsun
SCCA C Sedan – Don Devendorf, Datsun
USAC Sprint Cars – Pancho Carter
USAC Midgets – Mel Kenyon
Australian Formula Ford – Terry Perkins
Swiss Hill Climbing Championship – Roland Salomon
German Formula Vee – Wolfgang Klein
German Formula Super Vee – Bertram Schaffer
German Hill Climbing Championship – Willi Bergmeister
East German Touring Cars, 1300 cc – L.Thomas
Danish Formula Ford 1600 – Henrik Spellerberg
British Formula Vee – Brian Urlwin
Ecuadoran Championship – Heran Ampudia
Venezuelan Formula Ford – Juan Cochesa
Chilean Formula 4 – Juan Carlos Silva
Moroccan Formule Nationale – Gerard Cantarel
ARCA – Ron Hutcherson and Dave Dayton
NASCAR Modified – Jerry Cook
Rhodesian Saloon Cars – Richie Maine
IMCA Sprint Car – Chuck Amati
French Hillclimbing: Jimmy Mieusset
British Hillclimbing: Mike MacDowell
South African Formula Vee – J. Knez
South African Formula Ford – B. Tilanus
Scottish Supertox – Malcom Paterson
Scottish Saloon Stocks – Hamish Buchanan
Formula Caribbean – Mike Atwell

Driver fatalities during the year in racing incidents: Peter Revson, Helmut Koinigg, Silvio Moser, Jose Carlos Garcia del Castro, Eitel Mazzoni, Senikichi Omura, Billy Joe Gay, Burt Sonner, Johnny Cash, Paul Dewald, Seiichi Suzuki, Dave Skari, Ken Tibbs, Robert Bushley, Stan Trumbower, Dom Miuccio, Gip Gibson, Jon Thorney, Chris White, Leo Ingebrigtsen, Geoff Coles, Maurice Phillips, Robert

Bunselmeier, Joe Gregory, Stephen Tarigo, Ron Barber, Phil Scragg, Manuel Bobbio, Esteban Capkovic, Gerardo Carreno,

Formula 1:

- Drivers participating for the first time: **Jacques Laffite, Jean-Pierre Jabouille, Hans Joachin Stuck, Teddy Pilette, Gerard Larrousse, Richard Robarts, Bertil Roos, Lella Lombardi, John Nicholson, Carlo Facetti, Helmut Koinigg, Guy Edwards, Dieter Quester(*), Jose Dolhem, Leo Kinnunen, Larry Perkins, Ian Scheckter, Tom Pryce, Ian Ashley, Mike Wilds**
- Drivers who won for the first time: **Niki Lauda, Jody Scheckter, Carlos Reutemann**
- First win, manufacturers: (none)
- Drivers who won for the last time: **Denis Hulme**
- New manufacturers: **Hesketh, Penske, Parnelli, Amon, Token, Trojan, Lyncar, Maki**
- Last time **BRM** is on podium (**Beltoise**, second in South Africa)
- No less than 56 drivers actually start a F1 championship race during the year, and a few more attempted to qualify without success. This is in sharp contrast to other categories, where money is very tight and many competitors drop out or halt plans altogether.
- A record number of new makes joins the Formula 1 circus. Of the 8 new makes, only **Hesketh** and **Penske** would win a race apiece and none lasted in the long term. **Hesketh** would make as far as **1978**, **Penske** and **Parnelli** until **1976**, **Lyncar** and **Maki** until **1975**, **Amon, Token** and **Trojan** did not survive the season, although the **Token** would resurface as the **Safir** in **1975**.
- A Japanese driver participates in a Formula 1 race for the first time. It happened at the non-championship Race of Champions. The driver is **Noritake Takahara** and the car, a **March**.
- **Dijon-Prenois** is used for the first time as a Formula 1 venue. This means the French GP had three different venues in the last three seasons.
- Last season for Firestone tires in Formula 1. It has never been back.
- **Jorge de Bagration**'s attempts to race in Formula 1 fail again. The naturalized Spaniard, born a Georgian Prince, intended to race a **Surtees** in the Spanish Grand Prix. The entry is allegedly lost by the organizers, then found, but somewhere down the line he gives up on the idea.
- **Motoharu Kurosawa** said to be almost certain **March**'s number 2 driver. It did not happen.
- An Argentine bank said to offer US$150,000 to get **Luis di Palma** a Formula 1 seat. It did not happen.
- **Claudio Francisci** is just one of many drivers to try the Finotto **Brabham**.
- **Jacky Ickx** wins his last Formula 1 race, the non-championship Race of Champions, under pouring rain. It was his only win in a **Lotus**.
- A non-championship race is run in Brasilia, Brazil's capital, as inauguration of the racetrack. The winner is **Emerson Fittipaldi**. It is also the only F1 race his brother **Wilson** does in **1974**. Later on, the President of the Brazilian Racing Confederation (under intervention) at the time Army General **Eloy Meneses**, states it was the government's intention to move the race from **Interlagos** to **Brasilia**. It never happened.
- **Denis Hulme** wins his last GP, at Argentina. Denis had led a total 436 laps in his F1 career but he only led a total of 4 laps in his last two wins (Sweden, **1973** and Argentina, **1974**). A grand total of 20 km!

- A Finn driver is entered in Formula 1 for the first time: **Leo Kinnunen** gets a **Surtees** TS16-Ford but the season is not a happy one. He is also known for being the last driver to wear an open faced helmet in Formula 1.
- **Chris Amon** allegedly declines an offer to join **Brabham**, in respect for the folks who supported him in his newly formed Formula 1 team. One can only imagine what **Chris** would have done with the BT44…

Other categories:
- **Alfa Romeo** begins the World Manufacturers Championship season well, with a 1-2-3 in Monza and the winners are **Merzario** and **Andretti**. However, this was the last success of the season and **Matra-Simca** sweeps all before it. **Alfa** quits with a few races remaining.
- **Jacky Ickx**, already considered one of the top sports cars drivers of the day, actually raced for **Alfa Romeo, Matra-Simca** and **Gulf** in the **1974** season. He only won with **Matra-Simca**.
- The 9 Hours of **Kyalam**i finally achieves World Championship status in **1974**…except that it is a 6-hour, rather than 9-hour race, the renamed 1000km of Kyalami. The contest was duly won by **Matra-Simca**'s **Pescarolo-Larrousse** and it is also the team's final race.
- **Pescarolo/Larrousse** also won at **Le Mans**, despite a 46-minute stop to fix the transmission.
- **Matra-Simca** fielded 4 cars at **Le Mans**, including a new model, the MS680. This would turn out to be the car's single race and it ended in retirement.
- A **Ferrari** prototype did race at Le Mans…fielded by NART. The car was called a 312B, actually a **Ferrari** Can-Am car with a 3-liter engine. Drivers were **Andruet/Zeccoli**, who finished 9th.
- Formula 3 adopts a 2.0 liter regulation. Fields in England are abnormally small and **Brian Henton** wins both championships, in a works **March**. From this point until the demise of original Formula 2 in **1984**, both categories used 2-liter engines, although the F-3 were much less powerful, based on street car power plants.
- Several British F-3 races are poorly supported, almost club racing affairs, allowing drivers such as **Prince Nicholas Von Preussen, Pedro Passadore, Jose Espirito Santo** and **Tony Rouff** to come to the fore.
- A large number of Brazilians also drive in British F3, seeking to emulate **Emerson Fittipaldi**: **Alex Ribeiro** is the only one to make real impression, winning on three occasions. The others are **Jose Pedro Chateaubriand, Mario Moraes, Luis Moraes, Marivaldo Fernandes, Julio Caio, Teleco** and **Jan Balder**.
- A rare Indonesian driver also appears briefly in British Formula 3, **Hanu Wiano**. Many entry sheets spelled his name **Harry Wiano** and some news outlets incorrectly identify him as Indian.
- **Alpine Renault** simply walks away with the European 2 Liter Championship, winning all championship races.
- **Johnny Rutherford** wins the Indy 500 for the first time, driving a works **McLaren**. **McLaren** also won its maiden Formula 1 championship that year.
- **Hans Stuck** appears a sure bet for the European F2 championship but Frenchman **Patrick Depailler** gathers momentum and wins the championship, the fourth won by a Frenchman. **Depailler** had been third in the last two editions.
- Many races are cancelled worldwide as a result of the oil crisis in the wake of the Israel-Arab war of **1973**.
- The SCCA decides to drop the Can-Am, after a poor 5-race season. The season is dominated by the **Shadow** Team and **Jackie Oliver**, who wins 4 races.
- A **Lola** T70 was on the grid in the last traditional Can-Am race in **1974** and finished 12th, in front of other "younger" competition. This car type, driven by **John Surtees**, won the first edition of the championship in **1966**.

- In the wake of the oil crisis, hundreds of races are cancelled or postponed. The Portuguese government actually outlawed racing for a while.
- Looking to the East: Five formula 1 cars had a "demonstration race" held in **Fuji**, Japan, in November of **1974**. Expenses were paid by some Japanese businessmen: the participants were **Emerson Fittipaldi (McLaren), James Hunt (Hesketh), Jody Scheckter (Tyrrell), Ronnie Peterson (Lotus)** and **Carlos Reutemann (Brabham)**. **Peterson,** who seemed the only one taking things seriously, won the event.
- The **La Guacima** racetrack is inaugurated in Costa Rica. The winner of the main race is Salvadoran **Eduardo Melendez**, in a **BMW**. It was a truly international event with drivers from the USA, Mexico, Panama, El Salvador, Honduras, Guatemala and Colombia. There were races for different classes of touring cars as well as Formula Ford and Formula Vee races.
- The **La Chinita** racetrack is inaugurated in Venezuela. There were events for Formula Ford, won by **Bobby Dennet** and for touring cars. Drivers from several other countries also took part in the festivities: England, USA, Italy, Portugal, Canada, Sweden, Ecuador, Colombia, Mexico, Brazil and Peru.
- **Emerson Fittipaldi** wins an IROC race at Riverside, the only non-US driver to win in the series during the 70s.
- A new Touring Car Championship is established in Europe, to right the wrongs of the ETCC. The Trophee de l'Avenir for Group 1 was created with the best intentions but had little effect on the racing world.
- Canadian **Earl Ross** wins a NASCAR Winston Cup race at **Martinsville**.
- 2.0 **Ford** Escorts frequently beat more powerful 3.0 **Ford** Capris in touring car races, including the ETCC.
- The driver with the least chance of winning the inaugural Brazilian Super Vee title walks off with the crown. **Marcos Troncon** did only four of the events, won a single heat of the twelve he took part but scores two wins on aggregate which give him the title one point ahead of **Francisco Lameirao** and future Formula 1 driver **Ingo Hoffmann**.
- International racing in Bahamas reportedly back on track. However, the rumor is just a rumor. International races for Group 3 cars, a revival of 60s Bahamas races, fail to materialize.

1975

Champions
Formula 1 (Drivers): Niki Lauda
Formula 1 (Manufacturers): Ferrari
European Formula 2: Jacques Laffite
British Formula 3: Gunnar Nilsson (BP)
Italian Formula 3: Luciano Pavesi
German F3: Ernst Maring
Swedish Formula 3: Conny Ljungfeldt
World Manufacturers Championship: Alfa Romeo
Interserie: Herbert Muller
European 2 Liter Championship: Chris Skeaping
USAC Indy Car: A.J. Foyt Jr.
European Formula 5000: Teddy Pilette
American Formula 5000: Brian Redman
Tasman Cup: Warwick Brown
South African Formula 1: Dave Charlton

NASCAR: Richard Petty
IROC: Bobby Unser
European Touring Car Championship: Sigifried Muller/Alain Peltier
British Saloon Car Championship: Andy Rouse, Triumph Dolomite
DRM: Hans Heyer
DARM: Edgar Doren
European GT Championship: Hartwig Bertrams
Australian Touring Car Championship: Colin Bond
Australian Gold Star Championship: John McCormack
Australian Formula 2: Geoff Brabham

A very popular win, Hunt's maiden GP in Holland. Photo by Pieter Kamp.

New Zealand Gold Star Championship: Graeme Lawrence
New Zealand Saloon Car Championship: P. Fahey
Brazilian Formula Ford: Clovis de Moraes
Brazilian Formula Super-Vee: Francisco Lameirao
Brazilian Prototypes: Luiz Pereira Bueno (B), Mauricio Chulam (A)
Brazilian Touring Cars: Paulo Mello Gomes (B), Amadeo Campos (A)
Argentinian Formula 2: Miguel Angel Guerra
Argentinian Formula 4: Miguel Angel Guerra
Argentinian Turismo de Carretera: Hector Gradassi
Trans-Am: John Greenwood
IMSA Camel GTO: Peter Gregg GTU: Bob Sharp
Japanese Formula 2000: Kazuyoshi Hoshino
Fuji Grand Champion: Noritake Takahara
British Formula Atlantic: Tony Brise (John Player), Ted Wentz (Southern Organs)
Canadian Formula Atlantic: Bill Brack
Mexican National GT Championship: Memo Rojas, Sr.
Irish Formula Atlantic: Patsy McGarrity
European Formula Super-Vee: Mikko Kozarowitzky
US Formula Super-Vee: Eddie Miller
European Hill Climb Championship: Mauro Nesti
Spanish Championship: Juan Sanz de Madrid

Formula 1430: Luis Canomanuel
Swedish Touring Cars: Rune Tobiason
Belgian Championship: Jean Xhenceval
Dutch Touring Car Championship: Rob Slotemaker/Huub Vermeulen
Austrian Championship: Hans Fink
Swiss Championship: Markus Hotz
Peace and Friendship Cup (Formula Easter): Milan Zid
Estonian Championship (F2): Madis Laiw
Polish Championship (F-Easter): Jozef Kielbania
French Formula Renault: Christian Debias
European Formula Renault: Rene Arnoux
Danish Volvo 142 Cup: Jorgen Poulsen
Norwegian Formula Vee: Edvard Haug
Dutch Formula Ford: Jim Vermeulen
German Formula Ford: Wolfgang Locher
European Formula Vee: Kalle Jonsson
BARC Formula Ford: Geoff Lees
British Formula Ford 2000: Derek Lawrence
BRSCC Formula Ford: Geoff Lees
Formula Italia: Bruno Giacomelli
BARC Saloon Car Championship: Jock Robertson
BRSCC/BRDC/MCD Saloon Car Championship: Jock Robertson
Portuguese Speed Championship: Group B; Roberto Giannone
Portuguese Speed Championship: Touring, Clemente da Silva
Greek Speed Championship: Tassos "Javeris" Markus
Greek Hill Climb Championship: Tassos "Javeris" Markus
Formule Bleue (Citroen): Phillipe Jaffrenou
Porsche Cup: Claude Haldi
SCCA Formula A - Jerry Hansen, Lola
SCCA Formula B – Bobby Rahal, March
SCCA Formula C – Dirk Wrighston, Brabham
SCCA Formula Super Vee – Fred Phillips, Elden
SCCA Formula Vee – Mike Frangkiser, Lynx
SCCA Formula Ford – Tom Wiechmann, ADF
SCCA A Sports Racing - Jerry Hansen, Lola
SCCA B Sports Racing – Mike Hall, Lola
SCCA C Sports Racing – Jim Trueman, Bobsy
SCCA D Sports Racing – Kendall Noah, Ocelot Suzuki
SCCA A Production – Frank Fahey, Chevrolet Corvette
SCCA B Production - Bob Tullius, Jaguar
SCCA C Production – Bob Sharp, Datsun
SCCA D Production – John McComb, Triumph
SCCA E Production – Terry Visger, MGB
SCCA F Production – Ken Slagle, Triumph
SCCA G Production – Jerry Barker, Triumph
SCCA H Production – Jim Miller, Austin Healey
SCCA A Sedan – Jim Crittenden, Chevrolet Camaro
SCCA B Sedan – Dave Frellsen, Datsun
SCCA C Sedan – Damon Pleasant, Datsun
USAC Sprint Cars – Larry Dickson
USAC Midgets – Sleepy Tripp
USAC Silver Crown - Jimmy Caruthers
Euro Cup Renault 5 – Alain Hubert
Australian Formula Ford – Paul Bernasconi

Swiss Hill Climbing Championship – Markus Hotz
German Formula Vee – Jorg Plankenhorn
German Formula Super Vee – Keke Rosberg
German Hill Climbing Championship – Egon Evertz
East German Touring Cars, 1300 cc – K.P.Krause
Danish Formula Ford 1600 – John Nielsen
British Formula Vee - Ian Flux
STP Formula Ford Championship – Patrick Neve
Venezuelan Formula Ford – Oscar Notz
Moroccan Formule Nationale – Rene Gabana
ARCA – Dave Dayton
NASCAR Modifieds – Jerry Cook
Rhodesian Sports Cars – Isaac Codron
Rhodesian Saloon Cars – Richie Maine
IMCA Sprint Car – Bill Utz
French Hillclimbing: Jimmy Mieusset
British Hillclimbing: Roy Lane
Uruguayan Touring Cars – Gustavo Trelles
South African Formula Vee - U. Pettersohn
South African Formula Ford – R. J Scott
Scottish Supertox – Les Clark
Scottish Saloon Stocks – Robert Bruce
Formula Caribbean – Mike Atwell
Russian Formula Libre – Guran Digebuadze

Driver fatalities during the year in racing incidents: Mark Donohue, Neville Johnston, Bill Spencer, Jim Devitt. Russell Mendez, Alex Drust, James Rogers, John Buzzard, Bernardino Franceschini, Jack Cornell, Marv Peterson, Danny Burdette, Walter Czadek, Hank Wise, Jeff Sikes, Lawrence McCard, George Brockbank, Ernie Davis, Walter Neubauer, Warren Tope, Lorraine Peck, Wim Boshuis, Gerard Glenadel, John Gall, Steve Howard, B.J. Swanson, Earl Lowe, Tiny Lund, Tom Vance, Joe Towles, Bob Zwenke, Glen Snider, Nelson Dario Poggio.

Formula 1.

- Drivers participating for the first time: **Torsten Palm, Alan Jones, Tony Brise, David Morgan, Jim Crawford, Guy Tunmer, Jo Von Lanthen, Bob Evans, Roelof Wunderink, Hiroshi Fushida, Brian Henton, Harald Ertl, Michel Leclere, Brett Lunger, Damien Magee, Tony Trimmer, Renzo Zorzi**
- First wins: **Vittorio Brambilla, Jochen Mass, Jose Carlos Pace, James Hunt**
- First win, manufacturers: **Hesketh**
- Drivers who won for the last time: **Vittorio Brambilla, Jochen Mass, Jose Carlos Pace, Emerson Fittipaldi**
- New manufacturers: **Fittipaldi, Williams, Hill**
- Although **Niki Lauda** won the championship in convincing style, a total of 9 drivers won races. Besides Lauda, only Emerson Fittipaldi wins more than one race. The others to win are **Jochen Mass, Jody Scheckter, Carlos Pace, Carlos Reutemann, Vittorio Brambilla, James Hunt** and **Clay Regazzoni**.
- **Jean-Pierre Jarier** and **Shadow**'s performance in South America amazes the world. **Jarier** wins pole for both events but luck is not on his side. He fails to start in Argentina, after a component failure in warm-up and in Brazil, while leading with a huge cushion, a fuel metering unit fails and he retires seven few laps from the

end. In spite of this beginning and **Tom Pryce**'s pole in Britain and win in the Race of Champions, **Shadow**'s season is a fiasco.
- At the time, there are rumors that Cosworth had given **Shadow** a special unit for testing purposes, with no explanation as to why that team was chosen.
- The Brazilian **Fittipaldi** team debuts in Argentina, normally referred as Copersucar in the first few years. Initially the team tries to do as much as possible in Brazil, including building components, which proves to be a bad decision. The season is a steep learning curve and the car is not competitive.
- An Argentinian Formula 1 car is supposed to debut as well, the **Berta** for **Nestor Garcia Veiga** but it never appears in **Buenos Aires** or elsewhere. It resurfaces later in the season as a F-5000 car in the US Series, without impressing.
- **BRM** changes name to **Stanley-BRM**
- **Montjuich** (Barcelona) is used for the last time as a Spanish GP venue. A confusing race, with many leaders and accidents is ended before the half-way point, when leader **Rolf Stommelen** goes off the track, killing five people
- For the first time, half points are awarded for F1 races, twice, at Spain and Austria. The Austrian race was red flagged due to a deluged that came over the Oesterreichring.
- The winner at Austria was **Vittorio Brambilla**, in what turned out to be the only GP win by an Italian driver during the decade. It was also the first time the works **March** team won a race. Right after receiving the checkered flag, an over enthusiastic **Vittorio** lost control of the car and spun, ending up with a badly twisted nose.
- Goodyear is the sole tire supplier in Formula 1.
- A non-championship F1 race is held in **Dijon**, called the Swiss Grand Prix. The winner, appropriately, is **Clay Regazzoni**.
- **Graham Hill** retires for good, in the **Monaco** Grand Prix.
- After the pretty agitated race in **1974**, Monaco GP organizers limit the number of starters to 18. As a result many drivers do not qualify for the race.
- **Shadow** tries **Matra** engine, **Hill** considers **Alfa**.
- After the season is over, **Graham Hill** and young promise **Tony Brise** die in an airplane crash along with other Hill team members. This spells the end of the team as well.
- First **Williams** podium. In a race of attrition, **Jacques Laffite** finishes second in Germany. This also allows **Gijs Van Lennep** to score **Ensign**'s first point. The Dutchman was also the first to score a point for a **Williams**-built car, in **Zandvoort, 1973**.

Other categories:
- **Alfa Romeo** wins the World Manufacturers Championship for the first time but not as a works team. The cars are run by **Willi Kauhsen**'s team (WKRT). **Alfa** won seven times, 4 times with **Arturo Merzario** (3 driving with **Laffite**, 1 with **Mass**) and three times with **Pescarolo/Bell**.
- The only challenge to **Alfa** comes from **Alpine-Renault**, which wins at **Mugello** (**Larrousse/Jabouille**) but has no luck elsewhere. The **Renault** engine is a turbo.
- **Derek Bell** also wins his first Le Mans and becomes a bona fide top sports car driver. His teammate, **Jacky Ickx**, wins his second race (the first was in **1969**) and until **1982**, wins another four times, becoming the win record holder until the 2000s.
- The car driven by **Bell**, a **Gulf** GR8 (also known as **Mirage**) had a special low consumption Cosworth engine, which averaged about 7 mpg, almost twice the mileage of a Formula 1 engine.

- For the first time since the World Manufacturers Championship was established, **Le Mans** is not part of the World Manufacturers Championship, the ACO sets its own regulations.
- Half of the 55 cars on the Le Mans grid were **Porsche** Carreras
- A Senegalese driver, **Daniel Thiaw**, attempts to start the Le Mans race. **Daniel** was entered in a **Ford** Capri that does not show up, then as a reserve in a **Porsche** 911 that started but never took part. It was a good effort, talked about to this day, 43 years later.
- **Nino Vacarella** wins the Targa Florio one last time. No longer a world championship event, **Nino** partners **Arturo Merzario** and the duo overpowered the weak 2-liter prototype competition. They drove an **Alfa Romeo**.
- After only two races, the European 2 Liter Championship is cancelled for good. There is little support, no sponsor, so another championship falls prey to a bad economic climate. Many organizers cancelled their races early in the season. **Chris Skeaping** is named champion but FIA does not recognize the crown.
- Tico **Martini**'s team wins the European Formula 2 championship with **Jacques Laffite**, in great style. French drivers finish first through fifth in the final standings.
- **Ford** Brazil puts together a "Champions Tournament" to celebrate the launch of the 4-cylinder Maverick. In addition to several Brazilian drivers, including **Carlos Pace** and **Alex Ribeiro**, F-1 driver **Vittorio Brambilla** is invited, as well as drivers from several South American countries, namely, Argentina, Uruguay, Paraguay, Chile, Venezuela, Peru and Ecuador. It becomes a rare occasion in which drivers from all over the continent compete together. **Pace** wins one race, Argentine **Carlos Garro** the other.
- The Long Beach Grand Prix is run for the first time, as a Formula 5000 race, in preparation for the **1976** World Championship event. The first winner is **Brian Redman**. The event is star studded, with **Jody Scheckter, Tony Brise, Chris Amon, Vern Schuppan** among other regulars **Mario Andretti, Al Unser** and **David Hobbs**. **Schuppan** finishes second in an **Eagle**.
- An European Formula 3 championship is held for the first time. It is a short one and the first champion is Australian **Larry Perkins**, who had already attempted to race in Formula 1 the previous season.
- In the British BP Super Visco Formula 3 Championship, **Gunnar Nilsson** and **Alex Ribeiro** fight hard all season, although teammates at **March**. Nilsson is also a major presence in Formula Atlantic.
- As a communist government takes over Angola, motor racing collapses in the country. Angola had for many years a very lively racing scene, with many foreign drivers competing in some races.
- On the subject of Angolan races, **Emilio Marta's Ford** GT 40 still competes and wins a round of the Angolan championship that year!
- The last edition of the European Formula 5000 Championship is held. In the upcoming year, it would become a Group 8 Championship, accepting Formula 1, Formula 2, Formula 5000 and even Formula Atlantic racers.
- **Dale Earnhardt** races at NASCAR's Winston Cup for the first time.
- **BMW** takes part in the IMSA Camel GT Championship and wins 5 races, including **Sebring**.
- **A.J. Foyt** has an excellent USA season, winning seven races. **Tom Sneva** wins for the first time in the championship.
- The 1000th **Lola** racing car is produced. It is a **Lola** T340 Formula Ford.
- Yugoslav driver **Francy Jerancic** tries to qualify a **Surtees** for several races of the European Formula 2 championship without much success. He would later on participate in local Austrian Formula Libre races in **1977**, plus make occasional appearances in the Interserie.

- Hong Kong's **John McDonald** has a stellar season in Asia, winning at **Macau, Batu Tiga, Penang** and **Phillipines Grand Prix**. He drove a **Ralt**.
- The final race of the Brazilian Formula Super Vee championship had 41 cars on the grid, still a record for single seaters in the country. The race was won by **Eduardo Celidônio** but the champion was **Francisco Lameirão**, who had raced in England and Portugal in **1970**.
- Italian **Renzo Zorzi** wins the **Monaco** Formula 3 race in a rare **GRD** with **Lancia** engine. He actually inherited the win because on the road winner **Conny Andersson** is handed a one minute penalty for an infraction. Curiously, **Renzo** was born on the same date as **Emerson Fittipaldi**, who by then had been world champion twice.
- **Roy Lane** wins for the first time in the British Hill Climb championship. He would become the top winner in that series in years to come.
- South African Formula 1 is done. After many years running the only Formula 1 championship outside of Formula 1, South Africa changes course and adopts Formula Atlantic for **1976**. The final race is won by **Ian Scheckter** and there are only 8 starters.
- Argentine Formula 1 in crisis: only three races are run during the season, so no champion is declared.
- **Porsche** 917s race for the last time in the Interserie and win the championship. **Alfa Romeos** and **Mirages** also take part in a few races.

1976

Champions
Formula 1 (Drivers): James Hunt
Formula 1 (Manufacturers): Ferrari
European Formula 2: Jean-Pierre Jabouille
European Formula 3: Riccardo Patrese
British Formula 3: Bruno Giacomelli (Shellsport), Rupert Keegan (BP)
Italian Formula 3: Riccardo Patrese
German F3: Bertram Schafer
Swedish Formula 3: Conny Ljungfeldt
World Manufacturers Championship: Porsche
World Sportscar championship: Porsche
Interserie: Herbert Muller
USAC Indy Car: Gordon Johncock
Shellsport Group 8: David Purley
American Formula 5000: Brian Redman
Tasman Cup: Warwick Brown
South African Formula Atlantic: Ian Scheckter
NASCAR: Cale Yarborough
IROC: A.J. Foyt
European Touring Car Championship: Jean Xhenceval/Pierre Dieudonne
British Saloon Car Championship: Bernard Unett, Chrysler Avenger
DRM: Hans Heyer
DARM: Johann Weishedinger
European GT Championship: Toine Hezemans
Australian Touring Car Championship: Allan Moffat
Australian Gold Star Championship: John Leffler
Australian Formula 2: Graeme Crawford
New Zealand Gold Star Championship: Ken Smith

New Zealand International Championship: Ken Smith
New Zealand Saloon Car Championship: J. Nazer
Brazilian Formula Ford: Jose Pedro Chateaubriand
Brazilian Formula Super-Vee: Nelson Piquet
Brazilian Touring Cars: Bob Sharp (B), Vital Machado (A)
Argentinian Formula 1: Pedro Passadore
Argentinian Formula 2: Miguel Angel Guerra
Argentinian Formula 4: Hector de Rossi
Argentinian Turismo de Carretera: Hector Gradassi
Trans-Am: George Follmer
IMSA Camel GTO: Al Holbert GTU: Brad Friselle
Japanese Formula 2: Noritake Takahara
Fuji Grand Champion: Noritake Takahara
British Formula Atlantic: Ted Wentz
Canadian Formula Atlantic: Gilles Villeneuve
Irish Formula Atlantic: Patsy McGarrity
European Formula Super-Vee: Mika Arpiainen
US Formula Super-Vee: Tom Bagley
Central American Championship: Kikos Fonseca
Mexican Formula Ford Championship: Memo Rojas, Sr.
European Hill Climb Championship: Mauro Nesti
French Super Tourism: Jean-Pierre Beltoise
French Formula Renault: Alain Prost
Spanish Championship: Manuel Juncosa
Formula 1430: Pere Nogues
Belgian Championship: Alain Semoulin
Dutch Touring Car Championship: Jan Lammers/Huub Vermeulen
Dutch Formula Ford: Michael Bleekemolen
Austrian Championship: Sepp Manhalter
Peace and Friendship Cup (Formula Easter): Jiri Cerva
Peace and Friendship Cup (Touring Cars): Milan Zid
Soviet Formula 1: Vladimir Grekov
Estonian Championship (F1+2): Henry Saarm
Bulgarian Championship: Georgi Malkanov
European Formula Renault: Didier Pironi
Danish Volvo 142 Cup: Jorgen Poulsen
Danish Formula 3: Jac Nelleman
German Formula Ford: Tibor Meray
European Formula Vee: Dan Molin
BARC Formula Ford: Rod Bremmer
British Formula Ford 2000: Ian Taylor
British Formula Ford: David Kennedy
BRCSS Formula Ford: David Kennedy
Formula Italia: Roberto Campominosi
BARC Saloon Car Championship: Jeff Allam
BRSCC/BRDC/MCD Saloon Car Championship: Danny Albertson
Portuguese Speed Championship: Group A: Edgard Moreira Fortes
Portuguese Speed Championship: Group B: Antonio Onofre
Greek Hill Climb Championship: Giorgos Moschous
South African Formula Ford 1600: Desire Wilson
South African Formula Vee – P. Morrison
Renault 5 Cup: Mauro Bald
Porsche Cup: Bob Wollek
SCCA Formula A - Jerry Hansen, Lola

SCCA Formula B – Bobby Brown, March
SCCA Formula C – Michael Gilbert, GRD
SCCA Formula Super Vee – Herm Johnson, Lola
SCCA Formula Vee – James Brookshire, Agitator
SCCA Formula Ford – Dennis Firestone, Crossle
SCCA A Sports Racing - Jerry Hansen, Lola
SCCA B Sports Racing – Carl Thompson III, Lola
SCCA C Sports Racing – Fred Stevenson, Bobsy
SCCA D Sports Racing – Jeff Miller, Wynnfurst Kohler
SCCA A Production – Gene Bothello, Chevrolet Corvette
SCCA B Production – Howard Park, Chevrolet Corvette
SCCA C Production – Elliott Forbes-Robinson
SCCA D Production – Paul Newman, Triumph
SCCA E Production – Terry Visger, MGB
SCCA F Production – Dick Blizzard, Alfa Romeo
SCCA G Production – Joe Hauser, Datsun
SCCA H Production – Todd Wheeler, Austin Healey
SCCA A Sedan – Randy Blessing, Chevrolet Camaro
SCCA B Sedan – Elliott Forbes Robinson, Datsun
SCCA C Sedan – Dick Davenport, Datsun
USAC Sprint Cars – Larry Dickson
USAC Midgets – Sleepy Tripp
USAC Silver Crown – Billy Cassella
Euro Cup Renault 5 – Yves Fremont
Australian Formula Ford – Richard Carter
Swiss Hill Climbing Championship – Eugen Strahl
German Formula Vee – Rudi Niggemeier
German Formula Super Vee – Dieter Engel
German Hill Climbing Championship – Ludwig Nieberger
VW Scirocco Jr. Cup – Manfred Winkelhock
East German Formula B8 – Ulrich Melkus
East German Touring Cars, 1300 cc – L.Thomas
Danish Formula Ford 1600 – Soren Aggerholm
British Formula Vee – Tim Flynn
Chilean Formula 4 – Juan Carlos Silva
Chilean Turismo Nacional – Rodrigo Cana Correa
ARCA – Dave Dayton
NASCAR Modifieds – Jerry Cook
Rhodesian Formula Vee – Mike Wesson
Rhodesian Sports Car – Isaac Codron
Rhodesian Saloon Cars – Derick Henderson
IMCA Sprint Car –   Ralph Parkinson
Norwegian Formula Vee – Edvard Haug
British Hillclimbing: Roy Lane
International Supermodified: Steve Gioia Jr.
Australian Sports Sedan: Allan Moffat
French Super Tourism: Jean Pierre Beltoise
French Hillclimbing: Michel Pignard
Uruguayan Touring Cars – Gustavo Trelles
Scottish Superstox – Bill Pullar
Scottish Saloon Stocks – Robert Bruce
Russian Formula Libre – Vladimir Grekov

Driver fatalities during the year in racing incidents: Babe Sneva, Alex Wittwer, Ron Reguia, Fernando Cuevo, Ron Keister, Rene Spengler, Raul Salerno, Dennis Schumann, Gary Bott, Mary Lou King, Kai Berner, Jim Adamson, Jim Golden, Billy Wertz, Brian Wallace, Len Pehrlich, Barry Kettering, Andre Haller, Richard Sutherland, Randolph Thomas, Sonny Allen, Rod Ferree, Larry Kirkpatrick, Ernst Raetz, Richard Hendershot, Calvin Gilstrap, Jukk Reintam, Doug Hjermstad, Jim Matthews, Mark Freed, Jen-Pierre Coubault, Mike Vella, John Wingfield, Ed Losinski, John Hubbard, Dave Miller, Ron Dawson, Bob Toleman, Daniel Lawson, Michael Giddings

FORMULA 1

- Drivers participating for the first time: **Ingo Hoffmann, Patrick Neve, Boy Hayje, Jac Nelleman, Connie Anderson, Warwick Brown, Alex Ribeiro, Gunnar Nilsson, Masahiro Hasemi, Kazuyoshi Hoshino, Hans Binder, Masami Kuwashima, Emilio de Villota, Emilio Zapico, Otto Stuppacher, Alessandro Pesenti-Rossi, Loris Kessel, Divina Galica, Brian McGuire, Karl Oppitzhauser, Noritake Takahara**
- Drivers who won for the first time: **John Watson**
- First win, manufacturers: **Penske**
- New manufacturers: **Ligier, Kojima**
- First Bridgestone tire participation in F1. Japanese Dunlop tires are also used.
- First GP in Asia
- Japanese drivers manage to qualify for a GP for the first time, for the only driver to attempt this at the championship level (**Hiroshi Fushida**), did not come close to qualifying. Two of them, **Masahiro Hasemi** and **Kazuyoshi Hoshino** do very well, the latter climbing to third at one point in a private **Tyrrell** 007.
- Tall air boxes are gone. GP fans enjoy the tall air boxes in three races of the **1976** season. By Spain, the tall air boxes are gone, including the huge implement famously appearing on the **Ligier**. As a result cars lose another element of differentiation, for air boxes came in many different shapes and sizes since adopted in **1971**.
- **Masahiro Hasemi**, the Japanese driver supposedly scored the fastest lap in his home race drove the **Kojima**. The organizers corrected this a bit later, assigning the fastest lap to **Laffite**. To this day many sources still indicate that Hasemi had the fastest lap.
- Bearded **John Watson**, who promised to cut off his beard whenever he wins a first GP, does as promised, in Austria. The win came at the same place where **Penske** driver **Mark Donohue** died the previous season.
- A 6-wheel Formula 1 car is used for the first time. The **Tyrrell** P-34 lasts another season but there didn't seem to be any competitive advantage using six instead of 4 wheels.
- American **Ted Wentz** claims that he would be in the GP circuit in **1977** driving a **March**. It never happens. Such plans were often announced in the 70s.
- Former **Ensign** sponsors HB Bewaking Alarmsystems convinced a British Court that the team had failed to live up to its promise of a competitive car in **1975** and therefore, the car was theirs! So the **Boro** came to be. Every inch an **Ensign**, **Larry Perkins** could do very little with it in **1976**. At least he was not sued by the sponsors.
- Something about Sweden: **Tyrrell** again finishes 1-2 in Sweden, with the same drivers, **Scheckter-Depailler**. This turns out to be a 6-wheeler's F1 only win.
- **Rolf Stommelen** drives a 3rd **Brabham-Alfa** in Germany and finishes 6th, earning his last Formula 1 point.

- The race is also notable for **Chris Amon**'s amazing 3rd place starting grid in the **Ensign** and the resurgence of **Lotus** and **Mario Andretti** as a factor.
- **Lotus** actually starts the year in apparent disarray: it fields no less than four drivers in the first two races: **Peterson, Andretti, Evans** and **Nilsson**. Eventually it settles on **Andretti** and **Nilsson**.
- **Tyrrell** sells some of its 007s to privateers. **Pesenti-Rossi** does a few races, while **Otto Stuppacher** fails to qualify. He almost got a chance to start in Italy but had left the track. The one **Tyrrell** 007 that does well is **Hoshino**'s, in Japan, which climbs up to 3rd place in the deluge conditions.
- As **Niki Lauda** makes a surprising come back in the Italian GP to defend his title, **Ferrari** also fields a third car for **Reutemann**. The best of the Maranello lot is **Regazzoni**, who finishes second behind **Peterson**'s **March**.
- Sponsor issues: in addition to prophylactic Durex, which sponsors **Surtees**, girlie magazine **Penthouse** and rolling paper **Rizla** sponsor one of the **Heskeths**. BBC refuses to air Formula 1 broadcasts because of the "indecent" **Surtees** patron.

Other categories:
- FISA divided endurance racing in two: a Silhouette, Group 5 Championship (World Manufacturers Championship) and a Group 6 Championship (World Championship of Sports Cars)
- **BMW** fields a proper challenge to **Porsche** in the World Manufacturers Championship, in the form of a 3.5 CSL against the 935. Even a turbo version appears at the end of the season. **BMW**s win three times, to **Porsche** four wins. However, at the end of the year **BMW** decides to drop the 3.5 CSL in favor of winning the Division 1, for 2-liter cars, where it faces no competition.
- In the World Sports Cars Championship, **Porsche** takes all, in spite of a heated challenge from **Alpine-Renault**, which is fast but does not win any races. **Alfa Romeo** also takes part in some events. A number of "name" drivers race in the **Alpine Renault** during the year, including **Jody Scheckter** and **Patrick Depailler**.
- **Porsche** also takes the non-championship 24 Hours of Le Mans, with drivers **Jacky Ickx** and **Gijs Van Lennep**. The latter retires after the race.
- The Le Mans **Porsche** win is the first by a turbo car.
- The ACO includes new categories in the 24 Hours of Le Mans. In addition to a GTP category, contested by the likes of **Inaltera-Ford**, two NASCAR cars take part in the race, a **Ford** Torino by **Dick Brooks/Dick Hutcherson** and a **Dodge Charger** for **Hershell McGriff/Doug McGriff**. The endeavor is not met with success. A category for IMSA regulation racers is also created, which lasted a few years.
- A **Peugeot**-engined **WM** takes part in Le Mans. The factory gives unofficial, behind the scenes support to the outfit, which had been trying to qualify for the race since **1971**.
- In spite of the variety, there were no **Ferrari**s on the **Le Mans** field for the first time since World War II.
- The **Inaltera** of **Pescarolo/Beltoise** finishes 8th in its **Le Mans** debut.
- **BMW** also takes the race more serious than before, fielding six cars.
- **Renault** enters the Formula 2 championship as an engine supplier. The French engines equip the **Martini** and **Elf** teams and win most races and finish 1-2-3-4 in the Championship.
- **Alfa Romeo** wins for the last time an overall race in the European Touring Car Championship, with **Amerigo Bigliazzi** and **Spartaco Dini**.
- British Leyland fields a works team of **Jaguars** in the European Touring Car Championship. Although fast, the cars fail to win and the Luigi Team wins the crown, with Belgians **Jean Xhenceval** and **Pierre Dieudonne**.

- **Al Holbert** wins the IMSA Camel GT championship driving a **Chevy Monza** in most races.
- The South African Formula 1 championship is replaced by Formula Atlantic. In fact, just a few of the cars were actual Formula 1's, which normally won, the ever smaller fields boosted by Formula 2 and Formula 5000 cars.
- Too late! The **Dodge** engined **Shadow** wins a U.S. F-5000 event, with **Jackie Oliver**, at **Road America**. It is the first time a **Chrysler** engined F-5000 car wins anywhere. The championship is dropped by the SCCA at the end of the year, morphed into a new Can-Am.
- **Cosworth** cometh. After dominating Formula 1 for many years, the **Cosworth** engine comes to Indycar. Little by little it replaces the venerable but dated, **Offenhauser** engine. Al Unser wins for the first time with this engine at **Pocono**. The writing is on the wall.
- **Arturo Merzario**, better known as an **Alfa, Ferrari, Abarth** and Formula 1 driver, had a rather unusual mount in the 24 Hours of Daytona: a NASCAR Style **Dodge** shared with **Ed Negre**.
- **Janet Guthrie** makes her first attempt at qualifying at the Indy 500 but DNQ. She did start a Champ Car race at **Trenton**, to get mileage. She promised to be back and become the first female Indy 500 driver.
- **Janet** also debuts at NASCAR, doing 5 races. In **1977** she would take part in 19 races.
- The last edition of the American Formula 5000 Championship is held. For the upcoming season, SCCA decided to revive the Can-Am series, by placing sports cars bodies on the Formula 5000 cars and accepting 2-Liter sports cars.
- Busy man: **Derek Warwick** races in no less than 63 Formula Ford events during the year, winning about half of them. Most drivers do not do that in a whole career!
- **Bill Elliott** debuts in NASCAR. He would become the category's most popular driver.
- **Cale Yarborough** wins the first of his three straight Winston Cup. **David Pearson**, who ran a limited schedule, wins more races.
- The very last edition of the **Targa Florio** is run. The winners are local drivers "**Amphicar**"(**Eugenio Renna)/Armando Floridia**, in an **Osella**.
- The Brazilian government outlaws racing in the entire country, claiming it is a waste of gasoline. The president of the Brazilian Confederation actually convinces the military government that not holding races would result in more gasoline waste!
- The racing community joins hands to help the victims of the Friuli (Italy) earthquake. A couple of races are organized with Alfasud and **FIAT** 131 cars at **Varano** and many prominent drivers of the day come to lend their support: **Lauda, Scheckter, Peterson, Regazzoni, Laffite, Brambilla, Pace, Jones, Fittipaldi, Merzario, Kessel, Ertl** (both he and Laffite refused the reimbursement of the airline ticket), **Giacomelli, Lombardi, Zorzi, Flammini, Munari, Cambiaghi, Agostini** and **Cecotto**, among many others. Some F-1 teams also make donations and the event is a success. **Merzario-Paolo Galli** win the Alfasud race, in which famous drivers are matched with Alfasud series regulars. **Regazzoni-Pianta**, win the 131 race.
- A new club sports racing category, Sports 2000 is created. It is indeed inexpensive for the time. A **Lola** T490 chassis cost £4,750, an engine goes for £850. Lola produces 99 of these cars between **1976** to **1979**.
- **Herbert Muller** wins his third straight Interserie, driving a 2-Liter **Sauber**. He did not win a single overall victory, unable to beat the likes of **Reinhold Joest** in a Turbo **Porsche** 908/4 and **Peter Hoffman** in an old Can Am **McLaren**. Scoring for the 2-liters was separate from the larger cars.

1977

BRM attempted a full-time return to Formula 1 in 1977 but it did not work out (Photo Teddy Pilette collection)

Champions
Formula 1 (Drivers): Niki Lauda
Formula 1 (Manufacturers): Ferrari
European Formula 2: Rene Arnoux
European Formula 3: Piercarlo Ghinzani
British Formula 3: Stephen South (Vandervell), Derek Daly (BP)
Italian Formula 3: Elio di Angelis
German F3: Peter Scharman
Swedish Formula 3: Anders Olofsson
World Manufacturers Championship: Porsche
World Sportscar Championship: Alfa Romeo
Can-Am: Patrick Tambay
Interserie: Helmut Bross
USAC Indy Car: Tom Sneva
Shellsport Group 8: Tony Trimmer
South African Formula Atlantic: Ian Scheckter
NASCAR: Cale Yarborough
IROC: A.J. Foyt
European Touring Car Championship: Dieter Quester
British Saloon Car Championship: Bernard Unett, Chrysler Avenger
DRM: Rolf Stommelen
DARM: Walter Struckman
Australian Touring Car Championship: Allan Moffat
Australian Gold Star Championship: John McCormack
Australian Formula 2: Peter Larner
New Zealand Gold Star Championship: Dave McMillan
New Zealand International Championship: Keke Rosberg
New Zealand Saloon Car Championship: J. Nazer
New Zealand Production Car Championship: I. Tulloch
Brazilian Formula Ford: Arthur Bragantini
Brazilian Formula Super-Vee: Alfredo Guarana Menezes

Brazilian Touring Cars (D3): Amadeo Campos
Brazilian Touring Cars (D1, class C): Edgard Mello Filho
Argentinian Formula 1: Pedro Passadore
Argentinian Formula 2: Miguel Angel Guerra
Argentinian Formula 4: Juan Jose Reybet
Argentinian Turismo de Carretera: Juan Maria Traverso
Trans-Am: Ludwig Heimrath
IMSA Camel GTO: Al Holbert GTU: Walt Maas
Japanese Formula 2: Kazuyoshi Hoshino
Fuji Long Distance: Katayama Racing
Fuji Grand Champion: Tetsu Ikuzawa
Canadian Formula Atlantic: Gilles Villeneuve
Irish Formula Atlantic: Patsy McGarrity
European Formula Super-Vee: Arie Luyendyk
US Formula Super-Vee: Bob Lazier
Central American Championship: Kikos Fonseca
European Hill Climb Championship: Mauro Nesti
French Super Tourism: Jean-Pierre Beltoise
French Formula Renault: Joel Gouhier
Spanish Championship: Juan Onoro
Formula 1430: Miguel Molons
Belgian Championship: Raymond Raus
Dutch Touring Car Championship: Henri van Oorschot/Huub Vermeulen
Swiss Championship: Markus Hotz
Peace and Friendship Cup (Formula Easter): Karel Jilek
Peace and Friendship Cup (Touring cars): Oldrich Brunclik
Soviet Formula Easter: Toomas Napa
European Formula Renault: Alain Prost
Estonian Formula Easter: Boris Eylandt
Polish Championship: Marcin Biernacki
Danish Special Saloon Championship: Jorgen Jensen
Danish Formula 3: Jac Nelleman
Dutch Formula Ford: Marteen Henneman
USAC Mini Indy (Super-Vee): Tom Bagley/Herm Johnson
BARC Formula Ford: David Leslie
Brush Fusegear Formula Ford: Nigel Mansell
Dunlop Star of Tomorrow Formula Ford: Willy T. Ribbs
BRSCC Formula Ford: Chico Serra
Formula Italia: Siegfried Stohr
British Formula Ford 2000: Rad Dougall
MCD British Formula Ford: Trevor Van Rooyen
BARC Saloon Car Championship: Derrick Brunt
BRSCC/BRDC/MCD Saloon Car Championship: Derrick Brunt
Portuguese Speed Championship: Group A: Edgar Fortes
Portuguese Speed Championship: Group B: Robert Giannone
Coupe de L'Avenir Prototypes: Phillippe Streiff
Porsche Cup: Bob Wollek
SCCA Formula B – Kevin Cogan, Ralt
SCCA Formula C – Bill Anspach, Chevron
SCCA Formula Super Vee – Steve Ovel, Lola
SCCA Formula Vee – Mike Frangkiser, Lynx
SCCA Formula Ford – Dave Weitzenhof, Zink
SCCA A Sports Racing - Jerry Hansen, Lola
SCCA B Sports Racing - Ed Abate, Lola

SCCA C Sports Racing – Giuseppe Castellano, Lola
SCCA D Sports Racing – Jeff Miller, Wynnfurst
SCCA A Production – Steve Anderson, Chevrolet Corvette
SCCA B Production – Howard Meister, Porsche
SCCA C Production – Logan Blackburn, Datsun
SCCA D Production – Tom Robertson, Lotus
SCCA E Production – Terry Visger, MGB
SCCA F Production – Tom Collier, Triumph
SCCA G Production – Mike Pinney, MG
SCCA H Production – Todd Wheeler, Austin Healey
SCCA A Sedan – Randy Blessing, Chevrolet Camaro
SCCA B Sedan - Stuart Fisher, Mazda
SCCA C Sedan – Dick Davenport, Datsun
SCCA Showroom Stock A – D. J. Fazekas, Datsun
SCCA Showroom Stock B – Tom Kersey, Alfa Romeo
SCCA Showroom Stock C – Douglas Farrow, Mercury Capri
USAC Sprint Cars – Sheldon Kinser
USAC Midgets – Mel Kenyon
USAC Silver Crown – Larry Rice
Euro Cup Renault 5 – Mauro Baldi
Asian International Challenge – Steven Millen
Eire Championship - Patsy McGarrity
Australian Formula Ford – John Smith
Swiss Hill Climbing Championship – Markus Hotz
German VW Cup – Georg Lensing Hebben
German Formula Vee – Norbert Gross
German Formula Super Vee – Dieter Engel
German Hill Climbing Championship – Richard Sutter
East German Formula B8 – Wolfgang Gunther
East German Touring Cars, 600 cc – Hans Dieter Kessler
East German Touring Cars, 1300 cc – Peter Mucke
Danish Formula Ford 1600 – Klaus Pedersen
British Formula Vee – Dave Greenwood
Chilean Formula 4 – Juan Carlos Silva
ARCA – Conan Myers
NASCAR Modifieds – Jerry Cook
Rhodesian Formula Vee – Mike Wesson
Rhodesian Sports Car – Royce Love
Rhodesian Saloon Cars – Reg Lombard
IMCA Sprint Car – Bill Utz
International Supermodified: Jim Shampinee
British Hillclimbing: Alister Douglas-Osborn
Australian Sports Sedan: Frank Gardner
French Super Tourism: Jean Pierre Beltoise
French Hillclimbing: Christian Debias
Uruguayan Touring cars – Luiz Etchegoyen
South African Formula Vee – B. Smith
South African Group A – Mrs. J. Charlton/Sarel van der Merwe
Scottish Superstox – Les Clark
Scottish Saloon Stocks – Robert Bruce
Scottish Hot Rod – Hamish Buchanan

Driver fatalities during the year in racing incidents: Tom Pryce, Max Stewart, Bobby Isaac, Brian McGuire, Dave Peterson, Alexander Elvy, Franz Abraham, Len

McDonough, David West, Mike Swangler, Slava Starostenko, Jack Helget, Andino Coppari, Francois Burdet, Johnathan Canning, Aleksandr Lebeev, Vladislav Ondrejik, Moyto Valencia, Osvaldo Riera, Steve Bartram, Ted Kallos, Matthias Schafer, Pepe Llona, Jose Luis Gallo, Peter McCabe, Manuel Cunha, James McElreath Jr, Clemente Ribeiro da Silva, Mario Oscar Mazzoy, Preston Humphries.

FORMULA 1

- Drivers participating for the first time: **Gilles Villeneuve, Ricardo Patrese, Bruno Giacomelli, Patrick Tambay, Michael Bleekemolen, Hans Heyer, Mikko Kozarovitsky, Rupert Keegan, Lamberto Leoni, Danny Ongais, Hector Rebaque, Giorgio Francia, Bernard De Dryver, Andy Sutcliffe, Kunimitsu Takahashi**
- First wins: **Jacques Laffite, Gunnar Nilsson, Alan Jones**
- First win, manufacturers: **Shadow, Ligier, Wolf,**
- Drivers who won for the last time: **James Hunt, Gunnar Nilsson**
- New manufacturers: **Wolf, Lec, Renault, Apollon, McGuire**
- Last appearances by **Stanley-BRM** in the world championship.
- **March** announces it will quit Formula 1. **Max Mosley** sells his stake in the company and decides to be **Bernie Ecclestone**'s political/commercial sidekick full-time.
- A large number of **March 761's** is fielded by a number of private teams, with little effect.
- **Gunther Schmidt**'s **ATS** enters Formula 1 for the first time. At first, it fields the old **Penske** chassis, driven by **Jean-Pierre Jarier**. It actually scores (6th place) in the first race. No further success is forthcoming.
- **Renault** fields a turbo-engined formula 1 for the first time, driven by **Jean-Pierre Jabouille**, in the British GP. **BRM's** place in F1CA is given to the French constructor.
- The Japanese Grand Prix is held for a second time, then dropped from the schedule for many years. Last time the **Kojima** Formula 1 is raced. **Hoshino** started 11th in one of the cars.
- New game in town, veteran leaves: in this season, Michelin becomes a tire provider for the first time (Great Britain) and Dunlop starts its last GP (Japan)
- Brazilian driver **Carlos Pace** dies in a plane accident in Brazil. The plane was owned by another Brazilian, former driver **Marivaldo Fernandes**, who raced briefly in British Formula 3 in **1974,** who also dies in the accident.
- **Danny Ongais** races an Interscope entered **Penske** PC-4 in Canada and US. Grand Prix.
- **Hans Stuck** qualifies the **Brabham-Alfa** 2nd in Watkins Glen and drives away from the field under the rain, although he loses use of the clutch very early on. He lasts until lap 14, when an accident ends a very promising outing.
- Although **Ronnie Peterson** and the 6-wheel **Tyrrell** never came to terms, the fast Swede still squeezes a fastest lap in the U.S. Grand Prix East.
- Highly rated Canadian **Gilles Villeneuve** debuts in Formula 1 in the British Grand Prix, in a **McLaren**. He starts 9th and finishes 11th, generally giving a good account of himself.
- Ferrari politics: After winning the championship, **Niki Lauda** walks out on **Ferrari**, after the U.S. Grand Prix. He claims to have a bout of gastric flu but sources said he was truly upset with the dismissal of his mechanic **Ermano Cuogh**i and the fielding of a third **Ferrari** in Canada, to be driven by **Villeneuve. Chris Amon**, who managed the Canadian in the **Wolf** Can Am team, had called **Enzo Ferrari** early

in the year to recommend **Gilles**. Thus comes to an end a very successful, if rocky, relationship.
- The **Matra** engine wins for the first time in the World Formula 1 Championship. It happens in the Swedish Grand Prix, where **Laffite** and **Ligier** also win for the first time, thus, three first time wins. **Gunnar Nilsson**, the winner of the previous race, the wet Belgium GP, had also won a Grand Prix for the first time, albeit in a **Lotus**-Cosworth.
- A small constructor could still see some moments of stardom in the 70s. Under the rainy confusion of the Belgian Grand prix, **David Purley** finds himself in third place in the **Lec-Ford** for a few laps (some swear he led). **Brambilla** leads a few laps on the **Surtees** and finishes fourth.
- At **Anderstorp, Jackie Oliver** does a final Grand Prix for **Shadow**, replacing **Patrese** who is on Formula 2 duty elsewhere.
- **BRM** starts a race for the last time in South Africa. **Perkins** finishes 15th and last. A number of other drivers attempted to qualify the hapless car during the season, with no luck.
- **Hans Heyer** starts the German Grand Prix in the **ATS**, although he was not even first reserve. He is disqualified.
- An over subscribed entry list leads RAC and BRDC to hold a pre-qualifying session for 14 drivers two days before the actual qualifying for the British Grand Prix. The fastest is **Gilles Villeneuve**, who was entered in a third **McLaren**.
- **Jody Scheckter** wins Cosworth's 100th Grand Prix in **Monaco**.
- **Patrick Tambay** is a bit of a sensation driving a Theodore entered **Ensign** in the second half of the season. He scores five points and is hired by **McLaren** to replace **Mass** in **1978**.

Other categories:
- At **Le Mans Jacky Ickx** is placed in another **Porsche** factory car after the car he is sharing with **Henri Pescarolo** retires and manages to catch the **Alpine-Renaults** from very far behind. The **Haywood-Barth** car had spent one hour in the pits early on the race and was in 41st place when it went back racing.

Barth in the pits, Le Mans 1977. It was left to him to bring the sick car home. (Jurgen Barth collection)

- **Ickx** drove scintillating stints at night and was in the right place when the **Alpine-Renaults** failed, in spite of **Jabouille-Bell**'s efforts. **Ickx** wins sharing the car with **Hurley Haywood** and **Jurgen Barth**, the first recognized 3-driver team to win **Le Mans**. **Ed Hugus** reportedly had driven the **Rindt-Gregory** car for the **1965** win but the information is wildly disputed to this day.
- The winning **Porsche** takes the flag at walking pace. A disintegrating piston sends the car to the pits in the last half hour of the race. Approaching 24 hours, **Jurgen Barth** is sent out to drive the car very slowly and carefully for two more laps, which does the trick.
- The **Peugeot**-engined **WM** finished 15th at Le Mans this time.

- DRM adopts Group 5 regulations and a year-long battle between **Rolf Stommelen** and **Bob Wollek** bodes well for the future. However, the hype is only sustained for a few seasons.
- **BMW** decides against properly opposing **Porsche** for overall honors in the World Manufacturers Championship and drops the 3.0 CSL in favor of 2 liter 320.
- **Alfa Romeo** wins all eight races of the World Sports Cars Championship. Wins are split evenly between **Arturo Merzario** and **Vittorio Brambilla**, while **Jean-Pierre Jarier** shared two of **Merzario**'s wins. The championship is very poorly supported and a couple of races have single digit starters.
- The new Can-Am debuts to mixed reviews. In the first race of the season, top driver **Brian Redman** has a severe shunt and is sidelined. The winner is relative unknown **Tom Klausler**, in a peculiarly bodied **Schkee**. **Chris Amon**, who was supposed to drive the **Wolf** car, retires for good and hires **Gilles Villeneuve** as his replacement. The second race is also won by a relative unknown, Formula Atlantic driver **Don Breidenbach. Patrick Tambay** takes over the **Redman** seat and wins convincingly. Nice but not quite the Can-Am.
- **Lella Lombardi** races in NASCAR. Belgian driver **Christine Beckers** also tries it.
- **Arturo Merzario** wins an Interserie race driving the turbo **Alfa Romeo**. After that, the sports **Alfas** are retired once and for all.
- **Harald Ertl** debuted a **Toyota** Turbo Group 5 car in the DRM, a car that would be taken over by champion **Rolf Stommelen** the next year. **Ertl** did not miss the recalcitrant ride, in fact became DRM champion driving a **BMW** in **1978**, while **Rolf** suffered with the car that was no match to the 935s. However, **Ertl** did win a non-championship race with the car at **Zolder,** in **1977**.
- *Autosprint* reports that F1 driver **Jean-Pierre Jarier** had won the 6 Hours of **Dakar**, sharing a **Porsche** with **Raymond Tourol,** who had already won the race in **1975**. A very traditional African race, dating back to the 50s, it is a shame no one reports properly on the history of this race.
- The winner of the Indy 500 is no other than **A.J. Foyt**, who thus becomes the first 4-time winner.
- **Tom Sneva** posted the first 200 mph plus lap at Indy. **Tom Sneva** wins Penske's first USAC (Indy car) title.
- After a few years away, Europeans come back to the Indy 500. **Clay Regazzoni** managed to qualify but retired. **Teddy Pilette** fails to qualify. It should be noted that in those days, many more than 33 drivers tries to qualify for the race, in fact, sometimes there were more people out than in the field.
- **Lamberto Leoni** wins the **Misano** race of the European Formula 2 in a **Ferrari** engined **Chevron**. In spite of the win, **Ferrari** does not get very excited about the Trivellato team feat and this is **Ferrari**'s last win in the category. **Leoni** never repeats the form, as well.
- The Austrian Formula Libre races of the late 70s, which basically included F2, F3 and SuperVees, every once in a while had a surprise visitor from another country. Even mysterious Greek driver named **Christos Katsogiannos** is entered at the Pfingstpokalrennen. He and his mount, a Super-Vee **Kaimann,** never show up. His name does not appear anywhere else.
- **Jac Nelleman** wins the Danish GP for F-3 yet again. This time, the event has an international flavor with drivers from Norway, Sweden and Holland in attendance.
- The **Macau** Grand Prix morphs from a Formula Libre race into a proper single-seater race. The winner is **Riccardo Patrese**, in a **Chevron**. In addition to him, **Alan Jones** and **Vern Schuppan** also raced.
- **Pilbeam** wins for the first time as a marque. The **Pilbeam** cars would become the top winner in British hill climbing, eventually venturing into other areas, including sports cars.

- Peruvian drivers in Europe were a rare sight in the 70s but **Jorge Koechlin** drove an **Argo** in British and European Formula 3, without much distinction.
- Meanwhile, **Jan Lammers** learns the ropes in a Formula 3 **Hawke** in European Formula 3.
- Another large Brazilian contingent came to drive in Formula 3 in Europe: **Nelson Piquet, Mario Pati Jr.** (son of then Brazilian GP race director), **Aryon Cornelsen, Fernando Jorge** and **Mario Ferraris Neto**. Of these only **Piquet** succeeded. He was also the only one to choose to race exclusively in the European championship.
- **Ian Ashley**, who had done Formula 1 in **1976**, steps down to Formula 3, racing a **Lola**. The car is not successful, so he goes back to Formula 1, where he has a nasty crash in Canada, driving a **Hesketh**.
- The Canadian Formula Atlantic championship becomes a truly international championship. In addition to the obvious Canadians, Americans such as **Steve Saleen, Bobby Rahal, Price Cobb, Jeff Wood, Tom Gloy** and **Kevin Cogan** race in the series, plus Finn **Keke Rosberg**, Venezuelans **Juan Cochesa** and **Francisco Romero** and New Zealanders **Dave McMillan** and **David Oxton**. GP drivers **Jacques Laffite** and **Patrick Depailler** drive in the **Trois Rivieres** and **Quebec** city events, **Eddie Cheever** appearing in the latter. **Didier Pironi** races in **St. Felicien**.
- A team of capable Argentines and an Uruguayan races 1.3 **Alfa Romeos** in the European Touring Car Championship, usually winning the class. Among the drivers used were **Juan Pablo Zampa, Eugenio Breard, Nano Parrado, Eduardo Marques** and **Jorge Serafini**. The effort, sponsored by Argentine cigarette maker 43 70, is enthusiastically covered in the Argentine press.
- The ill-fated **Jaguar** effort at the ETCC manages a fourth place in **Silverstone**'s Tourist Trophy (**Derek Bell/Andy Rouse**). The team also places second at the **Nürburgring but** that is not enough to save the British Leyland program.

1978

Champions
Formula 1 (Drivers): Mario Andretti
Formula 1 (Manufacturers): Lotus
European Formula 2: Bruno Giacomelli
European Formula 3: Jan Lammers
British Formula 3: Nelson Piquet (BP), Derek Warwick (Vandervell)
French Formula 3: Alain Prost, Jean Louis Schlesser
Italian Formula 3: Siegfried Stohr
German F3: Bertram Schafer
Swedish Formula 3: Anders Oloffson
World Manufacturers Championship: Porsche
European Sports Car Championship: Reinhold Joest
Can-Am: Alan Jones
Interserie: Reinhold Joest
USAC Indy Car: Tom Sneva
Shellsport Group 8: Tony Trimmer
South African Formula 1: Ian Scheckter
NASCAR: Cale Yarborough
IROC: Al Unser
European Touring Car Championship: Umberto Grano
British Saloon Car Championship: Richard Longman, Mini
DRM: Harald Ertl

DARM: Klaus Niedzwiedz
Australian Touring Car Championship: Peter Brock

By 1978 road races were far in between. This is the start of the Braling Road Race in Purbalingga, in Indonesia. Lambertus Van Vreden in the Honda number 11. Photo Therry Van Vreden collection.

Australian Gold Star Championship: Graham McRae
New Zealand International Championship: Keke Rosberg
New Zealand 2 Liter Saloon Championship: B. Platt
New Zealand Production Car Championship: B. Lloyd
Brazilian Formula Ford: Amedeo Ferri
Brazilian Formula Super Vee: Alfredo Guarana Menezes
Argentinian Formula 1: Luis di Palma
Argentinian Formula 2: Agustin Beamonte
Argentinian Formula 4: Eliseo Salazar
Argentinian Turismo de Carretera: Juan Maria Traverso
Trans-Am: Greg Pickett
IMSA Camel GTX: Peter Gregg GTU: Dave White
Japanese Formula 2: Kazuyoshi Hoshino
Japanese Formula Pacific: Masahiro Hasemi
Fuji Long Distance: Katayama Racing
Fuji Grand Champion: Kazuyoshi Hoshino
Canadian Formula Atlantic: Howdy Holmes
Irish Formula Atlantic: Eddie Jordan
European Formula Super-Vee: Helmut Henzler
US Formula Super-Vee: Bill Alsup
European Hill Climb Championship: Jean-Marie Almeras
Spanish Championship: Carlos Jodar
Formula 1430: Juan Alonso de Celada
Swedish Touring Cars: Lei Nilsson
Belgian Championship: Claude Bourgoignie
Dutch Touring Car Championship: Henri Van Oorschot/Claude Bourgoignie
Swiss F3 Championship: Patrick Studer
French Super Tourism: Lucien Guitteny
French Formula Renault: Philippe Alliot
Eire Championship: Eddie Jordan
Ulster Trophy: Mike Nugent
Central American Championship: Carlos Cromeyer

Czech Championship: Frantisek Valovic
Peace and Friendship Cup (Formula Easter): Uli Melkus
Peace and Friendship Cup (Touring Cars): Vlastimil Tomasek
Soviet Championship (Formula Easter): Raul Sarap
Estonian Championship (Formula Easter): Raul Sarap
Hungarian Championship: Dezsoe Kiss
Danish Special Saloon Championship: Jorgen Jensen
Dutch Formula Ford: Ed Brower
USAC Mini Indy (Super-Vee): Bill Alsup
British Formula Ford 2000: Mike White (BARC), Syd Fox (MCD)
BRSCC Formula Ford: Ken Acheson
British Formula Ford: Ken Acheson
Formula Italia: Rodolfo Bellini
BARC Saloon Car Championship: Gerry Marshall
BRSCC/BRDC/MCD Saloon Car Championship: Gerry Marshall
Benelux Formula Ford 1600: Thierry Boutsen
Porsche Cup: Bob Wollek
SCCA Formula A – Stuart Forbes-Robinson, Lola
SCCA Formula B – Jerry Hansen, March
SCCA Formula C – Jim Trueman, March
SCCA Formula Super Vee – Mike Yoder, Lola
SCCA Formula Vee – Doug Courtney
SCCA Formula Ford – David Loring, Eagle
SCCA A Sports Racing - Jerry Hansen, Lola
SCCA B Sports Racing – Gary Grove, Chevron
SCCA C Sports Racing – Jeff Miller, Lola
SCCA D Sports Racing – Dave Leeson, LeGrand
SCCA A Production – Elliott Forbes-Robinson, Chevrolet Corvette
SCCA B Production - Andy Porterfield, Chevrolet Corvette
SCCA C Production – Frank Leary, Datsun
SCCA D Production – Trom Brennan, Datsun
SCCA E Production – Robert Overby, Porsche
SCCA F Production – Jack May, Triumph
SCCA G Production – Mike Pinney, MGB
SCCA H Production – Wlly Hicks, Austin Healey
SCCA A Sedan – Randy Blessing, Chevrolet Corvette
SCCA B Sedan – Dave Frellsen, Datsun
SCCA C Sedan - Dick Davenport, Datsun
SCCA Showroom Stock A – D.J. Fazekas, Datsun
SCCA Showroom Stock B – Don Knowles, Saab
SCCA Showroom Stock C – Bob Jordan, Chevrolet Vega
USAC World of Outlaws – Sheldon Kinser
USAC Sprint Cars – Tom Bigelow
USAC Midgets – Rich Vogler
USAC Silver Crown – Pancho Carter
Euro Cup Renault 5 – Wolfgang Schutz
British Formula Vee – John Holmes
Australian Formula Ford – John Wright
Swiss Hill Climbing Championship – Andre Chevalley
Swiss Championship – Eugen Strahl
Swiss Renault Cup – Hanspeter Velliger
German Sports Cars – Mario Ketterer
German VW Cup – Walter Struchan
German Formula Super Vee – Helmut Henzler

German Hill Climbing Championship – Volker Dietrich
East German Formula B8 – Heiner Lindner
East German Touring Cars, 600 cc – Helmut Assmann
East German Touring Cars, 1300 cc – Peter Mucke
Danish Formula Ford 1600 – Klaus Pedersen
Chilean Formula 4 – Juan Carlos Ridolfi
Romanian Speed Championship – Nicolae Leu
Romanian Hillclimbing Championship – Niculai Mihalescu
ARCA – Marvin Smith
NASCAR Modifieds – Richie Evans
Rhodesian Formula Vee – Mike Wesson
Rhodesian Sports Car – Royce Love
Rhodesian Saloon Cars – Les Kerwin
French Hillclimbing: Jean Marie Almeras
Australian Sports Sedan: Allan Grice
International Supermodified: Steve Gioia Jr.
British Hillclimbing: David Franklin
South African Formula Vee – G Gouws
South African Formula Ford – M. Hoffman
South African Group A – G. Piazzo-Musso
Scottish Superstox – Gordon McDougall
Scottish Saloon Stocks – Robert Bruce
Scottish Hot Rod – Les Kay
Irish Formula Ford – Michael Roe

Driver fatalities during the year in racing incidents: Ronnie Peterson, Polin Nellen, Antonio Marino, Tiit Skobelev, Jack Murphy, Sonny Easley, Alberto Beguerie, Gianfranco Riccitelli, Antonino Leone, Sammy Sauer, Thomas Shaffer, Jack Burch, Jon Fairchild, Samson Osborn, Buddy Barris, Jim Smith, Dick Tobias, Fernando Latrubesse, Carl Janssen, Ibert Corrieri, Bill Baker, C.H. Whorton, Lowell Woss, Silvio Martinez, Mike Waltz, Taavi Johvik, Bruno Nefe, Peter O'Reilly, Janito Campos, Buddy Taylor, Tommy Thompson, Charly Kiser, Kurt Bronson, Vincent Cannizzaro, Fred de Sarro, Sonny Eaton, Mike Grbac.

FORMULA 1

- Drivers participating for the first time: **Nelson Piquet, Keke Rosberg, Didier Pironi, Bobby Rahal, Gimax, Eddie Cheever, Rene Arnoux, Derek Daly, Beppe Gabbiani, Geoff Lees, Alberto Colombo**
- New manufacturers: **Arrows, Merzario, Theodore, Martini, ATS**
- Drivers who won for the first time: **Gilles Villeneuve, Patrick Depailler**
- Drivers who won for the last time: **Mario Andretti, Ronnie Peterson**
- **Mario Andretti** is the decade's first champion to have won the first Grand Prix of the year.
- **Surtees** leaves the Formula 1 World Championship for good at the end of the season. It would still try to remain afloat in the Aurora Championship. **Rene Arnoux** is the driver of the last **Surtees** entry in Formula 1, in Canada.
- Michelin becomes **Ferrari's** tire supplier. It wins the second time out.
- **Arrows** is formed by former **Shadow** personnel, including **Jackie Oliver** and **Tony Southgate**.
- **Riccardo Patrese**, in the new **Arrows**, leads in South Africa, the team's second race. **Arrows** is subsequently ordered by a British Court to stop using the car, which is deemed to be a copy of the **Shadow**. The other team driver, **Gunnar**

Nilsson, is found to have cancer and his place is taken by **Rolf Stommelen**, who brings Warsteiner beer sponsorship.
- The **Shadow**s, however, show none of the pace of the **Arrows**, in spite of having two experienced and fast drivers, **Regazzoni** and **Stuck**.
- Later on **Patrese** finishes second in Sweden, is lifted to status of "next big champion", until being accused of causing the Italian Grand Prix accident that killed **Peterson**. He is placed on probation by FIA. From heaven to hell in a single season.
- **Ronnie Peterson** dies in the hospital from injuries sustained in the Italian Grand Prix.
- **Gunnar Nilsson** eventually dies from cancer, October 20. In a little more than a month Sweden lost its top two drivers.
- The Swedish Grand Prix is held for the last time. The **Brabham Alfa Romeo** appears in this race with a fan in the back, which the team claims it is placed there for cooling purposes. The car readily shows form it had not shown until then, in fact wins the race and it is outlawed, although it keeps the win.
- **Lotus** tries to develop the Getrag gearbox that does not require a clutch for gear changes but gives up, sticking to the known quantity, the Hewland gearbox.
- For the first time in the decade, the **Monaco** Grand Prix is the first European race of the season.
- Facing competition from Michelin, Goodyear begins supplying certain teams with special rubber. **Fittipaldi** is one of the teams that receives these special tires and has, by far, its best season.
- Among other results, **Fittipaldi** finished second in the Brazilian Grand Prix, for the first time held in Rio and it was the best Goodyear shod car. The team raced the spare car.
- **Renault** scores its first points in the U.S. East (4th, **Jean-Pierre Jabouille**).
- After a wonderful U.S. Grand Prix subbing for the deceased **Ronnie Peterson** at **Lotus**, **Jean-Pierre Jarier** does it even better, scoring pole in Canada and running away with the race, until cooling problems cause his retirement.
- In this same race, **McLaren** appears with Lowenbrau beer, blue livery. The brand is also owned by Philip Morris, Marlboro's manufacturer.
- **Williams** scores its first fastest lap in Canada.
- Two future world champions debut in the season, **Piquet** and **Rosberg**.

Other categories:
- The World Sports Car Championship loses World status and becomes an European championship. It is won by **Reinhold Joest.**
- **Tom Sneva** manages to win the 18-race USAC Indycar championship without winning a single race. **Danny Ongais**, who won five times, never got close to **Sneva** on points.
- The championship also had two rare races in England, in **Silverstone** and **Brands Hatch**, won by **A.J. Foyt** and **Al Unser**.
- **Al Unser** wins the **Indy** 500 for the third time but also wins the two other 500 mile races in USAC's calendar. He uses a **Lola**.
- **Penske** debuts its first Indycar and wins in the first season.
- Australian **Alan Jones** is hired to replace **McLaren** bound **Patrick Tambay** at the Haas Can-Am team. He wins the series handsomely. The runner up is also an Aussie, **Warwick Brown**, who drove for Belgian team VDS.
- **Alpine-Rena**ult finally wins at **Le Mans**, with **Jean-Pierre Jaussaud** and **Didier Pironi**. This turns out to be the last race of the Renault turbo-prototype program, so that **Renault** turbo prototypes actually won their first (**Mugello, 1975**) and last race (**Le Mans, 1978**).

- The **Renault** effort allegedly costs the manufacturer £ 1 million. There were 4 **Alpine-Renaults**, plus 2 **Renault** engined **Mirages** on the track.
- The crew **Ickx-Pescarolo** was not successful at Le Mans. Their **Porsche** breaks again and **Ickx** is placed on the top **Porsche** 936, the **Wollek-Barth**. The trio does finish second but fails to push the French car into an error.
- In Formula 2, **Alex Ribeiro** embarrasses the might of **BMW** at the **Nürburgring**, winning the Eifelrennen in a basically unsponsored **March** with a **Hart** engine. Unfortunately, the good form does not continue for the rest of the season.
- **Bruno Giacomelli** does win a record 8 races of the European Formula 2 Championship in the works **March-BMW**.
- **Claude Ballot-Lena** does a couple of races in NASCAR, in **1978** and **1979**.
- Don't be fooled: the winner of the **1978** Italian Formula 3 championship, **Siegfried Stohr**, holds Italian citizenship.
- A smallish, two-race Argentinian F2 Temporada is held at the end of the year. The races were all supported, although champion **Giacomelli** was not around in the first. **Marc Surer** won the Mendoza race for **March** and Brazilian **Ingo Hoffmann** actually won in his final appearance in Formula 2. The South American F2 exercise was never repeated, although there was a F3 Temporada in **1979 and** a South American regulation Formula 2 was created in the 80s.
- The Brazilian Oil Board had actually prohibited the holding of a F2 race in **Rio**, that would be part of this Temporada, concerned about oil consumption…
- **Jacques Laffite** takes part in the **St. Ursanne** hill climb in Switzerland. He finished fourth in a **Martini**.
- **Cale Yarborough** completes a hat-trick, winning the NASCAR title for the third straight time.
- IMSA champion **Al Holbert** decides to go to NASCAR. He does not do well. Next he tries the Can-Am.
- Still winning after all these years: no longer a factor in the ETCC, the **Ford** Capri continues to win elsewhere. An example wins the 24 Hours of **Spa**, with **Teddy Pilette** and **Gordon Spice**. That is the last edition of the race in the old circuit.
- Hungarian driver **Janos Kiss** takes part in a local Austrian Formula Libre race at **Oesterreichring**. That is as close as a Hungarian got to Formula 1 during the decade.
- The Swiss F3 championship is introduced. Races comprise of circuit racing and hill climbs and are mostly held in Italy and France, given circuit racing prohibition in the country. **Lola** Formula 3 cars did very well in the second season, most unusually.
- As a celebration for the 25th Anniversary of the **Macau** Grand Prix, organizers put together a Race of Giants. A bunch of old timers (and some not that old), take part in the race, including **Emmanuel de Graffenried, Prince Bira, Jack Brabham, Phil Hill, Mike Hailwood, Bob Unser, Denis Hulme, Stirling Moss** and **Jacky Ickx**. Ickx wins with certain ease but everybody had a jolly nice time. Including **Teddy Yip**.
- **Anatolie Kozyrchikov** wins an ice race in Moscow, in a **Moskvich**.
- Formula Skoda is established in Czechoslovakia.
- **Teddy Pilette** manages to score a fastest lap in the **BRM** P207 at Oulton Park. This was BRM's last fastest lap.

1979

Champions
Formula 1 (Drivers): Jody Scheckter
Formula 1 (Manufacturers): Ferrari
European Formula 2: Marc Surer
European Formula 3: Alain Prost
British Formula 3: Chico Serra (Vandervell)
French Formula 3: Alain Prost
Italian Formula 3: Piercarlo Ghinzani
German F3: Michael Korten
Swedish Formula 3: Slim Borgudd
World Manufacturers Championship: Porsche
Can-Am: Jacky Ickx
Interserie: Kurt Lotterschmid
USAC Indy Car: A.J. Foyt Jr.
CART Indy Car: Rick Mears
Aurora Series: Rupert Keegan
South African Formula Atlantic: Ian Scheckter
NASCAR: Richard Petty
IROC: Mario Andretti
European Touring Car Championship: Carlo Facetti/Martino Finotto
British Saloon Car Championship: Richard Longman, Mini
DRM: Klaus Ludwig
DARM: Hermann Behrens
Australian Touring Car Championship: Rob Morris
Australian Gold Star Championship: Johnnie Walker
Australian Formula 2: Brian Shead
Australian Sports Sedan: Allan Grice
New Zealand International Championship: Teo Fabi
New Zealand 2 Liter Saloon Championship: R. Cook
New Zealand Ford Escort Series: R. Williams
Brazilian Super Vee: Mauricio Chulam
Brazilian Formula Ford: Arthur Bragantini
Brazilian Stock Car: Paulo Gomes
Argentinian Formula 1: Jorge Omar del Rio
Argentinian Formula 2: Miguel de Guidi
Argentinian Formula 4: Gustavo Sommi
Argentinian Turismo de Carretera: Francisco Espinosa
Argentinian Formula 1 Campeana: Alfredo Coronel
Trans-Am: John Paul
IMSA Camel GTX: Peter Gregg   GT: Don Devendorf
Japanese Formula 2: Keiji Matsumoto
Japanese Formula Pacific: Takao Wada
Japanese F3: Toshio Suzuki
Fuji Grand Champion: Satoru Nakajima
Fuji Long Distance: Advan Racing Team
British Formula Atlantic: Ray Mallock
Canadian Formula Atlantic: Tom Gloy
New Zealand: Mike Finch
Irish Formula Atlantic: Gary Gibson
Irish Formula Ford: Colin Lees
European Formula Super-Vee: John Nielsen

US Formula Super-Vee: Geoff Brabham
European Hill Climb Championship: Jean-Marie Almeras
Procar series: Niki Lauda
Spanish Championship: Miguel Arias
Belgian Championship: Jean Marie Martin
Dutch Touring Car Championship: Claude Bourgoignie
Swiss Formula 3 Championship: Beat Blatter
Formula 1430: Manuel Vallis I Biesca
French Super Tourism: Dany Snobeck
French Formula Renault: Alain Ferte
French Hillclimbing: Guy Frequelin
Formula Skoda: Jan Kacer
Peace and Friendship Cup: Vaclav Lim
Peace and Friendship Cup (Touring Cars): Vlastimil Tomasek
Soviet Formula Easter: Aleksandr Medvedchenko
Hungarian Championship: Dezsoe Kiss
Dutch Formula Ford: Hans Wolker
USAC Mini Indy (Super-Vee): Dennis Firestone
British Formula Ford 2000: David Leslie
British Formula Ford: David Sears
British Hillclimbing: Martyn Griffith
BRSCC Formula Ford: Terry Gray
BARC Formula Ford: David Sears
European Formula Ford 2000: Adrian Reynard
Formula Italia: Rodolfo Bellini
BARC Saloon Car Championship: Nick Baughn
BRSCC/BRDC/MCD Saloon Car Championship: Nick Baughn
Portuguese Speed Championship: Group A Rufino Fontes
Portuguese Speed Championship: Group B Antonio Pinto de Barros
Porsche Cup: Klaus Ludwig
SCCA Formula Atlantic – Tim Coconis, Ralt
SCCA Formula Vee – Wayne Moore, Zink
SCCA Formula Ford – Dave Weizenhoff, Zink
SCCA Formula Continental – Tom Pomeroy, Argo
SCCA A Sports Racing - Jerry Hansen, Lola
SCCA C Sports Racing – Tom Foster, Tiga
SCCA D Sports Racing – Dave Leeson, LeGrand
SCCA B Production – Andy Porterfield, Chevrolet Corvette
SCCA C Production – Paul Newman, Datsun
SCCA D Production – Lee Mueller, Triumph
SCCA E Production – Robert Overby, Porsche
SCCA F Production – Steve Johnson, Triumph
SCCA G Production – Bob Griffith, MG
SCCA H Production – Catherine Kizer, MG
SCCA A Sedan – Dan Moore, Ford Mustang
SCCA B Sedan – Bill Coykendall, Datsun
SCCA Showroom Stock A – Ron Christensen, Saab Turbo
SCCA Showroom Stock B – Don Knowles, Saab
SCCA Showroom Stock C – Sammy McSpadden, VW
USAC World of Outlaws – Sheldon Kinser
USAC Sprint Cars – Greg Leffler
USAC Midgets – Steve Lotshan
USAC Silver Crown – Bobby Olivero
Euro Cup Renault 5 – Luigi Calamai

EFDA Formula Ford 1600 Euro Series – John Village
British Formula Vee – Glenn Hay
Australian Formula Ford – Russell Norden
Swiss Hill Climbing Championship – Fred Amweg
Swiss Championship – Werner Wenk
Swiss Renault Cup – Rolf Fuhrer
German Sports Cars – Wilfred Gullet
German VW Cup – Heinz Friedrich
German Formula Super Vee – Frank Jelinski
German Hill Climbing Championship – Herbert Strenger
East German Formula B8 – Heiner Lindner
East German Touring Cars, 600 cc – Klaus Schumann
East German Touring Cars, 1300 cc – Jurgen Klapper
Danish Formula Ford 1600 – Jesper Villemsen
Danish Formula Ford 2000 - Soren Aggerholm
Chilean Formula 4 – Santiago Bengolea
Romanian Speed Championship – Andrei Bellu
ARCA – Marvin Smith
NASCAR Modifieds – Richie Evans
Rhodesian Formula Vee – Trevor Gilbert
Rhodesian Sports Cars – Royce Love
Rhodesian Saloon Cars – Ray Yeo
International Supermodified: Doug Heveron
Scandinavian Super Vee – Kurt Thiim
South African Formula Vee – K. Heath
South African Formula Ford – Graham Duxbury
South African Group A – G. Piazzo-Musso
Scottish Superstox – Bill Pullar
Scottish Saloon Stocks – Bob Jones

Driver fatalities during the year in racing incidents: John Morgan, Jean-Claude Fontaine, Pete Walker, Roberto Antoniazza, Mike Shaw, Terry Vaughn, Larry Brandon, Russell Gray, Terry Turbak, Fraus Meuwissen, Vladimir Trushin, Jim Doughty, Rimantas Kesminas, Roger Larson, Darryl Dawley, Dick Stoneking, Darl Ellis, Tim Kuykendall, Sonny Thompson, Evert Seal, John Draucker, Paul Salisbury, Mark Munroe, Darrell Wurban, Rob Slotemaker, Les Nailor, Lloyd Beard, Arnold Horner, Chris Murphy, Alfredo Roman Gines

FORMULA 1

- Drivers participating for the first time: **Elio de Angelis, Jan Lammers, Gianfranco Brancatelli, Marc Surer, Patrick Gaillard, Marc Surer, Ricardo Zunino**
- New manufacturers: **Kauhsen, Rebaque**
- Drivers who won for the first time: **Jean-Pierre Jabouille**
- Drivers who won for the last time: **Jody Scheckter, Patrick Depailler, Clay Regazzoni**
- First win, manufacturers: **Williams**
- First champion from the African continent, **Jody Scheckter**.
- **Jackie Stewart** is allegedly offered US$2.5 million to drive for **Brabham** in 1980, as replacement for the departing **Niki Lauda**. He declines. **Nelson Piquet** is confirmed, allegedly for US$ 50,000. Bernie was happy with the outcome.

- **Ligier** appears the world beater in South America, **Williams** dominates the end of the season but **Ferrari** ends up winning both the drivers' and manufacturers' title.
- The now Ford-engined **Ligier** qualifies 1-2 in both Latin American races and **Laffite** wins both. **Laffite** also scored four poles in the first six races.
- **Patrick Depailler**, the other **Ligier** driver, has a hanggliding accident and is sidelined for the rest of the season. There is great speculation about his replacement but **Jacky Ickx** ends being hired and disappoints in his last Formula 1 season.
- **Renault** scores its first pole in the high altitude of **Kyalami**. It is the first turbo pole in Formula 1.
- **Renault** then wins its first Grand Prix, in France. It is also the first time a turbo-engined car wins in Formula 1.
- **James Hunt** retired midseason, after showing little form in the **Wolf**. **Keke Rosberg** is hired to drive the rest of the season. The team closed at the end of the year and its equipment is sold to **Fittipaldi**.
- **Alfa Romeo** comes back as a works team this season, debuting the heavy looking 177 model in Belgium (**Giacomelli**). It had been away as a Formula 1 constructor since **1951** but **Alfa** engines had powered some South African specials in the 60s, plus **McLaren, March and Brabham** cars in the 70s.
- **Brabham** uses the **Alfa** engine for the last time in the Italian Grand Prix, where **Alfa Romeo** fields a car for **Brambilla**. In Canada, the Ford-engined **Brabham** shows much more speed than the **Alfa** version and **Piquet** starts from the first row in Watkins Glen.
- **Hector Rebaque** debuts his eponymous car. The **Rebaque** is only used in the last 3 races of the season (and the decade) and then retired.
- **Clay Regazzoni** ends up winning William's maiden F-1 victory. It happens at **Silverstone**, where **Jones** scores the team's first pole. **Alan Jones** follows that up winning four times in the second half of the season.
- As he did in **1977**, **Niki Lauda** leaves his team before the end of the season. This time, he retires from the sport. We all know how that played out. The **Lauda-Brabham** tie-up left a lot to be desired, especially in **1979**.

Other categories:
- An official trio wins **Le Mans** for the first time. The winning car, a Kremer **Porsche** 935 is driven by **Klaus Ludwig** and two of the **Whittington, Bill and Don**. The American brothers would, a few years later, be indicted and convicted on drug smuggling and money laundering charges. **Ludwig** did a large chunk of the driving.
- It is the slowest **Le Mans** since **1958**. In fact, the winning car did 530 miles less than the **1978** winning **Alpine-Renault**.
- The second placed car, also a **Porsche** 935, is driven mostly by **Rolf Stommelen** but also by actor **Paul Newman** and **Dick Barbour**.
- The same two trios (**Ludwig/Whittington/Whittington** and **Stommelen/Barbour/Newman**) also finish 1-2 in **Watkins Glen**.
- **Bob Wollek**, who drove for Kremer for many seasons, leaves the team and joins Gelo, which got the upper hand against Kremer the previous seasons. **Klaus Ludwig** leaves Gelo and joins Kremer. Kremer wins all but one DRM race. **Wollek** does win three World Championship rounds, though.
- The World Manufacturers Championship is in obvious trouble. Group 6 cars are allowed to race to boost up the grids.
- **Don Whittington** ends up winning the World Challenge for Endurance Drivers, a weird concoction of Group 5 and Showroom Stock races in Europe and the USA.
- The last race of the year is the very one-off 6 Hours of **El Salvador**. A few Americans and one Guatemalan join a field of Salvadorans, in the first international

event in the Central American country. It comes at the worse possible time, for the government was toppled the same week. **Don Whittington** wins the race with Salvadoran **Enrique "Jamsal" Molins**, in a **Porsche**.

- **Lella Lombardi** becomes the first woman to win a World Championship event outright, the **Enna** 6 Hours, with **Enrico Grimaldi**, driving an **Osella-BMW**. She would win again at **Vallelunga**, with **Giorgio Francia**.
- **Lancia** returns to racing big time. The Monte-Carlo debuts in **Silverstone** and wins the Group 5 category of the **Enna** 6 Hours (**Patrese-Facetti**), behind **Lombardi-Grimaldi**
- No less than **Stirling Moss** and **Denis Hulme** share a **VW**, in the Benson & Hedge 500, in **Pukekohe**, New Zealand. Neither were yet done with motor racing.
- Grass roots sponsorship: French racing magazine Auto-Hebdo raises money from readers in support of **Patrick Gaillard's** Formula 2 efforts. Driving a **Chevron** in four races, the Frenchman does not disappoint, posting a 5th place in **Pau** and 5th at **Hockenheim**.
- **Giacomo Agostini** shifts to the Aurora Formula 1 Championship, after a bad time in Formula 2. Although he did much better than in the previous category, driving a Williams, earning a second in **Snetterton** and two 3rd places, it was still a far cry from his all-conquering motorcycle days. He would finish the decade without a car racing win under his belt.
- **1979** is the first season for the Brazilian Stockcars championship, which would eventually become Brazil's top category. Initially no more than a **Chevrolet Opala** one-make series, supported by GM, this was the only top large engine category left in Brazil for many years, which may explain its popularity. GM's financial support in early years also meant good drivers, including a returning from Europe **Ingo Hoffmann**. **Paulo Gomes**, who also had international experience (Formula 3 and Le Mans) wins the title.
- **Richard Petty** wins his last NASCAR title, the fifth of the decade. Driving **Chevrolets** and **Oldsmobiles**, this time. He also scored his last pole.
- As for **David Pearson**, he is hired back by the Wood Brothers team and wins the Southern 500 in a **Chevrolet**.
- **Dale Earnhardt** wins the first of many Winston Cup races, at **Bristol**
- **Penske** cars win many Indy races, including the **Indy 500**.
- **Patrick Racing**, rather than insisting on building its own cars, also orders **Penskes**.
- Indycar is divided. Most prominent teams sided with newly formed CART, while a shorter championship is run under USAC, whose main supporter is **A.J. Foyt**. The Indy 500 remained a USAC property in this double series split but CART drivers were allowed to compete.
- **Rick Mears**, the first CART champion, is only the second Indy 500 winner to win the championship in the same season during the 70s. The other was **Al Unser**, in the first year of the decade.
- Unusually, 35 cars are allowed to start in the **Indy** 500. Normally 33 start.
- **Didier Pironi** races a **Kojima** Formula 2 car in the J.A.F. Grand Prix. European drivers regularly participated in Japanese F-2 races but rarely driving Japanese machinery.
- Even a Brunei Grand Prix took place during this surprising decade. The race in **Bandar Seri Bagawan** was won by **Peter Marshall**, in a **Ralt**.
- South Africa changes the engine specification of its Formula Atlantic championship. The **Ford** engine is dropped, **Mazd**a adopted instead.
- An Interserie race is held at **Most**, Czechoslovakia. This is the first Western European Championship race held in an Eastern European country other than ETCC, in the entire decade.

- A large number of Argentinian drivers try European Formula 2 during the season: **Ricardo Zunino, Ariel Bakst, Oscar "Cocho" Lopez, Miguel Angel Guerra** and **Juan Maria Traverso**. The best of the lot was **Guerra**, who scored 8 points. Incidentally, **Traverso** was a major Turismo de Carretera ace and scored two points.
- The European Formula 2 Championship ends in anticlimactic form: **Brian Henton**'s team appeals the disqualification from the **Enna** race, which, if overturned, would make him champion. In the end, the FISA (Italian Federation) upholds the disqualification and **Marc Surer** is confirmed champion months after the end of the championship.
- A team of **AMC** Spirits takes part in the 24 Hours of **Nürburgring**. The best, driven by **Gary Witzenberg-Lyn St. James** and **Jim Downing**, finished 25th. The other car, driven by **Amos Johnson/Dennis Shaw/James Brolin**, finished 42nd.

Lammers driving the Shadow at Long Beach, 1979. The car had an aggressive and colorful livery but it was not fast. (Kurt Oblinger)

DRIVERS

For some, nationality variety is not a 70s forte. In fact, nowadays we are rather used to seeing drivers from exotic Indonesia, Malaysia, Russia, China, Saudi Arabia all over racetracks, places with little or apparently no racing activity 40 years ago. While now you can probably count drivers from more than 50 different nationalities driving in top racing series in the world at any given time, back then most top level drivers hauled from a pool of less than 20 countries, which does not mean there were no racers in other countries. There were, in some surprising corners, too.

The idea that racing was restricted to a very few countries is further ingrained by the literature. Take the excellent book *Encyclopedia of Motor Sport*, from 1971. A very authoritative reference work, its entries included drivers, racetracks and car makers from "all over the world". The only mention to a Brazilian or Brazil in the entire book was the Emerson Fittipaldi entry, still a novelty in Europe. To most people, there was no motor racing in Brazil, which was not true. There were tracks, race car builders and actually a very talented generation. In a short 3 seasons, Brazil suddenly got on the radar, with a world champion, top drivers, international events and even a GP of its own. Other countries were no so lucky and remained on the sidelines, mere footnotes. I tried to make most footnotes represented here, as applicable.

Motor racing in the 70s was very much a regional sport, as discussed elsewhere in this book. There were tons of Russians driving racing cars but not at Le Mans or Formula 1 or the Indy 500. There where Indian drivers and Indian motorsport, there were Indonesian and Malaysian drivers, Costa Rican and Trinidadians practicing the sport and racetracks being built and maintained in unimaginable places. For more on that, check the Venues and Local Scene chapter.

The proliferation of organized championships, commercial sponsorship, TV, Formula 1's growing brand awareness, all contributed to larger number of drivers from different countries trying their luck at the international level. Back then Formula 2 and the ETCC were, after all, regional championships and USAC a national US championship. Racing became truly international years later.

This is not, of course, a comprehensive list. It is very subjective and I might draw some heat from it. I did include a largely unknown Icelandic Formula 3 driver and a Yugoslav who attempted to make it in Formula 2 in 1975 and perhaps I have left a few German, Italian and American drivers who were hot shoes in lesser disciplines and had won dozens, even hundreds of races. But the fact remains that the Icelandic driver was the country's absolute top driver of the day, by default perhaps and maybe the American with tons of sprint car races under his belt would not make the top 50 in a more qualitative assessment of his own country's drivers pool.

Therefore I tried to include drivers from as many nationalities as possible, to show racing's regional aspect and how motor racing was indeed practiced in a great many countries. Many of these drivers did not compete in Europe or the USA at all but were regionally relevant on their own, remembered and venerated as heroes to this day. It might come as a surprise that there were relatively major races in Peru, Panama and Singapore but in my view, this is due to the very idea of "anglo" relevance carried over from the 60s.

Anglo-Saxon drivers simply dominated car racing in the 60s. Drivers from England, Scotland, Australia, New Zealand, America and South Africa generally got the best drives and the ensuing headlines. Somewhat weak generations of Italian, French and German drivers just made matters worse. However, by the end of the 60s, Swiss, Belgian, French, German, Austrian, Swedish drivers were gathering momentum at the highest level and the scene became much more international. Commercial sponsorship and TV coverage also made this possible. Part of this skewed view is that most racing literature of the day was produced in England and America and writers concentrated on racing in English speaking countries, having no interest figuring out what a Brazilian or Japanese race report said. As a result, the South African Formula 1 championship's relevance is a bit overblown; after all, the only South African driver to be truly internationally successful in that era never even raced in that series.

In the 70s there were still large numbers of relevant British and American drivers. For one thing, the British scene was prolific during the decade and British drivers also took part in races in the Continent and in the US. Stateside, there were many well run professional championships, such as NASCAR, USAC, Can-Am and Trans Am, that allowed talent to brew, in addition to hundreds of amateur/semi-professional tournaments for a large range of categories.

Some names might cause some surprise, such as Sir Stirling Moss, who still raced occasionally in contemporary events and veterans such as Masten Gregory and Umberto Maglioli. Rally drivers such as Walter Rohrl, Simo Lampinen, Sobieslav Zasada, Shektar Mehta and Bjorn Waldegaard also made some forays into circuit racing and hill climbing. While Indonesian Hanu Wiano and Singaporean/Malaysian Sonny Rajah at least attempted to race in Europe, albeit unsuccessfully, some drivers from more exotic places who never raced in major centers are included to boost up variety, for they had relevant success in their countries or region.

Another consideration is misspelling. A note appeared in a Brazilian racing magazine when Alex Ribeiro was invited to race in Japan, a first for Brazilian drivers. At the time I first read the note, I saw no problem with it. As I reread it, some 30 odd years down the line, I noted that every single Japanese driver's name was misspelled on the note...There is also the issue of transliteration. Greek motorsport is not among the best in the world, yet, the name of George Moschous pops up here and there. He owned an Alfa Romeo T33 prototype, among other cars and won lots of races and hill climbs in the 70s. At least two reputable sites refer to him as P. Moschous, other sources as Mouchous. Transliteration is also a problem with Eastern European languages, so there are issues with Russian, Bulgarian, Yugoslav, Ukrainian, Belarusan, names.

Unfortunately, a lot of information from more exotic places is in very short supply and often times, conflicting. The 6 Hours of Dakar is a very traditional car race in Africa and often noteworthy European drivers have participated, specially during the 70s. Finding even a list of the winners of this race was a daunting task, partially achieved as of the date of writing (I am still missing 1978). I tried it in both English and French, to no avail but will not give up. The Senegalese Federation did answer a message, promised to help but I am still waiting...

Even perceived ultimate success can be mistakenly noted, decades later. Ecuadoran drivers Guillermo Ortega, Fausto Merello and Lothar Ranft who were heroes in regional racing, had a very successful outing at the 1973 Le Mans 24 Hours, driving a Porsche 908 to 7th. This is treated as almost a win by Ecuadorians, yet, many reputable sources indicate this took place in 1974.

There were only a couple of instances of eponymous drivers in this list. There was both an East German and West German driver named Klaus Ludwig in the 70s, the latter extremely successful. There were also two Bob Sharps. One of them was the American known for fast Datsuns and Nissans that raced in both professional and amateur racing during the decade. Bob was a fast driver himself but among others, Paul Newman and Sam Posey also drove for his team. The other Bob Sharp was a successful Brazilian touring car driver in the 70s who has become an automotive journalist.

Curiously, a few drivers that raced in the USA in the 70s raced officially as Cubans. They were obviously not living in Cuba at the time but I suppose nationalist fervor made them use their nationality of birth.

There are mentions of Haitian drivers in the literature but given that I was unable to find their names, I have not listed Haiti.

Although Puerto Ricans did have American nationality in the 70s, drivers from the island were normally identified with the abbreviation PR in American race results. Hong Kong was also part of Britain but the few drivers from the enclave appearing on results were usually identified with HK. As this adds to diversity and the regional characteristic of the sport, I left this little indiscretion linger on.

Still on the subject of nationality conflicts, certain drivers were born in one country, yet, hold other nationalities. Keke Rosberg, for instance, was born in Sweden, to Finnish parents who happened to be studying there when Keijo was born. There have been suggestions that American Mario Andretti, who was born in Italy, would in fact be a Croatian...Well, borders in 1940 were not what they are today. The village where Mario was born was indeed Italian territory in 1940, after the war it was annexed by Yugoslavia, now Croatia. John McDonald was actually born in England but is listed as a Hong Kong driver. Mike Beuttler was born in Egypt but is listed as British. In latter days, Hans Joachin Stuck is listed as Austrian, yet in the 70s he always used German citizenship. Franz Konrad is also listed as German and Austrian, Val Musetti as both Italian and British. Lastly, Roberto Guerrero is now known as American but he was a full-fledged Colombian in the 70s. I am positive there are a few dozen examples among the lesser known drivers.

There is outright confusion about the nationalities of certain drivers. Jan Bussell, who won the Macau GP of 1971 (and also 1968) is listed in some places as British, others as Malaysian and even Singaporean. Given his last name, I decided to stick to British until proven wrong, even though the Singaporean press included him in a list of graded drivers appointed by the Singaporean federation. The case of Sonny Rajah is also emblematic. Sonny is highly praised by elements of the Malaysian press as Malaysian and by the Singaporean press as Singaporean. As a result, his nationality appears as Malaysian in some sources and Singaporean in others. As Singapore is a city state located within Malaysia, part of the Malay Federation until becoming independent in 1965, I figured that Singaporeans who are not ethnic Chinese (thus, Malay) also got (or could claim) Malaysian citizenship. So he is listed as both, to be fair to both countries.

As for generational name choices, I do not remember a single driver in this list with the name Sebastian (or Sebastien), a very popular name in this generation in many cultures, languages and countries, including France. Yet there were loads of Jean-Pierres and Alains in France, which seem to have fallen out of grace.

Last but not least, Prince Bira, Phil Hill and Emmanuel de Graffenried are listed because they took part in the Race of Giants held in Macao, 1978, to celebrate the 25th Anniversary of the Race. I saw it fit to consider this a bona fide contemporary, racing event for active and highly competitive contemporary drivers such as Bobby Unser and Jacky Ickx also participated.

There is no hierarchy in the list, I have made them alphabetical to avoid controversy. Enjoy.

ALGERIA

Major international achievement: French champion, touring cars less than 1.6 lieetrs, 1977 (Fiorentino)

Bernard Fiorentino
Miloud Khalfi

ANDORRA

Antonio Puig Delivol

ANGOLA

Emilio Marta
Helder de Souza
Herculano Areias
Jose Reboucas
Mabilio de Albuquerque

ANTIGUA

Major international achievement: British F3 win in 1974 (Tyrrel)

Jimmy Fuller
Mike Tyrrel

ARGENTINA

Major international achievement: GP wins (Reutemann)

Agustin Bramonte
Alberto Scarrazini
Angel Monguzzi
Ariel Bakst
Benedicto Caldarella
Carlos Garro
Carlos Jarque
Carlos Marincovich
Carlos Reutemann
Carlos Ruesch
Eduardo Copello
Eduardo Crovetto
Eduardo Marques
Emilio Bertolini
Enrique Benamo
Esteban Fernandino
Eugenio Breard
Francisco Espinosa
Guillermo Kissling
Hector Gradassi
Janito Campos
Jorge Cupeiro
Jorge de Amorrortu
Jorge Omar del Rio
Jorge Recalde
Jorge Serafini
Jorge Ternengo
Juan Maria Bordeu
Juan Maria Traverso
Juan Pablo Zampa
Luis Di Palma
Miguel Angel de Guidi
Miguel Angel Guerra
Nasif Stefano
Nestor Garcia Veiga
Norberto Pauloni
Oscar "Cacho" Fangio
Osvaldo Bessia
Osvaldo Lopez
Pablo Brea
Ricardo Zunino
Ruben Alonso

AUSTRALIA

Major international achievement: GP Wins (Brabham, Jones)

Alan Grice

Alan Jones
Alfredo Costanzo
Allan Moffat
Andrew Miedecke
Bob Jane
Bob Muir
Brian McGuire
Brian Muir
Brian Shead
Buzz Buzzaglo
Colin Bond
Dave Walker
Frank Gardner
Frank Matich
Garrie Cooper
Geoff Brabham
Graeme Crawford
Hank Woelders
Horst Kwech
Ian Geoghegan
Jack Brabham
Jim Richards
John Goss
John Harvey
John Leffler
John MacCormack
Johnnie Walker
Kevin Bartlett
Larry Perkins
Leo Geoghegan
Max Stewart
Niel Allen
Norm Beechey
Paul Bernasconi
Peter Brock
Rob Morris
Russell Skaiffe
Terry Perkins
Tim Schenken
Vern Schuppan
Warwick Brown

AUSTRIA

Major international achievement: World Champion (Lauda, Rindt)

Dieter Quester
Franz Konrad
Hans Binder
Hans Royer
Harald Ertl
Hans Fink
Heinrich Wiesendanger
Helmut Koinigg

Helmut Marko
Jo Gartner
Jochen Rindt
Johannes Ortner
Joseph Schnabl
Karl Oppitzhauser
Karl Wendlinger (father)
Kurt Rieder
Markus Hottinger
Niki Lauda
Otto Stuppacher
Peter Peter
"Pierre Chauvet"
Rudi Lins
Sepp Manhalter
Walter Pedrazza

BAHAMAS

Robin Ormes

BARBADOS

Andrew Philipps
Doug Maloney
Lincoln Waterman
Mike Atwell
Ralph "Bizzy" Williams
Ralph Johnson

BELARUS

Anatolie Alchimovich
Valerie Ankuda

BELGIUM

Major international achievement: GP wins (Ickx)

Alain Dex
Alain Peltier
Alain Semoulin
Albert Vanierschot
Bernard De Dryver
Chris Tuerlinx
Christian Melville
Christine Beckers
Claude Bourgoignie
Claude de Wael
Daniel Herregods
Eddy Joosen
Gustave "Taf" Gosselin
Herve Regout
Hughes de Fierlant

Ivo Grauls
Jacky Ickx
Jean Blaton "Beurlys"
Jean Pierre Gaban
Jean Xhenceval
Jean-Claude Frank
Jean-Michel Martin
Marc Duez
Maurice Dantinne
Noel Van Assche "Pedro"
Patrick Neve
Philippe Martin
Pierre Dieudonne
Raijmond Van Hove
Raymond Raus
Rene Tricot
Teddy Pilette
Thierry Boutsen
Thierry Tassin
Yves Deprez
Yvette Fontaine

BOLIVIA

Dieter Hubner
Helmut Seng
Oscar Crespo
Rene Rocha

BRAZIL

Major international achievement: World Champion (E. Fittipaldi)

Abilio DIniz
Alcides Diniz
Alex Ribeiro
Alfredo Guarana
Antonio Carlos Avallone
Antonio Castro Prado
Arthur Bragantini
Bird Clemente
Bob Sharp
Camilo Christofaro
Carlos Pace
Chico Serra
Ciro Cayres
Clovis de Moraes
Edgard Mello Filho
Eduardo Celidoneo
Emerson Fittipaldi
Fausto Dabbur
Fernando Ribeiro
Bolivar di Sordi
Fernando Jorge

Francisco Lameirao
Francisco Landi
Fritz Jordan
Jan Balder
Jayme Silva
Jose Giaffone
Jose Maria Ferreira
Jose Pedro Chateaubriand
Jose Renato Catapani
Leonel Friedrich
Lian Abreu Duarte
Luis Pereira Bueno
Luis Siqueira Veiga
Marinho Amaral
Mario Ferraris Neto
Mario Pati Jr.
Marivaldo Fernandes
Mauricio Chulam
Maurizio Sandro Sala
Nelson Piquet
Nilson Clemente
Norman Casari
Paulo Gomes
Pedro Mufatto
Pedro Victor de Lamare
Placido Iglesias
Rafaelle Rosito
Raul Boesel
Roberto Moreno
Ronald Rossi
Wilson Fittipaldi Junior

BULGARIA

Georgi Malkanov
Georgi Seraminov
Hinov Kaltcho
Josef Csercoti
Rad Uzunov
Ricard Grujev

CANADA

Major international achievement: Grand Prix win (G. Villeneuve)

Bill Brack
Bill Robertson
Dave MacConnell
Earl Ross
Eppie Wietzes
George Eaton
Gilles Villeneuve
Horst Kroll
Jacques Bienvenue

Jacques Couture
Jacques Villeneuve
John Cannon
John Cordts
Klaus Blytzek
Ludwig Heimrath
Maurice Carter
Norm Ridgley
Rainer Brezinka
Richard Spennard
Rudy Bartling

CHILE

Major international achievement:
Argentine F-4 Champion: Salazar

Boris Garafulic
Claudio Ibarra
Eduardo Kovacs
Eliseo Salazar
Jaime Vergara
Juan Armando Band
Juan Gac
Luis Gimeno
Rodrigo Gama
Santiago Bengolea
Sergio Santander

COLOMBIA

Major international achievement: IMSA placings (de Narvaez)

Camilo Mutis
Francisco Lopez
Honorato Espinosa
Jorge Cortes
Mauricio de Narvaez
Pedro de Narvaez
Ricardo Londono
Roberto Guerrero
Roberto Morales

COSTA RICA

Major international achievement: IMSA participations (Fonseca)

Jorge Valverde
Kikos Fonseca
Roy Valverde

CUBA

Manuel Garcia

Juan Montalvo

CYPRUS

Zekia Redjep

CZECHOSLOVAKIA

Borivoj Korinek
Jan Kacer
Jaroslav Bobec
Jiri Cerva
Jiri Micanek
Jiri Rosicky
Jiri Smid
Karel Jilek
Milan Zid
Oldrich Brunclik
Vaclav Lim
Vladimir Hubacek
Vladislav Ondreijek
Vlastmil Tomasek
Zdenek Halada

DENMARK

Major international achievement:
Formula 1 participations (Belso, Nelleman)

Arne Hojgaard
Henrik Spellerberg
Jac Nelemann
Jens Ingvorsen
Jens Winther
John Nielsen
Jorgen Herlevsen
Jorgen Jensen
Jorgen Poulsen
Kurt Thiim
Lars Viggo Jensen
Ole Vejlund
Poul Erik Jensen
Preben Kristofersen
Tom Belso
Torkhild Thyrring

DOMINICAN REPUBLIC

Adriano Abreu
Carlos Lazaro
Chuck Fleishawer
Horacio Alvarez

Horacio Alvarez, driving a Toyota, was a major Dominican ace. (unknown author)

Jacinto Peynado
Jaime Rodriguez
Jose Arzeno
Luiz Garcia
Luiz Mendez
Rafael Aguayo
Tony Canahuate

ECUADOR

Major international achievement: 7th place in Le Mans, 1973 (Ortega/Merello/Raft)

Alfredo Vinueza
Andres Chiriboga
Fausto Merello
Fernando Madera
Franklin Perez
Guillermo Cisneros
Guillermo Ortega
Herman Lascano
Lothar Ranft
Louis Larrea
Miguel Vignolo

EL SALVADOR

Major international achievement: win 6 Hours of El Salvador, 1979 (Molins)

Alex Caceres
Carlos Cromeyer
Carlos Moran
Eduardo Barrientos
Edardo Melendez
Enrique Molins (Jamsal)
Francisco Zablan (Fomfor)

ESTONIA

Boris Eylandt
Enn Grifell

Henri Saarm
Juri Terenetski
Madis Laiv
Peep Lansoo
Toivo Asmer
Tuini Teesalu

FINLAND

Major international achievement: Formula 1 participations (Kinnunen, Rosberg)

Hans Laine
Keke Rosberg
Lasse Sirvio
Leo Kinnunen
Mika Arpianen
Mikko Kozarowitsky
Pauli Toivonen
Rauno Aaltonen
Simo Lampinen
Taisto Saario

FRANCE

Major international achievement: GP Wins (Cevert, Beltoise, Depailler, Laffite, Jabouille)

Adam Potocki
Alain Couderc
Alain Cudini
Alain Ferte
Alain Prost
Alain Serpaggi
Anne-Charlotte Verney
Bernard Darniche
Bernard Mange
Bob Wollek
Christian Debias
Claude Ballot-Lena
Claude Swetlik
Dany Snobeck
Didier Pironi
Francois Cevert
Francois Lacarrau
Francois Mazet
Francois Migault
Francois Servanin
Fred Stalder
Gerard Delpalanque
Gerard Larrousse
Guy Chasseuil
Guy Ligier

101

Henri Greder
Henri Pescarolo
Herve Labedan
Herve Leguellec
Jacky Haran
Jacques Almeras
Jacques Coulon
Jacques Henry
Jacques Laffite
Jean Claude Andruet
Jean Louis Schlesser
Jean Luis Lafosse
Jean Ragnotti
Jean Rondeau
Jean-Marie Almeras
Jean-Marie Jacquemin
Jean-Pierre Beltoise
Jean-Pierre Cassegrain
Jean-Pierre Jabouille
Jean-Pierre Jarier
Jean-Pierre Jaussaud
Jean-Pierre Maillard
Jean-Pierre Nicolas
Jean-Pierre Paoli
Jimmy Robert Mieusset
Joel Gouhier
Johnny Servoz Gavin
Laurent Ferrier
Marie-Claude Beaumont
Max Mamers
Michel Leclere
Michel Pignard
Michelle Mouton
Pascal Fabre
Patrick Dal Bo
Patrick Depailler
Patrick Gaillard
Patrick Perrier
Patrick Piget
Patrick Tambay
Philippe Alliot
Philippe Colonna
Philippe Jafrenou
Philippe Streiff
Phillippe Bochet
Pierre Francois Rousselot
Pierre Maublanc
Raymond Tourol
Rene Arnoux
Rene Metge
Richard Dallest
Xavier Lapeyre
Yves Courage
Yves Sarrazin

GEORGIA

Jakov Wart Patrikov
Michael Longinov
Tengis Sacharow

GERMANY, EAST

Fredler Radlan
Hartmuth Thassler
Heinz Melkus
Klaus Ludwig
Manfred Berger
Peter Mucke
Ullis Melkus

GERMANY, WEST

Major international achievement: GP win (Mass)

Albrecht Krebs
Alois Roppes
Anton Stocks
Armin Hahne
Axel Plankenhorn
Bertram Schaffer
Bodo Jahn
Christian Danner
Clemens Schickentanz
Dieter Basche
Dieter Glemser
Dieter Hegels
Dieter Kern
Dieter Schornstein
Dieter Spoerry
Edgard Doren
Egon Evertz
Erich Breinberg
Ernst Furtmayer
Ernst Kraus
Erwin Kremer
Ferfried Von Hohenzollern
Frank Jelinski
Franz Gschwendtnen
Fritz Mueller
Georg Loos
Gerhard Holup
Gerhard Koch
Gerold Pankl
Gunther Steckkonig
Hannelore Werner
Hans Dieter Dechent
Hans Georg Burger

Hans Hermann
Hans Heyer
Hans Joachin Stuck
Hans Peter Joisten
Harald Grohs
Harald Menzel
Hartwig Bertrams
Helmut Bross
Helmut Kelleners
Herbert Hechler
Hermann Behrens
Horst Godel
Hubert Hahne
Jochen Dauer
Jochen Mass
John Winter (Louis Krages)
Jorg Obermoser
Jurgen Barth
Jurgen Neuhaus
Karl Heinz Becker
Karl Heinz Quinn
Karl Von Wendt
Klaus Frtizinger
Klaus Ludwig
Kurt Ahrens
Leopold Von Bayern
Manfred Mohr
Manfred Winkelhock
Mario Ketterer
Michael Korten
Michael Weber
Peter Hennige
Reinhard Stenzel
Reinhold Jost
Roland Binder
Rolf Stommelen
Rudi Lins
Sepp Greger
Sigifried Muller
Tibor Meray
Toni Fischaber
Volkert Merl
Walter Rohrl
Waltraud Odenthal
Willi Deutsch
Willi Kauhsen
Wolfgang Locher
Wolfgang Schutz

GREAT BRITAIN

Major international achievement: World Champion (Stewart, Hunt)

Adrian Reynard

Alain de Cadenet
Alan Minshaw
Alan Rollinson
Alistair Walker
Andy Sutcliffe
Barrie Maskell
Bernard Unett
Bernard Vermillo
Bev Bond
Bill McGovern
Bill Sydenham
Bob Evans
Bob Salisbury
Brian Hart
Brian Henton
Brian Redman
Brian Robinson
Chris Craft
Chris Skeaping
Clive Santo
Colin Vandervell
Cyd Williams
Damien Magee
Dave Morgan
David Hobbs
David Piper
David Prophet
David Purley
David Sears
Derek Bell
Derek Lawrence
Derek Warwick
Derrick Brunt
Divina Galica
Frank Sytner
Geoff Lees
Gerry Birrel
Gordon Spice
Graham Hill
Guy Edwards
Ian Ashley
Ian Flux
Ian Grob
Ivan Dutton
Jackie Oliver
Jackie Stewart
James Hunt
James Weaver
Jan Bussell
Jim Crawford
Jock Robertson
John Bright
John Burton
John Cleland

John Cooper
John Fitzpatrick
John Handley
John Lepp
John Miles
John Surtees
John Watson
Jonathan Williams
Keith Holland
Kenneth Acheson
Malcolm Guthrie
Martin Brundle
Martin Raymond
Mike Beutller
Mike Hailwood
Mike Parkes
Mike Wilds
Mike Young
Mo Harness
Nigel Mansell
Norman Dickson
Peter Gethin
Peter Westbury
Piers Courage
Ray Allen
Ray Mallock
Richard Longman
Richard Scott
Ritchie Attwood
Robbin Widdows
Robs Lamplough
Roger Heavens
Roger Williamson
Roy Pierpoint
Rupert Keegan
Russell Wood
Stephen South
Steve Thompson
Stirling Moss
Stuart Graham
Syd Fox
Terry Gray
Tiff Needell
Tim Brise
Tom Pryce
Tom Walkinshaw
Tony Brise
Tony Dean
Tony Dron
Tony Lanfranchi
Tony Trimmer
Trevor Taylor
Trevor Twaites
Valentino Musetti

Vic Elford

GREECE

Major international achievement:
Giorgos Aposkitis raced in Italian Formula 3

Aposkitis' Formula 3 mount (site rally.gr)

Alekos Kotzamanis
Aris Loudimis (Asterix)
Christos Katsogiannos
Giannis Meimardes (Mavros)
Giorgos Aposkitis
Giorgos Moushos (George Mouschous)
Johnny Pesmazoglu
Konstantinos Samaropoulos (Nino)
Makis Saliaris
Pavlos Madentzsis
Pericles Fotiadis
Philip Antoniades
Tassos Livieratos (Sirokos)
Tassos Markus (Javeris)

GUATEMALA

Oscar Diaz
Pedro Cofino

GUYANA

David Reid
Eric Vieira
Roy Taylor

HOLLAND

Major international achievement:
participation in Formula 1 (Van Lennep, Hayje, Bleekemolen, Wunderink)

Arie Luyendyk
Boy Hayje
Cees Siewertsen
Ed Swart
Eddy Fresco
Gijs Van Lennep
Han Akersloot

Hans Deen
Hans Wolker
Henri Van Oorschot
Huub Rothengatter
Huub Vermeulen
Jan Lammers
Jim Vermeulen
Lambertus van Vreden

Van Vreden was a Dutch expatriate who raced in Indonesia. Photo Therry Van Vreden collection.

Leen Verhoeven
Liane Engemann
Marteen Henneman
Michael Bleekemolen
Nico Chiotakis
Rob Slotemaker
Roelof Wunderink
Toine Hezemans

HONG KONG

Major international achievement: Wins in Macau GP (McDonald)

John MacDonald was a real Asian hot shoe in the 70s. Here he drives a Brabham BT 40 in Macau, 1973. Photo by Jose Santos.

Albert Poon
Herbert Adamczyk
John McDonald
Peter Chow
Theodore "Teddy" Yip

HUNGARY

Dezsoe Kiss
Gal Pal
Janos Toth
Lanos Szaboki

ICELAND

Major international achievement participation in British Formula 3 (Thorodsson)

Sverrir Thorodsson

INDIA

A. Josephpherson
Dr. Cesare Rossi
Kinny Lal
Kumar Chanadityasinhji
Mahajarkumar of Gondal
Nazir Hossein
Ravi Kumar
Rishi Kumar
Sundaran Karivardhan
Vicky Chandhok
Vijay Mallya

INDONESIA

Major international achievement: Participation in British Formula 3 (Wiano)

Andi Yustana
Aswin Bahar
Beng Soeswanto
Chepot Hanu (Hanny) Wiano
Hengik Iriawan
Robert Silitonga
Tinton Suprapto

IRELAND

Major international achievement: Participation in British Formula 1 (Daly)

Alec Poole
Alo Lawler
Bernard Devaney
Brendan McInerney
David Kennedy

Derek Daly
Eddie Jordan
Gary Gibson
Martin Birrane
Michael Roe
Patsy McGarrity

ITALY

Major international achievement: GP Win (V. Brambilla)

Andrea de Adamich
Alberto Colombo
Alessandro Pesenti-Rossi
Amphicar (Eugenio Renna)
Andrea de Cesaris
Anna Cambiaghi
Armando Floridia
Arturo Merzario
Beppe Gabbiani
Bruno Giacomelli
Carlo Facetti
Carlo Giorgio
Claudio Francisci
Corrado Fabi
Corrado Manfredini
Cosimo Turizio
Domenico Scola
Duilio Ghislotti
Duilio Truffo
Edoardo Loaldi
Elio di Angelis
Ennio Bonomelli
Enrico Pinto
Enzo Corti
Eris Tondelli
Ernesto Brambilla
Francesco Cerulli-Irelli
Gabrielle Serblin
Gaudenzio Mantova
Giacomo Agostini
Giancarlo Gagliardi
Giancarlo Martini
Giancarlo Naddeo
Gianfranco Brancatelli
"Gianfranco" Trombetti
Gianluigi Picchi
Gianpiero Moretti
Gimax (Carlo Franchi)
Giorgio Francia
Giorgio Pianta
Giovanni Salvati
Girolama Capra
Guido Dacco

Guido Pardini
Ignazio Giunti
Lamberto Leoni
Lella Lombardi
Luigi Moreschi
Mario Casoni
Martino Finotto
Massimo Sigala
Maurizio Flammini
Mauro Baldi
Mauro Nesti
Michele Alboreto
Michele di Gioia
Nanni Galli
Nino Vacarella
Noris (Giacomo Noioli)
Odoardo Govoni
Oscar Pedersoli
Pal Joe (Gianfranco Palazolli)
Pam (Mario Pasotti)
Piercarlo Ghinzani
Piero Monticonne
Piero Necchi
Pino Pica
Pooky (Vincenzo Cazzago)
Rafaelle Pinto
Renzo Zorzi
Riccardo Palleti
Riccardo Patrese
Roberto Campominosi
Roberto Marazzi
Rodolfo Bellini
Sandro Munari
Siegfried Stohr
Spartaco Dini
Tambauto (Giuseppe Tambone)
Teo Fabi
Teodoro Zeccoli
Umberto Grano
Victor Coggiola
Vittorio Brambilla

JAMAICA

Corne D'Oyen
Geoffrey De Pass
Paul Chong
Peter Moodie
Richard Machado
Richard Melville

JAPAN

Major international achievement: Formula 1 participation (Fushida,

Hasemi, Kunimitsu Takahashi, Hoshino, Kuwashima)

Haruhito Yanagita
Harukuni Takahashi
Hiroshi Fushida
Hiroshi Kazato
Hiroyuki Hisagi
Jiro Yoneyama
Kazuyoshi Hoshino
Keiji Matsumoto
Kenji Takahashi
Kitano Yuan
Kunimitsu Takahashi
Masa Sakai
Masahiro Hasemi
Masami Kuwashima
Mitsuba Kurosawa
Motoharu Kurosawa
Noritake Takahara
Satoru Nakajima
Takao Wada
Tetsu Ikusawa
Tokomishu Urushibara
Toshio Suzuki
Yasumiri Toshimori
Yojiro Terada
Yoshimi Katayama

KENYA

Davinder Singh
Jim Russel
Shekhar Mehta
Vic Preston

LATVIA

Argot Liepa
Arnold Dambis
Uris Belmers

LIECHTENSTEIN

Major international achievement: Formula 1 participation (Von Opel)

Manfred Schurti
Rikki Von Opel

LITHUANIA

Antanas Jurjavicjus
Jonas Dereskjavicius
Stasis Brundsa

Vilius Roshukas

LUXEMBOURG

Major international achievement: 24 Spa hours win (Demuth)

Carlo Keller
John Lagodny
Nico Demuth
Nicolas Koob
Pit Weirig
Roman Feitler

MALAYSIA

Major international achievement: Participation in European racing (Rajah)

Chong Kim Fah
Gary Chua
Harvey Yap
Percy Chan
Sonny Rajah (also listed as Singaporean)
Tony Maw

Sonny Rajah in Macau. Photo by Jose Santos.

MALTA

Aldo Laferla
Alex Zammit
David Anastasi
Joe Anastasi

MEXICO

Major international achievement: GP Win (Rodriguez)

Andreas Contreras
Carlos Solis
Daniel Muniz
Fidel Martinez
Fred Van Bueren Jr.

Guillermo "Memo" Rojas, Sr.
Gustavo Bolanos
Gustavo Helmut
Hector Rebaque
Horacio Richard
Ignacio Baleguero
Jaime Perez
Johnny Gerber
Jose Marron
Josele Garza
Juan Carlos Bolanos
Juan Izquierdo
Luis Iglesias
Manuel Cardona
Michael Jourdain
Miguel Muniz
Pedro Rodriguez
Ramon de Izaurieta
Roberto Gonzalez
Roberto Quintanilla
Rolando Quintanilla
Ruben Novoa
Sergio Tabe

MONACO

Lionel Noghes

MOROCCO

Albert Benchaya
Charles Geeraerts
Christian Diot
Gerard Cantarel
Idrissi Ahmed
Jacques Berenger (aka Beranger)
Le Tahitien
Manuel Rodriguez
Max Cohen Olivar
Rene Gabana
Robert Lassus
Robert Sibony

MOZAMBIQUE

Carlos Prata Antunes
Fernando Capela

NEW ZEALAND

Major international achievement: GP Wins (Hulme)

Bert Hawthorne
Brett Riley
Bruce McLaren
Chris Amon
Dave McMillan
David Oxton
Denis Hulme
Graeme Lawrence
Graham McRae
Howden Ganley
John Nicholson
Ken Smith
Mike Thackwell
Peter Hull
Rob Wilson
Richard Hawkins
Steve Millen

NORWAY

Arne Steshorne
Arne Teig
Edvard Haug
Gudmund Fornes
Gunnar Bergersen
Iver Nederberg
John Haugland
Martin Schanche
Ola Rustad
Olav Ronningen
Per Bakke
Per Eklund
Per Sundet
Ray Fallo
Stener Svartrud
Trond Shea

PANAMA

Major international achievement: Le Mans Participation (Teran)

Henry Schwartz
Patricio Janson
Rodrigo Teran
Tony Janson

PARAGUAY

Major international achievement: win in Argentine F2 race in Rafaela, 1976 (Risso)

Alfredo Jaegli
Hector Risso
Juanbi Gill
Roberto Bittar

PERU

Major international achievement: British Formula 3 participation Koechlin

Arnaldo Alvarado
Eduardo Dibos
Federico Pitty Block
Francisco Schettini
Guillermo Arteaga
Henry Bradley
Jorge Koechlin
Ulderico Ossio

PHILIPPINES

Arthur Tuason
Dante Silverio
Louei Camus
Joey Bundalian
Jose "Pocholo" Ramirez
Narciso de la Merced

This is Joey Bundalian driving an Australian Elfin at Macau, 1973. Photo by Jose Santos.

POLAND

Major international achievement: IMSA participation: Potocki (Formula 2)

Adam Potocki (double citizenship, French)
Adam Smoranski
Aleksander Oczokowski
Andrei Wojcieckowski
Frank Ksawery
Janosz Kiljancik
Jozef Kielbania
Ksawery Frank
Lech Jaworowicz
Longin Bilak
Marcin Biernacki
Otto Bartkowiak
Richard Kopczyk
Robert Mucha
Sobieslav Zasada
Zbigniew Sucharda

PORTUGAL

Major international achievement: British F3 win (Espirito Santo, 1973)

Americo Nunes
Antonio Peixinho
Antonio Pinto de Barros
Antonio Portela Morais
Bernardo Sa Nogueira
Carlos Gaspar
Carlos Mendonca
Carlos Santos
Clemente da Silva
Ernesto Neves
Francisco Manuel Baptista Filho
Francisco Santos
Joaquim Felipe Nogueira
Jorge Pinhol
Jose Espirito Santo
Jose Lampreia
Luis Fernandes
Manuel Nogueira Pinto
Mario de Araujo Cabral
Mario Goncalves
Miguel Correia
Miguel Lacerda
Pedro Queiroz Pereira
Orlando Goncalves
Robert Giannone

PUERTO RICO

Major international achievement: IMSA participation (Febles)

Bonky Fernandez
Diego Febles

RHODESIA

Major international achievement: Formula 1 participation (Love)

Freed Godard
Isaac Codron
John Love
Mike Wesson
Royce Love

ROMANIA

Florin Popescu
Genu Cristea
Zoltan Timay

RUSSIA (SOVIET UNION)

Boris Karpov
Eduard Markovskie
Jukk Rentam
Michael Iwow
Nikolai Kazakov
Nikolai Rogoshin
Oleg Lysenko
Raul Sarap
Sergei Panasenko
Thomas Napa
Viktor Klimanov
Vitali Bogatyrev
Vladislav Barkowisk
Vladmir Grekov
Yuri Andreev
Yuri Markov
Yuri Terezkie

SENEGAL

Major international achievement: Participation at Le Mans (Thiaw)

Daniel Thiaw

SINGAPORE

Anne Wong
Ching Boon Seng
Harold Lee
Lee Han Seng
Lionel Chan
Richard Tay
Sonny Rajah (*)
William Lyou

SOUTH AFRICA

Major international achievement: World Championship (Jody Scheckter)

Basil Van Rooyen
Bobby Olthoff
Brian Von Hage
Bruce Van Der Merke
Dave Charlton
Desire Wilson
Eddie Keizan
George Santana
Guy Tumner
Ian Scheckter
Jack Pretorius
Jody Scheckter
John McNicol
Kipp Ackermann
Meyer Both
Mike Ackermann
Nols Nieman
Peter Parnell
Peter de Klerk
Rad Dougall
Roy Klomfass
Sarel Van der Merwe
Tony Martin
Trevor Van Royen
Willy Ferguson

SPAIN

Major international achievement: Participations in Formula 1 (Soler-Roig, Villota, Zapico)

Alex Soler-Roig
Carlos Jodar
Emilio de Villota
Emilio Zapico
Federico van de Hoeven
Fermin Velez
Francisco Torredemer
Jesus Pareja
Jorge Babler
Jorge Caton
Jorge de Bagration
Juan Fernandez
Juan Juncadella
Juan Sanz de Madrid
Juan Villacieros
Luis Canomanuel
Manrico Zanuso
Manuel Juncosa
Manuel Vallis I Biesca
Miguel Arias
Paco Josa
Pedro "Pere" Nogues
Rafael Barrios
Salvador Canellas

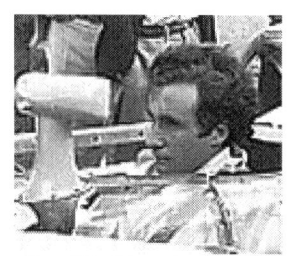

One of Spain's main drivers of the 70s was Jorge de Bagration, a Georgian prince. Unknown author.

Jesus Pareja
Jorge Babler
Jorge Caton
Jorge de Bagration
Juan Fernandez
Juan Juncadella
Juan Sanz de Madrid
Juan Villacieros
Luis Canomanuel
Manrico Zanuso
Manuel Juncosa
Manuel Vallis I Biesca
Miguel Arias
Paco Josa
Pedro "Pere" Nogues
Rafael Barrios
Salvador Canellas

SRI LANKA
Major international achievement: David Pieris' win in Madras Grand Prix of 1974 (India)

David Pieris
Jeffrey Mason
Leslie de Silva
Priya Munasinghe
Rohan Wijesekers
Shanthi Gunaratna

David Pieris was Sri Lanka's top car driver of the 70s. Pieris collection.

ST. VINCENT

Lennox Gonsalves

SWEDEN

Major international achievement: GP wins (Peterson, Nilsson)

Ake Anderson
Anders Oloffson
Bengt Eckberg
Bengt Tragardth
Bertil Roos
Bjorn Steenberg
Bjorn Waldegaard
Bo Emmanuelson
Boo Brasta
Claus Sigurdsson
Conny Anderson
Conny Ljungfeldt
Eje Elgh
Freddy Kottulinsky
Gunnar Nilsson
Hakan Dahlqvist
Henri Spellerberger
Ingvar Carlsson
Jan Lungdarth
Joakin Bonnier
Kenneth Leim
Leif Nilsson
Picko Troberg
Reine Wisell
Rune Tobiason
Slim Borgudd
Stanley Dickens
Sten Gunnarson
Thomas Lindstrom
Tomas Kaiser
Tommy Brorsson
Torsten Palm
Ulf Norinder
Ulf Svensson
Kenneth Persson

SWITZERLAND

Major international achievement: GP Wins (Regazzoni, Siffert)

Andre Wicky
Angelo Pallavicini
Bernard Cheneviere
Charly Kiser

Charly Schirmer
Claude Haldi
Clay Regazzoni
Cox Kocher
Dieter Spoerry
Dominique Martin
Emmanuel de Graffenried
Enzo Calderari
Eugen Strahl
Freddy Lienhard
Fredy Link
Gerard Pillon
Giordano Regazzoni
Hebert Mueller
Jean-Claude Bering
Jo Von Lanthen
Joseph Siffert
Jurg Dubler
Karl Foitek
Loris Kessel
Marc Surer
Marco Vanoli
Markus Hotz
Patrick Studer
Paul Blancpain
Paul Keller
Peter Sauber
Peter Schetty
Peter Zbinden
Rene Herzog
Rudi Jauslin
Silvio Moser
Urs Zondler
Walter Brun
Xavier Perrot

THAILAND

B. Bira

TRINIDAD & TOBAGO

Davey Maraj
Frankie Boodram
Gordon Gonsalves
Simon Gilmore

TURKEY

Serdar Bostanci

UKRAINE

Aleksandr Duryshev

URUGUAY

Major international achievement:
Participation in British F3 (Passadore)

Alberto Branca
Alberto Buffa
Daniel Luzardo
Gustavo Trelles
Hector Mera
Luiz Etchegoyen
Nano Parrado
Pedro Ken
Pedro Passadore

USA

Major international achievement: World Champion (Andretti)

A.J. Foyt Jr.
Al Holbert
Al Unser
Art Pollard
Benny Parsons
Bill Alsup
Bill Gubelmann
Bill Scott
Bill Whittington
Billy Vukovich, Jr.
Bob Bondurant
Bob Earl
Bob Garretson
Bob Sharp
Bobby Allison
Bobby Isaac
Bobby Rahal
Bobby Unser
Brad Friselle
Brett Lunger
Buddy Baker
Cale Yarborough
Cecil Gordon
Charles Mendez
Charlie Glotzbach
Charlie Kemp
Chuck Parsons
Dale Earnhardt
Dale Whittington
Dan Gurney
Danny Ongais
Danny Sullivan
Darel Dieringer
Darrel Waltrip

Dave Marcis
David Causey
David Heinz
David Pearson
David Weir
Dennis Firestone
Dick Barbour
Dick Brooks
Dick Simon
Dominic Dobson
Don Breidenbach
Don Devendorf
Don Whittington
Donnie Allison
Eddie Cheever Jr.
Elliot Forbes-Robinson
Elmo Langley
Fred Lorenzen
Gary Bettenhausen
George Dyer
George Follmer
Gordon Johncock
Gordon Smiley
Gregg Pickett
Gus Hutchison
Hershell McGriff
Hideo Fukuyama
Hurley Haywood
James Hylton
James King
Janet Guthrie
Jerry Hansen
Jim Adams
Jim Busby
Jim McElreath
Jimmy Caruthers
Jodi Ridley
Joe Castellano
Joe Leonard
Joe Milikan
John Greenwood
John Morton
John Paul
Johnny Rutherford
Kenper Miller
Larry Dickson
Lee Roy Yarbrough
Lennie Pond
Lloyd Ruby
Lothar Motschenbacher
Lou Sell
Luigi Chinetti Junior
Lyn St. James
Mario Andretti

Mark Donohue
Masten Gregory
Mel Kenyon
Mike Keyser
Mike Mosley
Milt Minter
Monte Shelton
Morgan Shepherd
Neil Bonnett
Orlando Costanzo
Oscar Kovelesky
Pancho Carter
Paul Newman
Pete Halsmer
Pete Hamilton
Pete Lovely
Peter Gregg
Peter Revson
Phil Hill
Price Cobb
Ray Elder
Rich Vogler
Richard Childress
Richard Petty
Ricky Mears
Ricky Rudd
Rocky Moran
Roger Mandeville
Roger McCluskey
Ron Grable
Sam Posey
Sam Sessions
Scooter Patrick
Sheldon Kinser
Spike Gelhausen
Steve Krisiloff
Steve McQueen
Swede Savage
Ted Wentz
Terry Labonte
Tim Coconis
Tim Richmond
Tom Bagley
Tom Gloy
Tom Klausler
Tom Sneva
Tony Adamowickx
Tony Bettenhausen
Tony Cicale
Tony Rouff
Wally Dallenbach
Willy T. Ribbs

UZBEKISTAN

Voldemar Hlojan

VENEZUELA

Major international achievement:
Participation in Formula 2 (Cochesa)

Armando Capriles
Edgardo Soares
Ernesto Soto
Francisco Romero
Johnny Ceccoto
Juan Cochesa
Julio Cesar Hidalgo
Luis Zereix
Oscar Notz
Roberto "Bobby" Dennett

Roberto Gonzalez
Roberto Quintanilla
Winston Chelby

YUGOSLAVIA

Major international achievement:
Participation in Formula 2 (Jerancic)

Branco Abdul Halik
Dagmar Suster
Drago Regvart
Dusan Todorovic
Francy Jerancic
Goran Strok
Milutin Gravilovic
Robert Lang
Sead Ali Hodzic

SIGNIFICANT DRIVERS OF THE DECADE

Top lists are always controversial. Somebody is always left out, especially Top 100, Top 50 and Top 10 lists. At the end of the day, lists are generally subjective. Thus, rather than ranking, I provided a sampling of some of the drivers who had significant impact on the sport during the decade, in my opinion. Number of wins is not the only criteria: NASCAR driver **Jody Ridley** had won hundreds of races in the 70s before joining the Winston Cup late in the decade and most people have no idea who he is. Some geographical consideration is given and some of your favorites might be missing. This is not meant as a comprehensive or absolute list and it is alphabetical, so that it is clear it is not a ranking. Some entries are slightly longer than others: **Jackie Stewart**'s is much shorter than **James Hunt**'s. It so happens that the **Hunt** story is much more dramatic and interesting.

A.J. FOYT

Foyt was still a topline USAC driver in the decade. The beginning was not auspicious, for in the first three seasons of the decade he won a single race in his **Coyote-Foyt(Ford)**. However, with time he began winning with greater frequency, racking up seven victories and the **1975** championship. He crowned that surge in competitiveness with his fourth **Indy** 500 win, in **1977**. During the **1979** USAC/CART split, **Foyt** sided with USAC and won that title easily. **Foyt** also drove in other USAC divisions during the decade, as well as NASCAR, where he was always the most successful USAC representative but never doing full seasons, winning five times during the 70s. He was the second winningest Indy driver of the decade, with 24 victories. **Foyt** also drove sporadically in Formula 5000 and won IROC twice (**1976** and **1977**).

AL HOLBERT

Al **Holbert**, son of **Bob**, was a prominent GT and Sportscar driver of the 70s. His main focus was IMSA Camel GT, a championship which he won in **1976** and **1977** driving a **Chevrole**t Monza. **Holbert** started his career in **1971** and was runner-up in the **1973** Trans Am driving a **Porsche**, which he continued to drive in IMSA. In **1978 Holbert** unsuccessfully tried a NASCAR career, which did not last beyond that season. Late in **1978 Holbert** moved into the Can Am series, winning a race and staying on. **Holbert** also raced in two editions of the IROC and drove an **Inaltera** in the **1977 Le Mans**.

AL UNSER

Al finished the decade in top order. The USAC champion in **1970**, plus winner of the **Indy** 500 in **1970** and **1971**, **Al** won not only the **1978 Indy** 500 but also the two other 500-mile races on the calendar and also won the last CART race in the **1979** calendar, driving the new **Chaparral**. He did this in different teams, too. In addition to his USAC/CART driving, **Unser** also drove very competitively in the US Formula 5000 series, IROC (he won the **1978** title). He was the winningest Indy Car winner of the decade, with 27 wins.

ALAN JONES

Australian **Jones** was already racing in Europe in **1970** and it took a while for him to impress in Formula 3. That he did in **1973 and** a season of Formula Atlantic in **1974** showed a star in the making. By **1975** Jones was in Formula 1, at first driving a Stiller **Hesketh**, then a **Hill**. The Australian driver also began driving in Formula 5000 races in Europe and the USA, winning in both arenas and ultimate Formula 1 success came in **1977**, in Austria. A Can-Am champion in **1978, Jones** realized his full potential in **1979**, when **Williams** came up with a very fast challenger and he won four GPs. He also raced sporadically in sports cars and also drove in the IROC and Procar series.

Photo by Rob Neuzel

ANDREA DE ADAMICH

Andrea de Adamich's two most prestigious wins were in Alfa Romeos in the World Championship of Makes, here in Brands Hatch. (Photo by Gerald Swan)

Andrea was an **Alfa Romeo** driver during the decade, who won prototype and touring car races on occasion for the Milanese marque. His finest hours came in **1971**, when he won two World Manufacturers Championship races, driving with **Pescarolo** (**Brands Hatch**) and **Peterson** (**Watkins Glen**), plus many placings. He was not successful driving **Alfa** engined **McLarens** and **Marches** in Formula 1, in **1970** and **1971** but scored his first points finishing fourth in the **1972** Spanish

Grand Prix for **Surtees**. He took his Ceramica Pagnossin sponsorship to **Brabham** in **1973**, finishing fourth in Belgium. The accident caused by **Jody Scheckter** in the British GP essentially finished **Andrea**'s GP career but he did return for a last season with **Alfa Romeo** in the **1974** World Manufacturers Championship, finishing 2nd in Austria and posting several 3rd places. **Andrea** also occasionally drove in Formula 2, placing well in some races, drove in the European 2-Liter Championship and ETCC, winning the **Nürburgring** race of **1970** in an **Alfa**. He also drove in the Interserie, Can-Am and domestic sports car races.

ARTURO MERZARIO

Merzario was a top sports car driver in the 70s, winning in the World Manufacturers Championship, Interserie, European 2 Liter Championship, World Sports Car Championship, Hill Climbs and also stand-alone races, driving for **Ferrari, Alfa Romeo** and **Abarth**. He did not have the same success in single seaters, although he scored on his debut for **Ferrari** in **1972** (Britain) and on four other occasions in Formula 1. Perhaps two optimistic, **Merzario** designed his own Formula 1 car, which he actually managed to qualify a few times. **Merzario** was the main contributor to **Alfa**'s winning World Manufacturers Championship campaign of **1975**, winning four times, plus won four other races in the World Sportscars Championship of **1977**. Little Art also drove in Hill climbs, Formula 2, GTs and Touring Cars, earning good places in all categories.

BOB WOLLEK

Wollek's single-seater career fizzled in **1973**, after two very good seasons in Formula 2 driving for **Ron Dennis**' **Rondel** team. He had started the decade driving in Formula 3 and won occasional sports car races in France driving Alfa P33, Lola T70 and Chevron 2-liter cars. He did find his place in the motoring world when he started racing **Porsches** in **1974**, winning the **Porsche** Cup three straight years and winning races in the DRM, World Championship of Makes, Interserie, European GT Championship, mostly driving Zuffenhausen cars. He became a true global star, earning the nickname "Brilliant Bob".

BOBBY ALLISON

Allison was one of the top NASCAR drivers of the decade, having won 41 races, 21 of them in **1970-1971**. He did have a 67-race winless streak later on the decade but resumed his winning ways. **Allison** drove for a variety of manufacturers during the decade, **AMC, Chevrolet, Plymouth, Ford** and **Dodge**. **Allison** also tried USAC (Formula Indy) racing for **Penske**, entered a Can-Am race but did not start and was also an IROC participant, winning 4 races. He and his brother **Donnie** had a famous fight with **Cale Yarborough** in the **1979 Daytona** 500 which brought much media attention.

BOBBY UNSER

Al's older brother **Bobby** was mostly **Eagle**'s works driver in USAC during the early 70s, winning his second Indy 500 in **1975** driving for that team. He remained a very competitive driver in the course of the decade and won six races in CART's debut season, in **1979**, driving for **Roger Penske**. **Bobby** won 15 races during the decade and he also won the second IROC season, **1975**.

Photo by Rob Neuzel.

BRIAN HENTON

Henton soldiered on in British lower categories for many years until finding ultimate success by dominating both British Formula 3 championships in **1974**. An eventual Formula 1 participant during the decade, driving briefly for **Lotus** in **1975**, Henton also found success in Formula 2, winning for **Boxer** and **March**, almost winning the **1979** Formula 2 Championship, were it not for his disqualification at **Enna**.

BRIAN REDMAN

Redman was a true professional who raced in many categories and scenarios during the decade: Formula 1, Formula 5000, Sports Cars, 2-Liter Sports Cars, Can-Am, Interserie, ETCC. He drove for **Ferrari, Porsche, Alfa Romeo, Chevron, Mercedes, McLaren, Surtees, BRM, Shadow** and won many Formula 5000 races in the USA (and three championships) and Europe. He could win both sprints and long-distance races, showing great versatility. On the downside, he had two major shunts in the decade, at the **1971 Targa Florio** and **1977 St. Jovite** Can Am round, both of which sidelined him for a while

BRUNO GIACOMELLI

A great success in Italian lower categories and British Formula 3, **Giacomelli** became the winningest driver in the European Formula 2 championship during the decade, winning 11 races in **1977** and **1978**, including eight races and the championship in the latter year. At first a **McLaren** F-1 driver, soon **Giacomelli** was signed by **Alfa Romeo's** Formula 1 works team but no success came his way. The Italian also won in the ETCC, driving a **BMW** Italia car.

BUDDY BAKER

Second generation **Buddy** is mostly remembered for his large frame, more suitable for a defensive American football player than a race car driver. Notwithstanding, **Baker** was one of the fastest and most popular drivers of the 70s, winning a total of 15 NASCAR races. **Ford** fans remember him well, for he was one of the few drivers that stuck to the brand mid-decade, racing for Bud Moore and won with it. He also drove **Oldsmobile, Chevy** and **Dodge** cars and drove for Petty Enterprises in the beginning of the decade. He also raced in the IROC.

CALE YARBROUGH

Cale Yarborough is mostly remembered for being the first NASCAR driver to win three straight championships, from **1976** to **1978**. **Cale** drove for **Junior Johnson** in these seasons and was the category's second winningest driver of the decade, with 52 wins. He drove a number of cars early on the decade (**Plymouth, Ford, Mercury** and **Chevy**) and tried his luck in USAC in **1971** and **1972** with mixed results. He came back to NASCAR in **1973** and finished both the **1973** and **1974** seasons in second place, switching to **Johnson**'s team mid-season. **Yarborough** also drove in the IROC, winning for races but no championships.

CARLO FACETTI

Facetti was already a veteran in **1970**, at the time linked with **Alfa Romeo**'s works team, Autodelta. **Facetti** raced in prototypes (World Manufacturers Championship and Interserie) and ETCC, where the **Alfa** was no longer competitive for overall wins in **1971** but good enough for class wins, often with **Facetti** on the winning crews. **Facetti** also drove in hill climbs, in minor races all over the world (Brazil, Senegal), Interserie and in the European 2 Liter Championship. His first full season with Autodelta's prototype team was **1974**, paired with De **Adamich**, when they finished 2nd once and 3rd on occasion. That year, **Facetti** attempted to qualify the **Finotto Brabham** in the Italian Grand Prix, without success. His future during the decade was inextricably linked with **Finotto** and they shared many ETCC wins driving **BMW**s, earning the title in **1979** and also a **Porsche** 935.

CARLOS REUTEMANN

Lole was one of the prominent Formula 1 drivers of the decade, having driven for **Brabham, Ferrari** and **Lotus**. He managed to get pole for his Formula 1 debut, a very rare feat, in a car that was not that competitive. **Carlos** was also the fastest driver of the beginning of the **1974** season but suddenly and strangely the **Brabham** performance dropped mid-season, recovering towards the end of the season. **Reutemann** was also very fast in Formula 2, where he raced from **1970** to **1972** and drove **Porsche, Ferrari** and **Alfa Romeo** in the World Sportscars Championship, from **1971** to **1974**. He also appeared in the Procar series.

CHRIS AMON

Amon's move to **March** from **Ferrari** for the **1970** season was indicative of the many mistakes the driver made when changing teams. His last three truly competitive seasons in the championship were **1970** to **1972**, although he stayed on in mostly uncompetitive rides until **1976**. One of the drives of the decade was **Amon**'s race in **Clermont Ferrand, 1972**. He earned pole in his **Matra** and drove away from the field, until a puncture dropped him to 8th. He came back, got as far as 3rd place and very close to 2nd placed man **Fittipaldi**. Following seasons with **Tecno, Amon, BRM, Ensign** and **Williams** did not yield much in terms of results and a brief time with **Tyrrell** did not impress the boss. Amon raced and won, in Formula 5000 and Touring Cars (for BMW), won two non-championship Formula 1 races during the decade and also drove **Ferrari** and **Matra-Simca** sports cars and **BMW** saloons at Le Mans and the World Championship.

CLAY REGAZZONI

Regazzoni's breakthrough year was **1970**, when he became a top Formula 2 driver for **Tecno**, which resulted in his being hired by **Ferrari's** Formula 1 team. **Clay** won the Italian Grand Prix for the team on his debut year and finished third in the championship, enough to raise his stature to that of Italian hero. His next two seasons were not great and a move to **BRM** in **1973** did little to improve matters. In his return to **Ferrari** in **1974**, **Clay** led the championship many times and came to **Watkins Glen** with great chances of winning a first title. He remained a couple more years at **Ferrari**, then drove for **Ensign** and **Shadow** and was surprisingly picked up by **Williams. Regazzoni** then won the marque's first GP, in England. **Regazzoni** also raced in sports cars (**Ferrari** and **Alfa**), winning for the former, GTs (**De Tomaso**), Formula 5000, Formula 2, Procar and even Formula Indy, starting the **1977 Indy 500**.

Photo by Rob Neuzel

DANNY ONGAIS

Ongais was a Hawaiian drag racing driver who worked his way into Formula 5000 in the 70s, who had the good luck of finding a great sponsor, **Ted Field**'s Interscope company. **Fields** would lead the Hawaiian to loftier heights, at USAC, IMSA and even Formula 1. Although Ongais' Formula 1 entries in a **Penske** and **Ensign** in **1977** and **1978** were not successful, he did win many IMSA races in **Porsche**s and no less than five USAC races in a highly competitive **1978** field.

DARREL WALTRIP

Waltrip was an emerging NASCAR talent who came to the fore in **1975**, driving Gatorade sponsored cars for the Di-Gard team, after racing as a team-owner for a few years. He began his winning ways that season and would not stop winning until the end. In total, **Waltrip** won a total 22 races during the decade, becoming a major force in NASCAR and he also raced in the IROC.

DAVID HOBBS

Hobbs never got ultimate success in Formula 1, although he got a final crack in the category driving the 3rd **McLaren** in some **1974** races. Notwithstanding, he remained a top driver during the decade, driving in Formula 5000, Can-Am, Indy, World Championship of Makes, IMSA, NASCAR, earning many victories in three continents, driving the likes of **Lola, McLaren, Ferrari, BMW, Matra-Simca**, etc. He won the **1971** US Formula 5000 title.

David raced Formula 5000 cars all over the world during the 70s.

DAVID PEARSON

David Pearson was one of the seventies stock car luminaries. While **Richard Petty** deserved a lot of credit for winning 87 races and five titles during the decade, **Pearson** won no less than 47 races, running restricted schedules almost every season, while King Richard ran full schedules. In fact, **Pearson** was the winningest driver in both **1973** (11 races) and **1976** (10 races) but running a restricted schedule could never get near the title. That did not matter: **Pearson** had already won three NASCAR titles and he tended to win the most important and richer races. **Pearson** also drove in four editions of the IROC, never winning a race.

DENIS HULME

Hulme began the decade the unquestioned leader of the **McLaren** Can-Am and Formula 1 teams, due to the death of **Bruce McLaren**. **McLaren** continued its domination of Can-Am, in fact, **Hulme** won the championship in **1970 but** in Formula 1 the team had lost its way. However, a revitalized **Hulme** won in South Africa in **1972** and was in the hunt for most of the championship. He raced near the front in **1973** and **1974** but not sufficiently to justify filling a most competitive seat. **Hulme** retired from F1 in **1974**. **Hulme** won 11 Can-Am races in the decade and 3 Grand Prix (plus one non-championship race), also drove in the first IROC, bringing his international career to a close, also raced in the **Indy** 500 but continued to race in the Antipodes.

DEREK BELL

Bell insisted on his single-seater career in **1970**, driving in both Formula 2 (runner-up in the championship) and Formula 1 (**Surtees**) trying sports cars for the first time at **Le Mans**. Eventually, he saw the light and focused on sports cars and tin tops. While success driving **Surtees** and **Tecno** Formula 1's was elusive, Bell won races in **Abarth, Mirage, McLaren, Alfa Romeo** sports cars, **BMW** touring cars, **Penske** in Group 8 and also drove in Formula 5000, Interserie, the **Jaguar** ETCC challenger, the Tasman Cup. That set the tone for a very successful decade.

Photo by Rob Neuzel

DIDIER PIRONI

A major star in Formula Renault, **Pironi** was brought into the **Martini** Formula 2 team for the **1977** season and performed well finishing 3rd in a competitive season, winning one race. He was immediately hired by **Tyrrell** for **1978**, at the time sponsored by Elf, which generally resulted in French drivers getting the best shot for a seat. **Didier** scored only 7 points to team leader **Depailler**'s 34 but impressed sufficiently and was retained for **1979**, matching **Jarier**'s score, 14. **Didier**'s greatest success of the decade was the **1978** Le Mans win with **Jean-Pierre Jaussaud**, which turned out to be **Alpine-Renault**'s only **Le Mans** win. The Frenchman had previously driven a **Porsche** 934 with **Wollek** and **Beaumont** in the **1976 Le Mans** and was also part of the **Renault** team effort at **Le Mans** in **1977**. **Pironi** also raced a **Kojima** in the Japanese Formula 2 Championship, raced in the Procar series and drove in the **Trois-Rivieres** Formula Atlantic race.

DIETER GLEMSER

Glemser was one of the most successful touring car drivers of the decade, winning many ETCC and DRM races, plus some World Manufacturers Championship class wins, always driving **Ford**s. A florist by trade, the driver was a major presence in European touring car races from **1970** to **1974**. He decided to retire from the sport in the aftermath of an accident in **Macau**, in which he was involved and resulted in the death of a spectator.

DIETER QUESTER

Although **Quester** is mostly remembered for his ETCC championship titles (won in three different decades, by the way) and longevity, he was actually very versatile, winning in Formula 2, 2-Liter, World Manufacturers Championship and IMSA, both long distance and sprint races. Mostly a **BMW** driver, **Quester** also drove **Ford, Abarth, Osella** and **Chevron** during the decade, as well as a **Surtees** in the **1974** Austrian Grand Prix and in Formula 2. He was considered for a **March** Formula 1 ride in **1971** but the deal fell through. He also drove in the **1979 BMW** Procar Series.

EMERSON FITTIPALDI

Emerson was a major star of the decade, winning not only two world Formula 1 championships but also won a number of races in Formula 2, Formula Ford, sports car, IROC. He tried his hand in **Porsche** 917s in the World Manufacturers Championship and Interserie and even tried a **McLaren** Indy car at the height of his fame. After a fast rise to fame in **1969, Emerson** moved to Formula 2, driving a **Lotus**, impressing right away. In no time he was picked up by the **Lotus** Formula 1 team, for which he won his fourth Grand Prix start. While **1971** was not great, in **1972** Emerson mounted a great challenge, winning the title, which he repeated in **1974**, by then driving for **McLaren**. A move to his brother's **Fittipaldi** team dampened the Brazilian's success during the decade, although **Emerson** finished 2nd in the **1978** Brazilian Grand Prix. His best racing result in **1979** was 3rd in the **BMW** Procar race in Monaco.

EMILIO DE VILLOTA

Spanish race car drivers were not generally successful in the 70s – the Spaniards preferred motorcycle to car racing even then. **Emilio**'s early exploits in touring cars and single seaters were not very promising, including a badly timed attempt to qualify for the **1976** Spanish Grand Prix but eventually **Emilio** became one of the main British Group 8 stars, winning races in **Lyncar, McLaren** and **Lotus** during the decade.

FRANCOIS CEVERT

Cevert was being groomed to be **Jackie Stewart**'s replacement at **Tyrrell** but an accident at the last Grand Prix of **1973** resulted in the Frenchman's death. **Francois** replaced the retiring **Johnny Servoz-Gavin** in the **Tyrrell** team in **1970** and stayed there until his untimely death. **Cevert**'s best season was **1971**, when he won the US Grand Prix (in the very same place where he would die), finishing 3rd. In addition to Formula 1, **Cevert** was a successful Formula 2 driver, won the **Ollon-Villars** hill climb, drove for **Matra-Simca**'s prototype team, winning a single race, also doing a whole season of Can-Am in **1972**, winning a race. He also drove **Ford** touring cars sporadically.

FRANK GARDNER

Gardner was a very fast Australian driver that somehow was overlooked by Formula 1 teams. Early in the decade, he was **Lola**'s development driver, greatly responsible for the success of the marque. He continued to race competitively, becoming the **1971** European Formula 5000 champion, drove and won in the Tasman Cup and raced mostly **Chevy** Camaros in touring car races in the rest of the decade.

GEORGE FOLLMER

Follmer was a major figure in the U.S. scene during the decade, racing in Can-Am, Trans-Am, Formula 5000, NASCAR, USAC, IMSA. He is best remembered for winning both the **1972** Can-Am and Trans-Am titles and being one of two drivers who won races in both the old and new Can-Am. Follmer also did a season in Formula 1, in **1973**, driving for new team **Shadow and** actually scored in his first two starts, including a very promising third in the Spanish Grand Prix. Unfortunately, his performance dropped afterwards and that was the end of his Grand Prix career. Follmer also drove for the **Porsche** factory team in long-distance events and drove in the IROC, winning a round.

Photo by Rob Neuzel

GERARD LARROUSSE

Larrousse started the decade as a major sports car exponent and ended as **Renault**'s team manager. Larrousse won **Sebring** and **Nürburgring** races for the Martini team in **1971** and was a major factor in **Matra-Simca**'s two world championships, winning nine races, including the **73** and **74 Le Mans**. He also won the **Mugello** round of the **1975** World Championship in an **Alpine**, with **Jabouille**. Gerard won many European 2 Liter events, drove for **Bonnier**'s **Lola** team in **1972**, drove for the Ford Works team, won a Formula 2 race for Elf in **1975** and had a single Formula 1 start to his name, in the **1974** Belgian G.P..

GIJS VAN LENNEP

Van Lennep was a leading sports car racer in the 70s, who won **Le Mans** twice, in **1971** and **1976**, in addition to the last World Championship edition of the **Targa Florio**, all in **Porsches**. Van Lennep also had success in single-seaters, having won the **1972** European Formula 5000 championship and earned both **Williams** and **Ensign**'s first points in Formula 1. Van Lennep also drove for **Abarth, Lola, Mirage, Alfa Romeo** and also took part in European 2-Liter, Interserie and European GT championship events. He retired after his **1976 Le Mans** win.

GILLES VILLENEUVE

Villeneuve was already impressive in Canadian Formula Ford in **1971** and graduated to the new Formula Atlantic series in **1975**, finishing 5th with a single win. He came back full strength in **1976**, winning both the CASC and IMSA series, racking up 8 wins, impressing pundits in both sides of the Atlantic. Villeneuve came back for more in **1977**, earning three wins and the crown and was hired by the Wolf Can-Am team to replace the retiring **Chris Amon**. Amon recommended

Gilles to **Enzo Ferrari** and after a great debut for **McLaren** in the British Grand Prix, **Villeneuve** was hired by **Ferrari**, eventually replacing the departing **Lauda**. With a highly entertaining and fast driving style, **Gilles** won four Grand Prix during the decade and was in the running for the **1979** title. He also drove **BMW**s in long distance events.

GORDON JOHNCOCK

The winner of the **1973** Indy 500 and **1976** USAC title, **Gordon** was one of the main USAC stars of the 70s, having won 12 races and always featuring well in the results, at first fielding his own cars, eventually driving for Patrick Racing where he found success, including a **1973 Indy** 500 win and 1976 USAC Crown. **Johncock** also took part in a few NASCAR races, as well as Formula 5000 and IROC.

GRAHAM MCRAE

The New Zealander was simply the king of Formula 5000 in **1972**, winning the Tasman Cup and the US Formula 5000 Championship and coming very close to winning the European title as well. **McRae**, who would eventually build his own **McRae** cars, also won the **1971** and **1973** Tasman Cups but his form dropped somewhat later in the decade, although he could still win races. A single Grand Prix for **Williams, 1973** and an **Indy** 500 start in the same year were not successful. He eventually drove his **McRae**s in the new Can-Am, when Formula 5000 folded.

The McRae won races in Europe, North America and Australasia. Photo by Rob Neuzel.

GRAHAM HILL

Hill was no longer a top Grand Prix driver in **1970**, yet he remained in the category until **1975**, by then running his own team. His major accomplishment of the decade was winning the 24 Hours of **Le Mans** of **1972**, with **Pescarolo**, becoming the only driver to win the F1 title, the **Indy** 500 and Le Mans, the goal now sought by **Fernando Alonso**. Hill was still fast enough to win non-championship Formula 1 races (Daily Express, **1971**) and Formula 2 races (Monza Lottery race of **1972**) during the decade. His pivoting to team ownership began in **1973**, with a **Shadow**, then setting up the **Hill** team, first with **Lolas** (**1974**) and later his own proprietary **Hill** chassis (**1975**). The promising team was destroyed in an airplane death that was bringing **Hill**, team driver **Brise** and other team personnel back into England. **Hill** also drove in Formula 2 early in the decade and also took part in the IROC.

GUY EDWARDS

One might question this driver's inclusion in this list. **Guy** did win in sports cars, Formula 5000 and Group 8, raced at **Le Mans** but his Formula 1 career with **Lola**, **Hesketh** and **BRM** was far from stellar. Notwithstanding, **Edwards** had a knack for obtaining good sponsorship deals and became rather influential in that area of the sport.

HANS HEYER

It is unfair that many will only remember **Heyer** for his illegal start in the **1977** German Grand Prix in an **ATS**, that resulted in disqualification. That is because **Heyer** was one of Europe's top touring car and sports cars drivers of the 70s, having won the DRM title several times, the ETCC title in **1974**, in addition to winning several World Manufacturers Championship races for Gelo. He drove mostly for **Ford** but also drove **BMW, Porsche** and achieved some fame driving the **Mercedes-Benz** 300 that finished 2nd in the 24 Hours of **Spa** of **1971**. He was also involved in AMG's efforts later in the decade.

HANS JOACHIN STUCK

The son of famed driver **Hans Stuck,** who raced from the 20s to the 60s, **Hans Joachin Stuck** caught the attention of pundits by winning the first edition of the 24 Hours of **Nürburgring**, in **1970**. He followed that up with many race wins driving **Ford** and **BMW** in the DRM (he won the first edition), ETCC and World Manufacturers Championship. Eventually he graduated to Formula 2, being runner-up in the **1974** series. He impressed at first in Formula 1 but the promise was never fulfilled. In F-1 he raced for **March, Brabham, Shadow** and **ATS**, his best season being **1977**, when he scored two podiums and led under the rain in **Watkins Glen**. **Stuck** remained mostly a **BMW** man during the decade, adding IMSA and Procar to his list of successes and his Formula 1 career ended with the closing of the decade. He also raced **Opel, Chevrolet** and **Ralt** cars during the 70s.

HECTOR LUIS GRADASSI

Argentina's Turismo de Carretera is a very tough category and championship, in existence even before the Formula 1 championship. Its main exponent of the 70s was **Hector Luis Gradassi**, a **Ford** works driver who won the title in **1972, 1974, 1975** and **1976**. Early in the decade, TC races were mostly very dangerous and long road races, often in dirt roads, plus some circuit races. By the end of the decade, the championship was being transformed into an all-circuit championship but **Gradassi** remained effective.

HELMUT MARKO

Marko or **Lauda**? For most observers, the one Austrian driver that was likely to replace **Jochen Rindt** as the country's hero was **Marko**, who after a learning season in **1970**, won the **1971** 24 Hours of **Le Mans** with **Van Lennep** and the European 2 Liter Championship, in addition to Formula 2 and Touring Car drives. He got his first Formula 1 rides with **BRM**, where he stayed in **1972**. Excellent sports car rides in **1972** with both **Alfa Romeo** and **Ferrari** augured well for the future. In the French GP, for the first time using the **BRM** P160 and starting in the top 10, **Marko**'s helmet was hit by a stone thrown by a car in front, blinding the driver in one eye and ending a very promising driving career.

HENRI PESCAROLO

Pescarolo was pretty much set on a Grand Prix career in **1970** but he was dropped by **Matra** at the end of the season, in spite of a podium at **Monaco**. The rest of his Formula 1 career was not successful, in spite of chances driving **Williams**' and works **Marches, Iso-Marlboro, BRM** and **Surtees**. Notwithstanding, he began a highly successful top level sports car career winning at **Brands Hatch** for **Alfa Romeo** in **1971**. He followed that with his first of three **Le Mans** wins for **Matra-Simca** and successful campaigns for the same team in **1973** and **1974** and **Alfa Romeo** in **1975**. **Pesca** also had a successful season winning three World races for Kremer in **1978**, although his **Le Mans** outings with the **Porsche** works were unlucky. He also raced **BMW** touring cars, **Motul** Formula 2, 2-liter **Lola** sports cars, all with distinction.

Pescarolo (on right) in other fast company at Le Mans, 1978: Bob Wollek on the far left and Jurgen Barth next to Wollek. (Jurgen Barth collection)

HERBERT MULLER

Muller's biggest moment of the decade was winning the last edition of the **Targa Florio** that was valid for the World Championship, in a **Porsche** Carrera. **Muller** was also second at **Le Mans** in **1971** (**Attwood**) and **1974** (**Van Lennep**), 3-times Interserie champion (**1974-1975-1976**), Muller won several races in his own

Ferrari 512, drove in the Can-Am and even dabbled in Formula 2.

Muller's roofless Ferrari 512 in the Can Am

HIROSHI KAZATO

Kazato had a premature death driving in a domestic sports car race in Japan, a major loss, for he could potentially develop into a star. The Japanese raced a **Lola** T222 in the entire **1971** Can-Am season, earning a best 5th place at **Road America**. He then shifted his focus to Europe, in Formula 2. At first **Kazato** drove a **March**, in **1972**, then managed to lead a race at **Hockenheim**, in **1973** in a **GRD-Ford**. He scored 3 points in **1972** and 4 points in **1973**.

Photo by Rob Neuzel

HURLEY HAYWOOD

Haywood is mostly known as an American GT driver, **Peter Gregg**'s partner in many IMSA and Trans Am races but he also won many races on his won. He was also part of the **Porsche** works crew that won the **1977 Le Mans**, from 41st place in the beginning of the race. **Haywood** also drove **Porsches** in Can Am and participated in Formula Super Vee, attempting to qualify for the **1979 Indy** 500 without success.

JACK BRABHAM

Brabham began **1970** the best possible way, winning the South African Grand Prix. He was consistently fast during the GP season but luck was not on his side and he gave away two Grand Prix to **Jochen Rindt** in the last lap. **Jack** also drove for **Matra-Simca** in prototypes, for whom he won the 1000 km of Paris and drove one of his cars in the **Indy** 500, leading one lap. At the end of the season, he packed his bags up and left **Ron Tauranac** to run the **Brabham** team. Jack continued racing in endurance events in Australia/New Zealand late in the decade, sharing rides with other stars such as **Stirling Moss** and **Denis Hulme**.

JACKIE OLIVER

Oliver was a Shadow driver for much of the 70s. He also drove the Dodge engined Formula 5000 car. Photo by Rob Neuzel.

Oliver began the decade with a split program, doing Formula 1 for **BRM**, with a best 5th place and driving the Ti22 in the Can-Am. He was much more successful in the Can-Am, finishing second in the first race of the year, following that with several other good placings. For **1971, Oliver** was hired to replace **Kinnunen** in the JW Team, partnering former **BRM** teammate **Pedro Rodriguez** in the World Manufacturers Championship, winning at **Daytona, Monza** and **Spa**. He was dropped from the team before the end of the season, after a misunderstanding but still managed three wins. He also did three F-1 races for **McLaren** this season, continuing to race in Can-Am, moving to **Shadow**. The rest of his racing career would be spent at **Shadow** and a single race for **BRM** (British Grand Prix, replacing **Ganley**, under discipline). He did the whole **1972** Can-Am series, with a best 2nd place at **Mid-Ohio**. **Shadow** entered Formula 1 in **1973** and **Oliver**'s best race was in **Canada**, where he finished 3rd after leading. He also raced in Can-Am, the season best a second in **Laguna Seca**. In **1974 Oliver** was back in the Can-Am, finally dominating the series with four wins. In **1975** and **1976 Oliver** drove a **Shadow-Dodge** in the U.S. Formula 5000 championship, winning one race at **Elkhart Lake** and won the **Mosport** World Sports Car race in the Can-Am **Shadow**. Largely retired by **1977, Oliver** did two final Formula 1 races, in the non-championship Race of Champions (5th), then in Sweden, finishing 9th, pursuing managerial duties thereafter, first at **Shadow**, later at **Arrows**.

JACKIE STEWART

Stewart retired at a relatively young age and certainly could have expanded his outstanding curriculum a bit more. He was extremely fast in his last season, **1973** and his talents were still on demand in **1979**, when **Bernie Ecclestone** allegedly offered him a huge retainer to take the departing **Lauda**'s seat at **Brabham**. **Stewart** stuck to his retirement plan and his last Grand Prix was Canada, **1973**. To his credit, he is ranked second in Grand Prix wins during the decade, despite taking part in only four seasons. **Stewart** also raced in Formula 2, Can-Am and the European Touring Car Championship, where he lent sponsor **Ford** a hand to raise the championship's reputation. He spent the rest of the decade as a TV motorsport commentator.
Photo by Rob Neuzel

JACKY ICKX

Ickx was one of the ultimate stars of the decade, winning in Formula 1, Formula 2, Prototypes, Can-Am, Touring cars, DRM. He won at **Le Mans** 3 times during the decade, won the Bathurst 1000, was runner-up in Formula 1 in **1970** and drove for **Porsche, Matra-Simca, Alfa Romeo, Mirage, Ferrari, Lotus, Ford, BMW, Lola, McLaren, Williams, Ensign, Ligier**. He was no longer a factor in Formula 1 in **1976** but was the ultimate endurance driver: he could be just as fast in sprints, such as short DRM races, as at **Le Mans**, where he was consistently fast for many hours. His **1977** drive in this race was epic.

Jacky Ickx won 3 of his Le Mans wins in the 70s. This is his 1975 mount, a Mirage, shared with Derek Bell. Photo Jurgen Barth collection.

JACQUES LAFFITE

Laffite began his racing career late. In **1970** he was still racing in lower French categories, although he was already 27. He progressed well, his big break coming in **1973**, when he won the French Formula 3 title and featured well in British races. He was immediately fast in Formula 2 in **1974** winning races and finishing 3rd in the championship. He was also given a chance in Grand Prix racing by **Williams** that same season. He followed that up with the Formula 2 title and 7 wins in **1975**, a steady F1 ride and first podium with **Williams** and 3 race wins for **Alfa Romeo** in the World Manufacturers Championship. **Laffite** was chosen as Ligier's Formula 1 driver for **1976**, where he stayed for the rest of the decade. There he won his first Grand Prix in Sweden, **1977** and the first two races of the **1979** season, finishing the season in 4th place. **Laffite** also raced **Alpine-Renault** prototypes at **Le Mans** and elsewhere, drove **Chevrons** in Atlantic races, raced in occasional hill climbs, took part in the Procar series and also drove the **Ligier-Maserati** in several **Le Mans** editions and the **1974** World Championship.

JAMES HUNT

A quick driver, with a reputation for being crash prone, thus the nickname "Shunt", **Hunt** had driven in Formula 3 in **1970** and **1971**, winning quite a few races but no championship and crashing often. His move to Formula 2 in **1972** with **Hesketh** Racing was inconclusive, so when **James** appeared in the **1973** Race of

Champions driving a secondhand **Surtees**, many were surprised. There were more surprises to come: his patron bought him a brand-new **March** for **Monaco** and suddenly the long-haired Brit began showing speed, maturity and results, all at once. He scored in his second race, after a few races he had his first podium and earned a second at **Watkins Glen** just behind **Peterson**. Soon **Hunt** was hot property, getting rides in the ETCC, Formula 5000, World Manufacturers Championship and although **1974** was not a bright season, he began **1975** well with a second, then won in Holland. There were some bad news on the way, when **Hesketh** withdrew support after the end of the season but **Hunt** got the break of a lifetime, replacing the departing **Fittipaldi** at **McLaren**. Fast all **1976** season, **Hunt** won six races in spite of disqualifications and political troubles and won the championship in the last laps of the last race, after a season long battle with **Lauda**. The great form would not last long, though. **Hunt** won three more races in **1977** and was still competitive but the fire seemed gone in **1978**. A move to **Wolf** in **1979** did not seem to restore his motivation, so **Hunt** quit mid-season. Some say it was too much partying, others claim **Hunt** (and many others) did not like ground effects. Whatever the reason, **James Hunt** makes an interesting character study.

James was fast, a star, bad boy, all into one, who lost interest in the sport way too early. Photo by Rob Neuzel.

JANET GUTHRIE

To the same extent that **Lella Lombardi** was a major female representative in the sport in the European arena, **Janet** broke several gender barriers in America. First woman to race in Indy cars, first to try to qualify in the Indy 500, first to actually qualify for the Indy 500, first to finish in the top ten in the Indy 500, first to qualify in the top 5 for an Indy car race, first woman to race in the **Daytona** 500, first female driver to lead a NASCAR race. Her results might not seem as impressive as **Lella**'s but she was just as important, especially in the "macho" environments of 70s NASCAR and Indy.

JEAN XHENCEVAL

Xhenceval was a Belgian touring car specialist, who rose to fame in **1976**, when he won the ETCC with **Pierre Dieudonne**. After that **Xhenceval**, continued to win several other major touring car races and also raced **BMW** and **Ferrari** at **Le Mans**. He raced mostly **BMW**s during his career.

JEAN-PIERRE BELTOISE

Beltoise was France's most prominent Formula 1 driver in **1970**, when he got a nice helping of points driving the V12 **Matra** but his reputation took a dip in the wake of the **1971** Buenos Aires 1000 km race, where he was blamed to cause **Ignazio Giunti**'s death. He was eventually hired by **BRM**, winning the make's last two races, including the **1972** Monaco Grand Prix. He was supposed to be the driver of the **1976 Formula 1 Ligier-Matra** but **Laffite** got the drive instead. Out of Formula 1, **Beltoise** kept busy, driving in hill climbs, French championship races, Formula 2 but was also a major part of **Matra**'s two successful World Manufacturers Championship campaigns, winning four races with **Jarier** in **1974**. **Beltoise** also drove **BMW**s in French Supertourisme, **Inaltera** and **Ligier** at Le Mans.

JEAN-PIERRE JABOUILLE

Jabouille was already driving a **Pygmee** in Formula 2 in **1970** but ultimate success in the category only came in **1976**, when he won the championship in a **Renault**-powered **Elf**. Before his tie-up with **Renault**, **Jean-Pierre** had driven **Lolas** in the 2-Liter Championship, **Matra-Simca** at **Le Mans** (3rd in **1973** and **1974**), **Williams** in Formula 1. His history with **Renault** began in **1973**, when he drove the **Alpine-Renault** in the European 2-liter championship, continuing the next season. He then drove the turbo version of the prototype in the World Manufacturers Championship in **1975**, winning on debut and continued in this set-up challenging **Porsche** in **1976**. He led the **Renault** assault at **Le Mans** from **1976** to **1978** and appeared to be on the way to a win with **Derek Bell** in **1977 but** the car broke. He made history becoming the first driver to start, lead, get a pole and win a Formula 1 race in a turbo car and had been partially credited with the design of some of **Renault**'s race cars.

JEAN-PIERRE JARIER

Jarier was in Formula 3 in **1970**, ascending to Formula 2 in **1971**. He rented a **March** for the Italian Grand Prix, a bit prematurely, for his Formula 2 form was not impressive at the time. He raced in both Formula 2 and 3 in **1972**, then came back as **March**'s factory driver in Formula 2 in **1973**. He did extremely well, winning the championship and seven races with authority, while in Formula 1 it was another story. He was hired by **Shadow** in **1974**, was third at Monaco, then in **1975** showed a lot of speed in the South American races, scoring poles in both races and leading in Brazil. He did well in Brazil again in **1976** but then his performance fizzled. By **1977** he was at **ATS** but also drove for **Ligier** and **Shadow**. His Formula 1 career was revitalized when he was called to replace the deceased **Ronnie Peterson** at **Lotus**, in the last two races of **1978**. He did extremely well and came very close to winning the Canadian Grand Prix. He was then hired by Tyrrell for **1979**. While **Jarier**'s tally of Formula 1 wins is zero, the Frenchman did win several races for **Matra-Simca** in the **1974** World Manufacturers Championship and for **Alfa Romeo**

in **1977** and was a frequent presence in **Renault**'s sports car team, at **Le Mans** and elsewhere. "Jumper" also raced **Porsche** GTs, **Shadow** in the Formula 5000 and in the old and new Can-Am.

JEAN-PIERRE JAUSSAUD

Jaussaud was France's Formula 3 champion in **1970** but already considered old for Formula 1. Notwithstanding, he persevered, graduating to Formula 2, where he became runner-up in the **1972** Championship. He was never given a chance in GP racing, continued driving in Formula 2 and Sports Cars, achieving great success at **Le Mans**, first for **Matra-Simca**, (3rd in **1973**), **Mirage** (3rd in **1975**) then winning **Alpine-Renault**'s sole victory in this race (**1978**) with **Didier Pironi**.

Jaussaud was fast in all types of cars but was bypassed by Formula 1. (Photo by Gerald Swan)

JIMMY ROBERT MIEUSSET

Jimmy Mieusset was a major European hill climb exponent of the decade, who dabbled in circuit racing as well, going as far as the European Formula 2 Championship. In fact, **Mieusset** used a variety of Formula 2 cars in his hill climbing activities (**Pygmee, March, Ralt, Alpine** and **Martini**) and was both French and European hill climb champion. He was the second winningest European championship driver of the decade in this specialty.

JOAKIN BONNIER

By **1970 Bonnier** was no longer a competitive Formula 1 driver and so he retired his old **McLaren** from the category in **1971**. However, he was still quite a competent sports car driver, having won the initial European 2-Liter Championship in **1970,** after a season long battle with **Brian Redman** in a Chevron, also racing and winning races in many countries. As **Lola**'s agent for the continent, **Bonnier** set up a team to race 3-liter **Lolas** powered by Ford Cosworth engines in the **1972** World Manufacturers Championship. The team had good drivers, was competitive on occasion but not enough to beat **Ferrari** which was at the top of its game in this season. It was in one such cars that **Bonnier,** in his early 40s, found death while lapping a back marker at **Le Mans. Bonnier** also raced in Can Am, Interserie and Formula 5000 between **1970** and **1972**. The team continued in business until **1973**.

JO SIFFERT

Popular **Jo Siffert** had an untimely death in **1971**, after his best Formula 1 season. The Swiss driver was one of the main sports cars drivers of his generation, having won races in the World Manufacturers Championship for **Porsche** in **1970** and **1971**. **Siffert** drove for **March (1970)** and **BRM (1971)** in Formula 1, winning the Austrian Grand Prix of **1971**. He also drove competitively in Formula 2, for **BMW** in **1970** and **Chevron** in 1971 and Can Am in these two seasons, doing much of the development work on what would become the dominating **Porsche** 917-10.

Siffert was sorely missed at tracks. BRM might have had a different fate, had he survived a late 1971 crash at the race of Victory in Brands Hatch. Photo by Rob Neuzel.

JOCHEN MASS

Mass was one of Germany's Grand Prix hopes of the decade and he had a decent shot at **McLaren**. **Mass** had mixed single-seater and touring car activities early in the decade, mostly driving **Ford** and **March** cars and was the ETCC champion in **1972**. In **1973** he was signed by **Surtees** to head its Formula 2 assault and he did well to finish the season's runner-up. His graduation to Formula 1 at **Surtees** was not successful but he ended **1974** as **McLaren**'s third driver and was promoted to second in **1975**. There, he won half points for a Spanish Grand Prix victory, the first GP win by a German since **1961**. In the next seasons he was an obvious number two to **Fittipaldi** and **Hunt** and in **1978** he was hired by **ATS**, then **Arrows** in **1979**. The German did find greater success in Sports Cars, driving and winning for **Willi Kaushen** in **1975** and then for the **Porsche** works team as of **1976**, winning many races, often with **Jacky Ickx**.

JOCHEN RINDT

During the decade **Rindt** only raced in **1970** and became the first and so far, only posthumous Formula 1 champion. His **1970** season consisted only of Formula 1 and a restricted Formula 2 schedule, a category he utterly dominated in the 60s, plus a sports car race in Buenos Aires. There were rumors that **Rindt** intended to retire at the end of the season (he was only 28), for he considered the **Lotus** cars too fragile. Most unusually, all his title season F1 points came from wins and he got two of those wins on the last lap, at the expense of the same driver, **Jack Brabham**.

JODY SCHECKTER

Scheckter, pictured here in a 1973 photo by Rob Neuzel, was already winning races in South Africa in **1970** and in **1971** had made it to Europe, immediately winning in Formula Ford and Formula 3. In **1972** he was **McLaren**'s F-2 driver, winning a race and getting a shot in Formula 1, impressing. In **1973** he had a very busy season, in Europe and in the United States (he won the US Formula 5000 championship) and had several crashes in Formula 1. Notwithstanding, **Tyrrell** hired him and managed to tame the South African's wild instincts, so that by mid-season he was performing properly. After a somewhat disappointing three years at **Tyrrell, Jody** impressed at **Wolf** and ended runner up to **Lauda** in **1977**. After a so-so **1978, Jody** was hired by **Ferrari** for **1979**, where he finally became world champion. **Scheckter** also drove in Can-Am, ETCC, World Manufacturers/Sportscars Championship, PROCAR, driving cars such as **Ford, BMW, Porsche, Alpine-Renault, March.**

JOHN FITZPATRICK

Fitzpatrick was one of the main closed-car drivers of the decade, having won several races in touring cars, GTs and Group 5. Not a lover of single-seaters or any open race car, **Fitz** won the European GT Championship twice, ETCC races, the 1000 km of Bathurst and World Manufacturer Championship races. He drove **BMW, Ford, Porsche, Jaguar, Holden, Alfa Romeo.**

JOHNNY RUTHERFORD

The Texan was one of the major USAC superstars of the decade, having won the Indy 500 in **1974** and **1976**, both times for **McLaren**, although he did not win the championship in this decade. **Rutherford** won Indy car races in every season of the decade starting in **1973**, when he joined **McLaren,** having previously driven for Patrick. He also drove in NASCAR, IMSA long distance races, Formula 5000 and IROC and internationally in the Bathurst 1000.
2-time Indy winner Rutherford. Photo by Rob Neuzel.

JOSE CARLOS PACE

Autocourse, in its 1973-74 edition, rated **Pace** the 4th best Grand Prix driver of the season, on the strength of his point scoring-fastest lap performances at Germany and Austria, plus some other outings in the so-so **Surtees** TS14. The greater heights were never reached. **Pace** managed a single Grand Prix victory, at **Interlagos, 1975** and only 5 other wins in lower categories during 6 and a half seasons of international racing, all of them in **1970-71**. Some reckon **1977** would be his year but an airplane crash took his life. **Pace** raced in the World Manufacturers Championship (2nd at Le Mans in **1973**), Can-Am (**1972**) and sports cars.

KAZUYOSHI HOSHINO

Hoshino was little known to Westerners in **1976** and then he burst into the Formula 1 scene, working his way up to third in a Bridgestone shod old **Tyrrell** 007 in the Japanese Grand Prix. **Hoshino** raced relatively little outside of Japan, having a very long career and could have been one of the greats. In the 70s, he won the Japanese Formula 2000/Formula 2 title three times (**1975**, **1977** and **1978**), winning 11 races, plus the Fuji Grand Champion title in **1978**. He was fast and effective in all types of race cars.

KEKE ROSBERG

Finn **Rosberg** won many Formula Vee and Super Vee titles and races before graduating to Formula 2 with the **Toj** team in **1976**. He impressed and was soon hired all over the planet, Can-Am and Formula Atlantic in North America, Formula 2 in Europe, Formula Pacific in New Zealand, winning everywhere he went. He even won in Formula 1 right off the bat, in the freak Daily Express race of **1978**, managing to keep his slow **Theodore** on the road while almost everybody else spun out under heavy rain. Further Formula 1 participations during the decade, in **Wolf** cars for Theodore, **ATS** and **Wolf**-works did not yield any results but **Keke** had left his mark in the world of racing.

Keke Rosberg rose to prominence in Formula Super Vee. Photo by Paul Kooyman

KLAUS LUDWIG

As many 70s drivers, **Klaus** began his career driving touring cars in his native country in the 60s. He continued on that path in the early 70s, joining the DRM in **1973**, driving at first a Division 1 **Ford** Capri. His first victory in that championship was in the **1974** Preis der Nationen, in a **Capri** and on the strength of many other results, he was the best placed Division 1 driver in the final table. In **1975** he drove both Division 1 Capris and Division 2 Escorts and finished 2nd in the points, winning in both categories (Eifelrennen (Div. 2), Preis de Nationen (Div. 1) and Preis von Baden-Wurttemberg (Div.1). He also raced in the ETCC, winning at **Jarama, 1974**, While continuing to successfully drive in the DRM Division 2, **Ludwig** attempted to break into single-seaters, joining the Formula 2 Kauhsen team, which fielded **March**-Harts in **1976** and **Kauhsen (Elf)-Renaults** in **1977**. This was mostly a failure, with few points scored in **1976** and none in **1977**, despite using the previous year's champion car. **Ludwig** joined the Loos team for **1978**, winning the DRM race at **Hockenheim** and also in the World Manufacturers Championship. His ultimate success came in **1979**. Now driving for Kremer, **Ludwig** won all but one race of the DRM and also won the 24 Hours of **Le Mans**, doing most of the driving and sharing a car with the **Whittington** brothers. He also won at **Watkins Glen** with the same teammates. There is life after single-seaters, as he would prove well into the 90s.

LELLA LOMBARDI

Lella was the first and still only female driver to score points in Formula 1, 0.5 point in the **1975** Spanish Grand Prix. Additionally, she was the first female to win overall a FIA World Championship circuit event, winning the World Sportscars events at **Enna** and **Vallelunga** in **1979**. In addition to these exploits, during the decade she also raced in Le Mans, Formula 5000 (placed 4th in the **1974** Championship), Group 8, Formula 3, Touring Cars, GTs, Interserie and even NASCAR.

LEO KINNUNEN

What is **Kinnunen** doing on this list? Formula 1 followers will remember his unsuccessful attempts to break into the Grand Prix world with an open-faced helmet in **1974**, in a privately entered **Surtees**, forgetting that he was one of the few drivers who mastered the **Porsche** 917, a powerful beast that was not easy to drive, requiring great skill. He won four races in the World Championship of **1970** partnering **Pedro Rodriguez** but then won three straight Interserie championships driving the even more powerful Turbo **Porsche**. Not a small feat.

LUIS RUBEN DI PALMA

Most racing connoisseurs might barely remember **Di Palma** but the fact is, this Argentine driver won championships in Turismo de Carretera, Argentine Formula 1 and Prototypes in the 70s, driving powerful cars in a very competitive environment. He made few inroads into International racing, including a **Berta** race at **Nürburgring, 1970**, USA Formula 5000 driving the **Berta** and long distance races in a GT **Ferrari** with fellow Argentine **Garcia-Veiga**. Definitely one of the major talents of the decade.

LUIZ PEREIRA BUENO

Bueno won many races in this Porsche 908/2 in 1971-72. Photo by Rogerio da Luz.

What is a driver who drove a single GP race, finishing next to last, doing in this list? **Bueno** won six Formula Ford races in England in **1969**, figuring he was too old to pursue an international career. He came back to Brazil and driving a down on power **Bino** prototype he won many races against stronger opposition in **1970**. He graduated to a **Porsche** 908, winning many races in **1971** and **1972** but in fact, would win in just about any type of car: Formula Ford, Division One Touring Cars, highly tuned Touring Cars and Brazilian prototypes. One of the few drivers in South America that could keep up with **Di Palma**.

MARIO ANDRETTI

The 70s can be called **Andretti**'s "European years", for that is where he focused most of his attention. In Formula 1, **Andretti** drove a private **March** in **1970**, then was hired by **Ferrari** for **1971**, winning his first race in South Africa. Besides a win in the non-championship Questor Grand Prix, no more prominent results came from this association in **1971-1972**. He came back to Formula 1 late **1974**, driving a **Parnelli** throughout **1975** (and a final race in **1976**). The car was just average and **Andretti** joined **Lotus** for **1976**. There, he found the proper environment to thrive, winning the **1976** final in Japan, followed by four races in **1977** and six in **1978**. **Andretti** was definitely the fastest driver of these two seasons but the American's performance in F1 dropped after **1979**. **Andretti** also had impressive performances in long-distance races. He was part of the crew that won the **Ferrari** 512's only World Championship victory in **Sebring, 1970** and won four races with **Jacky Ickx** in the **1972** season, also in a **Ferrari**. In **1974** he also won the 1000 km of **Monza** with **Merzario**, for **Alfa Romeo**. **Andretti** continued to race in the USA during the decade but he was not very lucky in USAC. Making huge efforts to race in both Formula 1 and USAC, **Mario** won a total of three races during the decade, although he remained very fast and popular and did not lead a single lap in the Indy 500. At USAC he raced **Hawks** and **McNamaras** in **1970**, winning at **Continental Divide**, continuing with the main set up in **1971**, with no wins. From **1972** to **1975** he raced for Parnelli Jones, leading several races, winning a single race in **Trenton, 1973**. He changed teams yet again, driving **McLaren** and **Penske** chassis for Penske, winning a single race at **Trenton, 1979**. In Formula 5000, he was more successful, winning eight races and finishing runner-up to **Brian Redman** in **1974** and **1975**. **Mario** also won a dirt track title in **1974**, drove occasional Can-Am races in **Ferrari** and **McLaren** cars, won the **1979** IROC title and took part in the Procar series.

MARK DONOHUE

In addition to being a very fast and technical driver, **Donohue** was also an excellent engineer, the perfect partner for **Roger Penske**. He raced in most major U.S. series during the decade: Can-Am, USAC, NASCAR, Trans-Am, Formula 5000, IROC and also managed to finish 3rd in his Formula 1 debut, in a **McLaren** in the **1971** Canadian Grand Prix. His **1971** races in the **Ferrari** 512 M were legendary. He won the **Indy** 500 in **1972**, won NASCAR races in the unloved **AMC** Matador, the **1971** Trans-Am in the **AMC** Javelin, destroyed the opposition in the **1973** Can-Am and retired after winning the **1973/74** IROC. He only failed to win in the AMC engine Formula 5000 challenger but got close: 2nd place. **Penske** decided to go Formula 1 racing in **1974** and got **Donohue** on board. Things did not go as planned in **1975** and the team bought a **March**, leaving the troublesome proprietary PC-1 chassis aside for a while. In Austria, **Donohue** lost control of the **March**, went off the road, in a seemingly innocuous accident. He was conscious leaving the car but a headache turned into a coma and coma into death. A sad state of affairs which happened too often in Formula 1 during the decade.

MARTINO FINOTTO

Most racing enthusiasts might have difficulty remembering **Finotto** but he was one of Europe's most prominent touring car drivers of the decade, eventually winning the ETCC in **1979**, sharing the title and many race wins with **Facetti**. **Finotto** also drove the Jolly Club **Porsche** 935 on occasion, finishing second in the Daytona 24 Hours of **1977** and placing well elsewhere, including wins in local Italian races. **Martino** also fielded a **Brabham** BT42 in the **1974** Formula 1 Championship, which enabled drivers such as **Facetti, Koinigg, Larrousse** and **Lombardi** to debut in this championship.

MAURO NESTI

Italian **Nesti** was the king of European hill climbing in the 70s, winning dozens of races for the European and Italian Hill Climb championships and elsewhere. He drove mostly a **Lola-BMW** 2-liter prototype but also raced **Chevron**. He made sporadic forays into circuit races but these were relatively rare.

MIKE HAILWOOD

Hailwood was a former champion motorcycle rider who had tried 4 wheels in the early 60s, deciding to return to 2 wheels. He made a permanent shift to 4 wheels in **1970**, choosing to drive in the European Formula 5000 championship. There he won races and was chosen by **John Surtees** to join his Formula 1 team late in **1971**. In his debut for the team, **Hailwood** did splendidly leading and almost winning the Italian Grand Prix of **1971** and early in the **1972** season, he led convincingly in the **1972** South African Grand Prix. He followed that up with **Surtees**' best result in a World Championship event, 2nd in the Italian Grand Prix and best score ever, 13 points. During the same season **Hailwood** drove for **Surtees** in Formula 2 and won the championship. The highlight of the **1973** season was a win with **Bell** in the 1000 km of Spa, driving a **Mirage-Ford** and no points in Formula 1. **Mike** had a wonderful opportunity, when a sponsor dispute forced **McLaren** to run a third car in **1974**. He scored quite a few points in the initial races of the year and was doing well, when an accident at the **Nürburgring** brought to a halt his season and car racing career. He would still do some bike races during the decade. **Hailwood** took part in **Macau**'s Race of Greats of **1978**.

NELSON PIQUET

Piquet's stature in Brazil grew suddenly with the establishment of Formula Super Vee, in **1974**. An unknown driver, he won the **Cascavel** race and was in the running for the title in the final race. In **1975**, he had the fastest car but broke almost everywhere and ended with merely 2 points. It all came good in **1976**, when **Nelson** won six of ten races and packed for Europe. At first he decided to race in the European Formula 3 Championship, winning two **1977** races late in the season. For **1978**, he shifted to the British series, winning the BP Championship. He debuted in Germany driving an **Ensign**, followed by some rides in an old BS Fabrications **McLaren** M23. Before the end of the season, **Brabham** hired the youngster. Life in the **Brabham-Alfa Romeo** was not easy in **1979**, the Brazilian scored some points, however, as soon as the Italian engine was dropped, **Brabham** became incredibly competitive. **Piquet** also won a round of the Procar championship in **1979**, the beginning of a long relationship with **BMW**.

NIKI LAUDA

In **1970, Lauda** was an up-and-coming Austrian driver who raced **Porsche** sports cars and **McNamara** formula 3s, without great distinction. Nonetheless, he joined Formula 2 in **1971**, then borrowed US$ 100,000 from a bank to finance a seat in the **March** Formula 1 team for **1972**, for whom he debuted in the **1971** Austrian Grand Prix. An obvious number 2 to **Peterson, Lauda** made little impression in Formula 1 but won occasionally in Formula 2, including the British Formula 2 title. **Lauda** also did some touring car and DRM races for **BMW** in **1973**, winning the first race of the ETCC season and the 24 Hours of **Nürburgring**. By then he was racing in the **BRM** F-1 team, where he was number 3 driver. Although he got only 2 points during the season, he raced impressively in many places, leading the Canadian Grand Prix under difficult conditions. Surprisingly hired by **Ferrari**, **Lauda** became a top GP driver overnight, finishing 2nd on his debut for the new team, leading and scoring poles for most **1974** races, although the 312B3 reliability was not good. **Lauda** continued to race and win in touring cars, moving to **Ford** for a large retainer and in **1975** achieved his goal, winning the Formula 1 title, earning five wins for **Ferrari**. He was the favorite for the **1976** title, winning most races in the beginning of the season, then he had that terrible fiery crash at the **Nürburgring**. He amazed the world by coming back in the Italian Grand Prix a little over a month after receiving last rites but at that point **James Hunt** had the upper hand. By quitting the Japanese Grand Prix on the early stages, **Lauda** just sealed his fate. **Lauda** did remain at **Ferrari** and won the title a second time in **1977** but felt the team belittled his abilities and left before the season was over, joining **Brabham**. At **Brabham**, all **Lauda** managed was two wins under controversial situations in **1978** and the **Alfa Romeo** engine was definitely not a championship contender proposition. He remained a further season but despite of a huge retainer on offer, he left the team before the season was over, choosing instead to run his own airline. This last season **Lauda** ran and won the Procar series, winning three races. **Lauda** also won an European 2-Liter Championship race in a **Chevron**, in **1971** and minor races in a **Porsche 910** in **1970**.

NINO VACARELLA

The Sicilian hero had been driving on a part-time basis since the 50s and his career was obviously coming to a close. Notwithstanding, he had three significant victories during the decade. For **Ferrari** he won the 512's only World Championship victory at **Sebring, 1970** (with **Andretti** and **Giunti**), then he won the **1971 Targa Florio** with **Hezemans**, for **Alfa Romeo and** won it one last time in **1975**, with **Merzario**. He also drove the best placed **Alfa** in the **1972 Le Mans** (4th, with **De Adamich**) and had several good placings in **1970** to **1972** (2nd at **Monza, 1970**, 3rd at **Sebring, 1971**, 2nd at **Oesterreichring, 1971**, 3rd at **Sebring, 1972**). **Nino** also won the **1970 Cefalu** hill climb in an **Abarth** and drove for Autodelta's touring car team sporadically. He retired after the **1975 Targa** win.

PATRICK DEPAILLER

Depailler was an excellent performer, who perhaps disappointed **Ken Tyrrell** who was used to **Stewart**'s domination. A Formula 2 driver in **1970**, **Patrick** returned to Formula 3 in **1971**, winning the French Championship, then came back to Formula 2, finishing the European Championship in 3rd place twice (**1972, 1973**), the last time driving a French **Elf**. For **1974** he was a **March** works driver and won the championship. By then he was already a **Tyrrell** full-time driver in Formula 1 (he debuted for the team in **1972**), playing second fiddle to **Jody Scheckter** in the first two seasons in the team (**1974, 1975**). In **1976**, **Patrick** at times seemed to have the upper hand over **Scheckter** driving the 6-wheel **Tyrrell** and scored often, finishing second many times. After **Jody**'s departure, **Depailler** became the number 1 driver and got his single **Tyrrell** victory in the **1978 Monaco** Grand Prix, at one point leading the championship. **Patrick** joined **Ligier** in **1979** and seemed on the verge of a breakthrough season, winning the Spanish Grand Prix. However, a hanggliding accident sidelined him for the rest of the season. Outside of Formula 1, **Depailler** drove in **Le Mans**, for **Matra-Simca** in **1973** and for **Alpine-Renault** in **1977-1978** and for **Ligier** in **1971**. **Depailler** also drove for the **Alpine-Renault** challenge to **Porsche** in the World Sportscar Championship and won the **1972** Formula 3 **Monaco** race and drove in the Trois Rivieres Formula Atlantic race many times. He even found the time to drive in local French events as late as **1977**.

PATRICK TAMBAY

Tambay climbed up the Formula Renault ladder of the early 70s, finishing 9th in **1972** and 2nd in **1973**, reaching Formula 2 in **1974**. He raced in this category until **1976**, finishing 2nd in **1975** (tied with **Leclere**) and 3rd in **1976**, driving the **Elf** in **1974**, a **March** works car in **1975** and a **Martini** in **1976**. His reputation reached greater heights in **1977**, due to sterling drives in a Theodore sponsored **Ensign** in Formula 1 and the Can-Am Series title. He was hired by **McLaren** for the **1978** Formula 1 season, without the expected success, scoring only 8 points. In **1979**, great damage was done to his reputation, as a whole season with five **McLaren** variants (M26, M28, M28B, M28C and M29) yielded not a single point. **Tambay** was also part of the **1977-1978 Alpine Renault Le Mans** effort.

PEDRO RODRIGUEZ

Pedro Rodriguez only raced in two seasons in this decade, **1970** and **1971** but left a major impression. In **1970** and **1971 Rodriguez** was recognized as the best sports car driver in the world and his handling of the difficult **Porsche** 917 was simply sublime. As a result, he won most races in both seasons, while also winning the **1970** Belgian Grand Prix, **BRM**'s first win since **1966. Pedro** also impressed greatly in a **BRM** Can-Am car and even raced in NASCAR. Never turning down a chance to drive, **Pedro** died in an Interserie sports car race, driving a **Ferrari** 512 at **Norisring, 1971.**

Pedro Rodriguez could drive a 917 like no one else. Sadly, he died in 1971. (Photo by Gerald Swan)

PETER GETHIN

Gethin was a fast driver and also very lucky. Three of the most amazing wins of the decade were his: the **1971** Italian Grand Prix, where the top five were covered by less than a second, the **1973** Race of Champions, the first time a Formula 5000 car beat a Formula 1 field and the **1972 Pau** Grand Prix, where he beat **Depailler** with a gap of less than a second after an hour and half. He also won the **1970** European Formula 5000 Championship and the **1974** Tasman Cup (the only outsider to do so in the 70s) and was one of two drivers to win races in both the old and new Can-Am. His Formula 1 career never took off, in spite of his **Monza** success. He drove for **McLaren, BRM** and **Lola** in this category and also drove **Chevron** sports and Formula 2 cars. He was the winningest driver in European Formula 5000

Gethin: fast, skillful but also very lucky. Photo by Rob Neuzel.

PETER GREGG

Most of "Peter Perfect" numerous wins were driving **Porsche** 911 and 935 cars during the 70s. Having competed since the early 60s, **Peter** was a major driver in the Trans-Am's lower category, until the IMSA series came about. **Peter** soon took control of it and except for a season driving **BMW**'s in **1976, Gregg**'s success came mostly in **Porsche** products in that series. He also raced in Can-Am in **1973** and had successful entries at **Le Mans**, winning the group 5 category with **Ballot-Lena** in **1977** and placing 3rd in **1978** in a works **Porsche** 936.

PIERRE DIEUDONNE

The Belgian, who was also a journalist, became better known as **Jean Xhenceval**'s partner in the **BMW** Luigi during the decade, although he did race in Formula 3 in **1975**, earning some good results in a **March-BMW**. **Dieudonne** and **Xhenceval** won the **1976** ETCC title dominating the last half of the season and the pair also tried their hand driving **Ferraris** at **Le Mans**. **Dieudonne** also raced in the Formula Atlantic series in New Zealand.

RENE ARNOUX

Arnoux, a trained mechanic, enrolled in the Winfield racing school at **Magny-Cours** in **1972** and won the European Formula Renault Challenge in **1973**, with seven wins. **Arnoux** then tried Formula 5000 prematurely, in **1974**, without much success and debuted in Formula 2, finishing 4th at **Nogaro**. He then joined the **Martini** team and won the new European Formula Renault Championship, with eight wins. Next, he joined the **Martini** Formula 2 team in **1976**, finishing second, then winning the **1977** title. His Formula 1 debut took place in **1978**, initially in the Martini team and then a couple of races for **Surtees**, after the French team decided to leave the category without finding success. **Arnoux**'s big break came in **1979**, having been hired by **Renault** finishing 8th in the championship, with three podiums, starring in an epic fight with **Gilles Villeneuve** in the French Grand Prix. **Arnoux** also shared a semi-works **Alpine-Renault** with **Pironi** in the **1977 Le Mans**.

RICHARD PETTY

King **Richard** won an amazing 87 NASCAR races during the decade, as well as five NASCAR championships. In the first two years of the decade alone, **Petty** won an astounding 39 races. One must consider that at the time NASCAR calendars comprised almost 50 races and **Petty** was one of the few drivers that raced the whole season. **Richard** drove **Chrysler** products (**Plymouth** and **Dodge**) until **1979**, when he shifted to **Chevrolet**. **1979** turned out to be **Pett**y's last title. Outside NASCAR, **Petty** drove in the IROC, without great distinction.

RICK MEARS

Mears is a rare case of a top driver who came from the world of off-road racing. The Californian then joined the short-track circuit around **1973**, competing in the **Pikes Peak** Hill Climb (3rd in **1974**, winning in **1976**). In **1976** he joined the Indy car circuit driving an old **Eagle-Offenhauser** in **Ontario**, then a Sugai **Eagle** for two more races. He remained at Sugai early in **1977** and after failing to qualify for the Indy 500, he drove for Theodore Racing, getting his first top five at **Milwaukee**. One of **Roger Penske**'s best virtues has been spotting talent, so he hired **Mears** to share the third **Penske** entry with **Mario Andretti** in **1978**. **Mears** immediately finished 5th in the first race of the year, then won in his fourth start for the team, at **Milwaukee**. He would also win at **Atlanta** and **Brands Hatch**, finishing 9th in points, in spite of not doing the whole schedule. In CART's first year **Mears** won the **Indy** 500, plus **Trenton** and **Atlanta**, getting his first Indy car title. **Mears** also took part in one edition of the IROC.

ROLF STOMMELEN

Stommelen was a major racing figure in the 70s. He began his career racing **Porsches** in hill climbs and circuit races but by **1970** he became an **Alfa Romeo** driver. **Rolf** was often the fastest **Alfa** driver for the next five seasons but never won a race for the Milanese make, in prototypes or touring cars. His first Formula 1 season in **1970** for **Brabham** yielded a podium but then his luck run out in the world's top racing category, in spite of a great run in the non-championship **1971** Argentine Grand Prix. **Rolf** did win many races in Germany, with **Ford** and **Porsche** cars and won an extremely competitive **DRM** title in **1977**. A return to Formula 1 with **Arrows**, after **Gunnar Nilsson** was found to suffer from cancer, yielded no results, so **Rolf** was back to his beloved Sports Cars, where he raced for the rest of his career.

RONNIE PETERSON

An amazingly fast driver, perhaps the fastest of the decade, who was able to overcome almost every car`s flaws, **Ronnie** just failed to win the Formula 1 championship a couple of times. He did entertain crowds during the decade, his driving style being the stuff of legend. He raced **Lotus, March, Alfa, Ferrari, BMW, Tyrrell** cars winning in Formula 1, Formula 2 and Sports Cars with great effect. In the **1971** season alone, **Peterson** was runner-up in Formula 1, won the Formula 2 championship and won the 6 Hours of **Watkins Glen** for **Alfa Romeo**. **Ronnie** was picked for the **Ferrari** sports car team, for **1972**, winning at both **Buenos Aires** and **Nürburgring**. Although **Ronnie** won only 10 GPs, he led 707 laps (ranked 4th in the decade) and had 14 poles, 9 of them in **1973**. He also drove in the IROC. His death in Italy, **1978**, the stage of his most memorable victories (**1973, 1974** and **1976**), was a terrible event, casting a very sad end to a wonderful career.

TEDDY PILETTE

Pilette is mostly remembered for his two European Formula 5000 titles, in **1973** and **1975**, in fact, he was a major global Formula 5000 exponent from **1971** until **1976**, having raced in the Tasman Cup and the American championship as well, always for the Belgian team VDS. He had a single Formula 1 start in a **Brabham**, in the **197**4 Belgian Grand Prix and eventually he was hired to try to qualify the **BRM** for a few races in **1977**, without success. **Pilette** also drove VDS' **Lola** T70, at **Le Mans** and the Makes Championship, a **McLaren** in the Interserie and was a frequent presence in the 24 Hours of **Spa**, winning it in **1978** with **Gordon Spice** in a **Capri. Teddy** also attempted to qualify for the **1977** Indy 500. He also raced a **Ferrari** 512 at **Le Mans**, in **1978**, with famed 60s Belgian privateer "**Beurlys**" and drove the **BRM** P207 in the **1978** Aurora Series.

TIM SCHENKEN

Australian **Schenken** was considered world champion material in **1968** but he never got a proper Formula 1 ride, although he won in almost all other categories in which he competed. **Schenken** was given a chance in the weak Frank Williams entered **De Tomaso** in **1970**, with no results but a **1971** ride at **Brabham** looked promising. There **Schenken** got his only Formula 1 podium, in Austria but then he moved to **Surtees**. Big **John** and **Tim** did not gel, although Tim occasionally qualified near the front and all he got was 2 points from the first race. In **1973** Schenken was without a Formula 1 ride. He did race once for **Williams** in **1973**, then, after a **Rondel** Formula 1 berth did not materialize, he got his final Formula 1 rides at **Trojan** and a third **Lotus** in the U.S. Grand Prix in **1974**, without success. Elsewhere, **Tim** was a driver in demand, who delivered. He was a top Formula 2 driver from **1970** to **1974**, winning two European races, a few non-championship events and generally placing well. He was part of the **Ferrari** sports car team in **1972** and **1973**, winning at **Buenos Aires** and **Nürburgring** in **1972**. He also drove in the European GT Championship, Interserie and DRM, racing **Porsches** for Gelo until **1977** and also took part in the World Manufacturers Championship driving **Mirage** and **Porsche** Carreras, winning the GT class three times in **1974**. He was also part of the failed **Jaguar** effort in the **1977** ETCC. **Tim** began a partnership with **Howden Ganley**, forming **Tiga** racing cars in **1975**, which was mildly successful into the 80s, although a planned **Tiga** Formula 1 car never raced.

Tim Schenken won in everything except formula 1. Here his mount is a Formula 2 Brabham (Photo by Gerald Swan)

TOINE HEZEMANS

During the decade, Dutchman **Hezemans** won no less than three FIA championships, the ETCC of **1970** and **1973** and the European GT Championship of **1976**. He drove for **Alfa Romeo, BMW, Ford, Porsche, Abarth, Chevron** and won races for all of them, including the **1971 Targa Florio** and races in the American and European continents. He also participated in the DRM, World Manufacturers Championship, European 2 Liter Championship and the **1979** Procar Championship.

Hezemans was featured in this BMW advertising campaign in his native Holland

TOM SNEVA

By **1977**, Team Penske was eager to win its first USA title. Having given up on Formula 1 dreams after a successful **1976** season, Penske had been fielding cars in the USAC championship for the likes of **Mario Andretti, Mark Donohue, Bobby Allison** and **Gary Bettenhausen** for years but in spite of a few wins, the team had failed to win a championship. **Tom Sneva** obliged, not once but twice. **Tom** had been driving for **Penske** since **1975**, having started in Champ Cars back in **1971**, in uncompetitive rides. He won his first USAC race in **1975** in **Michigan** and then won the **1977** and **1978** championships for **Penske**. The problem was that out of

32 races comprising these two championships, **Sneva** won only two, in fact won the **1978** championship without a single victory. This economical approach to championship winning did not cut well with **Penske**, who dropped the driver for the **1979** season, hiring instead **Bobby Unser**. **Sneva** was hired by the Sugaripe team, finishing second in the **1979** Indy 500. **Sneva** also raced stockcars, modifieds and drove in the IROC.

TONY BRISE

Brise was a wasted talent, who died in an airplane with team owner **Graham Hill** in **1975**. He won in Formula Ford, Formula Three and Formula Atlantic and his races in the **Williams** and **Hill** in **1975** showed great potential. Like **Bellof** in the 80s, here was a driver with great potential to be world champion who died prematurely.

TONY TRIMMER

One of the decade's major injustices was that **Trimmer** never got a proper crack at Formula 1. Incredibly fast in Formula Ford and Three, **Trimmer** did race for **Lotus** in a non-championship race in **1971** but was never given a chance in the world championship by the team. A fourth place in the **1973** Race of Champions in an **Iso Marlboro** was not enough to convince Formula 1 teams and **Tony**'s first chance was driving the woefully slow **Maki** in **1975** and **1976**. Eventually **Trimmer** managed to get rides in the British group 8 championships, winning the **1977** and **1978** titles in a **Surtees** and **McLaren** and many races. The cars were not sufficiently fast for qualification in the British Grand Prix, for proper tires and competitive engines were not made available to privateers. He raced in Atlantic, Formula 5000 and did **Le Mans** for **Dome** during the decade.

UMBERTO GRANO

Grano was a touring car driver, pure and simple. He did race sports cars sporadically but his focus was driving tin tops during the decade. As works teams drifted away from the ETCC later on the decade, **Grano** won the **1978** ETCC title and many races, becoming one of the championship's most successful drivers in the decade.

VIC ELFORD

Elford was considered a major sports car driver in the late 60s, who had very few Formula 1 opportunities. He was in the **Porsche** Salzburg and Martini teams, in **1970** and **1971**, winning three races in **Porsche** 908-3 and 917, with **Ahrens** and **Larrousse** (2). He also drove the **Chaparral** fan car in the Can Am and was a star in the **1970** Trans Am but his only Formula 1 ride of the decade came in Germany, **1971**, in a **BRM**. He raced briefly for **Alfa Romeo** in **1972**, drove a **Ferrari** Daytona to GT class win in the **1973 Le Mans**. He also drove **Chevron**, **Lola** and **March** cars in the European 2–Liter Championship, winning two races in this championship, did NASCAR and also raced a Formula 2 **Chevron**, retiring in **1974**. He was briefly a team manager for the **ATS** team in **1977**.

VITTORIO BRAMBILLA

Brambilla was already a Formula 2 driver in **1970**, still occasionally racing in Italian Formula 3, driving at first a **Birel-Alfa Romeo**, then a **Brabham-Ford**, in which he won the **1972** championship. In **1973**, with sponsorship from Beta Tools, he did very well in the European Formula 2 championship, winning two races in a **March-BMW**. He scored 44 points to **Mass**' 42, which would give him the runner-up position, except that he had to drop the points from the B Division **Salzburgring** race. **Vittorio** also drove a **BMW** in the ETCC and **Osella Abarth** in the European 2 Liter championship. **Brambilla** brought Beta sponsorship to the **1974 March** Formula 1 team, scoring his first point in that season. **Vittorio's** best F-1 season was **1975**, when he led multiple races, scored a pole in Sweden and had a half-win in Austria. He continued at **March** in **1976** but the team was overcrowded with 4 drivers at one point and although he qualified well, there were few results to speak of. His last two full seasons of Formula 1 were spent at **Surtees** and although he led briefly in Belgium, **1977**, he scored few points. An accident in the **1978** Italian Grand prix sidelined him for most of **1979** but he came back for three races in the new **Alfa Romeo F-1** late in the season. **Brambilla** also had a successful season driving for **Alfa** in the **1977** World Sportscar Championship, winning four races and drove a **Lancia** sporadically in the Silhouette championship and drove at **Trois Rivieres** . **Brambilla** was mostly known for an aggressive and messy driving style but the truth is, he was the single Italian driver to win a Formula 1 race in the 70s.

WILSON FITTIPALDI JUNIOR

Wilson followed younger brother **Emerson's** path, seeking an European career. He had actually attempted this all the way back in **1966** but the promised help did not materialize. In his second try, he chose Formula 3 as his entry category and got four wins during the season, including the Coupe de Salon in France. At the end of year, **Wilson** took part in the Brazil Cup, winning a race in a **Lola T70**, then won the early **1971** Brazilian Formula 3 Tournament, in a **Lotus**. He had an early incursion into Formula 1, driving a **Lotus** in the Non-championship Argentine Grand Prix of **1971** but spent the rest of the season driving in Formula 2. **Wilson** scored a total of 16 points, finishing the championship in a good 6th place. For **1972**, he was hired as **Brabham**'s 3rd driver in Formula 1, the high point being the non-championship Brazilian Grand Prix, which he led at the start. He continued at **Brabham**, scoring 3 points in **1973** and very nearly got a podium in **Monaco**. At the end of the season **Wilson** decided to build the first and still only, Brazilian Formula 1 car, the **Copersucar-Fittipald**i. The car debuted in **1975** and the team had a steep learning curve during the season, **Wilson** accumulating the functions of driver and team manager. He decided to quit driving, as the team hired brother **Emerson** for **1976**. **Wilson** also drove in the European 2-liter championship, Interserie, World Manufacturers Championship and won a non-championship Formula 2 race at **Misano**.

Wilson Fittipaldi was also very fast in sports cars, Photo by Rogerio da Luz.

VENUES AND LOCAL SCENES

This is an overview of circuit (tracks and street circuit) racing, whatever little was left of road racing, plus hill climb venues used in the 70s. This means you are not going to find information on karting, rallying, autocross, rallycross, sprints, slalom, off-roading or drag racing venues here. The list for hill climbs is not comprehensive, although I have added dozens of new venues in this revised edition and I hope to have done a good job with Argentine road race venues, which are numerous as well.

Venues are listed by country, in turn listed in alphabetical order. There are a few sites with particularly good specifics of most of these tracks (track length, width, actual location), although I have seen some wrong information here and there. The most important and active venues during the decade are listed. In the case of the United States, the listed tracks are, of course, a short sample of actual places where racing took place during the 70s. There were literally hundreds upon hundreds of short dirt and paved tracks, some of them less than half a mile long, where grass-roots racing took place, where sprint cars, midgets, stock cars of all persuasions and modifieds battled dozens of times a year. The list would go on forever but I added quite a few dozen more in this revision. A large number of such tracks no longer exist, having been gobbled up by real estate developments or shopping centers a long-time ago. Some still exist as ghosts, which is a shame. Just so that you get a notion of dimension, the NASCAR **1976** Annual indicates that NASCAR had sanctioned no less than 133 championships all over the country in 1975, besides the main Winston Cup and NASCAR West. And that is only NASCAR. ARCA and other regional, smaller sanctioning bodies were responsible for a large number of other tracks and championships, while USAC run a number of other championships for midgets, sprint-cars and stock-cars as well. Many of the tracks involved were small, dirt tracks, located far in the hinterland, in places you did not imagine exist.

There are some eye grabbing things in the list. First of all, you may be surprised with the large number of venues in Angola, which had a very lively local scene until **1975**. Some of these circuits (the majority of which were not proper racetracks but street courses) welcomed international drivers, who fought for victory against the likes of **Antonio Peixinho**, a Portuguese national who drove an **Alfa P33** and **Emilio Marta**, who drove a **Ford GT 40** until **1975**. Once the Communists took over Angola (and also Mozambique) the racing bug died off – or rather, was killed.

Morocco had a very lively international racing scene back in the 50s, even hosted a Formula 1 championship event but by the seventies the fervor had died off somewhat. The country did have a very enthusiastic representative in international racing, **Max Cohen-Olivar** who was already racing in the 70s. Senegal had the 6 Hours of Dakar, there was some racing in Rhodesia (now Zimbabwe) and of course, South Africa had thriving motor sport way before it got TV (which finally happened in **1976**). Racing also took place in Zambia, Kenya, Ethiopia/Eritrea and Mozambique.

Argentina may also come as a surprise but it should not. **Juan Manuel Fangio, Froilan Gonzalez** and others were successful in Europe for a good reason. Argentina's racing was very well organized and structured, with the Fuerza Libre championship running since the 20s and then Turismo de Carretera taking over as the main category. This provided the background for not only the large number of venues all over the country but also the large number of constructors, engine tuners and component manufacturers.

In addition to the venues, I have also provided information about the local racing scene for each listed country and basic data on international events held there. You will find that some information is very vague, simply because extraordinarily little of it is available or information was deemed untrustworthy. For one, a site mentions "formula 1 style racing" taking place in Kenya in the mid-70s, hardly believable. Formula Vees, not F-1, mixed in with touring cars in Libre events in that country, a far cry from Formula 1. Not everything you read is fact in the world wide web, with racing it is no different.

Getting a better feeling for the local racing scenes of all of these countries is important, because very little contemporary information was available at the time in books or magazines concerning the vast majority of them. As the sheer volume of racing in the USA and England was tremendous, there was a tendency to over emphasize racing in these countries to the detriment of others. Allow me to give you an example. Barrie Gill was an excellent writer of automotive books and annuals and in the early 70s he wrote a yearbook called *Motor Sport Yearbook*, a very good alternative for folks who could not buy *Autocourse* because of cost. Towards the end of the book, he mentioned racing outside the major centers. On page 299 of the **1974** edition the subject of South America arises. Lumping Brazil and Argentina together has always been a problem, offensive to the proud sense of identity of people from both countries. A large picture of Brazilian **Antonio Carlos Avallone** driving his sports car in **Interlagos** appears on the book, properly identified as that year's champion. In the text Gill not only says that **Luis di Palma**, an Argentine, had won that same Brazilian championship that very year but also calls **Oreste Berta** Brazilian! Honest mistakes both but it must have ignited the ire of Brazilians and Argentinians alike. Additionally, reference is made to Formula Vee as an active category in Brazil, a category that did not even exist in the country since late **1969** and would only return in **1975**.

San Marino had a first hillclimb in 1956, repeated a few times but the exceedingly small country was well known for rallyes, such as the San Marino Rallye and the 10 Ore Notturne and later on, for a Formula 1 Grand Prix held at Imola. It is interesting to note that speculation about such an event began in the early 70s but it took quite a bit of time to get off the paper.

Finding information on racing in certain countries has been exceedingly difficult and often inconclusive. I looked for evidence of circuit racing activity in Thailand, in both English and Thai and the farthest I got was a site with photos of quarter-mile races (like dragster), involving small sedans and even station wagons. Most pictures seem to be from 1987, thus out of the scope of this book. The single venue mentioned is Siam Park, near Bangkok and passing mention is made to circuit racing and rallying, with no further clues.

Iceland is a peculiar case. There was motorsport activity in the country but not the modalities covered by this book. In 1966, the first quarter mile (drag race) was held in the country. And a year before, even an auto racing modality was created in the country, the quite extreme Formula Off-Road As off-road racing is not covered by this book, Iceland is left out but it is worth noting that the first Formula Off Road champion was crowned in the 70s, in 1979 and the category has been exported.

Algeria is also a curious case. There was quite a bit of mWajor racing in the French colony during the 30s and that continued after World war II, in venues such as Bouzreah, Staoueli, Murdjardjo and Constantine. Strange as it may seem, racing continued during the Algerian Independence War, which ran from 1954 to 1962. After the war, car racing activities came to a screeching halt. This is actually a pattern in African countries. Most racing in African countries was done by colonialists and expatriates and once countries became independent, the activity was stopped.

As for Lebanon, a first hill climb was organized in **1951**, at a yet unidentified location and the Rallye of Lebanon was first held in **1968**. In fact, the Rallye was held four times during the decade but I have been unable to find results for the hillclimb in English, French and Arabic. Given the political turmoil that involved the country during most of the decade, it is quite possible no hill climbs were held. The Tal al Rumman hillclimb in Jordan was first held in 1962, in Jarash and it still exists. I was unable to find whether races were held during the 70s, thus, I have not included Jordan in the list. The oldest confirmed race I found was 1986, when Jordan prince Abdullah came second.

Who said that fake news is a recent development? Around Christmas, 1971, a report appeared in a British magazine of a Bermuda Can-Am race. Real connoisseurs would immediately realize it was fake, considering some of the outrageous claims made on the report. Winner Revson was said to have driven a 9.8 Turbo Chevrolet McLaren M8C, yielding about 1,500 HP, while Gijs Van Lennep drove a March with DAF Variomatic transmission and Ronnie Peterson, who was 2nd, drove a 2.6 Offy Can Am McLaren. Trouble was, some people might insist, to this day, that the race did take place, as did some other racing publications at the time. I did not find any real racing at Kingsley Field, the alleged venue.

REGIONAL OVERVIEW

Some comments about the different regions of the world are in place before embarking on country reviews, to give you an idea of the state of the sport in different regions during the decade.

WESTERN EUROPE

Western Europe, namely England, West Germany, Italy and France were the epicenter of global racing in the 70s. Additionally, most formula 1 races were held in Western Europe, many important race car manufacturers were located there, a large number of the prominent sponsors were based there and even most car makers involved in racing were based in the continent. Many European championships had world status, such as Formula 2 and drivers from all over the world tried to advance their careers by going to Europe, especially Britain. Other prominent racing countries in the Continent were Austria, Netherlands, Spain, Sweden, Belgium, while other countries such as Portugal, Greece, Ireland, Denmark, Finland, Norway, Luxembourg, Turkey, Malta and Switzerland had less impressive racing scenes. Even tiny Andorra, Liechtenstein and Monaco had racing but I found no evidence of it in larger Cyprus, San Marino and Iceland, besides motor sports not covered in this book, such as rallies and drag racing. Hillclimbing was much more important than today, with hundreds of races in several countries, many contested by Formula 2 (and even Formula 1 cars) and should be mentioned.

EASTERN EUROPE

Europe was divided during the entire decade and although Czechoslovakia, Hungary and Yugoslavia had some interaction with Western racing, the Soviet Union (Russia, Belarus, Ukraine, Estonia, Lithuania, Georgia, Latvia), East Germany, Poland and Bulgaria had their own local and regional races, mostly with locally built cars and engines and regulations. Romania had a relatively strong rally scene but also had circuit racing, including championships. Other Soviet republics and Albania might have had amateurish racing but I found no evidence of it.

NORTH AMERICA

The USA had, by far, the largest racing scene in the world, with hundreds of venues, some of them holding weekly races and a huge number of categories and formats catering to all tastes. It was also the only country to feature two grand prix in the same season during the decade. Many of these championships were contested by foreign drivers from all continents. Canada is a larger country but less wealthy and much less populated, so that racing was not as widespread. Rallying and hill climbing, two modalities that were very popular in Europe, had very little traction in North America, although the Pikes Peak hillclimb was already a very traditional event.

CENTRAL AMERICA AND CARIBBEAN

A surprising number of countries in this region had racing activities during the 70s: Mexico, Panama, Costa Rica, El Salvador, Dominican Republic, Jamaica, Trinidad, Puerto Rico, Barbados, Honduras, Guatemala. There was quite a bit of regional interaction and drivers from countries with no record of venues, such as Haiti, Antigua and Cuba participated in regional races. Needless to say, getting facts about these races is quite difficult, although videos and photos appear here and there.

SOUTH AMERICA

Argentina and Brazil were the two most important racing centers in the area. Argentina deserves special mention given the large number of constructors that built cars and even proprietary engines. Brazil's racing was boosted by Emerson Fittipaldi's world titles but both countries were heavily affected by the world economic crisis of the second half of the decade, which caused the demise of quite a few categories and championships. Most other countries in the region had car racing in one shape or form: Colombia, Venezuela, Peru, Ecuador, Chile, Paraguay, Uruguay, Bolivia, Guyana. Only Suriname and French Guyana seem left out. Nearby countries had a fair amount of interaction but efforts to bring Brazil and Argentina together failed greatly.

AUSTRALIA/NEW ZEALAND

By 1970 racing in the Antipodes was fairly developed and both Australia and New Zealand could proudly boast of having worthy World Champions. The far away continent's racing scene could live well in isolation even after the Tasman Cup became redundant, with a large number of categories and venues. Touring car's prestige increased towards the end of the decade, to the detriment of single seaters. The region also had a number of very capable constructors.

ASIA

Asian racing developed greatly in the 70s, mostly driven by Japan's economic and automotive industry success. There were Japanese championships for large number of categories, including single seaters, sports cars and touring cars and a Grand Prix was held for the first time in Asia in 1976. A number of "Grand Prix" were held for Formula 2, Formula Pacific and Libre in the region, in Macau, Philippines, Singapore, Malaysia, Indonesia and even Brunei, often contested by drivers from Hong Kong, Japan, Australia, New Zealand, Europe and the USA and tracks were built. India was another story. Far from the Far East and from the Western World alike, India had some racing, with some interaction with drivers from Sri Lanka. I found no evidence of racing in South Korea and not surprisingly, in China or Soviet Asia.

AFRICA

From the 30s to the 60s, a number of African countries held circuit racing events, including Libya, Tunisia, Algeria, Egypt, Congo and Madagascar, none of which featured in the racing radar in the 70s. As African countries got their independence starting in 1960, many stopped holding racing events, mostly contested by wealthy expatriates who left in droves. Yet, there was racing in the continent, specially in the South, where South Africa ruled. The site of the only African Grand Prix and other international events, the country even had its own Formula 1 championship until 1976 and Rhodesia, Zambia and Mozambique benefitted from that success. Angola also had a healthy racing scene until 1975 and Morocco in the North, Kenya in the East and Senegal in the West also held racing events. Ethiopia/Eritrea benefited from its early connections with Italy. Curiously, Nigeria was not in this noticeably short list. It should be noted that rallying was practiced in a few other places such as Ivory Coast, Madagascar, Burundi, Egypt, Tanzania and Uganda. There is some reference to circuit racing in Tanzania but no actual confirmation and data. The Tanzania 1000 was a rally, not a race.

MIDDLE EAST

Nowadays the Middle East attempts to make itself a name in the racing world, with a few world class venues and races and even drivers of some renown. That was not so in the 70s and the only racing activity I found there was the failed attempt to hold a Formula 2 race in Israel, in 1970. Allegedly, the idea was the inclusion of Israel in the Formula 1 calendar. My research continues on hill climbs in Lebanon and Jordan.

COUNTRY-BY-COUNTRY

Andorra

A tiny country with a population of just a few thousand, one would not expect much in terms of racing activity in Andorra. However, set in mountainous territory, it would be fair to expect hill climbs. At least two such venues were used in the 70s, Coll de la Botella actually hosting a round of the European Hill Climb championship in **1979**.
Hill Climbs: Coll de la Botella
Cortails d'Encamp

Angola

It may surprise many that the former Portuguese colony of Angola had a very active racing scene since the 50s, in fact, in a way it was stronger than Portugal's, with a large number of circuits and later on, purpose-built tracks. Racing was considered the 2nd most popular sport in Angola as of the 60s. Unfortunately, it all stopped in **1975** as a socialist revolution took over the newly liberated country and war ensued. The **Luanda** and **Benguela** racetracks were inaugurated in **1972**, actually before Portugal had inaugurated a purpose made track (Estoril) and all others were street circuits. Angolan races comprised of sports cars, GTs and touring cars. Among others, a **Ford** GT 40 competed in the country until **1975**, plus there was **Antonio Peixinho's** famous **Alfa** P33, a host of **Lolas** and **Porsches**, plus **Ford Escorts** and **Capris, BMWs, Camaros, Mini-Coopers** making up the numbers. Many Portuguese drivers, such as **Peixinho**, did a lot of their racing there, sharing spoils with local drivers, while many Europeans, South Africans and even Brazilians made the long trek to race in the country. There was even a locally built prototype, the **Chana**, built in **1972,** based on a Lotus.
International races: there were many international races in Angola in the course of the 70s. The inauguration of Luanda racetrack stands out.
Main race: 6 Hours of Nova Lisboa
Tracks:

Benguela (street course)
Benguela (track)
Huambo (street course)
Huila (street course)
Luanda (track)
Malange (street course)
Mocamedes (street course)
Nova Lisboa (street course)
Novo Redondo (street course)
Quipungo (street course)
Sa de Bandeira (street course)
Senhora do Monte (street course)
Songo (street course)
Sumbe (street course)
Uige (street course)

Angola had a healthy racing scene until 1975. Photo author unknown.

Argentina

Argentina became famous in racing circles in the 50s, when **Fangio, Gonzalez, Marimon, Mieres** and **Menditeguy**, among others, raced successfully in Europe and elsewhere. This international success did not continue into the 60s but by the 70s the country had a proper hero again, **Carlos Reutemann**. In spite of the several Temporada races for Formula 3, Formula 2 and Sports Cars, held since the 60s, knowledge of the local Argentine racing scene was at best scant in Europe and the USA, although the Italian magazine Auto Sprint covered the country with some frequency early on the decade. The fact is that Argentina had a highly active racing community since the 20s, with high level championships, first Fuerza Libre and then Turismo de Carretera (TC) in the 40s. While the road racing characteristics of the TC and Turismo Nacional categories was retained for most of the decade, there were many purpose-built racetracks all over the country. In fact, TC only started to become a track championship by **1977**, while some road races were still held. Argentina had its own Formula 1, single seaters with engines up to 4 liters, more similar to F5000 than F1. The category unfortunately ended in **1979**. It also had Formula 2 and Formula 4, a major Sports car championship until **1973** and Touring car championships. A Formula 4 race in Buenos Aires, 1970, had no less than 102 entries, which shows the strength of the sport early on the decade. It is important to note that most domestic Argentinian racing was done with cars and engines built in Argentina, which helped the development of the sport but endurance events were held with international brands such as BMW. Besides the national championships, there were regional races of a more subdued, club racing character, held in smaller tracks. There were even local single seater series, such as Formula Entrerriana and Limitada Santafesina, in addition to Midget racing. In tracks near the border, it was common for Brazilian, Uruguayan and Paraguayan drivers to compete. Argentina also influenced racing in other countries, such as Chile, Peru and Uruguay, nearby and as far north as Colombia and Ecuador, and manufactured whole cars, engines and components for all South American countries, including rival Brazil. In fact, dozens of constructors built race cars in Argentina during the decade but as in the rest of the world, these were not long lasting endeavors – by the end of the decade there were just a few left. The Rafaela 500 was the biggest oval car race outside the USA. The country's top race car builder, Berta, fielded a prototype in the 1000 km of Nürburgring of 1970 and then attempted to crack Formula 1 in 1975. Eventually the F1 Berta showed up in Formula 5000 races in the USA.

Argentine built prototypes raced in different countries during the 70s. The Berta with Luis di Palma won many races early in the decade.. (Alejandro de Brito)

International racing: Argentina hosted Formula 1 and World Manufacturers Championship races. It also hosted a Sports Car Temporada in **1970** (discussed in the end of the book), a non-championship Formula 1 race in **1971**, a couple of

USAC races at the Rafaela oval in **1971**, an international Formula 2 (European class) in **Cordoba** in **1971**, a mini, 2-race Formula 2 Temporada in **1978** and mostly a failed attempt to a Formula 3 Temporada in **1979**. Brazilian, Peruvian, Chilean, Paraguayan and Uruguayan drivers often competed in Argentina and some even won top Championships.

Main Races: Gran Premio de Turismo Nacional, Gran Premio Argentino (not to be confused with the Grand Prix of Argentina), 1000 km of Buenos Aires
Tracks:

Alfredo Fotabat (Zapala)
Alta Gracia
Aristobolo del Valle
Autodromo del Oeste
Balcarce
Buenos Aires
Ciudad de Rio (Cordoba)
Comodoro Rivadavia
El Challao
El Zonda (San Juan)
Eldorado
Eusedio Marcilla (Junin)
Las Flores (Buenos Aires)

Los Barrancos (Mendoza)
Los Condores (Cordoba)
Maggiolo (Santa Fe)
Murphy
Nueve de Julio
Oscar Cabalen (Cordoba)
Pergamino (Buenos Aires)
Posadas
Rafaela
Salto
San Martin (Tucuman)
Teodolina
Viedma

Road race venues:

Capilla del Monte-Cordoba
Circuito El Challao-Cerro de la Gloria
Concepcion-La Rioja
Jesus Maria-La Cumbre
San Juan-Calingasta
Vuelta de 25 de Mayo
Vuelta de Arrecifes
Vuelta de Azul
Vuelta de Bahia Blanca
Vuelta de Bragado
Vuelta de Chacabuco
Vuelta de Chivicoy
Vuelta de Cordoba
Vuelta de Coronel Probles
Vuelta de Hughes
Vuelta de La Montana

Vuelta de La Pampa
Vuelta de La Plata
Vuelta de Laboulaye
Vuelta de Laprida
Vuelta de Las Flores
Vuelta del Norte
Vuelta de Olavarria
Vuelta de Pergamino
Vuelta de Rioja
Vuelta de Salta
Vuelta de Salto
Vuelta de San Miguel del Monte
Vuelta de Santa Fe
Vuelta de Tandil
Vuelta de Vledma
Vuelta de Zapata

Roberto Mouras' Chevrolet won six straight Turismo de Carretera races in 1976. It was called the Golden 7. Photo author unknown.

Australia

Unquestionably, **Jack Brabham** put Australia on the racing map, much like **Fangio** did for Argentina before and **Emerson Fittipaldi** for Brazil, afterwards. However, there was also a healthy racing scene in Australia much before **Brabham** grabbed the headlines. In the 70s it was no different, although the influx of Australian drivers in European and American racing had somewhat decreased by the end of the decade, Australia continued to offer a number of championships for different types of cars, such as Formula 5000 (officially called Australian Formula 1), Australian Formula 2 and 3, Formula Vee and Ford, Sports Cars and Touring Cars. Australia was the last country to hold on to the Formula 5000 category, for the category was still active in **1979**. Much of interest on Australia's and New Zealand's scene came from the Tasman Cup of the sixties. Many European and American drivers made the long trip to the Antipodes to drive in a series of eight races, reportedly to be much fun for all involved. By **1970**, however, the big names were gone and the Tasman Formula (2.5-liter engine cars) gave way to Formula 5000, until **1975**. Some Europeans continued to come, such as **Mike Hailwood, Ulf Norinder, Ron Grable, Derek Bell, John Cannon, Teddy Pilette, Peter Gethin** and **Sam Posey** but by **1975** no foreigners were on the grid and the international atmosphere was gone. The long distance between Australia and the major racing centers of America and Europe had always prevented its insertion in international series, until greater financial influx from sponsors and TV and better logistics allowed Australia to have its proper Grand Prix. However, somewhat like Argentina, many Australian race drivers were completely happy with their local racing, which was organized, with many venues and events, plenty of competitors and reasonably profitable. As far as lower formulae were concerned, Australia was one of the earlier adopters of Formula Ford. In the beginning, only Australian built race cars were allowed in the category, which resulted in a large number of constructors joining the more established marques such as Elfin. Formula Vee was also popular and a large number of constructors also built cars locally. Formula 3 had no championship but was also a category in the country, even though European regulations were not followed, like Australian Formula 2. Most action took place in Eastern Australia, the wealthier, more populated and cosmopolitan are of the country. However, there was quite a bit of racing activity in Western Australia, in dirt and asphalt tracks that resembled a bit American grass roots racing, as well as Waneroo. A number of categories and cars were used, some of them resembling the British Stock car scene, others resembling American Modifieds but also races for larger sedans, including vintage and more modern Holdens, Hot Rods, midgets, small sedans such as Hondas and Minis. Quite a few of these speedways disappeared during the decade.

Australia is also noteworthy for the large number of home-bred racing car makes such as **Birrana, Mildred, Elfin** and **Matich**, some of which were exported to Asian countries and the U.S. as well and a number of sports cars.

1972 advertisement showed the balance of power in Australian racing in the early 70s.

Main races: 1000 km of Bathurst
Tracks:
Adelaide
Amaroo Park
Archerfield
Baskerville
Bathurst
Bencubbin
Bunbury
Calder
Golsworthy
Hume Weir
Lakeside
Laverton
Mallala
Oran Park
Phillip Island
Roebourne
Sandown Park
Surfers Paradise
Symmons Plains
Waneroo Park
Warwick Farm
Winton
Hill climbs:
Amaroo
Dapto
Golden Bar
Highclere
King Edward Park
Lakeland
Lakeview
Morwell
Mountain View
Mt. Corop
Mt. Cotton
Mt. Leura
Mt. Panorama
Mt. Tarrengower
One Tree Hill
Poatina
Silverdale
Tamworth

Austria

Austria was mostly a footnote in the world of car racing in the 60s, although **Jochen Rindt** was reckoned to be a very fast driver since the middle of the decade, the true king of Formula 2 and a Le Mans winner. It took a while for him to win his first GP but that he did in **1969**. In **1970** he became World Champion, dying before he knew it. Then another Austrian, **Niki Lauda**, won two more titles, in fact also won the largest number of F1 races in the decade and also scored the most poles and fastest laps. With several circuits and hill climb venues, Austria had plenty of breeding ground for its drivers to hone their skills. The **Oesterreichring** hosted races for a number of international championships, **Salzburgring** for others, while **Tulln Langenlebarn**, an airfield, hosted F2 races until **1972**, by which time it had proved to be inadequate for that level. It should also be noted that **Johannes Ortner** and **Dieter Quester** were also successful Austrian drivers during the decade, the former winning the European Hill Climb Championship twice and the latter, the ETCC. **Helmut Marko** seemed to be on path to a very successful career when a stone blinded one of his eyes at **Clermont-Ferrand, 1972**. An Austrian championship was held during the decade and although often identified as a Formula 2 championship, it was more of a Formula Libre affair, for Formula 3, Formula Super Vee and Formula Ford also participated and drivers from places such as Hungary, Yugoslavia and Greece competed sporadically. Austrian tracks were also used for rounds of the Swiss championship. Touring car races were also held in the country.

International Racing: Austria hosted F1, F2, European Formula 3, World Manufacturers Championship, European 2-liter Championship, European Hill Climb Championship, Interserie.

Tracks: Aspern Salzburgring
Innsbruck Tulln-Langenlebarn
Oesterreichring
Main Hill Climbs: Alpl Gargelen
Dobratsch Rechbergrennen

Bahamas

What a difference a few years make…until 1966, the Bahamas was a top racing spot, drawing top talent from Europe, the US and Australia/New Zealand. Then it all ended quite abruptly but the purpose had been achieved, helping make the Bahamas a top international travel destination. Notwithstanding, racing continued at Oakes Field until at least 1973. Not unsurprisingly, more details about such obscure events have not been found.
Tracks: Oakes Field

Barbados

The Bushy Park track was inaugurated in **1971**. Like nearby Trinidad there was quite a bit of racing activity in the island during the 70s, with exchange and participation of drivers from other islands and Guyana. In addition to touring car racing, which included small engined cars from European and Japanese manufacturers, races for Formula Caribbean single seaters were held in the country, which involved cars with engines up to 1.6 liters. This regional championship was won by Barbadian driver Mike Atwell in 1974 and 1975. The Terrapin race cars were built in Barbados and hero Ralph "Bizzy" used a VW based car which he called Foolishness.
Tracks: Bushy Park

Belarus

The races held in Belarus were the standard Soviet fare of the day: Formulas 1, 2, 3 and 4 (in the early part of the decade, later on, Formula Easter and Formula Junior) plus Touring cars. Events featured Eastern European block-built cars, including large numbers of Estonia single seaters in all classes.
Tracks: Borowaja
Minsk

Belgium

Belgium is a small country, however, it had witnessed a great amount of racing action during the decade, boasting three important tracks and a number of hill climb venues. The street races at Chimay were held until the early part of the decade but dropped due to safety concerns. In addition to the many international races, there have been Belgian championships for touring cars, Formula Ford, sports cars, in addition to several regional Benelux races with the participation of drivers from the Netherlands and Luxembourg. Additionally, races for German championships were also held at Zolder and there have been many standalone races during the course of the decade. The Spa-Francorchamps circuit was renovated in the 70s, due to safety concerns and also reduced in length. The Belgian Grand Prix venue was changed to Nivelles and Zolder as of 1972. Nivelles, a new circuit, was the direct opposite of Spa, a driver's favorite even after the renovation. Considered boring and bland, Nivelles did not survive long as a circuit. The 24 Hours of Spa continued to be the most important touring car race of the world, although it was not always included in the European Touring Car Championship. Several Belgian based race teams such as Luigi, Francorchamps, VDS were prominent in International racing, during the decade. Belgian drivers were especially successful in touring cars.

The 24 Hours of SPA was the world's top touring car race in the 70s. (Photo by Paul Kooyman)

Main races: 24 Hours of Spa, 1000 km of Spa, Grand Prix of Chimay
International races: a Formula 1 Grand Prix has been held in Belgium for almost every year of the decade, in three different venues. Additionally races were held for European Formula 2, European Formula 3, European Formula 5000, World Manufacturers Championship, European Touring Car Championship, DRM, Interserie, European 2-Liter Championship, European GT Championship.

Tracks: Chimay
Mettet
Nivelles
Spa-Francorchamps
Zolder

Hill-Climbs: Alle-Sur-Semois
Codroz
Fagnez
Fleron
Goensdorf
Herbeumont
Huy
La Reine à Houyet
La Roche/Samrée
Malmedy
Maquisart
Namur
Val Dieu

Brazil

Brazil is another country which rose from status of unknown to factor during the course of the 70s, mainly through the feats of **Emerson Fittipaldi**. It suffices to say that little was known in Europe or the USA about the local racing scene in Brazil in the beginning of the decade. In **1970** there were no championships but at least **Interlagos** was reopened after a very lengthy 2-year renovation and a new track was inaugurated at **Taruma**. An early season international Formula Ford tournament was held, with the intent of showing the racing world that Brazil was ready to host international races again. This was followed by a Sports Car Tournament (Copa Brasil) **(1970)**, Formula 3 (**1971**), Formula 2 (**1971**), then the Non-Championship Formula 1 race in **1972**. After getting on the F1 calendar, Brazilian organizers stopped holding international tournaments, the last ones being Copa Brasil and Formula 2 late in **1972**. In **1971**, the country had a more organized and rational schedule for the first time, with championships for Touring Cars (Division 3), Prototypes (foreign and domestic) and Formula Ford. There were still quite a few standalone races. In the following year, the prototype championship was divided in two, one for domestic, another for foreign cars. Long distance races for Division 1 (Group 1 touring cars) were introduced in **1973**. Formula Super Vee appeared in **1974** and it quickly became the main racing category in the country. The country was extremely affected by the two oil crisis (**1974, 1979**) which had severe effects on racing. As for venues, street races and dirt track racing were allowed for the last time in the decade in **1972**. Several new tracks appeared during the decade (**Brasilia, Goiania, Taruma, Guapore, Cascavel,** revamped **Jacarepagua**). Some dirt tracks operated in the Southern State of Santa Catarina and a single hill climb was held on the round to **Petropolis**, in **1970**.

Main Races: 1000 Miles of Brazil, 25 Hours of **Interlagos**, 500 km of **Interlagos**, 12 Hours of Porto Alegre, 1000 km of **Brasilia**

A rather mixed bag at a race start in Interlagos, 1970. A Richard Divila designed prototype, the Snob's,. Camilo Cristofaro's famous Chevrolet carretera, an old Maserati and a roof less BMW, nicknamed "casket". The BMW won. (Photo by Rogerio da Luz)

International racing: Brazil has hosted Championship F1 races since **1973**. Other international racing: Formula Ford Tournament (**1970**), Formula Three Tournament (**1971**), Formula Two Tournament also referred as Brazilian Temporada (**1971, 1972**), Brazil Cup for sports cars (**1970, 1972**), Brazilian Grand Prix, non-championship Formula 1 (**1972**), 500 km of Interlagos (sports cars, **1972**). Argentinian drivers often participated in races in Brazil, including a Formula 4 demonstration race in Taruma, **1971**. Italian drivers **Gianpiero Moretti, Corrado Manfredini, Carlo Facetti** and **Giovanni Alberti** took part in the **1970** 1000 Miles Race. A 2-race **Ford** Maverick 4-cylinder tournament was held in **1975**, with the participation of drivers from several South American countries, plus **Vittorio Brambilla**.

Tracks:
Anapolis (Street)
Belo Horizonte (Street)
Brasilia (Street)
Brasilia (Track)
Cascavel
Curitiba
Joacaba (Dirt)
Salvador (Street)
Hill Climb: Petropolis

Fortaleza
Goiania (Track)
Goiania (Street)
Guapore
Interlagos
Jacarepagua (Rio de Janeiro)
Taruma
Teresina (Street)

Brunei

A Brunei Grand Prix for Formula Pacific was held in **1979**. The Sultan of Brunei ruling during the entire decade was a known car enthusiast but the above race is the only found instance of an auto race in the Sultanate during the 70s. The full result has not been located, in spite of searches in many languages.
Tracks: Bandar Seri Bagawan

Bulgaria

Albena hosted rounds of the **1977** Peace and Friendship Cup, with the participation of many Bulgarian drivers in the Touring car section but only **Hinov Kaltcho** raced in Formula Easter. As usual, Czechs won both events. Bulgarian championships contested by Iron Curtain built cars, were also held.
Tracks: Albena

Trabants and other Eastern European cars were called into action in Bulgarian racing.
Author unknown

Canada

Given its proximity and affinity with the United States, one would expect Canada to have a well-developed racing environment in the 70s and that is indeed the case. It should be noted that Canada's orientation was towards road racing rather than oval racing. In the early part of the decade, as many as three Can-Am races were held in Canada every year. Although these were generally less well supported than the American races, they placed Canada on the world's radar, both during the traditional and the later iteration of the Can-Am. Formula 5000 races were also held in the U.S. Northern neighbor. A local Formula A/B championship was held in Canada in **1970**, called Gulf Canada Series, changing to Formula B from **1971** to **1973** and then Atlantic as of **1974**. This was indeed Canada's major contribution to international racing, displaying the talents of **Gilles Villeneuve**, among others. Eventually that morphed into a North American championship. Local races were also held for Formula Ford, Formula Vee, Sports, Honda Civic one-make championship, NASCAR sanctioned and Touring cars during the course of the decade. The Molyslip Endurance Championship was run from **1971** to **1979**. **International races**: A F1 Canadian Grand Prix was ran in most years of the decade. The country also staged rounds of the World Sports Car and Manufacturers Championships, plus USAC National Championship, IMSA, Trans-Am, Can-Am, U.S. Formula 5000 championships. The Canadian Formula Atlantic Championship eventually became an international championship of some stature, the Trois Rivieres race attracting some talented drivers of the age.

Quite a few race cars were built in Canada in the 70s, such as this Astur Formula Vee. My sketch.

Tracks:
Argentia
Atlantic
Debert
Deux Montagnes

Edmonton
Gimli
Halifax
Harewood Acres

Laval
Mosport
Mount Laurel
Nelson
Quebec City
Rockfield Airfield
Sanair
St. Croix

St. Felicien
St. Johns
St. Jovite
Shannonville
Trois Rivieres
Val Belair
Western Speedway
Westwood

Chile

Chilean Formula 2 in 1971. Notice the full stands. Photo author is unknown.

Given the proximity to Argentina, it is only expected that Chile's racing would be highly influenced by its Eastern more developed neighbor. In fact, carreteras raced in Chile as well, which looked like a cross between Argentine TCs and prototypes, some of them locally built, others entirely Argentine, plus there was road racing, like Argentina. There were races for Formula 2 and 4 single seaters, categories that had also been developed in Argentina, plus touring car races, for cars such as FIAT and Peugeot. Single make races for FIAT 600s were also run. Events were broadcast on TV and racetrack attendance was quite impressive. Seven people died from a crash between two Minis at a race in 1975, which resulted in the closing of Las Vizcachas for one year.
Main race: 6 Horas Chilenas, held at **Las Vizcachas.**
International racing: few truly international races were held but an Argentine Formula 2 regulation international tournament was held at **Las Vizcachas**, with participation of Argentine and Uruguayan drivers.
Tracks: Arica (Las Machas)   Las Vizcachas
Juvenal Jerado

Colombia

Colombia is a fairly large country, with a very mountainous topography. As a result, most racing had a regional character, although national championships were held. A variety of race cars were used in the decade, including **Alfa Romeo, Honda, DKW, Fiat, Ford, Simca, Corvette, Mustang, Porsche, Wartburg, Renault, Mini Cooper, Dodge, VW, Opel, Mercedes, Plymouth**, even an old **Studebaker** and single seaters, among others. There were categories from small engines (less than 1 liter) to larger engines above 3 liters. Some race cars were also locally built, including a very pretty **DKW** engined prototype. A single make **Renault** 4 Cup was run in the mid-70s. Given the topography, several hill climbs were run during the decade as well. Colombian drivers would often cross the border of both Venezuela and Ecuador to race in these countries. On a less cheery note, a certain **Pablo Escobar**, yes, that one, raced in Colombia. He was not a fast driver but on the strength of his persuasive tactics, was let to win on occasion. An effort was made to include Colombia in the international racing calendar early on the decade. Two international Formula 2 races were held in a spanking new Bogota track in early **1971**, one won by **Jo Siffert**, the other by **Alan Rollinson** but that did not develop in the long-term. There was also an attempt to hook up with the American SCCA professional Formula B series but the series itself folded.

International Racing: 2 Formula 2 events held in **1971**, SCCA Formula B events held in the country.

Tracks: Bogota Palmira
Buga Pasto
Cali Santa Elena
Las Palmas Tocancipa
Medellin

Renault fun in Bogota, sometime during the 70s. Photo author is unknown.

Costa Rica

Costa Rica had a fairly active racing scene in the 70s, in fact, it is the first place where I have detected serious pick-up racers, which had competed against regular cars since **1970**. Most races were run for small engine vehicles but some larger cars (*Turismo de Serie* and *Modificado*) were also used. There was a great degree of regional exchange with other near countries, like Panama, El Salvador, Guatemala and even Colombia and Costa Rican championships were also held. To give you an idea of the degree of regional interaction in Central America, the first winners of the 3 hours of Costa Rica, in **1975** were Costa Ricans **Roy**

Valverde and **Carlos Kikos Fonseca, Nissan** 280 Z but in **1978**, Panamanian **Rodrigo Terán** won the race in his **Porsche** 911 and in **1979** the spoils were taken by Salvadoran **Francisco Miguel "Fomfor"**, driving a **BMW** 3.0 CSL.
International racing: Panamerican Championship
Main race: 3 Hours of Costa Rica
Tracks: La Guacima

Czechoslovakia

Karel Jilek's MTX 1-03. Photo author is unknown.

Most racing enthusiasts will remember the Brno ETCC round, a 70s oddity, for it was the single Eastern European race consistently held for Western championships during the decade. There were also international Formula 3 races, including the **1970** race in which the likes of **Niki Lauda, Jurg Dubler, Helmut Marko** and even an American driver, **Peter de Merit**, competed. In fact, Czechoslovakia was unique in that Western Formula 3 cars such as **Lotus, Cooper, Tecno**, were used in its F3 championship in the beginning of the decade, while Poles, Soviets, East German and others remained loyal to communist single seaters, such as **Rak, Melkus** and **Estonia**. Czechoslovakians loved their racing and their **Skodas**, specially enjoyed when they beat the Soviet **Moskvich** and **GAS**, East German **Trabants** and **Wartburgs** in Touring Car races. There were many local events during the decade, including Formula Easter (Peace and Friendship Cup) rounds at **Most**. **Jaroslav Bobek** was a notable Czech driver of the day, winning on circuits and hill climbs, including the Peace and Friendship Cup and representing the **Skoda** team in international events. There were also races for locally built prototypes, such as the **MTX, Brixner, OM** and the nice looking **Gazela**, with various engines, from BMWs to Ladas. MTX also built single seaters. The **Skodas** in fact often beat other Eastern European makes in their class, such as **Wartburg, Moskvich, Lada, Polski-Fiat**. As far as the Soviet block goes, Czech racing was a cut above the rest. The large number of hill climb venues is also noteworthy. A Formula Skoda was adopted late in the decade.

International events: Czechoslovakia hosted ETCC races at **Brno** many times during the decade, plus an Interserie round was held at **Most** in **1979**. The **Ecce Homo** hill-climb enticed a few international drivers, mostly Austrian, German and Swiss, many of whom drove contemporary Formula 2 cars. There were many races with participation of drivers from other Iron Curtain countries.

Tracks: Brno (street course)
Havirov
Jicin
Most
Olomouc
Ostrava
Piestany (Slovakia)
Strambersky-Trojubelnik
Terlicko

Hill climbs:
Beroun
Boskovice
Bratislava-Pezinok (Slovakia)
Certina-Pec
Chumotov
Ecce Homo
Hladnov
Horni Jiretin
Hronov
Jicin
Mala Skala
Melnik
Nasledovic
Kokorin
Semily
Roznov pod Radhosten
Usti nad Orlice
Vitikov
Vranov
Vysker
Zaskali u Liberce
Zbecno-Sykorice

Denmark

Denmark did host a few international Formula 3 and Formula Ford races during the decade. Its circuits were short, not suitable for anything more substantial, however a European Formula 5000 Championship race was held there in **1973**, in which Danes **Tom Belso** and **Jac Nelleman** did well, 4th and 6th. Most Danish races were domestic or regional in scope, involving other Scandinavian participants. There was a Danish touring car championship and occasionally, international races were held, such as in August 8, **1970**, a race won by **Jens Winther**, in a **BMW**. **John Fitzpatrick** took part in this race in the smaller engine class. A Grand Prix of Denmark was run for Formula 3 cars from **1973** until **1977**. While Randy Lewis won the **1973** edition (held at **Roskilde**), Dane **Jac Nelleman** won from **1974** to **1977** (held at **Jyllandsring**) including a rare victory for a **Van Diemen** F-3 in **1976**. The country was one of the early adopters of Formula Ford. For a few years, there was a Danish **Volvo** 142 Cup in Denmark, one of the first one-make series of the time. As for international racing, a round of the European Formula 3 Championship was held at **Jyllandsring** in **1975**, won by **Terry Perkins**. A Danish Grand Prix for sports cars was run in 1970, won by **Jo Bonnier**.

International races: European Formula 3, European Formula 5000
Tracks: Djursland   Jyllandsring   Roskilde

Dominican Republic

Races were held at the former San Isidro air base, where the likes of **Horacio Alvarez, Rafael Aguayo, Jacinto Peynado, Jaime Rodriguez** and **Luiz Mendez** would use **Toyotas, Datsuns, Mitsubishis**, even a locally built, VW engined car called "**Super Deserter**". Occasionally, drivers from Puerto Rico would visit, bringing cars such as a **Ford** Escort and **Porsche** 911. In addition to circuit racing, there was street racing as well.

Tracks: San Isidro Air Base

East Germany

Some East German races attracted as many as 100,000 spectators (such as the Peace and Friendship Cup event of **1977**, duly won by local **Uli Melku**s). Like many other Eastern Europe countries, there was a number of races for Touring Cars and Racing Cars (single seaters), as well as Formula 3 early on the decade. Many a race was held with representatives from Poland, Czechoslovakia, Soviet Union, which featured mostly Eastern European built cars, including the local **Melkus**. Many rounds of the Peace and Friendship Cup were held at Schleizer-Dreieck and several East German championships were held during the decade.

Tracks: Bautzen   Frohburg
Bernau   Sachsenring
Dresden Hellerau   Schleizer-Dreieck
Hill Climbs: Luckendorfer

Ecuador

This Mustang Mach One, driven by Hermann Lascano "Nato" was a habitue in the Vuelta a la Republica de Ecuador, a road race. This photo is from 1973, when Hermann finished fourth (Photo reproduction authorized by Carlos Nunez)

Racing fever caught on after **1971**, in the wake of the first 12 Hours Marlboro, held at recently opened Yahuarcocha racetrack, an international event won by the **Adamowickz-Young Ferrari** 512. Races were held for touring and GT cars and there was a fair degree of regional racing, with drivers from Colombia, Venezuela, Costa Rica, Panama, Peru and Argentina visiting. The Vuelta a la Republica de Ecuador was a major road racing event. There had been some bad accidents at the Yahuarcocha track during the decade, resulting in death. Very competitive races for small pickup trucks were also held in the country during the 70s. Street races were contested in a fair number of venues. **Juan Cobo** built a front engine prototype, equipped with a small Honda engine, which was reportedly fast and won on occasion and other such cars were built in the country. There was also a single

seater category called Formula Nacional but at the time of writing little information was available.
Main race: 12 Hours Marlboro.

Tracks: Cuenca
Guayaquil
Machala
Manta
Quito
Riobanba
Salinas
Yahuarcocha

Road Race: Vuelta a la Republica

El Salvador

El Salvador racing basically consisted of touring and GT cars, such as **Porsche, Mazda, VW, Fiat, Alfa Romeo, Toyota, Datsun, NSU, Hillman, Mitsubishi,** even **Hyundai,** at the time a very exotic and unknown Korean import. El Jabali was only built in **1979** but racing was held in other unidentified venues. Salvadoran driver **Jamsal** won a touring car race in Spain, Jarama, in 1970 and often won Central American races.

International Racing: El Salvador hosted a World Endurance Driver's Championship race and rounds of the Central American Championship.
Tracks: El Jabali

England

England's contribution to 1970s motorsport is outstanding and the country firmly became the top producer of race cars and components of all types that were exported all over the world. That being said, the British club scene has always been very crowded, with multiple events being run for a large variety of categories every week: single seater, touring cars of all sizes, sports cars, historic (not covered by this book) plus hill climbs.

Most F1 cars of the 70s were built in England and many of those that were not had components built there. Among the most notable British cars of the decade was the 6-wheel Tyrrell P-34. (Alejandro de Brito)

The main domestic championships were Formula 3 (actually there were three of them for a while), several Formula Ford championships, including Formula Ford 2000, Formula 4, Formula Super Vee, Formula Vee, Formula Atlantic, the British Saloon Car Championship, assorted Sports Cars championships and Formula Libre events of all shapes and sizes. Additionally, there were dozens of specialized club championships for Minis, Lotus 7 and several other categories. One of the most peculiar racing categories in Britain was Stock Cars, simply because it has no connection whatsoever with the concept or idea of a stock-car in the U.S.A. or elsewhere. Some were garage specials made to look like old 30s, 20s coupes, which were quite popular with the crowds, others were Hot Rods and still others, beaten up sedans like Minis, Fords, Imps. Some of them are very awful looking and very tatty but they gave the world **Derek Warwick**, the category's 1973 World Champion! Always trend setting, a **Ford** Escort Mexico one-make championship was held in **1971,** which included races for other cars (all-comers) which were much fun. One-make championships would become a staple of worldwide racing in years to come. Most of the Formula 5000 events were held in England, so it is not surprising that the Championship that replaced it, the Shellsport Group 8 Championship (later Aurora Championship) was also England based. One of the most interesting categories in England in the 70s was Super Saloons, where touring cars were matched to unusually large engines, such as a DAF-Oldsmobile, VW Beetles with V8 Chevies, Skodas with V8 engines, etc. As a result of the sheer variety of categories and races, plus proximity and exposure to most Formula 1 teams, drivers from North, South and Central America, Asia, Africa, Australia/New Zealand and the rest of Europe flocked to England to race, hoping to climb the racing ladder and be discovered. Only a few succeeded, the vast majority returned home empty handed and a tad poorer. England was also the site of most non-championship Formula 1 races of the 70s.

International events: England has hosted races for F1, F2, European F3, Formula 5000, World Manufacturers Championship, ETCC, Interserie, European 2 Liter Championship, USAC National Championship, European Formula Super Vee.

Tracks: Aintree
Brands Hatch
Caldwell Park
Croft
Crystal Palace
Donington
Lydden Hill
Hill Climbs: Barbon Manor
Bodiam
Bouley Bay
Doune
Fintray
Great Auclum
Gurston Down
Harewood

Mallory Park
Oulton Park
Rufforth
Silverstone
Snetterton
Thruxton

Loton Park
Oddicombe
Pontypool Park
Prescott
Shelsley Walsh
Val des Terres
Valence
Wiscombe Park

Estonia

Estonia's major contribution to racing was the production of the Estonia race car, many hundreds of which were produced and distributed all over Eastern Europe during the decade. Soviet Formula 1, 2, 3 and 4 races (later on, Formula Easter and Formula Junior) were held in the country, obviously featuring vast numbers of

Estonias, as well as touring car competition (only Soviet cars). Estonian championships were also held during the decade.
Tracks: Miao
Pirita-Kose-Klostrimesta
Saug
Wana Wyida

Estonia's major contribution to 70s motor sports was the hundreds of Estonia single seaters built and raced during the period. (Madis Laiv archive)

Ethiopia/Eritrea

There was some racing in former Italian colonies in Africa during the 30s and that included Eritrea. The country was for some time taken over by Ethiopia, which includes the period in question. Therefore, even though Asmara is actually located in current day Eritrea, it was part of Ethiopia at the time. The major race of the period was the Gran Premio Automobilistico Expo 72, held in **1972**, which was attended by no less than Ethiopian emperor **Haile Selassie**. The winner of this race was Italian **Enio Bonomelli**, in a **Porsche Carrera**, followed by **Lino Rossi** in an Abarth 2000. A last race, the Gran Premio Asmara, was held in 1974, duly won by **Lino Rossi**. Then a long war came and Asmara races were no more. As for Ethiopian territory, racing began in the country in 1958 and there was a major rally there, the Highland Rally. No circuit or hill climbing information was found.
Tracks: Asmara

Finland

Finland has produced some excellent drivers but racing activity in the country in the 70s is surprisingly obscure and requires research in Finnish. The typical Keimola meeting of the 70s constituted of Group 1 and Group 2 touring car races for several categories, with several dozen of entries. The assortment of machinery used during the decade is greater than you would find most anywhere: **Simca**,

Alfa Romeo, Opel, Volvo, BMW, Ford, Fiat, Sunbeam, Mini, Datsun, Saab, Mercedes, VW, Chevy Camaro, Renault, Mustang, Citroen. The vast majority of the drivers from these meetings did not progress beyond domestic racing: in fact, pouring over much data none of the names sounded familiar. Usually these meetings also included a Formula Vee race, that could be local, a Scandinavian Cup event or even an European Championship event. A **1970** Formula Vee program contains some very familiar names, **Harald Ertl, Helmut Koinigg, Manfred Schurti, Bertil Roos,** while some of the Vee manufacturers are actually Finnish. The few international races, such as the Interserie races held at Keimola also included touring car races. There was also a long distant race, the touring car race Keimola 500, contested by teams of 2 drivers. The **1970** race included some well-known names such as **Rauno Aaltonen, Hannu Mikkola, P.Toivonen.** There was also a **M. Salo** (certainly not the **Mika Salo** of latter years)! In addition to the tracks, the city of Seinajoki held an early festival, which included sports cars and single-seater (Formula Vee) racing. Driver **Kai Berner** died in this event in **1976**. Keimola closed before the end of the decade.

International racing: Finland hosted races for the Interserie and European 2 Liter Championship in the early part of the decade. Additionally, European Formula Vee and Formula Super Vee championship events were held in the country. Standalone International F3 races at Keimola and Hameenlina held in **1970**.

Main race: Keimola 500
Tracks: Hameenlina (Ahvenisto)
Keimola
Seinajoki

The typical Keimola meeting comprised a number of categories, such as touring cars. This photo is from 1974. Photo by Jari Debner/Harry Hammaren

The typical Keimola meeting also featured Formula Super Vee races. The country hosted European, Scandinavian and local championship races. This photo is from 1974. Photo by Jari Debner/Harry Hammaren.

France

Automobile racing was created in France and many of the early exponents, such as **Peugeot, Panhard, Renault** and **De Dion**, were French firms. The country remained highly enthusiastic about the sport during the decade, with a large number of championships, teams, races and drivers, plus a large number of international events, which of course, included the 24 Hours of **Le Mans**. Formula 3 was run during most of the decade, while Formula Renault was also another important entry level category, a replacement (or shall we say, continuation) of Formula France that ended in **1971**. Touring car races were always run in France but a proper national championship began only in **1976**. There was a Sports Car Championship for many years, which included a vast variety of machinery and a number of standalone sports car races, mostly run as support races for championship events. Some French F1 and Sports cars drivers would often participate in these events, such as **Henri Pescarolo** and **Jean-Pierre Beltoise**. Another interesting championship was the Challenge Simca Shell, that ran from **1972** until **1974**. Another rarely spoken of category was Formule Bleue, single seaters equipped with 1-liter Citroen engines which operated until **1975**. There was also the Coupe de L'Avenir for Prototypes and Clubmans races were also held in the country. Coupe Gordini existed since **1966** and lasted until **1974** and it was the first long lasting one-make series. Additionally, by the end of the decade there were several one-make series in France, for Minis, VW, Simca, in addition to Renault. France's 70s hill climb scene was also extremely lively, with a huge number of races and venues and a French Hill Climb championship held during the course of the decade. During the 70s **Jimmy Robert Mieusset** was European Hill Climb champion twice and **Jean-Marie Almeras**, once. Other prominent hill climbers were **Michel Pignard** and **Christian Debias**. As for venues, **Paul Ricard (Le Castellet**) was an addition during the decade, inaugurated on April 18, **1970**. Often seen as the prototypical safe and modern circuit of the age, the track would host several editions of the French Grand Prix, plus a number of other races for other championships. Other tracks inaugurated during the decade were **Croix-en-**

Ternois and **Dijon-Prenois**, while **Clermont-Ferrand, Rouen-les-Essarts, Karland** and **Monthlery**, older circuits were being used less.
International Racing: During the decade France has hosted races for F1, F2, European Formula 3, World Manufacturers Championship, ETCC, European 2 Liter Championship, European GT Championship, European Hill Climb Championship.
Important Non-Championship races: 24 Hours of Le Mans, 1000 km of Paris

Among other things, many French cars were built in the 70s, including the Inaltera, here sitting in the Le Mans Museum. (Carlos de Paula)

Tracks:
Albi
Clermont-Ferrand (Charade)
Croix-en-Ternois
Dijon Airport
Dijon-Prenois
Folembray
Karland (Mireval)
La Chatre
Ledenon

Le Mans
Magny Cours
Monthlery
Nogaro
Pau (street)
Paul Ricard (Le Castellet)
Rouen-les-Essarts

Hill Climbs:
Abreschviller
Ac Lorrain
Aix-St Antonin
Ampus Draguignan
Angouleme-Serres
Ardus-Mirabel
Arette La Pierre St. Martin
Argeles-Gazost
Arry
Autun-Montjeu
Bagneres de Bigorre
Ballon D'Alsace

Beauxjolais
Bel Bouef
Belleau
Bellegarde
Bergeracois-Montbazillac
Bomerée
Bourbach-Le Haut
Boyeux-St. Jerome
Brides-Meribel
Buisson de Cadouin
Cabaretou
Cacharat

Caemieu
Cagnotte
Cannes
Caudie Col St. Louis
Chamrouse
Charnisay
Clermont Dessous
Col de Bayard
Col de l'Orme
Col St. Ignace
Col St. Pierre
Colombier
Courcoue sur Logne
Cosavy Valespir
Dunieres
Espallon
Eymoutlers
Flaine
Foret d'Auvran
Forez
Gaillac D'Aveyron
Gergeracois-Le Buisson
Glouneaux
Gouron-Caussols
Grignac
Haut-Cantal
Hautefage
Hautes Vosges
Hebecrevon
Irancy
L'Echelette
Lac d'Alfred
La Bachellerie
La Faucille
La Morte
La Pommeraye
La Roquette
Le Pertuis
Le Pin
Les Andelys
Les Baux
Les Gluneaux
Les Limouches
Les "S' de Treffort
Limonest-Mont Verdun
Lodeve
Lorne
Lure
Malvac

Mazamez
Millau-le-Buffarel
Miner
Monclair D'Agenais
Montaigu
Montauban Mirabel
Mont Dore
Mont Ventoux
Montbrison
Montgueux
Montmarquet
Montrevard
Monts de Jura
Murs
Neufchatel-en-Bray
Neuvy-le-Roi
Perigueux-Coursac
Perthuis
Poilly/Serein
Poissons
Quillan Le Portel
Rangiers
Revel St. Fereos
Roanne
Robert le Diable
Rodez
Saint Aubi des Coudrais
Saint Jean Du Gard/Col St. Pierre
Sainte Anne
Sainte Helene
Sancey
Saumur St Hilaire
Sewen
Soissons
St. Antonin
St. Baume
St. Cyprien
St. Geniez D'Ort
St. German sur Ile
St. Goueno
St. Maurice/Moselle
Tancarville
Tonerre
Treffort
Turckheim-Trois Epis
Urcy
Vence
Villeneuve Pujols
Vuillafans

Georgia

Peace and Friendship races, for Soviet touring cars and single seaters were held for the first time in Viljandi, Georgia, in 1979.
Tracks: Viljandi

Greece

Mouschos' Alfa Romeo won many races in Greece during the 70s. (unknown author)

A highly mountainous country, Greece had a hill climb scene but also a circuit racing championship. **Giorgos Moschous** destroyed his opposition with an **Alfa Romeo** TT33 prototype late in the decade, but a number of other prototypes raced in Greece at the time, including **Crossle-BMW, GRD, March, Grac-Renault, Chevron**. There was also a locally made prototype, the **Boufis-Alfa**, which was competitive. As for touring cars and GTs, there was a famous Corvette driven by **Johnny Pesmazoglu**, in addition to **Porsche 911, Datsun, Toyota, NSU, Alpine, BMW, Ford**. In **1971** the country prohibited racing on streets, because of an accident that killed famous local driver **Giannis "Mavros" Meimardes** in Rhodes. There were no permanent tracks per se but racing was still held in airports and off city centers. The Pititsa hill-climb was first run in **1973** and remains the most important event in the country. Please note that transliteration of Greek into English can be tricky, so the name **Giorgos Moschous** can appear as **George Moschos, Georges Moushous**, etc. **Johnny Pesmazoglu** sometimes appears as **Tony Pesmazoglu**. The same for the names of cities. I had to choose the best spelling at my discretion. Additionally, many Greek drivers had pseudonyms, so you might find them under that assumed name, rather than their real one.

Tracks: Chania
Corfu
Maritsa (Airport)

Hill Climbs: Dionysus
Lycabettus
Patras

Nea Smyrna
Rhodes
Tatoi
Pititsa
Riccona
Ritsonia
Voular

177

Tatoi race, 1971 (site rally.gr)

Guatemala

The Central American country was the site of local and regional racing. Salvadoran drivers often raced there and Central American championship races for touring cars were held in the country.
Tracks: Autodromo Mario Rivera

Guyana

When the decade started, racing had been taking place in Guyana for twenty years. After some years of turmoil and ensuing independence from England, the Guyanese were ready to resume racing by **1970** but that required revamping the South Dakota track. Funds were raised and the circuit reinaugurated in November of **1970**. In addition to teams from Guyana, there were British, Antiguan, Trinidadian and Barbadian teams. The race was featured in an *Autosport* article and was supported by BOAC (the forerunner of British Airways) which transported for free two cars for British drivers, the so-called Team Speedbird. Among others that raced in Guyana during the 70s are **Barry Williams, Robs Lamplough, Gordon Spice, Gabriel Konig** and **Richard Longman**. In addition to Mallock U2, Minis and a host of other European cars, there were locally built cars, one called "The Beast" was constructed by **George Jardim**, the other, the Royal Bank Special. The Terrapin, built in Barbados, also raced there. American Sprint cars that had been introduced in the country, with a specific class established for them. Between **1973** to **1975** there was a Caribbean Championship for these cars. **Diego Febles** from Puerto Rico also raced in Guyana, in his **Porsche Carrera**. In 1972, two Formula B races were held in Guyana, at Atkins Field, won by **Jimmy Fuller** and **Andrew Cheek**. After **1976**, due to the oil crisis, many of the people involved in the sport left the country and the racing scene quieted down until the end of the decade, while socialism loomed in the horizon.
Tracks: Atkins Field   South Dakota

Holland

The main motor racing venue in Holland during the 70s was **Zandvoort**, the seaside track very near the beach, which often suffered from sand accumulation. The track was used in a large number of international championships during the course of the decade but it was maligned due to two F1 deaths that occurred there in the early 70s (**Courage** in **1970**, **Williamson** in **1973**). The Dutch had run national and Benelux (with Belgium and Luxembourg) championships during the course of the decade, mostly for Touring Cars, Formula Ford, Formula Vee. There was also a one make series for **Chevrolet** Camaros, the Camaro Superstar Series. In **1979**, one of the main Dutch drivers, **Rob Slotemaker**, died in one of the series races, the "Trophy of the Dunes". Baarlo, Geleen, Woensdrecht (an Air Force Base) and Heerlen also held racing events during the decade.

International races: **Zandvoort** has hosted the Dutch Grand Prix, races for the European Formula 2 Championship, European Touring Car Championship, European Formula 5000 Championship, European Formula 3 Championship, DRM, European 2 Liter Championship, Interserie, European GT Championship, a large number of Benelux events. Rounds of the British Formula 3 championships were often held at Zandvoort.

A Dutch Formula Ford team from the 70s. Martin Fokkens and Wim Verboon are featured in photo by Jan Borsboom.

Tracks: Baarlo
Geleen
Heerlen
Welschap
Woensdrecht
Zandvoort
Hill Climbs: Vaals

Honduras

Races for the Central American Championship for touring and GT cars were held during the decades. Information is scant, although sources point out a location in Tegucigalpa, the country's capital.
Tracks: Tegucigalpa

Hong Kong

Hill climbs where held in a variety of places in Hong Kong during the 70s and there was even a Hong Kong Hill Climb championship. **Herb Adamczyk** and **John MacDonald** were the exponents in this championship, normally comprising of 4 events.
Hill Climbs:
Wong Nai Chong Golden Hill Brick Hill

Lye Yue Mun   Ha Tsuen

Hungary

Hungary was not known for much racing activity during the 70s, even though **Budapest** hosted a European Touring Car Championship in **1970**, never repeated. A Formula Vee support race was also held, won by Manfred Schurti. The country also hosted international races with exclusive participation of other Iron Curtain country drivers and hill climbs at Pecs. Hungarians sometimes raced in Austria.
Tracks: Budapest
Hill Climbs: Pecs

India

India's first races took place all the way back in **1907**. The country hosted domestic events, although drivers (and riders) from Sri Lanka did race there, bringing some international flavor to the races. These competitions were very popular, the Sholavaram races drawing crowds of as many as 70,000 people. There were some local heroes such as **Dr. Cesare Rossi** and his **Ferrari**, the **Maharkumar of Gondal, Vijay Mallya,** until recently **Force India's** owner and **Vicky Chandhok, Karun**'s father. Cars were mostly touring cars at the time but there were Indian prototypes in this period and some foreign sports cars. The Madras GPs of **1978** and **1979**, were won by **Kumar Chanadityasinhji** in a formula 5000 **Surtees-Chevrolet**. Locally produced **Hindustans** and **Premiers** were also raced at the track, located near Madras and the **Q`Marri** prototype that first raced in **1973**, competed until the 80s.

70s at Sholavaran. Mix of European GTs and Sedans, plus local specials such as Nazir Hoosein's Ford. Sri Lankan David Pieris' Ford adds international flavor. (Vicky Chandhok collection)

Tracks:
Alipore
Barrackpore
Calcutta (Kolkotta)
Sholavaram

Indonesia

A race start in Indonesia. Notice the grid girl identifying Lambertus Van Vreden in his Honda. The car appears in three different configurations in this book. Photo Therry Van Vreden.

Racing was not new to Indonesia, which had seen a surge in competitions since the 50s. In fact, Indonesian driver **Iriawan** had won the Malaysian GP of 1968. The sport did evolve greatly in the decade, though. The first purpose-built circuit appeared in Ancol Jaya, opened in 1970 and this is where Indonesia's first Grand Prix was held in 1976. The winner was **John MacDonald** and the race for Formula Pacific (Atlantic) was valid for the short-lived Rothman's International Series. The GP was the only one held in the decade. Other regional stars such as **Albert Poon** and **Sonny Rajah** also took part. Touring car races were also held in the circuit, contested by a number of drivers in European and Japanese cars. Dutch drivers living in the archipelago, such as **Lambertus Van Vreden, Frank Bruijn** and **Jacques de Steur**, competed in races, ranging from sprints, 6-hour races and road races. These took place in venues such as Pangkalan Kalijati Semarang, Serang and Purbalingaa Braling. Among the cars used in racing in the country was a **Matra** 530, which eventually received a **Honda** engine. The Pertamina racing team, sponsored by the Indonesian oil company, owned a stable of cars, which included Formula 2 cars used by drivers such as **Soeswanto, Wiano** and **Iriawan** in other Asian events. **Wiano** actually tried British Formula 3 in 1974 and is incorrectly identified in some racing literature as Indian. A curious fact is that some drivers appear in results with a single name, such as **Razief, Handartono** and **Hadiayarto** which was, in fact their full name! Many Indonesians back then were known by a single name and that included dictator Suharto. Additionally, a few prominent

181

figures raced (read politicians and their children) and faster drivers, including the Dutch drivers living in the country, were sometimes asked to let them win races...
Main race: Grand Prix of Indonesia
Tracks: Ancol Jaya Serang
Pangkalan Kalijati Semarang Purbalingaa Braling

Ireland

Ireland's tracks witnessed quite a bit of action during the decade, with championships for touring cars, Formula Libre, Formula Ford, Formula Vee and Formula Atlantic. Mondello Park hosted four European Formula 5000 races during the course of the decade and Irish drivers often took part in British races.
Main races: European Formula 5000
Tracks: Mondello Park Phoenix Park
Hill climbs: Craigantlett
Knockalla

Israel

Israel was supposed to have hosted a non-championship Formula 2 race in 1970. The German Automobile Club (ADAC) got a decent line-up to make the trek to Israel, which included the likes of championship runner-up **Derek Bell**, **Ernesto Brambilla**, **Peter Westbury**, **Tommy Reid**, **Brian Cullen, Mike Goth** in Brabhams, Tecnos for **Bruno Frey** and **Patrick Depailler**, **Xavier Perrot's** March and a **Pygmee** for **Patrick dal Bo**. As it transpired, the race, slated for a Saturday, did not happen. From the onset there was resistance when the Orthodox party protested in Parliament holding such an event during Shabatt. Then local authorities deemed the circuit unsafe, for allegedly there were many unexploded bombs throughout the circuit at Barnea beach. Barbed wire was also ineffective holding back overly excited Israeli fans. So the only race held was a supporting event for Formula Vees, won by Swede **Bertil Roos** followed by **Helmut Koinnig** and **Helmut Bross**. Other participants who achieved fame in the future were **Brian Henton, Harald Ertl, Manfred Schurti** and future **Porsche** boss **Manfred Jankte**, while a touring car race was also cancelled. Some sources say drivers "organized" a race in Jerusalem, in unidentified cars, which was won by **Derek Bell**. It is very unlikely this unofficial event did take place. There was talk of a **1971** GP but not surprisingly, that did not go very far. That sums up racing activities in the Middle East for the decade.

Track: Ashqelon

Italy

As one of the main producers of race cars in the world and also many fine racing drivers, Italy had no shortage of categories or racing, both for seasoned drivers and beginners. Formula 3 championships were run throughout the decade, as well as Formula Italia, a category that was run only in the 70s, in fact from **1972** to **1979**, which gave us **Bruno Giacomelli, Riccardo Patrese** and **Michele Alboreto**, among others. The country also had championships for Formula Ford, Formula Monza for cars equipped with FIAT 500 cc engines and Formula 850, for cars with 850 cc engines. A Sports Cars championship was run for many years, as well as touring car races for all levels of expertise. Italy also had the Alfasud Cup, Alfa's attempt to boost the poor image of the cars made in the South. Stockcars (the British kind) also raced in the country. Hill climbs were also very popular in the 70s, in fact the main hill climber of the decade was **Mauro Nesti**, who won dozens upon dozens of international events, even more domestic ones. In the beginning of the decade, there were also many stand-alone races, which tended to disappear in the course of the decade. Events for the Swiss championship were sporadically run in **Monza**, which is quite near the Swiss border. Besides **Monza**, other Italian tracks such as **Imola, Vallelunga, Misano, Enna** and **Mugello** also featured World and European events and Sicily's **Targa Florio** was a championship event until **1973**. **International racing:** During the decade Italy hosted races for F1 (Championship and Non-Championship), F2, European Formula 3, World Manufacturer's Championship, European 2 Liter, Interserie, ETCC, European Formula 5000, European GT Championship, European Hill Climb Championship.

Arturo Merzario was one of the main Italian drivers of the decade and also built his own F1 car. (Alejandro de Brito)

Tracks: Casale
Enna (Pergusa)
Ganzarri (Messina)
Imola
Magione
Misano
Monza
Mugello (track)
Mugello (road circuit)
Palermo

Targa Florio (Madonie, road circuit) Varano
Vallelunga

Main Hill Climbs:

Abriola-Sellata
Alghero Scala Piccada
Alpe Del Nevegal
Alta Garfagna
Amalfi-Agerola
Ascoli Piceno
Ascoli-Colle S. Marco
Bassano-Monte Grappa
Belmonte-Citta Di Alvero
Bolzano-Mendola
Bormio Stelvio
Bresannone-Sant'Andrea
Camucio-Cortona
Castellana (Orvieto)
Castell'Arquato-Vernasca
Castione Baratti
Castione-Presolava
Catania-Etna
Cefalu-Gibilmanna
Cesana-Sestriere
Colle della Maddalena
Colle S. Eusebio
Coppa Bruno Carotti
Coppa Carotti
Coppa Citta Volterra
Coppa del Chianti Classico
Coppa di Asiago
Coppa di Monopoli
Coppa Faro
Coppa Feraboli
Coppa Nissena
Coppa Orvieto
Coppa Paolino Teodori
Coppa Primavera
Coppa San Benedetto
Coppa Val D'Anapo Sortino
Cosenza
Etna
Fasano-Selva
Fornovo-Monte Cassio
Garessio-S. Bernardo

Giarre-Montesalico
Gubbio-Madonna della Cima
Iglesias
Macchia-Monte S. Angelo
Macerata
Malegno-Borno
Monte Acuto Campuomu
Monte Bonifato
Monte Eriche
Monte Kronio
Monte Pellegrino
Monti Iblei
Nicastro-Acquavona
Pedaria-Tarderia
Pieve St. Stefano-Passo Dello Spino
Ponte Corace-Tiriolo
Potenza
Rieti
Saccargia-Codrongiamos
Salita del Costo
Salita Val Martello
Salsomaggiore-S. Antonio
San Giustino-Bocca Trabaria
San Gregorio-Burcei
San Stefano-Gambarie
Sarnano-Sassotetto
Santuario di Graglia
Sillano-Ospedaletto
Stallavna-Boscochiesanuova
Svolte di Popoli
Tolmezzo-Verzegnis
Trapani-Monte Erice
Trento-Bondone
Treponti-Castelnuovo
Treviso-Cansiglio
Trofeo Luigi Fagioli
Turin-St. Martin-Le Haut
Valico dello Scopetonee
Verzegnis-Sella
Vittorio Veneto-Cansiglio

Jamaica

Races were held at Vernamfield throughout the decade. Some meetings had as many as 10 short races, which included races for various touring cars, sports cars and single seaters, which included the Caribbean-made Terrapin, mixed with the likes of European Brabhams. Some foreign drivers also raced there. Dominican and Puerto Rican drivers were invited to race in Vernamfield in **1972**. **Horacio**

Alvarez won his race in a **Toyota** 1000 and **Rafael Aguayo** also won his, in a special called **Super Deserter** that looked like a buggy. Also present was **Diego Febles**, from Puerto Rico, who also won his category. A hill climb was held at Albion.
Tracks: Vernamfield
Hill climb: Albion

Japan

Japanese racing blossomed during the 70s, specially as the country (and its automakers) were getting richer and more sophisticated. The Can-Am like prototypes of the 70s, that used to dice in the Japanese Grand Prix, such as the Isuzu R7 and McLarens, plus a host of locally built racers eventually were replaced by more nimble European 2-liter prototypes early in the 70s, which ran in the Fuji Grand Champion series, all races held at Fuji. Among the cars that raced in this series were **Chevron, Lola, GRD, March** and also the Japanese **Nova** and **Sigma**, the winning cars running **BMW** engines, although Toyota, Isuzu, Mitsubishi, Nissan, Mazda and Ford engines were also used. Even an Alpine-Renault entered a few races starting in 1975 and drivers such as **Marie Claude Beaumont, Bob Evans** and **Vern Schuppa**n made appearances. There was also a shorter Fuji Long Distance Series, which began in **1977**, for teams. Formula 2 (initially called Formula 2000) was adopted as the main single seater category, in addition to Formula Pacific later in the decade, which allowed Japanese drivers to contest races throughout Asia. Many European drivers raced in this championship, in fact, world champions **Jackie Stewart** and **John Surtees** won the Grand Prix of Japan for Formula 2 in **1970** and **1972**, respectively. Among the foreign drivers that raced in Japanese F2 (F2000) in the 70s are **Didier Pironi, Jacques Laffite, Alex Ribeiro, Hans Stuck, Beppe Gabbiani, Leo Geoghegan, Bob Muir, Danny Sullivan, Marc Surer, Peter Gethin, Brian Henton, Vern Schuppan, Dave McConnell, Eje Elgh, Rene Arnoux, Derek Warwick, Stephen South, Tony Trimmer, Keke Rosberg, Nick Craw, Larry Perkins, Gianfranco Brancatelli, Mike Thackwell, Derek Daly.** In addition to sports cars and single seaters, there were touring car races during the decade, initially dominated by **Nissan** Skylines, **Isuzu** Berets, **Hondas** S800**s**, **Toyotas** Coronas and Corollas, **Suzukis** and **Mazda** RX3, later replaced by Group 5, silhouette style cars, replaced by Super Silhouettes in **1979**. The long-distance races, as in Europe and US, combined sports and touring cars and as late as **1976, Porsche** 910 were still contesting local races in Japan. There was also an entry-level, 500 cc single-seater category.
Main Races: Fuji 1000 km, 6 Hours of Japan, Grand Prix of Japan (Formula 2000, Formula 2)

Fushida and Kuwashima dicing
Photo author unknown

International Racing: Formula 1. Many Japanese Formula 2 (F2000) and Sports Car races had foreign driver participation, so they are construed as international races.

Tracks: Fuji
Hokkaido
Mine
Suzuka
Tsukuba
West

Kenya

Local events were held in **Nakuru**, a dedicated racetrack,1.3 km long, which had been operational since the 50s. There were single seater races there during the 60s at least until the mid-70s, which included among others a locally created single seater called the **Sagoo Special**, equipped with a **Mercury** engine, which raced until 1969. Unidentified Formula Vees (likely South African) were often bundled in with **Fords, Vauxhalls, Renaults** and a number of other saloons. **Vic Preston**, well known in Rally circles, did race a **Brabham** there, although it is not clear which engine was used. Even a **Volvo** engined **Mini** graced the racetracks. Events with as many as 15 races were announced during the decade. There are uncorroborated reports of old 500 cc Formula 3 cars racing in the 70s and mentions of other racing venues. Another expert rally driver **Shekhar Mehta** also dabbled in circuit racing, driving a **BMW**, among other things.
Tracks: Embakasi   Nakuru (aka Langalanga)

Latvia

Soviet races at Bikernikie, in Riga, were generally well attended, with healthy grids for all usual Soviet categories: Formula 1, 2, 3, 4 (later on, Formula Easter and Formula Junior) and Touring cars. Races for the Lithuanian championship were also held in Latvia, before the Neman Ring was inaugurated in 1974.
Tracks: Bikernikie

Liechtenstein

The Vaduz-Triesenberg hill climb was held a last time in 1973, won by Silvio Moser in a Lola 2-liter prototype. The race was valid for that year's Swiss championship and featured cars such as Grac, Chevron and Saubers. There were slaloms in the tiny country, as well.
Hill climbs: Vaduz-Triesenberg
Ruggell-Schellenberg

Lithuania

A proper racetrack was inaugurated in 1974, the Neman Ring and races for single seaters and touring cars were held.
Tracks: Neman Ring

Luxembourg

One of the smallest countries in Europe, one would not expect a huge volume of racing activity in this land. However, Goodyear Europe built a high level track test in the country in **1967**, at Colmar Berg, which has, on occasion, been used for racing events. Its most important event was an Interserie race held in **1978**, won by **Reinhold Joest**, followed by **Bob Wollek**, both in **Porsche** 908/3. The track has also been used to host the Belgian Touring Car Championship during the 70s. Luxembourgian drivers would often race in nearby Germany, Holland and Belgium, holding national championship in tracks in those countries. In addition to touring cars, sports cars races were also held there and **Philippe Streiff** won a Coupe de l'Avenir sports car race at Colmar Berg in **1977**. Many hill climbs were held in different venues in the country as well.
International Race: Interserie race, **1978**. Belgian Touring Car Championship, **1977, 1979**
Tracks: Colmar-Berg Goodyear Test Track
Hill Climbs: Alle s/Semois
Berscheid
Ettelbruck
Helsdorf
La Roche
Lorentzweiler
Reisdorf
Wiltz

Macau

The Grand Prix of Macau was extremely important in the development of racing in Asia, having been held since the 50s, thus before Japan was on the motorsport radar. In the 70s, the race began attracting more European drivers, who enriched the field with Australian, New Zealander, Hong Kong, Indonesian, Singaporean, Pilipino, Malaysian and Japanese drivers, plus racers from Macau. While in **1970** it was still a free-for-all event, European and Australian Formula 2 cars such as **Elfin, Mildren** and **Dolphin,** mixed with GTs, small and large touring cars and Formula Vees, it grew on stature, entry quality improved vastly and by **1979** it was becoming the third most important street race in the world, after Monaco and Long Beach. **Dieter Quester** won the **1970** race in the Formula 2 **BMW**'s last race and Hong Kong's **John Macdonald** had a good run in **1971, 1973** and **1975**. In addition to the single-seater event, races were held for touring cars and motorcycles. The touring car races often featured cars rarely raced elsewhere, such as **Rover, Morris Marina, Subaru** and even **Mercedes**. In **1978** the Race of Giants, a celebration of the 25th anniversary of the race was held, with the participation of several important drivers of yesteryear, among them **Stirling Moss, Prince Bira** and **Toulo de Graffenried**.
Tracks: Guia

Early Macau Grand Prix races of the 70s included a variety of machines. In this 1972 photo, you see Harold Lee's Honda and Herbert Adamcyzk's Porsche. Photo by Jose Santos.

Malaysia

Malaysia had two racing venues and several international races were held in the country during the decade, with drivers from Hong Kong, Philippines, Indonesia, Japan, Australia, New Zealand and Singapore. A Grand Prix of Malaysia for Asian Formula 2 and Pacific was run in the country and touring car racing was also practiced in the country.
Tracks: Batu Tiga (Shah Allan/Selangor)
Penang

Malta

Joe Anastasi's lowered roof Mini. Photo by Joe Anastasi

Hill climbing had been practiced in the island since the 50s, continued in the 60s but faded, until the mid 70s, when an event began at Manikata. The enthusiasm eventually led to the founding of the Malta Automobile Federation in **1976** and the institution of a championship with multiple rounds. **Alex Zammit** drove the first single seater, a Formula Abarth, in the Qasam Barrani climb of **1977**. That enthusiasm fizzled in 1978, when the government failed to issue permits for further hill climbs. Road racing was prohibited in the country but there was drag racing and rallyes. Maltese drivers often raced in Sicily.

Hill climb: Bahrija
Manikata
Mizieb
Mtarfa
Nadur
Qasam Barrani
San Martin
Xwieni

Mexico

The Mexican local scene consisted mostly of GT, Touring car and Formula Ford races during the 70s. As the Mexican Grand Prix was cancelled in **1971**, never to return during the decade due to the **1970** race misbehaving crowds, the country lost both its major race and idol (**Pedro Rodriguez**) in the same year. Many of the drivers who had some impact in international racing, such as **Hector Rebaque**, **Fred Van Beuren IV, Johnny Gerber** and **Memo Rojas Sr.**, were also dominant in local racing. While there were races for more powerful and larger displacement cars such as **BMWs, Porsches, Corvettes, Mustangs** and **Camaros**, as in the rest of Central America, there were many races for small displacement sedans (called "pony", quite the opposite of the American pony cars) that included **VW Beetles** and **Japanese sedans.** Long-distance races were also held, the most important being the 1000 km of Mexico, which was included as an IMSA Camel GT round in **1974**. Veteran **Memo Rojas Sr.** won championships in Touring Cars, GTs and Formula Ford, during the decade. Formula Vee also raced in Mexico. There was a category called Formula 3 in Mexico, which had no connection with international Formula 3, as it used 1.3-liter engines, mostly Renault.

International races: a single Formula One Mexican Grand Prix was run during the decade. The 1000 km of Mexico was included as a round of the **1974** IMSA Camel GT season and Trans Am races were also held in the country in **1978** and **1979**. Formula B and Atlantic races were also held in the country.

Tracks:
Aguas Calientes
Hermanos Rodriguez (Mexico City).
Jalisco
Leon
Mazatapec
Monterey
Puebla
San Isidro

Monaco

Whether one likes it or not, the Monaco Grand Prix is by far the most glamorous car race of the world, in fact, it pioneered event marketing as a means of boosting a destination's standing. As TV coverage and reach became more widespread, the reputation of the race and the location only grew. The Grand Prix and during the 70s, the accompanying Formula 3 race, were the only racing taking place during the year, so there was no local scene to speak of. The only notable Monegasque driver of the era was **Lionel Noghes**, grandson of the race's founder, **Anthony**, often listed as a French driver. The Formula 3 race was also by far the most prestigious F-3 event of the year, often attracting close to 100 entries. A very notable Grand Prix of the era was **1972**, ran under a downpour, resulting in **Jean-Pierre Beltoise**'s single GP win and **BRM**'s last. It also lasted almost 2 and a half hours, a record for the decade.

Tracks: Montecarlo Street Circuit

Morocco

Morocco boasted a very lively international racing series during the 50s but by the 70s the importance of the sport in the country had diminished greatly. There was a Formula 3 championship in the early years of the decade and the GP de la Corniche remained an important event, albeit held sporadically, often contested by international drivers. The Casablanca GP of **1970** was won by **Claude Swietlik**, who often raced in Africa in the 70s. Races for sports cars, touring cars and formula 3 cars were held in the country during the decade and a Renault R5 Cup was held later on the decade. Some race cars were built in Morocco, such as the **Meli** and **Femenia** Formula 3 cars and the **Mertz-BMW** prototype. There was also a single seater category called Racers/Formula IV and it seems some cars were locally built – and looked downright dangerous. Many venues were used, including a hill climb.

Old cars such as this Porsche 910 still found usefulness in races in Morocco. This photo is from 1974. Andre Wicky. Author unknown.

Main races: GP de la Corniche
Kenitra
Marrakech
Meknes
Mohameddia
Nouasseur
Rabat

Tracks: Dar el Beida Ain Diab (Casablanca)
El Jadida
Tanger
Hillclimb: Gorges de Korifla

Mozambique

The Lourenco Marques track was inaugurated in **1962** and it was, for many years, included in the Springbok series, which attracted some top talent from Europe, in addition to the best South Africa had to offer in terms of Sports and Touring Cars. The country also hosted a number of rounds of the South African Formula 1 Championship but there was also local racing in Mozambique, basically for Touring Cars and GTs. Although the scene was not as lively as Angola's by the 70s, it was enthusiastic, nonetheless and it would not survive the decade for the same reason as Angola: independence from Portugal, followed by socialist fervor.
Main Race: 6 Hours of Lourenco Marques
Tracks: Lourenco Marques

New Zealand

At the onset of **1970**, New Zealand boasted three top level Grand Prix drivers, **McLaren, Hulme** and **Amon**. Additionally, during January every year, the racing community's attention was focused on New Zealand, where half of the Tasman Cup races were held every year. By **1979**, the country had not been properly represented in Grand Prix racing for years and the Tasman Cup was long gone, so all eyes were on young promise **Mike Thackwell**. A much smaller country and less populated than Australia, New Zealand nonetheless boasted many tracks and had championships throughout the decade.

The Begg was a Formula 5000 car built in New Zealand (unknown author).

The Tasman Cup champions from **1970** to **1973** were all New Zealanders, one should not forget. The main category in the beginning of the decade was Formula 5000, but as there were never enough cars of this category around, races were held with 2.5-liter old Tasman cars and 1.6 Australian Formula 2 cars, so in essence they were Formula Libre races. By **1975** the Tasman Cup was dead and New Zealand adopted Formula Atlantic, renamed Formula Pacific for obvious reasons. An international Formula Atlantic series was held in the latter part of the decade, which attracted the likes of **Keke Rosberg, Mikko Kozarovitsky, John Nicholson, Tom Gloy, Bobby Rahal, Danny Sullivan, Teo Fabi, Eje Elgh, Albert Poon** (and other Asian drivers), in addition to locals **Dave McMillan, Steve Millen, Ken Smith, Brett Riley** and **David Oxton**. Touring car races were also held in the country and Formula Ford was adopted as an entry level category early on the decade.

Tracks: Bay Park
Christchurch
Levin
Manfield
Pukekohe
Ruapana Park
Teretonga
Timaru
Wigram

Northern Ireland
An Irish Formula Libre series was held until 1973, at which point Formula 2 cars (the main staple of the series) became a tad expensive to run, so Formula Atlantic was adopted. Additionally, Formula Ford, Formula Vee and saloon car races were held and occasionally, Formula 3 races were held as well.
Tracks:
Bishopscourt   Kirkistown

Norway

Norway has never been known as a circuit racing paradise: this was rally territory, much more so even than Finland. However there was car racing activity in the country during the seventies. In addition to highly practiced ice racing, there were races for several categories of touring cars at Gardermoen Airport and Forus (usual mounts were the usual for the time, ranging from small **Fiats, NSUs, Saabs** and **Minis** to **Ford Capris, Volvos, BMWs, Skoda**, with some surprising **VW**

Beetles and old **DKW**s), plus Formula Vee championships. No international racing was practiced in the country, although one or another Swede like **Boo Brasta** showed up in some races, so that events were of a domestic nature. Many of the drivers that competed in asphalt, like **Trond Shea** and **Per Bakke**, also competed in ice racing and hill climbs. There were hill climbs in a large number venues, for touring cars and eventual Formula Vees.

Tracks: Forus
Gardermoen
Hill Climb:

Bjorkelangen	Honefoss
Elverum	Hurdal
Fagernes	Jaeren
Fetningslopet	Kongsberg
Fluberg	Larvik
Gjerdrumslopet	Lillehamer
Gjovik	Norefjell
Grenland	Oskrudveien
Hamar	Siggerud
Heistadmoen	Solvspretten
Hokksund	Trondheim

Panama

Panama's Rio Hato track held rounds of the Central American Championship during the decade. Among others, the Four Hours of Panama was held at the track. **Henry Schwartz** and **Rodrigo Teran** were the country's exponents and **Teran** made it as far as racing in the 24 Hours of **Le Mans**. Races were held for touring cars and GTs.

Tracks: Rio Hato

The first edition of the 500 km Viceroy, a prominent Central-American event at Rio Hato, Panama. Author unknown.

Paraguay

Landlocked Paraguay was a very poor country in the 70s. However, given its proximity to both Brazil and Argentina, which had lively racing scenes, the Asunción track of **Aratiri** saw action since the early part of the decade. Races were run for a variety of touring cars and sports cars. In **1973**, an Argentine Forrmula 1 race was held in Aratiri. The race was not valid for the championship and 12 cars took part. It was won by **Jorge Bianchi**, in a **Berta-Tornado**.
Tracks: Aratiri

Peru

Peru is a highly mountainous country, so that naturally, road races like **Camino de los Incas**, half race, half rally, were more adapted to the country's conditions. Nonetheless, the 6 Hours of Peru was run in many different venues in the 70s, contested by cars such as **Ford** Escort, **Lotus** Elan, **Toyota** Corolla and **Datsuns**. Although Peruvian drivers ventured abroad, international races were not common in the country. There were attempts to build local race cars in Peru during the 70s, such as the Kuntur P-1 and Proto-Rex, the latter a car built by the Araneta brothers. Both cars raced in the 6 Hours of Peru and both actually competed internationally, in Ecuador and Colombia. Peru also had Formula Vee races.

Main Race: 6 Hours of Peru, Camino de los Incas

Tracks: Agua Dulce
Atocongo
Campo de Marte
Canete (road race)
Collique
La Herradura
Pasamayo
Real Felipe
Santa Rosa

The Proto-Rex was one of a few race cars built in Peru during the 70s. (Unknown author)

Philippines

The Philippines Grand Prix, an international race, was created in **1973**, at the **Greenhills** track and international races were run in the country, for both single seaters and touring cars during the decade. Among the winners of this race were **John MacDonald** and **Graeme Lawrence**. Pilipino drivers often drove in other Asian countries, including the Macau Grand Prix. The Philippines government banned motorsport in the latter part of the decade, citing oil shortages.

Tracks: Green Hills   Luneta

Poland

In the early part of the decade Poland had events for race cars (single-seater), locally produced **Promot** and **Polonia**, most equipped with Ford engines, others with **Wartburgs**, as well as Touring cars. The smaller engine classes were dominated by **Polski-Fiats**, while in large engine classes there were **Alfas** and **BMW**s. Locally built **Syrenas** also appeared. By **1973**, faster machinery such as **Porsche** 911 were seen in Polish circuits and as in most of Iron Curtain countries, single-seaters were mostly **Estonias**. The **Torun** track hosted several rounds of the Peace and Friendship for Formula Easter and Touring Cars, towards the end of the decade. An international Formula 3 race was held in Szczecin, in 1970, with international drivers and cars.

Tracks: Orneta   Szczecin
Poznam   Torun

Portugal

The Palma was a Formula Vee built and raced in Portugal.

The high point of the 70s was the inauguration of the **Estoril** racetrack, in **1972**, Portugal's first specific purpose race circuit, but on the other hand, by **1973** the last international edition of the **Vila Real** street race was run, which was the most important race of the country. The authorities prohibited racing in the country for a while, in **1974**, in the wake of the oil crisis mixed with political ideologies. **Estoril** held a few Formula 2 Championship events during the decade, plus other events. The local scene consisted of races for sports cars, touring cars, Formula Vee and Formula Ford but national circuit championships were not held in 1974 and 1978. Veteran **Mario Cabral** continued to be the country's most important and internationally recognized driver, although **Ernesto Neves** won a number of

championships, before retiring in 1973, to an accident involving the owner of his racing team. Another highlight during the decade was the BIP Team that raced 2-liter **Lola** sports cars across Europe, with **Carlos Gaspar**. The team planned to go Formula 2 racing in **1974** but a new socialist government halted these "bourgeois" plans. There was also a proposed Portuguese Formula 1 car, the **Marinho,** which did not make beyond the planning stages. The Serra da Estrela hill climb was part of the European Hill Climb Championship. At any rate, Aurora produced a Formula Vee and created updated bodies for old Porsches such as the 908, which were raced until late in the decade.
Main Race: Vila Real
International Races: Formula 2, World Sports Car Championship, ETCC, European Hill Climb Championship.
Tracks: Costa Verde
Estoril
Monte Castelo
Vila do Conde

Vila Real
Hill climb: Rampa Da Falterra

Serra da Estrela

Puerto Rico

There was quite a bit of motor racing activity in the neighboring Bahamas in the 1960s and Puerto Rico took some advantage of the attention. A Grand Prix of Puerto Rico was held in 1962, with major drivers appearing but by the 70s the Bahamas Speed Week was long gone and Puerto Rico was no longer on the international radar. Notwithstanding, the local scene continued and the most prominent race was the 3 Hours of Caguas, where cars such as **Porsche, Corvette** and **Ford Capri** would fight for honors. The first edition of the event was held in **1978**, with the participation of teams from the US, Venezuela, Haiti, Trinidad, Panama, Costa Rica, Colombia and the Dominican Republic. **Anasco** and **Salinas** were other venues used by local racers during the decade. Drivers such as **Diego Febles** (born in Cuba), **Freije brothers**, **Roberto Bengoa** and **Bonky Hernandez** excelled.
Main Races: 3 Hours of Caguas
Tracks: Anasco   Caguas   Salinas

Rhodesia

Rhodesia's racing was basically tied to South African racing. In addition to rounds of the South African Formula 1 Championship, Rhodesia also hosted Springbok series races, for sports and touring cars and there races and championships held for Formula Vee, Sports Cars and Saloon (Touring) cars.
International races: South African Formula 1 and Springbok series.
Tracks: Bulawayo   Donnybrook

Romania

The country's forte was rallying but there were also speed races and championships in Romania. **Renaults** were particularly strong and the country, although part of the Iron Curtain, did not participate in the region's racing to any great extent. Drivers such as **Eugen Ionescu "Genu" Cristea**, who won many championships during the decade, **Zoltan Tomay** and **Florin Popescu** ruled the scene. Speed drivers also tended to take part in rallyes.

Tracks: Bucarest Pitesti
Cluj Napoca
Feleac

Racing in the streets of Bucarest, 1976. (Photo by Namtanu Valentin)

Russia

Let it be known that since the early part of the decade Russia had a Formula 1 championship! Not exactly what you are thinking but that is what they wanted us to think in the Western world. The cars were not close even to Argentina's F1 in terms of speed, eons from international F1, although engines had 3-liter capacity. These were **Wartburg, Gas** and **Moskvich** engined cars, mostly mounted on Estonia chassis, even though **Yuri Andreev** managed to sneak a **De Sanctis-Cosworth** in the category. **Moskvich** G5s were also seen during the decade, even though it was an older, **1968** car. There was also Formula 2, a Formula 3, a Formula 4 (**IzhJupiter** motorcycle engined) categories, plus Touring Cars. While the Czechs were more laid back about bourgeois machinery, Russians stuck to the party line and even touring car races featured mostly **Moskvich, VAS** and **GAS** – not even other Eastern European cars were allowed, so that Russian cars always won! Although Formula Easter had been established by **1974**, the Russians continued with their four-tier single seater set-up. The top category, Formula 1, had a newcomer in **1974**, the **MAD**, which joined the **Estonia** and **Moskvich** G5. Categories with small number of entries were consolidated in some events. By **1977**, the categories were changed to Formula Easter, Formula 3 and Formula Junior, which was really the new name for Formula 4.

Tracks: Luzhniki Neuskoe Koltso
Nami Nevaring

Russian purpose made race cars were built and raced in the decade, such as the Moskvich G5 (Yuri Terenetskyi archives)

Scotland

Lively Modified Sports Cars action at Ingliston, 1971. Photo by Colin Lourie

Considering that Scotland gave the world both **Jim Clark** and **Jackie Stewart**, one would expect a very intense, high level racing scene in the country. However, Scotland was mostly about club racing, before, in and after the 70s. This shows that a highly developed and intense local race culture is not necessary for the emergence of excellent drivers. **Ingliston** hosted races for single seaters, including Formula 3, Atlantic, Ford and Libre, touring and sports cars, including

197

BMW Counties one-make series and rounds of the British Saloon Car Championship. Some noteworthy outsiders like **Eddie Cheever, John Watson, Kenny Acheson, Norman Dickinson** raced there. **Knockhill**, the country's current top circuit, was inaugurated in **1974**, as a short 1.3 km motorcycle track, was eventually expanded hosting car races as well. The real bread and butter of Scottish racing was Stock Car racing, a bit different than U.S. practice. There were four basic categories: Supertox, weird looking, front engined contraptions equipped with a variety of engines, from **Ford** to **Mercedes**; Saloon Stocks, mostly small, tatty cars ranging from **Ford** Cortinas, Anglias, Escorts and Capris, Imps, Minis, **FIAT**, **VW** Beetles, old **Austins** and even a **Daimler** limousine; Hot Rods, nicer looking saloons; Formula 2 Stock-cars, smaller contraptions. Some of the cars were beat-up beyond recognition and the fairly detailed results found on a website do not identify the cars. Hundreds of cars took part in championships held in ovals all over the country and British and German drivers visited on occasion. Drivers from the discipline tended not to migrate to other more traditional racing and there was a group of stars, including **Malcolm Paterson, Kenny Ireland, Hamish Buchanan, Les Cay** and **Robert Bruce**. At any rate, the events were fairly animated, crowds of 8,000 common and there was some night racing.

Track: Armadale
Cowdenbeath
Crimond
Hednesford
Ingliston
Ipswich
Knockhill
Motherwell

Senegal

The 6 Hours of Dakar was held during the decade, often attracting European racers such as **Carlo Facetti, Raymond Tourol** and **Jean-Pierre Jarier**. Local drivers also participated in this race for touring and GT cars. Not much information could be found on other races in the country at the time of writing, except references that claim such races were held during the decade. The creation of the Paris-Dakar Rally simply made the 6 Hours unimportant.
Tracks: Dakar

Start of the 6 hours of Dakar, 1974.

Singapore

A Singaporean Grand Prix was held for Asian Formula 2/Pacific many times during the 70s, at the Thompson Street Circuit. Not as glamorous as today's iteration of the race, the races did feature local drivers, who often did well in Asian racing. As Macau, a city-country, it was not possible to close-off the roads for frequent racing.

Touring car events were also held there. Singaporean drivers also featured well regionally and are often referred as Malaysian.
Tracks: Thompson Street Circuit

South Africa

That South Africa was among the most important racing countries of the world in the 70s is unquestionable. Among other things, South Africa was the only country that had a true Formula 1 championship besides the World Championship, until the country wisely adopted Formula Atlantic for the **1976** season (Argentina and Russia had categories called Formula 1 that were not at all similar to international Formula 1). In fact, the number of Formula 1 cars in the championship was dwindling with every passing year and grids were always boosted by Formula 2 and Formula 5000 cars. The last South African "F1" race had only 8 cars on the grid. This oddity raised the country's prestige as a racing mecca, sometimes a tad exaggerated. Notwithstanding, besides **Jody Scheckter** who did not race in South African Formula 1 at all, many of the country's representatives are noteworthy, such as **Ian Scheckter (March** F-1 works driver in **1977), David Charlton, Eddie Keizan** (who briefly raced in Europe), **Guy Tumner, Tony Martin, Paddy Driver, Desire Wilson, Peter de Klerk, Basil Van Rooyen, Roy Klomfass** and others, who also raced successfully in neighboring countries such as Mozambique, Angola and Rhodesia. Besides its top series, there were also plenty of touring car races in the many South African racetracks: top former F1 star **Dave Charlton** left single-seaters in **1978**, choosing tourers instead. The Springbok series for sports cars was a popular year-end event, drawing many prominent international drivers, who were also able to race in neighboring Mozambique and Rhodesia but it did not survive beyond **1973**, another victim of the oil crisis.

South Africa was the only country to boast having a local F-1 series in the early 70s. Here David Charlton sorts out his problems at the 1972 South African Grand Prix. That is the car he used in the national championship (Photo by Russell Whitworth)

International racing: The South African Grand Prix was a mainstay of the Formula 1 calendar during the decade and the 1000 km of Kyalami were part of the **1974** World Manufacturers Championship. The Springbok series was run until **1973**.
Main Races: 9 Hours of Kyalami, 1000 km of Kyalami

Tracks: Aldo Scribante
Brandkop
Goldfields
Killarney
Kyalami
Pietermaritzburg
Welkom

Spain

In addition to many international events held during the decade, including Formula 1 Grand Prix, Spain boasted a reasonably developed domestic scene, with circuit races and hill climbs for sports cars, touring cars and even its own single-seater series, Formula 1430, named after a **Seat** model. Most Formula 1430 cars were built by **Selex**, a local manufacturer but a few other builders emerged during the decade. A number of venues were used, including Tenerife in the Canary Islands but Madrid's **Jarama** tended to concentrate most international and high-level races. A large number of hill climb venues were used during the decade and Montseny was a European championship fixture.

International races: In addition to the Spanish Grand Prix for Formula 1, Spain held races for the European Formula 2 Championship, European Formula 3 Championship, European Touring Car Championship, European 2 Liter Championship, European Hill Climb Championship.

Tracks: Alcaniz Guadalope
Circuito Calafat
Granollers
Jarama
Montjuich
Montserrat (Valencia)
Ofra
Tenerife (Street)

Hill Climbs:
Agua Garcia
Arrate
Bien Aparecida
Canencia
Castro de Beiro
Chantada
Coll Formich
Cruz Verde
Cuesta a Prades
El Fitu
Formigal
Galapagar
Garb
Gran Parada
Gruta de Las Maravillas
La Esperanza
La Mina
Mirador de Gulmar
Monte Jalzquibel
Montes de Malaga
Montseny
Morcuera
Naranco
Navarra
Nuestra Senora Los Angeles
Picos de Urbion
Piqueras
Puertito de Guimar
Puerto del Pico
Puig Mayor
Rabassada
Ricaveral
San Feiju de Codenas
San Felice de Codinas
San Miguel de Abona
Santo Emiliano
Sotillo
Trasiera
Urbasa
Veleta
Villaflor

Pepe Monsoon about to win a hillclimb in the Canary Islands, 1973 (unknown author)

Sri Lanka(Ceylon)

The Arpico Special Ford was much feared in the Indian Subcontinent. Photo Eshan Pieris collection.

Quite an isolated country, **Sri Lanka** (named **Ceylon** until **1972**), had some racing interaction with India, which had a more developed racing scene. Indians went to race in Sri Lanka and vice versa. The country's main exponent was **David Pieris**, who drove a feared **Ford** Special, called **Arpico**. **Pieris** not only won the Sri Lankan Grand Prix several times in the 70s but also won the Madras Grand Prix of 1974, in India. Sri Lankan meets, with enthusiastic crowds from 25,000 to 100,000 people, included motorcycle and car races. Most cars are called "specials" but seemed to be from highly to slightly modified street cars. A peculiarity of the

Sri Lankan GP, held at **Katunayake** airstrip, was that the co-organizer of the race was the Sri Lankan Air Force.
Venues: Katunayake

Sweden

Sweden produced many talented drivers in the 60s and 70s, following **Jo Bonnier**'s international path. The main domestic series was run for Formula 3 cars but there were series for Formula Super Vee, Formula Vee, Formula Ford, Touring Cars, Sports Cars, in addition to **Volvo** and **Camaro** one-make series. The country lost its two top drivers in **1978, Ronnie Peterson** and **Gunnar Nilsson**, which somewhat dampened the country's enthusiasm for the sport but there were many other aces such as **Reine Wisell**, **Conny Andersson**, **Eje Elgh**, **Anders Oloffson, Stefan Johansson, Boo Brasta** who featured well in local and international races. Anderstorp, where the Formula 1 Grand Prix was held, was located in a tiny town, with very little infrastructure. That might explain the demise of the race after the death of both **Peterson** and **Nilsson** in 1978. Sweden did have a healthy club racing scene in the 70s, in the form of the SSK Series. While in 1970 SSK events had about 10 entries, by mid-decade some events had as many as 250 participants. Dozens of categories were featured in SSK during the decade, usually, about 6 or 7 at any given time. There were usually 4 or 5 touring car races with engines of different sizes, races for Sports Cars (even a Porsche 917 raced in SSK for a few seasons) and a few single seater categories, mostly Formula Vee, Formula Super Vee and Formula Ford. Special categories called Formula 1300 and 1600 allowed Formula Fords and Vees to race against cars equipped with **BMW** and **Alfa Romeo** engines. Among other categories, there was a Ladies Mini Cup, a Renault R5 Cup, single make tournaments for Camaros and **Volvo**s and Sports 2000 was added later on the decade. Some established Swedish stars such as **Conny Andersson** and **Freddy Kottulinski** raced sporadically and some future stars, such as **Slim Borgudd** and **Eje Elgh** got their first taste of racing in SSK. Most drivers were Swedish but Norwegian, Danish, Finnish and even British drivers raced in the series. Several locally built sports cars such as the **Bodola** and **Minotte** raced exclusively in Sweden. Quite a few Swedish Formula Vees also raced in the series.

International races: the main race held in Sweden was the Swedish Formula 1 Grand Prix held there from **1973** to **1978**. Rounds of the European Formula 2 Championship, European Touring Car Championship, European Formula 3 Championship, European Formula 5000 Championship, European 2 Liter Championship, European Formula Super Vee Championship, were run in Sweden's many tracks during the decade.

Tracks: Anderstorp
Falkenberg
Karlskoga
Kinnekullering
Knutstorp
Mantorp Park

Switzerland

The country most famously banned circuit racing in the wake of the **1955** Le Mans disaster, although hill climbs were still allowed (!!!). Notwithstanding, there were many Swiss championships during the 70s for single seaters, Formula 2 then Formula 3, as well as sports cars, with races being held in neighboring France, Italy, Austria, Germany and even Liechtenstein, plus some hill climbs and slaloms held in Swiss territory. Many Swiss drivers, such as **Clay Regazzoni, Jo Siffert, Silvio Moser, Herbert Muller** and **Marc Surer** achieved notoriety in several disciplines, including Formula 1. There were many race teams and even car builders in the country during the decade, the most famous being **Sauber**.

Main Hill Climbs: Ayen Azere Oberhallau
Guggersbach Ollon-Villars
Gurnigel Payerne
Kerezenberg St Peterzell
Marchairuz St Ursanne

Sauber began building race cars in 1970. This is the C1 that raced mostly in hill climbs.

Trinidad & Tobago

Trinidad's racetrack **Wallerfield** had seen action since 1958, which intensified in the 70s as racing in the region evolved. Races at the track attracted fairly large and enthusiastic crowds, as one must remember entertainment options were few at the time, there and pretty much elsewhere. There were four Groups: 1 (unmodified cars), 2 (modified), 3 (modified and lightened) and 4 (single seaters). These Group 4 Formula Caribbean cars (**March, Ensign, Brabham**), used 1.3 to 1.6 liter engines. There is plenty of footage of races at the venue at the time, for apparently they had a deal with local TV. Lively races were run for touring cars, including local hero **Frankie Boodran**'s **Ford** Escort and other small sedans. Caribbean Championship races were also held there during the 70s, in fact there was plenty of interaction with places such as Barbados and Guyana.
Tracks: Wallerfield

Turkey

The first official rally in Turkey took place only in 1968 and rallying remained the most popular motorsport during the decade. There were, however, some circuit races in the country for touring cars, in at least two venues, nothing substantial or international. It is noteworthy that a Turkish car, the **Anadol,** raced in such events as well as in rallies. Other brands, most importantly **Renault** and **Ford**, also raced.
Tracks:
Karting
Tuzla

Ukraine

Many rounds of the Soviet Championship and the Peace and Friendship were held at Chajka. In fact, the track was by far the site of most Soviet Union events in the 70s.
Tracks: Chajka

Uruguay

Start of 6 hours of El Pinar, 1973 (Author unknown)

Uruguayans have always been enthusiastic about their racing, with a more laid-back approach than their neighbors Brazil and Argentina. Thus, the scene basically lived on the shadow of these two countries. Most regional races were touring car events, including European vehicles and Argentine products but there were categories such as Standard B featuring single-seaters made out of old car parts. While the re-inauguration of El Pinar in **1975** featured a race of Brazilian Division 3 cars (mostly highly tuned **VW** Beetles) rounds of Argentinian championships were held in Uruguay, including rounds for the top Argentinian Formula 1 category. One such race, valid for the 1976 championship was held at El Pinar and won by

Pedro Passadore. The **1977** race was not valid for the championship and it was also won by **Passadore.** Uruguay's top driver in the decade was indeed **Passadore**, who also raced in British and Italian Formula 3 in **1973** and **1974**. The Gran Premio 19 Capitales was a major road race.

International Racing: Argentine Formula 1
Tracks: El Pinar
Paysandu
Punta Fria
Rivera
Salto
San Jose
Tamarinas

USA

The sheer amount of racing done in the USA is overwhelming. In addition to being a country of continental proportions, it was by far the wealthiest, it had the top two car manufacturers in the world at the time, a very large population and commercial sponsorship had been widely practiced for many years. Add to that a very large number of venues and you soon realize you are talking about thousands upon thousands of races during 10 years. To make it simple, let's break it down into oval racing and road courses. There were hundreds of oval tracks in the country at the time, many of which are no longer in operation. Some have been the victim of urban sprawl, others remain ghost tracks. NASCAR and USAC were the two major exponents of oval track racing, one for touring cars (stock cars) and the other single seaters. In addition to running the Winston Cup and the National Championship, NASCAR and USAC were also sanctioning bodies, meaning they oversaw several other championships, tracks and drivers throughout the country. NASCAR had the Winston Cup but also ran NASCAR West, plus over 100 championships in racetracks across the country, for stock cars and modifieds. USAC, in addition to Indy cars, also had its own Stock Car championship, plus oversaw sprint cars and midgets all over the country. It also co-sanctioned the US Formula 5000 championship for a while. Additionally, ARCA also sanctioned mostly stock car races in several tracks all over the country. ASA, founded in 1968, also sanctioned racing at short tracks and there were other smaller and regional sanctioning bodies. By the way, many of these tracks were dirt tracks, a few paved. There were also small independent tracks by the dozens, which ran their own shows. Many of these held races every weekend, weather permitting, for local drivers. As for road courses, SCCA and IMSA were the sanctioning bodies. SCCA ran a few professional series, such as the Trans Am, Can Am, Formula 5000, Formula Super Vee and Formula B. All of these had their ups and downs, for SCCA was primarily a club for amateur racers – a huge club at that. In fact, it had thousands of members, who could choose about twenty categories that included Formula A (5000), Formula B (close to Formula 2), Formula C, Formula Ford, Formula Vee, A to D prototypes, A to H Production cars, plus GTs. The aim of these fine folks was competing in the Run-Off at the end of the year, in Road Atlanta, in Georgia, the Oscar of SCCA racing. IMSA was the newest of the sanctioning bodies, having started in **1971**. Its main championship was the Camel GTO and GTU championship (later GTX), a different take on the Trans Am concept. There was also a Showroom Stock category, races for small touring cars such as **Mazdas, AMC, Datsun, Alfa Romeo, BMW, Buick, Ford, Honda, Chevrolet, Oldsmobile**, plus an attempt to co-sanction the CASC Formula Atlantic series in **1976**, an arrangement which lasted a single year. IMSA made steady progress during the decade and although the main championship was dominated by **Porsche** cars as the European GT championship, **BMW's** challenge started in **1975** and a **Chevy** Monza won the championships in **1976** and **1977**. The calendar comprised long distance races such as the **24 Hours of Daytona** and **12 Hours of Sebring** and sprints.

Thousands of sprint car races were held in short tracks all over the US. Photo by Rob Neuzel.

International Races: All major U.S. professional races welcomed properly qualified foreign drivers, so in essence, they were all international. In fact, hundreds of drivers from Canada, South and Central America, Europe, Africa, Asia and Australia/New Zealand competed in US domestic races, mostly in road courses. Many 70s Can-Am and Formula 5000 titles were won by foreigners (**Hulme, Oliver, Redman, McRae, Scheckter, Hobbs, Cannon, Tambay, Ickx, Jones**) and even NASCAR had a surprising number of foreign drivers competing in the Winston Cup during the decade. The country also hosted Formula 1 Grand Prix during the decade (the only country to have two GPs from **1976** to **1979**) and World Manufacturers Championship races at Watkins Glen, Daytona and Sebring.

Main Races: Indy 500, Daytona 500, 24 Hours of Daytona, 12 Hours of Sebring
Tracks:

Airborne
Albany-Saratoga
All American
Allen County Coliseum
Altamont
Anderson
Angell Park
Ascot
Atlanta Motor Speedway
Augusta
Avilla
Baer Field Speedway
Beltsville
Berlin
Bloomington
Bowman-Gray Stadium
Brainerd
Brewerton
Bridgehampton
Bristol
Bryar
Cajon
California State Fairgrounds
Capital
Castle Rock

Catamount
Cayuga County Fair
Charlotte
Chase
Clovis
Columbia Speedway
Community Park
Coos Bay
Craig Road
Darlington
Davenport
Dayton
Daytona
Dells
Donnybrooke
Dover Downs
Duquoin State Fairgrounds
Eldora
Elko
Eugene
Evans Mills
Evergreen
Fairgrounds Raceway
Flamboro
Flat Rock

Fonda
Franklin County
Freeport
Fulton
Golden Sands
Greenville Pickens
Grundy County
Hales
Hallet
Hamburg Fairgrounds
Hartford
Hawkeye Downs
Heildelberg
Henry's
Hickory
Holland
I-70 Speeedway
Illiana
Illinois State Fairgrounds
Indianapolis
Indianapolis Raceway Park
International Raceway Park
Iowa State Fairgrounds
Islip
Jacksonville
Jantzen
Joliet
Joseph Meyer
Kingsport
Knoxville
Kokomo
La Crosse Fairgrounds
Laguna Seca
Lake Geneva
Lakewood
Lancaster
Langhorne
Langley Field
Lawton
Lee USA
Limaland
Lime Rock
Lonesome Pine
Long Beach
Lorain County
Madera
Madison
Manzanita
Martinsville
Metrolina
Meyer
Michigan
Mid America
Mid Ohio

Middle Georgia
Milwaukee
Minnesota State Fairgrounds
Missouri State Fairgrounds
Monadnock
Mount Clemens
Music City Motorsports
Myrtle Beach
Nashville
Nazareth
Nelson Ledges
New Asheville
New Bremen
New Egypt
New Smyrna
North Carolina
North Carolina Fairgrounds
North Wilkesboro
Oklahoma State Fairgrounds
Olathe Naval Air Station
Old Dominion
Ontario
Oswego
Owosso
Oxford Plains
Ozark Empire Fairgrounds
Pacific Raceway
Peotone Fairgrounds
Phoenix
Plainville
Pocono
Reading Fairgrounds
Redwood Acres
Richmond
Riverhead
Riverside
Riverside Parkway
Road America
Road Atlanta
Rockford
Rogue Valley
Rolla
Rolling Wheels
Sacramento
Salem
San Gabriel Valley
San Jose
Santa Fe
Saugus
Savannah
Sears Point
Sebring
Seekonk
Seelingsgrove

Seymour	Thunder Road
Shady Bowl	Toledo
Shangri-la	Tomahawk
Sharon	Trenton
Shasta	Tri-County
Sierra Mesa	Trumbull County
Skagit	Tucson
Smoky Mountain	Umatilla
South Bay	Utica
South Boston	Vallejo
Southside	Virginia International
Spanaway	Waterford
Sportsdrome	Watkins Glen
Springfield	Wausan Fairgrounds
Stafford	West Virginia International
Star	Westboro
Stockton 99	Williams Grove
Summit Point	Winchester
Talladega	Wisconsin International
Terre Haute	Wyoming County
Texas World	Yakima
Thompson	

Hill Climb: Pikes Peak

Among several series ran in the US during the 70s were single-make series. This is Mike White driving a VW Rabbit in the Rabbit Bilstein series, 1979. Photo Mike White collection.

Venezuela

Venezuela had an active local scene which included Formula Ford, Formula Vee, Touring Cars, Formula Libre. Although the country became more enthusiastic about motorcycle racing because of **Johnny Cecotto**'s achievements, there were attempts to get Venezuela into the international car racing circuit: an American Formula B event won by **Andrea de Adamich** in **1973**, plus a Formula Atlantic event won by Venezuelan **Bobby Dennet** in **1974**. Venezuela was also originally included in the Formula 2 Temporada of 1972 but in the end races were run only in Brazil. There were long distance races for touring cars, in which a variety of cars were used, such as **AMC** Hornet, **Opel, Ford Cortina, Renaults, FIATs**. Some old 50s **Ferraris** were still raced in Fuerza Libre, where competition could be a **VW** Beetle that really was a single seater covered by a Beetle body, Camaros, Corvettes and a **Lamborghin**i Miura. Venezuela also had Formula Ford and Formula Vee competition. Some Venezuelans ventured out of the country, such as **Oscar Notz**, who won Formula Ford races in Britain in the late 70s, **Juan Cochesa** who raced in both Formula Atlantic in North America and Formula 2 in Europe and **Ernesto Soto** drove in IMSA. There was interaction with neighboring countries, mostly Eastern Colombia and possibly Guyana. Some race cars were built in Venezuelan, such as the single seaters **Piovesan** and **El Gran Caribe** and the **Natalini Special**, a prototype.

Ernesto Soto was a top Venezuelan driver in the 70s. The car is Lotus 41. Photo provided by Enrique Soto.

Tracks: Autodromo San Carlos, Caracas
Turagua
Maracaibo (La Chinita)

Wales

Only club racing took place in Llandow throughout the decade, including saloons, Formula Ford and Formula Libre.
Tracks: Llandow

West Germany

Although **Michael Schumacher** and a host of other superior German Formula 1 drivers would appear on the scene many years later, Germany has always been a country with plentiful of motor racing action way before them. Germans always liked touring car races, which helps understanding the eventual popularity of the

DTM. During the 70s there were the DARM and eventually the DRM. The DARM was structured with many classes, while the DRM only had two divisions. The latter was at first a touring car championship, then in **1977** it adopted Group 5 (Silhouette) regulations, although some group 2 racers still made up the numbers. In the early part of the decade there were many stand-alone events, not only at the established tracks, **Nürburgring, Norisring** and **Hockenheim but** also in a number of airport (Flugplatz) tracks spread around the country. The number of such events diminished as the years went by. At a local level, there was a German Formula 3 championship for much of the decade, in addition to European and German Formula Super Vee and Vee, Formula Ford, Sports Cars and GTs, plus a large number of hill climb events all across the country. **Hockenheim** deserves special mention among tracks. The venue had a large quantity of major events during the course of 70s, in fact, as many as 3 rounds of the European Formula 2 Championship in a single year (an amazing total of 20 times during the decade), plus no less than 17 Interserie races.

International racing: Germany hosted, during the seventies, international racing for Formula 1, Formula 2, European Formula 3, Formula 5000, World Manufacturers Championship, World Sports Car Championship, Interserie, European 2-Liter Championship, European GT Championship, European Touring Car Championship, European Formula Super Vee. The DRM races always accepted foreign entries, in fact, some of its races were held outside Germany, like today's DTM.

Main Race: 24 Hours of Nürburgring, Marathon de la Route, 1000 km of Nürburgring

Tracks:
Augsburg-Muhlhalsen
Avus
Bremgarten (airport)
Burbach
Diepholz (airport)
Erding
Fassberg
Geilenkirchen
Hockenheim
Kassel-Calden (airport)
Kaufbeuren (airport)
Kunzelau-Niederstetten (airport)
Mainz Finthen (airport)
Mendig (Airport)

Neubiberg (airport)
Neuhausen
Niederstetten
Norisring
Nürburgring
Rheinhessen (airport)
Saarlouis (street)
Sembach (airport)
Sylt (airport)
Trier-Gruneberg
Ulm-Laupheim
Ulm-Leipheim
Ulm-Mengen
Wunstorf (airport)

Hill Climbs:
Altmuthal
Auerberg
Augusta
Bayerwald
Bruckberg
Dillkreis
Edelstein
Eggberg
Ellerburg
Eurohill
Frankenwald
Freiburg-Schaunisland
Griesbacher

Haldenhof
Happurg
Harz Bergpreis
Hauenstein
Heidelstein
Heilbronn
Homburger
Jura
Kalter Wangen
Kreuzberg Merzig
Landshut
Liztal
Lorch

Manberger	Shluchtern
Mickhausen	Schwabische Alb Neuffen
Mullacken	Schwan
Nibelungen	Sembach
Oberallgau	Spessart
Oberpfalz	Steribis
Ratisbona	Sudelfeld
Rheingau	Sutzhal
Rheingold	Taubensuhl
Rossfeld	Taunus
Rotenburg/Fulda	Ulm
Rusel	Unterfranken
Sackingen/Eggberg	Wallberg
Samerbergrennen	Wasgas
Sauerland	Zotzenbach
Schottenring	

The Barth/Doren not quite Porsche 935 finished 13th at the 1000 km of Nürburgring, 1977. (Jurgen Barth collection)

Yugoslavia

While Yugoslavia was a communist country in the 70s, Tito, the country's ruler, was not aligned with Moscow. This meant that although Yugoslavia was not entirely connected to the European racing world, the cars used in Yugoslavian races were not necessarily government mandated **Moskvichs** but rather, **Alfa Romeos, BMWs, Fiats, Fords, Renaults, Steyr Puchs** and Abarths, as well as local **Zastavas**. Formula Super Vee events were also run in Yugoslavia late in the decade, most cars used were Austrian **Kaimanns**. Some races had upwards of 81 cars fighting for a place under the sun in front of 10,000 people, such as in Lovcen, **1972**. Among the top drivers were **Robert Lang, Sead Ali Hodzic** and **Drago Regvart**. Sead actually tried British Formula 3 later in the decade, while **Regvart**,

211

whenever possible, would take part in ETCC races abroad, actually doing a full season in **1977**. **Francy Jerancic** was even more ambitious: he tried European Formula 2 in **1975**, without success, and tested a F-1 Surtees TS-16.

Tracks: Aranjelovac
Butmir
Gorhanci (Slovenia)
Kragujevac
Hill Climbs: Zagreb
Lovcen
Usce
Zagreb

Zambia

There was indeed racing in Zambia, previously known as Norther Rhodesia, which became independent in 1964, in two known venues, **Ndola Park** and **Lawrence Allen Circuit** and perhaps two others, **Bennets** and **Garneton**. The cars that raced there during the 70s were **Lotus Elan, Alfas, Ford Cortinas** and even a home-bred creation, the **Costa-Alfa Romeo**. The sports car was built by two Italian engineers **Remo** and **Alberto Costa and** had no competition, so it cleaned up between the late 60s to **1973**, when the two brothers (who also raced the car) sold it **Sergio Pavan**. A photo appears on the manufacturers section of the book.
Tracks: Lawrence Allen Circuit
Ndola Park

MANUFACTURERS

PRODUCTION CARMAKERS

This, I hope, is as complete as possible a list of production car makers that competed in racing worldwide during the 70s. As this book does not include Historic Racing, the likes of Bugatti and Vanwall will not be found in it. Cars that appeared only in rallies are also omitted. There is a separate – and much longer – list of specialty race car builders, right after this list.

In this second edition I expanded the information provided, indicating in which countries these car makes were raced. This is not by any means a complete list, for one thing, race reports and results often omit the vast majority of participants.

The reader will readily notice that the most widely used cars in racing were small engined, inexpensive cars such as **FIATs, Mini-Coopers, Imps, VWs, Toyotas, Renaults**. This is not because they were the best cars available but rather, they were affordable. They usually won their class but rarely won overall.

You will note names such as **Matra, Ligier** and **Lotus** in this list, for they also built road cars, besides their purebred racing activities. In fact, **Matra** had very ambitious plans to build a proper super car, which never came to fruition. So the Baghera and Djet constitute its main road car heritage.

There are some oddities in this list that deserve at least passing mention.

You will note both **Auto Union** and **DKW** in this list. Both brands were no longer manufactured anywhere by the beginning of this decade. Some **DKWs** could still be seen at racetracks as late as 1978, in Norway, earlier in Holland and Brazil and even in early European 2-Liter Championship races, which took in large number of GT cars to boost up the numbers. The **Auto Union** continued to race in Argentina, in the Turismo Nacional category. It so happens that these cars were branded **Auto Union** in Argentina and built by a company in Santa Fe, while sold as **DKWs** by Vemag in Brazil.

I found at least one instance of a British **Daimler** 250 starting races in the SCCA run-offs, mostly doing very well for several years. No sight of **Bentleys** or **Cadillacs**, cars that became common in racetracks in latter days. However, at least one **Rolls-Royce** Silver Shadow participated in an "all-comers" Escort Mexico Challenge touring car race in England in 1971. The world has changed, as luxury car builders now do want a sporting image, something they dreaded in the 70s. Even **Mercedes** was very careful about their motoring activities in the 70s, as you can see elsewhere in the book. If you are wondering about **Lincoln**, well, at least one raced in the Pikes Peak Hill Climb.

Some globally marketed mass producers, such as **Peugeot**, tried as much as possible to dissociate themselves from a circuit racing image, although **Peugeots** raced successfully in Argentina's Turismo Nacional category and in Uruguay and did very well in rallying. Many of the manufacturers represented in this list had no direct participation whatsoever in the preparation of cars.

Some companies that did build street going sports cars, namely **Maserati** and **Lamborghini**, are mostly absent from entry lists. As late as 1972 these cars were not homologated by the FIA as GTs, being produced in very low numbers and simply could not take part in Group 4 races; as prototypes they would be totally outclassed.

Yet I did find some instances were these cars appeared in racing.

One **Maserati** was an old 300S, which was fielded by **Salvador Cianciaruso** in a few long distance events in 1970 and 1971, in Brazil, sometimes with bodywork that prevented the car from being identified as a Maser. It was very slow. **Cianciaruso** ended up building a Formula Vee later on the decade, that won on occasion and looked a bit like a **Ferrari** 312 T. Dutchman **Henk Bosman** also fancied racing a **Maserati** Birdcage in assorted races in Europe, once allegedly equipped with an **Alfa Romeo** engine! There were always some phantom Le Mans entries, cars one knows little about and one such entry comprised a couple of **Maserati** Boras entered by ETS Thepenier for the 1973 race. Whether this was a serious entry one will never know, the cars never arrived, although Auto Sprint discussed the matter in a few articles. **Maserati** engines did equip **Ligiers** for a while.

As for the **Lamborghini**...Racing events in Brazil were still very sparse in 1970, even with the reopening of Interlagos. A riverside race against the clock was run in Sao Paulo. Among the entered cars was a **Lamborghini** Miura, owned by Alcides Diniz. You might recognize the last name. If you are wondering, **Alcides** was future Formula 1 driver **Pedro Diniz**'s uncle. Alcides and brother Abilio raced with great effect an **Alfa Romeo** GTAM in 1970 and 1971, winning two important races. **Alcides** did not win that day but his exploit merited inclusion in this book. A **Lamborghini** engine found its way into a **Furia** chassis in the 500 km of Interlagos international race of 1972, discussed further in the book. It is not clear whether this engine came from this car. Also in 1970, French driver Thierry Gore drove a Miura "barchetta" (with the roof cut off) in local French events, once earning a second place. Two **Lamborghinis** were entered at Le Mans. A Urraco was entered by Andre Wicky/Florian Vetsch/Aechlsimann for the 1974 race and a 400GT entered by **Paul Rily/Roger Leveve**, actually practiced but did not qualify with a time of 5m28s. A Miura also raced in Venezuela.

The old Masers were not the only old cars I found racing as contemporary racers. A **Studebaker** was still racing in Colombia in the early part of the decade and 50s **Ferraris** raced in Venezuela and a Traction Avant **Citroen** in India.

The names of Russian manufacturers are provided in different guises, because of transliteration issues. Often one sees **GAS** written as **GAZ**, **Volga** as **Wolga**, **VAS** as **VAZ** or **WAZ**! You get the drift. I have included the different spellings, so that you do not get confused and think they are different manufacturers. Although Soviet motorsport, as everything Soviet from this era, was very much shrouded in mystery, I managed to find reputable sources after a lot of hard work. Soviet cars ventured out West, **Moskvichs** ran at the 24 Hours of Spa and in British saloon car championships and raced in a few other places. The **Wartburgs** and **Trabants** were used mostly in East Germany but also elsewhere in the Iron Curtain and elsewhere and **Skodas** often ventured into Western racetracks, a few times winning their class. There was even a racing **Tatra** in their midst.

Hyundai was pretty much an unknown make in the 70s, so it is not surprising that they were not commonly found in racetracks. However, one of the last few races of the decade, the oddity-of-oddities, the 6 Hours of El Salvador of 1979, featured a Hyundai Pony among the delectable field of Salvadoran entries. It performed as expected. It did not finish last, though.

A sad part of the list is the reasonable number of British manufacturers which are no longer with us, the likes of **Sunbeam, Triumph** and **Rover**. The latter was mostly absent from top flight racing but it did take part in 1970s Marathon de La Route. An article in Motor Sport indicated that **Roy Pierpoint** would drive such Rover in the 1970 BTCC, however, the British driver chose a Camaro instead. **John MacDonald** did drive a **Rover** at the Guia Touring Car race at Macau, in **1973** and Rovers also appeared in club racing. A **Reliant** Scimitar did, however, come third in the inaugural race at the Yahuarcocha racetrack in Ecuador, in 1970.

Hong Kong's John MacDonald driving a Rover at Macau, 1973. Photo by Jose Santos.

I have included the Argentine **Torino** as a separate make, even though the car was made by IKA-Renault. IKA was the American Kaiser company that found its way into Argentina after failure in the USA and basically, it was a **Rambler**. But Argentines insist on the domestic breeding of the car, so here it is.

Some little cars that did very well during the early part of the decade were the Dutch **DAF**, German **NSU** and the **Simca** Rallye. The latter two were raced well into the decade and often beat cars with larger engines.

Some names appear in both lists, Production Carmakers and Specific Purpose Race Car Constructors, for the sole reason that they were different companies, altogether. The **ATS** appearing in this list is the sports car that was manufactured by the ill-fated **A.T.S.** company in the early sixties, which still took part in events in Italy in the early part of the decade and had nothing to do with the ATS Formula 1 team. The **Puma** in this list was a manufacturer of **VW, DKW** and **Chevrolet** engined sports cars (and even trucks) in Brazil, with no connection to the British single seater manufacturer.

Bottom line is, people raced what they had. In Costa Rica drivers were racing pick-ups (against cars) in 1970, Indians raced **Hindustans, Sipanis** and **Premiers** and there were "fun" races even for **VW** buses (Kombi) in Cascavel, Brazil

I did not take any wild guesses. The list of car manufacturers homologated by the FIA in 1972 includes names such as **Humber, Iso, Francis Lombardi, Murat, Singer** but I found no circuit participation for such cars during the 70s, or by latecomer **Kia**.

Abarth (Italy)
Most of the times, when you see Abarth on a race result, it really means an Abarth prepared FIAT. However, some Simca Abarths were still racing in the 70s, so including this as a separate marque is suitable. It should also be noted that Abarth, as a race car builder won the 1970 and 1971 European Hill Climb and 1972 European 2-Liter Championships. The Abarth race car division was sold to Enzo Osella in 1971.

Alfa Romeo (Italy)
Alfa Romeo touring cars were present in touring car races literally all over the world during the decade but as the GTA/GTV range (engines from 1.3 to 2.0 in size) became outdated, Alfas became a rarer sight. Alfa touring cars were raced in Austria, West Germany, Brazil, USA, Venezuela, Italy, Belgium, Holland, Sweden, Britain, Angola, Portugal, Spain, Colombia, El Salvador, Macau, Singapore, Hungary, Portugal, Czechoslovakia, Norway, Yugoslavia, Rhodesia, Mozambique, Poland, East Germany, Ecuador, Andorra, Switzerland, Finland, Peru, Canada, Uruguay, Paraguay, Senegal, Scotland, Chile, Indonesia, Zambia, Morocco, Malaysia, Singapore, Sri Lanka, Kenya, Malta, Romania, Ethiopia/Eritrea. The cars were also used in Group 5 and Group 4 events throughout the decade. The Alfetta sedan was tried in touring cars by Autodelta in 1973, albeit unsuccessfully and a Brazilian variant, called the 2300, raced sporadically in 1974 to 1976. The older 2600 model was still used in Italian local races early on the decade.

The Alfa Romeo GTA range raced – and won – in many different engine configurations during the 70s. Here a couple of 1300s in Zandvoort, 1970 (Photo Rob Petersen collection)

The GTV6 had better performance and won a ETCC event outright in 1976. Alfasud single make championships were also ran in Italy, Austria, Germany and

France and the model also appeared in championships such as the British Saloon Car Championship. The Montreal was sporadically used both in Europe, US GT events and even in Ecuador. Alfa Romeo was also a prominent player in sports car racing from 1970 to 1977, winning two world championships, in addition to Interserie races. Alfas also raced in Can Am, Trans Am and hill climbs. The 2.0 liter Alfa P33 was used in some European 2 Liter races. In Formula 1, Alfa engines were first used in McLaren (1970), March (1971), then Brabham (1976 to 1979). By 1979, Alfa had returned as a Formula 1 constructor. Alfa engines were also used in a host of Italian prototypes and race cars in a variety of countries, including Zambia. The Milanese company's engines were also used in Formula 3.

Alpine (France)
The Alpine road cars were very successful in rallying during the 1970s. The small Renault engined GTs were used in circuit racing and hill climbs worldwide, including the DRM and European GT Championship but powerless to beat the likes of Porsches and BMWs. Pure racing Alpines were also raced in Formula 3, winning many races early in the decade, the European 2-Liter Championship, destroying the competition in 1974 and most famously, won Le Mans in 1978, after three attempts.

AMC (USA)
AMC saw some success in racing early on the decade, as Roger Penske partnered with the company. AMC cars raced in NASCAR (Matador) and Trans Am (Javelin) and powered Formula 5000 cars, under the Penske banner and were also used in Formula Indy. The Javelins were also briefly used in the British Saloon Car Championship, in 1972 and 1973 and also in Scotland and Peru. An AMX raced in Ecuador. AMC Hornets, Pacer and Gremlin also raced (and won) in Showroom stock, SCCA, in Venezuela and even in touring car races in Europe.

Anadol (Turkey)
Anadol was a car produced in Turkey, equipped with Ford engines. Anadol STC16 models participated in whatever little circuit races that were held in the country but were successful in rallies.

Andino (Ecuador)
The Andino was a utilities vehicle built by Aymesa between 1972 and 1980. The Andino was an adaptation of the Vauxhall Beford BTV project and it was equipped with a 1.4 liter engine. Although it was more of a pick-up truck than car, the Andino participated in many Ecuadorean road races during the decade, often finishing last but finishing, nonetheless.

Aston-Martin (Britain)
The venerable British make appeared sporadically in racing during the 70s, coming back to Le Mans and the World Championship of Makes without much success. The AM V8 used by Robin Hamilton in 1979 was by far the heaviest car in the Le Mans race. It qualified last and was the 3rd car to retire, running in GTP. The car also raced at Silverstone. Aston Martins also raced in club racing in Britain and a vintage Aston mixed in with contemporary machines in Maltese hill climbs.

ATS (Italy)
Older road going ATS prototypes raced in Italy early on the decade.

Audi (West Germany)
Audi was far from a racing powerhouse in the 70s. The cars were underpowered, glorified VWs or DKWs. Still, during the course of the decade the Audi 80 got better as a race car and was often raced in smaller engine touring car categories, in places such as Germany, Italy, Austria, Czechoslovakia, Holland, Belgium, England, Yugoslavia, Portugal, France and Spain.

Austin (Britain)
Austins appeared in racing mostly as Minis, in touring car championships, hill climbs and club racing. See the entry for Mini, to find where the model was raced. Other make's models, such as the Marina, appeared in racing as well, without much success and A40s were raced in many places besides England, such as Guyana.

Austin Healey (Britain)
Austin Healeys were built until 1972. Yet, the cars remained competitive in SCCA racing throughout the decade, winning a large number of races and championships. To a lesser degree, the car was raced elsewhere in the world, with some success in Swedish club racing and was also used in Northern Ireland, Scotland, Australia and Holland.

A Scottish Austin-Healey, photo by Colin Lourie.

Autobianchi (Italy)
Autobianchis were raced in Belgium, Norway, Ecuador, Angola, France, Holland, Andorra, Switzerland and Italy track championships and also appeared widely in hill climbs. The Primula was also raced, although it was rarely seen in action

Authi (Spain)
The company built Minis under license in Spain and cars were fielded under that name.

Auto Union (West Germany)
DKWs were branded Auto Unions in Argentina and were raced in the country as late as 1972, although totally outclassed by then. Earlier an Auto Union won its class in the 1970 Gran Premio de Turismo in Argentina. At least one Auto Union also raced in Sri Lanka and A.U. engines were also used in Belgium, in prototypes.

Bertone (Italy)
Bertone Berlinettas, equipped with FIAT engines, raced in Italian events.

BMC (Britain)
BMC branded Minis were raced in many countries throughout the decade. As Minis were essentially the same car, I consolidated the model's entry under Mini.

BMW (West Germany)
BMW race cars were used in a large number of countries and won hundreds of races and quite a few championships. In addition to dominating the ETCC, BMW also raced in the DRM, World Championship of Makes, IMSA, Trans Am and some SCCA classes. BMWs appeared in racing worldwide, including Austria, France, Holland, Sweden, Italy, Britain, Belgium, Portugal, Canada, Spain, Angola, Brazil, Greece, Denmark, Norway, Andorra, Hungary, Switzerland, Finland, Czechoslovakia, Yugoslavia, Mozambique, Poland, Luxembourg, Macau, Australia, South Africa, Ireland, Singapore, Peru, Colombia, Morocco, Zambia, Puerto Rico, Chile, Romania, Uruguay, Indonesia, Scotland, Bolivia, Argentina, Mexico, Northern Ireland, Malta and, of course, West Germany. BMW engines also equipped a large number of prototypes all over the world, from Lolas and Chevron in Europe, to Furia in Brazil. BMW also fielded a proprietary works Formula 2 chassis in 1970, left the series in 1972 and then came back full power in 1973, powering at first only March, later on the likes of Martini and Osella racers. BMW engines were also used in Formula 3. BMW had a single make championship in England and most famously, promoted the Procar series in 1979, which staged the fastest GP drivers in qualifying against series regulars, in BMW M-1 cars.

Tony Lanfranchi in a BMW. Photo by Gerald Swan.

Bolwell (AUS)
The pretty Ford engined Bolwell Nagari raced in Australian events during most of the decade. The car was also successful, in fact, won the last Australian Sports car event of the decade.

Borgward (West Germany)
Borgwards were still raced in Argentina.

Buick (USA)
Buicks were raced almost exclusively in the USA, in NASCAR and other stock car series and also in IMSA Showroom Stock (Skyhawk). But a Buick was also raced in Colombia during the decade. Buick engines were also used in British hill climb specials.

Bulgar Alpine (Bulgaria)
Bulgarian car, licensed by Alpine, raced in native Bulgaria and East Germany.

Chevrolet (USA)
Chevrolet was the most successful manufacturer in NASCAR during the 70s but the brand also had success elsewhere. In Argentina, Chevies were often Ford's main competitor in Turismo de Carretera, while in Brazil, the Opala won many races in both Division 1 and 3, eventually running in a single-make series, called Brazilian Stock Car, starting in 1979. Chevrolets also raced in Showroom Stock, Trans Am, ARCA and several other stock car series in the USA. The Camaro was extremely successful in many countries, in the USA, Central and South America, Canada, Asia, Angola and used in touring car racing and hill climbing in Austria, Belgium, Holland, Sweden, Finland, Denmark, Australia, Britain, Norway, Ecuador, Luxembourg, Mexico, Argentina, France, Andorra, Barbados, Puerto Rico, Scotland, Guyana, Malaysia, as well as in the European Touring Car Championship. Chevrolet engines ruled in the old Can-Am until the arrival of the Porsche 917, conquered the single seater Can Am and was by far the most successful engine in Formula 5000 all over the world (US, Europe, South Africa and Australia/New Zealand), even winning a race in India.

Camaros raced worldwide, with much success, during the 70s. In this case, at Zandvoort, 1977 (Photo Rob Petersen collection)

Chevrolet engines also powered Argentine Formula 1 and prototypes, as well as Brazilian prototypes. The Vega engine was used for a while in European 2-liter racing and Corvettes were widely used in IMSA, Trans Am and SCCA racing, in addition to Le Mans and GT racing in Europe. As of the second edition, the IROC used Camaros. Among the Chevrolet models raced in the 70s were Camaro, Corvette, Chevelle, Opala, Vega, Chevette, Monte Carlo, Nova, Laguna, Monza, even old Corvairs.

Chrysler (USA)
At one point with operations in the major markets of the world (USA, UK, France, Spain, Australia, Argentina, Brazil), Chrysler collapsed during the decade. Cars built by the group were raced under the Dodge, Plymouth, Simca, Hillman, Sunbeam banners in most places. The nameplate Chrysler was used for Simca race cars in Spain and some Chrysler Hemis were enthusiastically raced in some European countries, including France. A Chrysler GTX (a Simca design that replaced the Chambord) appeared in a single race in Brazil, in 1970. Strangely, Dodge powered Avallone and Manta prototypes were referred as Avallone and Manta Chryslers in Brazil, rather than Dodge.

Citroen (France)
Citroens appeared sporadically in racing during the 70s. Every once in a while Citroens would be fielded in touring car races, most telling in the Tour de France but also in local French, Spanish, Italian, West German, Senegalese, Finnish, Norwegian, Chilean, Dutch, Argentine and Belgian races, even the Marathon de La Route. The cars also appeared in African races, in fact, Citroen's major circuit accomplishment of the decade was Lablanche's overall win in the 6 hours of Senegal in 1973, driving a Citroen SM. Meanwhile old Traction Avants still raced in India. Formule Bleue were Citroen powered single seaters. Additionally 2CV races were held in a few countries, such as France and Argentina, most for fun.

Clan Crusader (Britain)
The Clan Crusader was a small British constructor. The Crusader was raced in Scotland.

A Clan Crusader at Ingliston. Photo by Colin Lourie.

Colt (Japan)
Mitsubishis were occasionally branded Colts and raced as such.

Costin (Britain)
The Costin Amigo was used in some British club events.

Dacia (Romania)
Dacias were Renaults produced under license in Romania and were raced in Yugoslavia and also in Romania. In certain Romanian race results it is not clear if the car used was a Dacia or a Renault.

DAF (Holland)
The little DAF appeared in touring car championships in Belgium, Sweden, Italy, Norway, England, Indonesia, Portugal, and, of course, Holland. It gave Minis and FIATs a run for their money. A DAF Prototype came in 3rd in the 1971 Marathon de la Route. DAFs with large V8 engines were used in England's Super Saloon category.

A DAF 55 Marathon at Zandvoort, 1972. Driver is Dirk van der Pol (Photo Rob Petersen collection)

Daihatsu (Japan)
While in the 60s Daihatsu built purpose made race cars, by 1970 the company changed its focus immensely. A builder of very small engined cars such as the Fellow Max, Daihatsus were raced in Japan and elsewhere, fielded by optimistic privateers, without a major impact overall, unlike other Japanese manufacturers which advanced in production car racing internationally during the decade. In the tiny engine class, rarely used outside Japan (the maximum capacity was raised to 550 cc in 1978!), Daihatsu won 22 times out of 145 Japanese national touring races, losing to Suzuki and Honda.

Daimler (Britain)
Daimler 250 sports cars were used in SCCA racing, Britain and Australia. A Daimler limousine raced in Saloon Stocks in Scotland, although it is unclear what engine it used.

Datsun (Japan)
Datsun touring cars and GTs raced widely in Japan and Asia in general but the car was also successful in IMSA, Trans Am and SCCA racing. Datsuns were also used in Austria, Belgium, Sweden, France, Spain, Canada, Greece, Peru, Czechoslovakia, Portugal, Luxembourg, Macau, Scotland, Australia, South Africa,

Singapore, El Salvador, Peru, Puerto Rico, Mozambique, Mexico, Malaysia, Kenya, Singapore, Uruguay, Norway, Finland, Guyana, Jamaica, Barbados, Indonesia, Trinidad, Costa Rica, Britain, West Germany and Italy. Eventually, the name Datsun was dropped and Nissan adopted for all manufacturer's cars.

Leung's Datsun 240, in Macau, 1973. Photo by Jose Santos.

Davrian (Britain)

In front a Davrian, driven in British club racing. Photo by Colin Lourie.

Davrian was another small scale British builder of sports cars that was in business until 1976. Davrians used a number of small power plants, ranging from Mini and Imp to VW and were used in categories such as British Modsports. I located no records of Davrians racing outside of England and Scotland.

De Tomaso (Italy)
The Ford engined De Tomaso Pantera was seen in GT and Group 5 races throughout the decade and it was basically the only competition Porsche had in the European GT Championship. The Group 5 racers were used in the World Championship, Le Mans and DRM. De Tomaso Formula 1 and Formula 2 cars were also used during the decade. Photo on the next page.

De Tomasos raced in many countries during the 70s. This is Casoni's car in the Kyalami 9 hour race in 1973. Photo by Russell Whitworth.

Deep Sanderson (Britain)
Deep Sanderson GTs were still used in British club events in the beginning of the decade.

Diva (Britain)
Divas were used in Swedish club racing.

DKW (West Germany)

DKWs had not been built since 1967, yet they remained racing for a while. This example raced in Brazil. Behind it, a Ford Corcel (with obvious Renault DNA) (unknown author)

By 1970, DKWs had not been built for a few years, anywhere. Still, the 2-stroke cars resisted and some could still be seen in Brazilian racetracks as late as 1972, as well as Germany, Norway, Holland, Colombia, Ecuador, SCCA events in the USA, Morocco and other places. In fact, a DKW F12 was raced in Norway ice races as late as 1978! In Argentina the cars were branded Auto Union. A DKW Monza also raced briefly in the European 2-Liter Championship and a plaster bodied DKW powered prototype raced in Brazil. There was also a pretty looking DKW engined prototype used in Colombia, whose constructor and driver are unknown.

Dodge (USA)
Dodge stock cars won many races in the 70s, eventually dropping out as the company ran into trouble. Large engined Dodges also raced in the Trans-Am, Argentina's Turismo de Carretera and touring car races in Brazil. Small displacement Dodges were also used in Showroom stock and a version of the Hillman Avenger, sold as Dodge 1800 (Polara) raced briefly in Brazil. Dodge engines were also used in Argentine Formula 1 and in Formula 5000 and single seater Can-Am. Dodge engines were also used in Brazilian and Argentine prototypes, although in Brazil they were referred as Chrysler.

Elva (Britain)
Elvas were still raced in the 70s, some appearing in Swedish and American club racing and in places such as Austria, Malaysia and Germany.

Ferrari (Italy)
Ferrari racers graced the Formula 1 grids during the entire decade and top flight sports car racing until 1973. Customer 512 models were raced in the world championship and Group 7 races. Other Ferrari models, such as the Daytona (375 GTB), 250LM, Dino 206S, 512BB, 308GTB raced in GT, DRM, World Championship of Makes, IMSA, hill climbs, Le Mans and sports car racing all over the world. A Ferrari engined Formula 2 Chevron won a race in 1977 and Graeme Lawrence won the Tasman Cup in a 2.5 Ferrari in 1970.

FIAT (Italy)
Abarth tuned FIATs were widely used in touring car races, not only in Italy but all over the world and are often listed as Abarths in results. In Argentina, the locally built cars were raced in the Turismo Nacional class and in Brazil, a FIAT 147 single make series began in 1978. There was a single-make FIAT series in Finland as well. FIATs 124 and X1/9 were also used in GT racing. FIAT engines were also used in single seater series, such as Formula Italia and Argentine Formula 4 and low displacement prototypes, mostly in Italy. FIAT's were raced in Italy, USA, Brazil, Argentina, East Germany, Peru, Luxembourg, Belgium, Rhodesia, Mozambique, Poland, Australia, Norway, Britain, West Germany, Austria, Sweden, Holland, Greece, Denmark, Finland, Ecuador, India, Sri Lanka, South Africa, Colombia, Venezuela, Switzerland, Angola, Chile, Indonesia, Romania, Andorra, Scotland, Morocco, Kenya, Barbados, El Salvador, Puerto Rico, Zambia, Malta, Ethiopia/Eritrea, Malaysia, among other countries. FIAT derivatives were raced as SEAT, Lada, Zhiguli (Shiguli), Steyr Puch, Polski. FIATs were built by Murat in Turkey but I found no hard evidence of circuit racing Murats, although the cars were used in rallies.

FIAT Abarths were raced almost everywhere, often winning their class. Photo by Paul Rutten.

Fiberfab (USA)

The Fiberfab Avenger was a VW engine Ford GT 40 look-alike that was produced in the USA. Although I have no records of the car racing in the USA, at least one Fiberfab was used in Mexican long distance racing, with a beefed-up VW engine.

FNM (Brazil)

FNM built Alfa Romeos under license in Brazil. The FNM 2000 and 2150 were used in touring car races and their engines used in some prototypes, such as the Manta and the Furia.

FNMs were built in Brazil from 1960 to 1974. Photo by Rogerio da Luz.

Ford (USA)

It is almost impossible to write an abbreviated entry on Ford, given the breadth of its participation in worldwide racing during the 70s. Fords raced and won races, almost everywhere, with the noted exception of most Iron Curtain countries. Fords raced in USA, Germany, Britain, Argentina, Australia, Brazil, Belgium, France, Austria, Sweden, Norway, Holland, Ireland, Italy, Denmark, Czechoslovakia, Scotland, South Africa, Japan, Spain, Portugal, Colombia, Venezuela, Switzerland, Finland, Andorra, Macau, East Germany, Trinidad, New Zealand, Peru, Guyana, Chile, Greece, Yugoslavia, Jamaica, Costa Rica, Luxembourg, Rhodesia, Mozambique, Indonesia, Kenya, Canada, Mexico, Malaysia, Ecuador,

Morocco, Sri Lanka, Senegal, Turkey, Puerto Rico, Malta, Northern Ireland, Barbados and I am quite positive, in a few other countries. The most successful racing road going Fords were the Capri, Escort, Mustang, Anglia, Taunus, Zodiac, Torino (not the Argentine car), Thunderbird (USA), Falcon (Argentina, Australia and New Zealand), Maverick (Brazil, Venezuela but also in the USA), Lotus Cortina and even the small Fiesta, while oddities such as Granadas, Galaxies and Pintos were raced as well. Mustangs raced in the Trans Am, as well in various places in Europe, South America (specially Peru) and Australia. The Corcel raced in Brazil and Paraguay. Fords were successful in sprints and endurance races, club racing and Formula 1. The make was relatively not very successful in NASCAR during the decade, winning only 25 times but that was compensated by global success. There were single make series for touring Fords in a few countries. Ford engines also equipped a huge number of prototypes, GTs, single seaters and unnamed racing specials worldwide, in categories such as Formula 1, Formula 2, Formula 3, Formula Ford, Formula Ford 2000, Formula Indy, Formula 5000, Formula Atlantic, 2 liter sports cars, 3 liter sports cars, Can-Am, hill climbs, Sports 2000, Formula 1300, Formula F100, British/Scottish Stock Cars. Ford engines equipped the De Tomaso GT car, as well as the 1975 Le Mans winning Mirage and all race winners in the 1973 Formula 1 Championship. It should be noted that Ford engines used in Formula 1 and the World Championship of Makes were actually designed and built by Cosworth, so many might take exception to calling them Ford, which only paid the development bills. This also applies to turbo Cosworths used in Indy Car late in the decade, although early Indycar Fords were based on Ford blocks. Later on the decade, Ford engines were hard to find in categories such as Formula 2 and 3, replaced by the likes of BMW and Toyota.

The Ford Escort raced in dozens of countries during the 70s. (Photo Rob Petersen collection)

GAZ (GAS) (Russia)
Gaz 24 and 21 models raced in Soviet touring car races, that is, in Russia, Belarus, Latvia, Estonia and Ukraine. The make's engines were also used in Soviet Formula 1.

Ginetta (Britain)

Ginettas were raced in a few countries. Photo by Colin Lourie.

A small British constructor of GTs, Ginettas appeared a few times in racing during the 70s. They were particularly liked and used in Swedish club racing and were also raced in Germany, Scotland, Guyana, Malaysia and Switzerland. Ginetta also built Formula Fords.

Glas (West Germany)
Some Glas cars were still racing in German, Greek and Dutch events and hill climbs during the decade, even though by then the brand had been absorbed by BMW. Glas engined prototypes were also raced. A Glas was still raced in Angola as well.

GSM (South Africa)
GSM was a South African company that produced a sports car called Dart, which competed in the Springbok series and local events.

Hillman (Britain)

Hillmans also graced the racetracks. This Avenger raced at Macau, 1973. Photo by Jose Santos.

Hillman, by the 70s a Chrysler company, was well represented in the British Saloon Car Championship in the form of the Imp. Hillman Avengers also raced, sometimes branded as Dodges. Imps also appeared as Sunbeams. The make was raced in quite a few countries besides England, including Scotland, Ireland, Northern Ireland, Italy, West Germany, Ecuador, Sweden, Holland, El Salvador, Macau, Chile, Peru, Norway, Malta and Belgium

Hino (Japan)
Hino had built a racing car for the 1967 Japanese Grand Prix but the car was never allowed to start. Eventually, the company was sold to Toyota, stopped building cars, continuing only in the truck market. The Samurai ended up sold in the USA and raced in SCCA events. The car's buyer made many modifications and the car was actually successful, winning races in the early 1970s.

Holden (Australia)
Holden was GM's brand in Australia, where the cars were raced extensively during the 70s. Holdens raced in Australia, New Zealand, Macau, Jamaica, Guyana and Barbados. Holden engines were also used in prototypes and Formula 5000.

Here is a Holden Torana hard at work at Amaroo, 1977. Photo by Glenn Moulds.

Honda (Japan)

The 70s were the only decade in which no Honda engine appeared in Formula 1, since first appearing in 1964. Notwithstanding, small Honda touring and GT cars were used in the U.S.A, Britain, West Germany, Italy, Austria, Holland, Czechoslovakia, Colombia, Switzerland, Angola, Senegal, Mozambique, Chile, Norway, Macau, El Salvador, Paraguay, Finland, Ecuador, Northern Ireland, Belgium, Canada, Indonesia, Scotland, Australia, throughout the decade. By the end of the 70s, the manufacturer was planning a return to top level international racing, after their engines were successfully used in Japanese racing.

A tiny Honda 600 struggling to keep up with an Alfa Romeo. Macau, 1972 (Photo by Jose Santos)

Hyundai (South Korea)
The only places I found a Hyundai being used in competition during the 70s were El Salvador and Ecuador, where the Pony was raced.

Innocenti (Italy)
Innocenti built Minis under license in Italy and these were raced there and neighboring countries, like France.

Isard (Argentina)
Isard Argentina produced the Glas Isar in Argentina until 1965, under the name Isard 700. Some of the little cars were still being raced in the early part of the decade.

Isuzu (Japan)
Isuzu touring cars raced in Japan and the rest of Asia, appearing briefly in the Macau Guia race and were also used in Mozambique, Australia, Finland and South Africa. Isuzu prototypes continued racing in Japan and Isuzu engines were used in prototypes built by others.

Jaguar (Britain)
The Jaguar model E was raced in the US, by the Group 44 team and also raced in English, Scottish, Australian, Spanish and Swedish club racing, as well as Irish racing and Maltese hill climbs. Group 44 later prepared a XJ-S challenger for the Trans Am that raced in the US and Mexico. Most famously, a Jaguar works team contested the 1976 and 1977 European Touring Car Championships. The cars were fast, posted many poles, fastest laps and led many times but were fragile. British Leyland politics and ineptness did not help, so the program was scratched. Jaguars of unknown pedigree and age also raced in Sri Lanka and India.

Model E were raced in a few places, such as Scotland. Photo by Colin Lourie.

Jeep (United States)
Jeep mechanicals were used in Pikes Peak specials as well as Argentine regional categories.

Jensen Healey (Britain)
After the demise of the tie up with Austin, Healey entered into an agreement with Jensen. The cars achieved success in SCCA G production, winning two titles. Jensen Healey were also raced in Scotland.

Jensen Healey's were rare findings at tracks. Photo by Colin Lourie.

Jidé (France)
Jidé was a small builder of sports cars from France, which built a small number of racing and street cars from 1969 to 1974. Jidés raced mostly in France but also Morocco, where the cars were assembled. They used FIAT and Renault engines.

Lada (Russia)
Ladas were also branded Zhiguli and WAS. Beyond the Soviet Union bubble, Ladas popped up in Holland, Norway and Czechoslovakia, where competition was fiercer.

Lamborghini (Italy)
Lamborghini's were not produced in enough numbers to qualify for Group 4 homologation, so they would only appear as "prototypes" under rare situations. As mentioned, a Miura appeared in a race against the clock in Brazil, performing well and a Frenchman, Thierry Gore drove a Lambo barchetta in assorted minor events. A Lamborghini engined Furia also took part in the 500 km of Interlagos, in 1972 and Urracos were entered at Le Mans, ultimately not showing up. Early on the decade, Lamborghini Miuras raced here and there. Jack Tatenaeers/Gaston Daillien drove one in the Zolder 500 KM race in 1970 and Frank Littich drove one in Kaufberen airport race, the same year. The outings were not successful. A Miura also raced in Venezuelan events as late as 1976-77.

Lancia (Italy)
Lancia was much more successful in rallying than racing in the 70s but the Stratos finished 2nd in the Targa Florio in 1973 and was timidly tried in GT and Group 5 racing elsewhere. The Fulvia was prepared by some privateers and the Italian cars were raced in a few countries outside of Italy, such as the USA, Portugal, France, Switzerland, Czechoslovakia, Romania, Holland, Finland, Switzerland, Angola, Malta and Macau. The major advance by the Italian maker was the building of the Beta Montecarlo for Group 5 racing, which was able to win races outright by the end of the decade and appear in new markets at a top level.

Leyland (Australia)
Leyland, a British Leyland brand, built trucks and commercial vehicles in Britain but the name plate was used for cars in Australia. The company built the P76 during 1973 to 1975 and the large car was used in racing. The car's engine was also used in Formula 5000.

Ligier (France)

Ligier was basically known as a Formula 1 team but before that, it dabbled in sports cars and a street version of the JS-2 was sold in limited numbers. Ligier street cars used Maserati engine and a racing version used Cosworth. The car raced outside France, including in the 6 hours of Senegal. Vittorio Brambilla drove a Ligier in the 1973 Giro D'Italia.

Ligier in Senegal, 1974. Unknown author

Lincoln (USA)
Not really a racing brand, at least one Lincoln-engined car raced in the Pikes Peak Hill Climb.

Lorena (Brazil)
Lorena was a small manufacturer of a VW based GT in Brazil. A Porsche engine was also installed in one of these Ford GT 40 look-alikes. Very small numbers of this car were made and it raced briefly until 1971.

Lorenas were raced in Brazil until 1971 (Photo by Rogerio da Luz)

Lotus (Britain)
Lotus is better known for its exploits in Formula 1, although the company also built Formula 2, Formula 3, Formula 5000 and Formula Fords during the decade. Street legal Europa, Elan and Seven models were also prepared for long distance and sports car racing and a Group 5 Europa Silhouette also appeared, with little success. The Lotus Cortina, actually a Ford car, was still raced in many countries early in the 70s.

Lotus sports cars were used in quite a few countries. Photo by Colin Lourie.

Malzoni (Brazil)
DKW engined Malzoni GTs were still raced in 1970, although the car was very much outclassed by them. Some of these cars were also sold as Puma-DKWs.

Marcos (Britain)
Another British sports car specialist, whose cars appeared mostly in British, Scottish, Australian, Dutch, Guyanese and Swedish club racing and also sporadically in endurance races. A number of engines were used, including Volvo and Ford.

Maserati (Italy)
Maserati engines appeared in the Ligier and Citroen cars. Like Lamborghini, Masers were produced in very small numbers to qualify as GTs and were totally outclassed as prototypes. Still, old Maseratis appeared in places like Brazil and Holland, sometimes with different engines, in very optimistic programs. A team of Boras was entered for the 24 Hours of Le Mans of 1973 but were no shows.

Matra (France)
Given its racing success, it is easy to forget that Matra also built road cars but it did. Bagheras, 530s and Djets raced in minor events in France, Italy, Morocco, Indonesia and West Germany, overshadowed by the accomplishments of the purebreds. As of 1975, Matra became merely an engine supplier for the likes of Shadow and Ligier in F-1, while the street cars still showed up in minor events.

Mazda (Japan)

Rotary engine cars were seen as the future, by some, as failure, by others. Mazda was the only one that persisted and as far as racing goes, Mazda did rather well. Mazda sedans were raced in Japan, Britain, United States, France, Austria, Sweden, Italy, Holland, Czechoslovakia, South Africa, Angola, Macau, Northern Ireland, Ecuador, Indonesia, Singapore, Malaysia, Belgium, Rhodesia, Canada, Mexico, Australia, Trinidad and elsewhere, often winning its class. The Mazda engined Sigma was the first Japanese car to start Le Mans and a Mazda engined Chevron was raced in European 2-liter sports cars. Mazda engines also replaced Ford as South African Formula Atlantic's power plant. Mazda engines also equipped Japanese prototypes which raced exclusively in Japan, as well as single seaters. The RX7 model was launched late in the decade and was successful in GT racing.

Mazdas popped up in quite a few places. Katayama/Takeshi in South Africa. Photo by Russell Whitworth.

Melkus (East Germany)

The Melkus 1000 had a small production run during the 70s but not all cars raced, some were used as street cars so Melkus makes the list. The 2-stroke 1 liter engine was typical of East German cars of the era. Cars were raced in East Germany and other Iron Curtain countries and the builder also made pure racing cars, including single seaters.

Mercedes-Benz (West Germany)

Mercedes was making a slow warming up towards resuming racing activities in the 70s, through engine tuner AMG. A Mercedes 300 SEL famously took second place in the 24 Hours of SPA in 1971, driven by Hans Heyer and Clemens Schickentanz and appeared elsewhere, even winning a race at Norisring. In spite of the promise the program was scratched. Different models of Mercedes racers popped up in various places, such as Macau, the 24 Hours of Nürburgring, Belgium, France, Czechoslovakia, Finland, Sweden and even in Colombia and Peru, with no support from the factory. By the end of the decade, the stance had changed somewhat and a more nimble AMG Mercedes 450 SEL returned to the European Touring Car Championship, showing promise. However, one of these cars was even entered at Le Mans but did not qualify. It should be noted that updated versions of the Mercedes C111 were successfully used in record breaking activities, keeping the Mercedes reputation as high performance vehicles in the international public's eye.

Mercedes racers were a rare sight in the 70s. This example raced in Macau, 1971. Driver is unknown. Photo by Jose Santos.

Mercury (USA)
David Pearson won many NASCAR races driving Mercury product in the 70s. Given the American proclivity to badge engineering in the 70s, it is difficult to consider the Mercury as anything but a Ford with a different name. Mercury also appeared in other disciplines, such as IMSA (as the Capri) and even in the Swedish championship and Colombia. Sagoo, a Mercury engined single seater, raced in Kenya, but it seems only until 1969. Some sources claim the engine was actually a Lincoln.

MG (Britain)
Most MGs were sold in the USA and although the cars were raced in England and Ireland, it was in the SCCA amateur events that the small sports car found a home and many victories. Every once in a while they were used in endurance events on both sides of the Atlantic, without much success. MGs also raced in Sri Lanka, Malta, Trinidad, Scotland, Barbados, Guyana and Ecuador.

Mini (Britain)
The small Mini-Cooper (photo by Russell Whitworth) was one of the most widely used cars in racing in the decade. The car was built by many British Leyland companies, such as Austin, Morris, Wolseley and BMC and under license by Innocenti and Authi but by the end of the decade, Mini emerged as a separate nameplate. Several single make Mini championships were held in various countries such as Britain and France. Mini Coopers were raced in England, USA, Austria, Belgium, Holland, Sweden, Spain, Italy, West Germany, France, Denmark, Luxembourg, Indonesia, Norway, Angola, Portugal, Macau, Finland, Australia, Scotland, New Zealand, South Africa, Singapore, Ireland, Canada, Hungary, Yugoslavia, Rhodesia, Mozambique, East Germany, Colombia, Argentina, Brazil, Chile, Uruguay, Paraguay, El Salvador, Panama, Morocco, Sri

Lanka, Kenya, Malaysia, Malta, Trinidad, Guyana, Northern Ireland, Barbados, Japan, Philippines, Jamaica, Costa Rica, Malaysia

Minijem (Britain)
Minijems were small GTs that looked a lot like the Mini Marcos. The Mini engined cars were sold to the public but also raced in British club racing, in the Modsport series. The company changed owners many times.

Mitsubishi (Japan)
Mitsubishis were not widely raced but the make's cars were used in places like Macau, Dominican Republic, Sri Lanka, Spain and El Salvador, besides Japan. Mitsubishi engines also powered prototypes in Japan, such as Lolas in 1972, driven by Urusihara and Nagamatsu and Kazato's GRD in 1973

A Mitsubishi Galant in Macau, 1973. Photo by Jose Santos.

237

Morgan (Britain)
Morgan cars were sporadically raced in Group 5 but appeared with more frequency in SCCA, Australian, French, British club events and long distance races in the USA and Canada.

Morris (Britain)
Morris was one of British Leyland companies that produced the Mini and were raced in many countries. A list of countries is provided under "Mini". The Marina, a car with many detractors, was also used in racing.

The Morris Marina was an unloved car, yet, it was raced. This one was captured in Macau, 1973. Photo by Jose Santos.

Moskvich (Russia)
Moskvich models raced in Soviet touring car races, that is, in Russia, Belarus, Latvia, Estonia and Ukraine, as well as other Iron Curtain countries, such as Bulgaria. More importantly, though, Moskvichs raced in the ETCC at the 24 Hours of Spa and **Moskvich** 412 were used to great effect to win back to back touring car championships in England in 1972 and 1973. The cars were also raced in Norway and Scotland. The make's engines were also used in Soviet Formula 1, Formula 2, Formula 4. The make also produced a proprietary Soviet Formula 1 chassis, the G5. (Also transliterated **Moskvitch**)

Nathan (Britain)
Nathan was another British specialty constructor whose cars were raced in England and Scotland.

Nissan (Japan)
The Nissan nameplate was mainly used in Japan and the Far East and cars from this manufacturer were sold elsewhere as Datsuns during the decade. Notwithstanding, Nissan branded cars appeared in unusual places, such as in the 1970 Brazil Cup, in Angola, Canada, Greece, Barbados, Trinidad. Nissan engines powered prototypes in Japanese racing.

Nota (Australia)
Nota is an Australian constructor which built Clubman type cars, sold to the public. The company's purpose made race cars were used in the Australian sports car championship.

NSU (West Germany)
By 1969 NSU had been taken over by VW, although the Prinz continued to be produced until 1973. This little car continued to be raced all over the world throughout the decade, in touring car and hill climbing events, places such as

Holland, England, Austria, Italy, Denmark, Switzerland, West Germany, El Salvador, Czechoslovakia, France, Norway, East Germany, Greece, Belgium, Senegal, Chile, Argentina and Canada. The Wankel engined RO80 was seldom raced but picture is provided on page 35.

Henri van Oorschot's NSU at Zandvoort, 1973 (Photo, Rob Petersen collection)

Oldsmobile (USA)
While Oldsmobile cars were raced in the USA, winning 16 major NASCAR races but also raced in Ecuador. In the decade, the Oldsmobile engine was used in Formula 5000 outside the country, namely in Europe.

Opel (West Germany)

Opels were raced worldwide during the 70s. This one was raced by Danielle Plomteux in the 1970 Marathon de la Route. Photo Danielle Plomteux.

Opel was GM's company in Germany, plain and simple. Opels were generally beaten by Ford and BMW for overall wins but many folks prepared Commodores,

Mantas, Asconas, Kadetts and Rekords, which participated in touring car and endurance races all over the world, in Austria, Belgium, Holland, Sweden, Britain, France, Germany, USA, Yugoslavia, Canada, Italy, Peru, Denmark, Norway, Czechoslovakia, South Africa, Morocco, Luxembourg, Malaysia, Scotland, Spain, Portugal, Colombia, Venezuela, Ecuador, Switzerland, Northern Ireland, Finland, Angola, Trinidad, Andorra, Senegal, Macau and El Salvador. The cars were also used in hill climbs. The Opel GT, although quite hopeless against the Porsche 911, raced in GT an hill climb events on both side of the Atlantic, including the DRM. A well-supported race for all types of Opel models was also held in Germany early on the decade. The Commodore based Opala was produced in Brazil, sold as a Chevrolet and won many races.

OSCA (Italy)
At least one old OSCA 1000 still raced in the early 70s Targa Florio but soon became extinct in contemporary racing.

Panhard (France)
Panhards had not been built for a while when the decade began. Notwithstanding, a car referred as Panhard 850 participated in the category Racers/Formula IV in Morocco, in 1970. Just exactly what was this car, I doubt anyone alive will be able to tell. But it should have at least a Panhard engine, so the make is included here.

Peugeot (France)
Peugeot was not too fond of circuit racing in the 70s, finding Rallying to be a more suitable competition niche. Notwithstanding, some Peugeot tourers were raced and Peugeot engined cars appeared, among them the beautiful WM prototype. Eventually, Peugeot touring cars with official support were announced for 1980, with no other than Jean Pierre Beltoise doing the driving. A 204 model showed up in DARM late in the decade and Peugeots were raced in Chile, Canada and Kenya. In Argentina, it was a different story. Peugeots were raced and did well in TN, even in Turismo de Carretera and the engine was also used in Prototypes, Argentine Formulas 1 and 2. Peugeots also won many races in Uruguay.

Piper (Britain)
The Piper GT was still raced in a few places in the 70s, such as Sweden.

Plymouth (USA)
Plymouth, now a defunct Chrysler brand, was very successful in NASCAR racing in the decade and the car was also raced in Trans Am, ARCA and IMSA. Surprisingly, Plymouth Barracudas were raced in several countries in Europe, such as England, Sweden and France, as an anti-Camaro weapon, in Mexico. The Avenger raced in El Salvador.

Polonez (Poland)
This Polish car was raced mostly in Polish events but also made appearances in Hungary.

Polski Fiat (Poland)
Polski built Fiats under license in Poland. The cars were raced in Poland, Czechoslovakia and East Germany and even in Colombia and Ecuador. Polski engines were used to power Soviet Formula 2 cars.

Pontiac (USA)
Pontiacs raced in the USA, at NASCAR, IMSA, Trans Am but the Firebird also raced in places such as Holland and West Germany. Pontiacs were also raced in Ecuador.

Porsche (West Germany)
Porsches were raced in West Germany, USA, France, Italy, England, Belgium, Holland, Ireland, Denmark, Spain, Portugal, Sweden, Austria, Luxembourg, East Germany, Poland, Senegal, Angola, Morocco, Mexico, El Salvador, Canada, Brazil, Argentina, Japan, South Africa, Norway, Malaysia, Mozambique, Rhodesia, Finland, Macau, Venezuela, Puerto Rico, Andorra, Panama, Colombia, Switzerland, Ecuador, Australia, Greece, Indonesia, Guyana, Malta, Ethiopia/Eritrea and surely in many other countries. Porsche GT cars basically replaced Ferrari as the favorite GT race car in the 70s, being less expensive and easier to work on. Much of the winning was done by the Porsche 911 and derivatives (Carrera, 934, 912 etc) but other models, such as 908, 917, 917-10, 917-30, 935, 936, 914 and even older models such as the 356, 904, 907, 906 and 910 also won races and hill climbs overall and a huge number of class wins. Porsche engines also powered a number of prototypes and hybrids. It should also be noted that Porsche's vast application and fine tuning of turbo technology in both sprint and endurance racing during the decade drove widespread use of it in street racing and even Formula 1 by many other manufacturers. Large percentages of starters in the 24 Hours of Le Mans and other endurance races of the era were Porsches.

Large numbers of Porsches competed all over the world in the 70s. This is the Barth/Pesch 911 Carrera RSR that retired in Le Mans, 1974 (Jurgen Barth collection)

Premier (India)
Premiers were raced exclusively in India, mostly battling Hindustans.

This was the essence of racing in India in the 70s. Some prototypes up front and Premiers in the back. (Photo credit Vicky Chandhok)

Prince (Japan)
Prince had built the 380 race car in 1965, which was very successful in Japanese racing. Before the decade began, Prince had been sold to Nissan but at least one car was raced as a Prince 380 in the 1970 season.

Puma (Brazil)
Puma was a Brazilian manufacturer of a VW engined GT car. The car was widely raced between 1970 to 1972 but then disappeared from the circuits, for there was no GT category in Brazil. The car also raced briefly in Argentina in 1971. A car referred as a Puma also raced in Puerto Rico but I could not ascertain its identity.

Pumas raced all over Brazil early on the decade (Photo by Rogerio da Luz)

Rambler (USA)
By 1970 Rambler had been absorbed by AMC but old Ramblers were still raced in South American countries and Mexico.

Reliant (Britain)
Reliants were used in English club racing in the 70s and Reliant engines were widely used in Formula 750 in Britain. But the make's moment of international glory was coming 3rd in the inaugural race at Yahuarcocha track in Ecuador, 1970. The model used was a Scimitar. This model was also used in Australia.

Renault (France)
Renault was one of the major supporters of racing in the 70s, not only in France but also elsewhere. The R8 Gordini Cup was a single make category, in which many a French driver debuted, eventually replaced by the R12. The R5 championships began mid-decade, held in several countries besides France, such as Sweden. In the US the car was called Le Car, with a series of its own. A single make championship for Renault 4s was held in Colombia. Renault touring cars also raced in Argentina and were widely used almost everywhere besides France: USA, Austria, Belgium, Andorra, Holland, Sweden, Britain, Brazil, Spain, Italy, West Germany, Denmark, Norway, Canada, Andorra, Switzerland, Venezuela, Ireland, Chile, Colombia, Ecuador, Finland, Czechoslovakia, Yugoslavia, Rhodesia, Mexico, Scotland, Poland, Japan, Australia, Malta, Romania, Luxembourg, South Africa, Morocco, Senegal, Angola, Kenya, Uruguay, Turkey, Ethiopia/Eritrea. Renault engines powered Formula France, then Formula Renault. In top flight racing, Renault had very successful forays in Formula 3, Formula 2, 2 Liter Sports Cars, eventually winning Le Mans and fielding the first turbo Formula 1 challenger. Old 4CV's were still raced in the early 70s, in places like Morocco and even Brazil, were a VW engined example was raced as late as 1972. Old Dauphines and 1093 also appeared in races in many countries.

Renha (Brazil)
Joao Renha produced the GT Renha, a pretty VW engined car that was meant for limited production created by Herculano Ferreirinha, of future Heve fame. The car, also called Prototipo Renha, raced in a couple of hillclimbs in Petropolis, winning Division 4 once, albeit by default, appearing no further during the decade.

Riley (Britain)
The Elf was another Mini variant, which basically raced in England and Scotland during the 70s.

Rolls-Royce (Britain)
Believe it or not, even Rolls Royces were seen in club racing in England and there were plans to field a Rolls engine Formula 5000 car, which came to naught.

Rover (Britain)
There were plans to field Rovers in the 1970 British Saloon Car Championship in 1970, which did not come to fruition and instead, the car was raced in club events. A car did race and led in the 1970 Marathon de la Route and was then sold and raced in Australia, 1971. John MacDonald drove one in the Macau Guia race in 1973, while Alec Poole drove one in 1972, later taken to Barbados. Rovers were also used in Irish hill climbs. Rover engines were used in Formula 5000 and in Special Saloons such as a popular DAF-Rover.

Saab (Sweden)
It should be noted that Saab works cars won important rallies in the 70s. However, in racing and hill climbs Saabs rarely encountered success, even in their class. The noted exceptions were Ron Christensen's win in SCCA Showroom Stock A, in 1979, using a Saab Turbo and Don Knowles two Showroom Stock B titles in 1978 and 1979. The sporty Saab Sonnet was also used in racing. Saabs were raced in Sweden, Finland, Norway, Uruguay, Czechoslovakia, USA, Luxembourg, Belgium, Canada, Mexico, Poland, Australia, Ecuador and other countries.

SEAT (Spain)
In the 1970s, SEAT produced FIATs under license. The cars raced mostly in Spain but some appeared in Holland, Portugal, Andorra, Belgium and Poland. SEAT mechanicals were used in the Spanish category Formula 1430, which eventually became Formula SEAT.

Serenissima (Italy)
A Serenissima showed up in the 1000 km of Buenos Aires in 1970, disappearing quickly from the circuits after a poor performance. The setback made patron Count Volpi di Misurata give up on racing and car building once and for all.

Shelby (USA)
Shelbys GT350 were raced mostly in the USA but also appeared in European racing. AC Cobras sporadically still raced in early 70s events in the USA, Canada, Mexico and Sweden and won races.

Simca (France)
Most people will connect the name Simca to Matra, for Chrysler, who owned Simca, sponsored the French team from 1970 to 1974. However, there was as little Simca in Matra as there was Ford in Cosworth. Simca's small Rallye II and III, however, raced effectively throughout the decade all over the world. By the end of the decade, Chrysler Europe collapsed and Simca was bought by Peugeot and renamed Talbot. The large, 2.3 liter Simca Chambord derivatives still raced in Brazil until 1975. Simca single make series were run in France, both for Rallying and for Simca-engined prototypes, the Challenge Simca Shell (1972-1974). Simcas raced in France, England, USA, West Germany, Belgium, Norway, Austria, Netherlands, Italy, Denmark, Norway, Czechoslovakia, Japan, Spain, Portugal, Colombia, Chile, Brazil, Ecuador, Finland, Andorra, Macau, Luxembourg, Morocco, Senegal, Scotland, Argentina, Yugoslavia. The CG Simca, a prototype built for rallying, also raced in hill climbs, mostly in France.

Singer (Britain)
Singers were rare and few in the 70s but the Chamois was built until 1970 and was raced in Scotland. It was an Imp derivative.

Sipani (India)
Sipanis were raced in their native India. The Dolphin model was based on a Reliant Kitten model.

Skoda (Czechoslovakia)
Skodas were by far the Eastern European cars that raced in most countries during the 70s. In addition to racing in Czechoslovakia, Belarus, Ukraine, Poland, Hungary, Bulgaria and East Germany, Skodas also raced in the European Touring Car Championship, thus getting the chance to compete in England, Belgium, Austria, Italy, Holland, West Germany, as well as Finland, Colombia, Norway. Skoda also promoted a Formula Skoda championship during the decade and some prototypes and specials were built behind the Iron Curtain. Skodas with large V8 engines raced in Super Saloons in England and Ireland.

Steyr-Puch (Austria)
Steyr-Puch produced Fiats under license in Austria and the little cars were raced in a few other countries besides Austria, such as West Germany, Holland, Switzerland.

Studebaker (USA)
Studebakers had not been produced for a while by 1970, yet, they were still used in Colombian hill climbs and in Peru, early on the decade.

Subaru (Japan)
Subarus were rarely raced in the 70s but the make's cars surfaced in places like Japan, Macau, Ecuador, Kenya, Australia and Angola.

Subarus were rare in racetracks in the 70s. Photo by Jose Santos.

Sunbeam (Britain)

Imps were frequently used in smaller engined classes. Imps were also produced by Hillman. Photo by Colin Lourie.

Sunbeam Imps and Avengers appeared in touring car series and hill climbs in Austria, Ireland, Northern Ireland, Belgium, Holland, Luxembourg, Norway, Andorra, Panama, Switzerland, Scotland, Ecuador and England. GT Tigers were also raced in a few places. Eventually the name was dropped and Sunbeam, like all former European Chrysler brands, became Talbot. Photo on next page.

Suzuki (Japan)
Suzuki was mainly known as a motorcycle brand in the 70s but the make's cars also raced in a few places besides Japan, such as El Salvador, Norway, Chile and Macau. Suzuki engines were also used in SCCA D sports racers during the decade, winning many races and championships. Suzuki won many Japanese tiny car division races.

Syrena (Poland)
Syrena's racing career was restricted to Poland. Like the Trabant, it was a 2-stroke car.

Talbot (France/UK)
By 1979, the Chrysler European operations had been bought by Peugeot, so that brands like Hillman, Sunbeam and Simca all disappeared. As a result, models such as the Avenger, raced as Sunbeams and Hillmans until then, became Talbots.

Tatra (Czechoslovakia)
Tatras were used only in their native country, in hill climbs.

Torino (Argentina)
Torinos were a modified Rambler produced by IKA-Renault in Argentina, proudly called by Argentines their home bred car. Torinos were used in Argentina's grueling Turismo de Carretera category and a couple showed up in an international race in Brazil, in 1970 and were also raced in Uruguay, Peru, Chile and Ecuador.

Toyota (Japan)

In the beginning of the decade, small Toyotas were mainly an Asian oddity, a situation that was mostly changed by the end of the decade. Corollas, Coronas and Celicas were raced in a large number of countries, besides Japan, namely USA, Austria, Belgium, Holland, Sweden, West Germany, France, Denmark, Macau, Australia, Switzerland, Barbados, South Africa, Norway, Rhodesia, Scotland, Mozambique, Malaysia, Ecuador, El Salvador, Malta, Chile, Peru, Philippines, Greece, Canada, Indonesia, Argentina, Costa Rica. Additionally, Toyota engines powered a Sigma entry at Le Mans and a Group 5 Celica was entered in the 1978 DRM, driven by standing champion Rolf Stommelen. As of 1975, Toyota engines became the most prominent Formula 3 engines in Europe.

Toyotas raced in dozens of countries. This is a Celica at work in Macau, 1973. Photo by Jose Santos

Trabant (East Germany)
The 2-stroke Trabants are largely regarded as anachronic automotive jokes in the West but the fact is that the car was raced in East Germany, as well as Czechoslovakia, Poland, Hungary and Bulgaria.

Triumph (Britain)
Triumph sports and sedans were raced in several countries and the Dolomite was a very useful touring car. Triumphs were raced in England, France, Italy, Austria, Sweden, Holland, Spain, Portugal, Switzerland, Andorra, Scotland, Belgium, Colombia, Chile, Ecuador, Northern Ireland, Malaysia, Morocco, Norway, Canada, Sri Lanka, Kenya, Trinidad, Barbados, Guyana and Australia. Group 44 in the USA also built a TR8 used in IMSA racing, while a number of Triumph models (TR4, TR6, TR7, Spitfire) raced in SCCA's D and G production, winning many races and championships and TR3s were still raced as well.

Turner (Britain)
Turner built sports cars in small volume until 1966, however the cars continued to be raced until as late as 1979, in English and Scottish modsports.

TVR (Britain)
Several TVR models were raced in England, Holland and the USA, mostly in club racing and a model won the 1971 Shell Leaders hill climb championship in England, driven by Spotty Smith. The car was also raced by McDonald to win hill climbs in Hong Kong and also raced in Sweden and Australia.

Unipower (Britain)
Unipower GT production stopped in 1969 but some of the cars, powered by Mini engines, raced in many venues.

This Unipower was having some directional issues in Macau, 1973. Photo by Jose Santos.

Vauxhall (Britain)

Vauxhalls were mostly raced in Britain but also in countries such as Angola and Guyana.
Photo by Colin Lourie.

Vauxhall was GM`s brand in Britain but the cars were raced in a few other countries besides England, such as Scotland, Ireland, Northern Ireland, South Africa, Canada, Luxembourg, Norway, Belgium, Kenya, Puerto Rico, Guyana, Trinidad, Barbados, Portugal, Australia and Angola. It was not as popular as the Opel, GM's other European brand.

Volga (Wolga) (Russia)
Volgas were raced in the Soviet Union (Russia, Ukraine, Latvia, Estonia and Belarus)

Volkswagen (Germany)
VW was represented in touring car races early on the decade mainly by the Beetle, raced in West Germany, Belgium, Britain, Spain, France, Portugal, Luxembourg, Macau, Australia, El Salvador, Czechoslovakia, Switzerland, Finland, Holland, USA, Canada, Mexico, Brazil, Scotland, Paraguay, Uruguay, Indonesia, Ecuador, Andorra, Peru, Venezuela, Guyana, Chile, Barbados, Puerto Rico.

The 4-door VW 1600 was not widely used as a race car in Brazil. A 2.2 liter example actually raced in the first Copa Brasil, against the likes of Ferrari 512 and Porsche 908. The car's nickname was "Ze do Caixao", named after a horror movie director of ill repute. (Photo by Rogerio da Luz)

VW Passats were raced in quite a few countries, this one in England, 1974. (Photo by Gerald Swan)

The car was even used in Macau touring car races and in SCCA and Trans Am. In Brazil, a 4-door VW, the TL and the VW Brasilia were also used in touring car races, while the K70 was briefly used in Europe. Karmann Ghias, sold by VW in a few countries, were used as race cars sporadically. Eventually, water cooled VWs began appearing in racing in 1974, the Passat being first used in the British Saloon Car Championship. Later on the decade, the Polo, Golf and Scirocco became common. Single make series were staged for Golf (many countries in Europe), Rabbit (USA), Passat (Brazil) and VWs were also widely used in hill climbs. Formula Vee was a very popular entry level single seater series, with championships and chassis manufacturers literally all over the world. Formula Super Vee was a more selective category, championships held in West Germany, Scandinavia, Europe, Britain, Brazil, Yugoslavia and the USA. Given the easy and inexpensive preparation, VW prototypes were built and constructed all over the world.

Volvo (Sweden)
Although considered honest safe transportation even back then, Volvos were raced in many countries, mostly in Sweden, for obvious reasons but the cars also appeared in Belgium, Holland, Italy, Denmark, Norway, South Africa, Rhodesia, Ecuador, Colombia, Panama, Costa Rica, Portugal, Australia, Chile, Scotland, Morocco, Peru, Argentina, as well as SCCA and IMSA racing in the USA. There were single make Volvo series in Sweden, Finland and Norway. Even the old Volvo 544 continued to be raced in some places.

Wartburg (East Germany)
Wartburg touring cars raced in Eastern Europe (Czechoslovakia, Poland, Hungary, East Germany) but were used as far away as Colombia. Wartburgs also powered East German Formula 3 and Soviet Formula 1, 2, 3 and Formula Easter.

WAS (VAS) (VAZ) (Russia)
VAZ tourers were used in Soviet racing, in Russia, Latvia, Ukraine, Estonia and Belarus and also used to power Soviet Formula 2 and Formula 3 cars and later on, Formula Easter. VAZ cars were also branded Lada and Zhiguli (Shiguli). The cars were also raced in Czechoslovakia, Bulgaria, Hungary and East Germany.

Willys (USA/Brazil)
Willys-Overland's last operation, in Brazil, was taken over by Ford in 1966. Still, Willys Interlagos (a Brazilan built Alpine-Renault) was still raced in Brazil during 1970, eventually being totally outclassed. Even the clumsy Aero Willys, based on a Jeep platform, also raced sporadically, until at least 1971.

Wolseley (Britain)
Wolseley was another British Leyland brand that produced a Mini variant, with the brand`s typical grille, named Hornet. It raced in England and Ireland.

Yenko Stinger (United States)
Don Yenko prepared Chevrolet Corvairs that were sold as the Yenko Stinger. The car was still active in SCCA racing early on the decade.

Zastava (Yugoslavia)
Zastava, which built the Yugos that were sold in the USA in the 80s, were used in racing in Yugoslavia, Czechoslovakia, East Germany and even Belgium.

Zhiguli (Shiguli) (Russia)
These FIAT licensed cars were also branded Lada and WAS. As Zhiguli (also transliterated Shiguli), the cars raced in Hungary and East Germany.

SPECIFIC PURPOSE RACING CAR CONSTRUCTORS

This is a very long list, indeed. Even I was surprised, as I was compiling it. I tried to include just about everything in it, from Formula 1 manufacturers to hastily put together prototypes, with some exclusion criteria. Some race results make reference to a number of VW, Ford, Chrysler, FIAT Prototypes, with no specific name given to the contraption. As there is no way to tell whether VW Prototype A is the same as VW Prototype B and VW Prototype C, of if they are different creatures, I saw it fit to leave all of them off. I included only cars that were at least baptized with a specific name. These would number quite a few dozen cars.

For the very same reason, I stayed away from listing "Ford Special", "Chevrolet Special" and the like, for the sole reason that it is borderline impossible to differentiate one from the other. Indians fancied using the designation "Special", with a name before is, such as VR Special and Exide Special. I did not list these as manufacturers, for there are no surviving or identifying pictures of these cars, so that I can judge how special they really were. Perhaps in future editions I will find a way to include these properly, as long as I am able to ascertain the origin of the cars. At any rate, several such specials were simply ugly looking street cars with the roof taken off, nothing much special about them.

On the subject of names, I entertain no illusions that some cars received many different names, as they changed hands. One does not need to go farther than Formula 1 to see this, where a Boro was really a renamed Ensign, the Apollon and McGuire renamed Williams and the Safir a renamed Token, itself a Rondel project. In fact, a lot of racing car design was extremely derivative in the 70s, at least as far as chassis were concerned. The Duckham's prototype that raced in Le Mans was a reworked Brabham BT33 that Chris Craft raced sporadically and even the Amon Formula 1 was based on a Tecno design from 1973. The latter Formula 1 Merzario was a reworked Kauhsen and the 1976 Wolf-Williams was really a Hesketh 308C. So on, so forth. Racing cars were very often derivative or downright copies.

Therefore, maybe a few dozen (quite a few, maybe hundreds) are renamed cars, sometimes with no reason. Anthony Pritchard, in his 1972 Motor Racing Annual mentions the Tondelli. The owner, Italian Eris Tondelli, bought a Chevron and according to the author renamed it with no change to bodywork or mechanicals.

As motorsports became more professional and less "grass-roots" in the course of the decade, the proliferation of such "garagiste" specials diminished greatly and people simply bought well proven Osellas, Lolas, Marches, Reynards, etc.

A lot of French and Italian race results identify cars as Barchette or Barchetta. Before you jump the gun and believe this was a race car manufacturer, it isn't. It often refers to sedans and sports cars with the roof taken off, sometimes with some further modification to bodies, sometimes, none. A lot of these results do not identify the actual victimized car.

I looked over thousands of race results from all over the world to compile this list, and did independently. I suppose, with time more information will arise. I found that lots of available lists include only information from Western Europe, Australia/New Zealand and the USA, which I discuss elsewhere in this book. This is a shame, for in the 70s there were dozens upon dozens of race car makers in Argentina and Brazil who produced both single seaters and prototypes. Argentina is very impressive in that respect, for at one point it had four major championships featuring locally designed and built cars: Formula 1 Mecanica Nacional, Prototypes, Argentine F2, Formula 4 and even local single seater categories. Eastern Europe was also highly disregarded in most existing lists.

Although most of the cars in this list are British and American, racing cars have been built during the decade in Australia, Japan, France, Argentina, Austria, Switzerland, Italy, Spain, Brazil, Russia, Hungary, India, Ireland, Ecuador, New Zealand, Sweden, West Germany, East Germany, Holland, Canada, Czechoslovakia, Estonia, Dominican Republic, Chile, Kenya, Guyana, Greece, Angola, Zambia, Finland, Colombia, Poland, South Africa, Morocco, Peru, Venezuela, Bulgaria, Sri Lanka, Portugal, Belgium, Lithuania, Ukraine, Uruguay, Barbados, Denmark, Rhodesia, Mexico and I suppose, in every country where racing was happening. However, in the most exotic places cars tended to be named Ford Special, VW Special, etc, so they end up not being included here.

A large number of unnamed prototypes and specials raced all over the world, such as these cars in India. (Vicky Chandhok collection)

Needless to say, a large number of these makes are likely one-offs and could barely pass for a race car "manufacturer". The industry was pretty much dominated by the likes of **March, Lola, Ralt, Van Diemen, Chevron, Eagle, GRD**, while in the beginning of the decade grand prix makes **Brabham** and **Lotus** still made cars for customers for a number of categories. However, if we are to trust the figures, it does seem like **Estonia** (you guessed, an Estonian race car manufacturer) was a serious competitor for highest producer: during the decade no less than 369 Estonias were produced, which populated not only Formula Easter but also the Russian F1, F2 and F4 categories and hill climbs galore in Eastern Europe. But it is really difficult beating Lola in this respect: it produced 99 T490s Sports 2000, 104 T440 Formula Fords, 213 T340/342 Formula Fords, 56 T330/332/332C Formula 5000s, plus 101 T290/294/296 sports cars during the decade, in addition to low runs of several other models (Indy, Formula 1, Super Vee, Can-Am).

The Landar was one of many of hundreds of race car makers to make up the fields in the 70s. This one was driven by Stephen Lawrenson until 1976. It was equipped with a Broadspeed prepared Mini engine, thus generally outclassed in fields of 2-liter cars. Photo provided by Stephen Lawrenson.

RACING CAR CONSTRUCTORS LIST

161 Clubman (AUS)
Aardvark (USA)
AB (F)
AB (I)
Abbott (GB)
ABC (F)
Abrami (I)
AC (BR)
ACA (F)
ACE (AUS)
ACE (F)
ACG (F)
Acorn (GB)
Actet (UNK)
Adamas (GB)
Adams (AUS)
Adams (AUS)
Adeney (USA)
ADF (USA)
Adidas (E)
ADS (GB)
Aerofan (GB)
Agapiou (USA)
AGB (B)

AG-Bertinelli (I)
AGD (AUS)
Agitator (USA)
Agnesseens (B)
AGS (F)
Agshe (AUS)
Airoldi (I)
Alameda (CO)
Albatroz (BR)
Albert (A)
Albert (RA)
Albertinazzi (I)
Albizu (RA)
Aldon (GB)
Alexis (GB)
Alfa (USA)
Alfonsi (AUS)
Aljay (AUS)
Allan (GB)
Allegro (GB)
Allen (USA)
Allget (AUS)
Allison (AUS)
Allmeown (NZ)
Allross (NZ)
Alpha (GB)
Alton (AUS)
Altona (CDN)
Alton-Jaguar (GB)
Alvarez (RA)
Alvenius (S)
Amato (BR)
Amatol (AUS)
Ambivero (I)
Ambrose (GB)
AMC (BR)
AMCS (RA)
Amok (BR)
Amon (GB)
AMS (I)
Amweg (CH)
Amy (I)
Anco (GB)
Andre (B)
Andrew (AUS)
Andujar (RA)
Angood (GB)
Ansermin (CH)
Anson (GB)
Antares (USA)
Apal (B)
Apogee (GB)
Apollo (GB)
Apollo (J)

The Arpico was a modified Ford, prepared in Sri Lanka, that also won in India. Photo by Eshan Pieris.

The Arrows A1 in 1979. (Kurt Oblinger)

Apollon (CH)
Apolo (RA)
Applegate (USA)
APR (A)
Apy (E)
Aquarius (AUS)

Aquarius (GB)
Aquila (GB)
Arachnid (USA)
Aragano (BR)
Aramis (F)
Aranae (BR)
Arbyen (AUS)
ARC (F)
Arcam (F)
Archibald (NZ)
Arcos (GB)
Arcus (CZ)
Ardua (GB)
Arens/Schemann (D)
Argit (AUS)
Argo (GB)
Arguna (AUS)
Argus (AUS)
Arian (GB)
Ark-Sprite (GB)
Arno (NL)
Aron (S)
Arpa (F)
Arpico (SL)
Arrow (J)
Arrows (GB)
Art (GB)
Artford (GB)
Artog (CH)
ASCO (D)
ASD (GB)
Ash (CDN)
Ashdown (AUS)
ASK (SU)
ASP (AUS)
ASP (USA)
ASS (D)
Astap (GB)
Astech (USA)
Astra (GB)
Astur (CDN)
Asturo-Gepard (D)
Atecar (I)
Atlanta (USA)
Atlanta (USA)
Atom (AUS)
ATS (D)
ATS (I)
Attila (GB)
Au (D)
Aubits (GB)
Aucar (AUS)
Augusta (J)
Aulcor (AUS)

The Avallone was a Lola based prototype built in Brazil. They were equipped with Chrysler, Ford and Chevrolet engines, all pictured here. It also built Formula Fords and Super Vees. Photo by Rogerio da Luz

The Bino was a Merlyn copy that made the backbone of Brazil's Formula Ford during the 70s. Some Binos remained in competition well into the 80s, with a variety of bodies. The chassis was also used by Newton Pereira to build his Newcar Formula Super Vee car. Photo by Rogerio da Luz)

Aumec (RA)
Aurora (P)
Autoworld (USA)
Avallone (BR)
Avante (RA)

257

Avanti (AUS)
Avenger (USA)
Avia (CZ)
Avion (ZA)
Avispon Negro (RA)
AvS Shadow (USA)
Axone (F)
AZ (I)
Aztec (AUS)
Aztec (GB)
B Tracker (USA)
B&K Special (USA)
B&S (AUS)
Bacchus (AUS)
Bad Wander (J)
Badger (CDN)
BAE (AUS)
Baghira (CZ)
Bagnoli (I)
Balacco (RA)
Ballantyne (AUS)
Balle (AUS)
Balmar (F)
Bandido (AUS)
Bandido (CDN)
Bandini (I)
Bandit (AUS)
Bangalow (AUS)
Barcarr (USA)
Bardahl (AUS)
Barion (E)
Barlow (Rh)
Barnett (GB)
Baron (J)
Barp (AUS)
Barracuda (GB)
Barrelli (I)
Barrier (J)
Barton (GB)
Bassonette (GB)
Batellino-Pomodoro (RA)
Baufer (RA)
Bayspeed (AUS)
Bazeley (USA)
BBM (AUS)
BBM (F)
BC Razor (AUS)
BCJ (S)
BCM Phantom (AUS)
BDR (AUS)
Bea (USA)
Beach (USA)
Beagle (GB)
Beam (E)

The Brabham BT-45 (Kurt Oblinger)

The Carex was a Herald engined Indian prototype built in India. (Photo by Vicky Chandhok)

Beany (GB)
Bear (USA)
Beast (GU)
Beasy (AUS)
Beattie (IRL)
Beck (USA)

Beco (UNK)
Bee Gee (GB)
Bee Vee (AUS/S)
Befa (AUS)
Begg (NZ)
Behnke Condor (D)
Belchfire (USA)
Belcho (RA)
Bellasi (I)
Bellco (J)
Belloni (I)
Benamo (RA)
Benavidez (RA)
Benora (AUS)
Bepermoco (or Pepermo Koaco) (J)
Berati (AUS)
Berlinda (AUS)
Bernini (I)
Berta (RA)
Bertete (U)
Beth (AUS)\Beux (BR)
BFH (F)
BFT (CH)
Bignami (I)
Bingham (AUS)
Bini (RA)
Bino (BR)
Biota Monaco (GB)
Biraghi (I)
Birel (I)
Birrana (AUS)
Bishop (GB)
Bive (RA)
Bizzarrini (I)
BJ Special (USA)
Bladon (GB)
Bland (USA)
Blazicek (CZ)
Blomman (S)
Blum (USA)
BM (AUS)
BM Vee (S)
BMW (I)
Bobbin (AUS)
Bobek (CZ)
Bobsy (USA)
Bodola (S)
Bolar (GB)
Bolwell (AUS)
Bonetti (I)
Bonner-Powell (AUS)
Bono (AUS)
Bonzini (RA)
Boom (NL)

The Chana was a prototype built in Angola. It was based on a Lotus (Author unknown)

Chevrons were raced in a large number of countries during the decade. This one was used in a Formula Libre race in Scotland. Photo by Colin Lourie.

Bora (F)
Boral (AUS)
Borello (I)
Boro (NL/GB)
Borus (AUS)
Bosch (A)
Boufis-Alfa (GR)
Bouny (F)
Bourgealt (USA)

Bowin (AUS)
Bowren (AUS)
Boxer (USA)
Boyer (F)
Bozyck (RA)
BPG (GB)
BPS-Estonia (RU)
Brabasaki (USA)
Brabham (GB)
Brabota (USA)
Bradley (AUS)
Bradley (AUS)
Bradley (GB)
Bramhill (ZA)
Branca (I)
Brand X (USA)
Brandwood (USA)
Bratford (AUS)
Braun (A)
Bravi (RA)
Brawner (USA)
Bray (NZ)
Brazier (USA)
Brazil (S)
BRE (GB)
Bribo (AUS)
Brixner (CZ)
BRM (GB)
BRN (USA)
Brodsky (CZ)
Brogam (I)
BRP (GB)
Bruno (BR)
Brusadelli (I)
BRV (BR)
BS (CDN)
BS (DDR)
BSA (AUS)
BSC (AUS)
BSH (F)
BSM (RA)
Buchanan (AUS)
Bud Meadows Pinto (USA)
Buglioni (I)
Bugsy (USA)
Buland (AUS)
Buma (I)
Bunyip (AUS)
Burger (CH)
Burkhardt (D)
Burnaby (CDN)
Burnett (USA)
Butcher (AUS)
BWA (I)

The Costa-Alfa Romeo, a rare Zambian race car (author unknown)

BYC (USA)
Cabana (RA)
Cacador de Estrelas (BR)
Cadwell (USA)
CAE (USA)
Caflisch (CDN)
Caldwell (USA)
Caleffi (I)
Callegari (I)
Callet-Marcadier (F)
Cambal (CZ)
Camber (BR)
Cambron (AUS)
Cameron (AUS)
Camilo Especial (BR)
Campagnac (F)
Campo (RA)

Canale (I)
Canberra (USA)
Cancellieri (RA)
Cann (USA)
Canstel (AUS)
Capital (ZA)
Capoferri (I)
Capricornia (AUS)
Caracci Motorsports Special (USA)
Carex (IN)
Carillo (USA)
Carlboro (AUS)
Carlier (B)
Carman Apache (J)
Carroll (AUS)
Carsa (U)
Carter (USA)
Carter Corvette (USA)
Casaab (USA)
Casale (RA)
Casari (BR)
Cascavel Bi-Motor (BR)
Castelnau (F)
Castro (U)
Catellano (RA)
Caturo (GB)
Causey (USA)
CB (AUS)
CDSC (I)
CE1 (AUS)
Cebco (AUS)
Cecil (USA)
Cedac (F)
Cedoz (USA)
Cee Bee (AUS)
Celi (B)
Cenci (RA)
Census (GB)
Centaur (AUS)
Centaur (GB)
Centaur (USA)
Century (USA)
Cermak (CZ)
Cesca (F)
CG (F)
CGB (F)
Chamberlain (NZ)
Chamox (GB)
Chana (ANG)
Chaparral (USA)
Charkov (RU)
Charlie Brown (USA)
Cheales (ZA)
Cheetah (AUS)

264

The Super Deserter looks more like a buggy. The Dominican VW engined built racer raced regionally (Unknown author)

Dolphin Formula 2 car in Macau, 1972. Driver is Max Stewart. (Photo by Jose Santos)

Cheetah (CH)
Cheetah (USA)
Chelco (RA
Cheva (GB)
Chevitres (RA)

Chevitu (RA)
Chevron (GB)
Chilford (AUS)
Chill (AUS)
Chimba (USA)
Chimera (AUS)
Chimera (USA)
Chimo (CDN)
Chinook (CDN)
Chippala (AUS)
Chiro Special (USA)
Chivilo (RA)
Chiviuan (RA)
Chobon (F)
Christmann (D)
Cianciaruso (BR)
Cib (F)
Cicada (AUS)
Cicada (AUS)
Cicada (USA)
Ciceri (I)
Ciclon (RA)
Cigliotti (Cigliutti) (RA)
Cigo (I)
Cirrus (GB)
Citation (USA)
Clark (BR)
Claydon (GB)
Cloud Master (USA)
CM (GB)
CMS (AUS)
Coachwork (USA)
Coad (AUS)
Cobo (EC)
Cobra (BR)
Cobra (I)
Cobra (UNK)
Code (AUS)
Coffey (AUS)
Coldwell (GB)
Collector (GB)
Collignon (USA)
Colombo (I)
Colt (Indycar) (USA)
Colt (J)
Comando (CO)
Combus (F)
Comet (AUS)
Comet (J)
Competicion (RA)
Conchord (UNK)
Condor (AUS)
Condor (CDN)
Condor (D)

Australia's Elfin built single seaters and prototypes. (Photo by Glenn Moulds)

Debut of Ensign at Brands Hatch F3 race, 1971. (Photo by Gerald Swan)

Condor (GB)
Coniglio (J)
Connew (GB)
Consonni (I)

267

Consutinni (AUS)
Contender (GB)
Cooper (GB)
Coota (AUS)
Copyma (CH)
Cora (F)
Cordite (AUS)
Cordoban (E)
Corsa (USA)
Corsair (AUS)
Corsini (I)
Cosna (F)
Costa-Alfa (ZA)
Costello (USA)
Costin-Walker (GB)
Cougar (AUS)
Cougar (GB)
Cox (J)
Cox (UNK)
Coyote (USA)
Crance Special (USA)
Cravo (BR)
CR-CDS (I)
CRD (AUS)
Cres (USA)
Crespi (RA)
Crespo (RA)
CRM (I)
Crossle (IRL)
Crossley (GB)
Crosty (CDN)
Crown (USA)
CRS (D)
CRS (I)
Cruex (USA)
Crusader (USA)
CSP (F)
Ct3 (AUS)
CTG (GB)
Cuda (NZ)
Cunha (BR)
Cupido (CO)
Cuppes (CDN)
Cur (AUS)
Curtis (USA)
Cusson (F)
Custom (USA)
CVR (I)
Cyclo (AUS)
Cyclone (J)
D'Agnillo (RA)
D13 (USA)
Daasch-Volgt (DDR)
Daco (I)

The Fittipaldi FD-05 F-1 car (Kurt Oblinger)

Furias raced in Brazil from 1970 to 1973, using a vast array of engines: FNM, BMW, Chevrolet, Chrysler, Ferrari and even Lamborghini. (Photo by Rogerio da Luz)

Dagga (ZA)
Dagrada (I)
Dahmcar (D)
Daisy (GB)
Dallara (I)
Dalmac (AUS)
Dalshaw (AUS)
Dam (F)

269

Damper (USA)
Damsic (GB)
Dangel (F)
Danton (GB)
Daren (GB)
Darnval (F)
Dart (USA)
Darvic (GB)
Dasan (BR)
Dastle (GB)
Datalinski (GB)
Datford (AUS)
Dauphine (F)
Daveric (AUS)
Davey (RH)
David (GB)
Day & Night (J)
DB (AUS)
DBS (USA)
De Atley (USA)
De Cadenet (GB)
De Halb (AUS)
De Julius (CDN)
De Riu (I)
De Sanctis (I)
De Tomaso (I/RA)
De Villiers (ZA)
Deb (GB)
Debura (F)
Dee Vee (AUS)
Deka (AUS)
Del Giovane (I)
Delapena (GB)
Delta (AUS)
Delta (AUS)
Delta (AUS)
Delta (CZ)
Delta (GB)
Delta (I)
Dema (I)
Denmacher (USA)
Derichs (D)
Derrard (AUS)
Dervich (GB)
Deserter (Super) (DR)
Deserter (USA)
Destefano (RA)
Detmo (F)
Deutsch (D)
Devione (AUS)
Dewal SOS (AUS)
DEZ (ZA)
DF (F)
Di Tullio (RA)

GRD also built sports cars, besides single seaters. This is Tim Schenken in one, 1973. Photo by Russell Whitworth

The Hayhoe was not a success at Indy but added variety. Photo by Rob Neuzel

Diablesse (GB)
Dicer (USA)
Dickson (USA)
Dido (GB)
Diehl Special (USA)

271

Dieman (AUS)
Dieterbilt (AUS)
Dimep (BR)
Dingo (USA)
Dino (GB)
Diva (GB)
DLR (D)
DM3 Holden Cougar (AUS)
DMZ (I)
DNC (GB)
DNV (AUS)
Dobbin Sahara (GB)
Dolling (S)
Dolly Bee (S)
Dolphin (AUS)
Dolphin (USA)
Dome (J)
Domino (GB)
Dona (CDN)
Donadio (RA)
Donford (AUS)
Donnelly (ZA)
DP (ZA)
Dragon (USA)
DRC (DK)
DRE (USA)
DRL Hawke (USA)
DRM (AUS)
DRM-PRT (UNK)
Druid (GB)
Drummond (GB)
DRW (GB)
DTV (AUS)
Duba (CZ)
Dubury (USA)
Duck (USA)
Duckham (SF)
Duckhams (GB)
Ducret (CDN)
Dulon (GB)
Dunlop (I)
Duplo (BR)
Dupr (CZ)
Duqueine (F)
Durval (AUS)
Duval (USA)
Dynamotive (USA)
Dywa (I)
Eagle (AUS)
Eagle (J)
Eagle (USA)
Eagle Imp (AUS)
Easter (USA)
EB (AUS)

Heve made prototypes and formula cars in Brazil. Photo by Rogerio da Luz.

Huron built small engine prototypes but never quite made the big time Photo by Gerald Swan.

EBS (D)
Eckmann (ZA)
Eclipse (USA)
Ecosse (GB)
Ecosse (ZA)
Ecudire deDes Ford (AUS)
Edge (USA)

Edmonds (USA)
Edmunds (USA)
EHR (AUS)
Ehrlich (GB)
Eifelland (D)
Eisert (USA)
El Gran Caribe (YV)
El Opaco (CO)
El Toro (AUS)
Ela Tropex (ZA)
Elden (GB)
Elf (AUS)
Elf (F)
Elfin (AUS)
Elgar (BR)
Elina (F)
Elk (AUS)
Ellova (GB)
Elva (BR)
Elva (GB)
Elwyn (AUS)
EM (USA)
Emberton (GB)
EMC (GB)
Emiliani (I)
Emu (USA0
EMV (GB)
Endo (RA)
Engel (D)
Enlock (AUS)
Ennerdale (GB)
Enricone (BR)
Ensign (GB)
Epperly (USA)
Era 1 (BR)
Erfurt (DDR)
ERH (AUS)
ERJ (AUS)
Erjie (F)
ERM (GB)
ERS (ZA)
Escargot (AUS)
Escorial (ZA)
Esko (USA)
Espadon (F)
Espotti (RA)
Esqualus (also written Squalus) (BR)
ESS (ZA)
Essex (USA)
Esso Extra (J)
Estonia (EE)
Eta (ZA)
ETCO (E)
Etienne Aiger (I)

274

Kaimann Super-Vees and Vees were built under license in Brazil. The make was originally Austrian and also built a one-off Formula 2. (photo by Rogerio da Luz)

The King was driven by a few drivers at Indy, including Gary Bettenhausen. Photo by Rob Neuzel.

Eton (GB)
Eufra (D)
Excalibur (USA)
Excar (USA)

Exford (CDN)
Exide Special (SL)
Express (GB)
Exzotec (USA)
FA 101 (USA)
Fagioli (I)
Fairford (GB)
Falcon (J)
Falconer (USA)
Farina-Dison (GB)
Farrell (AUS)
Fatouros (AUS)
Fava (I)
FBA (NZ)
FD (F)
Feca (BR)
Fee (CH)
Feirense (BR)
Fejer Brothers (USA)
Felday (GB)
Felisatti (I)
Femenia (MO)
Ferraris (I)
Ferrea (RA)
Ferret (CDN)
Fiberkit (USA)
Fide (I)
Fielding (AUS)
Finesse (AUS)
Finley (USA)
Finvau (SF)
Fiore (USA)
Fireball (GB)
Fisanotti (RA)
Fischer (USA)
Fischetti (USA)
Fisher (GB)
Fitti (BR)
Fittipaldi (BR)
FJ (AUS)
Flamingo (AUS)
Flea (AUS)
Flying Anvil (GB)
Flynn (USA0
FM (AUS)
FM (I)
FM (RA)
FMG (ZA)
FMS (AUS)
FNC (GB)
Focus (GB)
Focus (S)
Foglietti (I)
Foolishness (BRB)

Foretti (AUS)
Formar (RA)
Formcar (USA)
Formisano (RA)
Formula Automotive (USA)
Forsgrini (USA)
Forwood (USA)
Fournier-Marcadier (F)
FP (AUS)
Fraber (I)
Franetti (I)
Franklyn (CDN)
Frantzen (USA)
Frattini (I)
FRC (USA)
Freudiger (CH)
Frimar (I)
Frisbee (USA)
Fronte (J)
Fronzelli (NZ)
Froya (AUS)
FST (AUS)
FTB (GB)
Fuber (GB)
Fuchs (D)
Fun King (ZA)
Funco (USA)
Furia (BR)
Furuya (J)
Fvee (USA)
FVW (BR)
FX Special (J)
G5M (RU)
GAD (AUS)
Galant P/RF (AUS)
Galaxia (P)
Gallen (UNK)
Galli (CH)
Gallo (RA)
Galloway (AUS)
Gandor (GB)
Gard (AUS)
Gardner (USA)
Gardos (AUS)
Garibotti (RA)
Gas (AUS)
Gason (BR)
Gaspa (J)
Gatorades (CDN)
Gatti (I)
Gauge (ZA)
Gazela (CZ)
Gazelle (GB)
GB (I)

GBA (I)
Gbelec (CZ)
GC (AUS)
GC (F)
GDS (I)
Geca (F)
Gecko (ZA)
Gem (GB)
Gemco (NZ)
Gemini (AUS)
Gemini (USA)
Gena (AUS)
Geneer Cheyenne (AUS)
Genie (USA)
Genovese (I)
Gentile (RA)
GEO (I)
Gepard (D)
Gerber SP2 (CH)
Gerhardt (USA)
Geri (F)
Gerrell (GB)
Gesca (F)
GFB (I)
Gian (BR)
Gideon (GB)
Giger (CH)
Gigi (I)
Giglio (I)
Giken Tokyo (J)
Gilbert (AUS)
Gilbert (USA)
Gilibertini (I)
Gillibiri (ZA)
Ginetta (GB)
Giom (CZ)
GiPi (I)
Gipsy (I)
Giripoka (BR)
Gissing (AUS)
Gitom (I)
Giuliani (I)
GJO (ZA)
GK (USA)
Glen Bryant (USA)
Glenadel (F)
GLH (NZ)
GLS (D)
GMC (I)
GMS (S)
Goblin (AUS)
Goddard (AUS)
Godfather Special (IN)
Golford (AUS)

The Kuntur was a pretty Peruvian prototype. The engine used in this prototype is not known but the car also raced internationally, in Ecuador, as well as in Peru. (Author unknown)

The Lolita was an Australian car. This one had an Alfa engine, driven by Vince Evans. Photo Glenn Moulds.

Goodman (AUS)
Gopher (GB)
Gordon (AUS)
Gough (AUS)

Govesa (BR)
Gozzoli (I)
GP (AUS)
GP (I)
GR3 (AUS)
Grac (F)
Graduate (AUS)
Grady (USA)
Graefentonna (DDR)
Grag (UNK)
Granger (AUS)
Grant (AUS)
Grantinni (AUS)
Graselli(I)
Graves (USA)
GRD (GB)
Greemax (AUS)
Green Ball (J)
Gremlin (GB)
Griffon (F)
Grigolo (RA)
Grimas (AUS)
Grizzly (USA)
GRM (I)
GRM (J)
Gropa (GB)
Gryphon (GB)
GSL (D)
GSR (I)
GTM (I)
Guellert (D)
Guepard (F)
Gug's (BR)
Guichaco (BR)
Guidi (RA)
Guisti (ZA)
Gulu (BR)
GV1 (AUS)
GWD (AUS)
Hadley Safari (AUS)
Haggis (GB)
Hahn (AUS)
Halcon (RA)
Halibrand (USA)
Haller (ZA)
Hamal (CZ)
Hamilton (AUS)
Hamlen (Hamlin) (GB)
Hammerschmied (A)
Hampe (F)
Hansen (S)
Hanter (ZA)
Hardman (AUS)
Hargal (AUS)

Lola built hundreds upon hundreds of race cars during the 70s, including this T310. Photo Lola Heritage.

Mantas raced with a variety of engines in Brazil and Paraguay (Photo by Rogerio da Luz)

Harp (AUS)
Harrier (GB)
Harrier (ZA)
Harris (GB)
Harris (USA)

Harrison (GB)
Hart (F)
Harvard (ZA)
HAS (SH)
Hauser (D)
Haval (CZ)
Havas (NL)
Hawk (USA)
Hawke (GB)
Hayashi (J)
Hayhoe (USA)
Hayman (CDN)
HD (USA)
HD13 (USA)
Hegglin (CH)
Heintzelman (USA)
Hela (CZ)
Helle (S)
Hema (F)
Henks Marves (USA)
Hepworth (GB)
Herber (CO)
Hering (CDN)
Hermes (GB)
Heron (NZ)
Herzig (A)
Hesch (D)
Hesketh (GB)
Heve (BR)
Hexagon (GB)
Hey (D)
Hibbit (GB)
Hick (A)
Hill (GB)
Hill (RH)
Hinotori (J)
Hipocampo (RA)
Hiro (J)
Hirondelle (B)
Hispakart (E)
Hite (USA)
HLM (USA)
HM Special (GB)
HMS (GB)
Hobson Special (AUS)
Hodge (USA)
Hogan (USA)
Hole (NZ)
Hollinger (AUS)
Hollingsworth (USA)
Holo (D)
Hook (AUS)
Hopkins (USA)
Horag (CH)

Horrocks (GB)
Horton (USA)
Hossack (AUS)
Hounskull (AUS)
HPB Ford Special (AUS)
Hrb (AUS)
HRS (GB)
Hrubron (F)
HS6 (AUS)
HTS (DDR)
Huarte (RA)
Huayra (RA)
Hudson (GB)
Huffaker (USA)
Hunter (AUS)
Huntsmann (GB)
Huron (GB)
Huron Spence (GB)
Hustler (AUS)
HVB (NL)
HVW (AUS)
Hybrid (GB)
Hyjumper (USA)
Hyperform (AUS)
Ian Davis Special (AUS)
Ibec (GB)
Ideal (BR)
Idra (I)
IDS (AUS)
Image (GB)
Imp (AUS)
Imp (B)
Impala (ZA)
Inaltera (F)
Incas (S)
Investor (USA)
IRW Hustler (GB)
Ishii (J)
Iso (F)
Iso Marlboro (GB)
Issert (USA)
Italdiesel (BR)
Iwakami (J)
Jabenti (AUS)
Jabro (USA)
Jackal (USA)
Jaco (GB)
Jagre (USA)
Jamaro (BR)
Jamun (GB)
Jane (AUS)
Jaraco (J)
JAS-Piranha (GB)
Javado (NL)

Javelin (GB
Javier (E)
JAX (J)
Jay Bee (AUS)
JBS (AUS)
JCB (F)
JCM (GB)
JDS (GB)
Jedda (AUS)
Jefa (F)
Jeff Special (SL)
Jeffrey (GB)
Jenine (AUS)
Jenkins (USA)
Jenoby (GB)
Jerboa (GB)
Jerri C (GB)
JGS (GB)
Jice (F)
JLW (GB)
JM Special (USA)
JMC Special (ZA)
JMF (F)
Joat (S)
Johnny Walker (GB)
Johnston (CDN)
Johnston (NZ)
JOLf1240 Special (J)
Jolus (AUS)
Jomax (AUS)
Jomic (GB)
Jomo (GB)
Jones (GB)
Jonmark (AUS)
Jonnez (F)
Josai (J)
Josefin (S)
Joy (USA)
JPE (F)
JR (BR)
JRM (F)
JRM (J)
JRM (NZ)
JS (F)
JSK (CZ)
JSM (F)
JSZ (F)
JTS (UNK)
JTS (ZA)
Juncoa (UNK)
Juncosa (E)
Junost (Ru)
Jurcik (CZ)
JV Mazda (AUS)

Brett Lunger in a F1 March (Kurt Oblinger)

The Martin was one of several British prototypes of the 70s. Photo by Gerald Swan

K2000/K3000 (UK)
Kaditcha (AUS)
Kaeffer (AUS)

285

Kaimann (A)
Kajiwara (J)
KAM (AUS)
Kanamoro (J)
Kanawer-Elrod (USA)
Kangaroo (USA)
Karasek (A)
Karringer (D)
Katano (J)
Katipo (AUS)
Kauhsen (GB)
KB Sprinter (AUS)
KE (J)
Kea (GB)
Keihan (J)
Keiyo (J)
Kellison (USA)
Kelly (CDN)
Kennedy (AUS)
Kenyon (USA)
Kerns (USA)
Kestrel (AUS)
KGB (GB)
Kiev (UK)
Kiki (USA)
Kilian (D)
Killroy (A)
Kincraft (GB)
King (GB)
King (USA)
Kingfish (USA)
Kingfisher (AUS)
Kinko (BR)
Kir-1 (J)
KISN Special (USA)
Kitchiner (GB)
Kitchmac (GB)
Kiwi (GB)
KK2 (USA)
Kleinig (AUS)
KLG (H)
KLT (USA)
KM (AUS)
KM200/300 (AUS)
KMW (D)
Knievel (USA)
Kniight (AUS)
Kobilan Special (USA)
Kobler (D)
Kogan (S)
Koike (J)
Kojima (J)
Komet (D)
Kondor (D)

Matich built single seater and sports cars. (Photo by Glenn Moulds)

Merlyns raced in a few categories, including Formula Atlantic. Photo by Gerald Swan

Kondou Special (J)
Koos (CZ)
Korwitzer (USA)
Kosaka (J)
Kotchie (GB)

287

Kovacs (H)
KR-1 (J)
Kramer (USA)
Krefel (AUS)
Kregol (AUS)
Krejci (CZ)
KS (J)
KSC (AUS)
KSR (NL)
Kubiena (CZ)
Kuether (DDR)
Kunimori (J)
Kuntur P-1 (PE)
Kurtis (USA)
Kuzma (USA)
Kuzma-Kenyon (USA)
Kvanti (SF)
Kwic (USA)
KY Special (J)
L&L (USA)
La Bomba (USA)
La Gallen (F)
Lab (I)
Labbe (F)
Ladi (RA)
Ladybird (GB)
Lahford (AUS)
Laki (I)
Lambert (USA)
Lamco (AUS)
Laminaire Special (USA)
Lamoureux (F)
Lampach (GB)
Lamplola (GB)
Lance (D)
Lance (USA)
Landar (GB)
Lapi (BR)
Lasear (USA)
Lasont (GB)
Launspach Mel (ZA)
Laycock (USA)
Lazerby (CDN)
Lazzat (BR)
LBM (S)
LBS (D)
LCR (A)
Le Bacq (UNK)
Le Chalutier (AUS)
Le Gallen (F)
Leah (GB)
Leavee (ZA)
Lec (GB)
Leda (GB)

In a single shot, the VW engined Newcar and Mili which raced in Brazil in the early 70s. Newcar also built a Super Vee that raced in 1974-75 (Photo by Rogerio da Luz)

Parnellis won Indy races but were not successful in Formula 1. Photo by Rob Neuzel.

Leda-Tui (GB)
Leecg (USA)
Leemas (GB)
Leffler (USA)

Leford GT (AUS)
Lefreve (USA)
Legalin (F)
Legrand (USA)
Legwood (CDN)
Lemas (GB)
Len Terry (GB)
Lenham (GB)
Lenham Hurst (GB)
Leningrad (RU)
Leon (NZ)
Leprechaun (AUS)
Leprechaun (USA)
Lepton (AUS)
Lesovsky (USA)
Leyba (USA)
Libra (AUS)
Libra (USA)
Liebre (RA)
Lightining Bug (CDN)
Lightning (USA)
Lightning 9AUS)
Limpet (AUS)
Lince (E)
Linnark (CDN)
Liswi (RA)
LJR (NZ)
Lloyd (GB)
LM Special (CDN)
LMT (D)
Lobbe (F)
Lobito (AUS)
Lodi (RA)
Loger (F)
Lois (YV)
Lola (GB)
Lolita (AUS)
Lomax (AUS)
Lombardi GP (UNK)
Lomin (AUS)
Lorelei (GB)
Lorenz (D)
Lotoy (D)
Lova (B)
Lowhad (AUS)
LS4 (S)
Lucalia (AUS)
Lucia (CZ)
Lucky (I)
Lucky Negri (I)
Luisvagen (BR)
LUL (BR)
Luzini (RA)
Lylec (Rh)

Polar made prototypes and single seaters in Brazil. Photo by Rogerio da Luz.

The Puma F3 car (Gerald Swan)

Lyncar (GB)
Lyndian (GB)
Lynx (AUS)
Lynx (USA)
MAC II Special (USA)
Macachin (RA)
MacGregor (AUS)

291

Macgregor (GB)
Maco (D)
Macol (E)
Macon (GB)
Madi (RU)
Madis (I)
Maegus (AUS)
Magee (AUS)
Maggot (GB)
Magnolia (AUS)
Magnum (AUS)
Magnum (CDN)
Maguire (USA)
Mahag (D)
Maier (D)
Maisonave (BR)
Maistegui (RA)
Maki (J)
Mako (AUS)
Mall (ZA)
Mallard (USA)
Mallock (GB)
Malloy (USA)
Malmark (AUS)
Malordy (A)
Mamba (ZA)
Mambo (F)
Mana (J)
Manatee (J)
Manhard (D)
Manos (USA)
Manta (AUS)
Manta (BR)
Manta (GB)
Manta (USA)
Mantis (GB)
Manx (AUS)
Manx (AUS)
Manx (USA)
Maraku (CZ)
MaralSP250 (NZ)
Marauder (F)
Marazzi (BR)
Marbell (F)
Marbo (USA)
Marcadier (F)
Marcellus (S)
March (GB)
Marcilio (BR)
Marco (BR)
Marcos (I)
Mark II (USA)
Marlen (ZA)
Marlin (GB)

Marlyn (GB)
Marnita (USA)
Marques (BR)
Marquiss-Magnum (GB)
Marrese (BR)
Marsico (RA)
Martare (NL)
Martin (GB)
Martini (F)
Martos (RA)
Martucci (RA)
Maru (USA)
Mascheroni (I)
Masquere (RA)
Mastery (J)
Matador (GB)
Mateju (SF)
Matich (AUS)
Matra (F)
Matta (I)
Mattel (USA)
Maubec (F)
Maurer (D)
Mavicapache (RA)
Mawer (AUS)
Maxim (J)
Maxwell (USA)
Maytaur (GB)
Mazron (USA)
Mazzili (I)
MC (BR)
MCB (I)
McBender (USA)
McCann (USA)
McElreath (USA)
McGregor (NL)
McGuire (GB)
McKee (AUS)
McLaren (GB)
McLeagle (USA)
McNally (GB)
McNamara (D)
McQueen (NZ)
McRae (NZ)
McReRo-ROGA (USA)
MCS (J)
MD (F)
MD (GB)
MDR (AUS)
Mean (B)
Mecca (J)
Mefisto (SF)
Meifa (RA)
Meiwa (J)

293

Mel (ZA)
Melesi (I)
Meli (MO)
Melkus (DDR)
Mellberg (USA)
Melton (USA)
MEP (F)
ME-PA (I)
ME-PRE (E)
Mercatelli ()
Mercury (GB)
Merlyn (GB)
Mero (RA)
Mertz (MO)
Merzario (I)
Meskowski (USA)
Messer (GB)
Meta-20 (BR)
MGK (CZ)
Michigami (J)
Mickey Mouse Special (GB)
Mickey Purser Special (GB)
Micron (GB)
Midon (AUS)
MIG (I)
Milano (AUS)
Mildren (AUS)
Milli (BR)
Milmor (GB)
Milua (AUS)
Minelli (BR)
Minho (BR)
Minning (USA)
Minos (AUS)
Minotte (S)
Mirage (BR)
Mirage (GB)
Mirage (GB)
Mirage (I)
Mispal (F)
Mistral (AUS)
Mistrale (GB)
Mistron (GB)
Mistry (GB)
Mitchell-Gano (USA)
MJM (AUS)
MKW (AUS)
Modus (GB)
Moleba (CDN)
Momo (I)
Momotaro (J)
Monaco (GB)
Monarch (AUS)
Monault (AUS)

The Repe was a Ford engined Brazilian prototype that was raced for a while in 1971. Photo by Rogerio da Luz.

Royale built both sports cars and single seaters, such as Formula 2, Formula 3, Formula Ford and Formula Atlantic. (Photo by Gerald Swan)

Mongoose (USA)
Mono (GB)
Monteverde (I)
Montore (RA)
Monza (USA)
Monza MG (AUS)
Monzeglio (I)

Moonraker (GB)
Moore (USA)
Moore (USA)
Morand (CH)
Moras (U)
Morbel (F)
Morcinek (CZ)
Morend (RA)
Morisson (F)
Moroni (I)
Morris (USA)
Morris (ZA)
Morton (US)
Mosden (ZA)
Motorlab (AUS)
MoTuL (D)
Motul (GB)
Moxon (AUS)
Moynet (F)
MP (BR)
MP (I)
MR (I)
MRA Riley (USA)
MRC (AUS)
MRD (I)
MRE (GB)
MS (AUS)
MS LANCIA (AUS)
MTX (CZ)
Muccini (I)
Mueller (BR)
Muggaroots (USA)
Multi (J)
Muma (D)
Mungo (CH)
Munro (NZ)
Murati (SF)
Murcia (CO)
Murphy Special (USA)
Murryay (USA)
Mutil (UNK)
MVW (AUS)
MWRisione (USA)
Myrtle (GB)
Mystere (GB)
Mystic (GB)
MZ (I)
Nadger (AUS)
Nakamura Special (J)
Nala (AUS)
Nala (E)
Nalman (AUS)
Nance (USA)
Narval (F)

296

Natalini (YV)
Nathan (GB)
National (AUS)
Nauticus (AUS)
Navajo (GB)
Navarro (RA)
Navarro (USA)
Navas (MO)
NCA (F)
NCM (F)
Nedloh (AUS)
Neisse (I)
Nejoh (AUS)
Nemesis (AUS)
Nemo (GB)
Nerus (GB)
Neugebauer (D)
Neutrino (USA)
Newcar (BR)
Newman-Draeger (USA)
Newton (AUS)
Nganti (AUS)
Niarce (J)
Nicewarmer (USA)
Nickie (USA)
Niegel (USA)
Nike (GB)
Niki (J)
Nimbus (AUS)
Nipama (I)
Nishiya (J)
Nisi (GB)
Nissen (AUS)
Nitra (J)
Noble (AUS)
Noble (NZ)
Nobuhiro (J)
Nola (AUS)
Nomad (GB)
Nord Ovest (I)
Nordic (GB)
Norseman (GB)
Nota (AUS)
Notso Triumph (AUS)
Nova (AUS)
Nova (J)
Nova (USA)
Novoa (MEX)
NTM (USA)
Nuitti (BR)
Numa (RA)
NWC (DK)
Nyarome (J)
Nymph (AUS)

OC-Capra (I)
Ocelot (USA)
Odin (AUS)
Odlins (NZ)
OF (AUS)
OK (BR)
Okamoto (J)
Oleari (I)
Olga (I)
Oli (BR)
Oliana (I)
Oly (USA)
Olympic (D)
Olympus (AUS)
Oma (I)
Omagon (GB)
OMS (I)
Onca (BR)
Orange (AUS)
Orbell (GB)
Orbit (ZA)
Ores (CDN)
ORI (J)
Orion (AUS)
Orion (D)
Orr (USA)
Ortega (CDN)
OSA (I)
Osborn (USA)
Osborne (USA)
Oscar (GB)
Oscar (J)
Osella (I)
Osmac (AUS)
OSO (I)
Osprey (USA)
Otokichi (J)
Oubury (USA)
Overdraft (GB)
P+G (CDN)
PAC (GB)
Pacer (GB)
Paci (CZ)
Pagani (RA)
Paganucci (I)
Paladin (GB)
Pale (CZ)
Paljar Mato (D)
Palliser (GB)
Palma (P)
Panda-JBM (F)
Pandora (AUS)
Panizza (RA)
Panizza (RA)

Tecno was very successful in F-2 and F-3, failed immensely in F-1. This is Regazzoni in the F2. (Photo by Gerald Swan)

The Turnham was an Australian sports car, here followed by an Elfin-Repco. Photo by Glen Moulds

Pankraz (D)
Pannis (CH)
Panther (AUS)
Panther (GB)
Paparusso (I)
Para (AUS)
Parnelli (USA)
Pascutti (RA)
Passalacqua (BR)

299

Passamonte (I)
Passanti (I)
Pastorello (I)
Patat (RA)
Pateco (BR)
Pati (BR)
Patinho Feio I (BR)
Patinho Feio II (BR)
Patinho Feio III (BR)
Patleijch (CZ)
Patterson (CDN/AUS)
Pauer (CZ)
Pauloni (RA)
Pavesio (I)
Pavi (I)
PBD (D)
PBF (GB)
PBS (USA)
PC (BR)
Pearsill (AUS)
Peat-Lola (USA)
Peco (ZA)
Pedler (AUS)
Pegasus (AUS)
Pegasus (AUS)
Pegasus Special (GB)
Pellero (F)
Pellin (I)
Penfold (GB)
Pennzoil Special (USA)
Penske (USA)
Pereyra (RA)
Performance Special (USA)
Perigee
Perigee (GB)
Perkins (AUS)
Pete Bill (AUS)
Phantom (AUS)
Phantom (AUS)
Phantom (AUS)
Phantom (BR)
Phantom (GB)
Phantom (J)
Phantom (USA)
Phenix (USA)
Philipp (USA)
PHM Papy (F)
Phoenix (CDN)
Phox (USA)
Pian (RA)
Pianetto (RA)
Pichi (D)
Pierce-GE (MEX)
Pilbeam (GB)

300

Piller (CH)
Pilotti (BR)
Pinetown (ZA)
Pink Panther (GB)
Piovesan (YV)
Piper (GB)
Pirana (AUS)
Piranha (AUS)
Pirolla (I)
Pitoco (BR)
Pixy (GB)
PMG (I)
PMS (ZA)
Polar (BR) Politoys (GB)
Polley (AUS)
Poponi (I)
Popot (F)
Porta (RA)
Porzio (D)
Pourciel (RA)
Pozzi (BR)
Pozzoni (I)
PP Special (BR)
Prad (AUS)
Prati (I)
Preditor (USA)
Prince (J)
Pringette Mistrale (GB)
Project (GB)
Project TC (GB)
Promot (PL)
Pronello (RA)
Prophet (USA)
Proton (AUS)
Proto-Rex (PE)
Protos (BR)
Provence (F)
PRS (GB)
PRT (UNK)
PSC (GB)
PT (BR)
PTSM (GB)
Pulsar (CDN)
Puma (AUS)
Puma (GB)
Purdi (USA)
Puzey (RH)
PV1 Berco (AUS)
PVB (GB)
PWS (AUS)
Pygmee (F)
Q'Marri (IN)
QGS (F)
Quartly (AUS)

Quasar (I)
Quasar (USA)
Question (GB)
Quick (UNK)
R&T (AUS)
R.E. (AUS)
Rab (AUS)
Race Craft (USA)
Race Queen (J)
Races (F)
Racewed (USA)
Radar (NZ)
Rader (GB)
Rae (GB)
RAF (CZ)
Rafaela (RA)
Raffo (GB)
Ragaiolo (I)
Raid (I)
Raithan (GB)
RAK (AUS)
Rak (PL)
Rally-TT (I)
Ralph (F)
Ralt (GB)
Rambler Edge (AUS)
Ramelli (F)
Ramini (RA)
Ramseyer (RA)
Ranger (AUS)
Rascar (USA)
Rassy (USA)
Rattebury (USA)
Rattler (USA)
Raven (AUS)
Raven (D)
Rawlson (AUS)
Ray (GB)
Raymond (I)
Rayner (NZ)
Rayton Special (GB)
RCA (USA)
Reader (USA)
Rebaque (GB)
Rebelle (AUS)
Rebman (AUS)
Rebo (I)
Red Devil (USA)
Red Vee (AUS)
Redex (GB)
Redline (J)
Redwing (AUS)
Reelac (GB)
Rees (USA)

302

Shadow F1 car at Long Beach, 1978 (Kurt Oblinger)

Tyrrell appeared as a constructor in 1970 (Kurt Oblinger)

Rego (NZ)
Regulus (J)
Reichmark (USA)
Reising (A)
Rejo (GB)
Rempel (USA)
Rennmax (AUS)
Renson (GB)
Rent-A-Hill Special (GB)

303

Renvogel (NL)
Renzini (I)
Reon (GB)
REP (F)
Repe (BR)
Repetto (I)
Requejo (RA)
Revell (AUS)
Revise (J)
Revoray (GB)
Rex (D)
Reynard (GB)
Reynolds (AUS)
RGB (I)
RGT (AUS)
Rheinland (D)
Rhubarb (NZ)
Riboto (GB)
Ricciardi (I)
Richev (AUS)
Rico (RA)
Riddell (AUS)
Rieger (D)
Riley (USA)
Rimco (USA)
Rina (EC)
Ringwraight (USA)
Rio (BR)
Riverside (J)
Rizzo (CH)
R-L (F)
RM (AUS)
RM (I)
Roadmaster (ZA)
Roadrunner (USA)
Roan (E)
Robe (AUS)
Roberts (AUS)
ROC (F)
ROC (UNK)
Roe (AUS)
Roger (CH)
Rohm (S)
Rollins Aero (USA)
Roma (AUS)
Romac (AUS)
Romero (RA)
Rondeau (F)
Rondel (GB)
Roosten (GB)
Roots-Kroupa (CZ)
Rorstan (AUS)
Rossi (RA)
Rostron (GB)

The Vollstedt was a not so successful 70s Indycar. Photo by Rob Neuzel.

The Wildcat won many Indy races in the 70s. Driver: Johnny Parsons. Photo by Rob Neuzel.

Roughcutter (GB)
Rousac (AUS)
Rousseau (F)
Rove (BR)
Royal (I)
Royal Bank Special
Royal Bank Special (GU)
Royal Special (J)
Royale (GB)
RPB (S)
RR (J)
RSM (S)
RSV (SF)
RT (AUS)
RTW (GB)
Rudeani (GB)
Rumas (I)
Russel Special (USA)
Rutherford (USA)
RWH (GB)
S&J (ZA)
Saav (I)
Sabel (USA)
Sabre (AUS)
Sabre (BR)
Sace (I)
Sachi (J)
Safety Breaker Special (USA)
Safir (GB)
Salatino (RA)
Salinas (RCH)
Sam (AUS)
Samantha (GB)
Samurai (J)
Sana (GB)
Sanderson (USA)
Sandstock (AUS)
Sanetti (I)
Santandrea (I)
Santilli (BR)
Saporoshez (DDR)
Sappo (DDR)
SAR (GB)
Saracen (GB)
Sarah GT (GB)
Sarak (GB)
Sark (UNK)
Sart (B)
Satti (BR)
Saturn (GB)
Saturn (ZA)
Sauber (CH)
Sauers (USA)
Sauter (CH)

Savage (J)
Savage (ZA)
Savey (F)
Sbarro (CH)
SBM (D)
Scabro (I)
Scabu (I)
Scamp (AUS)
Scaphoid (GB)
Scarab (GB)
Sceptre (AUS)
Sceptre (USA)
Schai (CH)
Schazum (AUS)
Schepers (B)
Schipper (NL)
Schkee (USA)
Schlesser
Schlusselklink (A)
Schmid - Kohlender (D)
Schmidt (D)
Schnee (USA)
Schrapnel (AUS)
Scimitar (AUS)
Scirocco (D)
SCM (ZA)
Scoffoni (RA)
Scora (F)
Scorer (AUS)
Scorpion (AUS)
Scorpion (AUS)
Scorpion (GB)
Scorpion (USA)
Scorpion (USA)
Scotcher (AUS)
Scott (AUS)
Scott (GB)
Scotti (I)
SE (J)
Sebring (AUS)
Sebring (BR)
Sebring (USA)
Sebring Special (AUS)
Seca (AUS)
Sederap (F)
SEG (DDR)
Seguin (F)
Sekai (J)
Selene (I)
Selex (E)
Sequeira (P)
Serenissima (I)
Sergio (RA)
Sesca (F)

Seyma (CH)
Seymour (USA)
Shadow (USA)
Shadow McGee (AUS)
Shadowfax (USA)
Shampine (USA)
Shamrock (USA)
Shannon (GB)
Sharp (AUS)
Sharp (NZ)
Shiden (J)
Shihala (USA)
Shirokuya (J)
Shores (USA)
Shortribs (USA)
Showcar (USA)
Shrew (AUS)
Shrike (AUS)
Shrike (USA)
Shuhei (J)
SIB (F)
SID (NZ)
Sidewinder (USA)
Sigma (J)
Sillvax (S)
Silnes (USA)
Silpo (BR)
Sinibaldi (I)
Sioux (AUS)
Slymper (S)
Smata (RA)
Smilin (S)
Smith (USA)
Smithfield (GB)
SMV (AUS)
Snob's (BR)
Sofia (I)
Solana Especial (MEX)
Sorbello (USA)
Sotro (RA)
Sovereign (GB)
Spartan (CH)
Spartan (GB)
Spartan (USA)
Sparton (GB)
Spectre (GB)
Spectrum (USA)
Speed Unlimited (USA)
Speedcraft Matador (GB)
Speedwell (E)
Spicar (I)
Spider (BR)
Spirit (USA)
Spook (GB)

Adfter a slow start, Williams became a force to be reckoned with in the late 70s F-1 (Kurt Oblinger)

Wolf raced for a short while in F1 (Kurt Oblinger)

Sportelli (USA)
Spreafico (I)
Sprint (USA)
Sprinter (AUS)
Spyder (USA)
Spyder (USA)

Squegon (GB)
Squite (AUS)
SRE (USA)
SRG (DDR)
SRS (J)
SRV (AUS)
SS (BR)
SSE (USA)
SSO (GB)
Stafford (GB)
Stag (AUS)
Stallwood (GB)
Stana (CZ)
Standfast (AUS)
Stanguellini (I)
Stanley-BRM (GB)
Stanton (NZ)
Stanton (USA)
Stapp-Sprint (USA)
Starfire (GB)
Stay (CZ)
Stealth (USA)
Stebro (CDN)
Steck (D)
Stellina (I)
Stevaux Wessler (BR)
Steve Sapp (USA)
Stewart (USA)
Sting (USA)
Sting (USA)
Sting (ZA)
Stinger (USA)
Stinger (USA)
Stirling (AUS)
Stoddard (USA)
Streaker (AUS)
Streamliner (USA)
Strider (CDN)
Sturdgess (GB)
Sturgeon (ZA)
Stylauto (I)
Suarez (U)
Sugai (USA)
Sugiyama (J)
Sunbeam Sports (AUS)
Sunoco (CH)
Super Sprint (BR)
Superbug (AUS)
Supernova (GB)
Surowka (CZ)
Surtees (GB)
Suzuki Bankin (J)
Swanseni (USA)
Swebe (S)

SWH (GB)
Swift (GB)
Swift (NZ)
Swift-Wright (USA)
Swiss Vau (CH)
Swiver (USA)
SWM (D)
Synnergism (USA)
T.P, (BR)
Tabra (AUS)
Tagliani (I)
Taipan (AUS)
Tallept-Estonia (RU)
Tallesin (NZ)
Tallisman (AUS)
Talon (GB)
Tamangueyu (RA)
Tamca (AUS)
Tangine (AUS)
Tappet (GB)
Targa (E)
Targa (NZ)
Tark (E)
Tarquin Minx (AUS)
Tasco (D)
Tasma (AUS)
Tasman (AUS)
Tasman (AUS)
Tasman (GB)
Tasman (ZA)
Tativale (BR)
Taurus (GB)
Taydec (GB)
Taylor McDonald (AUS)
Tchermoster (DDR)
Teac (J)
Techcraft (GB)
Technic (S)
Technica (J)
Technica Sur (RA)
Techno (UNK)
Tecma (F)
Tecni (CO)
Tecno (I)
Tee (AUS)
Tempest (AUS)
Tempest (GB)
Teo (USA)
Tequila (AUS)
Terapin (AUS)
Termini (F)
Terrapin (GB)
Terrapin (GB)
Terrick (GB)

Terrier (GB)
Terry (USA)
Tetranychus-Telarius (GB)
Thane (AUS)
The Old Nail (GB)
Theau (F)
Theodore (GB)
Thiele (I)
Thomas Special (USA)
Thompson Special (AUS)
Throwbridge (AUS)
Throwjm (AUS)
Thunder (J)
Thurner (D)
TI-22 (Autocoast) (USA)
Tiga (GB)
Tiger (AUS)
Tijuna (AUS)
Time (GB)
Tina (AUS)
Tiny Clanger (GB)
Tipke (USA)
Tirade (ZA)
Titan (GB)
TKN (GB)
TLE (USA)
Tobias (USA)
Toda (J)
Tognotti (USA)
Toj (D)
Tojeiro (GB)
Token (GB)
Tondelli (I)
Tonetti (I)
Tony (I)
Tornado (AUS)
Torpin (AUS)
Torralba (F)
Tortoise (J)
Total (USA)
Toti (I)
Toucan (GB)
TP-1 (BR)
Traco (D)
TRB (E)
TRC (USA)
TRC Imp (AUS)
TRE (AUS)
Treden (AUS)
Treford (AUS)
Trestle (USA)
Trevethan (AUS)
Trevis (USA)
Tri Ford (AUS)

Trick Fore (GB)
Tridem (AUS)
Triden (AUS)
Trident (AUS)
Trips (AUS)
Triton (AUS)
Trojan (GB)
Troyer (USA)
Trueno (RA)
TT Special (USA)
Tuan (AUS)
Tudor (AUS)
Tui (GB)
Tuppence A(US)
Turbos (AUS)
Turner (USA)
Turnham (AUS)
TXP (USA)
Tyoan (AUS)
Typhon (F)
Tyrrell (GB)
UBM (S)
UBS (D)
UFO (AUS)
UFP (F)
Union (RA)
Unser (USA)
Upsmalis (RA)
URD (D)
US Bong Products Special (USA)
Utz (D)
V2 (AUS)
Vairo (I)
Valaco (RA)
Valencia (AUS)
Valetti (I)
Valour (NZ)
Van Diemen (GB)
Van Hool (E)
Van Zyl (ZA)
Vaney (B)
Vanguard (USA)
Vargiu (I)
Variant (GB)
Varsity (AUS)
Vaugn (USA)
Vebo (S)
Vebra (GB)
Veegos (ZA)
Veemax (SF)
Veeva (USA)
Vega (RA)
Veglia (F)
Velax (S)

Vemo (ZA)
Venom (AUS)
Ventura (AUS)
Ventura (BR)
Ventura (USA)
Venture (USA)
Venus (USA)
Vermin (ZA)
Vesey (GB)
VF (CDN)
Viault (F)
Vicente (RA)
Vico (I)
Vidal (RA)
Vigezzi (I)
Vig-TB (BR)
Viking (GB)
Viking (S)
Village (GB)
Vincent Special (AUS)
Vinto (RA)
Viper (AUS)
Virage (GB)
Viro (GB)
Vista (GB)
Vista Bushwaker (USA)
Vitesse (GB)
Vixen (GB)
VM (CZ)
VMG1 (BG)
VNS (D)
Vogt (D)
Vogue (GB)
Volker (AUS)
Vollstedt (USA)
Voo Doo (AUS)
Votoupal (CZ)
Vounta (RA)
VR Special (SL)
Vulcan (AUS)
Vulcan (USA)
W3 (AUS)
Wagnon-Coulter (USA)
WAH (AUS)
Wainer (I)
Walch (D)
Walkye (CO)
Ward (USA)
Warlock (AUS)
Warp-Nine (GB)
Warren (GB)
Wasp (AUS)
Watanabe (J)
Watson (AUS)

Watson (USA)
WDC (AUS)
WDF (USA)
Weaver (USA)
Webster (USA)
Wedge (AUS)
Wedono (USA)
Wee (GB)
Weed (USA)
Weld (USA)
Welkom (ZA)
Wellanier (GB)
Wells (GB)
Wells-Coyote (USA)
Welsor (AUS)
Wessex (GB)
West (J)
Whatsyt (GB)
Wheatcroft (GB)
Wheeler (USA)
Whico (GB)
Whippet (GB)
Whiskey One (GB)
White (AUS)
Whitmore (AUS)
Widi (B)
Wilco (AUS)
Wildcat (USA)
Wildcat (USA)
Wilkie (ZA)
Williams (GB)
Williams (USA)
Williams (USA)
Williart (AUS)
Wilmer (AUS)
Wimhurst (GB)
Winkelman (UNK)
Wirra (AUS)
Witch (GB)
Witter (ZA)
Wiver (NL)
Wizard (GB)
WJ (AUS)
WM (F)
Wolf (GB)
Wolf Brayton (USA)
Woller (GB)
Wolverine (USA)
World (J)
Wortmeyer (AUS)
Woudhuizen (NL)
Wren (AUS)
Wright (AUS)
Wyatt (AUS)

Wynnfurst (USA)
Xenophan (GB)
Xpit (CDN)
Y&B (USA)
Yacker (J)
Yamato (J)
Yankee (ZA)
Young (J)
Young (USA)
Yukas (J)
Zagk (D)
Zago (I)
Zalfa (AUS)
Zamba (I)
Zanetti (I)
Zani (I)
Zarri (F)
Zebra Spider (CH)
Zedde (I)
Zee (GB)
Zeitler (USA)
Zepernick (DDR)
Zepheroo (AUS)
Zia (USA)
Zink (USA)
ZInkarella (USA)
Zircon (GB)
Zonker (USA)
Zoom (USA)
Zoor (USA)
ZX (AUS)

ENGINES:

The 70s were pretty much a Ford decade. Ford or Ford-badged engines won in a huge variety of racing series, worldwide. For obvious reasons, Ford engines equipped all cars in Formula Ford 1600, Formula Ford 2000 and most Formula Atlantic races, which during the decade exclusively used the Ford BDA engine (except in South Africa, as of 1979, which adopted Mazda engines). Ford or Cosworth engines won races in Formula 1, Formula 2, Formula 3, Formula 5000, Formula Libre, Group 8, Formula Indy, World Championship of Makes, European 2 Liter Championship, Interserie, NASCAR, European Touring Car Championship, DRM, British Saloon Car Championship, Trans-Am, IMSA Camel GT, Australian Touring Cars, Springbok Series, All-Japan Championship, Argentine Prototypes, Argentine Turismo de Carretera, Brazilian Touring Cars (Divisions 1 and 3), Brazilian Prototypes (Division 4), European GT Championship (equipping De Tomaso cars), European Hill Climb Championship, Dutch Touring Cars, Belgian Touring Cars, Austrian Touring Cars, in addition to several other championships worldwide. Additionally, Ford engined cars also won many of the important races of the decade: 24 Hours of Le Mans, Indy 500, 24 Hours of SPA, 24 Hours of Nürburgring, 1000 km of Bathurst, Brazilian 1000 Miles Race, 6 Hours of Peru, Vila Real, 1000 km of Kyalami, etc.

Curiously, although Ford is an American company, it did not win races in Can-Am, the reason for it being that the engines were very seldom used in that championship during the decade. Even in NASCAR, the 70s were not very kind for Ford: sister brand Mercury won many more races than Ford in the Winston Cup during the decade. Ford won a single IMSA Camel GT in the 70s. Ford also failed to win the two top American endurance races during the decade, the 24 Hours of Daytona and 12 Hours of Sebring. So not all was rosy for Dearborn.

Besides equipping literally hundreds of single seater and prototype chassis all over the world, the Ford street models that were more successful were the Capri, Escort, Falcon, Maverick, Thunderbird, Mustang, Lotus Cortina. Even the venerable race purpose Ford GT40 continued to be used during the decade. A bit obsolete for World Championship use, in 1970 the GT40 was still racing in various places such as Britain, France, Angola, Brazil. In fact, as late as 1975 a Ford GT40 was still winning races in Angola.

BMW engines also won many races, used in BMW cars but also equipping a variety of prototypes and single seaters in several categories.

The Porsche 911 (and derivatives thereof) was probably the winningest car model in the decade, used in races all over the world: Europe, USA, Canada, Mexico, Central America, Australia, Africa. Porsche engines also equipped a few non-Porsche chassis.

In the 70s the legendary Ford GT40 was washed up for big league racing. In lesser environments, it could still be fast. This one raced in Brazil until 1973, here driven by Wilson Fittipaldi Junior. Photo by Rogerio da Luz.

Chevrolet engines were used in the USA, Brazil, Argentina, Canada, equipped most Formula 5000 racers used worldwide, as well as most Can-Am cars. A Chevrolet model that deserves mention is the Camaro, used not only in the USA and Canada but also in a variety of settings such as Britain, Macau, Sweden, Holland, France, Ecuador, Colombia, Guyana, the Caribbean, Angola, etc.

Volkswagen engines were mostly used in Formula Vee and Formula Super Vee, however, prototypes using this manufacturer's engine were built in many countries. Volkswagen engines were also widely used in the Midget class, in the USA and elsewhere, as well as used in VW products.

A nice side view of a Lotus Europa racing in Scotland. Photo by Colin Lourie.

Other engine manufacturers that won races outright during the decade, besides the above include Ferrari, Alfa Romeo, Matra, BRM, Renault, Offenhauser, Toyota, Hart, Peugeot, Dodge, Mercedes Benz, MG, Healey, Triumph, Opel, FIAT, Mini, Datsun, Tornado, Holden, Hillman, Simca, Maserati, Chrysler, Mercury, NSU, Vauxhall, Sunbeam, AMC, Austin, Moskvich, GAS, VAS, Skoda, Volvo, Jaguar, Citroen, Honda. Motorcycle engines, such as Suzuki, Yamaha, Montesa, Ducati and Izh Jupiter also powered SCCA D sports racers, Soviet Formula 4 and Italian Formula K250 single seaters.

CATEGORIES AND CHAMPIONSHIPS

FORMULA 1 WORLD CHAMPIONSHIP

This book was not intended to be another Formula 1 book, while claiming to cover everything else - there are tons of these around. As a matter of fact, I decided against listing all GP races during the decade, Formula 1 results galore and that sort of thing. Actually, that is the one thing that Wikipedia does OK as far as auto racing is available: its Formula 1 historical coverage is quite competent, almost everything else is rather pitiful and incipient. There are literally tons of other books that cover the Formula 1 subject better than I could given book size limitations, considering the scope of coverage goes much beyond F1, including local racing in dozens of countries, such as India, Zambia and Guyana and all points between. Therefore the Formula 1 section is going to concentrate on some fun data strictly related to the decade, no more, no less. F1 decade highlights are provided elsewhere in this book. Now you can relax.

Ferrari was the top dog in 70s Formula 1 but its 1973 challenger was rather weak. Photo by Paul Kooyman.

GP winners during the decade

One noticeable feature of the 70s is that no driver dominated Formula 1 in the 70s, in the fashion that **Fangio** dominated the 50s, **Clark** the 60s and **Prost** the 80s. The competition was very close and the top 7 were quite bunched together:

1. Niki Lauda, 17
2. Jackie Stewart, 16
3. Emerson Fittipaldi, 14
4. Mario Andretti, 12
5. James Hunt, Ronnie Peterson, Jody Scheckter, 10
6. Carlos Reutemann, 9
7. Clay Regazzoni, Alan Jones, Jochen Rindt, Jacky Ickx 5
8. Denis Hulme, Jacques Laffite, Gilles Villeneuve 3
9. Patrick Depailler, Peter Revson 2
10. Jochen Mass, Vittorio Brambilla, Peter Gethin, Jean-Pierre Beltoise, François Cevert, Gunnar Nilsson, John Watson, Jose Carlos Pace, Jo Siffert, Pedro Rodriguez, Jack Brabham, Jean-Pierre Jabouille 1

In terms of nationalities, that works out as follows:
1. Great Britain, 28 (*)
2. Austria, 22
3. Brazil, 15
4. USA, 14
5. Sweden, 11
6. South Africa, 10
7. Argentina, 9
8. France, 8
9. Switzerland, Australia 6
10. Belgium, 5
11. Canada, New Zealand, 3
12. Italy, Germany, Mexico, 1
(*) This includes England, Scotland and Northern Ireland.

Laps in the lead 1970-1979, drivers:
1. N. Lauda, 1244
2. J. Stewart, 1148
3. M. Andretti, 798
4. R. Peterson, 707
5. J. Scheckter, 675
6. J. Hunt, 666
7. C. Reutemann, 622
8. E. Fittipaldi, 478
9. G. Villeneuve, 405
10. J. Ickx, 400
11. C. Regazzoni, 360
12. A. Jones, 227
13. J. Watson, 220
14. J. Rindt, 172
15. P. Depailler, 164
16. F. Cevert, 129
17. J. Brabham, 124
18. J. Laffite, 112
19. J.P. Beltoise, 97
20. D. Hulme, 96
21. J.P. Jarier, 79
22. P. Rodriguez, 67
23. P. Revson, 63
24. J. Siffert, 57
25. C. Pace, 50
26. R. Patrese, 37
27. J.P. Jabouille, 35
28. V. Brambilla, 32
29. C. Amon, 31
30. G. Nilsson, 21
31. J. Oliver, 16
32. H.J. Stuck, 14
33. R. Arnoux, 11
34. R. Stommelen, 8
35. M. Hailwood, 7
36. J. Mass, 5
37. P. Gethin, 3
38. T. Pryce, 2

Participations during the decade 1970-1979

Only three drivers managed to start at least one Formula 1 race in all of the decade's years: **Emerson Fittipaldi, Clay Regazzoni** and **Jacky Ickx**. None did full seasons in all seasons. **Mario Andretti** almost joined this exclusive club but he had no starts in **1973**.

Drivers with + after their name are those whose entire career took place during the 70s. A few drivers had already taken part in the F2 section of the German GP in the 60s.

1. Emerson Fittipaldi, 130
2. Clay Regazzoni, 128
3. Ronnie Peterson, 123+
4. Carlos Reutemann, 115
5. Niki Lauda, 113
6. Jody Scheckter, 99
7. John Watson, 94
8. James Hunt, 92+
9. Mario Andretti, 92
10. Jacky Ickx, 92
11. Patrick Depailler, 87
12. Jochen Mass, 85
13. Jean Pierre Jarier, 83
14. Jacques Laffite, 79
15. Hans Joachin Stuck, 74+
16. Carlos Pace+, Vittorio Brambilla, 72
17. Alan Jones, 67
18. Denis Hulme, Graham Hill, 63
19. Jean-Pierre Beltoise, 60
20. Arturo Merzario+, 57
21. Henri Pescarolo, 54
22. Rolf Stommelen+, 53
23. Chris Amon, 52
24. Jackie Stewart, 49
25. Francois Cevert+, 46
26. Tom Pryce+, 42
27. Mike Hailwood, 38
28. Riccardo Patrese, 37
29. Howden Ganley+, Patrick Tambay, Wilson Fittipaldi+, 35
30. Tim Schenken+, Brett Lunger+, Gilles Villeneuve, 34
31. Jean-Pierre Jabouille, 33
32. Jackie Oliver, Gunnar Nilsson+, Didier Pironi, 31
33. Peter Gethin+, 30
34. Andrea de Adamich, 29
35. Mike Beuttler+, 28
36. Peter Revson, 26
37. Jo Siffert, 23
38. John Surtees, 23
39. Reine Wisell+, 22
40. Hector Rebaque, Rene Arnoux, Nelson Piquet, 20
41. Harald Ertl, 19
42. Pedro Rodriguez, Ian Scheckter+, Rupert Keegan, 18
43. Nanni Galli+, 17
44. Keke Rosberg, 16
45. Mark Donohue+, Elio De Angelis, 14
46. Jack Brabham, Francois Migault+, Hans Binder+ 13
47. George Follmer+, Lella Lombardi+, Jan Lammers, Derek Daly, 12

48. Dave Walker+, Guy Edwards+, Larry Perkins+, 11
49. Rikki Von Opel+, Tony Brise+, Bob Evans+, Patrick Neve+, Alex Ribeiro+, Bruno Giacomelli, 10
50. Jochen Rindt, George Eaton, Helmut Marko+, Brian Redman, Dave Charlton, Vern Schuppan+, 9
51. Gijs Van Lennep+, 8
52. John Miles, Michel Leclere+, Renzo Zorzi+, David Purley+, 7
53. Alex Soler-Roig+, Derek Bell, 6
54. Skip Barber+, 5
55. Piers Courage, Ignazio Giunti+, Jo Bonnier, Brian Henton, Ian Ashley+, Danny Ongais+, 4
56. Bruce McLaren, Dan Gurney, Pete Lovely, John Love, Richard Robarts+, David Hobbs, Mike Wilds+, Eddie Keizan+, Roelof Wunderink+, Loris Kessel+, Alessandro Pesenti-Rossi+, Ingo Hoffmann+, Boy Hayje+, 3
57. Johnny Servoz-Gavin, Silvio Moser, Sam Posey+, Jackie Pretorius, Roger Williamson+, Tom Belso+, Helmut Koinigg+, Jim Crawford+, Emilio de Villota, Kazuyoshi Hoshino+, Noritake Takahara+, Bobby Rahal+, Patrick Gaillard+, Ricardo Zunino, 2
58. Peter De Klerk, Gus Hutchison+, Francois Mazet+, Jean Max+, Vic Elford, Chris Craft+, John Cannon+, Bill Brack, Luiz Pereira Bueno+, Graham McRae+, Paddy Driver, Teddy Pilette+, Gerard Larrousse+, Bertil Roos+, Leo Kinnunen+, Dieter Quester+, Eppie Wietzes, Jose Dolhem+, Guy Tumner+, Damien Magee+, Torsten Palm+, John Nicholson+, Dave Morgan+, Jo VonLanthen+, Conny Anderson+, Warwick Brown+, Masahiro Hasemi+, Hans Heyer+, Kunimitsu Takahashi+, Lamberto Leoni+, Eddie Cheever, Michael Bleekemolen+, Geoff Lees, Marc Surer, 1

A number of drivers unsuccessfully attempted to qualify for at least a single GP during the decade: Carlo Facetti, Andy Sutcliffe, Emilio Zapico, Otto Stuppacher, Masami Kuwashima, Tony Trimmer, Jac Nelleman, Brian McGuire, "Gimax"(Carlo Franchi), Willie Fergusson, Gianfranco Brancatelli, Alberto Colombo, Bernard De Dryver, Hiroshi Fushida, Giorgio Francia, Mikko Kozarowitsky, Beppe Gabbiani, Hubert Hahne, Peter Westbury.

Francois Cevert died just before his real big chance came. Photo by Rob Neuzel.

Poles, Drivers, 1970-1979
1. N. Lauda, 24
2. M. Andretti, 17
3. J. Stewart, 15
4. J. Hunt, R. Peterson, 14
5. J. Ickx, 10
6. E. Fittipaldi, 6
7. J. Laffite, C. Regazzoni, 5
8. J.P. Jabouille, C. Reutemann, 4
9. J. Scheckter, J. Rindt, A. Jones, J.P. Jarier 3
10. C. Amon, R. Arnoux, J. Watson, 2
11. T. Pryce, V. Brambilla, D. Hulme, C. Pace, P. Revson, P. Depailler, G. Villeneuve, J. Siffert, J. Brabham, 1

Fastest laps, Drivers, 1970-1979
1. N. Lauda, 16
2. C. Regazzoni, 15
3. J. Ickx, 11
4. M. Andretti, 10
5. R. Peterson, 9
6. J. Stewart, J. Hunt, 8
7. G. Villeneuve, 7
8. E. Fittipaldi, 6
9. J. Scheckter, C. Pace, 5
10. J. Brabham, P. Depailler, 4
11. C. Amon, C. Reutemann, J.P. Jarier, A. Jones, 3
12. R. Arnoux, J. Watson, J. Mass, F. Cevert, 2
13. J. Surtees, J. Siffert, J.P. Beltoise, H. Pescarolo, M. Hasemi, G. Nilsson, M. Hailwood, N. Piquet, 1

Constructors

Wins

1. Ferrari, 37
2. Lotus, 35
3. Tyrrell, 21
4. McLaren, 20
5. Brabham, 8
6. Williams, 5
7. BRM, Ligier 4
8. March, Wolf 3
9. Shadow, Hesketh, Renault, Penske 1

Poles
1. Ferrari, 41
2. Lotus, 37
3. McLaren, 18
4. Tyrrell, 14
5. Brabham, 7
6. Renault, 6
7. March, Ligier 5
8. Shadow, Williams, 3
9. Matra-Simca, 2
10. BRM, 2
11. Wolf, 1

Fastest laps
1. Ferrari, 45
2. Lotus, 23
3. Tyrrell, 17
4. McLaren, Brabham, 15
6. March, 6
7. Williams, 5
8. Ligier, 4
9. Surtees, 3

323

10. BRM, Matra-Simca, Shadow, Wolf, Renault, 2

11. Hesketh, Parnelli, Kojima, 1

Laps in the lead
1. Ferrari, 2648
2. Lotus, 1996
3. Tyrrell, 1425
4. McLaren, 895
5. Brabham, 744
6. March, 293
7. BRM, 267
8. Williams, 246
9. Ligier, 222
10. Wolf, 214
11. Hesketh, 88
12. Shadow, 50
13. Renault, 46
14. Matra-Simca, 39
15. Arrows, 37
16. Parnelli, 10
17. Surtees, 9
18. Hill, 8

Podiums
1. Ferrari, 96
2. Lotus, 71
3. Tyrrell, 69
4. McLaren, 64
5. Brabham, 36
6. March, 18
7. Ligier, 15
8. Wolf, 13
9. Williams, 12
10. BRM, 8
11. Hesketh, Shadow, 7
12. Matra, 5
13. Renault, 4
14. Penske, 3
15. Surtees, 2
16. Fittipaldi, Arrows, 1

Engines

Wins

1. Ford Cosworth, 99
2. Ferrari, 37
3. BRM, 4
4. Alfa Romeo, 2
5. Matra, Renault, 1

Poles
1. Ford Cosworth, 89
2. Ferrari, 41
3. Renault, 6
4. Matra, Alfa Romeo, BRM, 3

Fastest Laps
1. Ford Cosworth, 86
2. Ferrari, 45
3. Alfa Romeo, 6
4. Matra-Simca, 3
5. BRM, Renault, 2

Laps in the lead
1. Ford Cosworth, 5,998
2. Ferrari, 2,648
3. BRM, 267
4. Alfa Romeo, 267
5. Matra-Simca, 56

6. Renault, 46

Number of times venues were used in the 70s:
1. Monaco, Kyalami, Oesterreichring, Watkins Glen, Monza 10
2. Zandvoort, 9
3. Buenos Aires, Jarama, 7
4. Nürburgring, Zolder, Mosport, Interlagos, Anderstorp 6
5. Brands Hatch, Silverstone, Paul Ricard, 5
6. Hockenheim, Long Beach, 4
7. Dijon-Prenois, Montjuich, Nivelles, Spa-Francorchamps, Fuji, Clermont-Ferrand, Montreal, 2
8. Jacarepagua, Mont-Tremblant, Hermanos Rodriguez 1

Non-Championship F1 Races

In the early part of the decade non-Championship Formula 1 races were rather popular, especially in **1971** and **1972**. Then, as the calendar expanded to 15 races in **1973**, they decreased in number, to the point that only one such race was held in **1977** and **1978**. I have included in this list the Rothmans 50,000 (**1972**), which many authors do not consider a F1 race. While in fact it was open to even Formula-Indy, Can-Am and limitless specials, none of these cars showed up, so Formula 1 was top dog. **Chris Amon** never won a World Championship Formula 1 race but won two non-championship events, both of them 2-heat races.
1. Emerson Fittipaldi, 5
2. James Hunt, 4
3. Jackie Stewart, Chris Amon, John Surtees, Clay Regazzoni, Jacky Ickx, Peter Gethin, Niki Lauda, 2
4. Mario Andretti, Pedro Rodriguez, Graham Hill, Carlos Reutemann, Denis Hulme, Jean-Pierre Beltoise, Tom Pryce, Keke Rosberg, Gilles Villeneuve, 1

Top 6 in International Non-championship Formula 1 races during the 70s
Formula 5000 cars preceded by 5.0, Formula 2 cars preceded by 2.0

Race of Champions, Brand Hatch 03/22/1970	1st J. Stewart **March-Ford**	2nd J. Rindt Lotus-Ford	3rd D. Hulme, McLaren-Ford
	4th J. Brabham Brabham-Ford	5th G. Hill Lotus-Ford	6th P. Gethin, McLaren-Ford
Daily Express Trophy, Silverstone 04/26/1970	1st C. Amon **March-Ford**	2nd J. Stewart, March-Ford	3rd P. Courage De Tomaso-Ford
	4th B.McLaren McLaren-Ford	5th R. Wisell, McLaren-Ford	6th D. Hulme, McLaren-Ford
Gold Cup Oulton Park 08/22/1970	1st J. Surtees, **Surtees-Ford**	2nd J. Rindt Lotus-Ford	3rd J. Oliver, BRM
	4th H. Ganley, 5.0 McLaren-Chevy	5th T. Taylor, 5.0 Lola-Chevy	6th F. Saunders, 5.0 Crossle-Rover
Argentine Grand Prix, Buenos Aires 01/24/1971	1st C. Amon, **Matra-Simca**	2nd H.Pescarolo, March-Ford	3rd C. Reutemann McLaren-Ford
	4th D. Prophet 5.0 McLaren-Chevy	5th D. Bell, March-Ford	6th J. Siffert March-Ford
Race of Champions, Brands Hatch 03/21/971	1st C. Regazzoni, **Ferrari**	2nd J. Stewart, Tyrrell-Ford	3rd J. Surtees, Surtees-Ford
	4th T. Schenken, Brabham-Ford	5th H. Ganley, BRM	6th R. Allen, March-Ford
Questor GP, Ontario, USA 03/28/1971	1st M. Andretti, **Ferrari**	2nd J. Stewart, Tyrrell-Ford	3rd D. Hulme, McLaren-Ford
	4th C.Amon	5th T. Schenken,	6th J. Siffert,

	Matra-Simca	Brabham-Ford	BRM
International Trophy, Oulton Park 04/09/1971	**1st P.Rodriguez, BRM**	2nd P. Gethin, McLaren-Ford	3rd J. Stewart, Tyrrell-Ford
	4th H. Ganley, BRM	5th A. Rollinson, March-Ford	6th T. Trimmer, Lotus-Ford
Daily Express, Silverstone, 05/08/1971	**1st G. Hill, Brabham-Ford**	2nd P. Gethin, McLaren-Ford	3rd T. Schenken, Brabham-Ford
	4th P. Rodriguez, BRM	5th M. Hailwood, Surtees-Ford	6th H. Pescarolo, March-Ford
Jochen Rindt Memorial, Hockenheim, 06/13/1971	**1st J. Ickx, Ferrari**	2nd R. Peterson March (*)	3rd J. Surtees, Surtees-Ford
	4th H. Ganley, BRM	5th N. Galli, March-Alfa	6th S. Barber, March-Ford
Gold Cup, Oulton Park 08/21/1971	**1st J. Surtees, Surtees-Ford**	2nd H. Ganley, BRM	3rd F. Gardner, 5.0 Lola-Chevy
	4th A. Rollinson, 5.0 Surtees-Chevy	5th C. Craft, Brabham-Ford	6th M. Walker, 5.0 Lola-Chevy
Victory Race, Brands hatch, 10/24/1971	**1st P. Gethin, BRM**	2nd E. Fittipaldi, Lotus-Ford	3rd J. Stewart, Tyrrell-Ford
	4th J. Siffert, BRM	5th T. Schenken, Brabham-Ford	6th J. Surtees, Surtees-Ford
Race of Champions, Brands Hatch, 03/19/1972	**1st E. Fittipaldi, Lotus-Ford**	2nd M. Hailwood, Surtees-Ford	3rd D. Hulme, McLaren-Ford
	4th P. Gethin, BRM	5th T. Schenken, Surtees-Ford	6th J.P.Beltoise, BRM
Brazilian GP, Interlagos, 03/30/1972	**1st C. Reutemann, Brabham-Ford**	2nd R. Peterson, March-Ford	3rd W. Fittipaldi Jr, Brabham-Ford
	4th H. Marko, BRM	5th D. Walker, Lotus-Ford	6th L. Bueno, March-Ford
Daily Express, Silverstone, 04/23/1972	**1st E. Fittipaldi, Lotus-Ford**	2nd J.P. Beltoise, BRM	3rd J. Surtees, Surtees-Ford
	4th D. Hulme, McLaren-Ford	5th P. Revson, McLaren-Ford	6th P. Gethin, BRM
Gold Cup, Oulton Park. 05/29/1972	**1st D. Hulme, McLaren-Ford**	2nd E. Fittipaldi, Lotus-Ford	3rd T. Schenken, Surtees-Ford
	4th B. Redman, 5.0 Chevron-Chevy	5th V. Schuppan, BRM	6th R. Allen, 5.0 McLaren-Chevy
Gran Premio Rep. Italiana, Vallelunga 06/18/1972	**1st E. Fittipaldi, Lotus-Ford**	2nd A. de Adamich, Surtees-Ford	3rd N. Galli, Tecno
	4th M. Beuttler, March-Ford	5th H. Ganley, BRM	---
Rothmans 50,000 Brands Hatch, 08/28/1972	**1st E. Fittipaldi, Lotus-Ford**	2nd B. Redman, Mclaren-Ford	3rd H. Pescarolo, March-Ford
	4th G. Birrell, 2.0 March-Ford	5th J. Hunt, 2.0 March-Ford	6th J. Watson, 2.0 Chevron-Ford
John Player Challenge Trophy, Brands Hatch, 10/22/1972	**1st J.P. Beltoise, BRM**	2nd C.Pace, Surtees-Ford	3rd A. de Adamich, Surtees-Ford
	4th V. Schuppan, BRM	5th P. Gethin, BRM	6th J. Watson, March-Ford
Race of Champions Brands Hatch 03/18/1973	**1st P. Gethin, 5.0 Chevron-Chevy**	2nd D. Hulme, McLaren-Ford	3rd J. Hunt, Surtees-Ford
	4th T.Trimmer Iso-Ford	5th T. Dean, 5.0 Chevron-Chevy	6th J.P. Beltoise, BRM
Daily Express, Silverstone, 04/08/1973	**1st J. Stewart, Tyrrell-Ford**	2nd R. Peterson, Lotus-Ford	3rd C. Reggazoni, BRM
	4th P. Revson, McLaren-Ford	5th N. Lauda, BRM	6th G. Follmer, Shadow-Ford

GP Medici, Brasilia 02/03/1974	**1st E. Fittipaldi, McLaren-Ford**	2nd J. Scheckter, Tyrrell-Ford	3rd A. Merzario, Iso-Ford
	4th J. Mass, Surtees-Ford	5th W. Fittipaldi Jr., Brabham-Ford	6th H. Ganley, March-Ford
Race of Champions Brands Hatch 03/17/1974	**1st J. Ickx, Lotus-Ford**	2nd N. Lauda, Ferrari	3rd E. Fittipaldi, McLaren-Ford
	4th M. Hailwood, McLaren-Ford	5th C. Regazzoni, Ferrari	6th P. Revson, Shadow-Ford
Daily Express, Silverstone, 04/07/1974	**1st J. Hunt, Hesketh-Ford**	2nd J. Mass, Surtees-Ford	3rd J.P. Jarier, Shadow-Ford
	4th H. Pescarolo, BRM	5th F. Migault, BRM	6th J. Nicholson, Lyncar-Ford
Race of Champions Brands Hatch 03/16/1975	**1st T. Pryce, Shadow-Ford**	2nd J. Watson, Surtees-Ford	3rd R. Peterson, Lotus-Ford
	4th J. Ickx, Lotus-Ford	5th E. Fittipaldi, McLaren-Ford	6th Bob Evans, BRM
Daily Express, Silverstone 04/13/1975	**1st N. Lauda, Ferrari**	2nd E. Fittipaldi, McLaren-Ford	3rd M. Andretti, Parnelli-Ford
	4th J. Watson, Surtees-Ford	5th P. Depailler, Tyrrell-Ford	6th M. Donohue, Penske-Ford
Swiss Grand Prix, Dijon 08/24/1975	**1st C. Regazzoni, Ferrari**	2nd P. Depailler, Tyrrell-Ford	3rd J. Mass, McLaren-Ford
	4th R. Peterson, Lotus-Ford	5th J. Watson, Surtees-Ford	6th C. Pace, Brabham-Ford
Race of Champions Brands Hatch 03/14/1976	**1st J. Hunt, McLaren-Ford**	2nd A. Jones, Surtees	3rd J. Ickx, Williams-Ford
	4th V. Brambilla, March-Ford	5th C.Amon Ensign-Ford	6th T. Pryce, Shadow-Ford
Daily Express, Silverstone, 04/11/1976	**1st J. Hunt, McLaren-Ford**	2nd V. Brambilla, March-Ford	3rd J. Scheckter, Tyrrell-Ford
	4th T. Pryce, Shadow-Ford	5th J.P. Jarier, Shadow-Ford	6th G. Nilsson, Lotus-Ford
Race of Champions Brands Hatch 03/20/1977	**1st J. Hunt, McLaren-Ford**	2nd J. Scheckter, Wolf-Ford	3rd J. Watson, Brabham-Alfa
	4th Brian Henton, March-Ford	5th J. Oliver, Shadow-Ford	6th D. Purley, LEC-Ford
Daily Express, Silverstone, 03/19/1978	**1st K. Rosberg, Theodore-Ford**	2nd E. Fittipaldi, Fittipaldi-Ford	3rd T. Trimmer, McLaren-Ford
	4th B, Lunger, McLaren-Ford	5th R., Keegan, Surtees-Ford	--
Race of Champions Brands Hatch 04/15/1979	**1st G. Villeneuve, Ferrari**	2nd N. Piquet, Brabham-Alfa	3rd M. Andretti, Lotus-Ford
	4th J. Mass, Arrows-Ford	5th N. Lauda, Brabham-Alfa	6th E. de Angelis, Shadow-Ford
GP Dino Ferrari, Imola, 09/16/1979	**1st G. Villeneuve, Ferrari**	2nd J. Scheckter, Ferrari	3rd C. Reutemann, Lotus-Ford
	4th N. Lauda, Brabham-Alfa	5th R. Patrese, Arrows-Ford	6th V. Brambilla, Alfa Romeo

(*) Some sources say Peterson used a Ford engine, others say it was an Alfa Romeo engine

Formula 1 cars that never made it

The abundance of Ford Cosworth engines and ready availability of Hewland gearboxes gave hopefuls the false impression that building a Formula 1 challenger was an easy undertaking in the 70s. Thus a number of projects were announced and never made it to a F1 Grand Prix event.

New Zealander Howden Ganley decided to follow the steps of countrymen McLaren and Amon and build his F1 after retiring from the category in the wake of an accident with the atrocious Maki in Germany, 1974. The Ganley F1 was built but the world economy was not in very good shape in 1975 and there were no takers to pay the bills. So Ganley and Tim Schenken went into business, created Tiga which achieved success in a few lower categories.

Dydo Monguzzi announced a Dyna with Chevrolet engine in 1973, then a Cosworth engined car for 1979. It never made it to F-1, although the latter car was used in the Aurora championship. Even a bus manufacturer, Dutch Van Hool announced plans of a F1 challenger, which was stillborn in 1975.

Among the projects was the Portuguese Marinho, based on the relative success of the BIP sports car team. Sponsored by a bank, the Portuguese team decided to go Formula 1, even though drivers Carlos Santos and Carlos Mendonca, believed starting in Formula 2 would be more reasonable. Eventually, a socialist revolution took over the government in 1974, the bank was taken over by the government and that was the end of BIP. Then Bravo, Megre and Pereira decided to pick up the pieces and plans were announced for the 1975 season, postponed to a 1977 Spanish GP debut. In the end, there was no Marinho, as there was no BI.

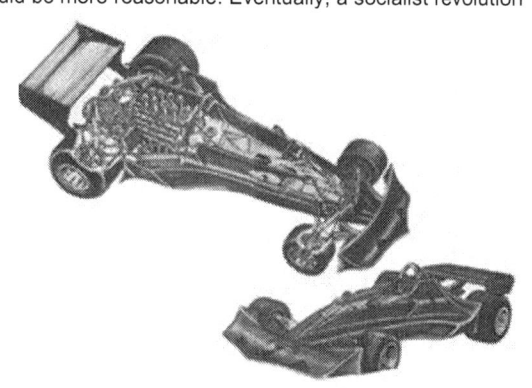

The Marinho Formula 1 never made it

The Berta was announced with some fanfare in South America, mostly disregarded elsewhere. Oreste Berta was a very talented builder of race cars in Argentina and the cars were supposed to debut in the Argentine GP of 1975. Berta had famously fielded a Cosworth powered prototype in the 1000 km of Nurburging of 1970, then Tornado powered Bertas in the Buenos Aires round of the World Championship of Makes in 1971 and 1972, initiatives that were not encouraging in terms of results. At first, there was talk of a proprietary engine, then changed to a more reasonable Cosworth-Hewland set up but coming January, 1975, there was no Berta F1 in Buenos Aires. The car ended up racing in the American Formula 5000 series, without much success.

In the age of the Cold War, public relations (or fake news) were important in the wider scheme of things and Soviets, eager to impress the world with their technological edge, every so often hinted they had a Formula 1 challenger in the works. There was a category called Formula 1 in the Soviet Union during most of the decade and the cars were powered by 3-liter engines. Reliable power figures were hard to come by in such a mysterious environment but it is highly unlikely such cars came even close to 300 HP. So Soviet Formula 1 remained behind the Iron Curtain.

As for more speculations, Italian magazine Auto Sprint wins the prize for the number of "projects" that appeared to be no more than wishes and wishful thinking of project "leaders". I suppose the English language literature did not absorb so much of this speculation, because of linguistic barriers, so that a lot of you are about to read will be news. Not surprisingly, a few of these "projects" involved Italian drivers or oriundi (Italian descendants) such as the Fittipaldi brothers and Mario Andretti and Italian constructors. Among the Formula 1 projects mentioned by Autosprint during the decade were:
- BRM to adopt Matra engines for the 1975 season;
- Lella Lombardi to race a McLaren in the 1976 season;
- McNamara, which built Formula 3 and Formula Indy cars, was said to build a F-1 car for 1972. Among the drivers slated to drive was German lady driver Hannelore Werner;
- Chaparral going Formula 1 racing;
- A GRD Formula 1 (and Indy) car was given as almost certain;
- A Rondel Formula 1 car was to appear in the 1973 season, to be driven by Bob Wollek and Tim Schenken;
- A 3rd McLaren was to use a Tecno engine in 1973; in 1971, the 12-cylinder engine, which had not yet even debuted, was said to be a possible power plant for Stewart (highly unlikely, given the load of money Ford paid the Scottish driver)
- Mike Keegan, father of Rupert and owner of British Air Ferries, was rumored in 1974 to be building a Formula 1 car to be driven by South African Roy Klomfass. The car was to be built by Hawke. Where exactly did Klomfass fit into the set up, is unclear, for BAF sponsored Rupert's early career racing.
- Honda slatted to equip Brabham cars in 1979;
- A BMW engine to appear in Formula 1 as early as 1974;
- Aubrey Woods to provide a proprietary engine to Hesketh;
- Merzario was said to drive the new Penske car in 1974. The magazine also placed him at BRM, Shadow and the private Finotto (Brabham) team. He raced in none of them.
- Leda/Granatelli for Graham McRae in 1973;
- Brian Redman is considered 95% sure as a Tecno driver for 1973.
- Niki Lauda is placed in a fourth Shadow for the 1973 season, while the same issue states he will drive a BRM! In fact, the magazine also placed Redman, Wisell, Bell, in addition to Merzario, driving for Stanley in 74. None of the actual 1974 drivers, Beltoise, Pescarolo and Migault, are actually mentioned in these early speculative reports.

However, I must say the most delicious rumor I found in Autosprint during the 70s involved the first Brazilian Formula 1 car and it deserves a long treatment, for it rarely appears on auto racing literature. Quite a large 1972 report claimed that Luis Antonio Greco would lead a new Formula 1 team, to be called Café do Brasil, in other words, sponsored by the Brazilian Coffee Institute, a governmental agency. The car was to be driven by Brazilian drivers, hinting at Carlos Pace and Wilson Fittipaldi and initially, the team would get its feet wet contesting Formula 2. Besides the Brazilian Coffee Institute, the article written by Gabriela Noris, said Petrobras and Varig would support the endeavor, which would cost 1 million dollars at first. The article also indicated that Ron Tauranac, who had sold Brabham to Ecclestone just a little before for allegedly £100,000, would design the car and 15 people would work in the England based outfit. Articles that appeared in Brazilian newspapers said that even Lotus, the year's champion, seemed to be afraid of the new team and some discomfort was caused with John Player Special, Emerson's sponsor, because Emerson was hinted to be inclined to join the team. Greco was, indeed, a very enterprising fellow, who led the Willys team after Christian Heins' death in

1963 and after Willys was taken over by Ford, all major Brazilian Ford racing projects of the 60s and 70s. Among other things, he built the first Brazilian Formula 3, the Gavea in 1965 and planned to bring the car to race in Europe (it did not happen but the car did race in the 1966 Argentine Temporada). He also introduced (and built) Brazilian Formula Ford (Merlyn copies) cars in 1971, ran Ford's semi works team in long distance racing between 1973 to 1976 and was involved in the Ford Corcel Tournament of 1970 and the 4-Cylinder Maverick Champions Tournament of 1975. But a few of his projects did not really take off, like the Formula Super Ford in 1975, or running a Ford GT40 in 1971 and 72. Both Pace and Wilson Fittipaldi had driven for Greco in their early days and even Emerson and Luiz Bueno had done so. As for the Brazilian Coffee Agency, it did provide personal sponsorship to Emerson, Wilson and Pace in their early Formula 1 careers (including 1972) but that commitment was likely rather insufficient to meet the costs of a whole 2-car Formula 1 team, with a proprietary chassis, no less. The article also hinted at a possible Brabham or Surtees buy-out, which would be a more sensible solution. The one astounding fact is that the contemporary Brazilian specialized press did not publish a single line about this "project" (articles did appear on daily newspapers, though) and neither do latter-day Brazilian historical blogs cover the subject, except my own blog. No Tauranac biographies mention this tie-up, so it seems that the pages of Autosprint were the only ones where the 1972 project appear as an almost certainty, even though the magazine's speculative team lists for 1973 do not list the Café do Brasil racer in either F1 or F2. In 1973 all Greco did was run Group 1 Fords in endurance racing and no further word was heard about Café do Brasil.

EUROPEAN FORMULA 2 CHAMPIONSHIP

This is how Formula 2 stacked-up in the beginning of the decade: in **1970**, Formula 2 was the ultimate category to be in for any driver who wished to become a GP racer. It was felt that it was just a matter of time before **1967** champion **Jacky Ickx** would win a F1 title (after all, he was runner up in **1969**), or **Jean-Pierre Beltoise** (**1968** title holder) would win a race. As for **1969** champion **Servoz-Gavin**, he also had great potential. Formula 2 races were highly competitive, more so than Formula 1 GPs and drew huge crowds. Top current GP drivers regularly took part in European and Non-Championship F2 races and were offered a little extra dough by organizers to ensure better gate receipts (after all, that is what lured **Jim Clark** to race at Hockenheim in **1968**). Some organizers were very satisfied holding only Formula 2 races, which were less expensive to run and sometimes more profitable than Grande Epreuves. The same could be said of teams. Entry lists were so huge in certain races that many drivers would not qualify. By **1979**, Formula 2 was still considered a logical stepping stone for drivers vying for Formula 1 fame, however, it was clear that it was not a champion grooming category. In fact, none of the 70s World Champions were Formula 2 champions, although **Jochen Rindt** was considered King of Formula 2 but would not score because he was a graded driver. Some of the decade's Formula 2 champions had in fact won European championship races: **Jackie Stewart, Emerson Fittipaldi, Jody Scheckter** and **Niki Lauda**. **Emerson** won his F-2 races by the time he was already a graded driver and he was not in F1 because of his Formula 2 performances. **Scheckter** won a single race and **Lauda** scored a race win finishing behind a graded driver. **Stewart** was a mega star and Formula 1 winner when he won in European Formula 2. As for other decade's champions, **James Hunt** was anything but successful in his short Formula 2 career in **1972** and early **1973**. **Mario Andretti** never raced in it. At best, winning a Formula 2 championship was good for grooming F1 runner ups: **Ickx, Regazzoni** and **Peterson** all won the F2 crown and were runner-ups in F1 during the 70s. The trouble was looming ahead: many drivers were choosing to simply skip Formula 2 altogether, which was the case of future world 80s champions **Jones, Piquet, Prost** and **Senna**. None of the five French drivers who won the European F2 Championship in the 70s would win the F1 title: the one Frenchman who did it a few times, **Prost**, mostly by-passed the category (he raced once in **1977**). Adding insult to injury, F2 cars were not all that cheap to run by **1979**: the stock block 1.6 engines of **1970** were replaced by race-specific 2.0 liters that required great attention and ensuing maintenance cost. Crowds were not all that great anymore and major GP stars generally had no reason to race in Formula 2: money in Formula 1 had become good, if not yet astronomical. The last GP star to win a European Formula 2 race was **Jochen Mass**, in **1977**. While the likes of **Arturo Merzario** and **Jean-Pierre Jarier** would do an odd F-2 race, they did it without any chance of shining and were not really top F1 drivers. Organizers were not queueing up to get dates, in fact, non-championship Formula 2 races were no longer held in Europe since **1976**. **Hockenheim** had to fill the gap that very season with 3 of the season's races.

In hindsight, we see that Formula 2 was in a clear state of decadence late on the decade. Nonetheless, it still served a purpose: in addition to the drivers already mentioned, many drivers who featured well in Formula 1 were 70s Formula 2 graduates: **Carlos Reutemann, Mike Hailwood, Jean-Pierre Jarier, Jean-Pierre Jabouille, Patrick Tambay, Jacques Laffite, Rene Arnoux, Didier Pironi, Eddie Cheever, Carlos Pace, Patrick Depailler, Hans Stuck, Jochen Mass, Vittorio Brambilla, Peter Gethin** to name a few. More recent F2 champs **Bruno Giacomelli** and **Marc Surer** could certainly expect very successful Formula 1 careers, one might think, but we all know how that went.

There was quite more variety of chassis manufacturers in the early part of the decade. **Brabham** was still the top manufacturer in terms of numbers in **1970** but there were also cars from **Lotus, Tecno, Pygmee, March, Chevron** and **Lola**, even the **BMW** factory cars and **Ernesto Brambilla**'s private **Ferrari Dino**. All of the above, except **Chevron**, **March** and sporadically, **Lola**, would be out of F2 by **1974**. Others would come and go, like **Surtees, McLaren, Martini, Elf, Tui, Boxer, Toj, GRD, Ralt, Motul, Modus, Osella, Wheatcroft**, during the course of the decade but the make that ruled F-2 was one that debuted this very **1970**: **March**. **March** won no less than 55 European Championship races during the course of the decade and numerically it was always the most abundant as of **1972**. **March**'s cars were relatively simple to run and engineer and lasted long. Some 732s were still running in the **1976** season, while many found homes in European hill climbs.

As for drivers, **Giacomelli** had an outstanding season in **1978** and a good one in **1977**, so he ended up the only double-digit race winner of the decade. All of **Emerson Fittipaldi's** six wins were earned as a graded driver. Others to do the same were **Jochen Rindt, Jacky Ickx, Jo Siffert, Jackie Stewart, Henri Pescarolo, Graham Hill** and **John Surtees**. **Hans Stuck, Ronnie Peterson, Jochen Mass, Francois Cevert, Tim Schenken** won races both as non-graded and graded drivers.

1970-1979 FORMULA 2 POINT SCORERS WHO DID NOT MAKE IT TO FORMULA 1

Formula 2 was conceived in the 40s as a steppingstone category to Grand Prix, replacing the 30s voiturettes. In the 60s, after some seasons in which only Formula 1 and Formula Junior existed as major single-seater categories in European racing, F2 came back in **1966** and an European Championship was created for **1967**. This championship ran non-stop until **1984**, when it was replaced by Formula 3000. Current Formula 2 only shares the name with the old 2.0-liter cars (the engine size from **1972** to **1984**, before that, 1.6 liter) and have much larger engine capacity and power. Additionally, while a large number of old-time Formula 2 participants, championship winners and point scorers and even some non-point scorers, made it to Formula 1 in the above-mentioned period, the same cannot be said of current GP2 (which was recently renamed Formula 2) drivers. Making to Formula 2 at present is not really a guarantee one will ever drive a F-1 car in the world championship. In fact, generally two, tops three Formula 2 graduates find rides in Formula 1 every year, while many Formula 2 drivers got the chance to drive at least once in F1 (such as **Jose Dolhem, Gerard Larrousse, Francois Mazet**, etc).

There are many reasons for that. First, in the 70s there were some privateer teams in Formula 1, whose business model involved renting drives to young (and not so young drivers). These teams often did not have stable driver lineups. Some works teams fielded more than two cars, as many as five and cars were made available to local drivers. Musical chairs were often played in the less wealthy teams, some of which could use as many as 10 drivers in the course of a season. More than 50 drivers attempted to qualify in the F1 fifteen races of **1974**, while a little over 20 get a chance in current formula 1.

On the other hand, two GP2 champions, **Lewis Hamilton** and **Nico Rosberg**, ended up world champions, while none of the Formula 2 drivers from **1967** to **1984** won the coveted Formula 1 title. In the period in question, **1970-1979**, three F2 champions were actually runner up in Formula 1 (**Ronnie Peterson** twice, **Jacky Ickx** and **Clay Regazzoni** once), while four other F2 champions managed to win more than one Grand Prix (**Patrick Depailler, Jacques Laffite, Jean Pierre Jabouille** and **Didier Pironi**). None of the F2 champions from **1978** to **1984** managed to win a single Grand Prix and of these, only **Bruno Giacomelli** led a single race. So one can say that Formula 2's relevance had diminished greatly during the course of the decade and many of the future F1 winners were graduating straight from F3 into F1, such as **Nelson Piquet, Alain Prost** (who participated in a single Formula 2 race in **1977**) and **Ayrton Senna**.

However, most Grand Prix champions of the period drove in Formula 2, such as **Jochen Rindt, Emerson Fittipaldi, Jackie Stewart, Niki Lauda, James Hunt** and **Jody Scheckter**. In the decade only **Mario Andretti** bypassed the category altogether, coming directly from Indycars when he entered Formula 1 in **1968**. While **Rindt, Fittipaldi, Stewart, Lauda** and **Scheckter** all won F-2 races, **Hunt**'s case was very peculiar. James only raced in the category in **1972** and early **1973** and did not do very well. All of this changed when he took the wheel of a Formula 1 **March** 731 in Monaco, **1973**. He scored a point in his second race, soon had a podium and by the end of the year, at **Watkins Glen**, had earned 2nd place a little over one second behind **Ronnie Peterson**, by far the fastest driver of the season. He quickly became a star, won his first GP in **1975**, the title in **1976** and as quickly as he rose, he faded. By **1979** his motivation was gone and **James** retired mid-year. Another driver who did not do very well in Formula 2 in 1972 but got some F1 drives in **1973**, in fact debuted in the same Monaco GP, was **David Purley**, on the strength of parental sponsorship by Lec Refrigeration. He did not do well like **Hunt** but this just shows that previous success in Formula 2 was not a requirement to make it to Formula One.

Gerry Birrel getting sideways at Crystal Palace, 1971. (Photo by Gerald Swan)

The object of this section is a quick analysis and history of the points scoring Formula 2 drivers from the **1970-79** period who did not make it to Formula 1 at all. It should also be noted that Formula 1 drivers regularly raced in Formula 2 until about **1976**, then with less frequency. Those that were graded drivers could not score points in the European championship, so often a 6th place score meant 8th or 9th on the road.

Before starting, a word about Formula 2 in the 70s. It was nothing like current F2, which comprises well funded and professional teams, with engineers, managers etc. In fact, way back when one could set up a basic 3-people team, buy a chassis and couple of engines, a trailer and a saloon and go Formula 2 racing. Even some "works", proprietary teams were very small operations, such as **Tui, Boxer** and **Pygmee**. As a result, by **1975, 76**, many of the races had over subscribed entries of as many as 45 cars, many of which were utterly uncompetitive. Some of these cars raced in hill climbs, domestic championships and Formula Libre events in England, France, Switzerland, Austria and Ireland (and later the Shellsport group 8 Championship) and every so often a driver from some of these more sedate disciplines managed to wrestle a point out of their humble participations and set-ups. By the end of the decade it was becoming much more difficult for some of these less structured teams to achieve success but a noteworthy, almost heroic performance was **Alex Ribeiro**'s win in the **1978** Eiffelrennen with a very minute and unfunded set-up.

For starters, let us talk about some of the important Formula 2 drivers who got no chance in Formula 1 at all.

Jean-Pierre Jaussaud had quite some experience by the time the decade began and by **1972** he was a top Formula 2 driver. In fact, he ended the season in second, winning two rounds and continued racing in the category until **1976**. A fast and very professional driver, **Jean-Pierre** was considered old in his runner-up season, 35 years old, in fact, so he never got a chance, even though **Jacques Laffite** debuted in Formula 1 when he was 31. Notwithstanding, **Jaussaud** did very well in sports cars, especially Le Mans, where he finished in the rostrum a few times (3rd with **Matra** in 73 and 3rd with **Mirage** in 75) until finding ultimate success winning the **1978** race for **Renault** (with **Pironi**) and **1980** for **Rondeau** (with **Jean Rondeau**). Thus **Jaussaud** became the only Frenchman to have achieved first time **Le Mans** wins for two French manufacturers. He also raced in touring cars with some success.

Jochen Rindt was known as the king of Formula 2 but did most of his winning in the 60s. Here he drives a Lotus at Crystal Palace, 1970. Photo by Gerald Swan.

Bob Wollek was also a Frenchman, although from the German speaking area of Alsace and raced in Formula 2 from **1971** to **1973**. He was heavily sponsored by Motul and brought that sponsorship to **Ron Dennis' Rondel** team. He won two rounds of the championship in **72** and **73** but at a time when French drivers won many F2 races and championships (French drivers won the title in **68-69** and then from **73** until **76**), that was not enough to raise much interest. He had a dispute with Motul and missed the chance of driving for Motul sponsored **BRM** in **1974**. **Wollek** ended up one of the top sports cars drivers of the world, having won dozens of races in many continents, having driven **Porsches, Lancia, Jaguar, Cougar, Matra, Toyota**. He never won **Le Mans**, however. *Autosprint* magazine speculated that **Wollek** would drive a Rondel F1 in 1973 and later, that Bob was being considered for the **Ligier** F1 drive in **1979**, to replace **Depailler** who had a hang gliding accident and had to sit out the rest of the season but this is the only source to speculate such interest, to my knowledge. **Ickx** ended up getting the drive.

Klaus Ludwig was involved in Formula 2 shortly, driving for the **Kauhsen** team in **1976/77** but the team was pretty much a failure. He gave up single-seaters and continued driving sports cars and touring cars and became one of the top drivers in these disciplines in the 70s until the 90s, including three **Le Mans** victories, DRM and DTM wins, in addition to several world championship races for the likes of Gelo, Kremer and Joest.

Maurizio Flammini was an Italian driver who won three European Formula 2 races in **1975** and **1976**, for **March** but never got a chance in GPs. After **1976** his career fizzled and mostly consisted of sports car races and odd F2 races.

Scot **Gerry Birrel** was reckoned to be **Francois Cevert**'s mate at **Tyrrell** for the **1974** season. Very much a **Ford** man, the British arm of the company was enthused with the prospect of a third Flying Scot excelling in F1. However, **Gerry** was good but clearly no **Clark** or **Stewart**. As it was, fate intervened and he died from a F2 accident in **Rouen**, in **1973**.

Among the period Formula 2 drivers who might have achieved stature in Formula 1 were Swede **Eje Elgh**, very fast in F3, who ended up having an excellent career in Japan; **Jacques Coulon** and **Colin Vandervell**, both of whom had very good seasons in **1973** and two Japanese drivers, **Tetsu Ikuzawa** and **Hiroshi Kazato**, who might have done well in Formula 1 under the right circumstances.

Here is a list of the **1970-1979** point scoring formula 2 drivers who did not make it to Formula 1, by that meaning at least attempt to qualify for a Formula 1 World Championship race. This list does not include the drivers already mentioned above:

Alistair Walker, Mike Goth, Tommy Reid, Peter Gaydon, Carlos Ruesch, Brian Hart, Patrick dal Bo, Claudio Francisci, John Wingfield, Dave McConnell, Sten Gunnarson, Bill Gubelman, Roland Binder, John Lepp, Hakan Dahlqvist, Richard Scott, Spartaco Dini, Peter Salisbury, Gabriele Serblin, Kurt Rieder, Jean-Pierre Paoli, Giancarlo Martini (who raced in non-championship F1 in a **Ferrari**), Alain Cudini, Duilio Truffo, Cosimo Turizio, "Gianfranco", Claude Bourgoignie, Carlo Giorgio, Sandro Cinotti, Ray Mallock, Roberto Marazzi, Willy Deutsch, Freddy Kottulinski, Markus Hotz, Juan Cochesa, Gaudenzio Mantova, Hans Royer, Luciano Pavesi, Patrick Bardinon, Piero Necchi, Rad Dougall, Juan Maria Traverso, Oscar Pedersoli.

Due to the very nature of Formula 2 (champions became graded drivers), there were no double champions.

Some more interesting facts about Formula 2:
- Formula 2 cars also raced extensively in European hill climbs, including the European Championship. They were also widely used in the South African Formula 1 Championship as grid fillers, as well as in the Shellsport and Aurora Group 8 Championships, that accepted Formula 1 cars as well. Formula 2 cars were the top racing category in Japan as of **1972** (initially called Formula 2000) and European regulation cars were also used in the **Macau** Grand Prix and other Asian races. Formula 2 cars were also used in the Swiss Championship and were the main cars in the Austrian Formula Libre Championship. F-2s were also used in British Formula Libre races, including **1972**'s Rothman's 50,000. America's Formula B, both professional and amateur, are often referred as Formula 2 but although some Formula 2 cars were used, regulations were closer to Formula Atlantic's than Formula 2. In fact, Atlantic's regulations were based on American/Canadian Formula B, not the other way around.
- International Formula 2 Tournaments were run a few times in South America: Colombia (**1971**), Brazil (**1971** and **1972**), Argentina (**1978**).
- Other categories that were named Formula 2 had their own set of rules and should not be construed as "real" FIA Formula 2. Argentine Formula 2, which also ran in Uruguay and Chile, was one such case. Soviet Formula 2 was even farther from European F-2: it used only Soviet made chassis and engines and were likely to be easily beaten by Western Formula 3s. Australian Formula 2 also had different regulations; these cars would also run in the Australian Gold Star championship and in the Tasman Cup and remained in 1.6 liter configuration during the course of the decade.

Driver wins (European Formula 2 Championship only), 1970s

1. Bruno Giacomelli, 11
2. Jean-Pierre Jarier and Jacques Laffite, 7
3. Emerson Fittipaldi, Hans Stuck and Ronnie Peterson, 6
4. Jean-Pierre Jabouille and Rene Arnoux, 5
5. Eddie Cheever, Jochen Mass, Michel Leclere, Patrick Depailler 4
6. Maurizio Flammini, Vittorio Brambilla, Derek Daly, Keke Rosberg, Brian Henton, Clay Regazzoni, Francois Cevert, 3
7. Jean-Pierre Jaussaud, Mike Hailwood, Henri Pescarolo, Tim Schenken, Patrick Tambay, Marc Surer, 2
8. Jochen Rindt, Derek Bell, Jo Siffert, Jacky Ickx, Dieter Quester, Graham Hill, Mike Beutler, Dave Morgan, Peter Gethin, Jody Scheckter, John Surtees, Reine Wisell, Roger Williamson, Jacques Coulon, Gerard Larrousse, Lamberto Leoni. Didier Pironi, Alex Ribeiro, Rad Dougall, Stephen South, Eje Elgh, 1

Wins by nationality
1. France, 43
2. Italy, 18
3. Britain, 13
4. Germany, 10
5. Sweden, 8
6. Brazil 7
7. USA and Switzerland, 4
8. Finland, 3
9. Austria, Australia, South Africa, 2
10. Belgium, Ireland 1

Constructors
1. March, 58
2. Martini, 14
3. Elf, 8
4. Lotus and Brabham, 7
5. Chevron, 6
6. Tecno and Surtees, 5
7. BMW, Ralt and Osella, 3
8. Motul, 2
9. GRD, McLaren and Boxer, 1

Venues
1. Hockenheim (D), 20 times
2. Vallelunga (I), Thruxton (GB) and Enna (I), 9
3. Rouen (F), Pau (F), 8
4. Nürburgring (D), Mugello (I), 6
5. Salzburgring (A), 5
6. Nogaro (F), 4
7. Mantorp Park (S), Albi (F), Estoril (P), Silverstone (GB), Donington Park (GB), 3
8. Montjuich (E), Tulln-Langenlebarn (A), Imola (I), Crystal Palace (GB), Karlskoga (S), Misano (I), 2
9. Jarama (E), Mallory Park (GB), Oesterreichring (A), Kinnekulering (S), Nivelles (B), Monza (I), Norisring (D), Zolder (B), Zandvoort (NL), 1

Most significant drivers in European Formula 2, year by year (**1970-1979**) (includes graded drivers, listed by performance, present and future stature)
1970 Clay Regazzoni (Champion) Jochen Rindt, Jackie Stewart, Derek Bell, Jacky Ickx, Emerson Fittipaldi, Dieter Quester, Jo Siffert, Tim Schenken, Hubert Hahne, Tetsu Ikusawa, Francois Cevert, Carlos Reutemann, Henri Pescarolo, Jack Brabham
1971 Ronnie Peterson (Champion), Carlos Reutemann, Emerson Fittipaldi, Dieter Quester, Francois Cevert, Tim Schenken, Graham Hill, Mike Beuttler, Niki Lauda, Wilson Fittipaldi Jr, Jean-Pierre Jarier
1972 Mike Hailwood (Champion), Jean-Pierre Jaussaud, Patrick Depailler, Emerson Fittipaldi, Jody Scheckter, Niki Lauda, John Surtees, Peter Gethin, James Hunt, Bob Wollek, Dave Morgan, Francois Cevert, Carlos Reutemann, Ronnie Peterson

1973 Jean-Pierre Jarier (Champion), Jochen Mass, Vittorio Brambilla, Colin Vandervell, Jacques Coulon, Henri Pescarolo, Bob Wollek, Patrick Depailler, Tim Schenken, Reine Wisell, Francois Cevert, Mike Beuttler, Tom Pryce, Ronnie Peterson, Emerson Fittipaldi
1974 Patrick Depailler (Champion), Hans Stuck, Patrick Tambay, Jacques Laffite, Tim Schenken, Jean-Pierre Jabouille, Michel Leclere, Gabriele Serblin, Tom Pryce
1975 Jacques Laffite (Champion), Patrick Tambay, Michel Leclere, Maurizio Flammini, Claude Bourgoignie, Gerard Larrousse, Jean-Pierre Jabouille, Giorgio Francia, Alessandro Pesenti-Rossi, Vittorio Brambilla, Brian Henton
1976 Jean-Pierre Jabouille (Champion), Patrick Tambay, Rene Arnoux, Maurizio Flammini, Alex Ribeiro, Hans Stuck, Hans Binder, Giancarlo Martini, Eddie Cheever, Keke Rosberg
1977 Rene Arnoux (Champion), Didier Pironi, Eddie Cheever, Jochen Mass, Keke Rosberg, Riccardo Patrese, Bruno Giacomelli, Brian Henton, Ingo Hoffmann, Alberto Colombo, Lamberto Leoni
1978 Bruno Giacomelli (Champion), Marc Surer, Manfred Winkelhock, Derek Daly, Keke Rosberg, Alex Ribeiro, Ingo Hoffmann, Alberto Colombo, Piero Necchi, Eje Elgh
1979 Marc Surer (Champion), Brian Henton, Eddie Cheever, Derek Daly, Rad Dougall, Bobby Rahal, Teo Fabi, Miguel Angel Guerra, Stephen South, Beppe Gabbiani, Eje Elgh, Alberto Colombo

WORLD MANUFACTURERS CHAMPIONSHIP, ALSO KNOWN AS WORLD CHAMPIONSHIP FOR MAKES/WORLD MAKES CHAMPIONSHIP

In the first year of the 70s this Championship almost rivaled Formula 1 in terms of prestige, for several GP drivers raced in the Manufacturers Championship, which had its own set of stars. Although some F1 races in **1969** were poorly supported – the French GP had merely 13 cars – the sports car championship always had healthy fields, although some cars were not very competitive at all, especially at the **Targa Florio** and the 1000 Km of **Nürburgring**.

There was great expectation that the **1970** would be a straight fight between **Porsche** and **Ferrari**, the only two manufacturers that decided to build 25 examples of their up to 5-liter 917 and 512 models, respectively. As it turns out, **Ferrari** never built 25 cars, it built 17 for homologation purposes but got a waiver from FIA, due to the large number of strikes that brought turmoil to the Italian industrial sector. The two **Porsche** works teams were John Wyer's Gulf J.W. Automotive Team and Porsche Salzburg, plus some privateer teams, like AAW, Gesipa, David Piper. **Ferrari** was represented by the works and several privateers, such as NART, Ecurie Francorchamps, Scuderia Filipinetti, Georg Loos, Escuderia Montjuich.

At the 24 Hours of **Daytona, Ferrari** was fastest (**Andretti, Merzario**) but the win fell onto **Porsche**'s lap (**Rodriguez, Kinnunen**). The same **Ferrari** duo had pole in **Sebring** and another **Ferrari** won the race (**Andretti-Giunti-Vacarella**), **Andretti** being called to complement the Italian crew. Score: 1-1. Rather unfortunately for Maranello, this was **Ferrari**'s last win in the year's championship. For one thing, **Porsche** enjoyed two car types: the 917 for faster tracks and the 908-3 for tighter places like **Nürburgring** and **Targa Florio**, where the 5-liter cars were a handful to drive. **Ferrari** only had the 512. **Porsche** won all remaining races of the championship, **Rodriguez-Kinnunen** winning another three races,

Gijs Van Lennep/Hans Laine Porsche 908 in the 1970 Targa Florio (Photo Rob Petersen collection)

Siffert-Redman three, **Ahrens-Elford** and **Hermann-Attwood** one each. **Porsche** won its first **Le Mans** in this season with the latter named pair, while **Ferrari**'s large works team self-destructed in the race. **Le Mans 1970** had a huge rate of attrition - only 7 cars were classified as finishers, while several others (many **Porsche** 911s) dragged along the track at a leisure pace. Very satisfied with how things turned out, **Hans Hermann** retired from racing on the spot. By the end of the year **Alfa Romeo** was showing enough pace to run with the leaders, finishing second in Austria (**De Adamich-Pescarolo**). **Matra-Simca** was also fast on occasion and won non-championship races in Argentina and France. Even Argentina's **Berta** prototype made a start at the **1970 Nürburgring 1000**, with **Di Palma/Marincovich**, equipped by a **Cosworth** engine rather than the regular **Tornado**. Older 5-liter cars, such as **Lola** T70s and **Ford** GT40s, still appeared but were rather outclassed by the new machinery. A **Ford** GT40 was inexplicably placed in the prototype class in the Austrian event.

As a result of the **1970** fiasco, **Ferrari** abandoned its 512 as a works car for **1971**, instead developing the 3-liter 312P, which turned out to be the right decision. Although the **Ferrari** prototype challenger was fast, it did not win a single race and it barely finished. **Porsche** again carried the crown, **Rodriguez** doing most of the winning again with **Oliver** (3 times) and once with **Attwood**. **Siffert** won at Buenos Aires with **Derek Bell**, making up 5 wins for J.W., while the Martini team's **Elford/Larrousse** won at **Sebring** and **Nürburgring** and **Marko/Van Lennep** at **Le Mans**. **Rodriguez**, the most outstanding **Porsche** 917 performer, died before the season was over driving a **Ferrari** 512 at a Norisring Interserie event. A nice surprise was **Alfa Romeo**, that won at **Brands Hatch** (**De Adamich-Pescarolo**), **Targa Florio** (**Vacarella-Hezemans**) and **Watkins Glen** (**De Adamich-Peterson**) and was very competitive elsewhere. A beautiful blue **Ferrari** 512 M was raced sporadically by **Penske** – it was fast but only finished at **Daytona** (**Donohue/Hobbs**, in 3rd) and was only entered in the American events and Le Mans (under the NART banner). The 312P only finished once in the top 6 (**Brands Hatch**, second with **Ickx/Regazzoni**) and the numerous privateer 512's (NART, Montjuich, Filipinetti, De Fierlant) generally did not do well: the 512's best results were second at Daytona (**Adamowicz/Bucknum**) and third at **Le Mans** (**Adamowicz/Posey**). In these two last years of 5-liter sports cars, an increasing number of 2-liter prototypes joined in to beef up the fields. Team VDS bravely soldiered on with its **Lola** T70 as long as it could. **Matra-Simca** continued developing its 3-liter sports car but its tragic involvement with the **Ignazio Giunti** death at **Buenos Aires** somewhat dampened the team's spirit and its appearances were sporadic. **Matra-Simca** did very well at Le Mans, running in 3rd place in the latter part of the event. **1971** was the end of the amazing 917s and 512s, who were then relegated to non-world championship service.

Matra-Simca conquered the 1973 and 1974 championships. This one sits in the Le Mans Museum. Photo by Carlos A. De Paula

Truth be told, the 917/512 era was a bit disappointing. According to figures provided by Porsche and Ferrari, a grand total of 42 of these monsters were produced (a figure that is somewhat disputed to this day), which could theoretically be pressed into service in World Championship races. However, save for Le Mans, where 17 of these cars raced in 1970 and 16 in 1971, the number of 917/512s at World Championship events was generally lower than 10, in one case, zero. See the table below:

1970

	Day	Seb	B.H.	Mon	SPA	TF	Nu	LM	WG	Oest
917	4	4	5	7	6	0	2	6	5	4
512	5	4	3	6	4	2	4	11	3	2

1971

	BA	Day	Seb	B.H.	Mon	SPA	TF	Nu	LM	Oest	WG
917	7	4	3	5	6	6	0	1	7	3	3
512	4	6	5	2	6	3	0	3	9	4	5

Although 917s were sold to several teams, quite often they were fielded only by the semi-works JW and Porsche Konstruktion in 1970 and JW and Martini Racing in 1971. The numbers of 512s curiously did not drop dramatically as the Ferrari works team dropped the type for the 1971 season, as more cars went into private hands, including the Penske team.

Most of the 917s handling issues were solved in 1969, even so, the car remained a powerful wild beast to tame, which might explain the low numbers of cars entered by less professional teams staffed by inexperienced drivers. The 512 was slower but more sympathetic to lack of talent and bravery but still fearsome.

As mentioned before, Porsche prepared and provided 908/3s for its semi-works teams for use in the tighter confines of the **Targa Florio** and **Nürburgring**. The few 917s that raced at the Nürburgring were used by private teams, with poor results, while the car never raced in the Targa Florio. The works **Ferrari** team entered a car in the 1970 Targa Florio, issuing a release explaining that it understood the car had no chance of victory and they were doing it only to allow **Vaccarella** to have some fun…In 1971 no 917s or 512 at all were entered in Sicily.

The 917, in spite of the wholesale disappearing act from tracks, remains one of the period's and racing's, more iconic cars with devoted throngs of fans, almost fifty years after retirement from the world scene. This romantic attachment to both cars creates an affective memory that simply did not take place: fields full of 5-liter sports cars from Maranello and Zuffenhausen dicing for hours on end, all over the world.

Porsche 917s and **Ferrari** 512s did race elsewhere in contemporary events for several years, in fact until 1976. They competed in the Can Am and Interserie, in different configurations, participated in Copa Brasil in 1970 and 1972, raced in many important standalone events at Vila Real, 1000 km of Paris, 500 km of Interlagos, 9 Hours of Kyalami, 12 Hours Marlboro (Ecuador), 6 hours of Jarama, 1000 km of Barcelona, 500 km of Imola, 1000 Miles of Brazil, 200 Miles of Fuji, Swedish Grand Prix and even less important events such as Swedish and SCCA club racing, Spanish and Swiss championship events, Italian hill climbs.

By 1971, 3-liter sports cars from **Ferrari, Alfa** and **Matra-Simca** were often beating 917s/512s in qualifying and **Alfas** in finishes and even some 2-liter prototypes threatened the more leisurely driven 512s.

That being said, from **1972** on, the future of big-time endurance racing lay on F1-engined prototypes, so ruled FISA.

In hindsight it is always easy to criticize decisions that went wrong. On the surface, everything was fine with the World Manufacturers Championship in the configuration it had in **1971**, yet, FISA had already decided to outlaw the 5-liter Group 5 monster machines with some advance and run the championship exclusively with 3-liter prototypes, which would be essentially Grand Prix racers with prototype bodies – basically the same idea that had been going around for a while (standardizing F1, Sports Cars and Indy Cars, with the same engine configuration, negotiations that collapsed in early 1970). While it is true that only a couple of manufacturers, **Porsche** and **Ferrari,** had built new generation 5-liter Group 5s and these would eventually become old, one gets the feeling that the decision was indeed hasty. Perhaps the 5-liters could contest the championship for a couple more years, ably backed up by 3-liter prototypes as had been the case hitherto. By **1971** the prototypes were no longer grid fillers. **Alfa Romeo** had won three races on merit, **Ferrari** was often the fastest car (even faster than the 917 and 512s), **Matra-Simca** showed promise and even updated **Porsche** 908s sprang surprises here and there. However, nothing indicated tons of manufacturers were ready and willing to produce a new generation of 3-liter machines either. Grand Prix teams were not in the healthiest of states and the last thing they needed was going endurance racing, where expenses were great, prizes tiny. By very definition, the Group 5s had on their side volume: to qualify for this group, a minimum of 25 machines had to be built, enticing production car manufacturers. Prototypes, on the other hand, could be singleton machines, enticing purpose built race car manufacturers.

The Mirage never reached the heights expected of JW but it won a championship race in 1973 and Le Mans in 1975. (Photo by Gerald Swan)

So, when the **1972** World Manufacturers Championship started, it appeared as if on the first year the contestants would be **Ferrari** and **Alfa Romeo**, with updated versions of their **1971** machines; **Joakin Bonnier**'s team with Cosworth **Lolas**; the announced J.W. Automotive **Gulf Mirage,** also with Cosworth engines but reported to change to Weslake power plants **and** a host of **Porsche** 908s which were still raceworthy, some with works support. **Matra-Simca** was inclined to do only **Le Mans**. So the grids lost a lot of the depth they had during the 5-liter era, the gone five liters were not replaced by 3 liters. 2-liter prototypes and GTs such as **Porsche** 911 and **De Tomasos** made up most of the grids, which often featured even Group 2 Touring Cars. Growing pains, it was hoped.

On the good side, both **Ferrari** and **Alfa Romeo** appeared in force initially, fielding mostly 3 cars per race and driver strength was solid. In those days, Formula 1 drivers often raced in other categories, for one, to increase their earnings. Additionally, testing was not as frequent as it is today, neither were sponsor commitments, there were less GPs, thus drivers were more available for racing. Thus a large number of the regular Grand Prix drivers contested at least a single race of the World Manufacturers Championship in **1972**: **Jacky Ickx, Mario Andretti, Clay Regazzoni, Tim Schenken, Ronnie Peterson, Carlos Pace, Peter Revson, Andrea de Adamich, Nanni Galli, Helmut Marko, Brian Redman, Arturo Merzario, Howden Ganley, Reine Wisell, Francois Cevert, Jean-Pierre Beltoise, Graham Hill, Chris Amon, Henri Pescarolo, Derek Bell, Rolf Stommelen, Wilson Fittipaldi Junior**.

From the onset it became obvious that **Ferrari** was the class of the field. **Alfa Romeo** had shown pace and reliability in **1971** but in **1972** it had neither. Only **Stommelen** consistently qualified close to the **Ferraris**, which ran away with the races. In some rounds, **Wisell** and **Larrousse** showed the Cosworth powered **Lolas** had promise, **Van Lennep** even posted the fastest lap at Le Mans in one such car but any challenge would never last more than a few laps. Additionally, at least one of the team drivers, **Hughes De Fierlandt**, was unable to match their professional teammates speed. The **Mirages** were not ready early in the season and at any rate, they were insufficiently fast to make the **Ferraris** tremble. As a result the championship became a **Ferrari** festival. The leading pair was **Ickx/Andretti** but **Schenken/Peterson** also won races and so did **Merzario, Munari, Redman, Regazzoni**.

Alfa Romeo was optimistic at the start of the year, fielding four cars in **Buenos Aires** but as the season went on, **Chiti**'s team became less sure of itself. After losing four straight races to **Ferrari, Alfa Romeo** did not appear in the home race at **Monza** and stayed away from **Spa** as well, two very fast tracks that favored the **Ferraris**. The strategy was a return in the roads of Sicily, in the **Targa Florio**, where **Autodelta** fielded four cars. **Ferrari**, on the other hand, entered a single car in the race, driven by junior driver **Merzario** and rally driver **Sandro Munari**. To **Alfa**'s desperation, it also lost this race, in spite of **Helmut Marko**'s Herculean efforts. **Alfa** ended up racing a couple more times, at the **Nürburgring and** at **Le Mans**, a race which **Ferrari** was to miss.

In the latter race, **Matra-Simca** fielded four cars, with very strong driver pairings, **Pescarolo/Hill, Cevert/Ganley, Beltoise/Amon** and **Jabouille/Hobbs**. **Alfa** was unable to challenge **Matra**, which finished 1-2 in the race. Even the Joest **Porsche** 908 finished in front of the fastest **Alfa** of **Adamich/Vacarella**.

In Austria, **Ferrari** entered four cars but surprisingly, the Cosworth powered **Mirage** and **Lola** posted the fastest qualifying times. In the race it was more of the same: **Ferrari** finished 1-2-3-4, with **Carlos Pace** and **Helmut Marko** on the driving strength.

So for **1973** it was expected that **Ferrari** would reproduce the same form, although **Matra-Simca** was to contest the whole season. The year turned out to be the absolute best of this era, with four manufacturers winning races on merit and **Matra** and **Ferrari** fighting to the end, although the uncertainties concerning the cancellation of the last race at **Buenos Aires** led to some criticism. However, there was no growth in entries, numerically or quality-wise, quite the opposite. **Alfa** entered only a few races with a single car. **Ferrari** fielded two cars most of the time, occasionally a third, with **Reutemann/Schenken**. Whatever remained of Ecurie Bonnier contested a couple of races and soon the 3-liter Lola was gone as well. **Mirage** fielded 2 cars in certain races and **Matra-Simca** fielded two, except at **Le Mans**, where it entered four cars once more. If FISA was expecting Grand Prix teams such as **Lotus, McLaren, Brabham**, et al to prepare prototype versions of their Cosworth racers, the intent failed miserably – none of them bit the bait. The only hope laid in **Porsche**'s renewed interest, in the form of the Carrera, which obviously focused on the future, rather the present of sports car racing.

Porsche ended up winning twice, at **Daytona,** with Americans **Gregg/Haywood** and at the **Targa Florio**, with **Van Lennep/Muller**. This would be the last **Targa Florio** valid for the World Championship and the second placed car was also a production-based vehicle, the **Lancia Stratos** of **Munari/Andruet**. . **Matra-Simca** won five times, always with the pair **Pescarolo/Larrousse**, even though **Cevert** was the hare in the team. **Ferrari** won twice, with **Ickx/Redman** and **Mirage** won a single time, at Spa, with **Bell/Hailwood**. **Alfa Romeo** was mostly uncompetitive, even though the new 12-cylinder car showed promise. Grand prix drivers still graced the fields, such as **Cevert, Beltoise, Reutemann, Ickx, Regazzoni, de Adamich, Stommelen, Pace, Hailwood, Amon** but the depth problem was still there. Races rarely had ten 3-liter cars, grids were still filled by myriad **Porsche** 911s and even smaller GTs and touring cars, while the Austrian round had merely

18 starters. The calendar, which had for years remained quite stable, had new, untraditional races in short tracks replacing the traditional dates.

For **1974**, **Ferrari** dropped out, although a prototype had been tested but **Alfa Romeo** promised a more consistent challenge to **Matra-Simca**. Things looked good at **Monza**, when **Alfa** beat an uncharacteristically unreliable **Matra** team, finishing 1-2-3. From the second round on, things were back to normal. **Matra** won everything in sight, including **Le Mans** for a third time and **Alfa**, like in **1972**, failed to enter the final races, when it became obvious that **Monza** was a flash in the pan. The year was difficult for racing in general, with the worldwide recession brought about by the oil crisis of **1973 and** endurance racing was strongly affected. There was no challenger to replace **Ferrari**, although **Mirage** appeared to be a solid proposition, not on the same league as **Matra**. **Matra**'s leading pair continued to be **Pescarolo/Larrousse** but **Jarier/Beltoise** also won many races and even **Jacky Ick**x shared a win for **Matra**, with **Jarier**. **Porsche** continued to develop the Turbo Carrera, which finished second in **Le Mans** but the car was not fast enough to beat the **Matras** overall. The end of the 3-liter formula loomed near, as **Matra** announced it was quitting the series at the end of **1974**. For **1976** the World Manufacturers Championship would be contested by a new breed of racers, the new Silhouettes, production based race cars such as the **Porsche Carrera**.

Although **Matra** was leaving, another French team, **Alpine Renault**, which had contested the European 2-liter championship in **1974**, announced it would participate in the championship with a new turbo challenger. However, Autodelta also announced it would pull out, thus killing any opportunity of a relevant championship. Eventually, former Interserie entrant **Willi Kauhsen** put together a deal to field the **Alfas** on behalf of the factory, with engineering support from the works. The first race of the championship was a **Porsche** benefit, with no Group 6 cars fielded at **Daytona**. The first round of the championship proper took place at **Mugello** and although **Merzario** scored the pole for **Alfa**, the race was won by the rookie **Alpine Renault**, with **Larrousse/Jabouille**. However, the **Alfas** proved superior, in fact won the remaining seven rounds, led by **Arturo Merzario** who won four races. The **Mirage** challenge vanished, the team deciding to do only **Le Mans**. In GELO colors, old **Mirages** did appear in **Monza** and **Nurburging**, where it finished second driven by **Schenken/Ganley**. **Reinhold Joest** had some support from **Porsche**, fielding a Turbo engined **Porsche** 908. Even 2-liter sports cars were becoming rare in the top results, so Group 4 **Porsche** Carreras featured strongly in the top 6 of most races. Even a Group 2 **BMW** finished third at Spa, so the formula was obviously not working.

In **1976** there would be a World Sports Car Championship, in which the 3 liter and 2-liter Group 6 cars could race, in addition to the World Manufacturers Championship, reserved for Silhouettes. As it turned out, the World Sports Car Championship would last a couple of years only but at least it would feature the **Porsche** works team in **1976**. **Porsche** had built a semi-new Le Mans challenger, the 936 and the Championship was ideal ground to develop the car. The opposition would come from **Alpine Renault** which had a strong team of drivers that featured **Jabouille, Depailler, Jody Scheckter, Laffite, Jarier**. **Alfa Romeo** appeared sporadically and there were still odd **Porsche** 908's, including **Joest**'s turbo powered example. This car ended up winning the **Nürburgring** round, when the 936 and **Alpines** failed. From then on, the works **Porsche** won everything, although **Alpine** scored most poles, and even **Alfa** scored a pole with **Brambilla** at **Salzburgring**. The **Mosport** round of the championship was so poorly supported that Can Am cars were allowed in to make up the numbers, so the overall winner was in fact **Jackie Oliver**, in the retired, non-regulation **Shadow Chevrolet**. A large number of 2-liter Osellas and even 1.3 liter prototypes made up the numbers. For **1977**, **Porsche** was gone again, having met its objective, which was to develop the 936 for **Le Mans**. **Alfa Romeo** was back with a full **Autodelta** works team but this was overkill. **Alfa** won everything, so the only interesting battle was between **Merzario** and **Brambilla**. Two of the rounds, **Estoril** and **Salzburgring**, had fewer than 10 cars on the gird, so FISA finally got the message and changed the status of the series to European level.

A Lola T212 in the Targa Florio. Photo by Lola Heritage.

Much was expected of Silhouette racing but car manufacturers did not embrace the concept. The first year, **1976**, turned out to be the most competitive. **Porsche** had the 935, supported by a number of 934/5s and 934s and **BMW** had the 3.0 CSL Group 5. The Bavarian manufacturer won three straight races (**Silverstone, Nürburgring** and **Oesterreichring**), with **Fitzpatrick/Walkinshaw, Quester/Krebs** and **Quester/Nilsson** and also fielded a Turbo **BMW** for **Ronnie Peterson**, which was fast but unreliable. **Ickx/Mass** won three races and **Stommelen/Schurti** one for the **Porsche** works team, winning the championship. Most of the races comprised of grid fillers in the form of GT cars (**Porsches, De Tomaso, MG**) and even Touring Cars (**Ford, Alfa Romeo, Opel, VW, Toyota, Chevrolet**), which were anything but Group 5 Silhouettes. A very fast **Lancia Stratos** was fielded by **Lancia** at **Vallelunga**, for **Brambilla-Facetti**. It qualified 3rd but retired and never raced again.

Any hope that the second year would be better than the first vanished when **BMW** announced that rather than continuing to develop the **BMW** 3.0 CSL Turbo, it would race the newer model 320, that had a much smaller engine, so that it was no match for the 935. At **Daytona**, the few 935's in attendance lost out to a 911 driven by **Haywood/Graves/Helmick**. At **Mugello**, there were no **BMW**s so **Porsche** filled the first 7 places with a variety of models (935, 934 and 911). At

344

Silverstone, at least the GELO and Kremer teams joined the works team and a Rudiger Faltz **BMW** 320i was fielded for **Peterson/Kelleners**, finishing 4th. There was an **Aston Martin** in the field as well, although it was not very fast. At **Nürburgring** the works team was beaten by GELO and Kremer, while **Surer** and **Winkelhock** finished third in a **BMW** 320i fielded by the works. At **Watkins Glen**, the **Porsche** works won again and the other German 935's did not show up. **Ronnie Peterson** and **David Hobbs** started second in a **BMW** entered by **McLaren** but that lasted a mere 20 laps. At **Mosport** the works **Porsche** team failed again, and winners **Wollek** and **Gregg** were disqualified, leaving the win to **Ludwig Heimrath** and **Paul Miller**. **Eddie Cheever** and **Gilles Villeneuve** finished 2nd after the winner's disqualification in a **BMW**. **Ickx** and **Mass** won again at **Brands Hatch**, their third win of the year and the best **BMW** could do was 8th, with **Winkelhock** and **Walkinshaw**. At **Hockenheim**, in a non-traditional two-heat format, it was time for **Bob Wollek** to win his first world championship race with **John Fitzpatrick** and **Claude Haldi**, in the Kremer **Porsche**. **BMW** finished 3rd with **Marc Surer** and **Eddie Cheever**. By **Vallelunga** the overall championship had gone **Porsche**'s way but **BMW** won Division 1, with very little competition. There were only three 935's on the Roman grid and the race was won by **Luigi Moreschi** and **Antonio Ferrari**. As in **1976**, most of the fields comprised of **Porsche** 911s, with a wide range of decidedly non-silhouette racers, which included **MGs, VW Golfs, Fiat X 1/9** and even the odd **Alfa GTA** which was not even competitive in the ETCC anymore. One cannot say that it was a memorable year but at least Kremer and Gelo managed to win and Max Moritz also had potential.

The news for **1978** were, if not bleak, indifferent. **Porsche** had no intention of running works cars in the entire season, while **BMW** insisted upon its quest to win the Division 1, where it had no competition, rather than putting together a car that could beat the **Porsches** for overall honors (by the way, such a car existed, the 320 Turbo that was developed in North America). There were more 320i's on the tracks, however, representing different countries: **BMW** Sweden, Italy, Switzerland, Belgium and Austria added color and a semblance of national rivalry. If only the strongest 935 privateers raced everywhere, there would be something to root for. And that is precisely what happened

In the 24 Hours of **Daytona** there were quite a few 935's, mostly cars which would be raced in the IMSA championship (Barbour, Interscope, Brumos, etc) but teams from Europe, such as Kremer, Konrad and Finotto also made the trek to Florida. Brumos won, with the trio **Stommelen/Hezemans/Gregg**.

The European season began in **Mugello** and Gelo won with **Hezemans/Heyer/Fitzpatrick**. **Bob Wollek** was teamed with **Pescarolo** in a Kremer car and there were other 935s from Konrad, Cachia, Rebai, Sportwagen, Coggiola, Schiller and Finotto, plus additional cars for Gelo and Kremer. The best **BMW** 320i was the Austrian car of **Quester/Bell** (3rd) and in total, there were six bimmers.

At **Dijon** the French pair **Wollek/Pescarolo** evened the score, bringing victory home in the Kremer car, in front of the fastest Gelo car of **Fitzpatrick/Heyer/Hezemans**. Two **BMW**'s followed in third and fourth, driven by **Francia/Cheever** and **Emanuelsson/Carlsson**.

At **Silverstone** the works spoiled the Gelo/Kremer party and won somewhat easily, **Ickx/Mas**s beating **Pescarolo/Wollek**. Both Gelo cars faltered and **BMW**s again came in third and fourth, this time **Grohs/Joosen** and **Kottulinsky/Hotz**. It should be noted that the "country" **BMW**s barely ever raced with the same pairings and drivers from different countries were often used in these cars.

Determined to win, Gelo took **Nürburgring** handily (**Ludwig/Heyer/Hezemans**), beating the Max Moritz example of **Schurti/Ickx**, with **Pescarolo/Wollek** not far behind. The 935's gave no chance for the **BMW**s to shine on home soil, for the best Bavarian car came in 6th (**Hottinger/Stuck**), ending on the same lap as the winner. As always, the **Nürburgring** race had a healthy field of 67, among them a **NSU Prinz**, a tiny car that was last made in **1973**.

In sharp contrast, the **Misano** race had only 19 starters, which included five **BMW 320is** and six **Porsche 935s**. Kremer evened the score again and **Wollek/Pescarolo** beat the locals **Coggiola/Monticone**. While both Gelo cars retired again, the best **BMW** came in fourth, the **BMW** Belgium example of **Neve/Grohs**.

The entry at **Watkins Glen** included many American based cars, including very fast **BMW 320i** turbos prepared by **McLaren**-North America, one of which qualified fifth (**Hobbs/Peterson**) but lasted a single lap. This car did well at IMSA and could beat the 935s. The European Gelo team won again (**Hezemans/Fitzpatrick/Gregg**) and a **BMW** came in third (**Stuck/Quester**). At least in **Watkins Glen** there was some variety. Whereas in other tracks it was all **Porsche** and **BMW**, a **Chevy Monza** came in fifth and a **Jaguar XJS** was placed seventh.

In **Vallelunga**, **Wollek** and **Pescarolo** again tied the scorecard and beat **Hezemans/Heyer/Fitzpatrick** and **Ludwig/Fitzpatrick/Hezemans**. While Kremer ran duos all year long, Gelo traditionally had been using three drivers since **1974**, **Fitzpatrick** and **Hezemans** often driving in two cars. Pit logistics must have been a handful but somehow it worked. The best **BMW** was **Surer** and **Kottulinski**, in 4th. Thus ended the **1978** championship, Kremer winning three times, Gelo three times, the works once and Brumos once. **Porsche** won Division 2 and **BMW** came out champion in Division 1. No surprises. Except for **Micangeli/Pietromarchi** (**De Tomaso**) and **Morton/Adamowick and Sahlman/Carradine** (**Ferrari**) brave 8th places in **Mugello** and **Daytona** and were noted elsewhere, the top ten in the other races were all **Porsches** and **BMW**s. Certainly not what FISA envisioned when the Silhouette Group 5 was created...

As usual, the **1979** championship began in **Daytona**. The field of 67 cars included some European challengers, including a Gelo car for **Wollek/Ickx** and **Gregg**, which qualified well but retired. In the end, it was the Interscope 935 of **Ongais/Field/Haywood** that won. A **Ferrari** (**Morton/Adamowickz**) in second was a refreshing sight, so were the two **Mazda** RX7s that arrived in 5th and 6th, the best example driven by **Terada/Katayama/Yorino**. These cars could not score World Championship points, though.

At **Mugello**, a smallish field of 18 started the race. There was no Kremer car and the **BMW** country 320 scheme was gone. To make a semblance of a race, organizers allowed several 2-liter prototypes to participate, indicating a tough year ahead. **Fitzpatrick/Schurti/Wollek** won over **Wollek/Ickx/Schurti**, both in Gelo 935s.

At **Dijon** the field was slightly larger but organizers not only allowed 2-liter prototypes but also the very strong **Porsche** 908/4 of **Reinhold Jost/Volkert Merl/Mario Ketterer** which won in convincing style. The Best Group 5 was the Gelo car of **Ickx/Wollek/Schurti**, followed by three other 935s, a 2-liter prototype and a Group 4 Porsche. 10 of the cars that started the race were prototypes.

At **Silverstone**, much of the same. Gelo won again, this time with **Fitzpatrick/Heyer/Wollek**, followed by the 3-liter **De Cadenet** prototype, a second string 935 and in fourth, a **Porsche** 911 Carrera! The championship was deteriorating fast and one can only commend Gelo for hanging on. There was light at the end of the tunnel in the form of the **Lancia Beta Montecarlo** driven by **Patrese/Rohrl**. It did not last long but at least it was something new.

The Kremer team made its first appearance of the year at the Nürburgring. **Klaus Ludwig** had been running away with the DRM and would eventually win the 24 Hours of **Le Mans** as well. Paired with **Plankenhorn**, he was defeated for the first time in the year, by **Schurti/Fitzpatrick/Wollek** in one of the Gelo cars. Although there were some Group 6 prototypes, the main one being the **Stommelen/Joest Porsche** 908/4, which did not finish, this time the 935s did well. The **Lancia** had not yet found its bearings and finished 18th, having a steep learning curve indeed.

The next round was **Enna**. There were a couple of things to cheer about after the race was over. **Lella Lombardi** had won her first World Championship race, a popular win, sharing a 2-Liter **Osella** with **Enrico Grimaldi**. Second, the **Lancia Beta Montecarlo** had finally finished a race well up, second on the road (**Patrese/Facetti**), first among the Silhouettes. But there were troubles. Only 12 starters, not a single **Porsche** 935 on the starting line. Besides the **Lancia**, the other Silhouettes were a **Ford Escort**, a **Fiat X 1/9**, a **De Tomaso Pantera** and a **Ferrari 308GTB**, which ended up fifth.

Things got slightly better in the **Watkins Glen** round, after all, there were tons of 935s racing in America, plus the usual variety provided in the American races, which included a **Triumph TR8**, an **AMC Javelin**, a **Datsun 280Z**, a **BMW** M1 and many Camaros and Corvettes. The winner was a European entry, although namely entered by the **Whittington** brothers: the **Porsche** 935K3 of **Ludwig/Bill/Don**. The best non-**Porsche** was the TR8 of **Bob Tullius** and **Brian Fursteneau**, in 8th place.

At **Brands Hatch** there was a **March** entered **BMW** M1 for **Winkelhock/Grob**, which qualified fourth but was the first retirement. There were some Group 6 prototypes, in fact, the race was won by **Joest/Merl** in the **Porsche 908/4**. Ludwig came back for another Group 5 win, sharing the car with **Plankenhorn,** while **Patrese/Rohrl** finished fifth on the road, third in Group 5. There were many **Porsche 911s**, a couple of **Lotus**, even a **Morgan 8** and a **Porsche 924** to add variety.

The final round of **1979**, thus, the decade's last, was held at **Vallelunga**. A reasonable number of cars started, 28, 13 of them Group 6 Prototypes. Again, **Lella Lombardi** came out the winner, this time paired with **Giorgio Francia,** impressively heading five other 2-liter prototypes. In seventh came a GT Porsche 911 and the winners of the Silhouette class, **Schornstein/Doren**, were only eighth. **Lancia** this time entered two cars, for **Pianta/Allen** and **Cheever/Rohrl**, which retired and the **March BMW M**1 was also there. None of the big German 935 teams showed up, so this was an obvious indication that Group 5 was dead.

347

In the beginning I mentioned that in the first year of the decade the World Manufacturers Championship had similar status as F-1. In the last year of the decade, nothing could be further from the truth. Whereas Formula 1 enjoyed good racing, star drivers, media coverage, good crowds, plentiful money and sponsors, plus technological development, the Manufacturers Championship had become a shadow of its former self. Whereas in the beginning of the decade 14 or 15 very competitive cars could be found in every field, by **1979** only four or five competitive cars could be counted to show in some rounds, if at all. And these were often cars that could not score points, because they were non-regulation prototypes.

While it is true that the world economy was not in a very good condition around **1979** and finding sponsorship was difficult, FIA failed to understand that simply allowing Group 6 cars to participate was not the answer. Creating a championship for these cars, run them all together, with a separate score from the Group 5's might have helped, because it is always easier to get a sponsor when the words champion or championship or winner are featured in the conversation or press clippings, even if you finish in 9th place. The World Challenge for Endurance drivers was a confusing affair, mixing several races of different categories of cars (Group 5, IMSA, Showroom Stock, European Touring Cars) which not a single driver would be able to attend, including a final race in El Salvador contested mostly by unknown Salvadorans, a few Americans and one Guatemalan. It would certainly have been better to keep separate scoring for drivers in the World Manufactures Championship as well, which would create greater interest among teams and drivers and facilitate sponsor hunting. This was done in the next decade, thankfully not too late.

Early decade **Le Mans** reports make very interest reading. Writers almost unanimously believed that the future of **Le Mans** laid on GT and Touring Cars, such as **Porsche** Carreras, **Ford** Capris and **BMW**s, which were appearing in larger numbers those days. They went as far as suggesting that public interest for cars such as fast **Ferrari, Matra-Simca** and **Mirage** prototypes was waning, with ensuing decreasing attendance. When the time of reckoning came for production-based cars to take over endurance racing, with the advent of Group 5, one learned that the obvious enthusiasm that existed in sectors of the specialized press and was allegedly shared by the public, was not shown by manufacturers, who mostly snubbed the Silhouette category and concept. In fact, the so-called road of salvation for endurance racing almost killed it in the late 70s, early 80s. **Le Mans** organizers, the ACO, did well to insist upon offering prototype classes during this period of turmoil.

RACE WINNERS, WORLD MANUFACTURERS CHAMPIONSHIP 1970-79
(INCLUDES WORLD SPORTS CARS CHAMPIONSHIP, 1976-77)

DRIVERS
1. Jacky Ickx (B), 19
2. Henri Pescarolo (F), 17
3. Gerard Larrousse (F) and Jochen Mass (D), 12
4. Arturo Merzario (I), 11
5. Pedro Rodriguez (Mex), 8
6. Bob Wollek (F), Brian Redman (GB), Jean-Pierre Jarier (F), John Fitzpatrick (GB), 7
7. Mario Andretti (US), Toine Hezemans (NL), 6

8. Derek Bell (GB), Rolf Stommelen (D), 5
9. Leo Kinnunen (SF), Jo Siffert (CH), Peter Gregg (US), Hurley Haywood (US), Jean-Pierre Beltoise (F), Manfred Schurti (FL), Vittorio Brambilla (I), 4
10. Vic Elford (GB), Jackie Oliver (3)(*), Ronnie Peterson (S), Tim Schenken (AUS), Jacques Laffite (F), Reinhold Joest (D), Hans Heyer (D), Klaus Ludwig (D), 3
11. Nino Vacarella (I), Richard Attwood (GB), Andrea de Adamich (I), Gijs Van Lennep (NL), Dieter Quester (A), Volkert Merl (D), Don Whittington (US), Bill Whittington (US), Lella Lombardi (I), 2
12. Ignazio Giunti (I), Kurt Ahrens (D), Hans Hermann (D), Helmut Marko (A), Clay Regazzoni (CH), Graham Hill (GB), Francois Cevert (F), Mike Hailwood (GB), Herbert Muller (CH), Jean-Pierre Jabouille (F), Tom Walkinshaw (GB), Albrecht Krebs (D), Gunnar Nilsson (S), John Graves (US), Dave Helmick (US), Luigi Moreschi (I), "Dino" (I), Danny Ongais (US), Ted Field (US), Mario Ketterer (D), Enrico Grimaldi (I), Giorgio Francia (I), Ludwig Heimrath (CDN), Paul Miller (CDN), 1

(*) Jackie Oliver won the 1976 Mosport race, which included several Can-Am cars to make up the poor field.

MANUFACTURERS
1. Porsche, 55
2. Alfa Romeo, 19
3. Matra-Simca, 15
4. Ferrari, 13
5. BMW, 3
6. Osella, 2
7. Gulf-Mirage and Alpine-Renault, 1

CARS THAT COMPETED IN THE WORLD MANUFACTURERS CHAMPIONSHIP 1970-79 (INCLUDES WORLD SPORTS CARS CHAMPIONSHIP, 1976-77)

What follows, I hope, is a complete list of the Manufacturers and models that competed in the World Manufacturers Championship between **1970** to **1979**. Not surprisingly, the top contributors in terms of models are **Porsche, Ferrari** and **Lola**. The latter also competed using a variety of engines, such as **Chevrolet, BRM, BMW, Ferraris, Alfa Romeo, ROC Chrysler, Abarth, Hart** and different **Cosworth** engine configurations, including 3-liter. The list is in alphabetical order and most of the prototypes without indication of engine were equipped with **Cosworth** power plants. It should be noted that some of the vehicles listed were mere touring cars, which at the discretion of some organizers such as the **Nürburgring 1000 km**, the **24 Hours of Daytona** and the **Targa Florio**, were allowed to run, perhaps vying for glory in the small engine touring car category. Most of these were rather hazardous to professionally raced prototypes and Group 5 racers but were a staple in the decade's long-distance events.

Abarth – 2000 SP, SE021, 1600 SP
Alfa Romeo – GTV, 33/3, Giulia Spl, GTA, 33/2, Giulia TZ, 33TT3, GTAM, Alfetta, 33SC12, 33TT12, Duetto, Montreal
Alpine Renault – A110, A441, A442

AMC – Javelin, AMX, Gremlin, Hornet
AMS – SF, 13, 273, 274, 175, 277
ASAM
Aston-Martin - AMV8
Astra - RNR 2
ATS-Ford
Audi 80
Austin – Marina
Austin-Healey – Sprite
Baufer-Chevrolet
Berta – LR
BMW – 2002, 2800CS, 3.0 CSL, 3.5 CSL, 320i, 1600, M1
Brabham-Climax – BT8
Cheetah – G601, G501
Chevrolet – Corvette, Camaro, Chevy II, Monza, Nova
Chevron – B16, B8, B19, B21, B23, B26, B31
Colt – Lancer
CR-CDS 1348
DAF – 555
Dallara-Ford 1600
Daren – MK2
Datsun – 510, 240Z, 280Z, 260Z, 280Z
De Cadenet Ford – LM
De Tomaso – Pantera
Deutsch-Porsche
Dome-Ford - Zero RT
Duckhams-Ford - LM
Dulon – LD11
Ecosse-Ford
Ferrari – 512S, 512M, 312P, 250LM, 375GTB, Dino 2065, 512BB, 312PB, 308GTB
FIAT – 124, X 1/9
Ford – GT40, Mustang, Capri, Escort, Cobra
Gigi-Lancia - P2
Giliberti – A112
Grac – ROC
GRD – S73, S74
Gropa – CM C
GSL-Porsche – BS910
Healey Repco – XR37
Huron – 4A
Inaltera-Ford
Jaguar – XJS
Jerboa BMC – SP
Kilan-NSU
KMW Porsche – SP30
Lancia – Fulvia, TSport, Zagato SP, Stratos, Beta Montecarlo
Ligier - JS3, JS 2
Lola – T70, T210, T212, T280, T290, T294, T282, T380, T390, T296, T297
Lotus – Europa, Lotus-BMW, Elan, Esprit
Marauder-Mazda
March – 73S, 74S, 75S, 76S
Martin – BM8
Matra (Matra-Simca) – MS650, MS660, MS670, MS670B, Djet, MS680

350

Mazda – M12A, RX2, RX3, Cosmo, RX7
McLaren – M8C, M20, M6B, M8F
MG – B, Midget, C, BGT
Mirage – M6, GR7
Momo-Carrero Opel
Morgan – Plus 8
Nomad - MK2
NSU - Prinz
OMS
Opel – GT, Commodore, Kadett
OSA-FIAT
Osca – 1000S
Osella (Abarth-Osella) – PA1, PA2, PA3, PA4, PA5, PA6, PA7
Pontiac – Firebird, Astre
Porsche – 917K, 906LE, 911S, 908/2, 908/3, 908/4, 910, 907, 914/6, 917LM, 911 Carrera, 935, 934, 936, 934/5, 911T, 930, 935-77, 935-78, 924, 935K3
Raymond-Ford
Renault – R12
Rex-Ford - SP1
Royale-Ford - RP17
Sauber – C5
Scorpion-Ford – JB4
Shadow-Chevrolet
Shelby – GT350
Sigma-Mazda – MC73, MC74
Simca – 1300
TOJ – SC03, SC04, SC302
Toyota – Celica
Triumph – GT 6, TR8
TVR – Vixen
UBS-Ford
Unipower - GT
Vogue-Ford SP2
Volkswagen – Scirocco, Golf
Volvo – 122S, 142

VENUES USED IN THE WORLD MANUFACTURERS CHAMPIONSHIP 1970-79
(INCLUDES WORLD SPORTS CARS CHAMPIONSHIP, 1976-77)

1. Nürburgring (D), 11
2. Watkins Glen (US), 10
3. Daytona (US), Monza (I) 8
4. Oesterreichring (A), Dijon (F) 7
5. Brands Hatch (GB), Spa (B), Le Mans (F), Vallelunga (I), 6
6. Mugello (I), 5
7. Targa-Florio (I), Enna (I), Silverstone (GB), 4
8. Imola (I), Sebring (US), 3
9. Buenos Aires (RA), Paul Ricard (F), Mosport (CDN), Salzburgring (A), 2
10. Kyalami (ZA), Hockenheim (D), Estoril (P), Misano (I), 1

24 HOURS OF LE MANS

The 24 Hours of Le Mans went through an interesting period in the 70s. Whereas in the 60s race wins were shared between only two manufacturers, **Ferrari** and

Ford, during the 70s **Porsche, Matra-Simca, Mirage** and **Renault** won races, all of them for the first time and two of these were French makes. As of **1975** the event was not a part of the World Manufacturers Championship for the first time since the inception of the championship, having adopted its own set of regulations. This liberty resulted in the creation of a new category, GTP, brief and rare appearances by NASCAR racers in Europe and an IMSA regulation class that allowed greater number of American entries. For a while it was the only top prototype race in the world, many of which were specially prepared for this race, such as the **De Cadenet** and **IBEC**. The famous race was also where Japanese pure race cars appeared for the first time in Europe (**Sigma-Mazda, 1973**), until then, only Japanese touring cars made appearances.

Porsche had been entering **Le Mans** races since the 50s but until **1969** it did not field the most powerful cars in the race, so it earned only class wins. The 917 was still unsorted in **1969** but by **1970** some of the aerodynamic flaws that made the car dangerous in its original form, especially at **Le Mans,** had been corrected and the type won both the **1970** and **1971** editions. Curiously, the top **Porsche** drivers of the day, **Siffert, Redman** and **Rodriguez**, did not win either edition: **Hermann/Attwood** and **Marko/Van Lennep** were the 917 victors at **Mans**. The **Ferrari** 512 was a good challenger but not enough to win the famous race.

The next three editions were won by **Matra-Simca**, which had decided to quit Grand Prix race in **1972** and concentrate on sports cars. **Matra**'s wins came at a hefty cost and even the French government helped with some funds. The **Ferrari** works team participated for the last time in the decade in **1973** and almost won the race, all three works cars leading at one point or another. The **1975** race, the first independent since the early 50s, was poorly attended and the regulations concentrated on fuel consumption, a concept that would be revised by FIA later on. The race marked **Ickx**' return to the highest place of the podium and it was also **Derek Bell**'s first victory in this race. The **Porsche** works came back in **1976** with the **Porsche** 936, a car that incorporated elements of the 908 and Can-Am 917, winning both the **1976** and **1977** editions. In the latter, the winning car had been as low as 41st, after a long stop, then **Jacky Ickx** was ordered to take it over, the **Haywood-Barth** car. As a result, **Ickx** matched the 4-win record of another Belgian, **Olivier Gendebien**, who until then was the winningest **Le Mans** driver.

Just like **Matra-Simca** before it, **Renault** decided to win **Le Mans** and invested millions in three campaigns, **1976** to **1978**. It came very close in **1977** but the **Bell-Jabouille** car broke down and left the coast clear for **Ickx**. Ultimately, the only **Renault** winning pair was **Pironi-Jaussaud**, in **1978** and **Renault** then left **Le Mans** to be conquered by others, focusing on Formula 1 from that point on. **Renault** had entered 4 works **Alpines** plus provided **Mirage** with **Renault** engines for that particular campaign.

Prototypes, including **Porsche** works cars and **Mirage**, failed tremendously in **1979**, in spite of very strong driving teams and a somewhat production-based car, the Silhouette **Porsche** 935 won at the lowest average since **1958**. Also noteworthy was **Paul Newman**'s 2nd place, also driving a **Porsche** 935.

Renault won at Le Mans the third time out. Then, dropped out, devoting its resources to Formula 1. This car can be seen at the Le Mans museum. Photo by Carlos A. de Paula.

Although a large number of **Porsche** 911 and derivatives raced during the entire decade, several manufacturers were represented at Le Mans during the 70s, including some works cars: **Ferrari, Alfa Romeo, Matra-Simca, Alpine-Renault, Lola, BMW, Ford, Datsun, Sigma, Dome, De Cadenet, Duckhams, Ligier, Chevron, Chevrolet, Dodge, Inaltera, WM-Peugeot, Mirage, Healey, De Tomaso, Grac, Moynet, March, Tecma, Lancia, Lenham, Cheetah, Aston Martin, Sauber, Osella, Rondeau, IBEC, Toj.** Many entries of cars from other interesting manufacturers, such as **Mercedes, Lamborghini** and **Maserati** never materialized.

In race reports from the **1974, 1975** era, journalists commonly insisted that the future of Le Mans laid on production-based cars, rather than the prototypes that generally prevailed. The Automobile Club de l'Ouest, the entity that promoted the race and set regulations, disagreed, in fact, it maintained prototype classes during the decade. The opinions of journalists and FISA was apparently wrong, for enthusiasm for the Silhouette formula was scant among manufacturers and development cost too much for privateers to bear. Only **Porsche** and **BMW** produced larger number of cars, **Lancia** came on board more seriously only in **1979**, while **Ford, Lotus** and **Toyota** Group 5 racers appeared in the DRM, hardly enough to come up with a competitive, 55-car field. So rather than ACO adopting FISA's and journalists point of views, by **1979** Prototypes were being allowed back in World Manufacturers Championship races.

De Cadenet built sports cars having Le Mans in mind, although it raced elsewhere. Photo by Paul Kooyman.

Podium feast in 1977: an epic win by Ickx, Barth and Haywood. Jurgen Barth collection.

The reason for the poor attendance in **1975**, often blamed on the fact that the public could not relate to prototypes, appears to be much different than fan demand for silhouettes. Traveling to races in **1975** had become an expensive ordeal for Europeans, specially Brits who attended the race in droves even when no competitive British entries were available and the absence of **Matra-Simca**, or any French car that was perceived to be a possible winner, or any works team, for that matter, might also have been more than a factor than love for tin tops. Curiously, **Ligier**, a French make **and** a closed car, did finish second...

It is also noteworthy that by **1978**, many of the crews comprised of three or even more drivers. Historically, Le Mans crews comprised two drivers. The **1977** edition of Le Mans was the first time a 3-driver crew officially won the race (it is claimed that a third driver drove the **1965** winner but officially, only **Rindt-Gregory** are credited with the win). Also curiously, the **1978** race was won by a two-driver team,

Pironi-Jaussaud. The first "intentional" three crew to win the race was **Ludwig-Whittington-Whittington**, in the last race of the decade.

Although it is easy to identify **Jacky Ickx** as the ultimate star of Le Mans in the 70s, closely followed by **Henri Pescarolo**, other drivers that deserve mention because of consistent excellent performances were **Gijs Van Lennep, Gerard Larrousse, Derek Bell, Jurgen Barth, Vern Schuppan, Francois Migault, Jean-Pierre Jaussaud, Jean-Louis Lafosse, Herbert Mueller, Reinhold Joest, Sam Posey, Alain de Cadenet, Chris Craft, Vic Elford, Nino Vacarella, Jean-Pierre Jabouille** and **Claude Ballot-Lena**. Also noteworthy performances are **Michel Pignard/Albert Dufrene/Jacques Henri**'s 2-Liter **Chevron** 6th place in **1976** and **Guy Chasseuil/Claude Ballot-Lena**'s 6th place in a **Porsche** 914/6 in **1970**. 2-liter prototypes were often entered and ran at **Le Mans** during the decade but most either broke down or finished low down the order, spending much time in the pits. As for the 914/6, a large of number of cars finished the **1970** race without doing enough laps to be qualified and the small engine car finished ahead of a large number of 911s. As for **Ballot-Lena**, he had no less than four class wins during the decade, quite an accomplishment.

Some other interesting **Le Mans** facts can be found in the section Highlights.

Top 6 at Le Mans during 1970-1979

1970
1. Hans Hermann/Richard Attwood, Porsche 917, 4,607 km
2. Gerard Larrousse/Willi Kauhsen, Porsche 917
3. Rudi Lins/Helmut Marko, Porsche 908
4. Sam Posey/Ronnie Bucknum, Ferrari 512S
5. Hughes de Fierlandt/Alistair Walker, Ferrari 512S
6. Guy Chasseuil/Claude Ballot-Lena, Porsche 914/6 (Winner GT up to 2 liters)
Fastest Lap: Vic Elford (Porsche 917), 3m21.0s

1971
1. Helmut Marko/Gijs Van Lennep, Porsche 917K, 5,335.31 km
2. Herbert Muller/Richard Attwood, Porsche 917K
3. Sam Posey/Tony Adamowickz, Ferrari 512M
4. Chris Craft/David Weir, Ferrari 512M
5. Bob Grossman/Luigi Chinetti Jr., Ferrari 365GTB4
6. Raymond Tourol/"Anselme", Porsche 911S (Winner GT)
Fastest lap: Jackie Oliver, 3m18.4s

1972
1. Henri Pescarolo/Graham Hill, Matra-Simca MS670, 4,691.km
2. Francois Cevert/Howden Ganley, Matra-Simca MS 670
3. Reinhold Joest/Mario Casoni/Michael Weber, Porsche 908/3
4. Andrea de Adamich/Nino Vacarella, Alfa Romeo 33TT3
5. Claude Andruet/Claude Ballot-Lena, Ferrari 365 GTB4 (Winner GT)
6. Sam Posey/Tony Adamowicz, Ferrari 365 GTB4
Fastest lap: Gijs van Lennep, 3m46.9s

1973
1. Henri Pescarolo/Gerard Larrousse, Matra-Simca MS670B, 4,853.945 km
2. Carlos Pace/Arturo Merzario, Ferrari 312PB
3. Jean-Pierre Jabouille/Jean-Pierre Jaussaud, Matra-Simca MS670B

355

4. Gijs Van Lennep/Herbert Mueller. Porsche 911 Carrera
5. Bernard Cheneviere/Juan Fernandez/Francisco Torredemer, Porsche 908/3
6. Vic Elford/Claude Ballot-Lena, Ferrari 365 GTB4 (Winner GT)
Fastest lap: Francois Cevert, 3m39.6s

1974
1. Henri Pescarolo/Gerard Larrousse, Matra-Simca MS670B, 4,606.571 km
2. Gijs Van Lennep/Herbert Mueller, Porsche 911 Turbo RSR
3. Jean-Pierre Jabouille/Francois Migault, Matra-Simca MS670B
4. Derek Bell/Mike Hailwood, Gulf Mirage Ford, GR7
5. Cyril Grandet/Dominique Bardini, Ferrari 365GTB4
6. Dave Heinz/Alain Cudini, Ferrari 365GTB4
Fastest lap: Jean-Pierre Jarier, 3m42.7s

1975
1. Jacky Ickx/Derek Bell, Gul Mirage Ford GR8, 4,595.577 km
2. Jean-Louis Lafosse/Guy Chasseuil, Ligier-Ford JS2
3. Vern Schuppan/Jean-Pierre Jaussaud, Gulf Mirage Ford GR8
4. Reinhold Joest/Jurgen Barth/Mario Casoni, Porsche 908
5. John Fitzpatrick/Gijs Van Lennep/Manfred Schurti, Porsche 911 (winner GT)
6. "Beurlys"/Nick Faure/John Cooper, Porsche 911
Fastest lap: Chris Craft, 3m53.8s

1976
1. Jacky Ickx/Gijs van Lennep, Porsche 936, 4,769.923 km
2. Jean-Louis Lafosse/Francois Migault, Mirage Ford GR8
3. Alain de Cadenet/Chris Craft. De Cadenet Ford
4. Rolf Stommelen/Manfred Schurti, Porsche 935 (Winner Group 5)
5. Derek Bell/Vern Schuppan, Mirage Ford GR8
6. Raymond Tourol/Alain Cudini, Porsche 911 RSR
Fastest lap: Jean-Pierre Jabouille, 3m43.0s

1977
1. Jacky Ickx/Hurley Haywood/Juergen Barth, Porsche 936, 4,671.630 km
2. Vern Schuppan/Jean-Pierre Jarier, Mirage Ford GR8
3. Claude Ballot-Lena/Peter Gregg, Porsche 935 (winner Group 5)
4. Jean Ragnotti/Jean Rondeau, Inaltera (winner GTP)
5. Alain de Cadenet/Christ Craft, De Cadenet Ford
6. Michel Pignard/Albert Dufrene/Jacques Henri, Chevron Ford
Fastest lap: Jacky Ickx, 3m36.50s

1978
1. Didier Pironi/Jean-Pierre Jaussaud, Alpine-Renault A442B, 5,044.530 km
2. Bob Wollek/Jacky Ickx/Juergen Barth, Porsche 936
3. Hurley Haywood/Peter Gregg/Jurgen Barth, Porsche 936
4. Jean Ragnotti/Guy Frequelin/Jose Dolhem, Alpine-Renault A442
5. Dick Barbour/Brian Redman/John Paul, Porsche 935 (winner IMSA)
6. Jim Busby/Rick Knoop/Chris Cord, Porsche 935 (winner Group 5)
Fastest lap: Jean-Pierre Jabouille, 3m34.2 s

1979
1. Klaus Ludwig/Bill Whittington/Don Whittington, Porsche 935K3, 4,173.930 km
2. Dick Barbour/Paul Newman/Rolf Stommelen, Porsche 935
3. Laurent Ferrier/Francois Servanin/Francois Trisconi, Porsche 935

4. Herbert Mueller/Angelo Pallavicini/Marc Vanoli, Porsche 934 (winner GT)
5. Bernard Darniche/Jean Ragnotti, Rondeau (winner Group 6)
6. Manfred Winkelhock/Herve Poulain/Marcel Mignot, BMW M1
Fastest lap: Jacky Ickx, 3m36.01s

EUROPEAN TWO LITER CHAMPIONSHIP

The first European 2-liter championship was contested in **1970** and many competitors used **Chevron** or **Lola** cars right from the start, although **Abarth** was a regular competitor. That year there were sporadic appearances by older **Porsches** and **Alfa Romeos**, in addition to other manufacturers, such as **Daren, Nomad, Astra, Focus, De Sanctis, Crossley**, with some GT/Touring cars such as **Lancia Fulvia, Porsche 911, Alfa GTA, BMW, Ford, Alpine Renault, Jerboa, Ferrari, Opel GT, Lotus and VW Porsches** making up the grids.

The very first edition of the championship was a straight fight between **Joakin Bonnier**, driving a **Lola** and **Brian Redman**, in a **Chevron**. **Bonnier** won four rounds, to **Redman**'s two victories. **John Burton** and **Vic Elford** also won races for **Chevron**, while **Abarth** won a single round with **Arturo Merzario**. The events were normally 2 hours in length, either single or two heat races, including rounds in France, Finland, Austria, Sweden, Germany(2), Italy (2) and Belgium. **Chevron** ended up carrying the makes championship, although **Lola**'s **Bonnier** took the drivers` title. A move by **Redman** on **Bonnier** in the last corner of the last race got **Chevron** the title. Among other drivers who raced that year were **Gijs van Lennep, Leo Kinnunen, Willy Kauhsen, Karl Won Wendt, Reine Wisell, Peter Schetty, Teodoro Zeccoli, Jonathan Williams, Dieter Quester, Johannes Ortner, Gerard Larrousse and Mario Casoni**. Although most of the British cars used **Cosworth** 1.8 liter engines, a Mazda 2 liter engined **Chevron** finished 6th in the Belgian round, while a **BMW** engined **Chevron** finished 4th in **Anderstorp**.

For **1971**, the championship continued to be a fight between **Lola** and **Chevron**, with **Abarth** always ready to pick a win, specially in Italy. The GT grid fillers were not present in most rounds, although the **Nürburgring** 500 continued to attract a large number of such cars. Among the 2-liter makes represented were **Martin, Daren, Dulon, Taydec, Redex, SAR, AMS and Gropa**. Austrian **Helmut Marko** was **Lola**'s main driver, while **Chevron** won races with **Toine Hezemans**, future world champion **Niki Lauda** and **John Hine**. **Vic Elford** and **Jo Bonnier** also won races for **Lola**, while **Merzario** won at **Vallelunga**, for **Abarth**. Among other drivers who contested rounds of the championship were **Jean-Pierre Jabouille, John Miles**, who had been sacked by the Lotus Formula 1 team the year before, **Gijs Van Lennep, Mario Casoni, Guy Edwards, Ronnie Peterson, Chris Craft, John Bridges, Bob Wollek** who became one of sports car racing's major stars in the late 70s, **Giovanni Salvati and Wilson Fittipaldi Junior**. **Lola** won the team championship, followed by **Chevron** and **Abarth**.

Merzario and his Abarth were the class of the field in the 1972 European 2-liter Championship and also raced in the World Championship for Makes. (Alejandro de Brito)

The **1972** Championship was handsomely won by **Abarth, Merzario** winning three rounds, **Toine Hezemans** and **Derek Bell**, one. **Dieter Quester** won a round, driving a **Chevron BMW**, John Burton carried the **Barcelona** round with a **Cosworth Chevron**, while **Jean Louis Lafosse** won the **Nürburgring** event in a **Lola** and **Gerard Larrousse** another, also in a **Lola**. Overall, **Abarth** finished ahead of **Chevron** and **Lola**. Some unusual makes around were **GRAC, Coldwell** and **KMW**. Among prominent drivers who contested the series were **John Watson, Nanni Galli, Vic Elford, Guy Edwards, Jo Bonnier** who died during the course of the year at **Le Mans, Carlo Facetti, Howden Ganley, Jody Scheckter, Bob Wollek and John Bridges**. At this stage, although the championship was considered interesting, it lacked financial support without a proper sponsor and crowds were generally poor.

The **1973** edition was won by **Chris Craft**, driving a **Lola** and many of the old supporters continued competing. **Arturo Merzario** won the **Eiffelpokalrennen** in **Nürburgring** in the newly named **Osella Abarth**, while **Vittorio Brambilla** won at **Enna**, for the same marque. The only **Chevron** win was at **Paul Ricard**, where **John Lepp** led a **Chevron** 1-2, followed by **John Burton**. **Craft** won at **Misano** and **Imola**, while **Guy Edwards** won the **Clermont Ferrand** and **Oesterreichring** rounds, both in **Lolas**. **Gerard Larrousse** won at **Montjuich**, with a **Lola BMW**. Other championship luminaries were **Toine Hezemans, Dieter Quester, Henri Pescarolo, Tim Schenken**, Italian hill climb star **Mauro Nesti, Dave Walker** in a **GRD**, American **Jim Busby, Jean-Pierre Jabouille, Vic Elford** and **Reinhold Joest**. A prominent newcomer as far as makes were concerned, was **Alpine Renault**. **March, GRD** and **AMS** also scored points during the year, so there was some further diversity as far as marques were concerned.

1974 was a hard year for racing in general and the European 2-liter championship was affected as well. The championship had seven rounds and it was utterly dominated by the **Alpine Renault** squad, which had on its driving strength **Gerard Larrousse, Alain Cudini, Jean-Pierre Jabouille** and **Alain Serpaggi**. **Cudini** won at **Paul Ricard**, while **Larrousse** won at **Clermont Ferrand, Pergusa** and **Mugello, Serpaggi** won at **Hockenheim** and **Jabouille** at **Misano** and **Jarama**.

Nothing was left for other manufacturers, which included newcomer **TOJ**, in addition to **Osella, Chevron, AMS, March, Lola** and **GRD**. As a result, top drivers that used to flock to the series in the past mostly stayed away, although **Merzario, Brambilla, Craft, Lepp** and **Lafosse** paid occasional visits and former **Lotus** F1-driver **Dave Walker** gave it a go in the **TOJ**.

The last year of the championship was **1975** and it was indeed a sad end. Several of the rounds were cancelled even before the championship started, still due to the **1974** oil crisis and the championship ended up with only two rounds. **Alpine Renault** had "graduated" to the World Manufacturers Championship with a turbo version of the 2-liter car, so it was all left to privateers. The two rounds that did take place were the **Brands Hatch** race won by **Obermoser** in the **TOJ and** a round at **Hockenheim**, won by **Martin Raymond. Chris Skeaping**, who had scored on both races was named champion and as less than six rounds were run, FIA did not recognize the championship. Some new makes appeared in those rounds, though: **Cheetah, Rex (Derek Bell)** raced one) and **Sauber**, which eventually would make it to Formula 1. 2-Liter sports racers continued racing all over Europe, in track and mountain climb races. In hindsight, although the racing was often spirited, the cars looked good, with no series sponsor and generally bad promotion by organizers, the 2-Liter Championship was doomed to failure. Race attendance was never good and it dropped further in the latter years. For example, the 1972 Enna race a mere 717 paying viewers. Had it taken place during the age of multiple-channel and cable TV, perhaps its fate would have been different.

2-liter prototypes continued racing all over. The Italian championship was particularly strong, mostly contested by **Osellas**. 2 Liters continued to be used in club racing in England, in hill climbs all over Europe and they comprised a large part of the fields in the World Manufacturers Championship in **1975** and most entries in the World Sports Car Championships of **1976** and **1977**. Eventually, the Sports Car Championship became a European level championship, still contested mostly by 2-liter cars. When the Group Five Silhouette concept collapsed in **1979**, 2-liter Group 6 cars not only contested the World Manufacturers Championship races but also won overall on several occasions.

Win ranking, drivers
1. Arturo Merzario (I), 6
2. Jo Bonnier (S) and Gerard Larrousse (F), 5
3. Helmut Marko (A), Jean-Pierre Jabouille (F), 3
4. Brian Redman (GB), John Burton (GB), Vic Elford (GB), Toine Hezemans (NL), Chris Craft (GB), Guy Edwards (GB), 2
5. Niki Lauda (A), John Hine (1), Dieter Quester (A), Jean-Louis Lafosse (F), Derek Bell (GB), John Lepp (GB), Vittorio Brambilla (I), Alain Serpaggi (F), Jorg Obermoser (D), Martin Raymond (GB), Alain Cudini (F), 1

Fastest laps, drivers
1. Jean-Pierre Jabouille (F), 6
2. John Burton (GB), Gerard Larrousse (F), 5
4. Joakin Bonnier (S), Arturo Merzario (I), 4
5. Guy Edwards (GB), 3
6. Brian Redman (GB), Helmut Marko (A), Vic Elford (GB), Jorg Obermoser (D), 2
7. Nanni Galli (I), Chris Craft (GB), Toine Hezemans (NL), Carlo Facetti (I), Dieter Quester (A), Jody Scheckter (ZA), Howden Ganley (NZ), Bob Wollek (F), Richard Scott (GB), Derek Bell (GB), John Hine (GB), 1

Win ranking, manufacturers
1. Lola, 16
2. Chevron, 11
3. Abarth, 9
4. Alpine-Renault, 7
5. Toj, 1

Venues used
1. Paul Ricard (F), 5
2. Hockenheim (D), Nürburgring (D), Enna (I), 4
3. Salzburgring (A), Jarama (E), 3
4. Mugello (I), Silverstone (GB), Imola (I), Vallelunga (I), Montjuich (E), Misano (I), Clermont-Ferrand (F), 2
5. Hameenlina (SF), Anderstorp (S), Spa (B), Zandvoort (NL), Dijon (F), Oesterreichring (A), Brands Hatch (GB), 1

Cars and models that raced in the European 2-Liter Championship (1970-1975)
Please note that in the first two years of the championship, certain organizers allowed entries of Group 4 and Group 2 cars to boost grid size. These brands and models are listed here:

Chevron B6, B6/8, B16, B19, B21, B23, B26
Lola T210, T212, T290, T292, T294, T390
Abarth 2000S, 1000S, 2000 SP71, SE021
Porsche 911T, 910, 907, 906, 914/6
Alpine A110, A441, A440
Alfa Romeo 33/2, GTA 1600, TZ1, GTA J
Daren M2, Mk4
Ligier JS1
Astra NR2
AMS 1000 P. 273, 274
Lotus Europa. Elan, 62
Nomad Mk3
Focus P
Jerboa 1000
Lancia Fulvia
Austin Healey Sprite 110P
MG Midget 1300P
Unipower GT
De Sanctis 1000
ATS 1000, 1300 P
Osca 1000 P
Opel GT1900
Triumph Spitfire
Ferrari Dino 206S, P
BMW 2002TI

Ford Escort
Crossley
Cox GTM
Ark Sprite
NSU Spyder
Mercury Mk3
DKW Monza 1000 P
Actec GS
Gropa CMC
Taydec Mk2
Fournier-Marcadier
Martin BM8
Sar P
Dulon LN11P
Coldwell C14
Huron SP1, 72, 4A
Grac MT16, MT20
KMW SP20
March 73S, 74S, 75S
GRD S73
Dallara 1300
Osella PA1, PA2
TOJ SS02, SG03
Vogue SP1
Aldon
Sauber C4, C3
Rex SP1
Cheetah G501

CAN-AM

I saw it fit to separate the Can-Am in two, setting apart the original Group 7 category that ran until **1974**, from the Formula 5000 bodied cars of **1977-79**.

TRADITIONAL CAN-AM

If on the one hand the *Bruce and Denny* show made the Can-Am look boring, very few would argue that any other car racing Championship had its clout, charm and reputation in the late 60s. The cars looked wonderful, sounded wonderful and the prize money was wonderful. Too bad no one had come up with a design that would challenge **McLaren** properly in the years before **1970**, despite **Chaparral**'s and **Ferrari**'s best efforts.

McLaren continued its winning ways in 1970-71 but it all came to a halt in 1972. Photo by Rob Neuzel.

The **1970** season was almost a different story. The Can-Am season started late as always, in June and by then one half of the *Bruce and Denny* show was gone. **Bruce McLaren** had lost his life testing his latest creation at **Goodwood**, so another legend was called to fill his place, **Dan Gurney**. **Dan** did well to win the first two races of the year, then raced once more and quit. His place was taken by **Peter Gethin**, the Brit who was cleaning up in Formula 5000 also driving a **McLaren**. However, right from the start, there was a whiff of apparent change in the air. **Jackie Oliver** was second in the first race of the year, in the titanium **Ti-22**, **Peter Revson** had a very fast **Lola**, there was the **AVS-Shadow** with its weird tiny wheels and looking like a kart on steroids, as of the second race a challenger from **BRM**, plus the **Ford G7** with a host of guest drivers. Towards the end of the season there was a new car from **March**, driven by **Chris Amon** and the famous **Chaparral** fan car. There was even a very unsuccessful **Mac's it Special** 4-engined car at **Laguna Seca** in the hands of **Hiroshi Fushida**! As it was, **Hulme** won most of the races, although **Gethin** would win once and a surprised **Tony Dean** managed a single victory in **Road Atlanta**, in a 3 liter **Porsche** 908, when the works **McLarens** failed. Although **Hulme** did win the final race of the season at **Riverside**, he was followed by quite a lot of diversity, **Oliver's Ti-22**, a **BRM** (**Pedro Rodriguez**) and **Amon**'s **March**.

Old cars such as this McLaren M1 continued to be raced during the life of the Can Am. This car in fact raced in 1974! Photo by Rob Neuzel.

The major news for **1971** was **Jackie Stewart** had been signed to drive a L&M sponsored **Lola**. Additionally, **McLaren** changed **Peters**, hiring **Revson** instead of **Gethin**. This turned out to be a major coup, for **Revson** proved an ideal teammate for **Hulme** and the orange **McLarens** again won most races, while **Revson** carried the championship. **Stewart** did prevail a couple of times, in **St. Jovite** and **Mid-Ohio** but was way behind the **McLarens** in points at the end. **Oliver** had gone to **Shadow**, which adopted conventional wheels, while **Siffert** drove a **Porsche** 917K that looked very promising. **Donohue** appeared in the Penske **Ferrari** at the **Glen** and BRM drivers **Ganley** and **Redman** did well the few times the car appeared.

The story changed in **1972**, when the **Porsche** 917K **Siffert** had been developing turned into the fearsome **Porsche** 910/10K. The year started as usual, **Hulme** winning, followed by **Donohue**, who had scored pole in a **Penske**-run **Porsche**. **Donohue** then got hurt and his place in the Penske team was taken by **Follmer**. The American won at **Road Atlanta**, then **Hulme** won once more, the works **McLaren** last Can-Am win. From that point on the Penske **Porsches** would win almost everything, except for a **Donnybrooke** win by **Francois Cevert** in a private **McLaren**. **Shadow** was the third best car of the series and **Hobbs**' **Lola** T310 was a major disappointment, totally outclassed. **Follmer** won the title and **Hulme** was runner-up in his last Can-Am campaign.

It is fair to say that the expensive **Porsche** 917 killed the original Can-Am, even if there were seven of them in **Mosport** at the opening of the **1973** season. Although **McLaren** swept all before it for many years, customer **McLarens** could be bought by privateers and equipped with engines for a reasonable price. The **Porsche** turbos cost a lot more money and no one came up with an idea or product to properly challenge the German car for the season. The opposition was mostly old **McLarens, Lolas**, while **Shadow** had the updated DN2 for **Oliver** (also for **Hunt** and **Elford)**, which was utterly incapable of keeping up with the conquering teutonic engineering feat. Making matters worse, **Penske** had an exclusive updated **Porsche** 917, the 30K, that was the class of the field, so that **Donohue** totally dominated proceedings leaving even other **Porsches** behind. Other **Porsche** drivers that season were **Follmer, Kemp, Scheckter, Gregg, Haywood, Kauhsen, Redman**, the slower **Wiedmer**. The SCCA decided to spice things up by dividing races into a short sprint, then a final. It is not clear how that spiced anything up but at least **Mario Andretti** made some appearances in the sprints sharing a **McLaren** with **John Cannon**.

So it was no surprise that in the uncertain economic environment of **1974**, when sponsorship deals were falling through by the dozen, tracks cancelling race after race, plus a certain degree of SCCA ineptitude and panic, the traditional Can-Am had its final season in **1974**. Only **Mosport, Road Atlanta, Watkins Glen, Mid-Ohio** and **Elkhart Lake** went through with their longstanding commitments and a limited, last season began in **Mosport**. **Jackie Oliver** and **George Follmer**, in **Shadow**s, dominated and **Oliver** won the first four races. **Porsche** 917s raced a couple of times, **Brian Redman** almost winning **Mid-Ohio** in the Penske 30k, on a very slippery track that reduced the car's advantage – lucky **Shadows**! **Redman** had also raced the **Posey Ferrari** at **Watkins Glen**. The final race of the series was won by **Scooter Patrick**, in a **McLaren**. A telling sign of decadence: among the runners, there was a **Lola** T70, the model that won the first Can-Am back in **1966**.

Race winners, 1970-1974, Drivers
1. Denis Hulme (NZ), 11
2. Mark Donohue (US), 7
3. George Follmer (US), 6
4. Peter Revson (US), 5
5. Jackie Oliver (GB), 4
6. Jackie Stewart (GB), Dan Gurney (US), 2
7. Peter Gethin (GB), Tony Dean (GB), Francois Cevert (F), Charlie Kemp (US), Scooter Patrick (US), 1

Gary Wilson's Sting. Photo by Rob Neuzel.

Race winners, 1970-1974, Cars
1. McLaren, 21
2. Porsche, 15
3. Shadow, 4
4. Lola, 2

Fastest laps (1970-1974)
1. Denis Hulme, 12
2. Mark Donohue, Peter Revson, 6
3. Jackie Oliver, George Follmer, 4
4. Jackie Stewart, 2
5. Peter Gethin, Dan Gurney, 1

Venues used (1970-1974)
1. Mosport (CDN), Watkins Glen, Mid-Ohio, Elkhart Lake, Road Atlanta, 5
2. Edmonton (CDN), Laguna Seca, Riverside, 4
3. Donnybrooke, 3
4. St. Jovite (CDN), 2

Car types (and subtypes) that raced in the Can Am (1970-1974)
McLaren (M1C, M1B, M6A, M6B, M8B, M8C, M8D, M8E/D, M8F, M8FP, M12, M12A, M12B, M20, "Special")
Lola (T70, T70mk3b, T70mk3, T163, T165, T162, T160/163, T220, T222, T260)
BRM (P154, P167)
AVS Shadow and Shadow (Mk2, Mk3, DN2, DN4)
Porsche (908, 917, 917PA, 917K, 917/10, 917/10K, 917/30KL, 917/30K, Carrera Prototype)
McLeagle
Ti22
Mac' II Special
Moore Mk2
Rattenbury MK4B
Ferrari (512S, 512P, 512M, 712M)
Chaparral 2J
Ford G7A
McKee Mk6
March 707
Burnett Mk2
Genie Mk10
Terry T10
Alfa Romeo T33/3, T33/4
Hodges LSR
Sting GW1
Costello (SP7, SP8)

Among the drivers that raced in the Can-Am in the period (besides those mentioned in the text): **Herbert Muller, Bobby Allison, Mario Cabral, Hiroshi Kazato, LeRoy Yarbrough, Jean-Pierre Jarier, Eppie Wietzes, John Cannon. Pedro Rodriguez, Arturo Merzario, Sam Posey, Andrea de Adamich, Willy Kauhsen, Mike Hiss, Reine Wisell, Reinhold Jost, Alain de Cadenet, Tony Adamowickz, Oscar Kovelesky, Dick Barbour, Gijs Van Lennep, Graeme Lawrence, Bob Bondurant, Chuck Parsons, Helmut Marko, Jo Bonnier, Ritchie Attwood, Derek Bell, Jacky Ickx.** As the Watkins Glen Can Am happened on the same weekend as the 6 Hours of Watkins Glen, many World Championship challengers took part in these races, with no chance of winning.

The Costello was one of the least known Can-Am cars. Here driven by David Sevill-Back, at Mid Ohio, 1974. Photo by Rob Neuzel.

CAN-AM, SINGLE SEATERS (1977-1979)

1974 was a terrible year for the SCCA's pro division. It had lost the sponsorship for its Formula 5000 championship and cancelled it (then another sponsor signed-up and the series was back on track); the Trans-Am had become a laughable 3-race championship; and the Can-Am suffered the results of its excesses. Given the bad economy, the club had lost several of its amateur members as well, so revenue from entry fees and memberships was down. By the end of the year, the Can Am was dead, the Trans-Am in life support and Formula 5000 was a problem that needed a solution.

The truth is the SCCA had a very good brand on one hand and a sensible product for the times, on the other. The good brand was the Can-Am, which had prestige, charm and admiration of fans, while the good product was Formula 5000, which imposed technical and regulatory restrictions that made its cars much cheaper than the Group 7 Can-Am. While Can Am had an unrestricted engine formula, which resulted in the emergence of the **Porsche** 917-turbo, Formula 5000s used stock blocks, with clear limitations. It was highly unlikely any manufacturer would create out of the blue a 5-liter stock block, build thousands of units, just to dominate Can-Am. Incidentally, **Chevrolet** powered most Formula 5000 winners around the world since the beginning of the category, so as long as there were a few chassis manufacturers around, no one would notice it was almost a one-make formula in terms of engine.

The solution was ingenious, almost Solomonic in conception, however, poor in execution. Formula 5000 cars would be transformed into Can-Ams and in the process would receive sports car bodies to resemble the Can-Am cars of yore. Rather unfortunately, most cars continued to look like Formula 5000 cars, with appendages, true but failed to strike the imagination of most as "exciting". Clumsy would be a better was to define some of them. New chassis manufacturers did not sign up in droves, the only true novelty being the **Wolf-Dallara**, to be driven by **Chris Amon**.

However, what killed the Can-Am, in my view, was the inclusion of a 2-liter category. While that ensured larger grids and chassis variety, the speed, sound and look differential between the cars made the series look decidedly different and inferior to the old Can-Am. The series would survive well into the 80s but one can say it was at best mildly successful, just because it survived that long. Although there were usually three or four name drivers (generally driving for Haas and VDS), drivers from other major spheres of American racing such as NASCAR, USAC and Sports cars were not interested, because the money was not that good as well. For the public, the cars were slightly slower compared to Formula 5000, given the excess body weight.

In the 3 years covered, **1977** to **1979**, several very good drivers raced in the Can-Am "revival": **Patrick Tambay, Chris Amon, Gilles Villeneuve, Peter Gethin, Alan Jones, Warwick Brown, Elliot Forbes-Robinson, George Follmer, Jacky Ickx, Keke Rosberg, Bobby Rahal, Graham McRae, Al Holbert, Vern Schuppan, Jean-Pierre Jarier, Howden Ganley, Alain de Cadenet, Geoff Lees, Geoff Brabham, John McCormack, John Morton**. However, there were never enough such drivers on the track at the same time to spark extreme international interest. Times were different.

The initial season started in the worst possible way. **Brian Redman**, the top star who had won the last three Formula 5000 championships and was considered the favorite, had a huge accident in qualifying for **St. Jovite**, the initial race and was sidelined for the rest of the year. The other big name in the race, **Chris Amon**, qualified 2nd and was the first retirement. The winner ended up being Formula Atlantic driver **Tom Klausler**, in the unusually bodied **Schkee**, which at least did not look like a Formula 5000 with fenders. In **Laguna Seca**, Haas had not provided a replacement for **Redman, Chris Amon** had retired from racing for good and even the **Schkee** retired early from the race. The winner in the poorly supported race was also relative unknown **Don Breidenbach**. For **Watkins Glen, Haas** had brought **Tambay** to replace **Redman** and the Frenchman won. **Gethin** won the next round in the VDS machine, then **Tambay** won the rest of the season's races. **Villeneuve** usually qualified the **Wolf-Dallara** in the top 3 but did not finish the season, while a welcome addition was **Alan Jones** in a **Dodge**-engined **Shadow**.

The very same **Jones** was hired as **Tamba**y's replacement for **1978**, for the Frenchman was hired by **McLaren**'s Formula 1 team. VDS also changed drivers, **Gethin** having decided to retire and **Warwick Brown** was retained in his place, so there were two Australians in the top cars. **Jarier** was slated to drive the **Shadow** and two new "manufacturers" appeared, the **Spyder** and the **Prophet**. It should be noted that these two cars (plus the **Schkee**) were in fact **Lola** chassis with different bodies, so save for the **Shadow**, a **McRae, Elfin** or **Talon** here and there, almost everybody was running **Lolas**… The **Spyder** was driven by **Forbes-Robinson** and the **Prophet** was raced by **Follmer**. **Alan Jones** won most of the races but **Brown, Follmer, Forbes-Robinson** and **Holbert** also won. In the end, an Aussie 1-2.

The Haas team ruled the single-seater Can Am, just as it ruled American Formula 5000. This is Tambay in the T333, 1977. Photo by Lola Heritage.

For the last year of the decade, **Ickx** was brought in to replace **Jones, Geoff Less** to replace **Brown, Rosberg** was added by **Spyder, Rahal** replacing **Follmer** at **Prophet**. One worrying trend was that in several races the 2-liters were breaking into the top 6, indicating that a lot of the 5-liter cars were not very competitive or reliable. **Ickx** did what was expected of him, won the series and five races but some felt his effort was half-hearted. **Ickx** was no longer the extravagant **Jacky** of **1970**, certainly not as exciting to watch as a younger **Rosberg** but he did win the series comfortably over **Forbes-Robinson**. **Alan Jones** replaced **Ickx** in Mid-Ohio and won. One interesting car was Australian **John McCormack's McLaren** M23, which body did look more Can-Amish than most. It was not very competitive, though. This was also a sign of the times.

INTERSERIE

Several European championships emerged during the early seventies, many of which did not survive many years, including the European GT Championship and European 2-liter championship. The Interserie was not a FIA championship and maybe for that same reason, it survived until the early 2000s, although in the latter guise it had a much lower stature.

The Can-Am series, in which large displacement 2-seater sports cars competed, was a major success in the late 60s, often eclipsing Formula 1 in interest and even speed. In fact, many prominent European drivers contested the series, which was dominated by the **McLaren** team from **1967** to **1971**. Group 7 was created in England but no major championship for the category was created in the European continent, until the Interserie, in **1970**.

Billed as the European Can-Am, the Interserie never achieved the same success as the U.S./Canadian series. For one, prize money was not as abundant, so the series failed to attract major talent of the day. Additionally, the Can Am races often attracted more than 30 participants, at least until **1972**, while Interserie entries were numerically less impressive. As a result, one would often find 2-liter sports cars filling grids against 8-liter and turbo engined brutes, in addition to some drivers of questionable pedigree.

On the positive side, the Interserie provided a longer European lifeline for 5-liter Group 5 cars such as the **Porsche** 917, **Ferrari** 512, **Lola** T70 and **Ford** GT40, which were disallowed in the World Manufacturers Championship, as of **1972**.

In the early years, the series was mostly a **Porsche** benefit, initially with the 917 and 908 models, eventually with the 917 K variant. Despite this dominance, works teams from **Ferrari, Alfa Romeo** and **BRM** took part in some races. On the driver side, the Interserie attracted mostly German or Nordic drivers, although the odd Italian, French, British and South American drivers participated.

The first championship comprised of 6 rounds, with races held at **Norisring, Hockenheim** (two rounds), **Croft** (England), **Keimola** and **Thruxton**. The first champion was **Jurgen Neuhaus**, who drove a 4.5-liter **Porsche** 917, winning the initial race, plus the 5th round. **Gijs Van Lennep** came in second, also driving a **Porsche** 917. Providing some welcome diversification, **Helmut Kelleners** won a couple of races driving a **March 707-Chevrolet**, the same car type that **Chris Amon** used in the Can Am but did not win.

For **1971, Leo Kinnunen** began his run of success in the series. Driving a spyder adapted **Porsche** 917, **Kinnunen** won the series for three straight years. Having risen to prominence as **Pedro Rodriguez**'s teammate in the successful World Manufacturers Championship campaign of **1970**, Leo won the **1971** championship on the strength of many good placings and a single victory at home, in **Keimola**.

The score was curiously reflected in Swiss Francs rather than points, which clearly showed why major drivers such as **Jackie Stewart** shunned the Interserie in favor of Can-Am: **Leo** won only 81,000 Swiss Francs. Among other attractions, **Brian Redman** drove a **Chevrolet** powered **BRM** to two victories, while **Arturo Merzario** drove a works **Ferrari** to victory at **Imola**. Autodelta **Alfa Romeo**s also appeared at the **Zolder** round, driven by **Stommelen** and **Hezemans**. Peter Gethin also won a couple of rounds and was the runner up in the championship. Sadly, **Pedro Rodriguez** lost his life driving a **Ferrari** 512 in the **Norisring** round.

For **1972 Kinnunen** was even more competitive, winning a total of 6 out of 9 rounds, driving an upgraded 5.4-liter **Porsche** 917-10. Leo was not the only driver to be so equipped, as **Willi Kauhsen** also drove that model effectively. **BRM** took part in a few rounds, winning at **Nürburgring** and **Oesterreichring**, with **Howden Ganley** at the wheel. On the driving strength, there were less stars taking part in Interserie races, a pattern that was to remain until the end of the period. On the positive side, the calendar had expanded to 9 races.

The **1973** tournament was down to 7 races again and it was duly won by **Kinnunen**, who was by then racing a turbo **Porsche** 917-10. **Leo** won four races, while **Willi Kauhsen** took two, to **Vic Elford**'s one. The championship was a real **Porsche** party and the best placing by a non-Porsche was **Teddy Pilette**'s fourth place driving a turbo **McLaren** at **Nürburgring**. **Teddy** had a frightening accident with this car at **Zolder**, caused by suspension failure.

Willi Kauhsen was one of the Interserie stars, before embarking on a full-time career as team owner. Photo by Rob Neuzel.

In **1974, Herbert Muller** began his championship hat trick. Having been loyal to **Ferrari** until **1973**, for **74 Muller** changed to a **Porsche** 917-20 Turbo, winning the first of three championships. **Herbert** won half of the six races, the other three being shared by **Kauhsen, Kelleners** and **Kinnunen. Kelleners** won at the **Nürburgring** with a **McLaren. 1974** World champion-to-be **Emerson Fittipaldi** took part in that race, driving a **Porsche** 917-10 Turbo to sixth, after scoring the pole. Curiously, his former **Lotus** teammate **Dave Walker** drove a **TOJ** to fifth place. Point scoring was again adopted, to the detriment of Swiss Franc earnings.

The **1975** calendar comprised seven races and **Muller** was again the winner, having won two races to **Tim Schenken**'s three. **Tim** had been hired by **Georg Loos** and won the last three races of the year, also in a **Porsche** 917 Turbo. The **Willi Kauhsen** Racing Team, which was racing **Alfa Romeo**s in the Makes championship that year, took part in a few rounds, winning one of the **Hockenheim** races with **Jochen Mass** at the wheel and at **Kassel Calden** with **Derek Bell**. Also driving **Alfas** during the year, were **Henri Pescarolo** and **John Watson**. **Howden Ganley** also drove in a few races in a **Gulf Ford**, achieving 2nd place at the **Nürburgring**. The calendar was becoming almost entirely German, a single race held at **Zandvoort** bringing some international flavor to the series. Three of the races were held at **Hockenheim**.

From **1976** on, the Interserie changed its original focus, as Group 7 cars were fewer and fewer, except for a **McLaren** here and there. In fact, it was one such **McLaren** that won the initial race of the season, **Peter Hoffmann's** racer, which prevailed in **Kassel Calden**. At **Zolder**, a different story – the winner was **Martin Raymond** in a 2-liter **Chevron**, for the few larger capacity cars all failed to bring home the bacon that day. Meanwhile, **Herbert Muller**, used to overall wins in previous seasons, was accumulating points driving a 2-liter **Sauber-BMW**. At **Hockenheim** yet a different type of car won, this time **Reinhold Joest's** turbo **Porsche** 908/3, which preceded **Hoffmann** and **Muller**. At the **Nürburgring Joest** won again, followed by **Wollek** in a similar car but **Muller** won among the 2 liters. Scoring was done by category and the overall champion would be the driver who scored more points in his category. At **Mainz Finthen Obermoser** won in a DFV engined **Toj**, while **Muller** won his class once more. Another win in class at **Hockenheim** ensured **Muller**'s third title, even though **Joest** had won overall again.

In **1977** much of the same happened. **Helmut Bross** ran a 2-liter **Lola** but won only a single race overall at **Wunstorf**. **Obermoser** won at **Kassel Calden** in the 3-liter **Toj-Ford**, while **Derek Bell** appeared once more driving an **Alfa Romeo** T33/SC12, winning at **Avus**. **Obermoser** won at the **Nürburgring**, while **Joes**t was victorious with his **Porsche** at **Mainz Finthen**. The last race of the year was won by **Arturo Merzario**, driving the turbo **Alfa Romeo** appearing for the last time at **Hockenheim**. **Bross** won the title given his better performance in his category.

The **1978** season also had 6 races. The first round, at the **Nürburgring**, was won by **Giorgio Francia** in a 2-liter **Osella-BMW**, which finished less than a second in front of **Reinhold Joe**st. The German did win the next race, a rare international event held in the **Colmar Berg** track, in Luxembourg, a testing track for Goodyear Europe. In second came **Wollek** in a similar **Porsche** 908 turbo, run by the Kremer brothers. At a poorly supported event at **Wunstorf, Kurt Lotterschmid** won in **Deutsch-Porsche** special. By this point some Interserie race entries were decidedly 2nd class. At **Kassel Calden Wollek** won in the Kremer **Porsche** 908/3 over **Joest**. The positions were reversed in the last two races, at **Ulm** and **Nürburgring** and **Joest** came out the series winner, in addition to his European Sports Car title. The participation of two drivers of the caliber of **Joest** and **Wollek** was good for the championship but not enough to maintain its prestige as a prime international series.

The **1979** season had 7 rounds. **Lotterschmid** won the first race at **Wunstorf** in a 2-liter **Toj**-BMW. In second, **Lella Lombardi** in an **Osella-BMW**. The best 3- liter car came in 6th, 3 laps behind the leader. The sports cars score from the 1000 km of **Nürburgring** served as round number two, the winners being **Stommelen** and **Joest**, in a **Porsche** 908/3 turbo. **Peter Hoffmann** won the next race at the **Nürburgring**, in his trusty, if leisurely driven, **McLaren-Chevrolet**. The next race took place in **Most**, Czechoslovakia, a rare Western championship round held in an Iron Curtain country. The winner was **Norbert Pryzybilla** in a **Toj-Ford**. The race had a relatively large entry, although the only famous names were **Lella Lombardi** and **Harald Grohs**. At **Ulm Stommelen** raced and won again, while **Lella Lombardi** came in second and won her class. **Joest** won the next race at **Hockenheim**, followed by **Lotterschmid**, while there were separate races for the two divisions in **Kassel Calden: Hans Georg Burger** won the race for 2-liters, while **Stommelen** won again for the large cars. Not terribly exciting but then again, sports car racing was going through its worse period in Europe. For bad, for worse, the Interserie had survived the decade and for that it deserves praise. The series never really achieved its proposed billing as the European Can-Am but it did provide an enduring platform for large sports car racing in Europe, not a bad thing.

Race wins (1970-1979) Drivers:
1. Leo Kinnunen (SF), 12
2. Reinhold Joest (D), 9
3. Herbert Muller (CH), 5
4. Willi Kauhsen (D), 4
5. Derek Bell (GB), Helmut Kelleners (D), Jorg Obermoser (D), Rolf Stommelen (D), Tim Schenken (AUS), 3
6. Jurgen Neuhaus (D), Vic Elford (GB), Arturo Merzario (I), Brian Redman (GB), Howden Ganley (NZ), Peter Hoffman (D), Kurt Lotterschmid (D), 2
7. Gijs Van Lennep (NL), Peter Gethin (GB), Chris Craft (GB), Jochen Mass (D), Martin Raymond (GB), Giorgio Francia (I), Bob Wollek (F), Norbert Przybilla (D), Hans Georg-Burger (D), Helmut Bross (D), 1

Chris Craft in the 1970 Interserie. Photo by Pete Austin.

Race wins (1970-1979), by car
1. Porsche, 36
2. McLaren, 7
3. Toj, 5
4. BRM, Alfa Romeo, 4
5. March, Lola, 2
6. Ferrari, Chevron, Osella, Deutsch, 1

Venues used (1970-1979)
1. Hockenheim (D), 17
2. Nürburgring (D), 12
3. Kassel Calden (D), 5
4. Norisring (D), 4
5. Keimola (SF), Imola (I), Mainz-Finthen (D), Wunstorf (D), 3
6. Ulm (D), Zolder (B), Silverstone (GB), 2
7. Croft (GB), Thruxton (GB), Oesterreichring (A), Most (CS), Casale (I), Zandvoort (NL), Misano (I), Avus (I), Colmar Berg (L), 1

Prominent drivers who took part in the Interserie in the 70s: **Jurgen Neuhaus, Helmut Kelleners, Ronnie Peterson, Niki Lauda, Helmut Marko, Emerson Fittipaldi, Wilson Fittipaldi Junior, Pedro Rodriguez, Gijs Van Lennep, Teddy Pilette, David Prophet, Gerard Larrousse, Chris Craft, Arturo Merzario, Herbert Muller, Brian Redman, Joakin Bonnier, Vic Elford, Leo Kinnunen, Peter Gethin, Willi Kaushen, Derek Bell, Jochen Mass, Richard Attwood, Rolf Stommelen, Toine Hezemans, Andrea de Adamich, Reinhold Joest, Georg Loos, Henri Pescarolo, John Watson, Lella Lombardi, George Follmer, Nanni Galli, Brian Henton, Harald Ertl, Loris Kessel, Hartwig Bertrams. Giampiero Moretti, Clemens Schickentanz, Otto Stuppacher, Clay Regazzoni, Carlo Facetti, Mario Casoni**

Cars that raced in the Interserie 1970-1979: Porsche 908-1, 908-2, 908-3, 908-3 Turbo, 917, 917K, 907, 910, 906; Daren MK3, Chevron B8, B16, B19, B12, B21, B23, B26, B27, B31, Spectre, March 707, 717, 75S, 74S, 76S; Nathan; Lola T70 Ford and Aston Martin, T210, T212, T290, T222, T280, T282, T294, T292, T290,

T296, T390, T297, T380; Lotus 23 and 62; Saturn Martin; Ford GT40, Ford Capri; Ferrari 512M and 512S; Astra, Brabham, McLaren M12, M6, M8, M20, M1; Alfa Romeo T33/3, T33/12, T33/SC/12; BRM P167, P154; TOJ SC306, SC302, SC206, SC304, SC204, Karasek, KMW Porsche, Momo-Abarth, GRD S73, Behnke Condor, Abarth Osella, Abarth 2000SP, Cheetah, Rawlson Ford, De Cadenet, Rieger SP1000, GLS Porsche, REX SP, LBW 747, Grac MT14S, Martin BM9, MTX201 BMW, Lotus Europa Turbo, CRS 679, Sbarro 576, LBS 5, Osella PA7, PA6, PA5, PA4, Landar :RB, Martin BM9, Deutsch Special, Tecno Porsche.

EUROPEAN GT CHAMPIONSHIP

Today GT racing is in a healthy state the world over. We do live in more affluent times, quite a few dream cars are eligible to run in the category, plus there is plentiful more sponsorship money, which was not the case in the early 70s. However, the world of sports car racing has always been a struggle between bona fide, purebred racers, mostly called prototypes and GTs, which are basically racy, production based cars. Plus, there have been categories in between, such as the Group 5 of the mid 70s/early 80s and the 5-liter sports cars of the late 60s/early 70s, which required a minimum production run of 25 units.

FISA's thinking was to separate the production-based GTs from pure-breed sports cars in the early 70s. With the benefit of hindsight one might say the experience was anything but successful. The prototype (Group 6) era of the World Manufacturers Championship was not successful in terms of quantity of cars or field depth, while the European GT championship created for **1972** remained a near **Porsche** monopoly during the years in which the series was run.

There was some obvious concern about the large numbers of **Porsche** 911's that had been entered in the **1971 Le Mans**. In fact, the ubiquitous car was entered in many other races, as it was relatively cheap to run, reasonably competitive for long distance racing, often finishing ahead of faster, less reliable machinery such as 2-liter sports racers. However, these cars, that just a couple of years back were entered in the European Touring Car championship, were relatively slow in their **1971** guise, compared to powerful beasts such as the **Ferrari** 512 and **Porsche** 917 and it was by sheer luck that they did not cause any major accidents, specially because not all drivers were professional or very skilfull.

The European GT championship was run between **1972** and **1976**. I suppose FISA expected other GT manufacturers would jump on the GT bandwagon, for a theoretically large number of cars were eligible for the championship in 1972/1973. The *FIA Yearbook of Automobile Sport* lists the cars that were homologated in Groups III and IV. In the end, **Porsche** 911's dominated the series, only slightly disturbed by **De Tomaso** (with some Ford support), which challenged **Porsche** in **1972** and **1973** and Tour de France winners **Ferrari, Lancia** and **Ligier**. It is noteworthy that certain cars, which were obvious GTs, such as **Maseratis** and **Lamborghinis**, were not homologated by the FIA in **1972, 1973**, for they were produced in very small numbers, not enough to reach homologation, thus their absence from the GT championship.

By and large, the championship ended up a contest between teams, such as Kremer, George Loos (Gelo), Tebernum and Max Moritz, all German, with very little non-**Porsche** opposition ever racing. As any reasonable person would expect, **Porsche** 911's were the majority, although some interesting, low displacement cars such as **Alpines, Datsun 240, Opel GTs** did appear here and there, plus the odd **Ferrari Daytonas**. Occasionally, very discreetly driven and prepared **Chevrolet Corvettes** and **Camaros, Lancia** and **Lotus** were fielded as well.

Brit **John Fitzpatrick**, driving a Kremer 911 won the **1972** championship on the strength of five commanding victories, two at the **Nürburgring**, one at **Hockenheim**, one at **Monza** and one at **Estoril**. The **De Tomaso** challenge resulted in a win by **Herbert Muller** at **Nivelles**, plus other minor placings. The Tour de France, more of a Rally than a race, was included in the calendar and **Andruet/Biche** won it in a **Ferrari Daytona**. Several series heroes emerged this very first year, including **Claude Haldi, Claude Ballot-Lena, Paul Keller, Gunther Steckkonig, Clemens Schickentanz** and **Jurgen Neuhaus**.

The **1973** title was shared by **Ballot-Lena** and **Schickentanz**, both with 164 points. The drivers did have different final scores but because FIA made a mistake on its mid-year bulletin, the Federation decided to declare both drivers champions. No single driver dominated the series and **Haldi** and **Keller** did well again. **Fitzpatrick** raced up front but was not lucky that year, while another Brit, **Mike Parkes**, of **Ferrari** fame, scored for **De Tomaso** a popular win at **Imola**, his last win. Formula 1 driver **Clay Regazzoni** added more stature to the series and scored **De Tomaso**'s second win of the season at **Hockenheim**, in a one-off drive. **Sandro Munari** won the Tour de France for **Lancia**.

John Fitzpatrick won the Championship again in **1974**. The calendar was much shorter than in previous years, as the oil crisis affected most racing series in the world, with the sole exception of Formula 1 which seemed to thrive. This time **Fitz** won only three races and was closely followed by Swiss **Paul Keller** and German **Clemens Schickentanz**, who won a race apiece. **De Tomaso** showed well in the first heat of the first **Monza** race, won by **Mario Casoni**, thereafter evaporating from the series. On the driving side, new exponents appeared, such as **Tim Schenken, Reine Wisell, Gijs Van Lennep, Manfred Schurti, Bob Wollek** and **Rolf Stommelen**, who won the Intereuropa Cup at **Monza**. **Ligier-Maserati** won the Tour de France, with **Larrousse/Nicolas/Rives**.

Hartwig Bertrams, who often paired with **Schickentanz** in the long-distance races, won the **1975** title for Tebernum. The year marked the emergence of Gelo as a power to be reckoned with, fielding a strong team of drivers that included **Fitzpatrick, Schenken** and newcomer to the series **Toine Hezemans**. Reportedly there were 100,000 people watching the Gelo win the **Norisring** race, quite an audience. While Gelo accumulated victories, **Bertrams** accumulated points and his sole victory was at the 6 Hours of **Monza**. Formula 1 drivers such as **Arturo Merzario** and **Vittorio Brambilla** also appeared in the series, the latter sharing a Marlboro sponsored **Lancia** with **Facetti** at Monza. **Merzario** raced in two rounds, finishing 4th at **Misano** and 2nd in **Monza**. As for diversity of machinery, things got worse, for except for the **Lancia,** most non-**Porsches** just made up the numbers.

By this point, it was becoming clear that the European GT Championship made very little sense. Most of the top teams also contested the World Manufacturers Championship, where more powerful **Porsche** Carreras could often score top 5 results. The German championship was little by little gaining in stature as an international tournament, plus, the **1976** World Manufacturers Championship would be run to Group 5 specification, further diluting the resources of the teams and the reason for the championship.

Nonetheless, the championship was run one last time in **1976** and GELO came out far ahead of its main competitor, Kremer. **Toine Hezemans** won five races, including the first three of the year and was expertly backed up by teammate **Schenken**, who shared one win. **Bob Wollek** won his single race in the series, at **Imola** and other prominent drivers, such as **Klaus Ludwig, Hans Heyer, Derek Bell** and **Helmut Kelleners** also appeared well. The only interloper in a sea of **Porsches** was the lone **Lancia Stratos**, which did not do much in the hands of **Gianfranco Ricci**, except for a third place in the poorly support race at **Misano**, which was boycotted by the German teams, won by the strangely named "**Tambauto**".

In **1977** there was no more European GT Championship. The German Championship (DRM) was run to Group 5 specification, although many of the grid fillers in the larger division were in fact group 4 **Porsches**, the same happening to the World Manufacturers Championship. However, Group 5 was not a long-term success as well and by the end of the decade the "Silhouette" formula was pretty much dead.

Race wins, by driver
1. John Fitzpatrick (GB), 9
2. Toine Hezemans (NL), 6
3. Clemens Schickentanz (D), 5
4. Claude Ballot-Lena (F), 4
5. Tim Schenken (Aus), 3
6. Paul Keller (CH), Claude Haldi (CH), Hartwig Bertrams (D), Rolf Stommelen (D), 2
7. Jurgen Neuhaus (D), Herbert Muller (CH), Jean-Claude Andruet (F), Biche (F), Mike Parkes (GB), Clay Regazzoni (CH), Erwin Kremer (D), Sandro Munari (I), Mario Manucci (I), Gerard Larrousse (F), Jean-Pierre Nicolas (F), Johnny Rives (F), Bengt Ekberg (S), Tambauto (I), Bob Wollek (F), 1

Race wins by car
1. Porsche, 32
2. De Tomaso, 3
3. Ferrari, Lancia, Ford, Ligier, 1

Venues used
1. Nürburgring (D), Hockenheim (D), Monza (I), 5
2. Zeltweg (A), Imola (I), 3
3. Montlhery (F), Nivelles (B), Tour de France (F), Estoril (P), Norisring (D), Misano (I), 2
4. Zandvoort (NL), Thruxton (GB), Enna (Pergusa), Jarama (E), 1

Fastest laps, drivers:
1. Clemens Schickentanz (D), John Fitzpatrick (GB), 6
2. Jean-Marie Jacquemin (F), Toine Hezemans (NL), Jurgen Neuhaus (D), 2
3. Herbert Muller (CH), Mike Parkes (GB), Claude Ballot-Lena (F), Clay Regazzoni (CH), Mario Casoni (I), Claude Haldi (CH), Paul Keller (CH), Reinhold Joest (D), Rolf Stommelen (D), Derek Bell (GB), Helmut Kelleners (D), Reinhardt Stenzel (D), Tim Schenken (Aus), 1

IMSA CAMEL GT

IMSA was created by **John Bishop** in **1969** and its showcase GT series began in **1971**. In a short period of time, it became the premier road racing GT/Touring (non Stock-car) car championship in America. There are a few reasons for this fast rise to prominence. In the late 60s, Trans Am ruled supreme as a professional road racing GT/Touring car championship. Its structure base was simple: races for American pony cars (Camaros, Mustangs, Javelins), with large engines, plus races for 2.0-liter cars, generally European and Japanese cars. Trans Am's popularity stemmed mostly from manufacturer involvement, which had vanished by **1973**. The SCCA, which ran the Trans Am, also managed Can Am and Formula 5000, in addition to a membership of several thousand amateur racers who raced in dozens of categories in hundreds of races throughout the country. One might say it had its hands full but in addition to that, from the onset IMSA actually looked more like a professional version of SCCA's amateur races than the Trans-Am did. Thus, many drivers flocked to these races and while the Trans Am calendar of **1974** had only three races, IMSA's had 12, one of them with 65 cars on the track. The SCCA failed to see the threat and react accordingly and there were more pressing issues involving both the Can Am and Formula 5000 that required immediate attention. By the time it got back its bearings, IMSA was well established and perhaps the only reason why the Trans-Am survived was that little by little the main IMSA series was transitioning into more of an international sports car series, rather than a GT/Touring car series.

Among other goodies, the IMSA provided the platform for a vast variety of cars to race together, in fact, some European cars that were seldom raced in professional races in Europe in the 70s were used in the championship, such as the **De Tomaso** Mangusta, the **Alfa Romeo** Montreal, the **TVR** and **Jaguar** XKE. Drivers were taking notice, in fact, by **1974** former F-1 drivers **Skip Barber** and **Bob Bondurant** took part in races and then **BMW** contested the whole 1975 series with **Hans Stuck, Brian Redman, Allan Moffat** and **Sam Posey** on the driving force. IMSA had arrived.

IMSA (International Motor Sport Association) Camel GT Series was created by John Bishop in **1971**, so that it preceded the European GT Championship by one year. Quite appropriately, the winners of the first IMSA race, a 300-miler held in Virginia, were **Peter Gregg** and **Hurley Haywood**, in a **Porsche** 914/6. Both the brand and these drivers came to epitomize what IMSA was all about in the 70s. They were followed by a Corvette, then three other **Porsches**. **Dave Heinz** won the next two races in his **Corvette**, while **Gregg/Haywood** won the fifth. **Heinz** won the finale in **Daytona,** with co-driver **Yenko**, winning the maiden championship. The races were basically 200 miles to 3 hour long, in other words, not too long but not short, justifying the use of two drivers without boring people to death. The races consisted of five classes, two for GTs (GTO and GTU) and three for touring cars. A wide variety of machinery was used in that first season, the hallmark of IMSA during the decade: **Porsche 914/6, Chevrolet Corvette, Porsche 911, BMW 2002, Datsun 510, Audi 100 LS, FIAT 850, Opel Kadett, Austin-Healey Sprite, FIAT 124, Volvo P1800, AMC Javelin, Triumph TR4, Mini-Cooper, Chevrolet Camaro, VW, MGB, Ford Cortina, MG Midget, Shelby GT350, Simca, Lotus Elan, Alfa Romeo Giulietta, Sunbeam Alpine, Triumph**

Spitfire, Alfa Romeo GTV, Ford Pinto, Saab, Chevrolet Vega, Datsun 240Z, Ford Mustang.

The first race of **1972** brought the first taste of international flavor to the series. Mexicans **Juan Izquierdo** and **Daniel Muniz** won the 200 miler in **Texas** in a **Ford Mustang**, in front of **Gregg/Haywood**, who by then had adopted a faster **Porsche 911S**. With a longer, 10-race calendar, the fields continued very healthy. Longer races were added: a 6-hour race in **Mid-Ohio** and a 500 km event in **Watkins Glen**. **Porsches** won four times, **Corvettes** three times and **Camaros** twice. Among the winners that season were **Gregg, Haywood, Charlie Kemp, Greg Pickett, Jim Locke, Bob Bailey, Denny Long, Bob Baisley, Michael Keyser, Maurice Carter, Paul Nichter** and **Gene Felton**. No car or driver dominated the season, which was good for the series.

The Chevy Monza became a worthy IMSA challenger in 1976. Photo by Paul Kooyman

The 12 hours of **Sebring** were added to the roster as of **1973**. That, plus the **Mid-Ohio** 6 hours and a 500-miler at **Pocono** were the longer races. **Peter Gregg** and **Porsche** began their pattern of domination this season: **Porsche** won 8 of the races, while **Camaros** won twice. Peter "**Perfect**" as he was called, won six times, three of them with **Haywood**, while **Michel Keyser** did well and won twice for **Porsche**. **Camaro** winners were **Carter** and **Felton**.

Twelve races were on the calendar for the **1974** season, including the series' first international race, the 1000 Km of **Mexico**, held in October. New names began to show well, such as **Al Holbert, Ludwig Heimrath, Elliot Forbes-Robinson, Milt Minter**, who made life more difficult for **Gregg**, who still did well. While **Al Holbert** shared a win with **Gregg** in Mid-Ohio, **Milt Minter** won races in both a **Porsche** and a Greenwood **Corvette**. Other big names raced sporadically: **Brett Lunger, George Follmer, Bob Bondurant, Skip Barber, Bob Sharp**. A **BMW** 3.0 CSL was used for the first time, which could challenge for overall wins, as opposed to the BMW 2002 used until then. As for the Mexican race, the local crew of **Guillermo Rojas, Hector Rebaque** and **Fred Van Beuren** Jr. managed to beat the Americans, racing a **Porsche** Carrera. **Gregg** and **Haywood** retired from this race South of the border and other top series drivers, such as **Milt Minter** and **Ludwig Heimrath** did not do well. The winning trio raced two cars in the race, the second coming in 11th. While **John Greenwood** won the finale in his famous **Corvette, Gregg** won the series again. In fact, he also won the weakened Trans Am that season.

The big news for **1975** was the presence of the works **BMW** team. In the 24 Hours of Daytona, the **Posey/Stuck** and **Peterson/Redman** crews faltered, leaving the road clear to regular winners **Gregg/Haywood**. However, it was a very long, 17-race season that included 4 double headers in **Road Atlanta, Laguna Seca, Lime Rock** and **Mid-America** and a Canadian race at **Mosport and** BMW began to show its pace by winning at **Sebring** with **Brian Redman, Allan Moffat, Hans Stuck** and **Sam Posey**. While **Gregg** and **Holbert** continued winning in their **Porsches, Hans Stuck** got the second of his five wins in the 2nd Laguna Seca race, following up with a win in the 6-hour enduro at **Riverside**, with co-driver **Dieter Quester**. However, the big winner of the season was **Holbert**, with six and **Haywood** and **Greenwood** also won races but **Gregg** still got the title.

As the saying goes, if you can't beat them, join them, for **1976 Gregg** joined forces with **BMW**. The ploy worked at **Daytona**, where he shared the car with **Brian Redman** and **John Fitzpatrick**. In his book, **Redman** says that **Gregg** did very little of the driving but made sure he was handed the trophy for the win, blocking both hard working British drivers from photographers and onlooker's view. Be that as it may, the fact is that **Gregg** only won one other race in the **BMW**, at **Talladega** and **Holbert** continued in fine form, winning six races, **Sebring** in a **Porsche** with **Keyser**, the rest driving a 5.6 **Chevy Monza. Holbert** also came out on top in the championship table. Other winners included **Jim Busby**, who was the best **Porsche** runner in 3rd (with 4 wins), **George Dyer** and **Michael Keyser**. The double header experience of the preceding season was not repeated, and all races were held in the USA.

For **1977, Al Holbert** was the clear favorite and continued to race the **Chevy** Monza. However, at the 24 Hours of **Daytona**, which was also a World Manufacturers Championship round, **Porsche** still prevailed, **Haywood, Graves** and **Helmick** winning it in a Carrera RSR over the 935 of **Finotto, Facetti** and **Camathias. Porsches** also had a 1-10 at **Sebring** and that time the winners were **George Dyer** and **Brad Friselle**, while **Diego Febles**, from Puerto Rico, came in second, with co-driver **Hiram Cruz**. After the two major endurance events, **Al Holbert** had his year's first win in the **Road Atlanta**'s 100 miler. **David Hobbs** debuted the very powerful turbo **BMW** 320i and finished third. At **Laguna Seca, Danny Ongais** led a 1-3 **Porsche** 934/5 feast, followed by **Busby** and **Follmer. Hobbs** grabbed the pole. **Mid-America** was the site of the next race and **Al Holbert** resumed his winning ways, while **Hobbs** was the first retirement. A large number of entrants were no shows. **Holbert** prevailed at **Lime Rock** once more, followed by **Haywood** and **Dyer**. At **Mid-Ohio, Hobbs** won for the first time in the turbo 320i run by **McLaren** North America. The best a **Porsche** could do that day was an uncharacteristic 5th place (**Dyer**). The 8th round was another 100 miler at **Brainerd** and **Ongais** won again in the black Interscope **Porsche** numbered "00".

Holbert could only muster 3rd place but led the championship with a safe margin. The 9th round was the second **Daytona** race of the year and **Dyer** led the **Porsches** of **Haywood** and **Belcher**. **Sam Posey** was doing very fine driving a GTU category **Datsun** 260Z, winning several races. Separate GTU races were run at **Hallett** and **Sears Point**, won by **Maas** and **Aase**, both in **Porsches**. The GTO race in **Sears Point** was **Hobbs**' second race win of the season, ahead of **Holbert** and **Friselle**, in **Monzas** and **Follmer** in a **BMW** 3.0 CSL. The best **Porsche** was **Frank**'s 6th placed entry, meanwhile, **Forbes-Robinson** drove a rare **FIAT** 131 to 7th. Winding down towards the end of the championship, **Holbert** won again at **Pocono**, from **Frank** and **Haywood**. The 3 Hours of **Mid-Ohio** had **Jacky Ickx** among the entrants, who co-drove a Vasek Polak 935 with **McKitterick**. **Peter Gregg** won overall in another 935 but the model was not yet lawful in IMSA regulations, so the GTO winners were **Haywood** and **Hagestad**, in a **Porsche**. Also driving in the race was **Eddie Cheever**, sharing the 320i turbo with **Hobbs**. A second 100 mile race at **Road Atlanta** was also won by **Hobbs**, ahead of **Holbert** and **Haywood** and the GTO's again ran separate races from the GTUs: **Aase** in a **Porsche** prevailed in the lower category. The British **Hobbs** also won the second 100 mile at **Laguna Seca**, ahead of four **Monzas** (**Holbert**, **Friselle**, **Woods** and **Thomas**). The third **Daytona** race of the year, the traditional 250-mile final, was won by **Hurley Haywood** in a **Porsche**, ahead of **Kenper Miller** in a **BMW** 3.5 CSL. **Holbert** completed only 6 laps but won the championship. In my estimation that was the most interesting IMSA season of the decade.

The GTUs ran separate from the GTOs in many races in **1978** and many of the types of cars that usually appeared in GTU in the early days of the championship were running in large numbers in the Showroom Stock category. At **Daytona, Stommelen/Hezemans/Gregg** won over **Barbour/Schurti/Johnny Rutherford**, the USAC driver who sporadically did some GT races. **Febles** came in third, this time pairing with Irishman **Alec Poole**. Two major changes for the season were the acceptance of the faster **Porsche** 935s in the new GTX category (in addition to GTO and GTU) and the fact that twice champion **Al Holbert** decided to race in NASCAR, which certainly made matters easier for the competition. **Brian Redman** made his comeback winning at **Sebring**, sharing a Dick Barbour car with **Charles Mendez** and **Bob Garretson**. At the 6-hour race at **Talladega**, it became clear that beating the 935s would be very hard. **Gregg** and **Friselle** won in a 935, followed by **Bill** and **Don Whittington** and **Dick Barbour** and **Johnny Rutherford** in 935s. At **Road Atlanta**, **Hobbs** was in the first row with **Gregg** but the American won the race in his 935, followed by **Ongais**, **Shafer** in a **Camaro** and **Gianpiero Moretti** who had joined the series. **Hobbs** retired after 17 laps. The separate GTU race was won by **Dave White**. At **Laguna Seca**, **Follmer** won in a Vasek Polka 935, followed by **Haywood, Gregg** and **Hobbs**. **Frank Leary** won the separate GTU race in a **Datsun** 240Z. **Hobbs** had his first race win of **1978** at **Hallett**, followed by **John Paul** in a **Corvette** and **Moretti** in his Momo 935, **Aase** winning GTU. **Peter Gregg** resumed his victorious ways at **Lime Rock**, followed by **Bill Whittington** and **John Paul**. **Sam Posey** won the separate GTU race in a **Datsun** 260Z. With a smaller number of entrants than other races, the GTX, GTO and GTU raced together at **Brainerd**. **Gregg** won from **Moretti** and **Don Whittington** and five 935s were in the top 6. **Gregg** also raced solo in the 250-mile **Daytona** race, beating two other 935s (**Kearns/Minter** and **Don** and **Bill Whittington**). **Hobbs** and the turbo **BMW** had pole and won at **Sears Point**, followed by **Don Whittington** and **Moretti** who was having a nice helping of results, the separate

GTU race carried by **Leary**. **Gregg** won the GTX/GTO race at **Portland**, followed by **Moretti** again and **Bill Whittington**. **Aase** also won GTU for **Porsche**. The 250 Miles of **Mid-Ohio** was won by **Bill Whittington** and **Jim Busby** in a 935, followed by **David Hobbs** and **Tom Klausler**. The second **Road Atlanta** GTX/GTO race was won by **Gregg** who was utterly dominating the season, over the **Whittington** brothers **Don** and **Bill** and **Moretti**. The best non-935 was **Chris Cord** in 6th, in a **Monza**. **Don Devendorf** won the GTU race in a **Datsun** 240Z. **Gregg** closed a perfect season, much to his liking, by winning the 250-mile **Daytona** finale, ahead of **Danny Ongais** and 5 other **Porsche** 935s. **Carlos Moran**, from **El Salvador**, shared the 5th placed **Porsche** with **Heimrath**, in a race contested by drivers from Italy, Puerto Rico, Colombia, Dominican Republic, Venezuela and Britain, giving it a truly international flavor.

The **1979** season was pretty much the same: a **Porsche** 935 party. **Ted Field, Danny Ongais** and **Hurley Haywood** won in the Interscope **Porsche** in **Daytona** and **Akin/McFarlin/Woods** won at **Sebring**. Separate GTU races were ran in seven rounds, starting in **Road Atlanta**. While **Gregg** faltered in the Florida enduros, he won this short race with one lap gap. There were a few 935s in the field, **Don** and **Bill Whittington, Gianpiero Moretti, Charles Mendez, Ted Field, Preston Henn, Danny Ongais** and **Cliff Hearns**, plus the **Hobbs BMW**. Honestly, only **Ongais** and **Hobbs** could challenge **Gregg** on the same footing. At **Riverside** the **Whittington** brothers, **Don** and **Bill** won over **John Paul/Al Holbert** and **Follmer/Lunger/Bell**, while **Gregg** came in sixth, partnered by **Klaus Ludwig**, followed by **Stommelen/Redman/Barbour**, in a rare true field of stars. At **Laguna Seca**, the entry list was less star-laden and **Gregg** won again from **Hobbs** and **Ongais**, with **Devendorf** carrying GTU honors. **Hobbs** won at **Hallet** again, followed by **Gregg**, while **Aase** won GTU. Positions were reversed at **Lime Rock**, **Gregg** followed by **Hobbs, Posey** winning his home GTU race. **Gregg** also won at **Brainerd**, followed by **Hobbs** and **Field**, while the first American car was Canadian **Maurice Carter's** Camaro, in 6th. **Charles Mendez** and **Hurley Haywood** won the Paul Revere race in **Daytona**, followed by **Field/Ongais** and by **Peter Gregg** driving solo. The notorious duo **Gregg/Haywood** was reunited at **Mid-Ohio**, where they won from **Don** and **Bill**, followed by a **BMW M1** driven by **Jim Busby** and **Dennis Aase**. **Gregg** and **Devendorf** won their respective classes at **Sears Point** and **Portland**. Another enduro was held at **Road America**, a 500-mile race, which was won by **David Hobbs** and **Derek Bell**. They were followed by two 935s plus the **BMW M1**. **Gregg** and **Devendorf** went back to their winning ways in the second **Road Atlanta** round, while the **Whittingtons (Bill** and **Don)** had a 1-2 in the **Daytona** finale, in their most successful season. There were ten 935's in this race, including a rare appearance by Colombian **Ricardo Londono**, who would become semi-famous in his unsuccessful quest for Formula 1 stardom in the 80s. While in the enduros other 935 drivers could expect a chance to win, everywhere else **Gregg** ran away from the field, with the exception of **Hobbs** and **Ongais**. While the **Porsche** 935 raised the speed profile of the series, it was clear that faster drivers would be required to beat the **Gregg** steamroller. A change was needed. And it would come but time had ran out in the 70s.

WINS, DRIVERS, 1970-1979

(Only overall and top class)

1. Peter Gregg, 36
2. Al Holbert, 19
3. Hurley Haywood, 17
4. David Hobbs, 8
5. Michael Keyser, 6
6. Jim Busby, Hans Stuck 5
7. Dave Heinz, Brian Redman, George Dyer, Danny Ongais, Eliott Forbes-Robinson, 3
8. Bob Beasley, Maurice Carter, Gene Felton, Milt Minter, John Greenwood, Brad Friselle, Charles Mendez, Bill Whittington, Greg Pickett, 2
9. Or Constanzo, Don Yenko, Juan Izquierdo, Daniel Muniz, Charlie Kemp, Jim Locke, Bob Bailey, Paul Nichter, Tony de Lorenzo, Guillermo Rojas, Hector Rebaque, Fred Van Beuren Jr, Allan Moffat, Sam Posey, Dieter Quester, John Fitzpatrick, John Graves, Dave Helmick, Bob Hagestad, Rolf Stommelen, Toine Hezemans, Bob Garretson, George Follmer, Don Whittington, Ted Fields, Bob Akin, Rob McFarlin, Roy Woods, 1

WINS, MANUFACTURERS, 1970-1979
(Only overall and top class)

1. Porsche, 73
2. Chevrolet, 21
3. BMW, 16
4. Ford, 1

VENUES USED, 1970-1979
1. Daytona, 22
2. Road Atlanta, 12
3. Lime Rock, Mid-Ohio, 11
4. Laguna Seca, 9
5. Sebring, Talladega, 6
6. Sears Point, 4
7. Brainerd, Mid America, Pocono, 3
8. Portland, Ontario, Hallet, Charlotte, Virginia, 2
9. Road America, Bridgehampton, Summit Point, Texas, Donnybrooke, Watkins Glen, Bryar, Indy Raceway Park, Mexico City, Riverside, Mosport, 1

USAC/CART

One could say that the Championship Trail, as the Formula Indy USAC National championship was called back then, might have been the subject of the highest degree of change in the 70s and it all happened very quickly, in the last year and a half of the decade. If you followed the USAC championship closely, it was easy to conclude that the sanctioning body was pretty much set into its own, more traditional ways. The last major change took place in **1971**, when dirt tracks events were excluded from the calendar. From that point on, only events in asphalt, the vast majority in ovals, would be included in the schedule. This resulted in a much shorter schedule and closed the opportunity for dirt specialists to feature well on results. In the decade, things were changing in the world of motor racing, as extensively discussed elsewhere in this book. TV was becoming more of a factor, with the advent of cable TV and although the **Indy** 500 remained the top race in the country, the other events on the USAC schedule paid relatively little prize money and were not important in the wider scheme of things. The power base was changing and **Roger Penske** became not only the most successful team owner of the lot but also the most influential and demanding. The team owners wanted more money, more control, a good TV package, to be able to provide good exposure to their sponsors, which were also becoming more sophisticated. There was international interest in Indy style racing but USAC's old ways were getting on the way.

The way drivers ascended to Indy style racing was also changing. Whereas the vast majority of the USAC Championship drivers in the beginning of the decade came from a background of USAC sanctioned, short-track sprint cars and midgets, by the end of the decade drivers were hauling from Formula Super Vee and Formula Atlantic, many having started in karting. Although USAC hesitated to include road courses in the championship, all other parties involved seem to want it. The **Mosport** and the two English races of **1978** showed Formula Indy cars could do a nice job on road courses as well as ovals. Thus, was born CART, as a franchise system, which basically excluded the old style smalltime Indycar mechanic-owner, that comprised at least a portion of the fields but could not be expected to contest full seasons. That was part of the problem: except for the 500-mile races, many of the Champ Car rounds barely had 20 cars for most of the decade and strong teams were few: there were many proprietary chassis constructors, many of whom had no chance to win anything. That brought color but not strength.

Clay Regazzoni was a rare European presence at Indy during the 70s. Photo by Rob Neuzel

This added to USAC's almost folksy, laid back image. But times were changing and racing was now becoming big business. NASCAR was growing by leaps and bounds and the Indy racers were getting far behind in the eyes of the public, media and sponsors.

Thus a civil war erupted and in **1979** there were two championships: the more modern CART and the old style USAC. Most big teams, such as Penske, Chaparral, Patrick, McLaren, etc, sided with CART, while only **A.J.Foyt** among the biggies gave USAC another shot. There was a truce at Indy, where both camps competed. In the end CART won: it was more competitive, more modern, had better sponsors, more stars, while **Foyt** was carrying USAC on his back.

As mentioned, the number of races decreased starting in **1971**. There were only 10 races in the USA, plus two held in **Rafaela**, Argentina, in the beginning of the season. The venues during the rest of the decade were pretty much the same: **Indianapolis** (of course), **Pocono, Phoenix, Michigan, Ontario, Milwaukee, Trenton**, later on, **Texas**. By **1973**, there were some double header races, which increased the number of scoring events but the dates were few. And thus it continued for the rest of the decade, year in, year out.

In CART's first year, there were signs of change on the horizon, when **Watkins Glen** was added to the schedule. **Michigan, Trenton, Atlanta** and **Phoenix** sided with CART, **Ontario, Texas, Milwaukee** and **Pocono**, with USAC. **Indy** was technically a USAC race but valid for both championships. CART prevailed.

The Rascar was one of several dozen Indycar chassis builders that raced in the decade. Photo by Rob Neuzel.

For most of the decade, **Foyt,** the **Unser** brothers, **Johnny Rutherford, Gordon Johncock, Wally Dallenbach, Mario Andretti** ruled, while in the beginning of the 70s **Joe Leonard** and **Roger McCluskey** were factors, **Peter Revson** and **Mark Donohue** also featured well. There were a number of customary participants, such as **Billy Vukovich Jr, Mike Mosley, Gary Bettenhausen, George Snider, Steve Krisiloff, Pancho Carter, Johnny Parsons, Jimmy Caruthers, Al Loquasto, Spike Gelhausen, Lee Kunzman, Tom Bigelow**, who often had good placings, **Gary Bettenhausen** and **Mike Mosley** winning more than once. Established NASCAR drivers such as **Cale Yarborough, Donnie Allison** and **Bobby Allison** also drove in the USAC Championship during the decade. Newer names such as **Tom Sneva, Rick Mears** and **Danny Ongais** came to the fore by mid-decade. Sadly, little by little, the one-off constructors were disappearing unable to keep up with new race car technology, as **Penske** won a large number of races in **1979,** setting the tone for the future. Racing had become more scientific; trial and error plus a dose of practical intuition, a thing of the past.

In **1970,** most cars used the 4-cylinder turbo **Offenhauser** engine that had been used for decades. In **1976,** there was a change of paradigm, when the much more modern Turbo 8-cylinder **Cosworth** was used for the first time. By the end of the decade **Offys** were becoming a rarity. Compared to Formula 1, there was slightly more engine variety at USAC. In addition to the above-mentioned engines, **DGS, Foyt(Ford), Chevrolet, Ford, AMC,** (also appears as Rambler in some results) were used during the decade, in addition to **Pratt & Whitney** and **Allison** Turbines.

In the late 70s, Indy was again attracting foreign talent. This is Teddy Pilette, who attempted to qualify in 1977. (Photo Teddy Pilette collection)

USAC Race wins (1970-1979), by driver
1. Al Unser, 27
2. A.J. Foyt, Jr., 24
3. Johnny Rutherford, 16
4. Bobby Unser, 15
5. Gordon Johncock, 12
6. Danny Ongais, 6
7. Wally Dallenbach, Joe Leonard 5
8. Mike Mosley, Rick Mears, 4
9. Mark Donohue, Tom Sneva, Roger McCluskey, Gary Bettenhausen, Mario Andretti 3
10. Dan Gurney, Lloyd Ruby, Jim McElreath, Swede Savage, Billy Vukovich, Jr, 1

CART (1979)
1. Bobby Unser, 6
2. Rick Mears, 3
3. Gordon Johncock, Johnny Rutherford, 2
4. Al Unser, 1

Wins by car
USAC

1. Eagle, 32
2. McLaren, 26
3. Coyote, 21
4. Parnelli, 19
5. Colt, 12

6. Wildcat, 9
7. King, Penske 5
8. Lola, 4
9. Mongoose, McNamara, Gerhardt, 1

CART
1. Penske, 11
2. McLaren, 2
3. Chaparral, 1

ALL INDY 500 STARTERS AND RESULTS, 1970-1979

DRIVER	70	71	72	73	74	75	76	77	78	79
A.J. FOYT	10	3	25	25	15	3	2	1	7	2
AL LOQUASTO							25	28		
AL UNSER	1	1	2	20	18	16	7	3	1	22
ART POLLARD	30	26								
BENTLEY WARREN		23			23					
BILL PUTERBAUGH						7	22	13		
BILL SCOTT							23			
BILL SIMPSON					13					
BILLY VUKOVICH JR	23	5	28	2	3	6	31	17		8
BOB HARKEY		22		29	8	10	20			
BOBBY ALLISON				32		25				
BOBBY OLIVERO								25		
BOBBY UNSER	11	12	30	13	2	1	10	18	6	5
BRUCE WALKUP	29									
BUBBY JONES								21		
BUD TINGELSTAD		7								
CALE YARBOROUGH		16	10							
CARL WILLIAMS	9		29							
CLAY REGAZZONI								30		
CLIFF HUCUL								22	33	29
DAN GURNEY	3									
DANNY ONGAIS								20	18	4
DAVID HOBBS		20		11	5		29			
DENNIS ZIMMERMAN			8	19						
DENNY HULME		17								
DICK SIMON	14	14	13	14	33	21	32	31	19	26
DONNIE ALLISON	4	6								
ELDON RASMUSSEN						24		14		23
GARY BETTENHAUSEN	26	10	14	5	32	15	28	16	16	
GEORGE FOLLMER	31	15								
GEORGE SNIDER	20	33	11	12	28	8	13	24	8	33
GORDON JOHNCOCK	28	29	20	1	4	31	3	11	3	6
GRAHAM MCRAE				16						
GREG WELD	32									
HOWDY HOLMES										7
JACK BRABHAM	13									
JAN OPPERMAN					21		16			
JANET GUTHRIE								29	9	34
JERRY GRANT	7		12	19	10	30	27			
JERRY KARL				26	19	13			14	
JERRY SNEVA								10	31	31
JIM HURTUBISE			23		25					

384

JIM MALLOY	33	4							
JIM MCELREATH	5			23	6			23	20	35
JIMMY CARUTHERS			9	21	23	14				
JOE LEONARD	24	19	3	18						
JOE SALDANA									15	16
JOHN MAHLER			22					14	26	25
JOHN MARTIN			16	8	11	27	21			
JOHNNY PARSONS					26	19	12	5	10	32
JOHNNY RUTHERFORD	18	18	27	9	1	2	1	33	13	18
LARRY CANNON					24		17			
LARRY DICKSON		28							22	24
LARRY MCCOY						30	26			
LARRY RICE									11	19
LEE KUNZMAN			17	7				7		30
LEEROY YARBROUGH	19									
LLOYD RUBY	27	11	6	27	9	32	11	27		
MARIO ANDRETTI	6	30	8	30	31	28	8	26	12	
MARK DONOHUE	2	25	1	15						
MEL KENYON	16	32	18	4						
MIKE HISS			7	17	14	29				
MIKE MOSLEY	21	13	26	10	29	26	14	19	17	3
PANCHO CARTER					7	4	5	15	24	20
PETER REVSON	22	2	31	31						
PHIL THRESHIE									30	17
RICK MEARS									23	1
RICK MUTHER	8	21			27					
ROGER MCCLUSKEY	25	9	24	3	16	5	30	8	25	13
RONNIE BUCKNUM	15									
SALT WALTER			33	33	17	33	9		28	12
SAM POSEY			5							
SAMMY SESSIONS	12	27	4	28		17				
SHELDON KINSER						12	19	32	32	28
SPIKE GELHAUSEN							33		29	10
STEVE KRISILOFF		31	21	6	22	11	24	9	4	11
SWEDE SAVAGE			32	22						
TOM BAGLEY									27	9
TOM BIGELOW					12	18	14	6	21	14
TOM SNEVA					20	22	6	2	2	15
VERN SCHUPPAN						18				21
WALLY DALLENBACH	17	24	15	24	30	9	4	4	5	27

LAP LEADERS IN THE INDY 500 (1970-1979)

Not surprisingly, **Al Unser** also leads this list, by a wide margin, 534 laps to the second ranked driver's 219. **Gordon Johncock**, perhaps surprisingly is ranked 2nd. Another surprise, **Mario Andretti** did not lead a single Indy 500 lap during the 70s. A single foreign driver, **Jack Brabham**, led a single lap in 1970. In total, 1809 Indy 500 laps were run, for 3 editions were shortened, 1973, 1974 and 1976. Curiously, two of the shortened races were won by **Johnny Rutherford**. The shortest edition was 1976, at 102 laps, a little over one half the regular race distance. The non-winning driver who led the most laps was **Gary Bettenhausen**, who had a stellar 1972 driving a Penske **McLaren**. The winning driver who led the less, **Rick Mears**, at 25, who more than made up for it in latter years…
1. Al Unser, 534
2. Gordon Johncock, 219
3. A.J. Foyt, 201

4. Bobby Unser, 198
5. Johnny Rutherford, 175
6. Gary Bettenhausen, 138
7. Wally Dallenbach, 101
8. Danny Ongais, 71
9. Mark Donahue, 70
10. Rick Mears, 25
11. Joe Leonard, 21
12. Jerry Grant, 16
13. Swede Savage, 12
14. Tom Sneva, 7
15. Steve Krisiloff and Lloyd Ruby, 5
16. Mike Mosley and Pancho Carter, 3
17. George Snider, 2
18. Bobby Allison, Billy Vukovich Jr., Jack Brabham, 1

INDY 500 STARTERS, MANUFACTURERS (1970-1979)

Winning chassis (*)

MANUFACTURER	70	71	72	73	74	75	76	77	78	79
ANTARES			1							1
ATLANTA			2		1	1	1			
BRABHAM	1		2							
CECIL	1									
CHAPARRAL										1
COLT	2(*)	2(*)	1							
COYOTE	4	2	4	3	2	1	1	2(*)	2	
DRAGON							2	1	1	
EAGLE	8	6	8	19(*)	17	16(*)	16	7	6	3
FINLEY					1	1				
GERHARDT	4	2	1							
HAWK	2	1								
HAYHOE	1	2								
KENYON						1				
KING	1	2	1	1	1	2	1	1		1
KUZMA		3								
LIGHTNING							1	6	5	6
LOLA	1	2	3						1(*)	2
MCLAREN	2	4	6(*)	7	7(*)	7	7(*)	7	6	4
MCNAMARA	1	2								
MONGOOSE	2	2								
PARNELLI			3	3	1		1	2	1	3
PENSKE									4	8(*)
RASCAR						1		1		
RILEY					1	1				
SCORPION	1	1	1							
SPIRIT										1
VOLLSTEDT	1	2			1	1	1	1	1	1
WATSON	1							1	2	2
WILDCAT						2	2	4	4	

AMERICAN FORMULA 5000

Formula 5000 was an American concept, beginning life as SCCA's Formula A. The category continued to exist as Formula A for SCCA amateurs but the name Formula 5000, concocted by **John Webb** in **1969** was also adopted in the United States. While some European Formula 5000 drivers made the jump to Formula 1, adding some value to the European championship, grids in the American series were always larger and there was no comparison in terms of prize money: the U.S.

series paid that much more. Thus, the U.S. Formula 5000 championship attracted not only American and Canadian drivers but also drivers from several countries and continents: in fact, all championships in the 70s were won by non-Americans, although top U.S. drivers such as **Mario Andretti, Mark Donohue** and **Al Unser Senior** raced and did well in the series. Among others, drivers from **Britain, Australia, New Zealand, South Africa, Belgium, Argentina**, **Japan, Italy, Switzerland, France** raced in the American series.

Canadian **John Cannon** won the 13-race **1970** championship, racing against the likes of **David Hobbs, George Follmer, Gus Hutchison, Eppie Wietzes, Bill Brack** and **Ron Grable**. Mark Donohue also won a race in **Sebring**, driving a **McLaren-Chevrolet**. The shorter 8-race **1971** season turned out to be a straight fight between **David Hobbs** and **Sam Posey**. **Hobbs** won five races, to **Posey**'s one. **Brett Lunger** and Australian **Frank Matich** also won a race apiece. **Skip Barber** sporadically raced a DFV-engined **March** in the series.

Graham McRae, who seemed to rule Formula 5000 worldwide in **1972**, won the US series, initially in his **Leda**, eventually in his **McRae**. The championship had 8 races and some of the more generous promoters paid as much as US$ 20,000 to winners. No wonder that the grid for some races had as many as 40 entrants and among the drivers who raced that year were **Peter Gethin, Derek Bell, Brian Redman**, Australians **Kevin Bartlett** and **Bob Muir, Sam Posey, David Hobbs, Lothar Motschenbacher, George Follmer, Brett Lunger**. Also noteworthy was **Brian Redman**'s first win in the series, at **Riverside**.

Redman's strongest opponent in **1973** turned out to be young South African lion **Jody Scheckter**, who ended up champion driving both **Trojan** and **Lola**. After **Brian**'s win in the first race of the season, **Jody** had a run of four straight victories, which placed him in command of the championship. **Redman** attempted a reaction by winning the next four rounds but Jody managed the scoring situation well and became champion. Among the drivers that raced that season were **Mark Donohue, Peter Gethin, Vern Schuppan, Sam Posey, Tony Adamowicz, Brett Lunger, David Hobbs, Graham McRae, Johnny Walker** (from Australia), former F-1 driver **Tony Settember** and even **Clay Regazzoni** had a go. **Donohue** drove an **AMC** powered **Lola**, which went as far as finishing second.

With **Jody** gone for **1974**, things might have become easier for **Redman**…however, his new major opponent was no other than **Mario Andretti**. The season almost did not happen, because of the **1974** oil crisis and resulting loss of a sponsor. It started late in June, as a joint SCCA/USAC sanctioning arrangement and a short, 7-race calendar. As a result of the joint sanctioning, USAC drivers like **Andretti, Al Unser, Rutherford, Mosley** and **Johncock** appeared in the series. **Brian** won three race to **Mario's** three and **David Hobbs'** one. Among other luminaries that season were **Al Unser, Warwick Brown, Sam Posey, Graham McRae, Eppie Wietzes** and special appearances by **Mike Mosley, Johnny Rutherford, Lella Lombardi** and **James Hunt**.

Brett Lunger was a habitué in American Formula 5000 races. Photo by Rob Neuzel.

The **1975** season had 9 rounds, including a special street race in **Long Beach**. It remained a **Brian-Mario** show: **Brian** won four races, **Mario** four. The only other winner was **Al Unser**. All winners drove **Lolas**, which was the most common chassis by far. However, new offerings from **Talon, Eagle**, Argentina's **Berta** and a **Dodge** engined **Shadow** brought some variety to the races, which were run as two qualifying heats and a final. Fighting for other positions were **Jackie Oliver** (in the **Shadow**), **Eppie Wietzes, David Hobbs, Warwick Brown, Danny Ongais, Gordon Johncock, Graham McRae** and a promising young driver called **B.J. Swanson**, who unfortunately died during the season, at Mid Ohio. **Tony Brise** won a heat at **Long Beach** and was duly retained for the rest of the year, always showing great speed and maturity. Among other star drivers in that race were **Jody Scheckter, Tom Pryce, Chris Amon** in the **Talon**. **Vern Schuppan** finished an excellent second in this event, driving the **Eagle**.

Formula 5000 was run one last time, under joint SCCA/USAC sanctioning. As discussed elsewhere, the SCCA was going through rough times. It had killed the high appeal Can-Am series in **1974** but decided to revive it in **1977** as a fendered Formula 5000 category. Many felt that Formula 5000 had no appeal, there was even a running joke that for non-connoisseurs the name Formula 5000 sounded like medicine for hemorrhoids and Can Am was a much stronger brand. So that was the end of the category as a professional series. A 7-race series was put together for **1976**, under the same qualifying heat and final set-up. **Redman** continued to rule winning three rounds, even though **Al Unser** made him work hard for the crown, as **Mario** had done the two preceding years. In addition to **Unser**, who won a race, **Alan Jones** also won a couple of races, one driving a **Lola**, in the other a **March** 76-A and **Jackie Oliver** got the only **Dodge** win in the series. In addition to the regulars, the VDS team contested the season with drivers **Peter Gethin** and **Teddy Pilette**, finding the going a little tougher than Europe.

388

Brian Redman was the king of American Formula 5000. Photo by Rob Neuzel.

Race wins by driver (1970-1976)
1. Brian Redman (GB), 16
2. David Hobbs (GB), 9
3. Mario Andretti (US), 7
4. Jody Scheckter (ZA), 4
5. Graham McRae (NZ), Brett Lunger (US), John Cannon (CDN), 3
6. Ron Grable (US), Gus Hutchinson (US), George Follmer (US), Mark Donohue (US), Al Unser (US), Alan Jones (AUS), 2
7. Sam Posey (US), Frank Matich (AUS), Eppie Wietzes (CDN), Jackie Oliver (GB), 1

Wins by car
1. Lola, 36
2. McLaren, 9
3. Trojan, Surtees, 3
4. Lotus, Brabham, Leda, 2
5. McRae, Chevron, March, Shadow, 1

Venues used, 1970-1976
1. Road America, 8
2. Riverside, Mid-Ohio, Laguna Seca, 6
3. Watkins Glen, 5
4. Mosport, 4
5. Pocono, Edmonton, Seattle, Road Atlanta, Lime Rock, 3
6. Brainerd, 2
7. Long Beach, Ontario, Michigan, Sears Point, Dallas, St. Jovite, Sebring, 1

EUROPEAN FORMULA 5000

As a truly European championship, Formula 5000 was never very successful. Except for regular rounds in **Monza, Zolder** and **Zandvoort**, most races were run in Britain through the 70s. Fields rarely exceeded 20 cars, with many also-rans appearing in every round and there was always great attrition rate, because many components were off-the-shelf, not specific for racing. Notwithstanding, several drivers from the continent raced in the championship, in fact, a few made names for themselves in it, plus some championships and races were rather interesting and competitive.

Peter Gethin was by far the most successful driver in the history of the championship and during the decade, winning the **1970** title and featuring well in others. In fact, **Gethin** was the first of a few drivers to use F-5000 as a platform to enter Formula 1, being hired to replace **Bruce McLaren** in the **McLaren** Formula 1 and Can Am team in **1970**, in the wake of his second Formula 5000 success.

Mike Hailwood driving the works Lola T190. Photo by Lola Heritage.

By and large, the championship always suffered from a lack of competitors, as the mostly American power plants turned out to be expensive in Europe. Most Formula 5000 cars ran **Chevy** engines, while other engines such as **Ford, Rover** (3.5 liter) and **Oldsmobile** were used in the cars in Europe. (Other engines such as **Buick, Repco, AMC, Dodge**, were run elsewhere).

McLaren was the most successful manufacturer in the first two years of the Championship, soon replaced by **Lola**, which won most races after **1971**. **Surtees** was also a prominent fixture of the first few years of the decade. Besides these three manufacturers, several others raced in the European championship, including **Crossle, Talon, Trojan, Chevron, Kitchner, Leda, McRae, Begg, March, Connew, Brabham, Modus, Harrier, Hepworth, Conchord, Dulon, Nike, Harris, Beattie, Kincraf**t. Old Formula 1 cars, equipped with 5 liter and smaller engines were also run, such as **Cooper, Lotus, BRM, BRP** including a

McLaren M19 that raced in **1974** and **1975** and a one-off **Brabham BT43** that raced in **1975**.

In **1970**, **Howden Ganley** was the runner up to **Gethin**, who won 8 of the first 12 rounds, building enough of a cushion to yield the seat to **Reine Wisell**, who won three races in the car. Those were good days for the Formula, which also enjoyed drivers of stature such as **Frank Gardner, Mike Hailwood, Trevor Taylor** and **Graham McRae**. The races were run in two heats, some of them as short as 35 minutes. Besides **Zandvoort, Monza** and **Zolder**, races abroad were also run in **Hockenheim, Mondello Park, Salzburgring** and **Anderstorp**, making this by far the most international of all European Formula 5000 championships.

A welcome development for the category was the use of Formula 5000 cars in the Tasman championship in **1970**. In this first F5000 Tasman Trophy, some old style 2.5-liter Tasman racers, such as champion **Graeme Lawrence**'s Ferrari Dino and Formula 2 cars were mostly used but eventually, Formula 5000s would become the majority for a few years. Some Formula 5000 cars were also raced in the South African Formula 1 championship and Brazilian **Antonio Carlos Avallone**, who raced in the category in Britain in **1969**, built a **Lola** based F-5000 car, to be raced in Brazil but his enthusiasm for the category was not shared by others. He ended up putting fenders on the car and raced it a few times as a prototype in **1974**, somewhat predicting what would happen the U.S. Formula 5000.

Gethin, Ganley and **Wisell** were gone in **1971**, all of them racing in Formula 1, so it looked as though the principle of the category was right. However, Formula 5000 was never properly promoted in Europe, although it did enjoy Rothmans sponsorship in the early years and it did not help much when the cars were included as grid fillers in Formula 1 races such as Britain's International Trophy, Race of Champions and Gold Cup, which made them look very inferior to Formula 1 cars. Most up and coming talent still continued to run in Formula 2, although **Frank Gardner** and **Mike Hailwood** battled royally for the **1971** title, which was ultimately won by the Australian **Gardner**. Another welcome addition to the driver ranks that year was **Brian Redman**, who would become one of the formula's exponents in the next few years. An interesting event was the "hors concours" participation of the **Lotus Turbine 56B** at **Hockenheim**, driven to 2nd by **Emerson Fittipaldi**.

Dutchman **Gijs Van Lennep** won the **1972** title in a **Surtees**, even though he won only two races and both **Brian Redman** and **Graham McRae** proved faster. These two drivers were contesting the US Series as well and missed a few of the British rounds. They had good reason: although the US winners of some races could make as much as US$ 20,000, the European series paid winners a meager £750 to £1,500. If one was trying to make a living out of racing, the US was a better bet by far. The pattern continued: many short races, a few drivers of star quality and quite a few ill-repared grid fillers, many cars failing to start and little internationality.

Some of the more talented drivers, such as **Brian Redman** and **Jody Scheckter**, preferred to contest the U.S. series in **1973**, for although it featured fewer races, it was much better promoted. Holding Formula 5000 races outside of Britain proved a handful. An event at **Misano** was cancelled, even though drivers had come all the way from Britain, practiced and qualified. It was alleged that a 2-liter limit had been imposed by local authorities for racing in the circuit, on safety grounds. A race was run in Denmark, at **Jyllandsring**, the only international race for powerful single seaters held in that track during the 70s. The Belgian VDS team emerged as one of the best in **1973** and won the title with **Teddy Pilette**. In addition to Teddy, **Peter Gethin** also raced for VDS. **Gethin** also got the only win by a Formula 5000 car in a major mixed F1/F5000 race, in the then traditional European Formula 1 season debut race, the Race of Champions at **Brands Hatch**. While this happened because most Formula 1s failed that day, it is nonetheless an accomplishment.

By **1974**, things were getting tougher for motorsport in general, specially in England, so it was no surprise that the Formula 5000 championship also felt the impact. **Bob Evans** emerged a worthy champion on the strength of three straight wins mid-season, earning enough exposure to be hired by a Formula 1 team for **1975**, **BRM**. **Brian Redman** and **David Hobbs**, American Formula 5000 habitual drivers, took part early in the year and both won races. **Peter Gethin, Guy Edwards, Ian Ashley** and foreigners **Vern Schuppan** and **Tom Belso** also won, so that the 18-race championship had a great variety of winners. Four races were held outside of England, namely at **Zolder, Zandvoort, Mugello** and **Monza,** while races planned for **Imola** and **Casale** were cancelled. Among participants were Italian **Lella Lombardi**, who finished many races and placed 5th in the championship. Other notables were **Mike Wilds, Steve Thompson, Damien Magee** and **Roelof Wunderink**, while there were other special appearances by **Rene Arnoux, Derek Bell, Leen Verhoeven, Tony Trimmer, Boy Hayje** and **Eddie Keizan**.

Teddy Pilette was twice European Formula 5000 champion. Here he is driving a Chevron at Brands Hatch, 1973. (Photo Teddy Pilette collection).

The last bona fide European Formula 5000 championship took place in **1975 and Teddy Pilette** emerged the winner once more. Later in the season, the fields were very thin, and many cars failed to start, due to the poor standard of preparation. The second round, to take place at **Brand Hatch** was cancelled due to lack of interest. The reason given for **Redman**'s no show at the **Brands Hatch** March 31 round was a peculiar "driver resting", which shows the general mindset concerning the category. Few cars were entered in races and many had mechanical failures that prevented them from starting. It became obvious that something had to change, for filling a grid with race worthy, full 5.0 Liter Formula 5000 machines was becoming very difficult, if not impossible. As a result the 3.4 Ford Cosworth GAA power plant was already being used by some drivers in **1975 and Alan Jones** and **David Purley** won races with it. Many drivers won races: **Ian Ashley, Gordon Spice** (better known for touring cars), **Richard Scott, Bob Evans but** the VDS pair of **Teddy Pilette** and **Peter Gethin** did most of the winning and finished 1-2 in the standings. The swansong championship had rounds at **Zolder** and **Zandvoort** one last time, two continental markets where Formula 5000 got some traction. Among some surprising participations were **Alain Peltier, Ingo Hoffmann** (getting mileage in high powered machines in preparation for his **1976** Formula 1 ride) and **Chris Amon**, who failed to start a single race in the **Talon.** Perhaps very fittingly, **Peter Gethin** won the last European Formula 5000 Championship race ever, held at **Brands Hatch**, driving a VDS **Lola.**

A wonderful shot of Bob Evans in Brands Hatch, 1974 (Photo by Pete Austin)

In **1976** the European Formula 5000 championship became a Formula Libre championship, the Shellsport championship, which accepted Formula 1, Formula 5000, Formula 2 and even Formula Atlantic entries. The uncompetitiveness of many remaining Formula 5000 cars was obvious, as many Formula 2 cars were much faster, in spite of the great power differential. The Formula 5000s would be allowed until **1977** and thereafter, the championship was open only to Formula 1 and Formula 2 cars, being renamed Aurora AFX Championship. It would not last long, as well. Formula 5000 cars continued to be used in club Formula Libre and hill climbs in England for years.

Among the noteworthy drivers who raced in this championship were: **Peter Gethin, Emerson Fittipaldi, Trevor Taylor, Alan Jones, Jody Scheckter, Derek Bell, Brian Redman, Gijs van Lennep, Reine Wisell, Bob Evans, Chris Amon, Frank Gardner, Keith Holland, Teddy Pilette, Clay Regazzoni, Arie Luyendyk, Mike Hailwood, David Hobbs, Lella Lombardi, Graham McRae, Ulf Norinder, Morris Nunn, Gordon Spice, Tom Belso, Damien Magee, David Purley, Ian Ashley, Tony Trimmer, Ingo Hoffmann, Brett Lunger, John Watson, Guy Edwards, Vern Schuppan, Eddie Keizan, Tom Walkinshaw, Dave Walker, Mike Wilds, Richard Scott, Boy Hayje, Paul Hawkins, Tony Dean, Chris Craft, David Prophet.**

Races for the championship were run in: England, Italy, Netherlands, Germany, Ireland, Denmark, Belgium, Sweden

Race winners, 1970-1975
1. Peter Gethin (GB), 17
2. Graham McRae (NZ), 10
3. Brian Redman (GB), 8
4. Frank Gardner (AUS), 7
5. Bob Evans (GB), Teddy Pilette (B), 6
7. Ian Ashley (GB), 5
8. Mike Hailwood (GB), 4
9. Reine Wisell (S), Alan Rollinson (GB), David Hobbs (GB), Guy Edwards (GB), 3
10. Mike Walker (GB), Gijs Van Lennep (NL), Steve Thompson (GB), Brett Lunger (GB), Keith Holland (GB), David Purley (GB), Alan Jones (AUS), 2
11. Trevor Taylor (GB), Tony Dean (GB), Tom Belso (DK), Vern Schuppan (AUS), Gordon Spice (GB), Richard Scott (GB), 1

Wins by cars, 1970-1975
1. Lola, 39
2. McLaren, 21
3. Chevron, 15
4. Surtees, 9
5. Trojan, 5
6. McRae and Leda, 3
7. March, 1

Venues used, 1970-1975
(where country not indicated, GB)
1. Brands Hatch, 21
2. Mallory Park, 14
3. Oulton Park, 12
4. Silverstone, 9
5. Snetterton, 8
6. Thruxton, 6
7. Zandvoort (NL), Mondello Park (IRL), 4
8. Monza (I), 3
9. Zolder (B), Castle Combe, Hockenheim (D), 2
10. Anderstorp (S), Salzburgring (A), Nivelles (B), Mugello (I), Jyllandsring (DK) 1

SHELLSPORT GROUP 8 AND AURORA F1 CHAMPIONSHIP, (1976-1979)

The last few races of the **1975** Formula 5000 season indicated that a change was needed. Grids were small, entry lists were not awe inspiring and a few cars always failed to start, bringing down the numbers even more. That way the Formula 5000 championship morphed into a Group 8 championship sponsored by oil company Shell, that welcomed Formula 5000, Formula 1, Formula 2 and Formula Atlantic cars.

Many pundits felt that Formula 1's would run away with all races but that is not what transpired at first. For one, driving a Formula 1 on the edge is one thing, having to watch the engine and avoid accidents at all costs, quite another. Many of the Formula 1 entrants ran on very tight budgets, so in the end, the championship was won by **David Purley** on a **Chevron** with a 3.4 **Ford** engine. **Purley** totally deserved the championship, winning 6 races, although in the beginning, **Damien Magee** mounted a charge, also driving a 3.4 Ford **March** and winning twice. With time, **Damien**'s car was replaced by a **Penske** 3.0 DFV (F1) and **Magee** himself dropped from the team (**Derek Bell** taking his place).The rest of the winners were a mixed batch. **Alan Jones** won a race in a pure 5.0 **Lola-Chevrolet, Ray Mallock** won at **Snetterton** on a Formula 2 **March-BDX**, while **Brian McGuire** was the first to win in a F-1, a **Williams** FX4, followed by **Guy Edwards'** win in a **Brabham BT-42**. **Keith Holland** had the second pure Formula 5000 win of the year, at **Brands Hatch**. A number of Formula 1s ran that season, including a **Surtees** driven by ex-skier **Divina Galica**, who showed promise, the **Lyncar** driven by **Emilio de Villota**, a **Shadow** DN3 driven by both **Mike Wilds** and **Lella Lombardi**, while **Guy Edwards** also drove an **Ensign,** in addition to the **Brabham**. Finally, **Andy Sutcliffe** drove a RAM **Brabham** BT-44. An interesting car was the one-off **McLaren M25-Chevrolet**, driven by **Bob Evans**, 2nd in the Evening News Trophy, which had no less than 35 cars on the grid, followed by 28 in the next round, at **Thruxton**. So, one can say that Formula 1 cars disappointed in this first season and the 5000s showed they still had some life in them, while the championship did fine for a first-year experiment.

Trimmer leading the pack in his Surtees, in 1977 (Photo Tony Trimmer collection)

In **1977** the story was a bit different. A Formula 1 car, the weak **Lyncar** driven by **Emilio de Villota**, won the very first round. The excellent **Tony Trimmer** on a **Surtees** TS19 was on pole, a welcome addition to the series both the car and the driver. These two, plus **Brian McGuire** were the only F1s that started that initial race. The two true 5000s in the race, driven by **Keith Holland** and **Tom Belso** would have to work hard but **Holland** still managed to come second, **Belso** finished fourth (after **Trimmer**). **Edwards** won the second race on a **Ford** GAA **March**, followed by the much-improved **Divina Galica**, also on a **Surtees** TS-19, followed by **Belso** and **Holland**. At **Oulton Park, Derek Bell** drove the **Penske-**

395

Cosworth to victory followed by the F-5000 of **Bruce Allison**. **Val Musetti** won at **Brands** in a **Cosworth** GAA, so the score was GAA 2 x DFV 2. **Trimmer** only began winning in the fifth round, followed by a GAA, two **Chevrolets** and another GAA. The next round at **Thruxton** was won by **Tony Rouff** in the **Boxer** F-2 car, followed by **Edwards** and **Holland**. From round 7, **Trimmer** began to take firm control of the situation, winning the next two rounds, followed by another Formula 1 victory, this time **De Villota** now driving a **McLaren** M23. This was followed by another **Trimmer** win, then **De Villota** won again. In spite of so few Formula 1 in numbers, they clearly had the upper hand. **Edwards** won the next round joining the F1 brigade as well, replacing his **March**'s GAA by a DFV. Round 13 was won by **Trimmer**, while **Edwards** won the last race of the season with the DFV engined **March** again. So GAAs won twice, DFVs eleven times and a Formula 2 once. While the efforts of **Allison, Holland** and **Musetti** during the entire season were noteworthy and **Belso** ran out of funds, it became clear that Formula 1 machinery was necessary to win Group 8 races, so the F-5000s looked quite dispensable. **Trimmer** won the championship.

David Kennedy's Wolf at Zandvoort, 1979 (Photo Rob Petersen collection)

In **1978**, the Group 8 series changed sponsors and morphed into the Aurora AFX Formula 1 Championship. This meant the end of Formula 5000 cars in top level contemporary racing in England and also the elimination of Atlantics from the field. From that point on, only Formula 1 and Formula 2 cars would be allowed. The championship had evolved compared to the previous two seasons, there was more field depth and competition was good in some races, not so good in others (such as **Snetterton**), with grids also varying in size – the September race in **Thruxton** had 20 cars. There was still room for growth but progress had been made. The previous year's champion, **Tony Trimmer**, came back with a stronger car, a **McLaren** M23, while **Guy Edwards** drove a **March**. Italian **Giancarlo Martini** drove a few races and won one driving an **Ensign**. **David Kennedy** in a **Wolf** managed to win from a single appearance, while many drivers drove more than one car in the series: **Bob Evans** first drove a **Surtees**, then a second **John Cooper Hesketh** (**Cooper** drove another one as well); **Emilio de Villota** had the unique **McLaren M25** but also drove a **Boxer** Formula 2; **Geoff Less** won in an **Ensign** but also drove a F-2 **Chevron**; **Divina Galica** drove a **Surtees** (2nd in **Zandvoort**) and **Ensign**, **Val Musetti** drove a **March** and an **Ensign**, **Bruce Allison** drove a **March** and **Ensign**. **Teddy Pilette** had the unloved **BRM P207** and managed to squeeze one fastest lap out of it. **Mike Wilds** did very well in a Formula 2 **Ralt** (**Kim Mather** also deserves mention among Formula 2 runners) and a few outsiders drove one-offs, such as **Boy Hayje, Brett Lunger, Ray Mallock, Brett Riley, Geoff Brabham** and **Elio de Angelis**. The **Zandvoort** race added international flavor to the series. **Trimmer** won five of the 12 rounds, **Edwards** won twice, **Evans, Allison, Martini, Lees** and **Kennedy** won 1 round each. **Trimmer** finished first in the championship, followed by **Evans, de Villota and Edwards**.

Arguably the **1979** season was the best of the decade, since Group 8 was established. For one, grids preponderantly comprised Formula 1 cars and the only other remaining category allowed in the championship, Formula 2, took a very secondary position in the wider scheme of things. A number of F-1 car manufacturers were represented and the championship was won by a British driver that was considered hot property as recently as **1976, Rupert Keegan**. **Keegan** drove an **Arrows** A1 and his teammate was Argentine **Ricardo Zunino**. **Keegan** won five races, to **Zunino**'s single victory. His main opposition were Irishman **David Kennedy**, who drove a **Wolf** WR4 and won the first two races of the season plus a race at **Mallory Park** and Spaniard **Emilio de Villota**, who had acquired a **Lotus** 78 and won four races mid-season, leading the championship for a few rounds. The trio **Kennedy-Keegan-De Villota** all led the championship at one point.

Guy Edwards and **Bernard De Dryver** had a couple of unrecognizable RAM **Fittipaldi** F5As at their disposal and **Edwards** won the Aurora section of the Race of Champions in one of the cars. **De Dryver** managed three second places which were the ultimate high point of a mostly undistinguished career. The only other driver to win a race was American **Gordon Smiley**, who drove a **Tyrrell** 008, a **Surtees** TS20 and a **McLaren** M23, winning the final at **Silverstone**. Fast **Desire Wilson** also drove the **Tyrrell** 008 and led and had fastest lap in the first race of the year at **Zolder** but ended third on that race and elsewhere. Other interesting and constant entries were **Tiff Needell**, on the one-off **Chevron** B41, the only Formula 1 car produced by the make, which finished 2nd in **Zolder, Philip Bullman** in the ground effects **Surtees** TS20, **Giacomo Agostini** in a **Williams** FW06, **Neil Betteridge** in a **Tyrrell** 008. **David Purley** returned to racing, driving the **Lec** and a **Shadow** DN9 and **Val Musetti** drove both **March** and **Wolf** Formula 1 cars, while **John Cooper** had an **Ensign** as his new weapon. **David Leslie** also drove the **Chevron**. The best Formula 2 performance was **Derek Warwick**'s second in **Mallory Park** but **Norman Dickison** tended to win the category. The championship featured three races outside England, at **Zolder, Zandvoort** and **Nogaro**. The Aurora FX Series seemed to be on the right path.

TASMAN CUP AND AUSTRALIA

The Tasman Cup was one of the most prestigious series of the 1960s. Usually an 8-race series, with 4 rounds in New Zealand and 4 in Australia, the series attracted several Formula 1 drivers who came down under during the Northern winter to make some money, in the process having some fun. The likes of **Jim Clark, Jochen Rindt, Graham Hill, Phil Hill, Piers Courage, Derek Bell, Jackie Stewart, Richard Attwood, Pedro Rodriguez**, joined locals **Jack Brabham, Bruce McLaren, Denis Hulme, Frank Gardner, Chris Amon, Frank Matich, Graeme Lawrence** in races for 2.5-to-1.6-liter single seaters. However, as the official racing calendar stretched into the months of January and February, as of **1970** very few top stars were poised to make the trek down south, as Formula

5000 was adopted, replacing the 2.5-liter formula. In its original guise, the Tasman Cup would last until **1975**.

Under the new configuration, the **1970** Tasman Cup had four races in New Zealand and three in Australia. Although a few 5-liter cars raced in **Levin**, January 4th, the race was won by **Graeme Lawrence**, in a 2.4 **Ferrari** Dino. Only three foreigners started the race: Sweden's **Ulf Norinder**, Britain's **Derek Bell** and America's **Ron Grable, Norinder** placing 6th. **Frank Matich** won the next couple of races, driving a 5-liter **McLaren**, with foreigners doing better (**Bell** was second at **Pukekohe**, **Grable** 2nd in **Christchurch**). **Graham McRae** began his run of Tasman success at **Teretonga**, also winning at **Surfers` Paradise** in a 5-liter **McLaren**. The small engined cars placed 1-2-3 at **Warwick Farm**, the winner being **Kevin Bartlett**. The last race, at **Sandown Park** was won by **Niel Allen**. The winner of the championship was **Lawrence**, the **Ferrari** driver, who scored in 6 of 7 races.

John McCormack drove a variety of cars during the 70s, including this Elfin. Photo by Glenn Moulds.

The **1971** was the first of a hat trick by New Zealander **Graham McRae**, who would become the top global Formula 5000 driver in short course. Few Europeans were convinced to bring their cars half around the world, the exceptions being **Teddy Pilette, John Cannon, Keith Holland** and **Evan Noyes**. On the positive side, GP driver **Chris Amon** was entered in the series. **McRae** won three rounds, including the first race, **Allen** two, **Gardner** one and **Matich** one. **Amon** drove the unusual **Lotus** 70 equipped with a 5-liter **Ford** engine and also a 2.5 Cosworth engined **March** 701. The best performance by a foreigner was **Pilette**'s second place at **Sandown Park**.

If the Tasman Cup no longer attracted top Formula 1 drivers, at least top drivers from the US and European Formula 5000 championships drove in the **1972** series: **David Hobbs, Frank Gardner, Mike Hailwood, Teddy Pilette**. **McRae** won four races this time and the title again, while **Bartlett, Matich, Gardner** and **Hobbs** won one each. **McRae**'s mount was the **Leda** designed by **Len Terry**, however, cars built in New Zealand and Australia also featured well: **Matich, Begg** and **Elfin**.

398

The foreign contingent was rather weak in **1973**: from Europe came **Allan Rollinson** and **Steve Thompson**, from the USA, **Sam Posey**. **Noritake Takahara** fielded a 1.8 liter **Brabham** in the 2.0 liter category. **McRae** won three races, driving his own **McRae-Chevrolet,** while **John McCormack** won two rounds in the Australian **Elfin** and **Matich** one in his **Matic**h. Therefore, no less than six of the 8 races were won by locally made cars, which was rather impressive. The other two races were won by Europeans **Rollinson** and **Thompson**.

The high point of the **1974** Tasman Cup was the presence of the European Champion team, VDS, with its two drivers **Peter Gethin** and **Teddy Pilette**. Nonlocals finally got the upper hand, winning the title (**Gethin**), although the VDS duo only won three races (**Gethin** won two, **Pilette** one). On the negative side, the VDS team was the only international presence. Making matters worse, some races had small entry lists and the locally made cars were not as competitive as in previous years. **Johnny Walker, Max Stewart** and **Warwick Brown** all won races in **Lolas**, the sole win by a local car was **McCormack**'s in the New Zealand Grand Prix, driving an **Elfin**. **McRae**'s luck ran out and he retired from many races in his GM2.

Teddy Pilette was one of the few Europeans to appear often in Tasman races of the 70s.
(Photo Teddy Pilette collection)

By **1975**, the Tasman Cup had become a regional event. The only international star was **Chris Amon**, whose career appeared to be winding down anyhow, slotted to drive a **Talon**. The regulars were all there: **McRae, Lawrence, Walker, Stewart, McCormack, Brown, Smith, Bartlett. Warwick Brown** won two races and the title. **Graeme Lawrence** also won a couple of races, while **Graham McRae** got some of his luck back by winning the Lady Wigram Trophy. **Johnny Walker** also won a round and **Chris Amon**, most popularly, won the round at **Teretonga**, New Zealand. The last Tasman Cup race ever took place in **Sandown Park**, Australia on February 23. The winner was **John Goss**, driving a **Matich** with **Holden** engine. At least the series died with some Australian pride.

Australian Gold Star Series

The Australian Gold Star Series was Australia's top single seater championship during the decade, also called Australian Formula 1. While Formula 5000 cars raced in the championship and generally won, many of the entries raced Australian Formula 2 cars, so one cannot really call it a Formula 5000 championship. Several locally made cars were used in this championship, some of which raced in the Tasman Cup as well. An interesting variation was a **Leyland** engined **McLaren** M23 raced by **John McCormack** in **1976**, which won on occasion.

Australian built cars such as the Matich raced against European machinery in Australian Formula 5000. (Photo by Glenn Moulds)

FORMULA 3

The path of Formula 3's stature in the 70s was in direct opposition to Formula 2's. While the latter became decadent with time, the former rose in significance. In **1970**, Formula 3 were little screamers, nimble cars with 1-liter engines. Formula 2, on the other hand, had more powerful and sophisticated 1.6 engines and behaved more like the heavier Formula 1 cars. The standard of driving was more polished in F-2, after all, top GP drivers raced in the category with young hopefuls. In a sense, Formula 2 was a required step for a driver to graduate into Formula 1. For one thing, F3 races were quite wild, and it was a learning category, where drivers with very little experience learned the craft, often for many seasons. By **1971**, F-3 had adopted 1.6-liter engines, while Formula 2 went into a 2.0 configuration as of **1972**. In **1974**, F-3 also adopted 2-liter engines, which were not as powerful as F-2's because they were stock blocks and less tuned, whereas F-2 used more tuned engines. However, the huge difference existing in **1970** was no longer there.

In the early 60s Europe there was only 1.0-liter Formula Junior and 1.5 liter Formula 1, as the Intercontinental Formula never took off. By the mid-sixties, under the new 3.0-liter Formula 1 structure, Formula 2 and Formula 3 were reestablished. Many a driver began driving in 1.0-liter Formula 3 a couple of years after starting racing at all, soldiering on for a few years. The way people came into the sport had changed dramatically by the latter part of the decade. Many European 60s drivers began racing in hill climbs, local touring car meetings and even motorcycles. Some would drive a few years in these entry level disciplines, before venturing into single-seaters but other more enterprising and ambitious drivers would quickly go into Formula 3. There they acquired experience, eventually making the big jump to F-2, sports cars or... gardening.

Brands Hatch 1970, a full grid of screaming 1.0 liter F3s (Photo by Pete Austin)

Formula Ford changed the picture further in 1967, by introducing another entry level category even before F-3. Prior to the appearance of F-Ford, Formula Vee filled the same need but it was not almost generally adopted as FF eventually was. The evolution of karting, from a cute novelty into serious competition, took place in the latter 60s and was consolidated in the 70s. Most drivers seeking Formula 1 glory were no longer beginning on the hills or 2-wheels, as adults: they had been doing karting since their early teens, so by the time they reached Formula Ford, they had almost a decade of racing experience. Most spent one or two years in Formula Ford, then jumped to a Formula 3 that was much closer to Formula 2 than at the beginning of the decade. There you have it: the Formula 2 step was no longer necessary by the end of the 70s.

This meant that a lot of Formula 3 drivers were able to go directly into F-1. Take, for instance, **Emerson Fittipaldi**. In his native Brazil, he did very little racing, simply because there were very few races in the country. He won a Formula Vee title in **1967**, drove sports and touring cars, then he came to Europe, in **1969**. He did half a season of Formula Ford, won many races, jumped into Formula 3 mid-year, won a championship. While he did drive in F-2 early in **1970**, he was already considered a strong candidate for a F-1 seat, which materialized way before the F-2 season was over, at the British Grand Prix. This became the new benchmark: from Formula Ford in early **1969** to Grand Prix racing by mid-season, **1970**. In a sense, **Niki Lauda** did something similar. Racing in Formula 3 in **1970**, by the **1971** Austrian Grand Prix **Niki** was already in Formula 1. It should be noted that both

Emerson and **Niki** were very talented drivers, with plenty of innate skill, thus they were able to do this. Many other lesser men (and women) adopted the same goal with much less ability. It should be noticed that a lot of future world champions raced in Formula 3 at one time or another during the 70s: **Niki Lauda, James Hunt, Jody Scheckter, Alan Jones, Keke Rosberg, Nelson Piquet, Alain Prost** and **Nigel Mansell**. That is quite a line-up. Future Indy 500 winners, Indycar champions, F2 champions, Formula 5000 champions, European Touring Car Champions, World Sports Car champions, Can Am champions and dozens of other championships also raced in Formula 3 some time during the 70s.

This meant that Formula 3 championships rose in importance. The British championships were always very important and there were three of them between **1970** to **1973**. British F-3 hit a decade low in **1974**, partly due to the oil crisis, the new 2-liter engines and partly due to Formula Atlantic's rise in popularity with crowds and participants. In **1975** there was a single British F3 championship sponsored by BP, while from **1976** until the end of the decade, two British championships were run.

FIA also introduced an initially low-key European F-3 championship in **1975**, which became stronger with every passing year. It would soon become the most important Formula 3 championship of the world. Sweden, France and Italy already had Formula 3 championships in **1970** and Germany soon adopted the formula. The French championship ran until **1973**, being dropped in detriment of Formula Renault, then reinstituted in **1978**. There was also a Danish championship in **1976-1977**.

Although **Ford** engines ruled until **1974**, as of **1975 Toyotas** were the best of the lot. Among other engine types used were **Renault, Triumph** (a works team), **BMW, Alfa Romeo, Lancia**.

Manufacturers that participated in Formula 3 during the 70s, among others: **Brabham, March, Ralt, Chevron, Lotus, Tecno, Modus, Ehrlich, Dastle, Viking, GRD, McNamara, Ensign, De Sanctis, Martini, Alpine, Osella, Supernova, Narval, Royale, Palliser, Titan, Alexis, Abbot, EMC, Beagley, Tui, Vesey, Matra, Nemo, Puma, U2, Merlyn, GRAC, Pygmee, AGS, Huron, Elden, MRE, Derichs, Cooper, Maco, Branca, Gozzoli, Birel, URD, MP, Eufra, Emiliani-Dallara, Wolf-Dallara, Wheatcroft, Hawke, Selex, Toj, Sana, Quasar, Lola, Rheinland, Anson, Safir, Ray, Muma, Duqueine, Kitchener**,

East Germany ran its own version of Formula 3, with mostly **Wartburg**-engined **Melkus**. The Soviet Union also had a Formula 3 category which was run under its own regulations. Among the cars that raced in Soviet and Czech events were **Chelik, MGK, Melkus, Hamal, AVIA, Gbelec, Stana, Kondor, Arcus, Cermac, Kupr, Estonia**.

Most prominent drivers in FIA Regulation Formula 3, Year by Year
1970 Dave Walker, Tony Trimmer, Jean-Pierre Jarier, Niki Lauda, Mike Beuttler, Carlos Pace, Wilson Fittipaldi Jr., Torsten Palm, Giovanni Salvati, Jean-Pierre Jaussaud, James Hunt, Jean-Luc Salomon, Denis Dayan, Gerry Birrel, Francois Migault, Freddy Kottulinski, Harald Ertl, Jean-Pierre Cassegrain, Gerold Pankl, Gianluigi Picchi, Adelmo Fossati, Jimmy Mieusset, Sandro Cinotti, Helmut Marko

1971 Dave Walker, Roger Williamson, Bev Bond, Colin Vandervell, Jody Scheckter, Patrick Depailler, Giancarlo Naddeo, James Hunt, David Purley,

Brendan McInerney, Alan Jones, Barrie Maskell, Jochen Mass, Pierre-Francois Rousselot, Jean-Pierre Jabouille, Jacques Coulon, Conny Andersson, Jean-Louis Lafosse, Ulf Svensson, Francois Migault, Torsten Palm,

1972 Roger Williamson, Jochen Mass, Rikki Von Opel, Mike Walker, Andy Sutcliffe, Jacques Coulon, Vittorio Brambilla, Michel Leclere, Conny Andersson, Colin Vandervell, Torsten Palm, Russell Wood, Lucien Guitteny, Jean-Pierre Jarier, Pierre-Francois Rousselot, Bob Evans, James Hunt, Tony Trimmer, Patrick Depailler, Alberto Colombo, Alain Serpaggi, Maurizio Flammini, Tom Pryce, Pino Pica

1973 Jacques Laffite, Tony Brise, Alan Jones, Richard Robarts, Mike Wilds, Russell Wood, Ian Taylor, Carlo Giorgio, Hakan Dahlqvist, Jean-Pierre Paoli, Masami Kuwashima, Damien Magee, Alberto Colombo, Leonel Friedrich, Larry Perkins, Johnny Gerber, Bernard Beguin, Mo Harness, Sandro Cinotti, Tony Rouff, Brian Henton, Christian Ethuin, Alain Cudini

1974 Brian Henton, Giorgio Francia, Tony Rouff, Alex Ribeiro, Jose Espirito Santo, Conny Andersson, Alberto Colombo, Tom Pryce, Gaudenzio Mantova, Gunnar Nilsson, Pedro Passadore, Willi Deutsch, Luciano Pavesi, Ulf Svensson, Alessandro Pesenti-Rossi, Danny Sullivan, Dieter Kern, Hans Binder, Nicholas Von Preussen

1975 Gunnar Nilsson, Alex Ribeiro, Patrick Neve, Renzo Zorzi, Danny Sullivan, Larry Perkins, Terry Perkins, Conny Andersson, Freddy Kottulinski, Conny Ljungfeldt, Luciano Pavesi, Ernst Maring, Pierre Dieudonne, Ingo Hoffman, Richard Hawkins, Gaudenzio Mantova, Alessandro Pesenti-Rossi, Gianfranco Brancatelli, Dick Parsons, Bob Arnott

1976 Riccardo Patrese, Bruno Giacomelli, Rupert Keegan, Geoff Lees, Conny Andersson, Gianfranco Brancatelli, Jac Nelleman, Bertram Schaffer, Conny Ljungfeldt, Stephen South, Mike Young, Ian Flux, Thorkhild Thyrring, Boy Hayje, Jac Nelleman, Willi Siller, Geoff Brabham, Brett Riley

1977 Piercarlo Ghinzani, Geoff Brabham, Nelson Piquet, Stephen South, Derek Warwick, Eje Elgh, Anders Olofsson, Beppe Gabbiani, Derek Daly, Oscar Pedersoli, David Kennedy, Elio di Angelis, Tiff Needell, Piero Necchi, Stefan Johansson, Bertram Schaffer, Nigel Mansell, Patrick Gaillard, Ian Flux, James King, Mario Ferraris

1978 Nelson Piquet, Jan Lammers, Derek Warwick, Chico Serra, Michael Bleekemolen, Bobby Rahal, Patrick Gaillard, Teo Fabi, Anders Olofsson, Mauro Baldi, David Kennedy, Alain Prost, Jean Louis Schlesser, Siegfried Stohr, Bertram Schaffer, Oscar Pedersoli, Bertram Schaffer, Huub Rothengatter, Guido Pardini, Bruno Pescia, Marzio Romano, Ian Taylor, Philip Bulmann, Nigel Mansell, Tiff Needell, Rob Wilson, Pedro Nogues, Jorge Caton, Satoru Nakajima, Ian Flux
1979 Alain Prost, Michael Bleekemolen, Chico Serra, Andrea de Cesaris, Brett Riley, Mike Thackwell, Michael Roe, Slim Borgudd, Michele Alboreto, Richard Dallest, Mauro Baldi, Arie Luyendyk, Michael Korten, Piercarlo Ghinzani, Slim Borgudd, Thierry Boutsen, Franz Konrad, Jo Gartner, Riccardo Paletti, Roberto Campominosi, Guido Pardini, Hans-Georg Burger, Helmut Henzler, Phillippe Streiff, Guido Dacco, Nigel Mansell, Piero Necchi

Formula 3 race winners, 70s

In compiling this list, I decided to leave out most Eastern Europe Formula 3 races, for these were run to a different set of regulations. I also left out Swiss championship races that appear on some sites, as well as Moroccan races of 1970, for a couple of reasons. First, Moroccans continued to use 1-liter regulations after 1970, with a twist: the 1 liter limit was imposed to international cars such as Lotus-Fords, while locally produced cars could have larger sized engines! This means it really was not Formula 3 but rather, a local formula. Additionally, I could not get reliable information for all years. At any rate, Jacques Berenger seemed to be the king of Moroccan Formula 3 and deserves mention. Thus, I considered mostly British, French, Italian, German, Swedish and Danish championship races. Drivers from the following countries won Formula 3 races in the 70s: Britain, France, Germany, Italy, Denmark, Sweden, Japan, Holland, Belgium, Brazil, Uruguay, Portugal, Austria, Liechtenstein, Ireland, Australia, South Africa, New Zealand, Antigua, USA, Switzerland. Racers from a host of other nationalities raced in Formula 3 during the 70s, including Argentina, Spain, Peru, Venezuela, Greece, Iceland, Norway, Yugoslavia, Jamaica, Indonesia, Monaco, etc. I have also excluded Australian and Soviet Formula 3.

The top winners list is curious. **Dave Walker** won 25 races in 1970 and 1971 and his full F1 season in 1972 was a total failure. Poor **Roger Williamson** only had two Formula 1 starts and died in the second, while **Conny Andersson** never had a proper crack in the category. **Brian Henton** raced for a variety of Formula 1 teams, but his only measure of success was a fastest lap, not a single point earned. **Anders Olofsson** never even raced in Formula 1. **Piercarlo Ghinzani**, tied with **Nelson Piquet** at 14 wins, was never a real success in Formula1. So **Piquet** is the first driver in the list to have achieved outstanding success in Formula 1.
1. Dave Walker, 25
2. Roger Williamson and Conny Andersson, 23
3. Brian Henton, 17
4. Anders Olofsson, 16
5. Piercarlo Ghinzani and Nelson Piquet, 14
6. Alain Prost and Tony Brise, 11
7. Derek Warwick, 10
8. Rupert Keegan, Chico Serra, Torsten Palm, Michel Leclere, 9
9. Bruno Giacommeli, Gianfranco Brancatelli, Vittorio Brambilla, Gunnar Nilsson, 8
10. Guido Pardini, Derek Daly, Tony Trimmer, Alan Jones, Ian Taylor, Alex Ribeiro, Ulf Svensson, Jean Pierre Jaussaud, Giovanni Salvati, Teo Fabi, Michael Korten, Stephen South, Jacques Lafitte, 7

11. Wilson Fittipaldi Jr., Giorgio Francia, Carlo Giorgio, Rikki Von Opel, Alessandro Pesenti-Rossi, Patrick Depailler, Bev Bond, Mike Thackwell, Andrea de Cesaris, James Hunt, Alberto Colombo, 6
12. Beat Blatter, Riccardo Patrese, Conny Ljungfeldt, Richard Robarts, Larry Perkins, Tony Rouff, Hakan Dahlqvist, Elio de Angelis, Bertram Schaffer, Jan Lammers, 5
13. Brett Riley, Siegfried Stohr, Eddie Cheever, Rudolf Dotsch, Colin Vandervell, Fernando Spreafico, Jac Nelleman, Danny Sullivan, Mike Beuttler, Fred Kottulinski, Jurg Dubler, David Purley, Claudio Francisci, Willi Deutsch, Andy Sutcliffe, Carlos Pace, 4
14. Stefan Johansson, Oscar Pedersoli, Eje Elgh, Gerry Birrell, Luciano Pavesi, Giancarlo Naddeo, Jody Scheckter, Jochen Mass, Russell Wood, Jacques Coulon, Alain Serpaggi, Mike Walker, Beppe Gabbiani, 3
15. Jochen Dauer, Michael Bleekemolen, Patrick Gaillard, Geoff Lees, Mauro Baldi, Thorbjorn Carlsson, Hans Georg Burger, Geoff Brabham, Gunnar Nordstrom, Jean-Pierre Cassegrain, Gianluigi Picchi, Tom Pryce, Bob Evans, Pino Pica, Mike Wilds, Jean-Pierre Jabouille, Steve Thompson, Willi Sommer, Dieter Kern, Hans P. Hoffmann, Christian Ethuin, 2
16. Alceste Bodini, Bert Hawthorne, Mike Tyrrell, David Cole, Jean Johansson, Alan Harvey, Gustav Dieden, Richard Scott, Sten Axelsson, Rolf Riesen, Gerold Pankl, Peter Hanson, Cyd Williams, Jean Blanc, Giancarlo Gagliardi, Hans Binder, Jose Espirito Santo, Nicholas Von Preussen, Jean-Pierre Jarier, Chris Speaking, Heinz Lange, Delmo Fossati, Francois Migault, Bernard Lagier, Luigi Fontanesi, Patrice Compain, Sten Gunnarson, Sonny Eade, David Morgan, Carlos Bredenstein, Fabrizio Noe, Jorg Obermoser, Barrie Maskell, Renzo Zorzi, Patrick Neve, Pedro Passadore, Maurizio Flammini, Bruno Pescia, Masami Kumashima, Terry Perkins, Dieter Quester, Ingo Hoffmann, Alberto Viale, Sandro Cinotti, Jean-Pierre Paoli, Mo Harness, Paolo Bozzeto, Chris Barnett, Dyfred Roberts, Gaudenzio Mantova, Ingvar Carlsson, Severo Zampatti, Richard Hawkins, Hakan Airiksson, Marc Surer, Heinz Scherle, James King, Claes Siggurdsson, Didier Pironi, Mats Nygren, Leonard Verrelli, Richard Dallest, Helmut Bross, Carlo Rossi, Trevor Templeton, Michael Roe, Bernard Devaney, Ernst Maring, Jan Riddel, Nigel Mansell, Walter Lechner, Thierry Boutsen, Frank Jelinski, Piero Necchi, Rob Wilson, Enzo Coloni, John Bright, 1

Last but not least. If you take the time to inspect F-3 race results in Sweden during the 70s you might find a Ronnie Petterson racing there. He is not THAT Ronnie Peterson, I must warn you.

FORMULA ATLANTIC

John Webb, credited with the creation of Formula 5000 is also deemed the inventor of Formula Atlantic. As in the case of the larger engine capacity formula, **Webb** "borrowed" the concept from an American single seater category – in F-5000s case, Formula A, in Formula Atlantic's, Formula B. At any rate, Formula Atlantic soon positioned itself as a low-cost alternative to Formula 2 and a faster category than Formula 3. In fact, by **1974** Formula Atlantic became so popular in England that it almost destroyed Formula 3. The category's first season took place in **1971** and its first champion was Australian **Vern Schuppan. Vern** won six races, all of which took place in England. Other prominent drivers in that first season were **Cyd Williams, Tom Belso, Ray Allen.** In the next five years, the category was adopted in many countries of the world, often as the main local racing category. Canada adopted it in **1974**, replacing Formula B and it soon became the top Formula Atlantic Championship of the world, a truly international series that brought to the fore, among others, **Gilles Villeneuve** and **Bobby Rahal**, plus the famous **Trois Rivieres** race. IMSA also ran a season of Formula Atlantic in **1976**, concurrent with the Canadian series. The Canadian Championship became the North American Formula Atlantic Championship in **1978**, with races in the USA as well as Canada. Ireland also adopted Formula Atlantic in **1974**. South Africa replaced its Formula 1 championship with a Formula Atlantic series as of **1976**, initially using the **Ford** engines like everybody else, in **1979** replacing it with rotary **Mazda** power. New Zealand dropped Formula 5000 in **1976** and held an International Formula Atlantic (renamed Formula Pacific) series for many years, as a replacement of the Tasman Series, in addition to a domestic series. Formula Pacific, in turn, was adopted in many Asian countries, including Japan, allowing countries in the region to compete on equal footing. As far as England is concerned, one could say that Formula Atlantic peaked in the highly contested **1974** season, when two championships took place, the Southern Organs and the John Player, while Formula 3 lingered with almost club status. Among the drivers who raced that season were **Tony Brise, Alan Jones, John Nicholson, David Morgan, Jim Crawford, Ray Mallock, Ted Wentz**. Some of the same drivers, plus **Gunnar Nilsson**, also contested the **1975** championship but it soon became clear that there was not enough room for strong Formula 3 and Formula Atlantic championships in England. As Formula 3 was widely adopted as a FIA category in Europe, it regained its strength back in **1975**, to Atlantic's detriment. In **1976** Atlantics were accepted as entrants in the newly created Shellsport Group 8 Championship, while a smaller Indylantic championship was held. There would be no British Formula Atlantic championship in **1977** and **1978** and in **1979** it resurfaced, a much weaker category, with unknown drivers. Overseas, the category prospered, although adapted and renamed.

FORMULA FORD

Formula Ford was created in **1967**, certainly taking a cue from Formula Vee, the **VW** powered single seater category. It was meant to be a low cost, fun way for budding racing drivers to learn how to drive a race car competitively, yet faster than the Vees, get mileage and exposure. The cars were easy to engineer, and the short races were sometimes frightfully competitive. By **1970**, Formula Ford had already produced the likes of **Emerson Fittipaldi** and **Tim Schenken**, F1 drivers who were in Formula Ford just one or two seasons back. It was mostly during the 70s that Formula Ford spread all over the world: a European, an American and a South African championship, besides the British championships, already existed when the new decade started. And one by one, countries adopted the formula. Canada, Australia, Portugal, Denmark, Holland and Italy did in **1970**, Brazil, Austria and New Zealand in **1971**, Sweden and Germany in **1973**, Switzerland in **1979** Mexico and Venezuela also adopted the category. One can say that Formula Ford did become a world phenomenon in the 70s. The pattern that emerged was that drivers would go from karting to Formula Ford and then progress to higher categories. The British championships were so prestigious that drivers from different countries contested the championship, to learn the circuits in preparation for Formula 3. Some of these drivers were used to race cars with three times the power of Formula Fords in their countries but that did not matter. There were so many FF races in England alone that a foreign driver could do in a single season of Formula Ford more races than he did in his country, in his entire career.

The Formula Ford Festival, held in England since **1972**, has been the category's most prestigious event of the calendar and drivers from several countries entered the race every year.

Not all Formula Fords shared the same regulation, or even had truly **Ford** engines. Brazilian Formula **Ford**, for example, used the engine from the **Ford** Corcel. This **Ford** car was in fact **Willys-Overland's** "Project M", which **Ford** inherited when it bought the company in 1966. And the Project M's engine was in fact a **Renault** engine, rather than **Ford**.

Noteworthy manufacturers during the 70s have been **Van Diemen, Royale, Lola, Ray, Merlyn, Macon, Elden, Ray, Titan, Lotus, Brabham, Palliser, Talon, Crossle, March, Hustler, MacNamara, Autocraft, Bino, Avallone, Polar, Heve, Elfin, Birrana, Image, Cougar, Hawke, Bowin, Andrew, Wren, Mawer, Streaker, Elwyn, Micron, Dulon, Alexis, Nike, Tiga, PRS, Sark, Delta, Pulsar, Ferret, Xpit, GRM, Chinook, Gatorades, Magnum, Phoenix, Winkelmann.** Even Dan Gurney's **Eagle**, best known for Formula 1 and USAC racers, attempted to crack the Formula Ford market in **1977**. A Formula Ford called "**El Gran Caribe**" was built and raced in Venezuela. In terms of numbers, **Van Diemen** and **Lola** were the highest producers and exporters.

Lively Formula Ford action at Zandvoort, 1975. Among the lot, Huub Rothengatter in a Royale RP1. (Photo Rob Petersen collection)

Surprisingly, three of the Dutch FF series champions managed to make to Formula 1: **Boy Hayje, Roelof Wunderink** and **Michael Bleekemolen**. In fact the latter first attempted to race in F1 one year after winning the Dutch Formula Ford crown! Other notable 70s F-Ford champions who made it to Formula 1, besides those already mentioned, were **Tony Brise, Derek Warwick, Alex Ribeiro, Chico Serra, David Kennedy, Ken Acheson, Geoff Lees.**

FORMULA VEE/FORMULA SUPER VEE

Formula Vee was invented before Formula Ford, so it created the concept of a single-seater category powered exclusively by one manufacturer. **Volkswagen** engines were cheap, easy to work with and plentiful. Perfect for an entry level category for both amateurs and budding professionals. In their 1.2 and 1.3 iterations they were not extremely fast but that was the point. Soon Formula Vee became popular all over the world, adopted in countries such as USA, Canada,

Germany, Britain, Sweden, Norway, Finland, Denmark, Brazil, Ireland, Portugal, Peru, South Africa, Venezuela, Rhodesia, Kenya, etc.

With the advent of Formula Ford enthusiasm for Formula Vee slowed down somewhat but the category lingered on, in certain cases, to this day. **Volkswagen** in the 60s was somehow averse to racing but by the early seventies, management began to see it with different eyes. Thus Formula Super Vee was created, cars equipped with 1.6 engines, much faster, with aerodynamic appendages and greater appeal. The first championships were held in Europe and the United States, then championships followed in Germany, Scandinavia, Britain, Brazil, Yugoslavia. In Brazil's case it was the top single seater category, often referred as "The Brazilian Formula 1". **Volkswagen** often invested a reasonable amount on promotion, prize funds (the winner of the first European Super Vee got a US$2,000 check, while Atlantic's first champion that same year did not get a tenth of that). In the United States an Oval only Super Vee championship was established in **1977**, to groom drivers for Indy work, a precursor of present-day Indy Lights. **Emerson Fittipaldi**'s first single seater experience was in Formula Vee (he was Brazilian champion in **1967**) and was **Niki Lauda's**. **Carlos Pace** also raced and won in the category in the 60s. **Keke Rosberg**'s first steps in racing were in Formula Vee in his native Finland, soon became a Super Vee star, moving up to Formula 2. **Nelson Piquet** was Brazilian Super Vee (then called Formula VW 1600) in **1976**. Lots of other worthy 70s drivers did some of their early racing in either Formula Vees or Super Vees or both: **Jochen Mass, Manfred Schurti, Helmut Koinigg, Tom Pryce, Harald Ertl, Chico Serra, Freddy Kotulinsky, Jo Gartner, Mikko Kozarowitsky, Tom Gloy, Howdy Holmes, Arie Luyendyk, Geoff Brabham, Bertil Roos, Elliott Forbes-Robinson, Kenneth Persson, Ingo Hoffmann, Helmut Bross, Mac Surer, Helmut Marko, Klaus Niedzwiedz.**

The South African built GJO Vee in the 1971 South African Grand Prix support race. (Photo by Russell Whitworth)

Several manufacturers built Super Vees and Vees in the seventies, in several countries, including Germany, Sweden, Australia, Belgium, Portugal, Brazil, South Africa, Finland, Austria, United States, England, etc: **Lynn, Supernova, Zink, Tui, Zettler, Lola, Elden, March, Kaimann, Royale, Dynamotive, Lynx, Ralt, March, Austro, Mahag, Karringer, Mutil, Citation, Autodynamics, Beach, Fuchs, Veemax, Avallone, Polar, Heve, Muller, Newcar, Manta, Govesa, Pateco, Apal, Olympic, DRM, PRT, Malordy, Dahmcar, Zagk-Hansen, Schlesser, McNamara, Cianciaruso, Ventura, Pati, Nortii, RSV, Mateju, Hansen, Jukon,**

BM, Rohm, Blomman, GMS, FinVau, Formcar, Celi, Maco, Feca, Sebring, Oli, Squalus(Esqualus), Marques, Rio, Fitti, NCM, Marazzi, Dee Vee Ation, Smitifield, Stafford, Monaco, Ideal, Luisvagen, Gian, Alba, Passalaqua, Aranae, Nicke, Albatroz, Protos, Gason, Lapi, Enricone, JR, Era 1, Guichco, Taipan, Kvanti, SAKNAS, Swebe, Testudo, Minelli, Nillti, Incas, TP-01, Clark, Exford, Ducret, VF, Quick, Legwood, PSR, Strider, Badger, Altona, Franklyn, Kellison, GJo, among hundreds of others. If you are interested in racing car constructors of the 70s, I suggest you look for my other book on the subject, **Racing Car Constructors of the 70s**, that covers many Formula Vees, including the marques above.

An unidentified Formula Vee racer in Peru (unknown author)

George Kronegard driving a Super Vee T252 Lola. Photo by Lola Heritage.

OTHER SINGLE SEATER SERIES

A few other single seater series were run in different countries.

Formula 1430 was established in Spain in **1971** and eventually the name was changed to Formula SEAT. The Spanish company **Selex** provided most cars and Formula 1800 was established later on the decade.

The Cordoba was built for Formula 1430 work in Spain.

In Argentina, in addition to Argentine Formula 1 and Formula 2, there was Formula 4, basically **FIAT** engined single seaters. There were also regional single seater series, Formula Entrerriana and Limitada Santafesina, for example.

As for Formula 4 the name appeared in many countries besides Argentina, such as Morocco, Eastern Block, in addition to Britain but in a few places it had nothing to do with the original Formula 4 concept that arose in Italy in the mid 60s. Back then cars were single seaters equipped with motorcycle engines and the formula was adopted in a few countries, as an inexpensive entry level category. So F4 in Italy and Britain were pretty much the same thing circa 1966 but starting in 1970, the focus of this book, there was no more F4 by name in Italy, which adopted a Formula K 250, really Tecno go-karts with bodies and engines of 250 cc. These sometimes contested hill climbs with cars with much larger engines. As for Britain, small car engines, such as Imp and Ford were adopted in the first years of the decade but regulations were soon changed and 1 liter, former F-3 engines were adopted. The Eastern Block's F-4 was closer to the original concept and Argentina used small FIAT engines. Japan had its Formula Junior 360 category in 1970 but it used Honda and Subaru microcar engines. So it is borderline impossible to talk about Formula 4 in global terms.

France had Formula France in **1970**, single seaters with 1.3 Renault engine. Among the drivers racing that season were **Laffite, Lafosse, Cudini, Coulon, Haran, Ethuin, Serpaggi, Leclere**, while manufacturers included **Grac, Pygmee, Tecno, Martini, Arpa** and **Jefa**. The category would morph into Formula Renault. There was also Formule Bleue, single seaters equipped with 1-liter Citroen engines which operated until **1975**.

Italy had Formula Italia as of **1972** and it was a popular entry level category used by several drivers such as **Giacomelli, Patrese** and **Brancatelli** to begin their careers. Other Italian single seater categories were Formula Monza, for cars equipped with FIAT 500 cc engines and Formula 850, for cars with 850 cc engines. A huge number of constructors built cars for the last two categories.

Brazil had a failed attempt at a specific Brazilian single seater category, the patriotically named Formula Brasil. There was much discussion as to what would constitute this category, some suggesting even Corvette engined formula cars, FNM and Opala engined racers, in the end the few cars that showed up were former formula Vee cars equipped with 1.6 **VW** engines.

The Iron Curtain countries at first had Formula 1, 2, 3 and 4, ranging from most powerful to least powerful. By the end of the decade, it became a two-tier system, Formula Easter and Formula Junior. The Czechs raced European regulation Formula 3s in **1970** and the East Germans also had a Formula 3 category, mostly locally produced **Wartburg** engined cars. Later on, Formula **Skoda** was established in Czechoslovakia. While most cars were produced in Estonia (part of the Soviet Union at the time), single seaters were also produced in Poland, Eastern Germany and Czechoslovakia.

Japan's Formula 2000 was basically Formula 2 with a different name. Formula Pacific was Formula Atlantic with a different name. The latter basically copied the North American Formula B regulations and used Formula 2 cars. There was also a Japanese single seater category for cars with 500 cc engines.

A number of special single seater with large engines raced in British hill climbs and sprints. Britain was also known for many club level Formula Libre events during the course of the year. It should also be noted that a few British categories with "Formula" in the name were not single seater categories at all, such as Formula 750 (750 Formula), Formula 1300 and Formula F100.

Some might take exception to calling American Midget and Sprint cars single seaters but that is exactly what they are. Races for these cars were run by the dozens every week during the summer months in the USA and sprint cars were used in the few dirt races left in the 1970 USAC calendar. Midgets were also raced in other countries, such as Argentina and Guyana. Formula C was a U.S. category with engine size limited to 1.1 liters, run at SCCA amateur events, later replaced by the name Formula Continental.

TOURING CARS

It is almost obvious that all countries covered by this book had one type or another of touring car (saloon) category or races. Touring cars are the most basic form of race car one can get, ranging from cars with very basic to no preparation, to highly modified stocks and Group 5 racers. Here are some curiosities about touring car racing in the 70s:
- Although karting is almost exclusively the entry level racing category for youngsters, who now start in their pre-teen years, many 70s drivers still began their racing careers driving some type of touring car in local circuit events and hill climbs. There were hundreds, perhaps thousands of these events, year in and out, featuring cars ranging from 500 cc **FIAT**s to 7-liter **Plymouth** Hemicudas.

This is how an average touring car field of the early 70s looked: Alfa Romeos, Ford Escorts, Mini Coopers, BMWs, plus FIAT Abarths. Photo by Paul Rutten.

- Truly international or major touring car championships were few, so most championships were country specific, others regional in character.
- A vast range of cars have raced during the decade, including some makes which are no longer around. Worldwide, **Ford** and **BMW** tended to rule, for their cars were used by winning drivers in many countries, in all continents. **Ford** used several models to achieve this success, including the Capri, Escort, Falcon, Maverick, Mustang, Thunderbird, Torino. **BMW**s were mostly 3.0 CSL, 3.5 CSL, 320, 1600, 2002. **Alfa Romeo** and **Chevrolet** also won races in many countries.
- A notable exception to **Ford** and **BMW** dominance was the Soviet Union, where only Soviet or Iron Curtain-made touring cars were allowed to race.
- Some Soviet cars did race in Western Europe, though, **Tony Lanfranchi's Moskvich** even winning 3 minor saloon car titles in England.
- In certain countries with a varied motoring culture, touring car categories were considered the main category in the country, the notable cases being the USA (NASCAR) and Argentina (Turismo de Carretera). These, along with Formula 1 were (and still are) the longest running racing championships of the world.
- Certain car makes were mostly used regionally: **Volvos** were rarely raced elsewhere, besides Scandinavian countries; **Holdens** raced almost exclusively in Australia and New Zealand; **Skodas** were widely used in Czechoslovakia and Iron Curtain countries. **Peugeot**'s policy during the decade was to discourage the use of **Peugeot**s in circuit racing but the car was widely and successfully used in Argentina's Turismo Nacional category, where it often beat larger **FIAT**s and used in neighboring Uruguay to great effect.
- **VW** Beetles were surprisingly used in racing in several countries: Brazil's Division 3 Beetles were very fast and often beat the 4.1 liter **Chevrolet** Opalas; Beetles (**VW** 1302) often showed up in the **Nürburgring** rounds of the ETCC; Beetles were widely used in racing in Mexico and elsewhere in Latin and South America; VWs were also used in ice and circuit racing in Scandinavia and even raced in the under 2 liter division of the Trans Am.
- Japanese makers were rare in the beginning of the decade, except in Asia and Central America but by the end of the 70s they showed in greater numbers in most

countries. Other rarer Asian makes used in racing during the decade were **Suzuki** and **Hyundai** but they raced in surprising places such as the early **Macau** events and **El Salvador**.
- Many touring car races included several categories, with great speed differential between larger and smaller capacity cars and they always featured in hill-climbs, although they rarely won overall, losing out to single seaters, GTs and prototypes.
- Another notable development was the appearance of many one make series in several countries, a way to build a sporting image without losing to competitors. Among manufacturers running such championships during the decade were **Ford, Chevrolet, Volvo, BMW, FIAT, Alfa Romeo, Renault, VW, Mini**.
- The **NSU** Prinz, which production was discontinued in **1972**, continued to be raced in touring car events until the end of the decade. **DKW**s, which stopped being manufactured in **1967**, were still being raced well into the 70s in a variety of places.
- The Brazilian **Aero Willys** was rarely used car in racing, basically using a similar platform as the Jeep. Yet, one such car won its division in a local race in Brazil, in **1971**, driven by **Sady Abe**.
- **Trabants** were often raced in the Iron Curtain countries and won races.
- Touring cars also participated as a different class in many sports cars events, including the 24 Hours of **Le Mans and** even Formula Libre events.

NASCAR

Like Formula Indy, NASCAR was one of the categories that went through one of the most dramatic changes in the 70s. Unlike the single-seater championship, though, the major change took place very early in the decade, rather than later. **1971** was the last year of the old, romantic NASCAR, which already included top speedways such as **Daytona** and **Talladega** but also some very small-town dirt mile tracks. This resulted in a substantial reduction of races, from upwards of 50 to about 30, a major paradigm shift because it allowed a greater number of drivers to do the full schedule, necessary to win the championship. Not meaning to belittle **Richard Petty**'s achievements but one of the reasons why he amassed so many wins was the fact that he was one of the few top drivers to consistently run full schedules. As a result, in the first two years of the decade King **Richard** totaled no less than 39 wins!

Bobby Allison was one of NASCAR's stars in the 70s. Photo by Rob Neuzel.

This also meant that the days of drivers such as **James Hylton, Cecil Gordon, Jabe Thomas, Elmo Langley** who usually finished high up in the championship tables by running full schedules and getting intermediate positions, rarely winning, were numbered. In fact, by **1974**, **Cecil** was 9th and **Hylton** 11th, a far cry from the top 4 positions they were used to getting. Some drivers, like **David Pearson**, were never fond of full schedules even when it was reduced to 30. **Pearson** enjoyed the superspeedways, where money was better anyhow: in **1976** he won 10 times out of 22 starts, more races than champion **Yarborough**.

Like USAC, NASCAR relied on a core group of top racers, who were crowd pleasers, had legions of loving fans and were frequent winners: in addition to **Petty** and **Pearson, Cale Yarborough, Benny Parsons, Buddy Baker**, the brothers **Donnie** and **Bobby Allison, Dave Marcis, Leroy Yarbrough, Bobby Isaac** in the first years and later on, new stars like **Darrel Waltrip, Neil Bonnet** and very promising **Dale Earnhardt, Terry Labonte** and **Ricky Rudd** were the bread and butter of the championship.

The more limited schedule allowed NASCAR to negotiate a full TV contract, which in turn, allowed teams and drivers to sign major sponsorship deals. Whereas some races were seen only by the crowd on hand early on the decade, with TV millions of spectators were reached every week. **Daytona** and other bigger races were often shown on TV (many as condensed broadcasts, that is) but it was during the late 70s that NASCAR was on the path to changing the very definition of car racing in the USA: to millions car racing became NASCAR, to the detriment most of Formula Indy.

Cale Yarborough was a major NASCAR ace of the late 70s.

TV exposure also helped tracks offer better pay and better pay meant full grids: some of the smaller tracks would attract a little over 20 drivers still at mid-decade, plus many local drivers of questionable pedigree, compared to the recent 40-plus pros that race in the Cup. Interesting NASCAR financial issues are further discussed in the section Money.

Despite a somewhat unfair reputation as a closed club of mostly Southern drivers, a variety of foreigners tried NASCAR in the 70s: **Pedro Rodriguez, Rolf Stommelen, Vic Elford, Claude-Ballot-Lena, Jackie Oliver, David Hobbs** and even female drivers **Lella Lombardi** and **Christine Beckers**. Canadian **Earl Ross** also won a race during the decade. Additionally, major USAC stars such as **A.J.Foyt, Gordon Johncock, Johnny Rutherford, Gary Bettenhausen, Roger McCluskey, Wally Dallenbach, Bobby Unser, Tom Sneva, Salt Walther, Jim McElreath, Dan Gurney** had a few starts, while drivers specialized in other disciplines, such as **Al Holbert, George Follmer, Peter Gregg, Gene Felton, Elliot Forbes-Robinson, Lothar Motschenbacher, Sam Posey** and **Mark Donohue** also participated. The latter, in fact, won a race in a rare **AMC** Javelin in

1973. American female driver **Janet Guthrie** also did quite a few races in the second half of the decade, led a race and was the first woman to drive in the **Daytona** 500.

Surprisingly NASCAR was not as reticent as USAC against using road courses, in fact the **Riverside** races were very popular, the track used twice a year for the entire decade.

As for cars, only American ones competed. The most consistent winner was **Chevrolet,** while **Dodge** and **Plymouth**, both **Chrysler** products (most wins achieved a certain Mr. **Petty**) did very well until **1977**. **David Pearson** was the standard bearer for **Mercury**, a **Ford** product, but **Ford** branded cars did surprisingly badly during the decade, while the make won hundreds of races in all corners of the world.

In addition to the Winston Cup, the official name of the championship as of **1971** in deference to sponsor Winston, a cigarette maker, NASCAR also ran NASCAR West, stock car races run in West Coast tracks and sanctioned more than one hundred championships throughout the country, quite a herculean task.

Race winners, 1970-1979, drivers
1. Richard Petty, 87
2. Cale Yarborough, 52
3. David Pearson, 47
4. Bobby Allison, 41
5. Darrel Waltrip, 22
6. Bobby Isaac, 16
7. Buddy Baker, 15
8. Benny Parsons, 14
9. Donnie Allison, 8
10. Neil Bonnet, A.J. Foyt, 5
11. Dave Marcis, Pete Hamilton, 4
12. Charlie Glotzbach, 3
13. James Hylton, Ray Elder 2
14. Dick Brooks, Earl Ross, Lennie Pond, Dale Earnhardt, Leroy Yarbrough, Mark Donohue, 1

Race winners, 1970-1979, Cars
1. Chevrolet, 100
2. Dodge, 73
3. Mercury, 62
4. Plymouth, 52
5. Ford, 25
6. Oldsmobile, 16
7. AMC, 5

TOP TEN IN NASCAR'S GRAND NATIONAL/WINSTON CUP FINAL STANDINGS DURING THE DECADE
(Richard Petty was the only driver who placed in the top 10 in all seasons)

	70	71	72	73	74	75	76	77	78	79
BEN ARNOLD			10							
BENNY PARSONS	8		5	1	5	4	3	3	4	5
BILL CHAMPION		7								

Driver										
BOBBY ALLISON	2	4	2	7	4		4	8	2	3
BOBBY ISAAC	1									
BUDDY ARRINGTON									9	
BUDDY BAKER					6	7		7	5	
CALE YARBOROUGH				2	2	9	1	1	1	4
CECIL GORDON		3	4	3	9	6		10		
DALE EARNHARDT										7
DARREL WALTRIP						7	8	4	3	2
DAVE MARCIS	9				6	2	6		5	
DAVID PEARSON					3		9			
DAVID SISCO					10					
DEAN DALTON			9							
DICK BROOKS						10	10	6	8	
EARL ROSS					8					
ELMO LANGLEY	6	5	7	9		8				
FRANK WARREN	10	8								
J.D. MCDUFFIE			9		10					
JABE THOMAS	7	6								
JAMES HYLTON	3	2	3	4		3		7		
JOEL MILIKAN										6
JOHN SEARS			8							
LENNIE POND							5		7	
NEIL CASTLES	5									
RICHARD CHILDRESS						5		9	10	8
RICHARD PETTY	4	1	1	5	1	1	2	2	6	1
RICK RUDD										9
TERRY LABONTE										10
WALTER BALLARD		10	6	8						

Most races led
1970, Bobby Isaac, 35
1971, Richard Petty, 41
1972, Bobby Allison/Richard Petty, 30
1973, Cale Yarborough, 21
1974, Cale Yarborough, 26
1975, Richard Petty, 26
1976, Cale Yarborough, 28
1977, Cale Yarborough, 28
1978, Cale Yarborough, 28
1979, Darrel Waltrip, 26

Most laps led
1970, Richard Petty, 5,007
1971, Richard Petty, 4,932
1972, Bobby Allison, 4,343
1973, Cale Yarborough, 3,167
1974, Cale Yarborough, 3,530
1975, Richard Petty, 3,198
1976, Cale Yarborough, 3,771
1977, Cale Yarborough, 3,218
1978, Cale Yarborough, 3,587
1979, Darrel Waltrip, 2,218

The following drivers led at least one lap in the NASCAR main division during 1970-1979:

Bobby Isaac, Richard Petty, Bobby Allison, Charlie Glotzbach, Cale Yarborough, LeeRoy Yarbrough, Buddy Baker, David Pearson, Donnie Allison, Pete Hamilton, James Hylton, Dick Brooks, Benny Parsons, Neil Castles, Johnny Halford, Friday Hassler, Ron Keselowski, Dave Marcis, John Sears, Dr. Don Tarr, Jim Vandiver, Frank Warren, Fred Lorenzen, Bill Dennis, Elmo Langley, J.D. McDuffie, G.C. Spencer, Coo Coo Marlin, Joe Frasson, Bill Dennis, Hershell McGriff, Darrel Waltrip, Lennie Pond, David Sisco, Walter Ballard, Richard Childress, Earl Ross, A.J. Foyt, Dan Doughty, George Follmer, Gary Bettenhausen, Bob Burcham, Dean Dalton, Richie Panch, Jackie Rogers, Bruce Hill, Ray Elder, Henley Gray, Ed Negre, Terry Bivins, Neil Bonnett, Chuck Bown, Jimmy Means, Terry Ryan, Sam Sommers, Janet Guthrie, Skip Manning, Frank Warren, Ricky Rudd, Jimmy Insolo, Tighe Scott, Jim Thirkelle, D.K. Ulrich, Joe Milikan, Harry Gant, Terry Labonte, Bill Elliott, Grant Adcox, John Anedrson, Buddy Arrington, Al Holbert, Ronnie Thomas.

Pole positions

It is no secret to the NASCAR follower that pole positions mean less in NASCAR than in most other racing disciplines. Thus, it is not that surprising that the two winningest drivers of the decade, Petty and Yarborough, are not the top two pole winners. In fact, Petty won more than twice the number of poles he got during the decade. It is also not surprising that some pole winners, like **Friday Hassler** and **Larry Baumel**, are rather unknown even to die-hard NASCAR fans.

1. David Pearson, 56
2. Bobby Allison, 44
3. Richard Petty, 41
4. Cale Yarborough, 30
5. Bobby Isaac, 27
7. Buddy Baker, 23
8. Darrel Waltrip, 16
9. Dave Marcis, Neil Bonnett and Donnie Allison, 13
10. Benny Parsons, 12
11. A.J. Foyt, 9
12. Charlie Glotzbach, 8
13. Lennie Pond, 5
14. Dale Earnhardt, 4
15. Pete Hamilton, 3
16. James Hylton, Fred Lorenzen, Friday Hassler, Leroy Yarbrough 2
17. John Sears, Larry Baumel, Bill Dennis, George Follmer, Sam Sommers, J.D. McDuffie, Joe Milikan, Harry Gant, Dan Gurney, Gordon Johncock, Ramo Stott, 1

Some 70s NASCAR curiosities:
- 22 different drivers won NASCAR's top tier races in the 70s. Only one of them was foreign, Canadian **Earl Ross**.
- Consider that 29 drivers won Formula 1 races in the 70s (from roughly half the number of NASCAR races), you reach the conclusion that contrary to conventional wisdom, it was easier to win a Formula 1 race in the 70s than a NASCAR one!
- 469 drivers started at least one NASCAR Cup race in the 70s.
- 31 different drivers scored poles.
- 31 drivers also placed in the Championship Top 10 sometime during the decade
- Only **David Pearson** managed to score poles in all 10 seasons.
- 72 drivers managed to lead a NASCAR race during the decade, one of them a female, **Janet Guthrie**. This shows how much easier it is to lead a NASCAR race than winning it.

- **Richard Petty** took part in 326 races, won 87, (ratio of 3.7)
- **Cale Yarborough** took part in 245 races and won 52 (a ratio of 4.7). Cale was busy trying to make it as an Indycar driver during the 1971 and 1972 seasons and had a total of 9 NASCAR starts in those two seasons.
- **David Pearson** took part in only 168 races and won 47. His ratio (3.5) is actually better than **Petty**'s. His pole winning ratio is even better, a neat and even 3, in other words, he scored pole for every three races he started.
- **Yarborough** led the most laps in five seasons, to **Petty**'s three.

EUROPEAN TOURING CAR CHAMPIONSHIP

Granted that for most people outside Europe this championship had very little relevance, for as the name says, all races were run in Europe and most participants were European, after all. Looking at the results, a lot of the names were utterly unknown (including top winner **Umberto Grano**), except to the most acute racing observer. Not that many brands won overall and **BMW** tended to dominate over the course of the decade. That is all true, up to a certain extent. For one thing, given that touring cars are the most basic form of car racing, this championship allowed drivers of more humble dispositions and pedigrees, from several countries, to tell their grandchildren "I raced against **Niki Lauda, Jackie Stewart, Jochen Mass, Hans Stuck, Chris Amon...**", for until **1977** big names participated in ETCC races. Local drivers from Czechoslovakia, Spain, Portugal were able to race the cars in which they competed in their countries. Both the **Ford** Capri and **BMW** 3.0 CSL were developed in this championship and were used in racing worldwide, literally in all continents. This was also the only FIA circuit championship to have rounds in Iron Curtain countries, **Budapest** (Hungary) in **1970** and **Brno** (Czechoslovakia) in many editions. Additionally, the ETCC was the place where **Mercedes-Benz** made its first inroads back into circuit racing, in **1971** then **1978**, not an irrelevant thing, considering what it has done since then. Many brands raced in the championship, which included several classes as most touring car races did back on the day.

After being beaten by **BMW** in **1968** and **1969**, **Alfa Romeo** had a proper challenger for **1970**, in the form of the 2.0 Liter **Alfa Romeo** GTAm. On the driving strength, Autodelta had hired Dutchman **Toine Hezemans**, who won the very first race of the season, at **Monza**. The main challengers that day were **Glemser** and **Mazet** in a **Capri**, **Marko** and **Soler-Roig** in a **BMW** 2800 CS and also **Alfa** teammates **Spartaco Dini** and **Carlo Facetti**. There were rumors of a **Mercedes** comeback but that did not happen in **Monza** or elsewhere during the season. At **Salzburgring Soler-Roig** managed to beat **Hezemans**, followed by **Dini, Krammer** and **Christine Beckers,** while **Helmut Marko** won the smaller division in a **BMW** 1600. The next round turned out to be the only major car race held in Hungary during the decade, with the participation of Westerners. This **Budapest** round was also won by **Hezemans**, followed by **Glemser** in the Capri, then **Dini, Nanni Galli** and **Beckers** in the GTAms. There were no Hungarian drivers, but a few Czechs turned up in smaller **Alfas** and **Skoda**. **Hezemans** also won the **Brno** round, beating the **BMW** 2800 CS of **Kelleners** and **Huber**. There were eight Czech entries, the best a 1.3 **Alfa** that finished in 11th. In the Tourist Trophy, Australian **Brian Muir** won both heats on his Camaro but **Hezemans** managed to finish second, followed by **Gardner (Mustang), Galli, Glemser and Picchi**. 93 cars started the 6 Hours of **Nürburgring** and despite the presence of larger engine cars, including Capris, Opels, Mustangs, **Alfa Romeo** once more prevailed, this time driven by **De Adamich/Picchi**, followed by two other GTAMs, **Hessel/Schuller** and **Zecolli/Beckers**. A team of **Mazda** M10A coupe's finished 4-5-6, the best of the lot driven by **Yoshimi Katayama** and **Yves Deprez**, but the **BMW** 2800 CS of **Quester/Soler-Roig** and **Huber/Kelleners** did not start because of tire problems. Compensating for the **Nürburgring** fiasco, **Huber/Kelleners** won the 24 Hours of **Spa** for **BMW**, followed by **Pinto/Berger** and **Facetti/Zeccoli** in **Alfa GTAms**. A **Mazda** also finished an excellent 5th. **At Zandvoort**, championship leader **Hezemans** did not do well in front of his home crowd. He had pole but an accident took him out of the race, which was won by **Picchi**, followed by **Facetti** and **Furtmayer**, the latter driving a **BMW**. Making matters worse, Division 1 driver **Johann Abt** had overtaken **Hezemans** in points, 40 to 39. So the championship would be decided at **Jarama**. Autodelta tried to make **Abt**'s life more difficult hiring fast **Abarth** drivers to deal with him but in the end, it was unnecessary – **Abt** retired. **Hezemans** won the race and the championship in a 1-2-3-4 **Alfa** festival (**Picchi, De Bagration** and **Zeccoli/Beckers** followed the Dutchman). The best **BMW** was **Marko/Soler-Roig**, in 5th.

Toine Hezemans won the 1970 title in an Alfa Romeo (Photo Rob Petersen collection)

Autodelta had won the **1970** championship but the 2.0 Liter **Alfa Romeo** GTAm was clearly outclassed in **1971**, vis-à-vis the more powerful and better developed **Ford** Capri and **BMW** 2800 CS. **Toine Hezemans** did squeeze another overall win out of the car at **Monza**, the season's first race, beating **Quester/Basche** in the larger engined **BMW**. However, the season would belong to **Ford** Cologne and **Dieter Glemser**. **Ford** would race both Capris and Escorts during the season and **Glemser** started winning in the second round at **Salzburgring**, racing solo. A number of other drivers supported **Glemser**'s efforts at **Ford** that season: **Helmut Marko, Francois Mazet, Alex-Soler-Roig, John Fitzpatrick but** the German was on a class of his own: he won at **Brno** solo, shared the win at **Nürburgring** with **Marko**, won at **Spa, Paul Ricard** and **Jarama** with **Soler-Roig**. The best **BMW** could do was win at **Zandvoort**, driven by **Dieter Quester**. The **Paul Ricard** race offered a nice purse, thus attracting the likes of former world champions **Graham Hill** and **John Surtees**, who won the first heat in a **Ford** UK Capri, plus **Rolf Stommelen** and **Gerry Birrel** (who won the second heat), **Gijs Van Lennep**, **Gerard Larrousse, Rauno Aaltonen** and others. **Mercedes-Benz** 300 SEL 6.3 cars were fielded by AMG at **Spa** and **Paul Ricard**, which the factory insisted was purely a privateer affair. At the Belgian race the **Mercedes** finished second with

Schickentanz-Heyer, while the Merc's performance was not very good in France. **Hezemans** won the 2-liter class for **Alfa Romeo**, which also won the 1.3-liter class with **Picchi**. In the 2-liter class **Alfa** had to beat the fast Escort of **Fitzpatrick**. In addition to the above-mentioned drivers, other prominent participants during the course of the season were **Teddy Pilette, Helmut Kelleners, Nino Vacarellla, Jochen Mass, Niki Lauda, Jean Xhenceval, Christine Beckers, Umberto Grano, Liane Engemann, Carlo Facetti, Andrea de Adamich, Alain Peltier, Henri Pescarolo, Hans Stuck, Willi Kauhsen.**

Dieter Glemser's Ford Capri at Zandvoort, 1971 (Photo Rob Petersen collection)

1972 was a continuation of the previous season: **Ford** domination. In **Monza**, the traditional first round of the championship, the winners were **Jochen Mass** and **Gerard Larrousse** in a works Capri, followed by Belgians **Peltier** and **Xhenceval** in a **BMW** 2800. The top **Alfa Romeo, Facetti/Hezemans**, came in fifth place. At **Salzburgring**, there were two races, one for Division 1(lower capacity cars), won by **Carlo Facetti**, in a 1.3 **Alfa** GTA, while the race for Divisions 2 and 3 was won by **Dieter Glemser**, in a Capri, followed by **Stuck** (in a **Ford**), **Fitzpatrick** in the first **BMW**, two more **BMWs, Pankl** and **Heyer**. Drivers ran solo. It is interesting noting that while **Stuck** ran in a **Ford** that season, he would be associated with **BMW** pretty much for the rest of the decade. As for **Heyer**, the driver that became almost synonymous with **Ford**, was racing for **BMW** in **1972**. The next round took place at **Brno and** again, there were two races, for Division 1, won by **Gianluigi Picchi** in an **Alfa** and Divisions 2 and 3 won by **Glemser** in the Capri, followed by **Fitzpatrick**. At the **Nürburgring** 6 Hours, cars were again shared by crews. This was **BMW**'s first win of the season, **Hans Heyer/Rolf Stommelen** and **John Fitzpatrick** doing the honors. They were followed by **Mass/Larrousse** in the **Ford**. At the 24 Hours of **Spa, Ford** prevailed once more. The winners this time were **Jochen Mass** and **Hans Stuck**, followed by two other **Fords, Birrell/Bourgoignie** and **Glemser/Soler-Roig. Fitzpatrick** was again the best **BMW**, sharing the car with **Peltier** and **Ethuin. Ford** continued its dominance at **Zandvoort,** this time the winning crew comprising **Glemser/Soler-Roig/Mass**. The best **BMW** was driven

420

by **Niki Lauda/Gerold Pankl/Toine Hezemans**, in third. At **Paul Ricard**, the novelty was **Jackie Stewart** sharing a **Ford** Capri with his **Tyrrell** teammate **Cevert**. They came in second, being beaten by **Brian Muir** and **John Miles**. At **Silverstone, Mass** shared the winning Capri with **Glemser** and **Hezemans** came in second, this time driving a **Ford**. Some unusual entries were the 5th placed **Camaro** of **Thomas/Sanger** and **Birrane's Mustang**, which finished 7th. By then **Mass** had clinched the championship but he would still win another race, the **Jarama** 4 hours, sharing the car with **Soler-Roig** and **Larrousse**. **Ford** had soundly beaten **BMW** in the top Division but **Alfa Romeo** won the Constructors Cup, having won all rounds of Division 1.

1973 was without doubt the best ETCC season of the 70s. **BMW** obviously intended to win the championship again, so in addition to works cars, semi-works entries were ran by Alpina and Schnitzer year long. **Ford** underestimated the opposition and ran two to three Capris all season. The **Ford** team argued that the **BMW** 3.0 CSL's wing was an illegal aerodynamic appendage, but the Bavarian manufacturer had complied with homologation regulations. Truth be told that the **Ford** Capri was a difficult car to drive, while the **BMW** 3.0 CSL was easier. Although **Ford** managed to even field a car for **Jackie Stewart** and **Emerson Fittipaldi** at the **Nürburgring**, while the Scot also ran elsewhere, **BMW** had a very strong works team, with **Chris Amon, Hans Stuck, Dieter Quester, Toine Hezemans, Brian Muir**. Other **BMW** drivers during the season **were Jacky Ickx, Vittorio Brambilla, Henri Pescarolo, Niki Lauda, James Hunt, Bob Wollek, Jean-Pierre Jaussaud, Derek Bell and Harald Ertl**. **Ford**'s main drivers were **Mass, Glemser, Fitzpatrick, Larrousse**. In **Monza**, the **BMW** 3.0 CSL beat the Capri right off the bat, **Lauda** and **Muir** finishing first followed by **Mass** and **Scheckter**, in a **Ford**. **Stewart** drove with **Glemser** in this occasion and came in 10th. **Ford** managed to turn the tables around in the next two rounds, winning at the **Salzburgring** (**Glemser** and **Fitzpatrick**) and **Mantorp Park** (**Mass** and **Glemser**). By then, **BMW** was already using more powerful 3.3 and 3.4 liter engines, while the Capris had 3.0 liter motors. The best **BMW** in **Austria** was **Hezemans/Muir** (2nd), followed by **Brambilla/Jaussaud** (**BMW**). In **Mantorp**, **Hezemans** and **Muir** also came in 2nd, followed by locals **Boo Brasta** and **Bo Ljungfeldt**. The tide turned in **BMW**'s favor in the 6 Hours of **Nürburgring**: 1-2-3 (**Amon/Stuck, Hezemans/Quester** and **Lauda/Joistein**), the best Capri coming in 5th (**Ludwig/Ludwig-Weiss**), behind even **Spartaco Dini** and **Carlo Facetti** in an **Alfa** 2000. As for **Hezemans**, he won three straight races with **Quester**. His hat-trick began in the 24 Hours of **Spa**, where **BMW** beat the Capri of **Mass/Fitzpatrick**, followed by the **Opel** of **Tricot/Haxhe**. The Dutchman took over the lead of the championship he would never relinquish. He also won on home soil, at **Zandvoort**, followed by **Brian Muir** and **James Hunt**, in another 3.0 CL (with a 3.5 engine). **Hezemans** clinched the championship in **Paul Ricard**, followed by **Ickx/Hunt, Amon/Stuck, Brun/Cocher**, all in BMWs. The best **Ford** could do was 5th with **Jackie Stewart** and **Jochen Mass**. There would be another race in the season, the Tourist Trophy, which was won by **Derek Bell** and **Harald Ertl**, in a **BMW**, followed by **Mass** in a **Ford** and **Muir** in a **BMW**. At least **Ford** managed to win the category up to 2 liters, beating **Alfa Romeo** by one point but the overall manufacturer winner was **BMW**.

While **1973** was a high drama season, with plenty of star drivers, **1974** was tough on the ETCC, as it was with most racing worldwide. The season had a short 6 races, the season ending **Jarama** race had merely 13 cars on the grid. The 4 Hours of **Monza** was won by **Peltier/Lafosse** in a **BMW**, followed by four other Bavarian cars. The best **Ford** was **Heyer/Kautz**, in a 2.0 **Ford** Escort. **BMW** won again at

Salzburgring, this time **Ickx** and **Stuck** doing the honors, followed by 3 other **BMW**s. There were only 21 starters, including a few **Porsche** 911 to boost up the numbers. **Vallelunga** hosted the 3rd round and **Peltier/Lafosse** won again, followed by **Finotto/Mohr (BMW)**, then **Heyer/Krebs** and **Ludwig/Odenthal**, in **Ford**s. It should be noted that **Heyer** raced a 2.0 **Ford** Escort, which by then was consistently beating the larger engined **Ford** Capris. In fact, at the **Nürburgring Heyer/Ludwig** in the 2.0 Escort beat the star crew **Lauda/Hezemans/Glemser** in a 3.4 **Ford** Capri, in a race where **BMW** did not feature well. At **Zandvoort** a Capri won for the first time in the year, **Mass** and **Stommelen** beating the **Porsche** 911 of **Van Lennep/Bertrams** (not competing for points) and the **BMW** of **Slotemaker/Vermeulen (Huub)**. **Ford** had won the manufacturers championship, so the only thing left to be decided at **Jarama** was the drivers' title, the two contenders being **Heyer** and **Peltier**. In the end the **Ford** driver won, sharing a win with **Hezemans** and **Ludwig** in a Capri, followed by **Mohr** and **Hezemans** in a Escort. **Peltier** and **Lafosse** came in third.

The Jaguar in the 1976 Tourist Trophy. Photo by Richard Woods.

The **1975** ETCC was not an improvement over the **1974** series. There were only six rounds, mostly thin fields, little factory interest and scant competition. In fact, **Alan Peltier** and **Siegfried Muller** won the first two races and led the championship from the start, driving an Alpina **BMW** 3.0 CSL. The race at **Monza** had a smallish entry, although there were two Alpina **BMW**s and two Schnitzers. Zakspeed fielded an Escort for **Heyer/Finotto**, which finished second. The latter crew also finished second at **Brno**, followed by another Zakspeed entry (**Colzani/Mohr**), while a **Skoda** driven by **Milan Zid** and **Oldrich Horsak** finished fourth. **Dieter Quester** won at **Salzburgring**, paired with **Urs Zondler**, in a Schnitzer **BMW**, followed by **Peltier/Muller** and a Group 4 **Porsche** 911 which ran to boost up the field. The **Nürburgring** race always had a healthy entry and 60 cars started the race which was won by the Alpina crew of **Kelleners/Grohs**, followed again by **Peltier/Muller**. A 1.3 **NSU** finished fourth! The **Zandvoort** organizers accepted entries from quite a few Group 4 **Porsche** Carrera 911s, which finished 1-2-3 (winners **Hezemans/Schenken**). FIA did not like this, and the Dutch track was not included in the **1976** championship, as punishment to organizers. The best Division 2 was again **Kelleners/Grohs**, helped by **Stommelen**. **Peltier** and **Muller** clinched the championship in this penultimate round. At **Jarama**, a small field of fifteen cars raced and the **Herbert Muller** team **BMW** 3.0 CSL won, driven by Swiss drivers **Paul** and **Henrici Keller**. In second place came the Iberian trio **Emilio de Villota, Jorge de Bagration** and **Mario Cabral**, who drove a **Ford** Capri. **BMW** won all races.

The **1976** season had 9 rounds and the biggest news was the involvement of British Leyland, which was to field 5.3 **Jaguars** XJ in the series. The British cars were not at **Monza**, in fact, only showed up in **Silverstone**. However, a couple of Swedish entered Camaros made the life of the Luigi team a bit more difficult in Italy, although **Xhenceval/Dieudonne** won with a 7-lap difference, a 2.0 Autodelta Alfetta finishing third. At **Salzburgring** the Belgian team had a 1-2-3, the winners being **de Fierlandt/Neve**, followed by **Xhenceval/Dieudonne**. The positions were reversed at **Mugello**, although **De Fierlandt**'s co-driver was de **Wael**. The **Alfas** continued to have good performance, finishing 3rd and 4th. The result was repeated at **Brno** but still no sign of the **Jaguars**. In addition to **Skoda**s, there were Eastern **Zastava** and **ZAZ** racers in the field, boosting up variety. Luigi continued its winning ways at the **Nürburgring**, which was won by **Gunnar Nilsson/De Fierlandt/De Wael**. **De Fierlandt** was getting very close to his fellow Belgian teammates by that race. Luigi fielded three cars at the returning 24 Hours of **Spa** but faced defeat for the first time in the season. The winners **Detrin/Demuth/Chavan** drove a **BMW** for Ecurie Jemeda, while **Alfa Romeo** cars finished 2nd (**Andruet/Dini**), 3rd and 4th. **Alfa** did one better at **Vallelunga** and won the race with **Spartaco Dini/Amerigo Bigliazzi**, followed by two other **Alfas**. That day **Xhenceval/Dieudonne/Finotto** could only get 4th. However, the Belgians recovered their earlier form, winning the last two races of the season, at **Silverstone** and **Jarama**, sharing their car with **De Fierlandt**. The **Jaguar**'s debut only took place at the Tourist Trophy, at **Silverstone and** the car did not disappoint in qualifying, **Derek Bell** posting pole position. In the race, **Bell** led and also got fastest lap but the fast car lasted all of 39 laps. A British Leyland entered **Triumph** Dolomite did finish the race in 14th, driven by **Craft/Rouse**. Not surprisingly, the **Jaguar** was not at **Jarama**. In the end **Xhenceval/Dieudonne** ended worthy champions and Luigi Racing emerged as a new touring car force. *****

The **1977** season was promising. In addition to the Luigi car of **Xhenceval/Dieudonne** and sometimes **Joosen/De Wael**, there would be **BMW** 3.0 CSLs from Jolly Club (**Facetti/Finotto**) and Alpina (**Quester** and a number of guest drivers) and a two-car **Jaguar** team (**Bell/Rouse, Fitzpatrick/Schenken**). A number of fast 2.0-liter **BMW**s, the 2.0 liter **Bigliazzi** Alfetta, 1.6 VW Sciroccos and even a team of enthusiastic Argentine drivers running 1.3 Alfas guaranteed support for the lower classes, while there were still some **Ford**s appearing. At **Monza, Facetti, Finotto** and **Grano** won in a 3.2 **BMW** 3.0 CSL, ahead of **Merzario** and **Bigliazzi** in the Alfetta. One of the **Jaguar** did not start, the other retired, while the other **BMW** 3.0 CSLs all retired. Round two was the **Salzburgring** race and the winners were Austrian **Dieter Quester**, partnered by **Gunnar Nilsson** in the Alpina **BMW**. The fast 5.4 **Schenken Jaguar** got fastest lap, while **Bell** got pole but neither car finished the race. The 3rd round was back in Italy, at **Mugello**. This time the Luigi team won with **Xhenceval** and **Dieudonne**, followed by **Facetti/Finotto**. The **Jaguars** skipped this race. Another Italian venue came up next, **Pergusa** and **Facetti** and **Finotto** won again, followed by **Dieudonne** and **Xhenceval, Facetti** leading the championship over **Finotto**. **Jaguar** came back at

Brno and again, were fastest in practice and posted the fastest lap. However, **Facetti/Finotto** won again, while the best **Jaguar** came in 16th, the other retiring. At the **Nürburgring, Quester** began his charge. He once again had Swede **Nilsson** as his team mate and beat **Jaguar**, which once and for all had managed to end a race in the podium (**Bell/Rouse**), followed by **Heyer** and **Hahne** in a 2.0 Escort. The powerful **Jaguars** also got pole and the fastest lap in this race. At **Zandvoort Quester** had on his side local hero **Hezemans** and they won followed by **Xhenceval/Dieudonne** and **Hayje/Vanierschot**, all in BMW 3.0 CSL. Although **Facetti/Finotto** had the pole in this race, they were having problems finishing races at this point. As **Quester** won the next round at **Silverstone,** that time with **Tom Walkinshaw** and the Italians again retired, **Dieter**, with 80 points, was closing onto leaders **Facetti, Xhenceval** and **Dieudonne**, which had 87. **Jaguar** again finished a race, in 4th (**Bell/Rouse**), **Andy** also setting fastest lap. At **Zolder Quester** had another local driver help him out, this time Belgian **Patrick Neve** but **Xhenceval** and **Dieudonne's** consistency meant they led the championship by 2 points. At **Jarama** the winners were **Joosen** and **Grano**, followed by **Dieudonne** and **Xhenceval** in the other Luigi entry, **Facetti/Finotto** and **Quester** and **Walkinshaw**. Coming into the final race, **Quester** did what he needed. He came in second, driving with **Grano** and although **Facetti/Finotto** won again, it was too late. **Xhenceval** and **Dieudonne** had to drop points, meaning they got 129 gross points but had to deduct 10, leaving **Quester** the champion with 125. British Leyland had given up after the **Zolder** race but **Jaguar** would be back with a better set up in the next decade.

Without **Jaguar** and a non-returning **Quester,** who decided to race in the World Championship of Makes instead, the ETCC looked less promising than in **1977**. Luigi continued running two 3.0 CSL, Jolly Club fielded a car for **Facetti/Finotto**, **VW** Motorsport decided to seriously race the 1.6 Sciroccos, plus there was a team of 1.3 **Skodas** racing during the season. There were quite a few **Ford** Capris and a 5.7 **Camaro (Dron/Nelleman)** in the first race of the season, this time held at **Brands Hatch**. The winner was still a **BMW**, the **Grano/Walkinshaw** car followed by **Facetti/Finotto**. However, the nicest surprise of the year came in **Monza**, an AMG 4.5 **Mercedes** 450SLC entered for **Heyer/Schickentanz**, which finished 3rd. The winners of this race were **Facetti** and **Finotto**. At **Mugello, Umberto Grano** won his first race of the year, sharing his **BMW** with **Fitzpatrick**, followed by **Xhenceval/Uberti**. **Facetti/Finotto** also won at **Salzburgring**, where the **Mercedes** made its second appearance of the year, finishing 3rd. **Grano/Walkinshaw** won again at **Jarama**, while **Grano** won with **Xhenceval** at **Estoril and** then partnered by **Hottinger** at the **Oesterreichring**. A crew of Yugoslavian drivers, **Drago Regvart** and **Dagmar Suster** were doing very well with a **VW** Scirocco, often finishing in the top 6 and **Lella Lombardi** also featured well in some races driving a **FIAT** 128. **Facetti/Finotto** won again at **Brno**, followed by **Grano/Xhenceval**, while at the **Nürburgring BMW** had a nasty surprise, when the 2.0 Escort of **Schommers/Denzel** and **Hahne** beat all **BMW**s. The **Mercedes** also raced but retired early. By that point **Grano** led the championship, followed by **Facetti/Finotto**. This lead would only be enhanced further when **Grano** won **Zandvoort** with **Toine Hezemans,** clinching the drivers' championship. Belgians **Rajmond van Hove** and **Eddy Joosen** won the last two races of the season, at **Silverstone** and **Zolder. Mercedes** retired in the Tourist Trophy (**Schickentanz/Brian Redman**) and also retired at **Zolder**, in spite of starting third.

Another nice Capri shot. Photo by Paul Kooyman.

Although the **1979** season was very long, with 13 dates, there was nothing new. A planned Luigi Camaro only hit the track at the **Nürburgring** and aside for a team of well prepared 2-liter Zakspeed Escorts, the whole affair looked like another **BMW** 3.0 CSL year. In fact, in **Monza**, which again hosted the first race of the year, **Xhenceval/Dieudonne/Van Hove** won, over the two Zakspeed Escorts. At **Vallelunga**, guest driver **Bruno Giacomelli** made a rare appearance, which he would repeat a few more times during the season and won the race with **Grano** and **Joosen**, a performance that was repeated at **Mugello**. At **Brands Hatch**, **Van Hove**, **Xhenceval** and **Dieudonne** won, followed by **Niedzwiedz** and **Muller** in an Escort. Two **Skodas** came in 8th and 9th, winning their class. Fields were generally smaller in **1979** and **Jarama** was no exception. **Grano/Joosen** won, beating **Van Hove/Xhenceval/Dieudonne**, while locally driven **Chrysler** and **Seat** entries came in 5th and 6h. The biggest surprise of the **Oesterreichring** round was that a **BMW** 3.0 CSL did not win it – a **BMW** 530 did! However, an **Audi** GTE came in second, driven by **Nowak/Bergmesiter**. It should be noted that **Audi** was not a racing powerhouse in the 70s, so this is very significant. Things were back to normal as **Van Hove/Xhenceval/Dieudonne** won at **Brno**, in a Luigi 3.0 CSL, a round that had one of the largest entries of the year. At the **Nürburgring**, **Facetti/Finotto** finally won their first race of the season. The **Mercedes** did not race but the Luigi Camaro was there (**Neve/Peltier**, retired) and there were some interesting names in the race, such as **Markus Hotz, Harald Grohs, Manfred Winkelhock, Herbert Muller, Helmut Kelleners**, all in BMWs, while **Tom Walkinshaw** shared a **VW Golf** with **Richard Lloyd**. **Finotto/Facetti** won again at **Zandvoort** and **Salzburgring**, with obvious momentum from their last win. At Pergusa, **Van Hove/Xhenceval/Dieudonne** won and **Finotto/Facetti** were second. **Facetti/Finotto** returned to their winning ways in **Silverstone**, beating the 2-liter Escorts and 4 **Ford** Capris and finished off the season with a fine win at **Zolder**, followed by the fast **Audi** 80 GTE of **Nowak/Bergmeister**. Thus **Facetti**, a veteran of Touring car wars from the 60s, had finally won his first ETCC, becoming the decade's winningest driver with **Finotto** and **Grano**. It was not a wonderful season but nonetheless the champions deserved the win.

Driver wins, in the 70s
1. Carlo Facetti (I), Martino Finotto (I), Umberto Grano (I) – 12
2. Dieter Glemser (D) – 11
3. Dieter Quester (A), Toine Hezemans (NL), Jean Xhenceval (B), Pierre Dieudonne (B) – 10
4. Jochen Mass (D) – 8
5. Raijmond Van Hove (B), Eddie Joosen (B) – 6
6. Alex Soler-Roig (E) – 5
7. Alain Peltier (B), Hughes de Fierlandt (B), John Fitzpatrick (GB), Tom Walkinshaw (GB) - 4
8. Helmut Kelleners (D), Gunnar Nilsson (S), Hans J. Stuck (D), Hans Heyer (D) – 3
9. Gianluigi Picchi (I), Gerard Larrousse (F), Rolf Stommelen (D), Jean-Louis Lafosse (F), Klaus Ludwig (D), Sigifried Muller (D), Harald Grohs (D), Patrick Neve (B), Bruno Giacomelli (I), Brian Muir (AUS) - 2
10. Derek Bell (GB), Harald Ertl (A), Chris Amon (NZ), Amerigo Bigliazzi (I), Spartaco Dini (I), Urs Zondler (CH), Niki Lauda (A), Andrea de Adamich (I), Gunther Huber (D), Helmut Marko (A), John Miles (GB), Jacky Ickx (B), Paul Keller (CH), Heinrich Keller (CH), Claude de Wael (B), Jean-Marie Detrin (B), Charles Van Stalle (B), Nico Demuth (L), Markus Hottinger (A), Werner Schommers (D), Jorg Denzel (D), Armin Hahne (D), Harald Neger (A), Heribert Werginz (A), Roman Loibnegger (A) – 1

Several former and future F1 world champions raced in this series: **Jackie Stewart, Niki Lauda, Emerson Fittipaldi, James Hunt, Jody Scheckter, John Surtees, Graham Hill**, most of them in the superb **1973** season. Only **Lauda** won a race.

This was pretty much a European championship: only two drivers from another continent won races: **Brian Muir** from Australia, twice and **Chris Amon** from New Zealand, once.

Belgian drivers had an outstanding presence in this championship but only Dutchman **Toine Hezemans** won the championship twice in the decade (**1970, 1973**).

Venues used:
1. Monza (I), Nürburgring (D), Salzburgring (A) – 10
2. Zandvoort (NL) – 9
3. Jarama (E), Brno (CS) – 8
4. Silverstone (GB) – 7
5. Spa (B) – 5
6. Mugello (I) – 4
7. Paul Ricard (F), Vallelunga (I), Zolder (B) – 3
8. Estoril (P), Enna (I) – 2
9. Budapest (H), Mantorp Park (S) - 1

Overall victories by brand:
1. BMW, 61
2. Ford, 20
3. Alfa Romeo, 8
4. Chevrolet, 1

Car brands that raced in the ETCC during the 70s

Note that some cars, like the Mini and Imp, were raced under different brands.

BMW, Ford, Mercedes-Benz, Opel, Alfa Romeo, Chevrolet, Jaguar, Moskvich, Mitsubishi, Mini, BMC, Talbot, Lada, Skoda, FIAT, Toyota, Simca, Audi, VW, Triumph, AMC, Vauxhall, NSU, Steyr Puch, Austin, Morris, Sunbeam, SEAT, Plymouth, Chrysler, VAZ, Zastava, Subaru, DAF, Volvo, Saab, Honda, Citroen, Renault, Mazda, Datsun, Hillman, Porsche, Nissan

TROPHEE DE L'AVENIR/ TROPHEE TRANSEUROPE

In some corners it was felt that European Touring Car racing was going in a wrong direction in **1974**, in spite of the wonderful **1973** ETCC season and that changes were necessary, Thus, **Paul Frere** created the Trophee de l'Avenir, whose name was changed to Trophee Trans-Europe in **1978**, with a different set of regulations from the ETCC's Group 2, in other words, Group 1. While the intentions were good, one cannot say that the results were all that great. There was never a core group supporting either championship and many of the drivers who won races and even championships were relatively unknown. Race venues would come and go, although the Belgian tracks **Zolder** and **Spa** (including the 24 hours) were included. If anything, this series allowed a number of unusual cars winning overall races: **Opel, Toyota, VW Golf, Camaro**, although **BMW** 3.0 CSL and **Ford Capri** still did most of the winning. A race at **Estoril, 1975**, ended up with two Portuguese victors, **Pedro Cortes** and **Domingos Sa Nogueira**, which happened by default, for no foreign drivers bothered to show up. A race was held in **Kraljevo**, Yugoslavia, in **1976**, in which rare **Zastavas** ran. A popular win was **Jean-Pierre Beltoise/Jean-Pierre Jaussau**d's victory at **Albi, 1976**, by which time **Beltoise** no longer featured in international races. By **1979**, the Trophee TransEurope had been including ETCC races, albeit with a separate classification.

Race wins, Trophee de l'Avenir
1. Jean Xhenceval, Fred Frakenhout, Huub Vermeulen – 3
2. Tom Walkinshaw, 2
3. Marc Demoi, Alain Peltier, Mike Crabtree, Hughes de Fierlandt, Willy Braillard, Stuart Graham, Pedro Cortes, Domingos Sa Nogueira, Karl Mauer, Rainer Grun, Eddy Joosen, Loek Vermeulen, Johann Weisheninger, Dietmar Hackner, Jean-Michel Martin, Philippe Martin, Jean-Pierre Beltoise, Jean-Pierre Jaussaud – 1

Trophee TransEurope
1. Gordon Spice, 3
2. Fred Frankenhout, Klaus Niedzwiedz, Huub Vermeulen, Thierry Tassin, Tom Walkinshaw, Teddy Pilette, Loek Vermeulen, Henny Vermeulen, Jean Michel Martin, Herbert Kummle, Karl Mauer, Winnifried Vogt, Stuart Graham, Tiff Needell, Philip Martin, Herbert Werginz, Roman Lobnegger, Harald Neger, 1

TRANS AM

One could say that Trans Am had a hell of a ride in the 1970s. Almost matching the popularity of the Can-Am in the late 60s, with the advantage of interest by many car makers, the pony car wars entered the 70s at a healthy state: large grids, lots of talented, "name" drivers and cars from different factories winning. **AMC, Ford, Chevy, Dodge** and **Plymouth** all fought for a space under the Sun. As the decade continued, there were clear signs of decadence: the factories were gone, the likes of **Donohue, Follmer, Parnelli, Elford, Revson, Savage, Gurney, Titus** had left too and then **Porsches** were allowed in and began winning races in **1973**. This, of course, put Trans Am on a direct fight against IMSA. The trouble was, IMSA only had the Camel GT to think about, while the SCCA had to think about Can-Am, Formula 5000, plus hundreds of races with thousands of amateurs involving thousands of cars and dozens racetracks across the continental sized-country. Thus the Trans Am reached its lowest point in **1974**, when only three races were held. Things did pick up, with seven races being held in **1975**, 8 in **1976** and 11 in **1977** but IMSA's show grew in popularity and stature, while depth of the fields and interest on the Trans Am were not that great. However, the Trans Am survives to this day, so it is one of the longest running car racing championships in the world.

As said, until **1972** pony cars in the form of **AMC Javelin, Ford Mustang, Chevy Camaro** and **Pontiac Firebird** dominated. It should be noted that from **1970** to **1972** separate races were run for the under 2-liter category, that included a mix of **Alfa GTA** and **GTV, Datsun 510, FIAT 124 and Abar**th, **NSU 1000, Volvo 122, Mini Cooper, Renault Gordini, Triumph Vitesse, Chevrolet Vega, Lotus Cortina, Saab, Toyota 1600, Ford Escort and Pinto, BMW 1600 and 2002, Opel Manta** and even the occasional **VW Beetle**. By **1972**, the only star left was **Follmer**, who ended up champion (he also won the Can Am) and while certain races still had 40 cars on the grid (such as Road America, 1972), others had much less than 20. Through changes of regulations, **Porsche** began winning in **1973**, although Camaros still won most races. There was a resurgence of American power in **1975**, when **John Greenwood** won in his Corvette and **1978**, when **Chevrolet** Corvettes and Monzas gave a hard time to the **Porsche** 935s (**Greg Pickett** won that championship). In fact, from **1975** on the most common cars on Trans Am races were Corvettes. The **Porsche** 934 became available as of **1976** and was able to challenge the large engined Corvettes on equal footing. As for the small class division, they were simply added to the main race, to make up the numbers. So the Corvettes and 934's shared the road with **Minis, VW Sciroccos, Renaults** and **Alfas**. Among the drivers in this division were **Horst Kwech, Peter Gregg** and **John Morton** and even drivers with Formula 1 experience, **Sam Posey** and **Tony Settember**.

The Trans Am never had a truly international profile during the 70s. Brit **Vic Elford** won a race in **1970** and Canadians **Ludwig Heimrath** and **Maurice Carter** won races later on the decade. There were races in Canada, in several venues such as **Edmonton, Mont Tremblant, Sanair** and **Trois Rivieres** and races were held in **Mexico** in **1978** and **1979**. So, as expected, quite a few Canadian drivers who were not regulars raced in Canada and Mexicans in Mexico City. The Mexican brothers **Daniel** and **Miguel Muniz** did a full season in **1979** and Salvadoran driver "**Jamsal**" appeared in a Mexico round.

Race wins, drivers:
1. Peter Gregg, 12
2. George Follmer, 11
3. Mark Donohue, 10
4. John Paul, 7
5. Parnelli Jones, John Greenwood, Hurley Haywood, 5
6. Gregg Pickett, 4
7. Milt Minter, Bob Hagestad, Jerry Hansen, Monte Shelton, 3
8. Warren Tope, Carl Shafer, 2
9. Vic Elford, Walt Maas, Al Holbert, Bob Wollek, Tuck Thomas, Hal Shaw, Maurice Carter, Warren Agor, 1

Race wins, manufacturers
1. Porsche, 35
2. Chevrolet, 19
3. AMC, 15
4. Ford, 10
5. Pontiac and Datsun, 1

DRM AND OTHER GERMAN TOURING CAR CHAMPIONSHIPS

Before the DRM, there was the DARM, the Deutsche Automobil Rundstrecken Meisterchaft. In a nutshell, this was a touring car championship, with many classes, including GTs such as **Porsche** 911, **Alpine-Renault** and **Opel** GT. After the creation of the DRM, the DARM took a more second-class status and indeed, the majority of its participants during the decade were unknown to non-Germans. Notwithstanding, drivers such as **Jochen Mass, Georg Loos, Clemens Schickentanz, Leopold von Bayern, Edgard Doren, Reinhardt Stenzel** and some Austrian, Belgian, Swiss and Dutch drivers also took part. Although it was a German championship, races were held in **Zolder, Zandvoort** and **Salzburgring**, as well as some more obscure venues like **Neuhausen, Sylt, Saarlouis**. A vast array of cars competed, including **Porsche** 911, **Alpine-Renaults, Opels** of all types, **BMWs, Alfa Romeo, Corvettes, Shelbys, VW, NSU, FIATs, Minis, Fords, Imps, Simcas, Datsun, Autobianchi**, etc. A rare appearance by **Bob Wollek** yielded a victory in **Hockenheim, 1977**.

From the beginning the DRM had a more upscale feeling. The first season had 10 rounds, including two hill climbs at **Freiburg** and **Sauerland**. From the beginning, airport races at **Kassel-Calden, Wunstorf, Diepholz** and **Mainz-Finthen**, were common championship fixtures

The DRM started in **1972** and it only included two classes: Division 1 for large engine cars, Division 2 up to 2 liters. Initially for touring cars such as **Ford Capri, Ford Escort** and **BMW**s, **Porsche** 911s were also accepted and by **1977** it became a Group 5 Championship. By then, due to an intense battle between **Rolf Stommelen** and **Bob Wollek**, many people outside of Germany began paying attention to the championship. **Hans Stuck** (D.1) and **Harald Menzel** (D.2) were the winners of the first DRM race held during the Eifelrennen meeting. There were only three foreign drivers in this race: Holland's **Liane Engemann**, Austrian **Harald Ertl** and Britain's **Peter Westbury**. **Stuck** won the first five races in Div. 1, while in Div. 2, drivers such as **Schuler** and **Basche** shared the spoils with **Menzel**. **Stuck** won four more and came out the clear champion, driving a factory **Ford**. Among other noteworthy participants in the maiden season were **Frank Gardner**, in a **Camaro, Hans Heyer, Clemens Schickentanz. Alex Soler-Roig, John Fitzpatrick, Dieter Glemser, Jurgen Barth, Claude Haldi, Reinhold Jost, Jorg Obermoser** and **Jurgen Barth**.

John Winter and Franz Konrad at Zandvoort, DRM 1978 (Photo Rob Petersen collection)

The **1973** brought some new names, such as **Toine Hezemans, Brian Muir, Klaus Ludwig, Helmut Kelleners, Rolf Stommelen** and **Helmut Koinigg**. **BMW, Ford** and **Porsche** won Division 1 races, with no clearly dominant driver, while **Glemser** tended to dominate Division 2 with a **Ford Escort**, even though **BMW** also won rounds with **Stuck** and **Kelleners**. **Glemser** turned out the overall champion.

Rolf Stommelen was the star driver for **Ford** in **1974**, in Division 1 and among other new participants were **Niki Lauda, Derek Bell, Tim Schenken** and **Vern Schuppan**. The number of entrants varied wildly: in some events, Division 1 had more cars, in others, Division 2 had the upper hand. Many lesser known DARM runners raced sporadically and some races had a reasonable turnout of Swiss drivers. **BMW, Porsche** and **Ford** again shared the spoils in Division 1, while **Ford** and **BMW** won in Division 2. **Glemser** won overall, while **Ludwig** won among Div. 1 runners.

Bob Wollek, who would become such a big part of the **DRM**, joined it in **1975**. **Jochen Mass** was also a welcome addition, winning for **Ford** at the **Norisring**, where former F-1 driver **Reine Wisell** also drove. **BMW, Porsche and Ford** all won Division 1 races, although **Porsches** made up most of the fields. **Heyer** won the championship for the first time and runner-up **Ludwig** ran in both divisions. **Krebs**, a **BMW** driver, was the first among the big cars.

By **1976** the **Porsches** basically took over Division 1, to the point that in some races there were no cars from other manufacturers. Among winning drivers, there was variety, with **Hezemans, Wollek, Schenken, Kelleners** and **Neuhaus** winning races. However, a pattern emerged where Division 2 drivers usually won the championship overall and this happened again, **Heyer** winning once more. The best among Division 1 drivers was **Wollek**, who finished third.

This situation was reversed in **1977**, when **Rolf Stommelen** and **Bob Wollek** simply dominated proceedings: **Rolf** won five races to **Wollek**'s four and **Schurti**'s one and **Rolf** came out on top. In Division 2, things got tougher for **Ford**, for **BMW** made a strong effort of wrestling the championship away from the blue oval. And that it did, with newcomer **Manfred Winkelhock** leading his **BMW** Junior teammates but more importantly, beating **Heyer**. Even **Porsche** got involved in the smaller division, fielding a "baby" **Porsche** 935 for **Jacky Ickx**, at **Hockenheim**. Among some of the newcomers besides the above were **Marc Surer, Eddie Cheever, Ronnie Peterson, Peter Gregg, David Hobbs, Armin Hahne** and **Dieter Quester**. **Harald Ertl** also debuted a **Toyota** in Division 1. In this season, two races were held in Belgium, at **Zolder**.

Stommelen agreed to drive the **Toyota** in 1978, which was not a good idea. Gelo had hired **Hezemans** from Zakspeed and the Dutchman was the top team's racer, while **Fitzpatrick** and **Ludwig** also won for Gelo. **Wollek** won a few times for Kremer and **Schurti** for Max Moritz. This greater balance among Division 1 racers meant a Division 2 overall champion again, **Harald Ertl**, the first foreigner to win overall. The Austrian raced a **BMW** and so did another Austrian, **Markus Hottinger**, second in division 2. There were races at both **Zolder** and **Zandvoort**, which meant some one-off participations by local drivers like **Bourgoignie, Van Oorschot, Neve** and **Suykerbuyk**.

Wollek finally left Kremer for 1979, talking a drive at Gelo, while **Ludwig** joined Kremer. Poor **Bob** simply saw **Ludwig** walk away with the championship in the novel K-3 **Porsche** 935, winning ten times to **Wollek**'s single win. **Ludwig** became the undisputed champion, overall winner for the first time. Matters were more balanced in Division 2: **Ertl** was hired to partner **Heyer** in the Capris, while **Winkelhock** and **Hottinger** were the main **BMW** challengers. **Heyer** won Division 2 again. **BMW** M1's raced in Division 1 as well, in fact, both **Niki Lauda** and **Clay Regazzoni** drove these cars at the **Nürburgring** and **Mass** and **Stuck** also made appearances in the new Bavarian sports car.

The DRM ended the decade in a healthy state, indeed much better than the World Championship for the same type of car, Group 5. In fact, a decline would begin in **1980**, out of the scope of this book but the DRM would also set the template for the future DTM, that appeared in the next decade. Germans simply loved their touring cars, even when they were not really touring cars.

Winners (1972-1979), Drivers
1. Hans Heyer, 23
2. Klaus Ludwig, 19
3. Hans Joachin Stuck, 15
4. Bob Wollek (F), 13
5. Dieter Glemser, 9
6. Rolf Stommelen, Toine Hezemans (NL), Harald Menzel, 8
7. Jorg Obermoser, Harald Ertl (A), 7
8. Manfred Winkelhock, 5
9. Reinhardt Stenzel, Markus Hottinger (A), 4
10. Manfred Schurti (FL), Gerhard Schuler, Albrecht Krebs, Peter Hennige, 3
11. Dieter Basche, Helmut Kelleners, Tim Schenken (AUS), 2
12. John Fitzpatrick (GB), Klaus Fritzinger, Eddie Cheever (USA), Harald Grohs, Marc Surer (CH), Jochen Mass, Jurgen Neuhaus, Jacky Ickx (B), Helmut Koinigg (A), 1

Manufacturer wins, (1972-1979)
1. Ford, 60

2. Porsche, 48
3. BMW, 40

IROC

The International Race of Champions was a made-for-TV series put together by **Roger Penske** in **1973**, which aim was bringing together European stars and American top drivers from many disciplines (USAC, NASCAR, Formula 1 and US road racing) and decide who was best. An invitation-only affair, it was easy not to take the series seriously, although the pay was excellent: **Mark Donohue** won US$ 54,000 (or US$ 41,000, depending on source) in the maiden series, while **Mario Andretti** got a whopping US$ 75,000 in the last championship of the decade, all that from running in four sprint races.

In the first season, **1973-74**, the series used **Porsche** Carreras, while for the rest of the decade **Camaros** were used. The format of the 6th season (**1978-1979**) was slightly different: three qualifying races were held for 12 NASCAR, USAC and Road Racing drivers each and the top four from each of these races would advance to the finals, one race in an oval, ther other in a road racing track. Formula 1 drivers generally did not do well: only **Mario Andretti** won a title, although he was a USAC driver as well. Part of the reason is that Formula 1 drivers were not used to oval racing's more muscular approach to racing and drafting. **Jody Scheckter** placed last twice and 10th in one edition. **Emerson Fittipaldi** and **Alan Jones** were the best placed foreigners, with 5th places in **1974-75**, the former and in **1978-79** the latter.

As the final race always took place the year after the series began, the final race of the **1979-80** season falls out of the scope of this book, so it is not computed in wins. Curiously, **Cale Yarborough**, the joint top winner with 4 wins, never won a single championship, while **A.J.Foyt**, who won the series twice, got a single race win under his belt. **Richard Petty** never did particularly well. A single foreign driver qualified for the last season of the decade, Swiss **Clay Regazzoni**. **Emerson Fittipaldi** was the only foreign driver to win a race, in the **1974-75** season.

Participations:
1. Bobby Unser, Bobby Allison, Richard Petty, Gordon Johncock, A.J. Foyt – 5
2. Al Unser, David Pearson, Emerson Fittipaldi, Cale Yarborough, Johnny Rutherford, Mario Andretti – 4
3. Jody Scheckter – 3
4. George Follmer, Benny Parsons, James Hunt, Buddy Baker, Al Holbert, Darrel Waltrip, Tom Sneva, Neil Bonnett, Peter Gregg – 2
5. Mark Donohue, Peter Revson, Denny Hulme, Roger McCluskey, Ronnie Peterson, Graham Hill, Brian Redman, Jacky Ickx, Gunnar Nilsson, Alan Jones, Donnie Allison, Rick Mears, Don Whittington, Clay Regazzoni - 1

Wins:
1. Cale Yarborough, Bobby Unser and Bobby Allison, 4
2. Mark Donohue, Mario Andretti, 3
3. Neil Bonnett, Gordon Johncock, Darrel Waltrip, A.J. Foyt, Peter Gregg, Al Unser, Buddy Baker, Benny Parsons, Emerson Fittipaldi, George Follmer, 1

BMW PROCAR SERIES, 1979

The **BMW** Procar series was interesting for it gave the public the rare opportunity of seeing Formula 1 drivers driving something other than GP cars late in the decade, namely **BMW** M-1 sports cars. The races were held in the same weekend as European Formula 1 championship rounds, starting at **Zolder** and ending at **Monza**. Five guests cars were made available to best placed drivers from the first GP qualifying session, plus a number of series regulars, which included **Toine Hezemans, Dieter Quester, Hans Stuck, Albrecht Krebs, Markus Hottinger, Manfred Winkelhock** and others. **Niki Lauda** ended up winning three rounds (he was actually a series regular) and the championship. **Hans Stuck** also a series regular, albeit also a GP driver in the hapless **ATS**, won two rounds, **Elio de Angelis, Jacques Laffite** and **Nelson Piquet** won one each.

The contemporary Formula 1 drivers who raced at least once during the season were: **Elio de Angelis, Clay Regazzoni, Mario Andretti, Jacques Laffitte, Hans Stuck, Niki Lauda, Emerson Fittipaldi, Eddie Cheever, Jean-Pierre Jarier, Patrick Depailler, Nelson Piquet, Alan Jones, Didier Pironi, Carlos Reutemann, Jochen Mass, Bruno Giacomell**i.

SCCA AMATEUR RACING

On a good day, 70s SCCA race meetings were huge gatherings of enthusiasts ranging from large engined Can-Am and Formula A racers, smaller sports cars and single seaters, GTs and touring cars of all sizes. In these good days, hundreds of cars and drivers took to the track, all vying for a berth in the run-offs at the end of the year, where national champions were crowned. Some meetings were not as well attended and many categories were bunched together. Not all were unknown, or amateur drivers. To name a few, drivers such as Skip Barber, Bob Sharp, Elliott Forbes-Robinson, Bobby Rahal, Milt Minter, Kevin Cogan, Bob Tullius and a certain Paul Newman were among the decade's SCCA champions. It should be noted that some participants in SCCA's pro series, Can-Am, Trans Am, Formula 5000 and Super Vee, frequently raced in SCCA amateur events. The sheer variety of machinery in average SCCA meetings was astounding: from a few beasts such as Can-Am McLarens and Lolas and 5-liter formula A`s, to dozens of Formula Vees and one-off D Sports Racers, to cars rarely raced elsewhere such as the Jensen Healey, model E Jaguar, Daimler SP250, mixes of American, Japanese and European sedans and sports cars. Jerry Hansen, the SCCA's winningest champion (27 titles), did most of his winning during the decade, winning in Formula A, Formula B, A Sports Cars, B Sports Cars and A Production. Towards the end of the decade, some categories were renamed, Formula A dropped and even some of the production classes dropped and consolidated as GT classes for the 80s. Champions are listed in year highlights in the beginning of the year.

Here is a line-up of the 1970s SCCA amateur categories:

Formula A (from 1970 to 1978, no champion in 1977). This was the category that gave rise to Formula 5000 and actually survived the professional category.

Formula B (from 1970 to 1978, replaced by Formula Atlantic in 1979). These were equivalent to Formula 2. SCCA attempted to make a professional Formula B series, even holding events abroad, such as in Venezuela.

Formula C (from 1970 to 1978, replaced by Formula Continental in 1979). These were equivalent to Formula 3.

Formula Atlantic (1979). The category replaced Formula B in 1979.

Formula Super Vee (1970 to 1978). The same cars that raced in professional Super Vee were used in SCCA.

Formula Vee (1970 to 1979). The longest running SCCA single seater category, fields were usually large, racing close and some one-offs took to the track.

Formula Ford (1970 to 1979). Formula Ford was also popular. An Eagle won the national championship in 1978.

Formula Continental (1979) This category replaced formula C in 1979.

A Sports Racing (1970 to 1979). Cars such as the Porsche 917, McLaren and Lola Chevrolet raced in this category. Fields were generally small but awed the public anyhow. This is where Hansen did most of his winning.

B Sports Racing (1970 to 1978). This was roughly equivalent to European 2 liter prototypes.

C Sports Racing (1970 to 1979). Prototypes with 1.6 engines.

D Sports Racing (1970 to 1979). These were prototypes with motorcycle engines, very affordable.

A Production (from 1970 to 1978). Large sports cars such as Chevrolet Corvette, Shelby Cobra, TVR Griffith. A and B production and A Sedan were consolidated into GT-1 as of 1979.

B Production (from 1970 to 1979). Sports cars such as Corvettes and AC Cobras with smaller engines and cars such as Jaguar E, AMC AMX, Porsche 911S, Sunbeam Tiger, Ferrari 365

C Production (from 1970 to 1979) Sports cars such as Datsun 240/280, Porsche 911, Lotus Elan, Lotus Europa, Jaguar E, Porsche 914, Triumph TR6

D Production (from 1970 to 1979) Sports cars such as Triumph TR6 and TR7, Lotus 7, Datsun, Porsche 924, Jensen Healey, Ala Romeo 1750, Elva Courier, Yenko Stinger, Daimler SP250, Lotus Europa

E Production (from 1970 to 1979) Sports cars such as MGB, Porsche 356, 914, 912, Triumph GT6, Triumph TR3, Morgan Plus 4,

F Production (from 1970 to 1979) Sports cars such as the Triumph Spitfire, Alfa Romeo Spider, Saab Sonnet, MG Midget, Austin Healey Sprite, Volvo P1800, Alpine A110

G Production (from 1970 to 1979) Sports cars such as MG Midget, Alfa Romeo Spider, Austin Healey Sprite, MG Midget, Datsun 1600, Triumph Spitfire

H Production (from 1970 to 1979) Sports cars such as Fiat Abarth, Austin Healey Sprite, Morgan.

A Sedan (from 1970 to 1979) Large engined sedans such as Chevy Camaro, AMC Javelin, Ford Mustang, Pontiac GTO, Pontiac Tempest, Plymouth Barracuda, Ford Falcon, Dodge Challenger

B Sedan (from 1970 to 1979) Sedans such as Datsun 510, Alfa Romeo GTV, Mazda RX 3, BMW 1600, BMW 2002, Opel Rallye, Toyota 1600, Ford Pinto, Triumph Vitesse, Volvo, Fiat 124, Toyota Corolla.

C Sedan (from 1970 to 1978) Sedans such as Alfa Romeo GTA, Mini Cooper, Datsun 1200, Datsun B210, Ford Escort.

D Sedan (from 1970 to 1971) Small sedans such as Fiat Abarth and Mini Cooper

Showroom Stock A (from 1977 to 1979) Cars such as Datsun 280Z, Saab Turbo and Porsche 924.

Showroom Stock B (from 1977 to 1979) Cars such as Alfa Romeo Spider and Saab 99

Showroom Stock C (from 1977 to 1979) Smaller engine cars such as Mercury Capri, Chevrolet Vega and VW Rabbit.

BRITISH CLUB SCENE

The UK's territorial size is a fraction of the USA, so it would be unfair to expect the British Club Scene to be as large as US grass roots racing or even SCCA Amateur Racing. Notwithstanding, races for a large number of categories were held in British venues every year during the decade, some of them specific to the UK. Many prominent racers cut their teeth in club racing before moving on to more professional pastures. As some of these categories were quite inexpensive, they served as the stepping stone for a large number of drivers.

In general, individual club races were short affairs of about 15 minutes and the number of entrants could vary greatly from a very few to a great many.

One of the most unusual categories was Super Saloons, contested by hybrids, such as a **DAF** equipped with a 5-liter **Rover** engine, **Mini** equipped with a **Ford** V8, **VW** Beetle with a large **Chevy** engine, **Ford** Capris with **Chevy** engines, **BRM** engined Escorts, **Skodas** with **Ford** and **Chevy** engines and the Big Bertha and Baby Bertha **Vauxhalls** driven by **Gerry Marshal**. Some of these cars were extremely fast, entertained the crowds visually and audibly but could be awfully unreliable.

Races for a number of regular sedans, of different engine sizes, were also held in meetings, contested by a variety of **Fords**, throngs of **Minis** (and derivatives thereof, including Clubman) and **Imps**, some Camaros and a host of other cars. Old **Jaguar** 3.8s still raced in these events and even **Aston Martin** DB4s, not found elsewhere, appeared in select club events. As mentioned before, even a **Rolls Royce** was found in the tracks in 1971 and on the low end, **Wolseleys** were also raced. Some street legal GTs not raced anywhere else, such as **Davrians** and **Clan Crusaders**, also raced in club events. Some of the "saloon" events were single make races for the likes of **Ford** Escort Mexico and **Minis.**

Meetings also included a number of single seater races. At the top of the food chain were Formula Libre events, where Formula 5000 and old Formula 1 cars diced with Formula 2, 3, Atlantic and even sports cars. Some of these cars were old formula 1s, such as a **BRM** chassis mated with a 5 liter engine, most likely **Chevrolet**. Additionally, there were races for Formula Ford, Formula Ford 2000 later in the decade, Formula 3, Formula Atlantic, Formula Vee, Formula Super Vee, historics.

Although we associate the word Formula to single seaters, it should be noted that a few British club categories were called Formula but the cars were 2-seater sports cars. One such category was Formula 750 (or 750 Formula), a category dating back to 1949. Initially these cars were equipped with **Austin** 7 engines, which by the 70s had been replaced by **Reliant** engines. A huge number of one-off manufacturers appeared in this category. To make matters confusing, a motorcycle category called Formula 750 emerged during the 70s, so if you ever make an internet search about Formula 750, you must include the word "car". The category remains alive to this day, only now **FIAT** 1 liter engines have replaced the **Reliant**. The category was known for the low cost and gave rise to the 750 Motor Club, which holds dozens of meetings in England, for a number of categories.

Two other "formula" categories that were actually sports cars categories were Formula 1300 and Formula F100. Formula 1300 saw light of the day as 1172 Formula, back in 1953. Equipped with **Ford** engines of that size, eventually upgraded to 1200 and then 1300 cc, the name was changed to Formula 1300 by the 70s. A number of chassis were also created by practitioners of the discipline, although it is unclear how much original was found in Formula 1300 and Formula 750 cars. In all likelihood, they started life as something else, a new body panel added here and there and voilá, you have a spanking new race car make! Rather common practice in the 70s, I might add.

Formula F100 lasted a mere two years, **1970** and **1971** and more traditional car makers were involved, such as **Royale**, also equipped with **Ford** engines. The second and last champion was **Tom Pryce**, of future Formula 1 fame.

In addition to these categories, a number of sports cars/GT races were held for a variety of machinery, ranging from **Ferrari** 512 and **Ford** GT 40, to 1.6 liter prototypes, some from known manufacturers such as **Lola** and **Chevron**, others, one-off specials. The Modsport championship featured street legal sports cars rarely seen anywhere else, such as **Davrian, Turner, Marcos, TVR, Morgan,** which mixed in with more common **Porsche, MG, Lotus, Triumph** and **Datsun**.

In the latter part of the decade Sports 2000 was created and the "special" tradition diminished greatly.

EUROPEAN HILL CLIMB CHAMPIONSHIP

For most of the 60s, the European Hill Climb Championship was one of the few FIA championships in existence. As a result, top drivers and works teams from **Ferrari, Porsche, BMW** and **Abarth**, among others, took part. Additionally, a lot of F-1 and sports cars drivers began their racing careers in the mountains. By **1970** only **Abarth** was left and top driver participation dwindled, although **Jean-Pierre Beltoise** got the **Matra** V12 Formula 1 car's first win in a round of the **1970** championship and **Francois Cevert** won at **Ollon-Villars** in **1971**. Eventually, the championship developed its own set of stars, such as **Johannes Ortner, Mauro**

436

Nesti, Jimmy Robert Mieusset, Christian Debias, Michel Pignard, Domenico Scola, the **Almeras** brothers, etc. The star of the decade was surely **Nesti**, who won a large number of rounds (almost double the second ranked driver) plus dozens of local Italian events. Early on the decade, a large number of races was won by Formula 2 cars and later on, 2-liter prototypes tended to prevail.

Wins by driver (**1970-1979**)
(Only overall winners provided)
1. Mauro Nesti, 27
2. Jimmy Robert Mieusset, 14
3. Xavier Perrot, 6
4. Johannes Ortner, 5
5. Markus Hotz, 4
6. Max Mamers, 3
7. Roland Salomon, Michel Pignard, Eugenio Baturone, Mario Ketterer, Christian Debias, Willy Siller, Pierre Maublanc, 2
8. Jorge de Bagration, Antonio Zadra, Arturo Merzario, Rolf Stommelen, Jean-Pierre Beltoise, Mario Casoni, Francois Cevert, Silvano Frisori, Reinhold Joest, Fredy Amweg, Gabriele Ciuti, Jean Marie Almeras, Jose Trabal, Jean Louis Bos, Marc Sourd, Carlo Facetti 1

Venues used, 1970-1979
1. Montseny (Spain) Dobratsch (Austria), 10
2. Trento Bondone (Italy), 9
3. Ampus-Draguinan (France), St. Ursanne-Les Rangiers (Switzerland), 8
4. Mont Dore (France), 7
5. Freiburg-Schaunisland (Germany), Serra da Estrela (Portugal), 5
6. Mt. Veentoux (France), Cesana-Sestriere (Italy), 4
7. Rossfeld (Germany), Cosenza (Italy), Bolzano-Mendola (Italy), 3
8. Rieti (Italy), Ascoli (Italy), Col de la Botella (Andorra), Macerata (Italy), Potenza (Italy), 2
9. Ollon-Villars (Switzerland), Cefalu-Gibilmanna (Italy), Alpl (Austria), Puig Major (Spain), 1

In addition to the European Championship, local hill climbing scenes were very healthy in Europe. The French had a huge number of venues, in fact, multiple events were held on the same day during summer months. Formula 2 cars were commonly used in French hill climbs, in addition to many sports cars, GT and touring car classes. Italy also had a large number of events, from Sicily up to the North, only that Formula 2 and other single seater cars seldom took place. Another country with great hill climb tradition is West Germany, where single seaters were also raced. The British hill climbing series was isolated from the continent and even Formula 5000 cars and specific specials participated. Small countries such as Liechtenstein, Andorra and Malta were limited to hill climbs. Circuit racing was forbidden in Switzerland since 1955 but hill climbs were allowed. Other countries with a number of hill climbs were Czechoslovakia, Belgium, Luxembourg, Norway, Greece, Austria, Ireland, Spain, Hungary, Romania, Yugoslavia. Even Holland, known for its flat terrain, had a hill climbing event.

A number of other countries globally had hill climbs, the most notable being the Pikes Peak event in the US, part of the USAC Championship Trail until 1970. Other countries included Australia, Hong Kong, Colombia, Morocco, Jamaica, while

Brazil had a single event during the decade. Road races in Argentina, Peru, Ecuador, Bolivia and Chile often ran through mountainous terrain.

Hill climbing was very popular in Europe. Here is Michael Lochmann driving his BMW at Bressalone-S. Andrea (Michael Lochmann collection)

MONEY

The subject of money does not resonate well in certain circles but it stands to reason that motor racing was and it still is, an expensive endeavor, therefore money is a big part of understanding the changes that took place in the period. Not discussing the financial changes in motor racing during the decade would render this book useless and foolish.

Most crucially, financial figures are not readily available and when they are, they seem largely untrustworthy. For practical reasons, they are mostly omitted in 70s racing literature. Although celebrities love to flaunt money and possessions these days, in the 70s this was not considered proper behavior in most cultures. Additionally, it could lead one to trouble with taxation authorities, always eager to extract money from the wealthy, at an age with little to no control. Consider that the top tax bracket for capital gains in Britain in the mid-seventies was a whopping 98% and income tax, 83%, so you see why the subject was barely ever discussed in public forums. That is why drivers quickly began seeking tax asylum in places such as Switzerland and Monaco, where there was no income tax, once they started earning more substantial income.

Cigarette money paid a lot of bills in the 70s. This is Revson's Lola in 1970. Photo by Lola Heritage.

There was a clear change in driver activity behavior, from the first to the last year of the decade. In **1970**, Formula 1 drivers raced in several other categories, such as Formula 2, Formula 5000, Formula Indy, Sports Cars, Hill Climbs, Touring Cars, GT, NASCAR, Formula Libre, Formula Atlantic and often in their own national series. Reportedly, **Pedro Rodriguez** accepted driving in a minor **Norisring**

Interserie because he needed the cash and so did **Joakin Bonnier** at Le Mans, **1972**. In the end, both met their deaths in those races, although I am not suggesting any type of causal nexus. Even drivers who often were not real stars in Formula 1 but considered so in lesser circles, would race in places such as Japan, Singapore, Senegal, Angola, Mozambique, Venezuela, Ecuador, Brazil, India, Macau, in exchange for an airline ticket, hotel and some decent prize money, often treated as royalty. Some prominent drivers even won their last races in such opportunities, such as **Andrea de Adamich** who won a Formula B race in **Venezuela** in **1973**. "Star" drivers were often provided questionably maintained and old cars, under somewhat dangerous conditions but still soldiered on, for the additionally money was welcomed.

A very naïve commentator in a Facebook group said that drivers in the old days took more pleasure in driving than today's lot and that is why they raced all over, all the time! I made the mistake of commenting that drivers **needed** to race to make decent money because even in Formula 1 pay was meager. I got called all types of names by my guileless interlocutor but I knew I was right. Arguing with fools is a waste of time.

The book *Forza Amon*, by Eoin Young, indicates that **Chris Amon** was lured to drive for **March** in **1970** for two reasons: the team would use the Cosworth engine, which **Chris** insisted upon but also on the basis of a juicy US$ 100,000 retainer, very high for the period. It so happens that **Chris** allegedly never received the full amount, even though the book does not indicate how much he did receive. Thus he left the team after a season, seeking greener pastures. After the financial woes of **1970**, **Matra** had finally convinced **Amon** to drive for the team in **1971**, at the alleged retainer of £1,000 a week, which was a nice salary. At the end of **1972**, after the shutting down of the **Matra-Simca** F1 operations, it had been announced that **Chris** was being rehired by **March**. The book does not say it but something tells me that the matter of the unpaid **1970** retainer had resurfaced and all that is known is that **March** and **Amon** had a big fall-out. **Chris** ended up without a job until being hired by **Tecno,** which almost amounted to not having a job.

Most racing careers were short in the period, so a professional driver had to make money while he was on demand. This meant that Formula 1 drivers could be seen in lesser events, in a wide variety of settings. For instance, until **1978**, it was common for F-1 drivers to race in Formula 2, although graded drivers could not score championship points. Additionally, in spite of a diminished status, at the end of the decade the World Sports Car championship still managed to feature some Grand Prix greats, here and there. For instance, young **Riccardo Patrese** accepted **Lancia**'s invitation and joined the team, staying on board for quite a few years, into the 80s.

The **1973** *Encyclopedia of Motor Racing Greats* indicates that **Jackie Stewart** made between US$825,000 to US$ 1 million in **1971** – US$ 335,000 from a contract with Goodyear. It is widely mentioned elsewhere that **Jackie** was the first driver to make 1 million dollars in a season, largely paid by sponsors, which also included oil company Elf and **Ford**. There is obviously some advertising income from this, plus the income from driving a **Lola** in the Can-Am. So it is no surprise that **Stewart** was rarely seen outside the F1 world championship starting **1972**. Sponsor **Ford** managed to have him drive the unloved **Ford Capri** a very few times in **1972** and **1973**, once with other Formula 1 great **Emerson Fittipaldi** but **Stewart**'s **1971** Can-Am campaign was the last time the Scot ventured outside F-

1 and his sponsors' orbits on a consistent basis. He rarely raced in non-championship F1 races, which at the time were still common.

Not everybody made big bucks early on the decade. Highly touted **Clay Regazzoni** asked £63,000 to drive for **BRM** in 1972 and was offered £50,000. Brabham, on he other hand, offered him £30,000. He remained at **Ferrari** and who knows how much he made.

By the middle of the decade, fatter retainers were being negotiated, as TV exposure increased exponentially. Whether or not one likes **Bernie Ecclestone**, he was largely responsible for this. Sure, eventually he became a billionaire off Formula 1's back, some felt but he made lots of other millionaires along the way! Thus, by **1978**, top driver **Mario Andretti**'s Formula 1 retainer was reportedly about US$**900,000**, which allowed him to continue living in Pennsylvania and commuting on the Concord whenever his services were required in Europe.

In **1976** it was widely suggested in Brazil that **Emerson Fittipaldi** had been lured away from the proven **McLaren** team to the novice **Fittipaldi** squad by a retainer of one million dollars. The staggering figure at the time had been disclosed elsewhere as the team's budget for a year, which included cars, personnel and two drivers' salaries, including *Emerson*'s. It should be noted that in the mid 70s, remittance of foreign exchange was not the easy thing it is today and information about it is spotty and often unreliable. The process was extremely bureaucratic in countries such as Brazil as other South American countries which somewhat helps explain why many drivers did not go racing in more developed centers and focused on a regional and local career instead.

But not everyone made huge amounts of money in Formula 1, even recognized names. The book *Arturo Merzario Il Cowboy delle Corse* tells a funny story concerning **Ecclestone** and negotiations with drivers. When **Carlos Pace** died in an airplane crash in **1977**, a seat became available at **Brabham**, which at the time had **Alfa Romeo** engines. One of the drivers to talk to Bernie was **Hans Stuck**. The lanky German had asked a lofty retainer, which he deemed more suitable to his talents (and height), about US$ 100,000. In the middle of the phone conversation, Bernie said he had **Arturo Merzario** on the other line, who had agreed to drive for US$ 35,000. As **Art** was **Alfa**'s man, **Stuck** stepped down his demands and matched **Merzario**'s request. However, **Merzario** was never on the other line…

Merzario was also a character in another story that involves **Bernie** and sheds some light on the precarious state of F1 finances mid-decade. For **1973, Frank Williams** replaced sponsors for his Formula 1 team, changing from car model manufacturer Politoys to real car manufacturer Iso Rivolta and Marlboro. Iso Rivolta was an Italian maker of sports cars, which was also involved in the creation of the 50s Isetta. Marlboro needs no introduction. The set-up continued in **1974**, at which point Frank had hired **Arturo Merzario**, who, incidentally, had a private sponsorship deal with Marlboro. Resultwise, the **Merzario-Williams** tie up did relatively well, compared to Iso's previous season. The car even started one race in 3rd place and earned points in two occasions, including a 4th place in **Monza**. However, Iso Rivolta did go into bankruptcy during the year. In early **1975**, **Art** was back in a **Williams**, no longer bearing Iso's name. Then, driver and owner had a fall-out in the early part of the year, reportedly due to financial misunderstandings. Late in the season, at **Monza**, as **Williams** arrived at the track he is readily greeted by a Court bailiff, who had a Court order to seize the team's equipment. It turned out that **Williams** had not paid the promised **1974** retainer and **Merzario** sued. **Ecclestone** came to the rescue, lent Frank the money and **Williams** could go free, while **Merzario** raced the **Fittipaldi** on a one-off basis. In spite of the judicial intervention, **Merzario** was rehired by **Wolf-Williams** mid-season, **1976**, although Frank was largely out of the picture by then.

There are also some other stories involving **Williams** and **Bernie** during the 70s but some may be just that - stories. By the way, anything involving Bernie is blown out of proportion, for, like it or not, **Bernie Ecclestone** was a major, if not the major, promoter of change and power broker in motor racing during the 70s, thus subject to much envy. As he also managed to become extremely wealthy in the process, many books, articles, stories have been written about him, the so-called easy target, for people love to speculate about money and power. The book *The Secret Life of Bernie Ecclestone*, by Tom Bower, is a good example. Bower is a gifted story-teller, with a fluid style that is intriguing, leading the reader to connect the dots. The problem is the facts.

As any book about **Bernie**, it concerns largely money. It confirms the early 70s shaky state of Formula 1 teams in general, the low pay offered by organizers, the informality, cash payments, etc, even though some of the sweeping statements in the tome made seem a bit exaggerated. The section dealing with Bernie's early career in Formula 1, the chapters "Embryo" and "Squeeze", shows off Bower's writing skills but makes a troubling number of blundering mistakes that demonstrates the author is no Formula 1 expert, albeit a bestseller biographer.

Right at the start, he refers to **Jochen Rindt** more than once as "German". Although it is true that **Rindt** was born in Germany, racing literature unanimously refers to **Jochen**'s nationality as Austrian, in similar fashion as **Mario Andretti** is considered American. Call that an honest mistake, or perhaps, a dramatic attempt to link the deceased driver to Nazi Germany! Drama is a major requirement in sensationalist best-seller writing.

What follows below is a parade of "facts" that are patently incorrect, including trucidating a simple Italian expression ("È morto" is the right expression for "He is dead", not "È morte", which means "(it) is death"). These, by the way, are not obscure facts, in truth, any person with a fair knowledge of Formula 1 in the 70s would be able to pick up these mistakes right away. I will make reference to the page numbers in the paperback version:

- Page 54: author says that **Ron Tauranac** designs "enabled **Jack Brabham** to win the world championship three times since **1961** but after their third victory in **1966**, the cycle of failure…was apparently irreversible". Well, the world knows that **Brabham**, the team, won two world championships in the 60s, **1966** and **1967**. **Brabham**, the driver, did win three titles, in **1959, 1960** and **1966**, the first two driving for **Cooper**.
- Page 59: "After **1958 Lotus** had a winning spree of seven world championships". It is important to notice that in this section of the text, he is referring to **1971**. By that date, **Lotus** had won only four world driver championships. Maybe he is counting constructor titles as well? In this case he would be wrong too, because the sum would be eight. If **Emerson Fittipaldi**'s and **Mario Andretti**'s championships were added, the number would still be wrong…
- Page 60: he says that **March** had sold two models to **Ken Tyrrell** in **1969**. The truth is that the **Tyrrell** team started racing **March** cars in **1970** and there was no **March** formula 1 car in **1969**. The only existing **March** in **1969** was the 693 model,

a Formula 3 car driven by **James Hunt** and **Ronnie Peterson**, among others. Whether the actual sale took place in **1969** it is another matter – but the text does not really say that.
- Page 63: he refers to **Carlos Reutemann** as a world champion. **Carlos** was never a world champion, the only title he ever won was Argentine Formula 2 in **1969**.
- On page 65, the author says **Ken Tyrrell** was bonding with **Ecclestone** as family, a few pages later, on page 68, he says they had major disagreements, to the point one threatening to throw the other out the window! Well, I guess families do have major disagreements, so I will let this one pass.
- On that same page 65, there is reference to the non-championship Brazilian Grand Prix of **1972**. He has on the "plane crossing the Atlantic", **Frank Williams, Bernie and McLaren's Teddy Mayer**. However, **McLaren** did not take part in this race, so **Mayer** had no reason to be on that plane. Certainly **Teddy** did not go for a jolly ride, airline tickets to Brazil were extremely expensive at the time and the **McLaren** owner/manager was known to run a tight ship and avoid waste.
- On page 74, he calls **BRM** "the winning car for **Graham Hill**". Well, **Hill** did win a championship for **BRM** way back in **1962** but by **1970**, when **BRM** got Yardley sponsorship, **Hill** had been very far from Bourne for a while, since 1966, in fact.
- On the same page, he says that **BRM** lost Marlboro sponsorship in **1972**. That is wrong, **BRM** was sponsored by Marlboro in **1972** and **1973**.
- On page 77 he says the Canadian GP would return to **Montreal** in **1976**. The Canadian race was held at **Mosport**, Ontario, at the time.
- On page 80, he says that **Carlos Reutemann**'s replacement at **Brabham**, after the Argentine left in **1976** *would be* **Carlos Pace**. Well, the Brazilian had been in the team since **1974**, in fact had won a race in **1975**.
- On page 82, he says that coming into Japan, **1976**, the point difference between **Lauda** and **Hunt** was one point. That is not so. **Lauda** had 68 points, to **Hunt**'s 65. After Japan, the difference was one, in **Hunt**'s favor.
- On page 87, the writer says the **1977** Brazilian Grand Prix was in **Rio** – it was still held at **Interlagos**.
- On page 98, he makes reference to a non-existing **Ford** Formula 1 team – twice.

These are all simple facts that could have been easily checked in Wikipedia. They were obviously not and no motor racing historian has apparently read the manuscript. Therefore, any references I make to "facts" from this book will have the expression "allegedly" pegged to it. "Facts" in Bower's book can be trusted up to an extent. If we cannot trust easily checkable facts, how can we believe the insider scoop?

Brian Redman is very candid about financial issues in his excellent biography. He said that he refused an offer to continue driving for **Shadow** in Formula 1 in **1974** (in the wake of another driver death, this time, **Peter Revson**) because of poor pay. As he had learned that American Formula 5000 had been cancelled because of the oil crisis, he first agreed to drive for **Don Nichols**. Then, as the American Formula 5000 championship was back on, **Brian** gave up on F1, simply because **Shadow** paid very little and he could make much more money with less stress driving in America. He was a professional, after all! Indeed, **Brian**'s published F-5000 prize money in **1974** was US$81,150, rather substantial for a 7-race series. Remaining on the subject of **Brian's 1974** season, **Roger Penske** contacted **Redman** to drive his Can Am Porsche at Mid-Ohio. **Redman** agreed but asked for US$ 5,000 for a single race. **Penske** agreed but said "**Brian**, you're the most reasonable racing driver I ever met". Now **Brian** reckons **Roger** was being ironic, after all, this was a single race.

Redman in the Can-Am Penske Porsche. Photo by Rob Neuzel.

Bottom line is, actually finding out how much money drivers made in F1 prize money was a difficult exercise back on the day, the issue is simply avoided. The US Grand Prix purses were usually published and we find that **Emerson Fittipaldi** and **Francois Cevert** won US$50,000 for their **1970** and **1971** wins, while second place drivers got US$ 20,000. The US race was known to pay better, so we can safely assume that other races paid less, perhaps, much less. Surprisingly, we find, here and there, the prize money paid in non-championship F1 races. An article in the **1973** *Autocourse* lets us know that **James Hunt** made £2,500 from fifth place in the Rothmans 50,000, which technically was a Formula Libre race. In fact, **James** drove a Formula 2 in that race, which was also contested by Formula 1, Formula 5000 and even **Mario Casoni**'s sports **Lola**. Some wild specials were on the entry list but they never showed up, which suggested cars with Can Am engines and even larger. Building a car for a single race to possibly make £2,500 seemed a folly, though, in spite of the £50,000 promises...

The purses for another non-championship F1 race (which also included Formula 5000s), the Questor Grand Prix held in **Ontario**, California, **1971**, were published. So here are the top 8 and their respective earnings:

1. **Mario Andretti** ($39,400)
2. **Jackie Stewart** ($25,250)
3. **Denis Hulme** ($17,400)
4. **Chris Amon** ($14,350)
5. **Tim Schenken** ($13,550)
6. **Jo Siffert** ($12,050)
7. **Ron Grable** ($8,000) (First in Formula 5000)
8. **Peter Gethin** ($11,850).

The money was not bad in this race. Not Indy 500 level cash but not insubstantial, which explains the very healthy entry list. This was the exception, rather than the rule.

Let's place things on a better perspective. It is safe to assume that you, the reader, is a car enthusiast. So I provide below the sticker prices of a number of brand new automobiles in the United States, in **1974**:

Chevrolet Camaro – US$ 3,540
Dodge Dart – US$ 3,269
Ford Pinto – US$ 2,679
Ferrari 308 GT4 – US$ 24,550
Mercedes-Benz 450 SL – US$ 17,056
Rolls Royce Corniche – US$ 49,700

We conclude that the 81 grand Mr. **Redman** earned in Formula 5000 was indeed a nice piece of change. In fact, some Formula 5000 promoters were paying US$20,000 to race winners back in **1972**. We should consider, however, that **Brian** did not take the whole loot home. Part of the money went to mechanics, part to car owner and part to tax authorities. That explains why he still saw the need to drive in Can Am, Formula 1 and World Sports Cars, in other words wherever it was worthwhile and the pay, reasonable.

As for NASCAR, it has always published purses, in fact talking about how much money athletes make has been part of American culture for ages. Purses for Can-Am and the Indy 500 were widely disclosed at the time, which helps us monitor developments as the decade went on.

The total purses paid to NASCAR Grand National champions during the decade were as follows:

1970 – US$ 199,600
1971 – US$ 351,071
1972 – US$ 339,405
1973 – US$ 182,321
1974 – US$ 432,020
1975 – US$ 481,751
1976 – US$ 453,405
1977 – US$ 561,642
1978 – US$ 623,506
1979 – US$ 561,934

One notices right away that the **1973** champion, **Benny Parsons** made relatively little money, compared to other champions. Champions were not always the winners of the largest purses, in fact, that particular year four other drivers, **Yarborough, Pearson, Petty** and **Baker** made more money than **Benny**, who won fair and square on points but had less stellar race performances, having won a single race.

Not everybody made big bucks in NASCAR during those years, though. In some years, by the middle of the decade, very low purses were paid to back markers in some of the less important races – and there were quite a few on the schedule. **Bill Champion** (no pun intended, that was his real name) took home a meager US$ 280 for retiring after a single lap in **Nashville, 1975**!

A list of the total purses of the 50th ranked NASCAR drivers during the decade places this in a clearer perspective

1970 – US$ 4,505
1971 – US$ 3,685
1972 – US$ 3,435
1973 – US$ 5,270
1974 – US$ 8,585
1975 – US$ 8,020
1976 – US$ 3,010
1977 – US$ 9,490
1978 – US$ 6,202
1979 – US$ 11,695

It should be noted that in some years, drivers that ranked a little better, in 47th, 48th place, made even less, a little over US$ 2,000, which was not the stuff of dreams even back in the 70s. Therefore, the difference is huge between top and bottom.

Indy 500 winner purses were relatively steadier, in fact, the **1970** winner, **Al Unser**, made more money than the **1979** winner, **Rick Mears**. Here are the Indy 500 winner purses:

1970 – US$ 271,697
1971 – US$ 238,454
1972 – US$ 218,767
1973 – US$ 236,022
1974 – US$ 245,031
1975 – US$ 214,031
1976 – US$ 255,321
1977 – US$ 259,791
1978 – US$ 290,363
1979 – US$ 270,401

Indy 500 winner purses only grew in the 80s, in fact, **1989** winner **Emerson Fittipaldi** won US$ 1,001,604! I suppose CART's better handling of TV deals made all the difference, for during the 70s the race was still sanctioned by sleepy USAC who had lost its way. CART copied some of **Ecclestone**'s tactics from the early 70s.

Although the prize figures seem very enticing, it should be noted that an **Offenhauser** engine cost US$20,750 in **1970** (while a **Ford** Indy engine cost US$27,000) and a brand new **McLaren** Indy chassis cost US$50,000. Compare that to the £4,850 price tag for a **McLaren** formula 5000 in **1970**. Going Indycar racing on a competitive set up was not cheap!

As for Europe, in the first years of the Interserie, promoters ensured that prize money was prominently disclosed to the public, so that we learn that champion **Leo Kinnunen** had won 81,000 CHF, 115,500 CHF and 127,500 CHF (about US$32,400, US$ 46,200 and US$ 51,000) in his three championship years. Then, as decadence set in, scores were indicated in points. There was no reason to show off anymore, after all, the Interserie continued and the Can-Am had died...But then,

Can Am returned, by which time the Interserie was a shadow of its former self. These are the cycles of life, I suppose.

The **1970** Can Am winner, **Denis Hulme**, made US$ 50,000 for his troubles, whereas the **1974** series champion, **Jackie Oliver**, made US$68,900, in a shorter 5-race series. Compared to the Indy 500 and even to an entire season of NASCAR, this was little money. However, NASCAR calendars stretched close to 50 races in the decade's first year. For comparison purposes, the average annual income in the USA in **1970** was a little less than US$ 10,000, the median house price, US$ 26,700, so that US$ 50,000 was a nice sum, in fact it gave **McLaren** status as one of the best funded Grand Prix teams.

But Formula 1 organizers were rather stingy and race winners generally made a few thousand dollars in prize money, except for the US Grand Prix, which paid good starting money early on the decade. That explains why teams such as **Lotus, McLaren, Tyrrell** fielded extra cars in this race, which helped offset the high transportation costs.

As for sports cars drivers, money was not plentiful even at the top level. **Peter Gregg** made only $8,750 as **1974** Trans Am champion but that was a very short season indeed (only three races). In **1972** Trans Am champion **George Follmer** made US$26,800 and individual race wins paid US$4,000. Prize money in all IMSA categories was very insubstantial.

The book *Bob Wollek en marge de la glorie* contains an interesting photo of a cover letter from **Matra**, sent with the 5,000 Franc check given as payment for **Bob**'s participation in the 24 Hours. This was about 700 dollars. Granted that **Bob** was not yet a top sports car driver at the time but one can only imagine how much **Toyota** paid **Fernando Alonso** to be part of its team in 2018…Italian driver **Teodoro Zecolli** claims that in the early part of the decade, the usual prize money share of each endurance driver was 20% (there were two per crew, generally); the team would get 50%, mechanics, 10%. One presumes this was **Alfa**'s policy, for whom he drove but he claims the arrangement was pretty much universal in top level endurance racing.

In **1971**, the prize money paid to **Le Mans** winners was about US$ 13,000, roughly the amount a winner of a short Indy car race would make those days (other 500 milers paid substantially more but nowhere close the Indy 500 payout), while fifth place winners would take home about US$750. In other words, people did not race at **Le Mans** seeking money, there was little to be had. In its winning years, **Matra-Simca** spent between US$ 1 million to US$ 1.6 million a year, to field 4-car teams. In **1972**, the team raced four different cars, with various body-engine configurations. The ploy worked but it was a costly exercise and resulted in the demise of the Formula 1 team. In **Matra**'s last year, it fielded a brand new car, the MS680, which retired in its single race, although it posted the fastest lap. While in **1972 Le Mans** was **Matra-Simca**'s only prototype race of the year, the budget for **1973** and **1974** must also include (or amortize) the development of the cars for the year-long championships. In **1974 Matra-Simca** also had some sponsorship from cigarette manufacturer Gitanes but it should be noted that the French Government dished out US$ 300,000 for the worthy effort.

As for the amount of appearance, starting and prize money more famous drivers made driving in places like the **Trois Rivieres** Formula Atlantic Race, **Macau** Grand Prix, 1000 km of **Bathurst** (won by Le Mans winner **Jacky Ickx** in **1977**),

Japan Formula 2 races (**Stewart** won the Japanese Grand Prix in **1970**, **Surtees** in **1972**), plus domestic races, there was no information I could put my hands on. A lot of the money was paid in cash (as it was clearly admitted in the inauguration of the **Paul Ricard** racetrack in **1970**) and drivers were very secretive about disclosing these cash amounts, which probably went widely unreported. Additionally, double taxation could ruin a driver's pay day really fast. Some international events had relatively large attendances and being able to advertise an **Indy** 500, **Le Mans** champion and Grand Prix driver, or even an international driver on the bill surely sold additional thousands of tickets. Some of the foreign drivers that frequently raced in Angola in the early part of the decade, before communist takeover, were indeed European, not exactly famous, such as **Andre Wicky** and **Claude Swietlik**. **Raymond Tourol** was not a household name in international racing, in spite of good results at **Le Mans** but he was treated as a major star in Senegal's 6 Hours of **Daka**r, which he won more than once. In fact, in **1977** he was partnered by a real star, F1 hotshoe **Jean-Pierre Jarier**.

Most European touring car drivers did not make a great living off racing as well, contrary to NASCAR drivers. **Dieter Glemser**, a **Ford** factory driver from **1970** to **1974** and European and DRM champion, reckoned **Ford** paid him 2500 to 3000 Deutsche Mark (more or less US$ 680 to US$833) per race, plus travel expenses and lodging. That explains why he continued to be a florist throughout his racing career and did not rely on racing to put food on the table. On the other hand, **Ford** offered **Niki Lauda** a hefty 100,000 DM (about US$ 32,000) to lure him away from **BMW** Alpina late in **1973**. What made the difference was that **Lauda** was a promising Formula 1 driver, freshly signed by **Ferrari and** always a hard bargainer. Remember he still had a huge bank note to pay... **Ford** was on a spending spree at the time, also hiring **1973** champion **Toine Hezemans** from **BMW**, for a different reason: **Jochen Neerpasch**, **BMW**'s boss, offered the Dutchman a salary with a 30% deduction to keep him in **1974**. Some way to treat the current champion! As for prize money, little to no information is available. Some ETCC races, like **Monza**, would draw crowds of 40,000 plus people, **Nürburgring** and **Brno** drew even larger crowds but it seems very little of ticket sales ended up in drivers' pockets.

On the other hand, IROC champions could make a lot of money from relatively little work. In the first year of the series (**1973-1974**), champion **Mark Donohue** won no less than US$ 41,000 (some sources say over 50 grand), without spending a cent on the car. The catch was that IROC was an invitation only series and most invited drivers were American. Each of the colorful **Porsche** Carreras used in the maiden series were sold for US$21,500, so Penske lost no money on the made-for-TV series deal. One can only imagine how much these cars cost these days.

Major drivers, such as **Jean-Pierre Beltoise** and **Henri Pescarolo** often drove in the second string French sports car championship races of the day. **Dieter Quester** was a major international touring and sports car hero but every so often drove in the Austrian championship. At the height of his fame, in **1975**, **Jose Carlos Pace** traveled to Brazil a few times during the year to drive a **Ford** Maverick in long distance, Group 1 events, partnering **Paulo Gomes**. In fact, the duo won the championship and three races. **Jody Scheckter** would always find the time to drive in his country's 1000 km of **Kyalami**, in fact winning the race a few times during the 70s. They were international stars and definitely made more money than regulars.

Already an extremely well established star in **1971**, in fact a F-1 driver, **Mario Andretti** refused to leave his roots aside and in spite of a very busy season, drove in the Silver Crown sprint car competition, run in dirt tracks in U.S. Mid-Western Fairgrounds. I remind the reader that the USAC National Championship included assorted dirt tracks until **1970. Mario** also came back in **1973,** in fact, in **1974** he took the thing very seriously, winning three races and the championship. That was the end of his dirt track racing in the 70s, though.

In the early part of the decade, one could go racing on literally a shoestring. Sure, many people still do this today in amateur racing and entry level formulae, or the 24 Hour of Lemons here in the USA. But we are talking Formula 2, Formula 3, Sports and Touring cars, even Formula 1. The **Brabham** Formula 1 team had its first major sponsor, Martini, only in **1975** and still managed to be a topline team.

As for Formula Ford and Formula 3, many "teams" comprised a driver who doubled up as mechanic and team manager, a racing car, two engines, a street car plus a trailer, no different than the 50s impecunious drivers. Bear in mind we are talking about Western Europe, major championships. So it follows that most drivers needed to have a very good mechanical background in order to race, which is not the case today.

Even in Formula 2, in **1978** some entrants still lived a hand-to-mouth existence. **Alex Ribeiro** who had a very poor Formula 1 season with **March** in **1977,** went back to Formula 2 in **1978**. The team was he, a mechanic, a **March** car and Hart engines. No major sponsor. A devout Christian, **Alex** had the sayings "Jesus Saves" painted in different languages on the car and ended up getting some help from other Christians to continue racing. At the **Nürburgring,** of all places, **Alex** beat the full strength of **BMW**, represented by the **March** works team and Project Four. The challenge was not sustained the rest of the season, though. Prize money was not that great. In **1974**, Formula 2 paid about US$ 632.00 to race winners! Early on the decade, GP drivers reportedly made appearance money deals with organizers, to draw better crowds.

In fact, a large number of the Formula 2 entrants during the decade were of a simpler persuasion. A lot of them drove in the European Hill Climb championship, Austrian and Swiss championships, Group 8 and had very little to no sponsorship. At the top of the food chain were the works teams which used proprietary chassis and well-funded privateers such as Project Four and Fred Opert, which basically won everything, leaving scraps for others.

Professional Formula 3 teams, such as Project Four, Alan Docking, Euroracing, Unipart, Roger Heavens developed during the decade. These often ran multicar teams, had proper management, mechanics and even engineers and sponsorship money was put to good use. The structure of the successful Formula 3 teams of the future was formed in the mid to late 70s. To give you an idea, in **1979**, the budget to race in the British Formula 3 Championship was £ 3,000 per event, while total prize money was a mere £ 1,000 per round.

The fact is that prize money paid in lower categories was risible. The **1971** Formula Atlantic champion was slotted to get a mere £250! **Volkswagen**, never too fond of racing at the time, was a bit more lavish, offering the first Formula Super Vee champion £2,000. One should note that, at this time, things were much less expensive at this level. A Formula 2 FVA engine, very popular, cost £2,500. The BDA engine, used in the new Formula Atlantic category, cost half of that, which explains the initial hype.

The sponsorship fever that hit Europe, initiated in **1968**, spread all over the world and the vast majority of successful teams and drivers had sponsorship of some type. Argentina was a very peculiar case. The state oil company YPF paid most bills of the topline championships, meaning prize money and organization, although cars were sponsored individually. This came at a cost – no other oil companies could sponsor cars in Argentina, which caused a problem. As the **1974** oil crisis deepened and state oil companies in different countries mostly subsidized gasoline prices at the time, YPF being no different, the company was no longer full of cash and had to cut motor racing purses. This caused the immediate demise of the Argentinian Sports Car championship (many of the cars were sponsored by other oil companies before the YPF monopoly was established, such as Esso) and reduction of overall investment in the sport.

The extent of YPF's hold on car racing in the country is epitomized by a weird circumstance, in the **1972** Argentinean Grand Prix. The country was back on the F-1 World calendar for the first time since **1960** and you might have guessed that YPF was paying the bills. It did have some demands, though. The company wanted its logo appear in every car on the field, in the ring around the number, so except for **Reutemann**'s car, which was supported by YPF anyhow, the entire field had logos of two oil companies: YPF plus Shell, Elf, Agip, Fina, BP, Esso, Texaco. These were the days before tracks were overrun with throngs of lawyers, accountants, managers, media handlers, PR and trouble makers, so everybody agreed with such unusual situation. No major damage was done, because TV broadcasting of F1 races was still in its infancy, so the only people that saw this were those in physical attendance and readers of racing magazines, many of whom had no idea what YPF meant anyhow.

The Argentinean book *Auto Record 73* provides a very thorough report on driver earnings for some categories. We learn, for instance, that Turismo de Carretera's big money winner, **Nasif Estefano** (who had tried European Formula 1 in the early 60s, by the way), won 10,899,250 pesos moneda nacional. (Total prize paid in this category was 85,856,000 pesos). **Luis Di Palma** won 12,198,000 in Sports prototypes (69,326,375, total prize). **Angel Monguzzi** made 6,782,150 in Formula 1 (total prize 54,785,617), **Osvaldo Lopez** 3,070,468 in Formula 2, **Carlos Jaque**, 2,633,550 in Formula 4 and **Carlos Garro** 3,285,250 in Turismo Nacional. The amount paid to **Estefano**, converted to dollars would be around US$ 31,100. Note there were two official currencies in Argentina at the time, the peso moneda nacional and peso ley. If you use the peso ley conversion rate (around 10.50 to 1 USD) you would conclude that Argentina had the wealthiest racing scene in the world, which was not the case.

Ecuador is not known as a racing power house but when oil money started flowing in the early 70s, the little country began a love affair with the sport. The financial partner was not an oil company however but Marlboro. Not only did Marlboro sponsor the country's main race, the 12 Hours Marlboro but also the **Merello/Ortega/Hanft Porsche** 908 that finished 7th in **Le Mans, 1973**. The company also sponsored a team of **Surtees** Formula 2 cars for the Ecuadorians in **1974**. By the way, Marlboro in fact sponsored teams, individual drivers and championships all over the world, such as Argentina, Brazil, Macau, United States, all over Europe, in all almost all major categories, including Formula 1 and the World Manufacturers Championship.

In the **1975** season, Brazil, never known to have calendars that made sense, decided to reduce the number of dates, running Formula Ford together with

Prepared Touring Cars (Division 3) and Formula Super Vee with Prototypes (Division 4). The championships would have 6 dates, while Division 1, similar to European Group 1, had separate dates, after all, the races were long distance. The single seater series were respectively sponsored by **Ford** and **VW**, while the other two championships were sponsored by Caixa, a federal savings bank. For all intents and purposes, it worked well but it did not last long. Caixa decided to sponsor **Alex Ribeiro** in Formula 2, in **1976 and** the Division 3 and Division 4 championships were left on their own. The prototype championship did not come back at all, while the big banger class of Division 3 did not last beyond **1976**. This shows racing's very fragile state during the decade.

Brazilian *Auto Esporte* magazine actually addressed the subject thoroughly, with an article entitled "How much does it cost to race in Brazil", published in **1976**. The picture was not rosy. Formula Super Vee champion **Francisco Lameirao** earned Cr$121,173.63 (about US$16,500.00), during the season, however, his team's expenditures totaled Cr$719,000.00 during 1975 (roughly US$100,000), to cover payroll for a small staff, engines, parts, tires, transportation, fuel, etc. Tires, at the time imported, consumed a large percentage of the budget. The Formula Ford champion **Clovis de Moraes** made a bit more, having won a Maverick car in addition to prize money but it was obvious that one could not make money racing in Brazil and having a sponsor was essential to pay the bills.

Last but not least, top race drivers had been able to make money from advertising income for quite a while. This increased during the 70s, as commercial sponsorship became more prevalent and there was also an expansion of print and electronic media during the decade. Advertisements of drivers peddling a large number of goods and services appeared worldwide, as advertising agencies began to intensify marketing to young people. It should be remembered that unlike the current millennials, who in great numbers seem to think of cars and anything related to it (such as racing) enemies of mankind, in the 70s racing had a definitely young appeal. Many drivers, some of them not very famous but marketing savvy, were able to make a nice income as brand ambassadors and spokespersons, including for cigarette makers, which was even back then perceived as "not the right thing to do". As mentioned, Marlboro actually sponsored many drivers who did not necessarily drive Marlboro sponsored cars and in the US, Winston already sponsored the main NASCAR championship, which was called Winston Cup for many years, Hollywood was a major sponsor in Brazil, Lucky Strike in South Africa, Gitanes in France, 43 70 in Argentina, Colt in Finland, Memphis in Austria, West in Germany, etc. Hollywood actually had a number of advertisements published in Brazilian car magazines from 1971 until the demise of the team in 1976. The team's Porsche 908-2 appeared in ads way after it had been retired due to regulation issues. For a while Shelton, another Brazilian cigarette brand that sponsored Clovis de Moraes, winner of the 1972 Formula Ford title, attempted an advertisement war against Hollywood. Even drivers outside of Formula 1, such as Dutchman Toine Hezemans, were featured in print advertising from the likes of BMW. In fact, car manufacturers all over the world were not shy in promoting their racing success. Porsche frequently bought ads in major publications every time it won Le Mans, while Alfa Romeo bought ads in Singapore to promote Albert Poon's Asian success in its cars and British Leyland in Chile placed ads informing the public about the works team's win. Ford, Chevrolet, Renault, Datsun and other makes bought ads all over the world, in the USA, UK, France and elsewhere. A Brazilian ad for FIAT borders on the comical. The Italian company bought ads in conventional media promoting its dozens of wins during the 1978 season, forgetting one minor detail: FIATs only raced each other, in several single-make series in different regions of the country. The practice was old: Willys published many ads for its Gordini (Dauphine) car in the sixties, forgetting to say most were class wins, without any opposition. Not lies but not truth either. Read more about sponsors in the next chapter.

Marlboro paid lots of racing bills and driver salaries in the 1970s. (Kurt Oblinger)

SPONSORS

I could not write a book about racing in the 70s and leave out those who paid most of the bills – the sponsors. Most people will probably assume that only cigarette companies were involved in racing, given the high profile of sponsors such as Marlboro, JPS, Winston, Camel and Gitanes. But the fact is that a very wide range of industries were involved in racing sponsorship at the international, regional and domestic levels, all over the world. Some companies got a lot of bang from the buck they spent, with tons of advertising in various media, merchandising and promotions.

Back in the decade, **Ferrari** was not the only one to field works cars without any major sponsor decals decorating its racers. Works operations from the likes of **Ford, BMW, Alfa Romeo, Matra, British Leyland**, graced the racetracks without the benefit of major sponsorship. However, **Matra** received a large sum of money from the French Government to win Le Mans and **British Leyland** was a public company, so the deep pockets of governments often came into play, directly or indirectly. Nowadays, one rarely finds a race car without sponsor decals, specially at the highest levels, even works cars.

1977 1000 km of Nürburgring poster

This list is far from comprehensive. I hope it is an interesting sample of sponsors in the top categories. It lists mostly major sponsors and there were thousands of others. So if you think only cigarette companies were in the game in the 70s, you are dead wrong. The range is vast including companies in the following fields, besides tobacco: fuel, alcoholic beverages, non-alcoholic beverages, dairy foods, chocolate, perfumes, banks, car models, magazines, radio stations, stereo equipment, car dealerships, tools, preservatives, airlines, clothing line, jeans, refrigeration services, coffee, electronics, beef, car parts of all types, automotive magazines, cigarette (!) rolling papers, girly magazines, tiles, chicken, aluminum, watches, caravans (trailers), alarm systems, fabrics, weapons, sunscreen, eyewear, insurers, racetracks, funeral homes, export promotion, cigars, scooters, musical synthesizers, chemicals, construction, large and small appliances, real estate, newspapers, restaurants, sports teams, luggage, prunes, circus, hotels, heaters, bridal gowns, hairpieces, steel, drugstores, car rental, pizza chains, tires, cement, veal, radar detectors, boats, ice cream shops, temporary employment agency, etc. Even the city of Syracuse sponsored an Indycar, while a labor union, the Machinists Union, sponsored an Indycar team for many a year, into the 90s. The Republican Party sponsored Cale Yarborough's Indy car and a campaign for a 21st Constitutional Amendment sponsored Jerry Sneva in 1977.

Some sponsorship deals were unusual. For instance, Iso-Rivolta, a sports car manufacturer, sponsored a Formula 1 car, the **Williams**, with apparently no desire to suggest Iso made Formula 1 cars. At any rate, while sponsoring the car the company went bust, during **1974**, yet the **Williams** cars continued to be called Isos to the end of the season. Which does not mean that the sponsor paid the agreed amount, as you will find out elsewhere in this book.

Newsweek magazine sponsored a few teams, including **Keke Rosberg** in Formula 2 and so did girlie magazine Penthouse. In fact, the same car that was sponsored by that magazine in **1976** (the **Hesketh**), with a (dressed) pin-up girl, was also sponsored by a rolling paper manufacturer (Rizla). Plus there was a **Surtees** sponsored by a preservative brand, Durex. There was no political correctness in the world of F1 sponsors back in **1976**! The "indecent" sponsor led BBC to refuse broadcasting Formula 1 for a while.

Arturo Merzario is certainly not a superstitious man, for during the decade his car was sponsored by a funeral home, La Varesina! His car was also sponsored by Flor Bath, a semi esoteric brand of floral baths. Years before, his quick 2-liter **Abarth** carried stickers from weapon manufacturer **Beretta**, during the Silverstone race!

It is hard to fathom model car builders Minichamps and Spark as major sponsor of formula 1 teams in this day and age of multi-million budgets but model builders Norev, Matchbox, John Day and Politoys were major sponsors for **Surtees, March** and **Williams** cars in the 70s.

While Saudi money helped make **Williams** a top team and were quite a novelty when Saudia decals appeared on the **Williams March** in **1977**, this was not much of a lasting trend. After a few years, the Saudis dropped out. However, one of the **Williams** sponsors from the Saudi era is surprising: Bin Laden. Yes, that Bin Laden. Not Osama but his family, who owned the largest Saudi construction company at the time.

The Japanese little by little warmed up and were a fairly constant presence from the 80s on. Canon was an early presence, back in **1971** and a number of other company logos appeared in cars during the decade, Toshiba, Hitachi, Citizen, Fuji

Film, Nikon, Asahi-Pentax. **Teddy Yip** sponsored **Ronnie Peterson**'s car in **Long Beach, 1976**, the first time Chinese script appeared on a Formula 1 car.

Copersucar sponsored the Fittipaldi team during the 70s but would step out in 1980. (Kurt Oblinger)

Government agencies were also involved in sponsorship. Two **Brabhams**, in **1972** and **1973**, were sponsored respectively by the Argentine meat promotion agency (**Reutemann**) and the Brazilian coffee promotion agency (**Wilson Fittipaldi Jr.**). The latter also sponsored **Emerson** and **Pace's** helmets and it is claimed, almost had a F1 team of its own. Sometimes a country's export promotion agency would sponsor a driver from a different country, such as was the case of **Marie Claude Beaumont**, whose 2-liter **Lola** was sponsored by Ivorian Coffee. The Somali banana export agency was said to probe Italian teams, wishing to sponsor a Formula 2 team in 1973. It never happened. Swiss Cheeses sponsored many French drivers but also **Jo Bonnier**'s team, while Made in Britain was splashed all over **De Cadenet**'s car in the **1978 Le Mans**. Even the American GOP joined the party. The Republican party sponsored an Indy car for Cale Yarborough early on the decade.

Some unusual sponsors appeared in the 24 Hours of Le Mans, here and there. The restaurant Fouquet, which still exists in Champs Elysees, was a sponsor of the **Newman-Barbour-Stommelen** 2nd place car in **1979**. In **1978**, the **Whittington** brothers decorated their **Porsche** with the colors of Road Atlanta, the racetrack they had just bought. A **Lola** sponsored by "Macumba" also appeared in **1979**. In Brazil this is a form of voodoo. Scary stuff. But it was merely a cabaret in France. Not so bad.

It should also be noted that a number of companies from different fields sponsored entire championships, such as cigarette makers L&M in American Formula 5000, Winston at NASCAR, Camel at IMSA and Rothman's in European Formula 5000. British Formula 3 championships were sponsored by the likes of John Player,

Lombank, Forward Trust, Shellsport, BP Super Visco. Oil company YPF paid most of major Argentine racing bills early in the decade, as noted in the previous chapter and First National City Travelers Checks went into a shopping spree mid-decade.

While sponsors ensured the life of racing teams, at least in one case long litigation with a disgruntled sponsor is claimed to have caused the demise of a team. This involved the Belgian representative of Bang & Olufsen and the **Surtees** team. **John Surtees** claims that this litigation in British Courts drained his resources and energy and caused the ultimate closing of team **Surtees**.

Camel began its sponsoring activities in 1971. This is a 2-liter Lola. Photo by Lola Heritage.

At a more local level one could find mechanic shops, stores of all sizes and shapes, drive-in movies and a host of local businesses, who probably paid 500 bucks or less for the honor. NASCAR racers and Turismo de Carretera cars often carried dozens of minor sponsor decals, in addition to major sponsors. Very poorly done signage was often seen in less professional categories.

Ovoro is an Italian liqueur brand that sponsored a few cars in the 70s. It so happens that the company owner, Mario Casoni was also a driver, which made negotiations easier…This is a photo from Le Mans, 1975, when Casoni finished fourth, with Barth and Joest. The car is a Porsche 908-3 (Jurgen Barth collection)

70s Sponsors Sampler

21st Amendment
3M
AAW
Al Bilab
Alitalia
Alpine Stereos
Ambrozium
Amdahl
Antar
Arawak
Argentine Meat
Asahi Pentax
Atlanta Falcon
Auto Motor Und Sport
BAF
Banco Portugues do Brasil
Bang & Olufsen
Barclays
Bardahl
BASF
Belga
Beretta
Beta Tools
Bin Laden
BIP (Portuguese Bank)
Boraxo
Bosch
BP
Brahma
Brastemp
Brazilian Coffee (Café do Brasil)
Brooke Bond Oxo
Brumos
Bryant Heating and Cooling
Budweiser
Caixa
Calberson
CAM2
Camel
Campari
Candy
Canon
Capricorn
Castrol
Cebora
Ceramica Pagnossin
Citizen Watches
City of Syracuse
Coca-Cola
Colonial Bread
Colt
Coors Light
Copersucar

Creditum
Dairy Queen
Davia
Dinitrol
Direct Film
Domino's Pizza
Durex
Eifelland Caravans
Elf
Ellus
Embassy
Enny
Essex
Esso
E-Z Wider
F&S Properties
Fairo Drugs
Fernet Tonic
Filon
Fina
First National City Travellers Checks
Flame Out
Fouquet Restaurant
France Chauffage
Gatorade
Gelo
Genesee
Gilmore
Gitanes
Gold Leaf
Goodyear
Gosser
Gould
Grundig
Gulf
Haribo
Hawaiian Tropic
HB Bewaking Alarm Systems
Hermetite
Hertz
Heuer
Hitachi
Holly Farms
Hollywood cigarettes
Hy Gain
Iberia Airlines
ICI
Inaltera
Interscope
Isaura
Iso Rivolta
Ivorian Coffee

Jagermeister
Jesus Saves
John Day
Jorgensen
JPS
K&K Insurance
Kores
L&M
La Pierre du Nord
Lambretta
Lavazza
LEC Refrigeration
Lexan
Lexington
Liqui Moly
Lloyd's
Lowenbrau
Lucky Strike
Macumba
Mampe
Marlboro
Martini&Rossi
Matchbox
Mecarillos
Miller
Minolta
Mopar
Motorcraft
Motul
MS
Newsweek
Nikon
Norev
Norris Industries
Norton
Olsonite
Olympus Cameras
Ovoro
Parmalat
Pennzoil
Penthouse
Pepsi-Cola
Personal
Philippe Salvet
Polifac
Politoys
Pooh Jeans
Pronuptia
Provimi Veal
Purolator
Radio Luxembourg
Radio Montecarlo
Rastro
RC Cola

Red Roof Inn
Republican Party (USA)
Rizla
RMO
Rodenstock
Roland Music Synthesizers
Rotary Watches
Rothmans
Sadia
Samsonite
Sanyo
Saudia
Scaini
Schweppes
Searay Boats
Seiko
Sekurit
Shell
Simoniz
Singapore Airlines
Sin Mast
SKF
Skoal
Sugaripe
Sunoco
Swiss Cheese
Tabatip
Tag
Tergal
Texaco
Theodore
Thomson
Tissot
Toblerone
Toshiba
Travelodge
Truxmore
Ultramar
Unipart
Uni-Pex
University of Pittsburgh
UOP
Vaillant
Valvoline
Varig Airlines
Viceroy
Villiger
Voxson
Warsteiner
Weisberg
Wurth
Yacco
Yardley
YPF

THE WRITTEN PRESS AND ANNUALS

Let us face it. Motor racing coverage is mainly electronic these days. Newspapers, themselves a dying breed and specialized print magazines, do not cover racing like they used to and we, readers, do not consume the product as we used to. The few racing magazines that remain in print primarily publish articles and only Italian *Autosprint* continue to publish proper reports, with results, while France's *Auto Hebdo* does a good job. When this book comes out quite possibly the print version of British *Autosport* will be a thing of the past. During the 2020 pandemic, the publisher stopped publishing the print version and I reckon we will never see it on newsstands again. Let us see.

The problem with such a TV coverage model is that racing has become a product for immediate consumption. You watch one race today, then you watch another one and you forget everything very fast. As the entry lists are stable, there is almost nothing to differentiate from one race to the other. Grand events are basically the **Indy** 500 and 24 Hours of **Le Mans**, although the Germans love their decidedly non-championship 24 Hours of **Nürburgring,** the Grand Prix of **Macau** and the 1000 km of Bathurst remain healthy. Adding insult to injury, in the past 18 years or so domination has been the rule in top motorsports. **Michael, Vettel** and **Lewis** in F1, **Audi** in **Le Mans, Jimmy Johnson** in **NASCAR** and the **Sebs** in rallying.

It is not that I do not enjoy having five or six races to watch every week - I definitely do. I wish I could have watched all the racing I talk about in this book way back when but TV stations were few in most countries and auto racing transmissions were not the top priority in broadcasters' minds. Everything began to change when NASCAR got its first major TV deal in **1978** and even before that, **Bernie Ecclestone** was working towards turning Formula 1 into a proper TV product. That called, among other things, taking the **Nordschleife** and the old **Spa** off the schedule, venues which were totally improper for TV capabilities at the time. Technological advances, such as satellite availability and cost, were also at play.

It may come as a surprise, if you were not around in the 70s, that *Autosport* and *Autosprint,* both weeklies, were also the best magazines at the time, in terms of depth of coverage and detail. These magazines covered not only Formula 1 and other main championships well, they also included reports on racing across the world, their countries' local championships, providing lavish results for most events. *Motoring News* was a British newspaper that covered racing in great detail, specially British club racing and a must read for anybody in the racing business. As for *Motor Sport*, in spite of having **Denis Jenkinson** on staff, the magazine had poor quantitative coverage of racing activity across the world. One would find excellent articles during the 70s but a large portion of the magazine was devoted to classified advertisements for cars, which was a shame. However, one must pay the bills, always.

Remember that a lot of race reports were often given by phone, under complicated transmission conditions, or at best, telex. The fax machine already existed but it was extremely expensive, slow and not widely available and commercial email would only become available in the 90s. A lot of material, including rolls of film and actual reports, were shipped by post, airlines or diplomatic pouch. Now we complain that the internet is down for five minutes...

So it is an amazing thing that both *Autosport* and *Autosprint* were able to produce these magazines and put them on the newsstands that fast. I use to buy them in New York some five days after the weekend covered in the magazines.

The coverage provided by both magazines was complementary, in that Autosport tended to cover in detail racing in English speaking countries (Britain, USA, Canada, South Africa, Australia, New Zealand) including, of course, the British and Irish club scene and European and American racing in greater detail than the Italian magazine. Autosprint covered Italian race series but also, in the early part of the decade, the Argentine and Brazilian racing scenes. Additionally, Swiss, Austrian, Belgian, Spanish races were covered, with a summary result section that covered the prolific French hill climb scene. Both magazines included sporadic features on rarities such as Greek, Eastern European, Asian and African scenes, I suppose when there was space available.

The German magazines *Auto Zeitung* and *Auto Motor Und Sport* were rather stingy in terms of racing coverage space. For one, both of these magazines covered both racing and the automotive market, so there was not as much space as the other mentioned magazines, which were specialized in racing.

America's *Road and Track* contained some good articles but one cannot really say it covered racing. This was left to *Auto Week (previously Competition Press)*, at the time a weekly newspaper, which covered mostly racing. *Auto Week*'s coverage was very thorough, although it did not go into more exotic series and races, like the major European magazines. *National Speed Sport News*, a newspaper led by **Chris Economaki** covered American grass roots racing very well, although it was not readily available in many markets. *Stock Car Racing* covered NASCAR and other forms of Stock Car racing really well, plus there were other publications like *Auto Racing Digest* and *Formula* that contained some interesting information. *Motor Trend* and *Car and Driver* ran interesting racing articles every once in a while but they were really automotive magazines.

France's *Sport Auto* was well produced, featuring very good photographs and had good racing reports as well. *Auto Hebdo* provided coverage similar to today's and *Echappement* was also available to French enthusiasts. Argentina's *Parabrisas Corsa* covered Argentine racing very well, even the more obscure events but tended to be a bit negligent about racing elsewhere. There were other publications that covered racing in Argentina but they were not internationally available.

The two major Brazilian racing magazines of the 70s, *Quatro Rodas* and *Auto Esporte*, also had to share space in the publication, the former with automotive and travel, the latter, with automotive content. As a result, coverage suffered. There was a good balance of international and domestic racing but coverage of international events and categories was intermittent: three or four Formula 5000 reports in one month, nothing the rest of the year. As **Emerson Fittipaldi** became a successful Grand Prix driver, Formula 1 coverage expanded during the decade. *Grand Prix* was a true racing magazine, with very good photography but it did not last long. Its advertising base was restricted and I suppose, costs were high, given the quality. Specialized motoring newspapers were launched but never lasted too long.

A Swedish Motor Sport magazine cover

Racing magazines were published in several other countries

West Germany: Sport Auto, Rennsport Woche
Holland: Auto Visie, Motorsport Nieuws, Auto Kampioen
Portugal: Autosport, Motor
Venezuela: Mecanica Nacional, Fuerza Libre
Finland: Vauhdin Maailma
Ecuador: Carburando
Australia: Racing Car News
New Zealand: Motoraction
Sweden: Bilsport, Motor Sport, Racing Sport
Belgium: Sportmoteur/Motorensport, Retro, Virage
Japan: Auto Sport
Colombia: Motor
Angola: Revista do ACTA
Romania: Autoturism
Ireland: Auto Ireland
Chile: Estadio (actually a sports magazine, that often covered racing)
Denmark: Bil Nyt, Bilen Motor og Sport
Spain: Formula, Autopista
East Germany: Illustriert Motorsport
Hungary: Auto Motor
Poland: Motor
Mexico: Automundo
Yugoslavia: Avto Magazin (Slovenia), Sport Vozaci I Saobracaj (Croatia)

As for yearbooks, *Autocourse* was undoubtedly the best of the age. However, the result section of *Autocourse* as we know today only came to be in **1972**. One will be surely disappointed, buying earlier editions of the annual seeking the lavish results section of latter years. But even when the results section improved, there was never a constant set of results provided: one year, USAC Stock cars were included, then Canadian Formula Atlantic appeared, the Interserie soon was dropped out from the roster, South African Formula Atlantic considered worthy of inclusion, then excluded the next year. The **1974** edition only listed a couple of British Formula 3 events, while Formula Atlantic was thoroughly covered. As is almost always the case, there were tons of Formula 1 statistics, even Grand Prix race maps. The level of detail dropped according to importance. The yearbook, as most in the period, also covered rallies. There were obvious cost considerations were at play. The more pages a book has, the costlier it is. Current printing technology allows one to produce and prepare a book at a fraction of the cost and speed. That is why color photographs were few, not only in *Autocourse* but in almost every racing yearbook and book of the period. Generally, there was a short section of color panels in the more expensive books, if at all. Computer technology was not used in printing or production of books. This meant that a lot of people were involved in the process: the writer, hopefully some type of knowledgeable fact checker, a proof reader, an editor, the graphic designer, the typesetter and somebody who would check the type setter's work and sign off. Nowadays a writer is expected to do almost everything (sometimes even selling the books him(her)self).

Automobile Year, which was also published in French, *L'Année Automobile* and in other countries (*Ano do Automóvel* was published in Brazil during **Emerson**'s heyday) contained some racing information (mostly Formula 1 reports and articles on assorted series) results of FIA championships plus the Indy 500. Like some of the period's magazines, it had to share space with automotive industry and historical content.

A number of less costly yearbooks were also published in the period. **Barrie Gill** published yearbooks, first sponsored by John Player Special (*Motor Racing Year*) and then, by Marlboro (*International Motor Racing*). Gill's early yearbooks concentrated on some major championships (Formula 1, Formula 3, World Championship of Makes, European 2 Liter, Formula 5000), the American Racing Scene and Rallies, while simply overlooking others such as the European Touring Car Championship and Interserie, which were more "Continental" in character. There was reasonable coverage of other racing activity in England, with passing mention of club racing and most of these reviews tended to be on the economic side. The **1974** edition contained a nice attempt to cover racing in more exotic places, such as South America and Asia. The major flaw of Gill's *Motor Racing Year* was the inclusion, in every edition, of tiresome short reports of every Formula 1 Championship GP held from **1950** until the year in question, which consumed a large number of pages that could be better used providing results of the year's racing all over the world. As for the *International Racing Year,* the long review of GP results was gone but so was coverage of sports car racing. There was a nice section on up-and-coming drivers in the **1977** edition.

Anthony Pritchard, was the author of a condensed motoring encyclopedia but also published a nice yearbook series called Motor Racing Year from **1969** to **1973**. I managed to get my hands on the **1970, 71** and **72** editions. In addition to covering Formula One, **Pritchard**'s yearbooks contained complete articles on each event of the World Manufacturers Championship, as well as chapters on other important series of the season, such as F2, Can-Am, Interserie and European Two-Liter Championship. Interestingly, **Pritchard**'s yearbooks were virtually the only ones to contain detailed individual articles on the various extra championship Formula 1 events held at that time. In fact, other **1971** yearbooks, such as *Autocourse,* **Eddie Guba**'s yearbook and **Barrie Gill**'s *Motor Racing Year*, contained only (incomplete) results of the non-championship races - and nothing more.

Thus, Pritchard's **1971** Motor Racing Year (pages 138 to 141) was the only yearbook to contain a full report on the Jochen Rindt Gedachtnis-Rennen race, an extra championship race held at **Hockenheim**.

In this report, Pritchard emphatically says that **Ronnie Peterson** drove a **March** with an **Alfa Romeo** engine, instead of a Cosworth. It turns out that **ALL** other sources found on the Internet and outside (including the other yearbooks), provide a more traditional motorization, the Cosworth engine!!!

Pritchard, whose books generally contained no errors, insisted that **Peterson** drove chassis 6 in the race, with an **Alfa Romeo** engine. **Pritchard** was so thorough that he even indicated which chassis was being used by each driver even in the extra championship races. The "**Alfa Romeo** engine" information is contained in the entry list, in the body of text (where **Pritchard** says that **Peterson** had at his disposal the chassis 02, with **Ford** engine, as a reserve) and then super emphatically at the end of the article and in the result of the race. In fact, the last sentence of the report was "Peterson was almost a minute behind at the checkered flag but this was the best performance to date by Type 33-3 Alfa engined car". That is, the author makes a point of stressing that **Peterson** drove an **Alfa Romeo**-powered car! The race result again indicates the Italian motorization in the car!

The Autosprint race report of this race, won by **Jacky Ickx**, is the only other place that identifies the Alfa engine equipping **Peterson**'s car (fact or fake?). Was **Peterson** the author of a heroic act by taking a **March-Alfa** to second place in an F1 race?

It turns out that the report by **Pritchard** and Autosprint are the only places I found, on paper or online, that say that **Peterson** used the car with the **Alfa** engine and both are very emphatic about it. The site in tribute to **Peterson**, in Swedish, goes so far as to say that **Ronnie** practiced with the **Alfa** powered car in that race but ran with **Ford**. Autocourse, **Eddie Guba**'s and **Barry Gill** annuals and every other race result site list the **Ford** engine, instead of the Alfa.

Disillusions and myths aside, here are some considerations. First, if **Peterson**, the king of the second places in **1971,** came second at **Hockenheim**, the almost one minute that separated him from **Ickx** in such a short race makes me question whether the car was in fact equipped with the **Ford** engine. This huge gap could be an indication that the engine was the less swift **Alfa**.

But why would **Pritchard**'s and Autosprint's information be against that provided by the rest of the world? Did everybody else simply assume that the **March** used by **Peterson** in that race was the conventional **March-Ford** (or did the official result provided by organizers stated that and no one, besides **Pritchard** and Autosprint, probed further)?

What would have led **Pritchard** to make such a faux pas, if he was wrong and reiterate it in four different places in his otherwise flawless book? The fact is that **Pritchard** was a prolific author of several other motoring books, one of them not yet released, on a series of subjects. A highly respected and meticulous author. **Anthony** was the only person who could answer these questions. I say was because, unfortunately, he died of an accident recently.

So always healthily question any motoring information your gut tells is "unusual", because even work by knowledgeable authors could contain mistakes.

Eddie Guba's *Motor Sport Annual* had a nice, spacious layout, with many photographs, although the sequence of the book was confusing. It started with touring cars, then hill climbs, sports cars, then single seaters, back to a NASCAR table, back to Formula 2, 3, etc. The results section at the end was much better than what *Autocourse* had to offer at the time, with fairly complete results (or points tables) for almost every category covered, including Formula Super Vee rarely covered elsewhere.

The Germans tended to provide more coverage of Interserie and Formula Super Vee than other yearbooks, for obvious reasons, which is what you find in the

Autodrom yearbooks published in the German language. The books also covered the DRM, Formula 1 and 2, world Sports Cars but no mention whatsoever of the American racing scene. The particular flaw of the German published yearbooks, both the hard cover **Guba** titles and the *Autodrom*, is that they tended to fall apart with time, something that did not happen to British yearbooks.

FIA also published the *"Annuaire du Sport Automobile"* (*Year Book of Automobile Sport*), an almost pocket size book, that contained a lot of information other yearbooks did not have: regulations, names of graded drivers, official schedules for the upcoming season, list of homologated production cars. It also contained the layout of several tracks, an unusual and welcome feature.

NASCAR also published a nice pocket-sized yearbook containing the results of the preceding season's racing. It listed not only complete results of every Winston Cup race but also the final results of over 100 championships sanctioned by NASCAR all over the country. IMSA also published an annual during the decade, in a different format, while the SCCA and USAC apparently refrained from the practice – at least I have not seen one.

Several other countries published yearbooks as well. Although Portugal was not a hotbed of racing activity during the decade, **Francisco Santos** began publishing his yearbook "*Motores*" in the 70s. The journalist would continue publishing racing yearbooks for many years.

Argentina had an extremely thorough review of its domestic scene, in the form of *Auto Record*. In keeping with the proud and independent character of Argentine racing that lasts to this day, information on domestic racing is presented first, international racing (including Formula 1) towards the back of the book. The book contains full results of every Argentine national championship race, technical details on cars, points table and even an earnings table! The only flaw was the failure to include at least a summary of regional racing in the country, which was already very prolific.

Today's global general press basically overlooks racing events, in print and online form, with the exception of Formula 1, Indy 500 and NASCAR, or when a major accident occurs. Back in the 70s, regular newspapers all over often devoted large number of pages to domestic racing activities, with results, special features etc. And if you run a search on the American newspaper clipping site newspapers.com, which includes newspapers from the USA, England, Scotland, Australia and even Panama, you will see surprising mentions of even minor racing events popping up in newspapers in midsize to small American cities. Of course, such news were picked up on wire of news agencies such as AP and Reuters, in days when there was some vacant space on the newspaper, not because there was so much interest. Thus people somewhere in the Midwest of the United States could learn of **Tony Trimmer**'s latest win in 1970 British F3 or the news from a race in Southeast Asia. News were not always 100% accurate: names were frequently botched and **Lella Lombardi**, for one, was rechristened **Lola Lombardi** here and there. A lot of the information in this book has been picked up from newspaper clippings of dozens of countries, published on websites, blogs, forums and social media pages and even online clipping services. The site Eresourcesnib.gov.sg which contains clippings from newspapers in Southeast Asia, in English and local languages, gives an idea how a local driver would become a sports hero of the day. The exploits of driver **Sonny Rajah** are widely covered in a number of articles during the decade, which is not the case of the average local driver of the age.

MISCELLANEOUS

FEMALE DRIVERS

The 70s was an important decade for female drivers, with many prominent achievements in the European, American, African and Asian scenes. It all started in the 1970 Macau Grand Prix, when Singaporean **Annie Wong** beat a field full of men during the supporting touring car event. **Annie** remained a fixture of Southeast Asian racing during the decade. Little by little, female drivers were taken more seriously by males and the public. In long distance racing, the somewhat condescending practice of teaming women only with other women lost traction, as drivers such as **Lella Lombardi, Waltraud Odenthal, Lyn St. James** proved they were more than a match for their male counterparts. In solo racing, women raced in **Indianapolis**, returned to **Le Mans** and scored in Formula 1. The top exponents are listed below.

LELLA LOMBARDI

Lella Lombardi became the first female driver to score points in Formula 1, when she finished sixth in Spain, **1975**, driving a full season for **March**. As the race was stopped before half distance, she only got half a point. In addition to this, **Lella** became the first female driver to win a World Championship event, when she won a World Sportscar event at Enna in **1979**, sharing an **Osella** with **Luigi Moreschi**. She would also win a second time in the same year, at **Vallelunga**, driving with **Giorgio Francia**. **Lella** had a variety of rides in many categories. She did Formula 3, then Formula 5000, raced in Australia, Interserie, drove in the British Group 8 series, achieving some notable results. She raced **FIATs** and **Alfa Romeos** in touring cars, including the ETCC and even tried her hand at NASCAR! She raced at **Le Mans** a few times during the decade and among others, she raced an **Alpine-Renault** with **Marie Claude Beaumont** in **1975** (see below for more information about the season in that car), a **Lancia Stratos** with **Christine Dacremont** in 1976, an **Inaltera** with **Christine Beckers** in **1977** (11th overall, 5th in class). She was for sure the most accomplished female driver of the age.

MARIE CLAUDE BEAUMONT (CHARMASSON)

Marie-Claude's father <u>and</u> mother used to race in rallies in the 50s, so it is fitting that she loved the scene. Although she was mostly a (successful) rally driver, **Marie Claude** achieved fame in **1971** by becoming the first woman to be allowed to race at the 24 Hours of **Le Mans** since **1951,** for women had been barred from the race since the death of **Annie Bousquet** in the 12 Hours of **Rheims** in **1956**. Not only that, she raced a powerful Corvette in the race. **Marie Claude** also drove this car in the European GT Championship in **1972**. In a very short period of time, she had a varied career in 70s circuit racing. She raced a 2-Liter **Lola** in the European Championship of **1973**, won the Coupe de l'Agaci in **1974** driving a 2-Liter **Alpine** prototype, also won a couple of touring car races in **1974**, driving **Opels** in **Paul Ricard** and **Croix-en-Ternois**. In 1975 Marie-Claude was teamed with **Lella Lombardi** for a full World Manufacturers Championship season in a 2 liter **Alpine-Renault**, finishing 4th in **Monza** (class winners) and 6th in **Mugello**. They also raced the same car at **Le Mans**. Her attempt to race in Formula 2 at **Rome** was not successful, DNQ with an **Elf**. Her best **Le Mans** result was 19th, sharing a **Porsche** 934 with **Bob Wollek** and **Didier Pironi** in **1976**. She also won the very first French Supertourisme race, in **1976**, driving a **BMW** 3.0 CSL at **Monthlery**, achieving other placings during the course of the season. **Marie Claude** also won her class at **Bathurst, 1975,** sharing an **Alfa Romeo** with **John Leffler**. She also raced in hill climbs.

CHRISTINE BECKERS

Belgian **Beckers**, who also raced under the name "**Christine**" had been racing for a few years by **1970**. She did rallies, hill climbs and circuit racing and participated in many events. She was one of the prominent female drivers of the decade with many participations at **Le Mans**, including a class win in the **1974** 24 Hours of **Le Mans**, winning the 2-liter prototype class with **Yvette Fontaine** and **Marie Lourent**. She was 3rd in the **Nürburgring** round of the ETCC, with **Teodoro Zeccoli** in an **Alfa Romeo**, in **1970**, also finishing in the top 5 in five other occasions. She continued to drive for **Alfa Romeo** in **1971** and won races overall at **Dijon** and **Paul Ricard** in **1972**, plus raced a 2-Litre **Chevron** with **Roger Dubos**, at the Four Hours of **Le Mans** of **1971** and 1000 km of **Spa** of **1973**. During the decade, she was three times female driving Champion of Belgium, in **1970, 1972** and **1974**.

LIANE ENGEMANN

Dutch **Liane** raced in both touring cars and single seaters, in fact she had raced in F3 in **1969**. She was one of the drivers who participated in the BUA sponsored Formula Ford Tournament held in Brazil in early **1970**. **Lianne** also took part in the 24 Hours of Spa of **1970** sharing an **Alfa Romeo** with **Christine Beckers**, then raced a **Ford** Escort for a Dutch team the rest of the season. She raced **Alfa**s in the ETCC and Holland in **1971** and also drove at the **Targa Florio** in a **Porsche**, had a go in a 2-Liter **Abarth** Prototype in **Zandvoort**, finishing 7th. **Engemann** featured well in DRM races driving a **Ford** Capri in **1972**, finishing the championship's very first race in 4th. She retired in **1973**.

WALTRAUD ODENTHAL

Waltraud Odenthal was a German touring car driver who impressed greatly in early DRM races. **Waltraud** was the daughter of a **Ford** dealer, so her career was based spent driving **Ford** touring cars. She began the decade driving Escorts, by **1971** had upgraded to the larger Capri. **Waltraud** finished the very first DRM race ever in 5th place, behind another female driver (**Liane Engemann**), at the **Nürburgring**, where she finished fourth again later in the season. She also competed in the ETCC, often driving outside of Germany, such as in Austria, Sweden, Holland and Italy. In fact, she finished 5th in the **1973** Monza ETCC round, pairing with **Klaus Fritzinger**, another DRM **Ford** exponent. She continued with DRM and ETCC in **1974** and drove with **Klaus Ludwig** in **Vallelunga**, finishing fourth. From **1975** until **1977** she only raced in her native Germany, winning at **Mainz Finthen** overall and posting a touring car win at the **Ulm-Mengen** hill climb. She managed a fifth place in the **1976** DRM race at **Hockenheim**: to her credit, by then the **Ford** Capris were totally outclassed by **Porsches** in her class. She retired in **1977**.

DESIRE WILSON

South African **Wilson**'s major accomplishments would come in the 80s but she did enough in this decade to justify listing here. **Desire** started racing Formula Vees in South Africa, later changing to Formula Ford, becoming the **1976** South African champion in this category. As a result she got a scholarship to drive in Europe and won a Formula Ford 2000 race in **Zandvoort** in **1977**. She raced an **Ensign** in the Aurora AFX series in **1978**, posting one 3rd, one 4th and to 6th places. She also got rides in Sports 2000 and Super Vee. For **1979 Desire** got a **Tyrrell** 008 for the Group 8 series, actually leading and earning the fastest lap at **Zolder** but ended up third. She was seventh in the series, with four 3rd places and 2 fourths and placed 3rd in the Sports 2000 series.

DIVINA GALICA

Galica was an Olympic level skier, used to downhill speeds upwards of 125 miles per hour. For promoter **John Webb** she seemed a perfect match for one of his **1974** Escort celebrity races. **Divina** not only raced the Escort but also finished second and got the racing bug. She went to a race driving school and in the next couple of years continued racing in Escorts, finishing second in a ladies-only championship, in addition to doing some Formula Ford. The racing world was somewhat shocked when the British driver decided to race a **Surtees** TS16 Formula 1 car in the **1976** Shellsport Championship. One of the few drivers to race a Formula 1 car that season, **Divina** did reasonably well with a bad car and finished fourth in this first season. Perhaps a bit prematurely, **Divina** tried to qualify the TS-16 in the British Grand Prix without success. She also raced in Formula Ford 2000. For **1977** she had a better car, a **Surtees** TS19 and although she finished only 6th in the final table, she had a couple of impressive runner-up placings in individual races. She also raced in Sports 2000, finishing second in the championship. For **1978** she got a berth in the **Hesketh** team for World Championship racing but the car was very poor and she never qualified it. She did finish 2nd in **Zandvoort**'s Aurora race and drove in Canadian Formula Atlantic. In **1979** she raced a Formula 2 in the Aurora AFX Championship, once finishing in 5th place. **Divina** won 9 Sports 2000 races during the decade and continued racing into the 80s and 90s.

GABRIEL KONIG

Gabriel was a female Irish driver, don't let the name fool you. She did not go far up the ladder in her career, thus her name might not sound familiar but a couple of South American excursions are noteworthy. **Gabriel** was one of the drivers who raced in the BUA Formula Ford series in early **1970** and a nasty accident at **Interlagos** sidelined her for the rest of the season. She would find better luck racing in Guyana and Barbados, in **1972**, winning 3 races overall driving a **Chevrolet** Camaro, under the "Team Speedbird" banner. This was the same car she used in British Group 1 racing during the season, occasionally winning and posting fastest laps in Britain and her native Ireland. Eventually she moved to Guyana, where she continued to win races in a **Vauxhall** Viva.

HANNELORE WERNER

This German driver achieved notoriety by finishing 2nd in a non-championship Formula 2 race at the **Nürburgring, 1970**, won by **Xavier Perrot**. There were some very good drivers at the track that day, such as **Tim Schenken, Carlos Reutemann** and **Derek Bell**, so this was no fluke. She also showed well in

Formula 3 races in Germany in **1970**. **Hannelore** appeared and won, many other races, mainly in Germany in the 60s, including Formula Vee and a 24 Hour touring car race with **Rudiger Faltz**, in 1969, the forerunner of the 24 Hours of **Nürburgring**. She continued racing Formula 3 cars in **1971** (won at **Niederstetten**, second at **Bremgarter**). She was third in the Championship.

ANNE-CHARLOTTE VERNEY

During the 70s **Verney**, who lived in **La Sarthe**, where the **Le Mans** track is located, raced 6 times in the 24 Hours, always with creditable results. Her best was 1st in class in **1978**, sharing a Group 4 **Porsche** with **Xavier Lapeyre** and **Francois Servanin** but she also finished 2nd and 3rd once. She began her competition career driving rallies and also raced in other long distance events, including an outing in the 1000 km of **Paul Ricard** in a **Chevron,** with **Daniel Brillat**, while in **1976** she raced a **Porsche** 935 pairing with **Hubert Streibig** in several World Manufacturers Championship rounds. She also did other races with **Streibig** in **1977** and **1978**, including an outing in a 2-liter **TOJ** in **Monza**. She also raced in the 24 Hours of Spa of **1979**, in a Ford.

YVETTE FONTAINE

Belgian Fontaine had been racing since **1969** and by **1970** did a race for Autodelta, the **Alfa Romeo** works team. She was primarily a touring car driver, winning races and championships in her native country and often participating in races at **Spa**, where she finished 2nd in the **1975** 24 Hours. **Yvette** was also a class winner in the **1974** 24 Hours of **Le Mans**, winning the 2-liter prototype class with **Christine Beckers** and **Marie Lourent**. She finished 2nd in the GT class in **1975** (11th overall), sharing a **Porsche** with **Corinne Tarnaud** and **Anne Charlotte Verney**.

MICHELE MOUTON

Michele Mouton is best remembered as one of the top rally drivers of the eighties. However, before that **Mouton** shared a **Moynet-Chrysler/Simca** with other female drivers **Cristine Dacremont** and **Marianne Hoepfner**, winning the 2-liter prototype class in the **1975** 24 Hours of **Le Mans**. They finished only 21st but ahead of six other cars. This was **Mouton**'s only **Le Mans**.

JANET GUTHRIE

Janet raced small sports and touring cars from the 60s to the early 70s but then one day she decided she was going to be the first female driver in the **Indy** 500, when she accepted the challenge placed by Indy team owner **Rolla Vollstedt**. It did not take her too long to do it. She failed to qualify in **1976**, still learning the ropes but managed to qualify in **1977**, ending a creditable 9th in **1978**, She was also the first female to drive in the **Daytona** 500 and to lead a NASCAR race. Her first Indycar race took place in **Trenton**, for **Vollstedt**, in **1976**. Some of the guys did not like a woman in their midst, there was rejection from some corners but little by little got the respect she deserved, specially after finishing 15th in her NASCAR debut. She also started an Indycar race in 4th place (**1979 Pocono** 500) and finished fifth at Milwaukee. She retired at the end of that season.

Janet Guthrie did well at Indy, NASCAR and elsewhere. Photo by Rob Neuzel.

LYN ST. JAMES

Lyn became more famous for her outings at the **Indy** 500 in the 90s but she had in fact began racing in **1972**. Her major outings in the 70s were long distance races in the IMSA series, driving cars such as a Corvette and **Ferrari** 365 GT/4. She shared this latter car with two other women, **Bonnie Henn** and **Janet Guthrie**, in the 12 Hours of **Sebring** of **1979**. She also finished eighth (4th in class) in the Paul Revere event in Daytona that same year.

MOVERS AND SHAKERS

It would be perhaps unfair to write a book celebrating racing in the 70s and leave out the people who made things happen in the background. Drivers are important but so are team owners, managers and designers, in fact, most of the pivoting has happened because of these fine folks. As I do not want to ascribe any ranking and invoke the wrath of sensitive folks (there are many in racing circles, I have learned over the course of the years), the list will be in alphabetical order, by first name. Sure, a few hundred more people could be included and perhaps will be so in future editions. For the time being, here are a few. Please note that these are not meant as full biographies but rather, profiles that concentrate on the individual's contribution to 70s racing.

ALEXANDER HESKETH

The somewhat rotund **Lord** was called a breath of fresh air when he burst into the Formula 1 paddock in **1973**. The eponymous team had a **March** 731 and **James Hunt**, a rock star looking driver widely referred to as *Shunt* in the near past, plus a young designer called **Harvey Postlethwaite**. **Hesketh** had been **Hunt**'s patron for a short while and quickly decided that hanging around in Formula 2 was counter-productive. The combination **Hunt-March-Harvey** was sensational and before the year was over **Hunt** had been on the podium a couple of times. How could this be possible in an unsponsored atmosphere of utter cheerfulness, with beautiful models, good food and wine flying about? Well, **Hunt** and the Lord stayed together a couple more seasons, by which time there was a car named **Hesketh** that won a Grand Prix in short order. The Lord was wealthy but no **Onassis**, thus he pulled the plug late **1975**. The team continued a few more seasons with the same name, under the guidance of sometime Hesketh team driver **Bubbles Horsley** but it was never the same. It was very magical and very short.

BERNIE ECCLESTONE

Much has been written in this book concerning the importance of **Bernie Ecclestone** to Formula 1 and global racing. Quite simply, one can say there was racing before and after **Bernie**. He turned racing into a sound business and brand, a rich business and powerful brand at that. Although mostly concerned with Formula 1, **Ecclestone** influenced the way drivers, team owners, sponsors, media, politicians, promoters, track owners, manufacturers and even the public interacted. His tactics and actions have often been called into question but the fact is, he became very wealthy but so did hundreds of others since **1971**. He began the decade as **Jochen Rindt**'s buddy-advisor-manager and after the Austrian's death, he decided to stay in Formula 1, buying **Brabham** from **Ron Tauranac** in **1971**. He soon began negotiating deals on behalf of somewhat clueless and commercially naïve Formula 1 team owners and by the end of the decade had consolidated his position as "the man" in Formula 1. Read more about this in the chapters **The 70s – The End of the Romantic Era, Pivoting to Organization** and **Money**. Draw your own conclusions.

CARL HAAS

Carl Haas, no relation to the current **Haas** formula 1 team owner's, was **Lola**'s importer in the USA, besides having other business endeavors. Given the large number of cars sold in the country for Formula 5000, Formula Super Vee, Formula Ford, Prototypes, Can Am, Formula B, USAC, etc, **Haas** did brisk business. However, he is better known for owning the team that utterly dominated the American Formula 5000 championship from **1974** to **1976** (all won by **Brian Redman**) and then the revamped, single seater Can Am until the end of the decade (**Tambay, Jones** and **Ickx**). Most people will remember him from CART TV transmissions starting in the 80s, always chewing on a huge cigar as **Paul Newman**'s partner.

CARLO CHITI

After leaving **Ferrari** in **1962**, **Chiti** joined the failed **ATS** operation (no relation to the 70s/80s formula 1 team) and was eventually hired by **Alfa Romeo**, setting up **Autodelta**. Under his leadership, the team won the European Touring Car Championship in **1970**, with **Toine Hezemans** and the World Sports Car Championship in **1977**. By **1970 Alfa Romeo** had a 3-liter prototype that could challenge the **Porsche** 908-3 and **Matra-Simca**, finishing 2nd in the 1000 km of **Oesterreichring**. Autodelta's best year was unquestionably **1971**, when the **Alfas** beat **Porsches** and **Ferraris** fair and square in **Brands Hatch, Targa Florio and Watkins Glen**. The next three seasons yielded a single win at **Monza**, in **1974**, by then with a 12-cylinder Alfa engine. The **Alfa**'s most competitive year in the makes Championship was **1975** but the cars were run by the **Willi Kauhsen** team, not Autodelta. During the course of the decade the **Alfa** GTAM was no longer competitive against the **Ford** Capri and **BMW** 2800/3.0 CSL, so eventually **Alfa Romeo** had to be content with class wins in the ETCC, which it managed often. Alfa's forays into Formula 1 were also poor during the decade. As an engine supplier to **Andrea de Adamich**'s and **Nanni Galli**'s **McLaren** and **March** mounts in **1970** and **1971**, the 8-cylinder engines were always also-rans. Much hope was placed on the 12-cylinder that powered **Brabham** from **1976** until **1979** but the partnership yielded two wins, both under questionable circumstances: in Sweden with the fan car and in Italy, after the **Mario Andretti** and **Gilles Villeneuve** were handed 1 minute penalties. As **Brabham** gave up on the engine, Autodelta decided to set up its own Formula 1 team, which debuted in **1979**, with **Chiti** still at the helm.

COLIN CHAPMAN

Writing a short entry on **Colin Chapman** is almost embarrassing, given his outstanding contribution to race car design and the racing business in general. Many of the **Lotus** cars were not entirely designed by **Colin**: he used to have ideas which were conveyed to trained engineers such as **Maurice Phillippe**, which duly executed them. Allegedly, **Colin** had design ideas in the unlikeliest of places and these were put down on paper napkins, among other mundane things. The **Lotus** 72, which debuted in **1970** and won that year's championship, set the tone for early 70s single seater design, with its edge shape, side radiators and other goodies. Then, the **Lotus** 78 and 79 brought another revolution in the form of skirts, wing cars and ground effect. The 72 and 79 models resulted in 3 driver championships for **Lotus** during the decade (plus four manufacturer championships), so that **Lotus** was clearly one of the decade's main manufacturers. There were failures too: the 76 of **1974** and the Texaco Star Formula 2 of **1973** were dismal failures, the first one leading to an extended use of the 72 one additional, unintended year. **Colin**'s business approach was also very influential, for **Lotus** was the first team to use commercial sponsorship in Formula 1 in **1968**. **Lotus** stopped making race cars besides Formula 1 as of **1974**. **Chapman** would not survive much longer after the end of the decade.

COUNT RUDI VAN DER STRAATEN

Van Der Straaten was the owner and patron of the Belgian VDS team, one of the last truly privateer teams which did not depend on outside sponsorship at all. His team raced during the entire decade, starting as a sports car team in **1970**, fielding a **Lola** T70 in the World Manufacturers Championship and other races throughout Europe. The car was outdated by then but managed to win at **Vila Real** and also raced at **Le Mans** in **1971**. The team eventually bought a **McLaren** for Interserie racing, that was destroyed in a terrifying accident in **1973**. In **1971** the team found its true vocation: Formula 5000. The team won many races in this category, including 3 championships (European in **1973** and **1975**, with **Teddy Pilette** and Tasman Cup in **1974**, with **Peter Gethin**). When the European championship was discontinued, VDS moved its operations to the USA in **1976**. At first it was not very successful in Formula 5000 but as the category itself morphed into the new Can-Am, the team became the second most successful team in the category, with runner-up positions in **1977** (**Gethin**) and **1978** (**Warwick Brown**). The team continued in Can Am during the eighties, eventually building a proprietary chassis.

Team VDS's true vocation was Formula 5000. (Photo Teddy Pilette collection)

DAN GURNEY

Gurney was still capable of winning races as a driver, as he showed by capturing the first two Can-Am races of **1970** but time had come to hang his helmet. **Gurney**'s main influence in the 70s was as the owner of **Eagle**, the make that won no less than 32 USAC races during the decade, thus the top winner. In addition to that, **Eagle** attempted to crack Formula 5000 and even Formula Ford, although it was not successful in both endeavors. Many of the 70s Indy fields had a large percentage of **Eagles**, including the **Indy** 500s but by the end of the decade the make was overtaken by the likes of **Penske, Lola** and **McLaren**.

Dan Gurney raced very little in the 70s (but still won 2 Can Ams). His Eagles were for many years the most important Indy chassis. Photo by Rob Neuzel.

DAVID BALDWIN

David Baldwin was a **Lotus** engineer who became famous when his **Ensign** MN176 showed a great turn of speed in **Chris Amon**'s hand in **1976**. The car was an evolution of the **1975** car, also designed by the engineer and surged towards the front in many races during the **1976** season, earning a 5th in Spain and starting 3rd in Sweden and 6th in England. However, like **Lotus, Baldwin's Ensigns** tended to be fragile and **Amon** and later **Ickx**, had some terrifying moments in the car. **David** did not finish the season in the small British team, instead, joined **Fittipaldi**, where he designed the F5, which in its original form was not successful. It was very similar to the **Ensign** but its performance only improved after **Giacomo Caliri** and **Ralph Bellamy** revised the car for **1978**. By then **Baldwin** was long gone, in fact he left before the car ever raced. His next design was **1979**'s revised **Shadow** DN9, which was not successful.

DEREK BENNETT

Bennett was **Chevron**'s boss. The make had built successful single seaters and prototypes for a few years by **1970**, however, it was during the 70s, that **Chevron** achieved its greatest success and notoriety, with **Chevrons** racing and winning all over the world in Formula 2, Formula 3, Formula Atlantic, Formula 5000 and prototypes. There were plans to enter Formula 1 but in the end no **Chevron** ever raced in the World Formula 1 championship, although a F1 racer, the B41 was completed and ran in the Aurora Championship, the best result a 2nd by **Tiff Needell** in **1979**. **Chevron** prototypes won the first edition of the European 2-Liter Championship, in spite of a great challenge from **Lola**. **Chevron** 2-liter cars raced all over the world, winning races in European hill climbs, SCCA amateur races, Springbok races in South Africa and Japanese sports car races, plus a large number of class wins, including at **Le Mans**. Some of the make's cars were also equipped with 3-liter Cosworth engines, albeit not successfully. In Formula 2, **Peter Gethin** had a famous win at **Pau, 1972** and later in the decade, **Chevron**'s did well, in total winning six F-2 Championship races. **Gethin** also drove a **Chevron** in the only instance Formula 5000s beat Formula 1s in a mixed race, the **1973** Race of Champions. Eight of twenty Formula 2 point scorers in **1978** drove **Chevrons**. The make also won in Formula 3 during the decade, including the **1976** European Championship with **Riccardo Patrese**, plus **Teddy Pilette** drove a **Chevron** to victory in the **1973** European Formula 5000 Championship. **Derek Bennett** died before the end of the decade, in a hang gliding accident in **1978** and in short order the company closed, in spite of company director's **Paul Owens**' best efforts. The closing of the company severely affected **John Bridges**. You may recognize him as one of the main **Chevron** drivers early in the decade. It so happens that the "B" in **Chevron**'s name was given as recognition to **Bridges**, who invested a inherited lot of money in the company through the course of the years. The ultimate demise of **Chevron** was caused by a failed Can-Am Car deal with **Paul Newman**. As a result, **Bridges** lost his house and the family's farm.

DEREK GARDNER

Derek Gardner shot to prominence as the designer of **Tyrrell**'s early Formula 1 cars. His first design debuted in **1970** and although fast, it did not win. However, in the next season **Stewart** and **Cevert** won no less than seven of the championship's eleven races, raising **Gardner's** reputation accordingly. **Derek** continued with the team and designed the **1972** and **1973** challengers, which won another nine races in **Stewart**'s hands, plus the driver championship in **1973**. The decline came soon - the 007 was a good car but **Scheckter** and **Depailler** were no **Stewart** and were still inexperienced at the F1 level. In its three years racing (the third mostly in the hands of privateers), the car won only three races. For **1976**, Derek decided to revolutionize and produced the only 6-wheel formula 1 car that ever raced, the **Tyrrell** P34. The car raced in **1976** and **1977** and although it got many placings and a win in Sweden, **1976**, plus 3rd in the driver's and manufacturers championship in **1976**, it did not display any of the expected advantages vis-à-vis the traditional four-wheelers. The designer expected aerodynamic advantages, better braking with the smaller wheels, improved grip but none of this seemed to transpire and the idea was quickly cast aside, after two seasons. That was the last we saw of **Gardner** in Formula 1, who decided to pursue other engineering interests after falling ill. Starting **1971, Tyrrell** cars adopted the signature full-width nosecone, a concept which was copied under different shapes by **BRM, March, Hesketh, Williams, Ensign, Brabham, Trojan, Surtees, Amon, Tecno, Matra-Simca, Renault and** tried by others. In fact, **Tyrrell** dropped the concept in the 007 but resumed use of it in the P34.

DON NICHOLS

American **Nichols** was allegedly a CIA agent at one point or another and his team's logo was in fact a shady character. Be that as it may **Nichols' Shadow** team was a product of the 70s: it began in **1970**, it survived a few months into **1980**. It raced in Can-Am, Formula 1 and Formula 5000, winning in all categories but never in a sustainable fashion. The first **Shadow** was a weird Can-Am creature with tiny tires that made little impression on the field. By **1972, Shadows** looked more fearsome, although ultimate success still eluded the team, headed by **Jackie Oliver**. In **1973**, a **Tony Southgate** car was produced for Formula 1 and although it scored in the first two outings, including a podium, it was not a world beater. **Revson** was hired for **1974**, showed speed in South America but was killed in testing at **Kyalami** and the season was mostly unstable. The team did win its only championship that year, the Can-Am, with **Jackie Oliver**. The surprise came in **1975**: the DN5 was a very fast car, won three poles (including the first two races), almost won in Brazil. It was so fast that there were uncorroborated rumors it used a development Cosworth. But results were few, although it won the Race of Champions with **Tom Pryce**. The UOP sponsorship was lost for **1976** and **Shadow** was a shadow of its former self, pardon the pun. The team did win a race in Formula 5000 that season, with a **Dodge** engined car and the **Mosport** World Championship event, hors-concours. In **1977**, the team lost leader **Tom Pryce** in **Kyalami** as well but then **Alan Jones** was brought into the team, as well as **Riccardo Patrese**. Alan eventually won the first and only **Shadow** official F-1 victory in Austria but did not remain for the next season. There was a major convulsion in the **Shadow** camp in **1978**, which might have caused its ultimate demise. **Oliver**, plus **Southgate, Rees, Wass** and other key personnel formed **Arrows**, which was quick right away in **Patrese**'s hands but **Nichols** claimed the car's design was the same as the **Shadow**. A London Court ruling forced **Arrows** to come up with a new design but driven by **Stuck** and **Regazzoni**, two fast drivers, the **Shadow** showed none of the **Arrows** pace. The last full season was **1979**, with rookies **Jan Lammers** and **Elio di Angelis**, the team having fallen into terminal midfield to back marker status. It would survive a few races into the **1980** season, **Teddy Yip** was left to pick up the pieces and then **Nichols** packed up and went home, never to be seen in racetracks again.

ENZO FERRARI

A figure of mythical proportions: intransigent, fearsome, intimidating, conniving, polemic, genius, conspiratorial, dramatic, contemptible, crazy, difficult, enlightened, ill-tempered, sad, political, nasty, operatic. All of these adjectives and many more have been used to qualify **Ferrari**, whose footprint on the world of racing can be felt since the **1920s**. **Ferrari** had his own set ways: he had some contempt towards drivers, believed that his cars were what really matter, cared mostly about engines dismissing aerodynamics and the fine art of chassis design as secondary. While **Scuderia Ferrari** continued to race in sports cars and

Formula 1 until **1973**, a decision was made to drop long distance racing as of **1974**. As a result, **Ferrari** became the winningest Formula 1 team of the decade and remains a force to be reckoned with until today. He had his favorites: years after **Chris Amon** had left **Ferrari**, the *Commendatore* used to send him birthday cards. **Gilles Villeneuve** was also dear to him and his death deeply affected the old man who never got over the death of a beloved son. With others, like **Niki Lauda** and **Nino Vacarella**, the relationship was tenser, not much love being shared. In true Machiavellian tradition, **Ferrari** believed a high powered political environment would ensure good results. The ploy would work sometimes, at times failing miserably. The ensuing drama, which somewhat remains part of the company culture to this day, has been often entertaining for outsiders, for sure the source of many ulcers and maybe a few heart attacks for insiders. Be that as it may, **Ferrari** was the consummate image nurturer of the sport and much of the decade's color is directly or indirectly related to himself, his team and cars.

ENZO OSELLA

Osella worked for **Abarth** and when **FIAT** bought the company outright in **1972**, **Osella** acquired the race car operations. At first the cars were called **Abarth-Osella** but eventually, the name **Osella** was adopted. In addition to continue building sports cars, which were sold in large numbers all over Europe and elsewhere, **Osella** ambitiously launched his first Formula 2 car, the FA2, in **1974**. Among drivers who drove these early cars were **Arturo Merzario, Francois Migault, Hans Binder** and **Giorgio Francia**, the latter scoring 16 points in the **1975** championship. New versions continued to be released but it was only in **1979** that the **Osella** Formula 2 car became truly successful, **Eddie Cheever** winning three races and coming close to taking the championship. **Osella** also won its first two World Manufacturers Championship races in **1979**, with **Lombardi-Grimaldi** and **Lombardi-Francia**,

ERIC BROADLEY

Eric had been around since the late 50s and by **1970**, his **Lola** cars were well known worldwide. With the expansion of categories during the decade, **Broadley** made brisk business. There were **Lola** Formula 2, Formula 3, Super Vees, Atlantics, Formula Fords, 3-liter sports cars, 2 liter sports cars, Formula 5000, Can-Am (traditional and single seater), Indycars, sports 2000. **Lolas** were successful in almost every category, except for Formula 1. The constructor was in the category between **1974** and **75** and on and off in different decades, strangely always without success. Generally easy to engineer, **Lola** cars were the top winners in Formula 5000 and very successful in 2-liter prototype racing. Among the drivers that used **Lolas** in the decade was **Mauro Nesti**, the Italian hill climb specialist who won dozen of races during the course of the decade, plus **Brian Redman, Mario Andretti, Graham Hill, Jo Bonnier, Gerard Larrousse, Gijs Van Lennep, Bob Evans, Teddy Pilette, Al Unser, Rolf Stommelen, Frank Gardner, Jerry Hansen, David Hobbs, Vic Elford, Peter Revson.**

ERWIN KREMER

Kremer was a German Porsche driver and tuner who fielded cars in various championships with his brother, including the World Championship of Makes during the entire decade. **Kremer** cars won the European GT Championship, the DRM and became a regular winner when the World Championship of Makes went into a Group 5 configuration in **1976**. Kremer's peak was his version of the

Porsche 935, the K3, which ran an air/air intercooler instead of the air/water units used by Porsche works and won all but one race of the DRM, as well as the 24 Hours of Le Mans, in **1979**, a great closing of the decade. Among the drivers who raced for Kremer in the 70s were **Bob Wollek, Klaus Ludwig, John Fitzpatrick, Didier Pironi, Hans Heyer, Axel Plankenhorn, Marie Claude Beaumont, Guy Edwards, Jim Busby, John Winter, Egon Evertz, Peter Gregg, Dieter Schornstein, Reine Wisell, Clemens Schickentanz, Helmut Kelleners, Paul Keller, Jurgen Barth, Martin Raymond, Francois Servanin, Bill Whittington, Don Whittington**, and, of course, **Erwin Kremer,** who won a version of the Porsche Cup.

FRANK WILLIAMS

Who says that persistence does not pay? In **1970 Williams** was optimistic, after a wonderful **1969** season as a privateer with driver **Piers Courage**, which resulted in two second places in Grand Prix racing. For **1970** he had an exclusive design, the **De Tomaso**, which turned out to be dreadful. Adding insult to injury, **Courage** was killed in Holland. The next six, seven seasons must have been character building for **Frank**. There were the **Marches** of **1971**, in Formula 1 and Formula 2, **Marches** and **Politoys** in **1972**. That season **Pescarolo** destroyed many cars but **Pace** looked like a good bet but left before the end of the season. Then, the **Iso Marlboros** of **1973** and **1974**, that were the laughing stock of the field when they first appeared. Sponsorship problems resulted in the end of the Iso tie-up and the **1975** challenger was mostly a back marker, except for a lucky 2nd place in Germany. In **1976** he had a good sponsorship agreement, with Canadian millionaire **Walter Wolf** and no less than **Jacky Ickx** driving the promising ex-**Hesketh** 308-C. It did not turn out well. By the end of the year, **Williams** was booted out of his team, which would become **Wolf**, so the world looked bleak for **1977**. While **Wolf** turned out a winner, **Frank** went back racing with a private **March** in the hands of **Patrick Neve,** in a partnership with **Patrick Head**. A novelty and major coup was the inclusion of several Saudi sponsors in the car. For **1978, Frank** had **Alan Jones**, a more sound driver and a car designed by **Patrick Head**. In the course of two years, Frank had gone from bleak to world beater, for the **1979 Williams** was by far the best car in the field. So that persistence does pay, after all.

GEORGE LOOS

Wealthy **Loos** was a German gentleman driver, who founded Gelo Racing in **1970** and drove powerful **Ferrari** 512 in the World Championship and Can-Am **McLarens** in the Interserie. **Loos** decided to quit driving and concentrated on running teams of GT and sports cars during the rest of the decade. The Gelo team employed fast professional drivers like **Tim Schenken, Rolf Stommelen, Bob Wollek, John Fitzpatrick, Klaus Ludwig, Toine Hezemans, Clemens Schickentanz, Jurgen Barth, Manfred Schurti, Howden Ganley, Jochen Mass** and **Jacky Ickx**, Gelo won many DRM, Interserie, World Manufacturers Championship, European GT Championship races and even championships, running **Porsche** cars such as the 911, 934, 935, 917-10 but it also raced a **Mirage** in the **1975** World Championship. Gelo was known for running three-driver crews in long distance events, with a fast driver doing double duty in two cars. Gelo was pretty much a 70s phenomenon, for it would not survive much longer after **1979**.

GIAMPAOLO DALLARA

Dallara is today the most prominent race car constructor of the world. It all started in the 70s as well. **Giampaolo** established his company in **1972**, producing small engine prototypes that basically raced in Italy, eventually it was involved in the design of the **1974 Iso Marlboro** Formula 1 car as a consultant. In typical Italian style, **Dallara** provided consulting services to many others. **Dallara** was retained by **Wolf** to produce his first Formula 3 car the WD1, of which three units were built for the **1978** season, while one the cars continued to race as the **Emiliani** in **1979**. It was just a fair car back then but the constructor persisted. It was all a steep learning curve but he did learn well.

GORDON COPPUCK

Coppuck was the creator of one of the most successful Formula 1 cars of all time, the **McLaren** M23 but also the M24 and other preceding Indy cars that won many races during the decade. After serving in F1 dutifully, winning two championships, the M23 continued to race successfully, winning races in British Formula 1, including the title with **Tony Trimmer** in **1978**. Unfortunately, **Coppuck** did not repeat the M23 success with the M26, so the M23 was his peak. The M28 and M29 **McLaren**s were not successful and **Coppuck** was shown the door. In the 80s he was involved with the **Spirit** project.

GORDON MURRAY

Murray was a young South African engineer who happened to be a junior designer at **Brabham** when **Ecclestone** bought the team in **1971**. Back then, the lead designer was **Ron Tauranac**, Jack's old partner. Ron was first replaced by the more experienced **Ralph Bellamy**, who did early design on the BT37 but eventually **Gordon** took over altogether. A rather inventive and innovative designer, **Gordon**'s cars had distinctive looks. He began his triangular chassis configurations in **1973**, with the BT42, achieving great success with the BT44. The heavy and thirsty **Alfa Romeo** engine did not help the BT45 but by **1978**, the **Brabham** looked sleeker. **Gordon** borrowed the **Chaparral**'s fan concept and used it in the BT46, immediately winning in Sweden. The allegation that the appendage was not an aerodynamic aid, rather being used for cooling purposes, did not stick and the car was duly protested. The **Anderstorp** win was confirmed but the fan was outlawed from further participation. The **1979** BT48 was not a success, **Niki Lauda** got discouraged but by then **Nelson Piquet** had come into the team. **Piquet-Murray** would become the most memorable driver-engineer combo of the 80s. Murray also designed the **Duckham**'s Le Mans car, which was based on a **Brabham** BT33 chassis.

HARVEY POSTLETHWAITE

Harvey began his career at **March**, helping design the Formula 2 and Formula 3 cars in **1970**. He came into Formula 1 as part of the **Hesketh** team, in **1973**. He showed ability right away, managing to extract performance from the sluggish **March** 731, something even the works failed to do with **Jean-Pierre Jarier** on board. By **1974** he penned his first Formula 1 design, the **Hesketh** 308. The car had only a fair performance that year but the revised version of the 308 began **1975** well, finishing second in Argentina. Victory came soon, in Holland but that turned out to be **Hesketh**'s sole win. The 308C, with more daring and modern lines was actually a bad car. Lord **Hesketh** decided to stop burning his fortune in Grand Prix racing and the 308C's were sold to **Wolf-Williams** for **1976**. In spite of

Harvey's presence in the team and drivers such as **Ickx, Amon** and **Merzario**, the renamed **Williams** FW05 just got worse with time. Was **Harvey** a flash in the pan? Not so fast. The new **Wolf** challenger, unveiled to the public in November of **1976**, ended up winning on its debut. The car, driven by **Scheckter** won a couple more races and **Jody** finished championship runner-up. The ground effects **1978 Wolf** was not as good and there were no wins. At the end of the year **Jody** was gone. For **1979, Wolf** managed to wrest **James Hunt** away from **McLaren** but more trouble loomed ahead: the WR9 looked fast but it was not a world beater. **James Hunt** left mid-season, being replaced by **Keke Rosberg** but **Wolf** was not interested in running mid-field teams and closed the operation at the end of the year. Millionaires lose interest fast from new toys. But **Postlethwaite** had a long and influential career ahead of him, though.

JIM HALL

The fan equipped **Chaparral** driven by **Vic Elford** and **Jackie Stewart**, was a (fast) novelty in the **1970** Can Am which was soon outlawed because it was aerodynamically effective but allegedly dangerous. Hall spent most of the decade on the sidelines, although a futuristic F-5000 appeared in the hands of **Franz Weis** in **Lime Rock, 1971**. However, by the end of the 70s **Chaparral** was back with a very good Indycar design, in the hands of **Al Unser**, which began showing its real pace in **1979**. Ultimate success came only in **1980**.

JOCHEN NEERPASCH

Neerpasch was a **Porsche** factory driver in the 60s, who won on occasion and by **1970**, he had become **Ford** Germany's competition boss. Under his guidance, the **Ford** Capri was developed into a fast and winning car, although a bit difficult one to tame. After winning the **1971** and **1972** ETCC titles for **Ford**, **Jochen** was hired by **BMW** to become its competition boss, achieving immediate success with the **1973** title and the very fast (and easier to drive) 3.0 CSL. **Jochen** remained with the Bavarian manufacturer during the rest of the decade, developing, among others, the Group 5 BMW 3.0 CSL, the **BMW** 320 Group 5 which won many DRM races and also the **Procar** series, contested by **BMW** M1 sports cars.

JOHN BISHOP

John Bishop was the founder of IMSA, a sports car club/sanctioning body that began activities in **1969**. Under his guidance, the IMSA GT series (began in **1971**) became a force to be reckoned with, almost causing the demise of SCCA's Trans Am series. Among other things, **Bishop** realized the Trans Am somewhat alienated SCCA's large amateur core constituency, by placing little emphasis on the small engine capacity category. From the start **IMSA** races mixed pony cars such as Camaros and Mustangs, with Corvettes, **Porsche**s and European sedans of all sizes. Eventually, as the top category cars became much faster, IMSA also separated classes. In **1976** IMSA also tried holding a Formula Atlantic series in the USA, without much success.

JOHN SURTEES

John Surtees began and stopped building Formula 1 cars in the 70s. A very knowledgeable, practical engineer and an experienced and fast driver, he knew what he wanted in a race car but in hindsight, using the services of an experienced designer from the onset might have helped **Surtees** thrive. After achieving some success with his Formula 5000 cars in **1969**, **Surtees** launched his Formula 1 car in **1970**. The car did win a couple of poorly supported Gold Cup races in **1970** and **1971** but real success was elusive in the World Championship. **1972** was definitely the best year for the marque: it won the European Formula 2 championship (**Hailwood**), the European Formula 5000 Championship (**Van Lennep**) and it had its best result in the World F-1 Championship, 2nd in Italy (**Hailwood**), where the same driver almost won the slipstream battle of the preceding season. **Hailwood** also led in South Africa on speed and **Surtees** cars did very well in non-championship races. However, as of **1973 Surtees**' performance dropped, never properly recovering. Among other things, there was an influx of younger, talented designers such as **Murray** and **Postlethwaite**, while **Surtees** insisted on basically designing the cars himself. The TS19 of **1976** was credited to **Surtees** and **Sears** and if properly developed could have done better. Money was an issue as of **1974** and the team survived in Formula 1 until **1978**. A **Surtees** TS19 did win the **1977** Shellsport Group 8 Championship, with **Tony Trimmer** and **Surtees** tried to remain in competition one more year after leaving Formula 1, joining the Aurora Championship. Team **Surtees** would not survive the decade, though. A very long Court battle with an unhappy sponsor drew much of the team's financial resources and time, which **John** claims to have destroyed his team (and health).

JOHN WYER

John Wyer was a British team manager who achieved much success running a number of cars at **Le Mans** and long distance racing, including **Aston Martin** in the 50s and **Ford** GT40s in **1968** and **1969**. As a result, he reached an agreement with **Porsche** and his J&W Automotive ran **Porsche** 917 and 908 models in the **1970** and **1971** World Manufacturers Championship, as a semi-works entity. J&W won most races in these seasons, with drivers such as **Rodriguez, Siffert, Kinnunen, Bell, Redman** and **Oliver**. However no Le Mans wins were forthcoming in these two successful **Porsche** seasons. With the outlawing of the 917, **Wyer** resurrected the **Mirage** brand, still financed by Gulf sponsorship, in **1972**. Fast on occasion, the **Ford** engined **Mirage** only won a single championship race, at **Spa, 1973** (**Hailwood/Bell**), plus the **1975 Le Mans** race (**Ickx/Bell**). By that time, Gulf had bought the team, although **Wyer** remained as manager until **1976**, when he retired.

JUNIOR JOHNSON

Junior Johnson was a very successful driver on his own until **1966**, after being a moonshiner. Eventually he became a car owner and was successful for many a year. His great streak in the 70s was the 3 NASCAR Cup wins with **Cale Yarborough**, in **1976, 1977 and 1978**, with **Chevrolet**s. This was a major coup, something that not even **Richard Petty** had achieved, which only **Jimmie Johnson** (no relation) would emulate and better in the 2000s. After **1978**, the partnership fizzled and eventually **Darrel Waltrip** took up the helm, during the 80s.

KEN TYRRELL

A timber trader, Tyrrell raced in his youth, without much brilliance. He was at the right place at the right time, when he made a liaison with the young **Matra** concern and made a killing in Formula 3 and 2 in the **1966** and **1967** seasons. He also did the right thing leaving **Matra** for the **1970** season, although the **March** chassis proved to be insufficient for **Stewart's** immense talents. The Tyrrell proprietary chassis came in the end of the season and the **Tyrrell-Stewart** partnership was one of the most successful of the decade, albeit short. When **Stewart** retired and **Cevert** died, **Tyrrell** was in obvious trouble. Perhaps thinking of emulating the relationship he built with **Stewart, Ken** hired **Jody Scheckter**, the **1973** season's *enfant terrible*. **Jody** started slowly in the 006, allegedly a very difficult car to drive but once he got the 007, he was consistently on the pace and had a slight chance to win the title. Unfortunately, the **Jody-Tyrrell** tie up was not long lasting, in fact, it lasted all of three seasons. The decision to run a 6-wheel car in **1976** might have contributed to the ultimate fall-out. But in hindsight, one can say that **Tyrrell** was only in the top of the world between **1971** to **1973**. Wins after **Scheckter**'s departure were few and far and by the end of the decade the team, without Elf sponsorship which had gone to **Renault, Tyrrell** was pretty much a midfielder, although it was in the game until the late 90s.

LOUIS STANLEY

The first two years of the decade were reasonably good for **BRM**. **Pedro Rodriguez** scored many points in the Yardley sponsored car in **1970**, won a race and in **1971** the **BRM** team had won 2 of the last 4 Formula 1 races of the season and was ranked second in the constructor's championship. **Stanley** had a golden chance in **1972**, for then **BRM** had landed the enviable Marlboro sponsorship, allegedly to the tune of £100,000. It was not to be. It is not really clear whose idea was to run as many as five **BRM**s in Grand Prix, at a time that successful teams ran 2 cars. Adding insult to injury, **BRM** built its own engines and gearboxes and it used no less than 5 models that season: the P153, three variations of the P160 and the P180. The idea was to have a main team of **Beltoise, Ganley** and **Gethin** and several "country" teams (Marlboro-Austria, Marlboro-Spain, Marlboro-Holland). At one point, there was talk of eight **BRM**s hitting the tracks at the same time! By the end of the season, **BRM** had won its last Grand Prix, although Marlboro continued another season. **Stanley** still persisted with a 3-car set up in **1973** and although **BRM**s led races and had a pole, the writing was clearly on the wall. Eventually, Marlboro sponsorship was lost to **McLaren** and **BRM** would last another season as a serious team, even launching a new car, the Motul sponsored P201. The new car ran well on its debut, in South Africa, only to become less and less competitive as the season went on. **BRM** went on receivership by the end of **1974**. **Stanley** bought the assets of the team and ran it as **Stanley BRM** for a while, with no success. There were hopes the **Len Terry** designed P207, with Rotary watch sponsorship, could bring **BRM** back to dignity, if not glory. However, it was the end, **BRM** would never return to the Grand Prix, although it raced in the Aurora championship for a short while, driven by **Teddy Pilette**. **Louis Stanley** did squander a good chance back in **1972**, for sure.

LUCA DI MONTEZEMOLO

Luca di Montezemolo graduated from University in **1971** and the youngster was soon working for **FIAT**. **1973** was a very bad year for **Ferrari** in Formula 1 and only fair in Sports Cars. The team had not won a Formula 1 championship since **1964** and this made the **FIAT** group, which owned **Ferrari**, very jittery indeed. **Ferrari** was, after all, an Italian institution and its success was more important than Italian drivers winning races or championships. The young man, in this 20s, had been made assistant to **Enzo Ferrari** in **1973** and was appointed the Scuderia's team manager for **1974**, in spite of his lack of experience. **Luca** is widely credited with engineering the **Ferrari** turn around. In **1974**, the B3 was the fastest car, although it broke down often but it won three times and was in the running for the championship until the final race. The hard decision not to race sports cars seemed right: the Scuderia could concentrate on Formula 1 properly once and for all. Bringing back **Forghieri** and hiring **Lauda** were also good managerial moves. The **1975** T model was even faster than the B3, certainly more reliable and **Lauda** became champion with some ease. Having done his job, Luca was appointed for other top management positions at the **FIAT** Group and by **1976** had been replaced by **Daniele Audetto** as team manager, before reaching 30 years of age. A short but successful stint.

MAURICE PHILLIPPE

Phillippe goes down in history as the designer of one of the most successful and ground breaking Formula 1 cars of all time, the **Lotus** 72. In **1972**, already out of **Lotus**, he had the pleasure of being the designer of the winning cars of both the Formula 1 (**Lotus**) and USAC National Championships (**Parnelli**). **Maurice** also penned the **Parnelli** VP4 Formula 1 car that raced from **1974** to **1976**, without much success. His USAC designs for **Parnelli** continued to win, while his next Formula 1 design was the **1978 Tyrrell** 008, which won at **Monaco**. **Maurice** continued at **Tyrrell** in **1979** but the 009 was not a success, although it appeared to be a copy of the **Lotus** 79 (like **Williams** and **Ligier**, by the way).

MAURO FORGHIERI

Ferrari always had a relatively large team of engineers working on its Formula 1 cars, so saying that **Ferrari** GP cars were totally penned by **Mauro Forghieri** is a stretch of reality. After all, the team also had proprietary engines and gearboxes, plus a lot of politics. Notwithstanding, **Mauro** was the head designer and in the one year when he was not around, **1973**, the team foundered. **Ferrari** was the most consistent winner in Formula 1 during the 70s, failing to win only in **1973**. **Forghieri** was not known for much innovation but the transversal gearbox was his idea, featured in **1975**'s Ferrari 321 T.

MAX MOSLEY

Max Mosley was the M in **March,** which had grandiose plans for the decade. After debuting as a marque in **1969**, **March** was coming to GP racing with a works team, fielding cars for **Amon** and **Siffert**, plus customer cars for whoever had the cash. **Stewart** won the second time out but it was not to be. That was pretty much the history of **March** as a Formula 1 constructor in the 70s. There was **Peterson** in **1971**, **Hunt** in **1973**, **Brambilla** in **1975**, **Peterson** again in **1976** but only non-sustained flashes of brilliance. On the other hand, as a constructor of race cars, **March** did very well, specially in Formula 2, where it won the largest number of races of all in the decade. **March** cars were also very fast in Formula 3, Formula Atlantic and tasted more limited success in other categories such as 2 Liter Prototypes, Formula Ford, Super Vee and Formula 5000. **Mosley** was a former driver (not excitingly successful) that went as far as Formula 2, a lawyer, son of a prominent and polemic politician. After the dreadful **1977** Formula 1 season, **Mosley** decided his time would be better served as a full-time sidekick to **Bernie Ecclestone**, whom he had been assisting since his arrival in F1, so **Robin Herd** was left with **March**. Max' influence was great as a seller of race cars in the 70s, although some drivers had unkind words for his business tactics, such as **Alex Ribeiro** and **Chris Amon**. In **Alex**' book "*Mais que Vencedor*", the driver refers to then **March** owner as Mack Mouse, which kind of says it all.

MIKE PILBEAM

As far as Formula 1 is concerned, **Pilbeam** will be best remembered for designing the **BRM** P201, which showed some promise in **1974**, however, had poor performances in the next two seasons. **Pilbeam** set up his own business and began producing **Pilbeam** cars as of **1975**. His cars won a large number of British hill climbs beginning in the 70s and eventually produced sports cars as well. During the decade he also produced a Formula 2 (MP42) and Formula 3 (MP44) cars in **1979**.

MORRIS NUNN

Nunn was a former **Lotu**s mechanic and works driver, who decided to build cars, against all odds, in **1971**, after a Formula 5000 ride feel through. The Formula 3 **Ensign**, built by a 2-employee company, impressed in its maiden season and even more so in the second, when many cars were sold. Among its users was one **Rikki Von Opel**, who won many races and a British championship and decided to finance a DFV-powered challenger for the **1973** Formula 1 season. The first F1 **Ensign** was not fast and not particularly pretty, with a huge and long airbox. The team continued in **1974**, although **Von Opel** withdrew his support early in the season moving on to the much more promising **Brabham** team. During the rest of the season **Nunn** used a host of other drivers, without any success. For **1975**, the team got support from a Dutch alarm company, a new designer, **David Baldwin**, plus two Dutch drivers, **Van Lennep** and **Wunderink**, who shared the car. **Van Lennep** finished 6th in a high attrition rate at the **Nürburgring**, earning **Ensign**'s first point ever and late in the season **Chris Amon** was convinced to race the car. **Chris** must have seen potential, for he was back in **1976**, in what can be termed **Ensign**'s most promising season. The N176 was fast, **Amon** ran in the top 6 in a number of races and qualified an amazing 3rd in Sweden. However, **Baldwin** designed a fast but fragile car and **Amon** had a couple of nasty accidents during the season. After **Nürburgring** he quit the team but eventually Nunn got **Jacky Ickx** to jump on board, who also had a very nasty accident in **Watkins Glen**. For **1977 Nunn** got Tissot sponsorship and the services of **Clay Regazzoni**, let go by **Ferrari**. The Swiss scored on occasion and so did **Patrick Tambay** in a Theodore sponsored entry but the team seemed destined to the midfield. A number of drivers were used in **1978**: **Leoni, Daly, Ongais, Ertl** and there were occasional DNQs. **Ensign** can boast of giving **Nelson Piquet** his first Formula 1 ride in Germany but all it got was a single point from **Daly**'s 6th in the last race of the year. The **1979** challenger, driven by **Daly** and **Gaillard**, was a very ugly car with prominent, ghastly front radiators and rather ineffective. The end always seemed near but **Ensign** promised it would return in **1980** and return it did. Not for long, though. **Ensign** cars did rather better in the Aurora FX Championship, both **Lees and Martini** winning races in **1978**, which must have brought **Nunn** a smile.

ORESTE BERTA

Most Europeans and Americans are likely to say, **Oreste** Who? However, back in Argentina **Berta** is venerated as great, with good reason. Indeed **Berta** designs won in a vast range of categories, including Argentine Formula 1, Formula 2, Turismo de Carretera and prototypes. There were some forays into international racing during the 70s, at first at the **1970 Nürburgring** World Championship of Makes race, with **Luis Di Palma** and **Nestor Garcia Veiga** driving one of his prototypes powered with a Cosworth engine and then at Formula 1. The latter plans did not go as well, the Argentinian economy was a mess, so the **Berta** Formula 1 never took to the track. Eventually, it was transformed into a Formula

5000, without much success. In **1975** the **Berta-Hollywood Ford** basically destroyed its competition in the last Brazilian Division 4 prototype championship, while **Berta** cars and engines won many times in Argentina during the course of the decade, in several categories.

PATRICK HEAD

Head, like many other designers such as fellow Brit **John Barnard**, was a **Lola** alumnus, where he worked early on the decade. **Patrick** became a bit disillusioned with racing car design mid decade, deciding to design boats instead. That is until **Frank Williams**, whom he had met during his **Lola** days, decided to resurrect his **Williams** team in Formula 1, under the new name **Williams** Grand Prix Engineering and invited **Head** to be his partner. It should be noted that the first iteration of the **Williams** team, which ran from **1969** until **1976**, was bought out by **Walter Wolf** in **1976 and Williams** was booted out. At first, **Williams** ran a slow **March** 761 for **Patrick Neve**, without great success. For **1978, Head** penned his first car, the FW06 and little by little new driver **Alan Jones** extracted higher degrees of speed from it, finishing the late season US Grand Prix East in second place. In addition to having an excellent driver and good car, the team managed to convince a number of moneyed Saudi sponsors, including Saudia Airlines, Albilab, TAG and Bin Laden, to sponsor the team. For **1979** they had a team of experienced drivers, **Jones** and **Regazzoni** and an improved **Williams** car, the FW07, obviously based on the successful **Lotus** 79. **Williams** won its first race in Britain, with **Regazzoni** and **Jones** was the fastest driver of the second half of the season, winning four times. Thus started **Williams** most successful phase, which lasted the entire 80s until the late 90s.

RALPH BELLAMY

Australian designer **Bellamy** was involved in Formula 1 during the entire decade. He was credited as co-designer of the very successful and trend setting **Lotus** 78 of **1977**, designed the good **McLaren** M19 of **1971/72**, re-designed the mildly successful **Fittipaldi** F5A for **1978**, penned the so-and-so **Brabham** BT37 but was also responsible for the dreadful **Fittipaldi** F6 of **1979**, a very nice-looking car which could not be made to work in spite of **Emerson Fittipaldi**'s well known talents as a car sorter. He also worked on the **McLaren** M14 Indycar. As people tend to remember the later failure, than early success, by late **1979** he was no longer considered a top Formula 1 designer.

REINHOLD JOEST

Joest's driving career began in the 60s, however, his career as team owner and manager started in the 70s. By and large associated with **Porsche**, most famously driving the 917 Pig in **Le Mans, 1971, Joest**'s first major international win actually came in the 500 km of **Interlagos** in **Brazil, 1972**. By then, **Joest** had become the main entrant of **Porsche** 908-3's in the World Championship of Makes and the works lent him a hand here and there in the next four seasons, doing development work that would result in the 936. In **1972 Joest** actually finished **Le Mans** in 3rd place and 2nd in Monza, showing he deserved works support. During the course of the decade, **Joest** racing competed with 908-3 and 908-4 turbos in the World Championship of Makes, European Hill Climb Championship, Interserie, European Sports Car Championship and elsewhere, also fielding 936s and eventually racing Group 5 **Porsche** 935s as well. **Joest** had a short foray in Formula 2, driving a **Lola** unsuccessfully in **1976** and decided to concentrate on Sports Cars henceforth. His team would eventually become the most successful **Le Mans** winner, with 13 wins, all that from humble beginnings in the 70s.

RICHARD DIVILA

Although designing a Formula 1 car in the 70s was not such a complicated endeavor as today, when cars are designed by committees with dozens of members with multiple **PhD**s, it was not peanuts either. In that sense, Brazilian **Divila** did a commendable job designing the first two **Fittipaldi** Formula 1 cars, for he had no Formula 1 experience or top level design track record to rely upon. His previous designs were all race cars used in Brazilian local races: the 2-engined **Fittipaldi VW** Beetle prototype and the **Snob's Corvair** prototype that raced in **1969** and **1970**. His European experience was limited to engineering **Wilson Fittipaldi**'s Formula 2 cars. Much of the beautiful FD-01 design did not make it to the racetracks. His second design, the FD04 was better, actually scored points in six occasions in **1976** and **1977**, started the **1976** Brazilian Grand Prix in fifth place and scored the second fastest race lap at **Watkins Glen** before the rear wing fell off. **Divila** was not called back to design the F5 but his talents were noted by the Formula 1 paddock: **Divila** did built a long career as a sound race car designer into the next decades.

ROBIN HERD

Herd was a former **McLaren** designer, who decided to go on his own, forming **March** with **Max Mosley** and others. **Herd**'s duty was the design of Formula 1 cars, overseeing the design of cars for several other categories. **March**'s history of Formula 1 in the 70s started in **1970** as it ended in **1977**: with tons of cars on the entry lists. In **1970**, the works drivers were the experienced **Amon** and **Siffert**, while the **1977** drivers were the inexperienced **Ian Scheckter** and **Alex Ribeiro**. In **1970** the non-works cars included **Tyrrell**, plus cars for **Ronnie Peterson** and **Mario Andretti**. In **1977**, the privateers included RAM, F&S Properties, Merzario and **Brian Henton**. So while **March** won its second World Championship in Spain in **1970** (with **Stewart** in the **Tyrrell** car), in the **1977 Marches** were the laughing stock of Formula 1, most not qualifying for races. Mosley suddenly wanted out, more enamored with the power and money to be had running Formula 1 than managing a team and factory and **Herd** stopped fielding (or building) Formula 1 cars for a while, although most of the work on the **1978 ATS** was done by **Herd** and **March**. However, the team sold a hundreds of cars for Formula 2, Formula 3, Formula Ford, Formula Super Vee, Formula Atlantic, Formula 5000, Can-Am, Sports-Prototypes. It was the winningest Formula 2 car of the decade, so **March** did not need Formula 1 to survive. **March** cars won races in all continents during the decade and in spite of the Formula 1 failures, it was one the most successful constructors of the decade.

ROGER PENSKE

By **1970 Roger Penske** was a successful team owner, mainly in Trans Am. His team had won a world event at **Sebring** but more substantial success in the Can-Am evaded him, in spite of a race victory in **1968** and several in the USRRC. All that would change in the 70s. **Penske** became the man to beat seemingly all over. His entries won the **Indy 500**, several Indy races, championships, until, in the last year of the decade, a **Penske** made Indycar hit and conquered the tracks. By then he had also a successful **1976** season in Formula 1, winning a race with **John Watson**, simply walked away with the **1972** and **1973** Can-Ams, won NASCAR races with the unusual **AMC** Javelin and tried other disciplines, such as Formula 5000 (with an AMC engined car) and a beautiful **Ferrari** 512M that was fast but did now win as planned. **Penske** was also a major force in the formation of CART and the split from USAC which was very beneficial to Indy-style racing and put together the IROC. Unfortunately, in the midst of all this success, **Penske** lost his best friend and partner, **Mark Donohue**, who died in qualifying for the **1975** Austrian Grand Prix. One cannot have everything, I suppose.

Penske consolidated his relevance in racing during the 70s. Photo by Rob Neuzel

RON DENNIS

Dennis was a former **Brabham** mechanic who worked his way into fielding a strong team of **Brabham**s and then the proprietary **Motul**s in Formula 2, as the Rondel Team. Although the Motul sponsored team never won the championship, during the period **1971** to **1973** it won many races and among its drivers were **Henri Pescarolo, Tim Schenken, Bob Wollek, Tom Pryce, Graham Hill, Ronnie Peterson, Gunnar Nilsson, Carlos Reutemann, Jean-Pierre Beltoise, Jean-Pierre Jaussaud**. For **1974 Dennis** intended to make the big step into Formula 1 but poor economic circumstances led him to hold back on his plans. At any rate, the would-be Rondel Formula 1 car was eventually raced by others as the **Token** and **Safir** and it turned out to be a total dud. **Dennis** then set up the best organized non-works Formula 2 and Formula 3 team in the business, Project Four Racing, essentially setting the standard for future professional Formula 3 teams, which won many races with the likes of **Eddie Cheever, Ingo Hoffmann, Chico Serra, Stephen South, Derek Daly**. Eventually, in the 80s, **Dennis** big day would come, courtesy of Marlboro, which engineered the acquisition of the **McLaren** team, which **Dennis** expertly and successfully ran for many years.

RON TAURANAC

Aussie **Ron Tauranac** was **Jack Brabham**'s partner, so he took over the team when **Jack** decided to go back to Australia at the end of the **1970** season. He was also the team's designer. In **1971 Bernie Ecclestone** decided to plunge into Formula 1 and bought **Brabham** from **Ron**, allegedly for £100,000, although **Ron** wanted £130,000. **Tauranac** was supposed to stay on board as designer but the two men did not get along and **Ron** was soon shown the door. **Tauranac** continued in the industry, initially designing the **Trojan** T101 and T102 Formula 5000 cars, then the **Trojan** Formula 1 of **1974**, worked for **Williams** for a while but then re-established **Ralt** in **1974**, a car name he had used prior to joining **Brabham**. The marque soon became one of the top single-seater manufacturers of the world, the RT1 actually being used as a Formula 3, Formula Atlantic and Formula 2 car. **Ron** also designed a very conventional Formula 1 car for **Theodore** racing, for **1978**. The car even won a Formula 1 race, the Daily Express race under deluge conditions. This was the last **Tauranac** Formula 1 design.

TEDDY MAYER

With **Bruce McLaren**'s death, American attorney **Teddy Mayer, Bruce's** partner, had the difficult task of keeping the **McLaren** company afloat. **McLaren** was seen as a split Kiwi/American company. There was the Europe based GP side of it and then the American Can Am/Indy Car side of it. In **1970** and **1971 McLaren** was much more successful in Can Am than Formula 1: the team failed to score a F-1 victory in both seasons and the European based effort seemed to be fading. In **1972**, there was a change of fortune: new sponsor Yardley, plus fast American **Peter Revson** teamed with **Denis Hulme**, injected new strength into the team and a race was won in South Africa – **McLaren** was back. At Can Am, **Porsche** utterly crushed **McLaren**, although a **Penske** run **McLaren** won at Indy. The team reached a new level of performance with the release of the M23, which was used between **1973** to **1978** (only by privateers in this last year) and a tie up with Marlboro as of **1974** which lasted for over two decades. With the M23, **McLaren** won its first and second Formula 1 championship with **Fittipaldi** and **Hunt,** plus several races. The next design, the M26, was only fair and the last designs of the decade, the M28 and M29, were downright bad. **McLare**n reached another trough and there were rumors the company would become entirely American. Marlboro was not happy, no one was happy and **McLaren** was sold early on the next decade, a sale largely engineered by the sponsor.

TEDDY YIP

Hong Kong's **Teddy Yip** was an Indonesian born businessman of Chinese descent and enthusiastic supporter of motor racing for decades. He raced in the **Macau** Grand Prix himself until a ripe old age, without yearning to achieve results, just for the sake of participating. **Yip** also had many interests in **Macau** as well as elsewhere, including construction, hospitality, shipping, foods, etc. The name "Theodore Racing" appeared not only in Asian races but also in Indycar, Formula 5000 and Formula 1. Yip sponsored **Ronnie Peterson**'s car in the **1976 Long Beach** Grand Prix, the first time Chinese writing appeared on a Grand Prix car. By **1977**, he sponsored an **Ensign** for Frenchman **Patrick Tambay**, who managed to score five points, while greatly impressing. By **1978** he had commissioned a proprietary **Theodore** chassis from **Ron Tauranac** and the car won a race early in the season, the Daily Express race at **Silverstone,** run under extreme weather. In championship racing, in spite of the good services of **Keke Rosberg**, the **Theodore** was very slow and abandoned. He then bought and fielded some old **Wolf** chassis, to no avail. There was no Formula 1 **Theodore** team in **1979** but it would come back for a short while in the 80s but Theodore sponsored cars continued to race in Asia.

Teddy Yip also raced early on the decade. This is his trusty Porsche 906, in Macau, 1972. Photo by Jose Santos.

TONY SOUTHGATE

Southgate began the decade as the **BRM** designer, his first design being the P153. He also designed the P160 and P180, until **1972** and while his **BRM** designs won a total of seven races (including 4 official GPs), the dramatic environment at **BRM** was not among the best, in spite of lavish Marlboro sponsorship. By **1972** he had left to design the Formula 1 **Shadow**s, the first one being the DN1. The car got two podiums the first season, including one in the second race but it was not consistently competitive. **Tony** sprung a surprise on the F1 establishment with his DN5 design of **1975**, which got pole in both South American races and led commandingly in Brazil until late in the race. Again, consistency was not its forte and points were few. **Southgate** continued at **Shadow** until **1977** and his co-designed DN8 won the Austrian Grand Prix in **Alan Jones**' hands. In **1978** the **Shadow** set up collapsed and major personnel, including **Southgate**, formed **Arrows**, which showed a great turn of speed, leading its 2nd race in South Africa. A British Court deemed the car an illegal copy of the **Shadow** and the team was ordered to come up with a different designed (the designer had already been working on an alternative car, just in case). **Southgate** stayed at **Arrows** until **1979** and was replaced by **John Baldwin**. **Southgate** also did consulting work for **Chevron**, after **Derek Bennett**'s death.

WALTER WOLF

Canada's **Wolf** was part of a small club of enthusiastic wealthy people who self-financed entire Grand Prix teams in the 70s, which included **Lord Hesketh** and **Teddy Yip**. **Wolf** was by far the most successful, although his team lasted a little over three seasons. Initially, **Wolf** invested in the **Williams** team, in **1976**, which had bought the **Hesketh** 308C. The car was not very good and in spite of using fast and experienced drivers such as **Ickx, Merzario** and **Amon**, it was by far the worst non-privateer team. Late in the season, **Wolf** had bought the team from **Williams** and a new, **Postlethwaite** designed car announced in November. Driven by **Jody Scheckter**, the car won the first time out and the South African finished the **1977** championship in second. **Wolf** also had a Can-Am team, initially employing **Chris Amon** and later **Gilles Villeneuve** as drivers but the results were disappointing. A **Wolf-Dallara** Formula 3 driven by **Bobby Rahal** also appeared in **1978**. **Wolf**'s formula 1 success was not sustained, **Jody** had a poor **1978** season and **James Hunt** was hired for **1979**. It soon became clear that the motivated **James** of **1976** was long gone and by mid-season the British driver quit. His place was taken by **Rosberg**, who failed to score with the car, although showing some pace. At the end of the season, **Wolf** had had enough and sold the equipment, including the cars, to **Fittipaldi**.

Other 70s personalities who deserve mention are **Gerard Ducarouge, Bernard Boyer, David Yorke, Georges Martin, David Wass, Jean-Luc Lagardere, Andre de Cortanze, George Bignotti, Ray Jessop, Allan McCall, Ralph Firman, Giorgio Stirano, Manfred Jankte, Parnelli Jones, Syd Taylor, Pat Patrick, Michel Tetu, Bernard Didot, John Webb, Michael Kranefuss, Hans Dieter Decent, Huschke Von Hanstein, Len Bailey, Ken Sears, Tico Martini, Frank Dernie, Nigel Stroud, John Gentry, Martin Olgivy, Geoff Ferris, Franco Rocchi, Andy Swallman, Glen and Leonard Wood (Wood Brothers), Denis Jenkinson, Rob Walker, Bob Sparschott, John McDonald, John Coombs, Andy Granatelli.**

STANDALONE RACES AND SHORT RACE SERIES

As I mentioned in the beginning of the book, early in the 70s there were quite a few standalone races, in other words, events not connected to championships. These were often races open to multiple categories, international or domestic events. With time, as racing got more organized, sponsorship expanded and driver and team demands grew, the trend was the disappearance of some standalone events, which indeed happened.

Short race series were basically held in warmer climate during the northern hemisphere's winter. It gave drivers a chance to make some money during the off season, sun bathe, party a bit, but as Northern seasons grew in length and money got better, such series disappeared, in spite of a late attempt at reviving the Argentine Formula 2 Temporada in 1978.

STANDALONE RACES

BATHURST, 1000 KM

Throughout this book, you will see many mentions of the global **1973-1974** oil crisis that affected motor racing worldwide, causing the demise of many series and entire racing scenes, such as in the Philippines. There was definitely an adjustment and analysts from the era reckoned there were too many series chasing too few dollars, pounds, marks and yens, so natural selection claimed the likes of **Formula 5000**, the **European 2 Liter Championship** and the **European GT Championship**. As for **Formula 5000**, cars were expensive to run and in general, media exposure and prizes were not sufficient to keep semi reasonable fields going. In general, single seater categories often had to compete with more popular touring car championships in many countries and in many cases, such as the USA, Argentina, Brazil and Australia, tin tops won. While touring car racing had always been very popular in Australia, large single seaters were the undisputed top category early in the decade. But all that was changing and enthusiasm for **Formula 5000** dimmed, while touring car racing came to the fore.

So it is only fitting that a race such as the Bathurst 1000 would take over from the ashes of the Tasman Cup and Formula 5000. As in the other countries mentioned above, large touring car racing meant a fight between **Ford** and a **GM** product, in the Americas, **Chevrolet**, in Australia, **Holden**. This does not mean that only large engined **Ford** Falcons and **Holden** Toranas participated, for the occasional **Chrysler** Charger joined the party and smaller cars also took part. In the first edition of the 1000 classic held in **1973** (upgraded from a 500 km race known as Hardie Ferodo) there were several brands in lower categories, namely **Renault, Subaru, Alfa Romeo, Datsun, FIAT, Mazda, Honda** and **Mini**, in addition to **Ford** Escorts. So it was a bit different from the current Aussie touring car series.

The smaller fare could not dream of winning overall and in fact, the winners in **1973** were Canada born **Allan Moffat** and **Ian Geoghegan**, in a 5.7 **Ford**, followed by five 3.3 **Holden** Toranas. An **Alfa** took the B class, a **Mazda** the C class and a **Datsun** the A class. Only Australians and a few New Zealanders took part in the affair. **Ford** won again in **1974**, this time with **John Goss** and **Kevin Bartlett** but the more numerous and reliable **Holdens** had been fitted with 5.0 engines and ended 2nd to 5th. **VW** and **BMW** appeared for the first time, while the **Alfa** that finished 6th was disqualified. An **Alfa** took the B class, a **Mazda** the C class and a **Mini-Cooper** the A class. American **Bob Stevens** and German **Dieter Glemser** (pairing with **Moffat** in a **Ford**) added international flavor. **Holden** won its first "1000" in **1975**, a car driven by **Peter Brock** and **Brian Sampson**. The race began attracting more foreign drivers and **Marie-Claude Beaumont, Hiroshi Fushida** (who finished 5th), **John Fitzpatrick** (in an Alfa) and **John McDonald** took party. Former Australian Formula 1 driver **Tim Schenken** also participated but retired. A **Toyota** and a **Triumph** also made the race for the first time.

Fitzpatrick came back in **1976,** then driving a **Holden** and won the race with **Bob Morris**. **Holdens** finished 1st through 7th and the first Ford was not even a locally produced Falcon but rather, a Capri which won class C (an Escort won class B). Among the foreign contingent were **Beaumont** and Sir **Stirling Moss**, who shared a Holden with no other than **Jack Brabham** (they retired).

Ford added **Jacky Ickx** to the driving strength in **1977** and the Belgian and **Moffatt** won the race, a 1-2 for the Falcons. Some interesting foreign drivers took part. **Johnny Rutherford** and **Janet Guthrie** shared a Holden which crashed. The foreign contingent also included **Derek Bell** (class winner in an **Alfa**), **Henri Pescarolo, Basil Van Rooyen, Yoshimi Katayama, Satoru Nakajima** and **Rudiger Dahlhaler**, a couple of big names, others not so much. Holden went back to its winning ways in **1978**, driven by **Peter Brock** and **Jim Richards**. A Falcon came in 3rd, another in 5th, so it was not a disaster for **Ford**. **Jack Brabham** finished 6th in a **Holden** shared with **Brian Muir**. Foreigners **Derek Bell, Dieter Quester, Henri Pescarolo, Jacky Ickx, John Fitzpatrick, Rudiger Dahlhaler** and **Patrick Neve** all retired but kept the race on the spotlight. The last "1000" of the decade was won by **Peter Brock** and **Jim Richards** and **Holdens** took the first eight places! **Ford** was not even the first non-Holden, a **Toyota** was. The best **Ford** came in 14th. An **Isuzu** Gemini made the race, a car that was also branded **Holden** Gemini in Australia and a **Chevrolet** Camaro also raced. Among the foreigners a few new names, **Dick Barbour, Mark Thatcher, Kyoshi Misaki** and returnees **Pescarolo, Quester, Fitzpatrick and Bell,** none of whom did particularly well. In addition to touring car regulars, many other Australians and New Zealanders often connected with single seaters and international racing also took part in the 1000 km of Bathurst during the 70s, such as **Frank Gardner, Geoff Brabham, John Leffler, Johnny Walker, Tim Schenken, Larry Perkins, Vern Schuppan, Graeme Lawrence, Graham MacRae, Alfredo Costanzo** and **Warwick Brown.**

FRONTIERES GP, CHIMAY

The Grand Prix of Frontieres had been held in **Chimay**, Belgium since 1926 and thus, it was one of the oldest races in the world. Never a top event it was nonetheless, traditional, in fact the second most traditional Formula 3 race in the calendar. The story of the race in the 70s can be summarized in one name: **David Purley**. The British driver, not known for many wins in Formula 3, won all three editions of the Belgian race in the 70s. In his first win, **Purley** had to beat **James Hunt**, known as a fast but erratic driver back then, followed by local driver **Claude Bourgoignie**. It is true that **Purley** had very little opposition winning his second **Chimay** race win, in **1971**, for none of the top drivers from the British, French, Italian and Swedish championships raced in Belgium. After **Purley**'s **Brabham** came **Claude Bourgoignie**, followed by **Randy Lewis**. The swansong was decidedly much better and **Purley** had to work real hard with his **Ensign** to beat a large field that included **James Hunt, Tony Brise, Bob Evans, Alain Serpaggi, Christian Ethuin, Conny Andersson, Michel Leclere**. That was the last race through the streets of Chimay, which had become a very dangerous proposition, as Belgian **Ivo Grauls** died in the supporting touring car race in his famous Camaro.

IMOLA 500 km

The **Imola** 500 km was a sports car race not connected to any championship in **1970, 1972** and **1973**. It was held in September, after the world sports car season was over, so entries were usually healthy, attracting the likes of J.W., Autodelta and **Ferrari**. The **1970** race had 23 starters and the winner was **Brian Redman**, in a **Porsche** 917 followed by **Galli/De Adamich** in an **Alfa** 33, followed by three 908s. The **Ferrari** works was represented by **Merzario/Giunti**, who retired. There was no 500 in **1971** but the **1972** race was won by **Merzario** in a **Ferrari**, who won from **Ickx, De Adamich** and **Joest**. The race comprised two heats and a final. The **1973** event was won by **Derek Bell** in a **Mirage-Ford**, followed by **Stommelen** in an **Alfa** (the team's best result of the year, by the way), **Casoni** in a **Porsche** and **Facetti** in another **Alfa**. The entry was not as good as in previous years, including some **De Tomaso** GTs and second rate Italian entries. That was the end of the Imola 500 KM as a standalone race. However, races called 500 km of Imola happened in **1973** (valid for the European 2 Liter Championship) and **1976** (valid for the World Sportscar Championship).

INTERLAGOS, 500 KM

The 500 Km of **Interlagos** was the fastest race in Brazil, ran in the outer ring of **Interlagos**, not quite an oval but very fast nonetheless. For **1972**, there was a treat for Brazilians: it would be an International sports car race, with some recognizable names, besides the top Brazilian sports drivers of the day: **Reinhold Joest** in a **Porsche 908-3**, **Herbert Muller** in a **Ferrari 512**, **Gianpiero Moretti** and **Corrado Manfredini**, in Momos, **Angel Monguzzi** and **Rolando Nardi**, in Bertas, **Teodoro Zeccoli** and **Giovanni Alberti**, sharing an **Autodelta Alfa**, the main Portuguese drivers of the day (**Ernesto Neves, Carlos Santos, Artur Passanha**), some 2 liter prototypes, **Lionel Noghes** in a **Grac**, **Paul Blancpain** in a **Chevron**, lady drivers **Lella Lombardi**, in an **Abarth** and **Christine Beckers** in a **Lotus**. Among the Brazilians, **Luiz Pereira Bueno (Porsche 908/2), Marivaldo Fernandes (Alfa**

Romeo T33/3), Paulo Gomes (Ford GT40), Tite Catapani (Lola T210), Angi Munhoz (Porsche 907), Jaime Silva (Furia-Lamborghini), Nilson Clemente in a Brazilian **Avallone-Ford** and **Antonio Carlos Avallone**, in an **Avallone-Chrysler**, in addition to **Marinho Antunes' Lola T70**. The latter car burned to the ground, the second T70 to burn in Brazil's fastest race. **Silvio Moser** also non-started. The race was a straight fight between **Joest** and **Bueno**, with **Muller** looking on and the German ended up having his first major international win. Behind these three came, **Fernandes** in the **Alfa**, **Nilson Clemente** in the **Brazilian** prototype and **Blancpain** in the **Chevron**. In 1973 the race went back to its domestic DNA.

The formation lap of the 500 km of Interlagos of 1972 (Rogerio Luz)

1000 KM OF KYALAMI

The 9 Hours of Kyalami was the crown jewel of the South African Springbok series covered in the end of this chapter. In keeping with the times, the 9 hours was shortened into the 1000 km of **Kyalami** in **1974** and the first edition of this race was actually included in the World Championship of Makes a single time. Starting in **1975**, the race became a traditional season ending race for touring cars, generally attracting some international stars.

The **1975** edition, for instance, had entries from **Ford** Cologne, **BMW** and Autodelta, plus a Faltz-Alpina car. The winners were **Hans Heyer, Peter Hennige** and **Jochen Mass**, in a **Ford** Escort, which was followed by the works **BMW** of **Ronnie Peterson** and **Hans Stuck** and the Faltz car of **Derek Bell** and **Brian Redman**. The best **Alfa** could do was 7th place, for the Autodelta star line-ups of **Merzario/Dini** and **Ian Scheckter/Roy Klomfass** retired. Another Escort driven by **Mass/Ludwig** retired. In **1976** the positions were reversed and **Harald Grohs, Jody Scheckter** and **Gunnar Nilsson** won in a **BMW** 3.0 CSL. The Ford standard bearer was driven by **Heyer/Ludwig**, which was followed by **Reine Wisell/Stuart Graham** in a Camaro and **Merzario/Dini** in an **Alfa Romeo** Alfetta GTV. The best local pair was **Keizan/Ian Scheckter**, in a **BMW** 530, which came in 5th. Other interesting teams were **Hezemans/Schenken**, in an Escort and **Peterson/Fitzpatrick**, in a **BMW**, both of whom retired. **Jody** won again in **1977**, this time teamed with **Hans Heyer**, followed by **Toine Hezemans/Armin Hahne/Reinhold Jost**, both crews on Zakspeed Escorts. **BMW**s 320 came in 3rd (**Grohs/Hottinger**) and 5th (**Winkelhock/Surer**), while the South Africans **Lavoipierre/Martin** crew came in 4th in a **BMW** 530. **Stuck/Peterson** and **Ertl/Ludwig** retired their **BMW**s. The **1978** event lacked star crews and the winners were **Brian Cooke** and **Phil Adams**, driving a **Datsun** 140Y but **David Hobbs** (3rd) and **Mike Hailwood** (8th) brightened up the entry. 51 cars started the **1979** race, which was won by **Helmut Kelleners** and **Eddie Keizan**, in a **BMW** M1, followed by **Winkelhock/Stuck** in another M1, **Booysen/Goddard** in a **BMW** 530 and **John Watson** and **Jochen Mass** in yet another **BMW** M1. Other international drivers on hand were **Derek Bell, Markus Hottinger, Hans Georg Burger** and even **Peruvian Jorge Koechlin**, who finished 7th in a **BMW** 530. The race has been held on and off since the 70s.

MACAU GRAND PRIX

The Macau Grand Prix had been held since the 50s and it was a regional event in its formative years. In **1970** the event was still a hodge podge of cars, including Formula 2, sports cars (**Honda** RV800), GTs (**Porsch**e 911 and Corvette) and even a Formula Vee car. A certain **Teddy Yip** was in this field, driving a **Porsche** 906 but the most important driver was **Dieter Quester**, driving a works Formula 2 **BMW** making its last appearance, while Australian **Kevin Bartlett** also raced in a Mildren. **Quester**'s superior machinery resulted in a win, closing a chapter for **BMW**.

1972 Macau *JSantos*

VW Beetles also raced in the Macau touring car race. Photo by Jose Santos

The **1971** event was again regional in character, with less variety in terms of categories (no Formula Vees this time), although a **Porsche** 911 and a 906, a **Datsun** 240, a **Honda** and a **Lotus** Elan, mixed in with European and Australian single seaters. There were no Europe-based drivers on the field and a single

Australian (**G. Cooper**) but the GP was actually won by British expatriate driver **Jan Bussell** (in some results this driver appears as both Malaysian or Singaporean, so let us call him a citizen of the world).

The **1972** race had two Australians on the field, **Vern Schuppan** and **Max Stewart and** some grid filler sports cars (a **Honda, Yip**'s **Porsche** 906, **Adamczyk**'s 911, **Suzuki, Lancia** and **Datsun** entries) were still found. In the end, Hong Kong's **John Macdonald** won the affair in a **Brabham** BT36. **Quester** and **Schuppan** were both back in **1973** and **Graeme Lawrence** and **Leo Geoghegan** came from the Antipodes, while the rest of the field was all Asian. **MacDonald**, by then driving a **Brabham** BT 40, won again.

Schuppan returned for a third time in **1974** and this time won the race, followed by **David Purley**. Sports/GTs filled most of the last three rows of the grid but **Adamczyk**'s **Porsche** arrived in third place anyhow. **Schuppan, Purley, Bartlett** and **Stewart** all came back in 1975 and **Steve Millen** was a newcomer but the winner was again **Macdonald**, by then driving a **Ralt** RT1.

Jan Bussell appeared in Macau, 1972, in this Palliser. Photo by Jose Santos

The **1976** grid even had a Formula 1 regular, Australian **Alan Jones** in an old **March** 722. Other non-Asians were **Schuppan, Rupert Keegan, David Purley** and **Graeme Lawrence** and **Schuppan** came out the winner in his **Ralt**. There were still a couple of **Porsche**s on the grid, which gave the race the Libre feeling of yore but in **1977**, the Macau GP finally became a true single seater race. There were 23 cars on the grid and in addition to returnees **Schuppan, Lawrence, Bartlett** and **Jones**, other non-Japanese Asian drivers made the field, **Riccardo Patrese, Steve Millen** and **Andrew Miedecke** and two prominent Japanese drivers also raced, **Satoru Nakajima** and **Masahiro Hasemi**. Italian **Patrese** won in a **Chevron**.

By **1978**, Macau had adopted the 2-2 grid formation (it had been 3-2-3 until **1977**) and in addition to returnees **Jones, Patrese, Miedecke, Bartlett, Lawrence** and **Hasemi**, Europeans **Keke Rosberg** and **Derek Daly** and Americans **Brett Lunger, Skeeter McKitterick** and **Kevin Cogan** were also on the grid. The race became a much more international affair, to detriment of local Asian drivers. **Patrese** won again and the best traditional drivers could do was sixth.

In the last Macau GP of the decade there were only two Non-Japanese Asians on the grid: **Poon** and **Ramirez**, as **Sonny Rajah** had an accident and failed to start. The rest were all Europeans (**Patrese, Daly, Needell, Keegan, Rothengatter, Lees, Marshall**), Americans (**Cogan, Earl, Gloy, McKitterick**), Australian (**Miedecke and Schuppan**) and Japanese (**Hasemi, Nakajima, Misaki, Ida** and **Shimuzu**). Not surprisingly, none of the non-Japanese Asian drivers made the top six and the race was won by **Geoff Lees**. So the Macau Grand Prix is emblematic of the theme of this book, the pivoting from Romantic, early on the decade, to Organized in the end. While races in the early 70s were populated by local drivers from Macau and Hong Kong, plus exotic Indonesians, Pilipino, Malays, Singaporeans, driving a range of machines, late on the decade the profiles of both drivers and cars had changed substantially. **Albert Poon** from Hong Kong deserves mention, for he was the only driver to start all ten Macau GP races of the 70s.

The Macau Grand Prix weekend also included a touring car race, contested by a wide range of machinery, from expected Japanese cars (**Toyota, Honda, Subaru**) to **Rover, Morris, Mini Coopers, VW Beetles** and even a **Mercedes**, rarely seen in action in Asia. European champion **Glemse**r drove in this race a few times but an accident in 1974 that caused the death of a spectator led him to retire from racing.

MARATHON DE LA ROUTE

By far the longest race in the world, at 86 hours, the Marathon de La Route had seen better days when the race was held at the **Nürburgring** in August of **1970**. The novelty had worn off somewhat. There were 64 starters in that **1970** race and Porsche actually fielded a works team of 914/6s, for **Larrousse/Marko/Haldi, Waldegaard/Andersson/Chasseuil** and **Ballot-Lena/Steckonnig/Koob**. Not surprisingly, **Porsche** cleaned up, finishing 1-2-3 in the above order, for all other teams, except for a **Mini** Clubman entered by British Leyland, were privateers. The **Pierpoint/Enever/Baker** 4.3 **Rover** led for 16 hours but it retired and left the road open for the **VW-Porsches**. There were no huge manufacturer surprises, such as the **Torino**s and **Tatra**s that raced with distinction in the late 1960s but there was quite a bit of variety at hand: **BMW** 2002 and 2800, several **Opel** models (Kadett, Commodore, Rekord), **Datsun** 1600, **Daf** 55, **Volvo** 122S, **Ford** Capri 3000, **Fiat** 124, **Alfa Romeo** GTV, **VW** 411 and Beetle, **Citroen** DS21, **Peugeot** 204, **Simca** 110 S, **Triumph** TR6, **Renault** R8, **NSU** RO 80 and 1200, **Honda** S800, **Lotus** Elan, **Alpine** A110, plus a couple of **Porsche** 911. Besides the **Porsche, Rover** and **Mini** crews, the vast majority of the drivers were German and Belgian amateurs. The regulations required that teams had to complete as many laps in the last 12 hours as in the first 12, so consistency was a major deal.

The **1971** edition was the last Marathon and it went out with a bang, the race having been extended to a whopping 96 hours!!! Merely 39 teams showed up and only 16 finished. This time, there were no works teams. The French trio of **Jacques Henry, Jean-Luc Therier** and **Maurice Nusbaumer** won the race in an Alpine A110. Among the starters there was a **Ferrari** Dino driven by **Hughes de Fierlant, John Goosens** and **Yves Deprez but** it did not finish. A little **DAF** 55 prototype came in 3rd, driven by a Belgian crew, bringing this romantic race to an end.

Belgians Danielle Plomteux and teammates "Clyde" and Y. Erroelen finished 11th in the 1970 edition, in their Opel Commodore.

Here is Danielle Plomteux receiving her well-deserved prize.

MONACO FORMULA 3 GRAND PRIX

Theoretically, the Monaco Formula 3 Grand Prix should not be included in this section which lists standalone races that were not part of any championship. That is because in the 70s the Monaco Formula 3 race was part of the British Shellsport and John Player Championships, the Italian Championship and the European Championship, sometimes the race was actually included in two championships at the same time! However, the stature of the Monaco Formula 3 race was such that it stood out among dozens of Formula 3 races throughout Europe, to the extent that drivers that graduated to higher disciplines would still come back to try a Monaco win, like winners **Depailler** (72), **Pryce** (74), **Pironi** (77) and di Angelis (78). The Monaco race attracted large entries, close to a hundred, although quite a few never showed up. Participants from all European Championships entered the race and even some one-offs showed up.

Some interesting facts:

- the race was so competitive that the first **March** win in Monaco took place only in **1974**

- an unusual **Lancia** powered **GRD** won the race in **1975**. It never won again anywhere else.

- **Lionel Noghes**, grandson of the Monaco GP creator, failed to qualify for the **1970** race. He was the only Monegasque entered. Other Monegasque drivers did not fare better during the decade: **Damon Metrebian** and **Manolo Veladini** also failed to qualify.

- Even a Greek driver, **Giorgio Aposkitis**, was entered for the **1977** race but never showed up. Greek drivers rarely raced outside of Greece.

- **Jean-Pierre Jaussaud**, who raced in the 1970 event, was entered in the 1977 race. By then he was a more than an established driver, runner-up in the **1972 Formula 2** Championship but I guess he wanted something more in his resume. He deservedly got a **Le Mans** win in **1978** and another in **1980**!

- the race was not kind even to world champions to be. **Nelson Piquet** failed to qualify in both his attempts, **1977** and **1978**.

Winners:

1970, Tony Trimmer – Brabham-Ford
1971, Dave Walker – Lotus-Ford
1972, Patrick Depailler – Alpine-Renault
1973, Jacques Laffite - Martini-Ford
1974, Tom Pryce – March-Ford
1975, Renzo Zorzi – GRD-Lancia
1976, Bruno Giacomelli, March-Toyota
1977, Didier Pironi, Martini-Toyota
1978, Elio di Angelis, Chevron-Toyota
1979, Alain Prost, Martini-Renault

Prominent drivers who raced or attempted to qualify for the Monaco Formula 3 race during the 70s, besides the winners mentioned above: **Gerry Birrel, Jean-Pierre Jarier, Giovanni Salvati, Jean-Pierre Jaussaud, Ulf Svensson, Wilson Fittipaldi Jr., Mike Beuttler, Bob Wollek, James Hunt, Helmut Marko, David Purley, Jean-Pierre Jabouille, Roger Williamson, Rikki Von Opel, Bob Evans, Jochen Mass, Torsten Palm, Alan Jones, Lella Lombardi, Tony Brise, Vittorio Brambilla, Giorgio Francia, Masami Kuwashima, Mike Wilds, Brian Henton, Danny Sullivan, Alex Ribeiro, Larry Perkins, Piercarlo Ghinzani, Gunnar Nilsson, Arie Luyendijk, Patrick Neve, Ingo Hoffmann, Rupert Keegan, Pierre Dieudonne, Jean-Louis Schlesser, Ian Ashley, Boy Hayje, Riccardo Patrese, Huub Rothengatter, Anders Olofsson, Stefan Johansson, Geoff Brabham, Derek Daly, Geoff Lees, John Nielsen, Jan Lammers, Tiff Needell, Nelson Piquet, Derek Warwick, Bobby Rahal, Teo Fabi, Michael Bleekemolen, Howdy Holmes, Nigel Mansell, Andrea de Cesaris, Michele Alboreto, Mauro Baldi, Jo Gartner, Kenny Acheson, Slim Borgudd, Thierry Boutsen, Philippe Streiff, Eddie Jordan, Roberto Guerrero, Philippe Alliot.**

NÜRBURGRING, 24 HOURS

The Germans always liked touring car races, in fact, the European Touring car Championship was created by a German in the 60s, so it is only fitting that eventually two major touring car races were held at Nürburgring, plus a host of minor ones. The 6 Hours had been a staple of the European Touring Car Championship from the onset and an international race. The 24 Hour race was created as a domestic event, which attracted professionals and amateurs alike.

The first edition of the event was held in **1970** and 99 cars took the start, mostly German machinery, although some **Alfas, Fiats, Renault, DAFs** and other manufacturers were represented. The **1978** race actually had 113 cars at the start. **Niki Lauda**, by then a driver of some stature, was part of the winning crew in 1973. No races were held in **1974** and **1975**, due to the oil crisis. Eventually, GTs joined in the fun and **Porsches** won three events during the decade.

1970 – Hans Stuck/Clemens Schickentanz, BMW 2002
1971 – Ferfried von Hohenzollern/Gerold Pankl, BMW 2002
1972 – Helmut Kelleners/Gerold Pankl, BMW 2800 CS
1973 – Niki Lauda/Hans-Peter Joistein, BMW 3.3 CSL
1976 – Karl-Heinz Quinn/Herbert Hechler/Fritz Muller, Porsche Carrera
1977 - Herbert Hechler/Fritz Muller, Porsche Carrera
1978 - Herbert Hechler/Fritz Muller/Franz Geschwendher, Porsche Carrera
1979 – Herbert Kummle/Karl Mauer/Winfried Vogt, Ford Escort RS2000

PARIS, 1000 KM

The 1000 km of Paris, held at **Montlhery** usually attracted a good entry. Held at the end of the sports car season, it was as close to a Paris Grand Prix one could get. The **1970** race was won by **Matra** 660 driven by **Jack Brabham** and **Francois Cevert**. They were followed by **Juncadella/Jabouille** (**Ferrari** 512), **Larrousse/Ballot-Lena** (**Porsche** 908) and **Beltoise/Pescarolo** in another **Matra**. This was **Brabham**'s last race win. The **1971** event had quite a few 5 liter prototypes (**Porsche** 917 and **Ferrari** 512) and even **Alfa Romeo** entered two cars, none of which started. The winners were **Derek Bell** and **Gijs Van Lennep**, who were followed by **Larrousse/Kinnunen**, both in 917's. By **1972 Monthlery** was not in usable condition for top level racing, so the Paris race was held quite far, in **Rouen**! The winners were **Beltoise/Larrousse**, in a Bonnier **Lola** 3 liter, followed by a number of 2 liter cars. This was the last edition of the event.

Main drivers who raced in the 1000 km of Paris during the 70s: **J. Brabham, F. Cevert. J. Juncadella, J.P. Jabouille, G. Larrousse, C. Ballot-Lena, J.P. Beltoise, H. Pescarolo, A. de Cadenet, J. Neuhaus, W. Kaushen, H. Marko, C. Haldi, T. Pilette, P. Depailler, D. Bell, G. Van Lennep, L. Kinnunen, B. Waldegaard, R. Tourol, J.L.Lafosse, C. Amon, B. Wollek, R. Heavens, M. Casoni, F. Migault, J. Barth, A, Serpaggi, R. Stommelen, J. Coulon, J. Bridges, J Hine, J. Fitzpatrick, J.P.Jarier, J. Laffite, A. Merzario, M. Cabral, D. Purley, J. Leep, R. Jost**.

Cars that raced in the 1000 km of Paris during the 70s: Ford GT 40; Porsche 910, 908, 917K, 907, 914/6, 911; Matra-Simca MS 660; Ferrari 512 S and M, 365 GTB4; Chevron B8, B16, B21; Chevrolet Corvette; Lola T210, T212, T290, T280, T70; Alfa Romeo T33, De Tomaso Pantera, Martin BM8 and BM9; Taydec.

SWEDISH GRAND PRIX, 1970

This race only makes the cut because there were a few Formula 1 Swedish Grand Prix in the 70s, although this one was a sports car race. The **1970** event was the only Swedish GP with **Bonnier, Peterson** and **Wisell** on the grid, after all and **Niki Lauda** was also there, driving a **Porsche** 908. The 40 minute race in **Karlskoga** was a tad short for a Grand Prix, it must be said and in the end none of the Swedish big shots won it. Neither did **Gijs Van Lennep** or **David Piper** who had **Porsche** 917s. The winner was **Chris Craft**, driving a 3-liter Cosworth powered **McLaren** M8, which had already posted the fastest lap at **Vila Real**. Other notable drivers in the race were **Helmut Marko, Teddy Pilette, Guy Edwards, Jurgen Neuhaus** and **Alain de Cadenet**. A few weeks later, a Danish Grand Prix was held at **Jyllandsring** and **Bonnier's** Lola prevailed this time. Only 2-liter cars raced in Denmark.

TARGA FLORIO

Until **1973** the **Targa Florio** was a much expected event in the international calendar, part of the World Championship of Makes. The race through the streets of several Sicilian villages and roads, some not very well kept, was both exciting and dangerous. The long 72-km circuit resulted in 30 minute plus laps, so viewers only saw cars a few times. Notwithstanding, the event was prestigious and as long as local hero **Nino Vaccarella** had a car, Sicilians were happy. However, by **1973**, as 3-liter prototypes were way too fast and sophisticated for the Madonie circuit and efforts to control the Sicilian crowd were in vain, so the Targa Florio was dropped from the international calendar. It resisted a short while longer, as we shall see.

The event was held at the usual time of the year in 1974, a shorter 8-lap race and the winners were **Gerard Larrousse and Amilcare Ballestieri**, in a **Lancia**

Stratos, fielded by the works. 59 cars started and there were no pure large engine prototypes. The Silhouette like **Lancia**s were actually fielded as prototypes but prototypes they were not. **Larrousse** and **Sandro Munari** (in the other Lancia) were the only big names on the field and there was no Nino in sight, a bummer for the Sicilians.

That was all solved in **1975**. Not only was Nino back, paired with **Arturo Merzario**, he was also driving an **Alfa Romeo** T33/12 fielded by the works, rather than WKRT. The same two drivers had shared a **Ferrari** in 1973 but **Arturo's** early enthusiasm took the best of him, the car retired, resulting in a few unkind words from *Il Professore* in his book a few decades later. **Vaccarella/Merzario** were the only two name drivers on the field, the **Alfa** had no match besides the **Casoni/Dini** sister car that did not end a single lap, so the Italians won with a 20 minute cushion over "**Amphicar**"/**Armando Floridia** in a **Chevron**. The carefully driven **Alfa** lapped up to the 8th placed car, which gives an idea of its superiority. This was also **Vaccarella**'s last win and last race. There was one last event named **Targa Florio** in **1976** and it was an even more subdued affair. The race was won by "**Amphicar**"/**Armando Floridia**, this time in a 2 liter **Osella-BMW** and the only name driver was **Carlo Facetti**, who arrived in second place in a **Lancia** Stratos shared with **Gianfranco Ricci**.

VILA REAL

Vila Real is located in the Northern part of Portugal and racing had been taking place there since **1931**. By **1970**, activities comprised of a major race for sports cars, another one for touring cars and one for **Formula Ford**. Usually held during the summer, it cannot be said the event attracted extremely high quality entries but the event was equivalent to a Portuguese Grand Prix of the day, definitely Portugal's most important race.

The **1970** race, 500 km in length, was won by the VDS Team **Lola** T70 **Chevrolet** driven by **Teddy Pilette** and **Gustav Gosselin**. They were followed by five 2 liter prototypes, although other larger engine cars also started, including **Chris Craf**t, who drove a Cosworth powered Mclaren. The **1971** race was shorter and the winner was Spaniard **Jorge de Bagration**, in a **Porsche** 908. He was followed by the best Portuguese driver of the day, **Mario Cabral**, who drove a **David Piper Porsche** 917 and fought for the lead for most of the race with **Rene Herzog** in a **Ferrari** 512. The **1972** race was won by **Claude Swietlik**, who drove a 2-liter **Lola** and was able to beat **Carlos Gaspar**, who drove a 3-liter **Lola**.

The **1973** race was the last of the **Vila Real** international cycle and it was won by **Carlos Gaspar** in a BIP **Lola** 2 liter. Among the drivers were **Peter Gethin**, **Vic Elford** and **Jean Louis Lafosse**. The opening of the **Estori**l racetrack and the socialist revolution brought **Vila Rea**l to an end as a major international event.

Cars that raced at **Vila Real** in **1970-1973**: Lola T70, Chevron B6, Nomad Mk2, Porsche 906, Ford GT40, Porsche 910, Mclaren M8-Ford, Gropa BRM, Lotus 47, Lola T210, Chevron B16, Porsche 908, Porsche 917, Chevron B19, Martin BM8, Daren, Mercury-Ford, Abarth 2000, Redex, Ferrari 512, Porsche 911, Lotus 62, Datsun 1600, Porsche 907, Dulon Porsche, Lola T290, Lola T280, Chevron B21,

Abarth 3000, Porsche 914/6, Chevron B23, GRD S73, March 73S, Scorpion JB4, Porsche Aurora 2000, Porsche Carrera.

Mario Cabral drove a Porsche 917 in the 1971 edition of the Vila Real race. (Author unknown)

Non-local drivers who raced at **Vila Real** in **1970-1973**: **Teddy Pilette, Taf Gosselin, John Bamford, Ed Negus, Mark Konig, Roger Heavens, Mike Garton, Claude Larrieu, Willie Green, Julian Gerard, Mike Coombe, John Chatham, Paul Vestey, James Tangye, Chris Craft, David Weir, Willie Tuckett, Alain de Cadenet, Jorge de Bagration, Richard Knight, Martin Dendey, Ken Walker, Tony Birchenhough, Alan Fower, Everardo Ostini, Tony Goodwin, Mike Gribben, Rene Herzog, "Bing Jock", William Schereen, Peter Crossley, Martin Ridehalgh, Claude Swetlik, John Bridges, John Burton, Paco Josa, Peter Humble, Enrico Pasolini, Martin Raymond, Peter Hanson, Vic Elford, Peter Gethin, Jose Juncadella, Dave Walker, Jose Uriarte, Andrew Fletcher, John Blanckey, John Rulon-Miller**

TROIS RIVIERES GRAND PRIX, CANADA

As mentioned in the section on Formula Atlantic, the category was growing by leaps and bounds by **1974**, in the process almost driving Formula 3 to extinction in Britain. Additionally, the category was adopted in several other countries and continents, including **Canada**. The **Trois Rivieres** race existed since **1967 but** it was mostly a subdued regional affair. By **1974**, the race became a non-championship Formula Atlantic race, in fact, the most prestigious in the world. This status did not last for long, by **1979 Trois Rivieres** became just another round of the North American Formula Atlantic Championship.

In **1974**, in addition to the best Atlantic drivers in North America at the time, a few European hotshoes were convinced to race **at Trois Rivieres, Patrick Depailler, Jean-Pierre Jaussaud** and **Tom Pryce**, the latter two racing in the Fred Opert stable. Additionally, **George Follmer**, a highly experienced former Can Am and Trans Am champion and Formula 1 podium scorer, also added stature to the event. The winner was American **Tom Klausler**, who would eventually win the first race of the Single-Seat Can Am, driving a **Lola**. If you are wondering, yes **Gilles Villeneuve** was in this race as well but retired before completing a lap.

The second international **Trois Rivieres**, in **1975** had an even greater foreign presence. The winner was **Vittorio Brambilla**, who had just won the shortened Austrian Grand Prix, driving a Shierson **March**. Fred Opert fielded **Jean-Pierre Jarier** (2nd), **Jean-Pierre Jaussaud** (3rd) and **Jose Dolhem** (4th) in addition to Mexican **Hector Rebaque** who finished 5th. Other international drivers in the field were **Bertil Roos** (6th), **Dave Walker** (7th), **John Nicholson** (8th), **Damien Magee** (retired) and **Patrick Depailler** (retired). The best a local driver could do was 9th (**Seb Barone**) and **Gilles** had another accident and retired.

In the **1976** edition **Gilles** finally overcame his crashing proclivities and won over a field that included F1 champion to be **James Hunt** (3rd). Another future World Champion, **Alan Jones**, finished 2nd in an Opert **Chevron**. Other foreigners were **Vittorio Brambilla** (4th), **Patrick Tambay** (6th), **Hector Rebaque** (9th), **Bertil Roos** (12th), **Damien Magee** (retired), **Jose Dolhem** (retired) and Venezuelan **Juan Cochesa** (retired).

By **1977 Trois Rivieres** was no longer attracting large numbers of international drivers and only **Depailler** (3rd), **Jacques Laffite** (6th), **Cochesa** (11th) and **Keke Rosberg** (retired) were on the field. **Keke** does not even count, for he was a series regular. The winner was American **Price Cobb**, followed by **Howdy Holmes**.

The last International Trois Rivieres race took place in **1978**. The best foreign driver was **Didier Pironi**, who finished 3rd. **Arturo Merzario** was disqualified for overtaking under yellow flag and **Riccardo Patrese** did not even start, with electrical woes on the pace lap. At least the winner was Canadian veteran **Bill Brac**k, who had some Formula 1 experience.

It was good while it lasted. In **1979 Trois Rivieres** became just another humble round of the North American Formula Atlantic championship, the glamour gone forever.

SHORT RACE SERIES

ARGENTINE TEMPORADA

SPORTS CARS, 1970

Since the mid 60s Argentina had been holding international short series, first for Formula 3, then Formula 2 cars. For 1970, the Temporada comprised of two sports car races, the traditional Buenos Aires 1000 km and the Buenos Aires 200 Miles race, both held in January, because it was not possible to put together a reasonable Formula 2 field due to regulation changes. The Autodelta and Matra-Simca teams fielded works entries and a Piper Porsche 917 was also brought over. Additionally, armies of Porsche 908 and Lola T70s made up the rest of the field, truly international in character, which included many Formula 1 drivers such as Rindt, Oliver, Courage, Beltoise and Bonnier. A Serenissima was also entered for Jonathan Williams. Works teams Alfa Romeo and Matra shared the spoils. The French team won the most important and longer race, crewed by Beltoise/Pescarolo, while the shorter race was won by De Adamich/Courage. Argentine drivers were part of the teams arriving in 3rd, 4th and 5th in the 1000 km and generally did well. The Argentine Berta LR qualified well for both races but retired. The longer race became part of the World Championship again, in 1971, while the shorter race was a one-off. Several teams ran with solo drivers (**bold in the list below**) in the shorter event. The participants were:

BERTA LR:
L. di Palma/C. Marincovichi

PORSCHE 917:
D. Piper/B. Redman

FORD GT 40:
P. Brea/F. Serra
D. Martin/P. Forester

PORSCHE 908:
A. Soler-Roig/J. Rindt (in first race), J. de Bagration/C. Reutemann (in second race)
T. Dean/E. Copello
A. de Cadenet/C. Pairetti
J. Juncadella/J. Fernandez
H. Laine/ G. Van Lennep
H. Dechent/G. Koch/ (Koch teamed with A.Vianini in second race)
W. Kauhsen/H. Schultze
Masten Gregory
LOLA T70s:
T. Pilette/N. G. Veiga
R. Peterson/J. Cupeiro (Wisell teamed with Cupeiro in second race)
J. Oliver/C. Reutemann
J. Rey/E. Berney
J. Bonnier/R.Wisell
L. Morand/G. Pillon
C. Craft/R. Attwood
B. Smith/E. Swart
D. Prophet/C. Pascualini
T. Taylor/P. Gethin

SERENISSIMA
J. Williams/M. Montagnari

ALFA ROMEO T33/3
A. de Adamich/P. Courage
N. Galli/ R. Stommelen

MATRA SIMCA MS630
J.P. Beltoise/H.Pescarolo

The Argentine drivers in the event were Carlos Reutemann, Carlos Marincovich, Pablo Brea, Nestor Garcia Veiga, Andrea Vianini, Jorge Cupeiro, Carlos Pascualini, Eduardo Copello, Carlos Pairetti

The Serenissima made a final appearance in the 1970 Argentine Temporada (Alejandro de Brito)

FORMULA 2, 1978

The idea was reviving the Argentine and Brazilian Formula 2 Temporadas of the late 60s, early 70s, taking advantage of renewed South American interest on the category. In the 1978 championship, there were no less than three Argentines (**Ricardo Zunino, Miguel Angel Guerra, Ariel Bakst**) and two Brazilians (**Alex Ribeiro** and **Ingo Hoffmann**), the largest South American contingent in many a year. Plus there was talk of Turismo de Carretera's **Juan Maria Traverso** joining the mini-circus, which he actually did in 1979. Races in Argentina and Brazil were scheduled but Brazilian authorities, quite concerned with oil consumption in car races since 1976, did not allow the Brazilian races.

So in the end, a couple of races were held in Argentina, one in Mendoza, the other in Buenos Aires. March had cars for **Marc Surer, Teo Fabi** and **Ricardo Zunino** and the notable absentee in the first race was champion **Giacomelli**, who did appear in Mendoza. In addition to the March crew, the best F2 could offer was there: **Rosberg, Cheever, Lees, Dougall, South. Henton, Colombo, Gabbiani** (in the **Ferrari** engined **Chevron**) and even Formula 1 drivers **Clay Regazzon**i and

Jean Pierre Jarier, both former F2 champions. **Arturo Merzario** was slated to drive a Fred Opert **Chevron** but he never arrived.

The Mendoza race was dominated by the March works drivers **Surer** and **Fabi**, who finished ahead of **Colombo** and **Jarier**. In Buenos Aires, local driver **Zunino** inherited pole from **Giacomelli** but the winner turned out to be **Ingo Hoffmann**, who had been driving in Formula 2 since 1976, with no wins. This was in fact Ingo's last Formula 2 race, for he chose to resume his racing career in Brazil. **Regazzoni** came in 3rd, followed by **Ghinzani, Cheever** and **Ribeiro**. **Surer** and **Giacomelli** had accidents and did not start the race. There was talk of a 1979 F2 series but it came to naught. Instead, a Formula 3 series was put together but many races were cancelled and only Bahia Blanca and Balcarce actually happened. In a sea or Argentines and a couple of Uruguayans (**Pedro Passadore** and **Alberto Buffa**), the only foreigners were Italians **Michele Alboreto, Alberto Colombo** and **Corrado Fabi**. **Oscar Larrauri** won both races.

DESAFIO DE LOS VALIENTES, 1972

If trying to get Argentines to race Brazilians on a regular basis was difficult in the 70s, imagine getting drivers from several South American countries together. However, the Argentines managed to do just that, courtesy of **FIAT**, which promoted a couple of races called Desafio de los Valientes. One race was a street race between **Carlos Paz-Mina Clavero** and back. Rally drivers from Europe competed against Argentine specialists from Turismo de Carretera in equal **FIAT** 125s. **Jorge Recalde** won this race and the best European was **Simo Lampinen**, in fourth.

The track race was held at the **Buenos Aires** Circuit and it included drivers from Argentina, Paraguay, Uruguay, Peru, Chile and Brazil. Representing Brazil were **Jose Renato Catapani** and **Luiz Pereira Bueno**. A famous name ended up winning this race, **Oscar "Cacho" Fangio**, followed by **Canedo** and **Garcia Veiga**. **Catapani** was fourth, the best non-Argentine and **Bueno** finished in 6th place. It was a nice effort but never repeated.

AUSTRALIA'S ROTHMAN'S SERIES, 1976-1979

The Tasman Series had collapsed after a poor 1975 and Australians and New Zealanders decided to part company. Australians stuck to Formula 5000 for the rest of the decade and a 4-race series was put together for the last four years of the decade.

The 1976 series appeared to be a likely success, when 28 entries were received. In the end, an average of 17 cars actually showed up for races and the only two international drivers were Canadian **John Cannon** and **David Purley**. Eventually only the races at **Oran Park, Adelaide** and **Sandown Park** were held, while **Surfer's Paradise** was cancelled. **Vern Schuppan**, an Aussie with great experience in Europe and America, won the first race and was second in the two other races. New Zealander **Ken Smith** won the second race, **Cannon** the third. **Cannon** drove an older March, while the other two winners drove **Lolas**. Some old

Mclarens, locally built **Matich, Gardos, Cicada** and **Elfin** contested the series and engines were either **Chevrolet** or **Repco Holdens**. Top Australians like **Leffler, Bartlett, Goss, Allison** and **Walker** participated.

The surprise for the 1977 series was the participation of **Alan Jones**, the return of former Tasman Champions **Warwick Brown** and **Peter Gethin**, plus a Leyland engined **McLaren** M23 driven by **John McCormack**. Local **Beggs, Matich, Gardos** and **Elfins** were used, against **Lolas** and a **Chevron**. **Schuppan** drove an **Elfin** for the first time. There were more cars than 1976 and at first it seemed like the duo **Brown/Gethin** would dominate proceedings, finishing 1-2 in **Oran Park** and **Surfers Paradise**. At Sandown Park, **Max Stewart** won from future star **Alfredo Costanzo**, while **Alan Jones** prevailed over Brown in Adelaide. **Warwick Brown** won the series.

The 1978 series had a few surprises. **Graham McRae** was back, driving a **McRae** and the international drivers were **Keith Holland, John Cannon** in his trusty March 73A, **Don Breidenbach** and **John David Briggs**, who had raced in the single seater Can-Am in 1977. There was a rare **Brabham** BT43 for **Kevin Bartlett** and **Adams** and **Cicada** chassis to add diversity. In the end, **Warwick Brown** totally demolished the competition, winning all four races. **Schuppan** was second at **Adelaide** and **Surfers Paradise**, while **Garrie Cooper** was runner-up in **Sandown Park** and **Bruce Allison** did the honors at **Oran Park**. **Elfins** were second in three races and **McRae** managed a third place at **Oran Park**.

Australian built cars such as this Elfin did well in Australian Formula 5000 races. Photo by Glenn Moulds.

The news for 1979 was the inclusion of Formula 1 and Formula 2 cars, an obvious attempt to attract foreign entries. In the end only two foreigners took the bait, **David Kennedy** in a **Wolf** and **Geoff Lees** in an **Ensign**, both entered by Theodore Racing. A number of competitive local drivers took part, such as **Larry Perkins** (in an **Elfin**), **Alfredo Costanzo, Warwick Brown, Vern Schuppan**. American **Salt Walther**, who rarely raced outside the USA, drove a **McRae**. **Larry Perkins** won the series but none of the four races. **Costanzo** won at **Sandown Park** and

Adelaide, Kennedy won in the F-1 Wolf at Surfers Paradise and Brown at Oran Park. Thus ended a cycle, the last international Formula 5000 series in the world. Local Australian Formula 5000 races continued to be held a little longer.

BRAZILIAN SERIES

FORMULA FORD SERIES

Prior to **1970**, the best word to describe racing in Brazil would be amateurish. There were some serious and competent folks around but more often than not things were run by dilettantes. Planning was non existing, races were canceled with no prior warning, others added in the last moment, schedules were laughable pieces of fiction, the Brazilian Automobile Club (ACB) and the Brazilian Motor Racing Confederation (CBA) fought for control of the sport for many years, there were more rumors flying around than actual action. Yet, there was a lot of talent in the country, both in and out of the racetrack.

It took **Emerson Fittipaldi**'s success in Europe to make a lot of very important people see auto racing's potential in the country. There was much talk about hosting international Formula 2, Formula 5000 and Formula Ford series in Brazil during **1968** and **1969** but with **Interlagos** closed during these two years the likelihood of that occurring was close to zero. Conditions were perfect at the beginning of **1970** and it finally happened - an international single seater race series was held in Brazilian soil.

It did not happen overnight and it took planning and work. Two men stand out, **Antonio Carlos Scavone**, a one-time racer turned promoter and **Mauro Salles**, who engineered the event with the help of Emerson and other Brazilians in Europe. One very important player was BUA, a major British airline at the time, which was named sponsor by providing free transportation of the cars - by far the costliest element of the series. Globo TV network also began its long lasting involvement in racing by sponsoring the series and broadcasting it. The important thing is that save for BUA, unlikely to ever get involved in a Brazilian project after this, all parties involved seemed to think in-sync about the big picture and long-term, a novelty. The idea was not to make a fast buck and run, rather, invest on the future of international racing in Brazil. Today Formula Ford, tomorrow F3, then F2 and finally, Formula 1. Brazil had to prove it could do it.

Five races were scheduled in four different Brazilian tracks, during the European off-season. Two races were held in **Rio de Janeiro**, one each in **Curitiba, Fortaleza** and **Interlagos**. All races were run in real tracks, although out of the four only **Interlagos** had international grade facilities. Many cars were brought for Brazilian drivers, who did very well, considering the majority had never driven a Formula Ford before. The foreign contingent was led by British drivers **Ian Ashley, Ray Allen** and **Peter Hull**, those who stood better chance of beating the Brazilians. Among the foreigners, three would reach Formula 1 as drivers one day and one as a team owner. Brit **Ian Ashley**, Australian **Vern Schuppan** and Dane **Tom Belso** would all drive in F1 during the 70s, albeit briefly, while **Tom Walkinshaw** owned Arrows. The rest of foreigners were not well known but included two ladies,

Gabriel Konig and Liane Engemann. Clive Santo, Ed Patrick, Max Fletcher, Sid Fox and Toni Lanfranchi also took part. **Valentino Musetti**, a one-time stuntman, also drove in the series and during the 80s would drive a much modified **Fittipaldi** F5 to a win in the British Formula 1 series.

Emerson and **Wilson Fittipaldi** led the Brazilian group, which included, at one time or another, **Luiz Pereira Bueno, Marivaldo Fernandes, Milton Amaral, Norman Casari, Ricardo Achcar, Pedro Victor de Lamare, Francisco Lameirão** and **José Moraes Neto**. **José Carlos Pace** was a notable absence. Many different manufacturers were represented, **Lotus, Hawke, Titan, Merlyn, Macon, Royale, Lola**.

Bueno, fresh from a successful European season, won the very first heat of the series, in **Rio de Janeiro** but failed to finish the second heat, leaving **Emerson** an easy winner overall, followed by **Ray Allen**. **Ricardo Achcar**, the first Brazilian to win in Formula Ford, in **1968**, did not have an easy time here and elsewhere and never finished in the top 6, although he raced bravely.

Emerson did not do well in **Curitiba**, finishing 9th and 7th, leaving the way open to Brits **Ashley** and **Allen**. The best Brazilian was **1969** national champion **Marivaldo Fernandes**, who finished in 3rd and 2nd, finishing second overall. The **Fortaleza** stop had its share of organizational problems, expected of an area not used to major car races or international events of any type. It was included in the series, nonetheless. The track was also very short but no accidents happened and local fans were glad to see **Emerson** winning both heats again, followed by **Luiz Pereira Bueno**. The second **Rio de Janeiro** race was won by **Bueno**, followed by **Emerson Fittipaldi**. **Norman Casari** had a very noteworthy performance, finishing the first heat in 3rd place.

The final race was the reopening of the **Interlagos** racetrack. The grandstands were full and the atmosphere Grand Prix like. The 2 heats were won by **Emerson Fittipaldi**, followed by his brother **Wilson**, who did not shine until then. **Emerson** broke the Interlagos lap record, at 3m11.5s. In fact, the lap records of all other tracks were also broken during the series. **Francisco Lameirão**, had his single start that day and always ran in the top 6, finishing in 5th place. **Luiz Pereira Bueno** decided to race a **Lola** at Interlagos, leaving the **Merlyn** to **Lameirão** and must have regretted the decision for he underperformed at his home track. The final race had double score, so **Emerson** finished in first with 42 points, followed by **Ashley** (27), **Allen** (20), **Wilson Fittipaldi** (15), **Bueno** (15), **Fernandes** (7), **Hull** and **Casar**i (6), **Lameirão** (4) and **Walkinsha**w (3).

COPA BRASIL, 1970

While **Antonio Carlos Avallone's** dreams of becoming a top F5000 driver vanished in a nasty accident in the opening lap of the first **1970 Oulton Park** race, the driver developed his idea of staging an international series in Brazil, something he already wanted to do in **1969** - but had no venue. With **Interlagos** open for business, **Avallone** then had a top track to attract talent in Europe and got backing from Banco do Commercio e Industria de Sao Paulo.

Unfortunately, things did not quite work as **Avallone** expected. The **Avallone** run series did not have the same support as the **Scavone/Globo** single seater series, in fact it competed against them and this did show on the weak entry list. Additionally, the timing was not the best. At the same time **Avallone** was staging the Copa Brasil, in December, top European sports car racers were duking it out in South Africa, in the more established Springbok series. This meant very poor international entries.

However, **Avallone** had the support of the **Fittipaldi** brothers, who agreed to race VARIG sponsored **Lolas** in the series: **Wilson** drove a 5 liter T70 and **Emerson Fittipaldi** had a "tiny" 1.8 **Lola** T210. The recent winner of the US Grand Prix would have some trouble beating his brother and at least of powerful **Porsche** 908, driven by **Prince Jorge de Bagration**, the heir to the Georgian throne, naturalized Spaniard. Additionally, **Alex Soler Roig** was down to drive a less powerful **Porsche** 907 and **Antonio da Matta** was slated to drive the **Alfa Romeo** P33 that took part in the 1000 Miles.

For the first race, run in December 6, there would be no **Ferrari** 512S, which broke during qualifying. Additional international stars were Portuguese driver **Ernesto Neves** in a **Lotus** 47 and the Argentine **Jorge del Rio**, in an **Avante** prototype. Among the local crowd were **Camillo Christofaro**, back in action with his carretera, **Luiz Carlos Moraes**, with the **Porsche** 910, **Amat**o and his small engined prototype, **Celidonio** in the Snob's, **Silvio Montenegro** in a 4-door **VW**, **Jose Pedro Chateaubriand** in his Puma, **Nelson Marcilio** in a **Ford** engined Karmann Ghia, the Alfa GTA of **Graziela Fernandez** (the only lady driver in the Copa) and the **MC**-Porsche of **Raul Natividade**. It could be better, it could be worse.

Bagration posted a 2m57s time in practice and did well to win the race, followed by the other Spaniard, **Soler-Roig**. **Emerson** had a mid grid position, having no qualifying time and finished in fourth, right after **Da Matta** and the **Alfa**, posting a new record for **Interlagos**, 2m54.9s. In fact he almost beat the 3.0 liter **Porsche** of **De Bagration** but the car had to make a 7m37s stop to fix the fuel pump. Unfazed, **Emerson** drove the little **Lola** like a maniac and made enough ground to finish fourth, while his brother did not finish.

The second round had a few more cars entered. **Jayme Silva** was there in his **Furia FNM**, **Gianpiero Moretti** would try to start at last and a few more **Pumas**, **VWs** and an **AC prototype** made up the numbers. However, the two **Royales** that were promised for **Carlos Pace** and **Luiz Pereira Bueno** had not arrived, the Japanese **Nissans** were not there and both the **Da Matta Alfa** and the 910 **Porsche** were no shows. **Interlagos** had claimed another **Alfa** P33, for **Da Matta** crashed his car in practice beyond repair. **Casari** did not show up with the Brahma **Lola** T70 either.

The race start was delayed, to ensure the **512** would make it. It was pushed to the grid but when it mattered, the car did not move an inch. It ended up pushed to the pits, leaving the way open to the first race protagonists. **Emerson** had the pole but **Bagration** jumped ahead. However **Emerson** did not take long to pass the Spaniard and so did **Wilson**. **Emerson** made a rare mistake and was passed by his brother. **Wilson** made good use of his power and won ahead of **Emerson**,

Bagration, **Soler-Roig**, **Neves**, **Ternengo** (who alternated driving the **Avante**) and **Silva**, who, at 6th was the first Brazilian car.

Grid for Copa Brasil race, 1970. Emerson and Wilson in Lolas, Moretti in the Ferrari. Photo by Rogerio da Luz.

In the third race **Moretti** finally seemed to be able to make the start but the number of cars dwindled, in spite of the presence of the **Ferrari** and the **Nissan** Z 432 with **Yamaguita**. **Christofaro** and his carretera were gone and the gap between the pole position, **Emerson** and the last driver to post a time was a huge 48 seconds. **Emerson** posted 2m51.2s in qualifying followed by **Wilson** (2m54.2) and **Moretti** (2m55.1s) relegating the Spanish **Porsches** to the second row this time. However the weather did not cooperate and heavy rain meant the race was moved to a Tuesday - there simply would not be another weekend to reschedule the race. When the dry Tuesday came, **Moretti** jumped ahead and used the more powerful **Ferrari** engine to hold the **Fittipaldis** at bay. However **Emerson Fittipaldi** took the nimble **Lola** to new heights of speed, managed to pass **Moretti** and keep him at distance even on the straight lines. **Emerson** thus finished ahead of **Moretti**, **Wilson**, **Bagration** and **Soler-Roig**. **Jayme Silva** again had the best placed Brazilian car.

Come the final race and the Copa had three different winners. The grid for the final race had a few more cars, including the **Lola** T70 of **Norman Casari**, who finally made it, although he was over 20 seconds off the pace of **Wilson**'s similar car. **Camillo** was back, **Anisio Campos** had a **Porsche** engined AC, **Carlos Alberto Sgarbi** entered his **Opala** and **Masami Kuwashima** was now the **Nissan**'s driver.

510

The Argentine **Avante** prototype never posted a time in qualifying in all races, although it finished well on three occasions. **Emerson** lowered his own qualifying record and was about to give Brazilians a gift, two days after Christmas. In spite of the 5 liter **Ferrari, Emerson** again won, finishing in front of **Moretti, Bagration, Soler-Roig, Del Rio** and **Jayme Silva**, winning the Copa with a four point difference. Curiously, the Copa adopted points paying positions for the top eight (9-7-6-5-4-3-2-1). Copa Brasil was not a huge success by any stretch but at least **Emerson** managed to show he was a driver of great skill, beating much more powerful cars and claiming again **Interlagos**' lap record and the **Ferrari** did a couple more races after all.

COPA BRASIL, 1972

The last Brazilian international tournament of the 70s was a bit of a failure. After failing to convince Europeans and Americans to come to Brazil for a second Copa Brasil, in **1971, Antonio Carlos Avallone** did not give up and insisted on holding a second edition of Copa Brasil, to be held at **Interlagos** in late **1972**, announced with a bit of fanfare during the year. Two Group 7 **BRM**s were entered. There were rumors that **Ferrari** would send a car for **Pace**. Additionally **Tony Dean** and his **Porsche** 908, **Helmut Kelleners** in his Group 7 **McLaren, Brian Robinson, Trevor Twaites** and **David Purley** in **Chevrons** and **Brian Martin** in a **Martin** were given as certain entrants. There were so many interested drivers that there were two reserves, the **McLarens** of **Steve Matchett** and **Lothar Motschenbacher** and a **Berta** for **Luis di Palma**. Somewhere down the line there were reports that a ship that was bringing "many" cars to Brazil had sunk, which would explain the ultimate poor entry. In fact, the only entrant that claimed insufficient transportation insurance was provided for a car was **David Hepworth**, who had shipped a **BRM** in that sinking ship and sued **Avallone**, the organizer, in British courts.

Andrea de Adamich was one of the stars of the poorly supported Copa Brasil of 1972 (Photo by Rogerio da Luz)

The only actual foreign entries were **Willi Kauhsen**, in his **Porsche** 917-10, **George Loos** in a **McLaren, Albert Pfulhl** in a **McLaren** and **Andrea de Adamich**, in an **Alfa** T33-3. The fields were slightly boosted by a closed **Porsche** 917 for **Wilson Fittipaldi Junior**, plus a few foreign and domestic prototypes. Not even the local Hollywood, Greco and Jolly teams fielded their foreign prototypes. The races were shortened to 17 minute affairs, to ensure there were cars running at the end. **Wilson** won one race and the series, **Kauhsen** and **Loos** won the other races. A sad closing to the cycle of international tournaments in Brazil, that shows how difficult was running proper international races in South America in the early 70s.

INTERNATIONAL FORMULA 3 TOURNAMENT, 1971

The Formula 3 series, which occurred in January **1971**, was the second stage of the ultimate ambitious plan: hosting a Brazilian Grand Prix for formula one cars. In fact the dream was ever so close that during the F-3 series **Emerson Fittipaldi** drove the **Lotus** 49B that raced in Argentina, for a demonstration run at **Interlagos,** clocking 2m47.8s in the infield and 55.3s in the outer circuit. As for Formula 3, four rounds took place, the first three at **Interlagos**, a last race at **Tarumã** and a number of good European Formula 3 drivers were brought by sponsor Globo TV Network. Among them, Australian **Dave Walker**, a fast but sometimes controversial driver. Another Australian, who was to achieve much greater things later on the decade was also present: **Alan Jones**. British drivers in attendance were **David Purley, Tony Trimmer, Peter Hanson, Barrie Maskell, Mike Beuttler** and **Mike Keens**. Representing France was **Francois Migault**, while Italians **Giovanni Salvati, Claudio Francisci** and **Giancarlo Gagliardi** also fielded entries. The foreign contingent was completed with Swedes **Sten Gunnarson** and **Torsten Palm** and Swiss **Jurg Dubler**. A number of Brazilians were entered and the favorite were **Wilson Fittipaldi Junior** and **Jose Carlos Pace**. **Luiz Pereira Bueno** was down to drive a **Chevron**, **Jose Maria Ferreira** and **Ronald Rossi** had **Brabhams** and **Fritz Jordan** also had a **Lotus** at his disposal.

The Brazilians made the large public at Interlagos very happy, when they qualified for the first race 1-2-3 (**Fittipaldi, Pace, Bueno**), followed by **Dubler** and **Gunnarson**. **Wilson** followed his great qualifying effort with a win in the first and second heats. In the first heat, **Pace** managed to overtake **Wilson** a few times but was passed back every time. **Pace** finished second, followed by **Walker, Migault** and **Jordan**. **Bueno** raced in 3rd for a while but dropped back and finished eighth. In the second heat, **Wilson** again led every lap. **Bueno** recovered and by the 2nd lap was already in second, a position he held to the end. **Giovanni Salvati**, who was eighth on the first lap finished 3rd. **Pace** retired before completing the first lap. On aggregate the result was **Fittipaldi, Bueno, Walker, Purley, Salvati, Trimmer**. A racing incident between **Dave Walker** and **Fritz Jordan** had a bit of a row. **Walker** had really driven **Jordan** off the road and the Brazilian waited for the Australian to give him a piece of his mind. The **Lotus** works team requested the elimination of **Jordan** but eventually both drivers made peace - although **Walker** continued to make enemies during his Brazilian trek, as we shall see later.

Wilson Fittipaldi was also on pole for the second race of the series, this time followed by **Francisci, Pace, Salvati and Bueno**. The race was hotly contested although **Wilson Fittipaldi** led every lap of both heats - the action was behind him. In the first heat, several drivers were in 2nd (**Pace, Salvati, Bueno, Francisci**) and it was **Salvati** who finished second, followed by **Bueno, Walker** and **Palm**. The same happened in the second heat, only this time, it was **Walker**, ahead of **Maskell, Jordan** and **Palm**. On aggregate time, **Fittipaldi** finished in front of **Walker** and a surprising **Fritz Jordan**.

By the third race of the series, the foreign drivers had gotten the hang of the **Interlagos** racetrack and the top four qualifiers were all non-Brazilians (**Walker, Salvati, Trimmer, Francisci**). **Pace** was the best Brazilian, followed by **Bueno** (8th) and **Fernandes** (10th). **Wilson** did not record a time. In the heat, though, the story was different. **Wilson** was 9th in the first lap, 6th in the second, 5th in the 3rd, 3rd in the 4th and on the lead in the fifth lap, which he held to the end. **Walker**, who led one lap, had to be happy with his second place, while **Trimmer**, who led the first two laps, finished fourth. **Salvati** was third and **Marivaldo Fernandes,** who replaced **Hanson** and **Beuttler** in the **Chevron** finished in 6th place. The top Brazilians did not do well in the second heat, though. **Fittipaldi** had problems at the start and foreigners led every lap: **Walker** (1-2), **Salvati** (3-4-6-8-10) and **Dubler** (7-9). The winner was **Salvati**, driving a **Tecno**, who finished ahead of **Purley, Trimmer** and a trio of Brazilians, **Ferreira, Rossi** and **Wilson Fittipaldi**. On aggregate, the result was **Salvati, Trimmer, Purley, Fittipaldi, Dubler** and **Fernandes**.

A major disappointment in this series was the one driver who would eventually win the World Formula 1 championship - in fact, the only one to win more than one Grand prix out of the whole bunch: **Alan Jones**. He always raced in the back, failing to display the speed and fighting spirit he was known for in latter years.

A non-series F3 event was held in **Tarumã**, the second international race held in the venue in the short space of a month. Seventeen cars started the first heat, which was led initially by **Wilson Fittipaldi Junior** and **Jose Carlos Pace**, both of whom were passed by **Jurg Dubler**. The Brazilians soon regained their position but **Dave Walker** worked his way up to the front, passed **Pace** and finished the heat 1/10 of a second in front of the Brazilian. The two drivers also starred in the second heat, only with reversed positions. **Walker** shut the door on **Wilson** often and won with a gap of 2/10 of a second, winning on aggregate with the tightest of margins. At the end of the race **Wilson** walked up to **Walker** to complain about his driving, leading many to think the lanky Brazilian would resort to a more physical dispute resolution. The final result was **Walker, Wilson Fittipaldi Junior, Jose Carlos Pace, Tony Trimmer, Torsten Palm** and **Mike Keens**.

FORMULA 2

INTERNATIONAL FORMULA 2 TOURNAMENT, 1971

In November of **1971 Brazil** was getting ever nearer the dream of hosting a Formula 1 race and eventually, a World Championship event. The Formula 2 Series held in October and November of that year would be the last step in systematically proving that Brazil could host major auto racing events. The series put together by **Antonio Carlos Scavone**, with the help of Globo TV Network, comprised three events, two at **Interlagos** and one in Tarumã. Many of the best

Formula 2 drivers of the day went to Brazil: former world champion **Graham Hill**, F1 runner up and F2 Champion **Ronnie Peterson, Tim Schenken, Carlos Reutemann, Henri Pescarolo**, F2 race winner **Mike Beuttler, Jean Pierre Jarier, Reine Wisell, Bob Wollek, Peter Westbury, Claudio Francisci, Arturo Merzario, Giovanni Salvati, Spartaco Dini, Francois Migault** and **Carlos Ruesch**. Brazilians **Emerson** and **Wilson Fittipaldi, Jose Carlos Pace, Luiz Pereira Bueno, Ronald Rossi** and **Jose Maria Ferreira** were slated to drive in the event. Things did not work out well for **Bueno**, who got measles, so for the Sao Paulo events, **Lian Duarte** drove the car.

Things did not start well, for the first practice was suspended, due to nine missing spare part boxes, which did not arrive from Italy. Thus the qualifying and practice was postponed to Saturday. **Wilson** and **Emerson Fittipaldi** made good use of their knowledge of the track, qualifying 1-2 for the first race. Over 60,000 people cheered on **Emerson Fittipaldi**, who led from the start in the first heat but was later on caught by his brother and by **Ronnie Peterson**, both of whom passed **Emerson** on the 11th lap. **Wilson** finished first in his heat, followed by **Peterson, Emerson, Reutemann, Pace** and **Salvati**. In the 2nd heat, **Reutemann** jumped ahead but was soon passed by **Peterson** and eventually by **Emerson**. There was an intense dice between **Peterson** and **Emerson**, who fought every inch of the way. **Emerson** did win the second heat and on the aggregate as well and the final result was **Emerson, Peterson, Wilson, Reutemann, Salvati** and **Hill**.

For the second race, held one week later in **Interlagos, Emerson** qualified on pole, followed by **Reutemann, Schenken, Peterson** and **Salvati**. **Reutemann** started better but soon **Emerson** passed him. **Peterson** fell back at the start but soon recovered, breaking the **Interlagos** lap record at 2m42.6s but his **March** soon broke down and **Emerson** won again, followed by **Reutemann, Schenken** and **Wilson**. In the second heat, Reutemann again started better, while **Emerson** fell back to fifth. **Peterson** fixed his car during the interval and took part in the second heat, soon catching **Reutemann**. The race readily became a 3-way battle between **Peterson, Reutemann** and **Emerson** and the Brazilian won again, with the tiniest of margins, 3/10 of a second. On aggregate, **Emerson** finished first, followed by **Reutemann, Wilson, Beuttler, Hill** and **Ruesch**. The Brazilian drivers **Ronald Rossi, Jose Maria Ferreira** and **Lian Duarte** did not perform well at **Interlagos**.

The third Temporada race was held in **Tarumã** and the same drivers that dominated proceedings at Sao Paulo were at the top of the result sheet in the South: **Emerson Fittipaldi, Ronnie Peterson, Carlos Reutemann** and **Tim Schenken**. Among the entrants was **Spartaco Dini**, who shared the **Tecno** with **Merzario** and **Luiz Pereira Bueno**, who had at last overcome measles. This time **Schenken** qualified on pole but the Argentine was again the best starter. Among the leaders, in fifth place, was **Giovanni Salvati**, ahead of many fancier names. Eventually **Peterson** caught **Reutemann**, passed him but once more retired with damaged suspension. **Reutemann** thus won the first heat, ahead of **Schenken, Emerson, Pace, Wilson** and **Westbury**. Only twelve cars took part in the second heat and this time **Emerson** started better, followed by **Schenken** and **Reutemann**. **Pace**'s car failed to start and took off only after everybody had gotten away. **Salvati** soon worked his way up to fifth, chasing **Wilson Fittipaldi Junior**, while **Pace** drove frantically to get nearer the front of the pack. **Salvati** eventually tried to pass **Wilson** on turn 1 but missed the breaking point, losing the car, which almost hit **Wilson**'s and crashed violently onto the guard-rail. **Salvati** died on the spot, the first racing death at **Tarumã** and the first in **Brazil** that year. **Emerson** finished first on this heat but on the aggregate order was **Reutemann, Emerson, Pace, Wilson Fittipaldi, Westbury** and **Hill**. There were no podium celebrations that sad day and the stark reality of motor racing in the early 70s hit the happy Brazilians.

FORMULA 2 TEMPORADA, 1972

The second Brazilian Formula 2 Temporada was slated for the latter part of the year, with races in October and November. Originally, it was supposed to be a series of races in Brazil, Argentina and Venezuela but first, the Venezuela race was dropped and then the races in Argentina were cancelled. In the end, it turned out to be a 3-race affair, with three rounds at Interlagos (a Tarumã round was cancelled as well). As in **1971**, a number of top Formula 2 drivers raced in the event, some of whom were already Formula 1 drivers. The foreign contingent included F2 champion **Mike Hailwood**, Argentina's **Carlos Ruesch** and **Andrea de Adamich** in **Surtees**; **Bob Wollek, Tim Schenken, Henri Pescarolo** and **Ronnie Peterson** in Rondel **Brabhams**; **Jean Pierre-Jaussaud** in a **Brabham**; **David Morgan** in a **Chevron**; **David Purley, James Hunt, Clay Regazzoni, Jose Dolhem, Brett Lunger** in **Marches**. All cars had **Ford** engines.

A number of Brazilians drove in this Brazilian F2 Temporada. **Emerson Fittipaldi** came back for more F2 action, driving the sole **Lotus** on the field, while **Pace** also raced for **Surtees** and **Wilson Fittipaldi Junior** drove a **Brabham**. In addition to that, a host of other local drivers drove in what turned out to be the last F2 Temporada. **Pedro Victor de Lamare** rented a **March** 722 with Novamotor engine. The **Clay Regazzoni March** entered by Shell Arnold was driven in the second race by **Francisco Lameirão**, for the Swiss driver, still a **Ferrari** driver, was slated to drive in the 9 Hours of **Kyalami** sports car race, which he duly won with **Arturo Merzario**. Lian Duarte got a **Surtees** with a BDA/Hart engine, while **Silvio Montenegro** rented a **March** 722-BDA. **Montenegro**, more used to drive **VW** touring cars in Brazil, was totally out of his depth at this level and not surprisingly, retired after the tournament. **Luiz Pereira Bueno** was slated to drive but in the end did not get a car, a blow to the Brazilian contingent.

The first race pleased the partisan crowd very much, for idol **Emerson Fittipaldi** won in commanding style, with brother **Wilson** also on the podium, in third. **Wilson** actually qualified better than **Emerson**, with a time of 2m42s04, followed by a surprising **David Morgan** and then **Emerson**. In the first heat, **Emerson** jumped ahead of everybody, while **Morgan** dropped out of contention right away. **Emmo** was followed by a trio comprising of **Wilson, Schenken** and **Peterson**, who fought a mighty battle during the course of the heat. **Hailwood** was also in the thick of things until losing his engine. In the end it was **Emerson**, followed by **Schenken, Peterson, Wilson, Pescarolo, de Adamich, Hunt, Purley, Lian** and **Lunger**. In the second heat, **Schenken** and **Peterson** put the pressure on **Emerson**, who was overtaken by **Schenken**. **Emerson** still finished the heat in second place, followed by **Wilson, De Adamich** and the others. On aggregate, the result was:

1. Emerson Fittipaldi, Lotus

2. Tim Schenken, Brabham
3. Wilson Fittipaldi Jr, Brabham
4. Andrea de Adamich, Surtees
5. James Hunt, March
6. David Purley, March

Pace retired on the first heat of this race, after only two laps and the other Brazilians all finished above ninth.

Pace thoroughly made up for the disappointment of the first race, by winning both heats of the second race in great form. He led every lap of both heats and not even **Emerson Fittipaldi** could catch him on that day. The battle was for other places. The best of the lot was **Emerson Fittipaldi**, who finished the first heat in second and the second in third. **Pace** was followed in the second heat by **Emerson** in second and **Wilson** in fourth. There was a great rate of attrition among foreign drivers in this race. **De Adamich, Pescarolo, Ruesch, Morgan, Peterson** and **Hunt** did not start the second heat and **Schenken, Jaussaud** and **Purley** had an accident right after the start of the second heat. As a result, the less experienced Brazilians did well, as **Lamare, Lameirão** and **Montenegro** came in 8th, 9th and 10th. The only Brazilian who was not in the top 10 was **Lian Duarte**, who drove very well and should have finished in the top 6. The result of the second Temporada race was:

1. Jose Carlos Pace, Surtees
2. Emerson Fittipaldi, Lotus
3. Mike Hailwood, Surtees
4. Wilson Fittipaldi Jr, Brabham
5. Bob Wollek, Brabham
6. Jose Dolhem, March

The last Temporada series race ever was not kind on Brazilians - the only one in top 6 was **Wilson Fittipaldi** Jr, in sixth. **Pace** scored pole-position but had problems and finished 16th on the first heat. **Lamare** finished tenth and both **Emerson** and **Montenegro** retired. The first heat was won by **Pescarolo**, who had not shown much pace yet. He was followed by **Hailwood, Emerson, Schenken** and **Wilson**. **Pace** won the second heat handsomely, to the crowd's delight but that was not enough to bring him up the order, so he officially finished 8th. Behind **Pace** were **Hailwood, Schenken, Wollek** and **Regazzoni**. Unusually, on aggregate none of the heat winners were in the top 6. The result of this final international Formula 2 race held in Brazil was:

1. Mike Hailwood, Surtees
2. Tim Schenken, Brabham
3. Clay Regazzoni, March
4. James Hunt, March
5. Jean Pierre Jaussaud, Brabham
6. Wilson Fittipaldi Jr., Brabham

The **1972** Temporada was supposed to include races in **Cordoba, Tarumã** and **Buenos Aires** but the **Interlagos** rounds were the only ones actually run. Further attempts to hold Temporada races in Brazil, in **1973** and **1978**, came to naught.

COLOMBIA

FORMULA 2 RACES, 1971

It was a nice idea. Colombia dreamed of following Argentina's footsteps and transforming its Formula 2 Temporada into a bona fide Formula 1 event. Thus, a proper racetrack was built, the Ricardo Mejia Autodromo, to be inaugurated with an international field. Two races were slated for Bogota, one called the Gran Premio de la Republica de Colombia, the other, Gran Premio de Bogota. The field of 18 cars was reasonable, rather than stellar. Excellent drivers such as **Jo Siffert, Derek Bell, Rolf Stommelen** and former world champion **Graham Hill** did show up, while the 4-car **Tecno** team never made it. On the driving strength were **Enzo Corti, John Blades** and **Brian Cullen**, not exactly world beaters. Some unusual entries such as **Spartaco Dini's De Tomaso** and **Tetsu Ikusawa's Crossle** made the trek to the high altitude circuit but the winners were **Jo Siffert**, in a **Chevron** and **Alan Rollinson**, in a **Brabham**. The experience was never repeated, even though the organizers reportedly made a hefty US$200,000 profit, not an unsubstantial amount at the time. Colombia remained on the sidelines for the rest of the decade and the racetrack eventually closed.

NEW ZEALAND

PETER STUYVESANT SERIES, FORMULA 5000, 1976

By 1976 gone were the prestigious days of the Tasman Series jointly held in Australia and New Zealand for Formula 5000 cars. Australians and New Zealanders still tried to do it alone in 1976, each one putting their own international series. The four races at New Zealand were held in January, the regular rounds at **Pukekhoe** (New Zealand Grand Prix), **Manfield, Wigram** and **Teretonga**. The only European who made the long trip South was British Formula 5000 king **Brian Redman**, who had won the last two editions of the U.S. championship. Curiously, he was the only one driving a 2.0 liter car, a **Chevron-BMW**, while the rest had 5.0 liter cars, a mix of **Lola, Begg, Elfin** and **Katipo** chassis. The Pukekhoe round had 14 cars attempting to qualify but two 1.6 chargers did not make the cut. **Ken Smith** won his national Grand Prix, followed by Australians **Bruce Allison** and **Kevin Bartlett** and British **Redman** in the F2 car. At **Manfield** Brian showed even more speed, in a field of 11 cars and finished 2nd to Australian **Max Stewart**. **Allison** came 3rd and **Bernasconi**, 4th. At **Wigram,** a much maligned race in the British press, Smith came first again, followed by **Jim Murdoch, Bernasconi** and **Allison**. Smith confirmed his favorite status by coming second to **Graeme Lawrence** in the final race. **Bartlett** came 3rd, **Allison** 4th. Thus finished the last "international" series for Formula 5000 cars in New Zealand. As of 1977, Formula Atlantic (Pacific) was adopted, with more successful results.

NEW ZEALAND INTERNATIONALS, FORMULA ATLANTIC(PACIFIC) 1977-1979

The decision to shift to Formula Atlantics turned out to be a healthy one. For one, the fields were larger, with 16 cars on offering. Besides New Zealanders and Australians, there were drivers from Finland (**Keke Rosberg** and **Mikko Kozarowitsky**), USA (**Tom Gloy**), Hong Kong (**Albert Poon**), Indonesia (**Beng Soeswanto**). **Steve Millen** took the first round at **Bay Park**, while **Keke** won the next three (and the title) and **Tom Gloy** won the last race.

The experience was repeated in **1978**, with double headers and thus more races. 23 cars showed up for most races and **Rosberg** was back for more. Additionally, Americans **Bobby Rahal** and **Danny Sullivan** appeared, as well as Belgian **Pierre Dieudonne** in an Ehrlich and Australian talents, such as **Larry Perkins** and **Andrew Miedecke** also competed. **Keke** won six of the ten races in the Fred Opert **Chevro**n and the series but **Larry Perkins** also did well, winning two rounds. The other two races were won by New Zealanders, **Steve Millen**, who won again the initial race at **Bay Park** and **Brett Riley**, one of the **Manfield** rounds.

Keke was not back for **1979** but **March** entered a car for **Teo Fabi**, who won the first six races at **Bay Park, Pukekhoe** and **Manfield**, totally demolishing the competition. Other foreigners were **Larry Perkins**, Sweden's **Eje Elgh** and American **Jeff Wood**. The fields were smaller than **1979**, with around 14 cars on offering. At Teretonga, **Larry Perkins** took advantage of **Fabi**'s misfire in race 1 and 7th place in race 2, winning both races, while local driver **Dave McMillan** won the two races at Wigram. The New Zealand International series remained on the calendar until the mid 80s.

SOUTH AFRICA

SPRINGBOK SERIES

The Springbok Series was held late in the year, with races in South Africa, Rhodesia and Mozambique. The series also included the 9 Hours of Kyalami, which continued to be held as a shorter 1000 km race after the demise of the series. The 9 hours generally attracted a world class entry, in fact, the Ferrari works team won the event in 1970 (Ickx/Giunti), 1971 (Regazzoni/Redman) and 1972 (Regazzoni/Merzario). Unfortunately, the top European cars did not stay for the rest of the series, which was basically contested by 2-liter prototypes, GT and touring cars, mostly driven by local South African and in Mozambique, Mozambican drivers. A lot of the drivers who took part in the South African Formula 1 Championship drove in the series at one time or another. In the end, it turned out to be a fight between Lola and Chevron, although the latter had the upper hand. Future world champion Jody Scheckter had a great performance in 1971, winning one race. By 1973, the oil crisis had claimed its first victim, the series being cancelled after the second race. Springbok was no longer to be.

Antonio Peixinho/Arnold Chatz in an Alfa Romeo 1750 in the 1972 9 Hours. Photo by Russell Whitworth.

Cars that raced in the Springbok series: Ferrari 512, Porsche 917, Porsche 908, Chevron B16, Lola T70, Lola T210, Chevron B8, Ford Boss Mustang, Mazda M10A, Porsche 906, Ford Capri, BMW 2000, Renault R8, Nomad-BRM, Alfa Romeo GTAM, Alfa Romeo Berlina, Mini Cooper, Ecosse, Lotus 23, Volvo 142S, Mamba, Isuzu GT, Lotus Elan, Mosden, Bramhill, Datsun 1600, GRD S73, Porsche Carrera, Ferrari 312P, Chevron B19, Toyota Corona, Ford Escort, Alfa Romeo GTV, Sunbeam Tiger GT, Fiat 124, Chevy Firenza, Vauxhall Viva, FMG, March 73S, Chevron B23, Ferrari 365GTV, Datsun 240Z, Toyota Celica, Lola T280, BSM Dart, Gulf Mirage M6, BMW 3.5 CSL, De Tomaso Pantera, Ford Cortina, BMW 2002. Some of the cars were actually built in South Africa.

International drivers who drove in the Springbok series from 1970 to 1973: Brian Redman, Karl Von Wendt, Mike Hailwood, David Hobbs, Barrie Smith, Mark Konig, Paul Vestey, Derek Bell, Hughes De Fierlant, John Hine, Helmut Marko, Gijs van Lennep, Gerard Larrousse, Rudi Lins, Jo Siffert, Kurt Ahrens, Willy Kauhsen, Frank Gardner, Mike de Udy, Richard Attwood, Clay Regazzoni, Jacky Ickx, Mario Andretti, Howden Ganley, Tony Adamowickz, Mario Casoni, Dieter Glemser, Jochen Mass, Ed Swart, Guy Edwards, Chris Craft, Herbert Muller, Rene Herzog, Terry Clucker, Robert Grant, Willie Tuckett, Arturo Merzario, Gerry Birrell, Niki Lauda, Peter Gethin, Y. Katayama, Toshindri Takeshi, Antonio Peixinho, Brian Robinson, Frank Sytner, Ian Harrower, Peter Brown, Robert Grant, Reinhold Jost, James Hunt, Ian Grob, Kunimitsu Takahashi, Kenji Tohira, Hans Joachin Stuck, "Gero", Martin Birrane, Charles Lucas, Reine Wisell, Jean Louis Lafosse, Tim Schenken, John Nicholson.

Redman/Ickx in the same race. The 9 Hours were contested by powerful cars such as this Ferrari 312 P and more sedate touring cars such as the Alfa pictured above. (Photo by Russell Whitworth)

1970
Kyalami 9 Hours – Ickx/Giunti (Ferrari 512S)
Capetown 3 Hours – Redman/Attwood (Chevron B19)
Lourenco Marques 3 Hours (Mozambique) – Redman (Chevron B19)
Pietermaritzburg 3 Hours – Redman (Chevron B19)
Bulawayo 3 Hours (Rhodesia) – Redman/Love (Chevron B19)
Goldfields 3 hours – Redman/Attwood (Chevron B19)

1971
Kyalami 9 hours – Regazzoni/Redman (Ferrari 312P)
Capetown 3 Hours – Marko/Love (Lola)
Lourenco Marques 3 Hours (Mozambique) – Swart/J. Scheckter (Chevron)
Bulawayo 3 Hours (Rhodesia) – Hailwood/Driver (Chevron)
Goldfields 3 hours – Hine/Charlton (Chevron)
Pietermaritzburg 3 Hours – Love (Lola)

1972
Kyalami 9 hours – Regazzoni/Merzario (Ferrari 312P)
Capetown 3 Hours – Birrel/Mass (Chevron)
Lourenco Marques 3 Hours (Mozambique) – Birrel/Mass (Chevron)
Goldfields 3 hours – Birrel/Gethin (Chevron)
Pietermaritzburg 3 Hours – Mass/ Gethin (Chevron)

1973
Kyalami 9 hours – Joest/Muller (Porsche 908)
Capetown – Watson/I. Scheckter (Chevron)

BIBLIOGRAPHY

24 HEURES DU MANS, 1978, Publi-Inter S.A., 1979
24 HEURES DU MANS, 1979, Publi-Inter S.A., 1980
ADRIANSENS, TONY. **ALLEGERITA**, Corsa Research, 1994
ASH, DAVID. **GRAND PRIX ALMANAC**. Automobile Almanac Lt, 1974
AUTOCOURSE (several editions), Hazleton Securities Ltd
AUTO HEBDO, **LES 73 PILOTES FRANCAIS EN F1 1950-2018**, Auto Hebdo, 2018.
AUTODROM MOTORSPORTDOKUMENTATION (6, 7), Axel Morenno, 1974, 1975
BEUSQUET, PATRICE, **CHARADE LE PLUS BEAU CIRCUIT DU MONDE**. EDITIONS DU PALMIER, 2003
BEUX, MIGUEL. **A CURVA DO TEMPO**. Beux, 2017.
BOWER, TOM. **NO ANGEL. THE SECRET LIFE OF BERNIE ECCLESTONE**. Faber & Faber, 2011.
BRUSINI, ROMANO. **IL COWBOY DELLE CORSE**, Brusini, 2011
CASTO REY, HECTOR, **AUTO 73 RECORD**. Artekno Editora, 1973
CIMAROSTI, ADRIANO. **THE COMPLETE HISTORY OF GRAND PRIX MOTOR RACING**. Aurum, 1990
CLAUSAGER, ANDERS; CLARKE, R.M. **LE MANS "THE FORD AND MATRA YEARS" 1966-1975. Brooklands Books.**
CLAUSAGER, ANDERS; CLARKE, R.M. **LE MANS "THE PORSCHE YEARS" 1975-1982. Brooklands Books.**
COSTANDUROS, BOB. **DEREK BELL**. Kimberley's, 1985.
COWDREY, BERNARD. **FORMULA 5000, THE A-Z**. Book Marque Publishing, 1998.
CUTTER, ROBERT; FENDELL, BOB. **ENCYCLOPEDIA OF AUTO RACING GREATS**. Prentice-Hall, 1973
DIAZ, MARIA JESUS, Editor. **EL AUTOMOVIL EN ESPANA – ATLAS ILUSTRADO**. Susaeta
DOMINIQUE, VINCENT. **MATRA TOUTE L'HISTOIRE, TOUTES LES COURSES**. L'Autodrome Edition, 2017
FIA ANNUAIRE DU SPORT AUTOMOBILE 1973, FIA, 1973
GEORGANO, G.N. **THE ENCYCLOPEDIA OF MOTOR SPORT**. Viking Press, 1971
GERAERD, BERNARD. **LA DYNASTIE PILETTE**, Appach Prodution & Publihsing
GILL, BARRIE. **INTERNATIONAL MOTOR RACING, 1977**. Two Continents Publishing, 1977.
GILL, BARRIE. **JOHN PLAYER MOTORSPORT YEARBOOK**, 1972. Queen Anne Press, 1972
GILL, BARRIE. **MOTOR SPORT YEARBOOK**, 1974. Collier Books, 1974.
GIRAUD, GREG; LAMBOT, IAN; NEWSOME, PHILIP. **THE ROAD TO SUCCESS: MACAU GRAND PRIX**. Watermark.
GOLENBOCK, PETER; FIELDEN, GREG. **NASCAR ENCYCLOPEDIA**, Motorbooks Intl.
GUBA, EDDIE. **MOTOR SPORT ANNUAL 5**, Greenville, 1972.
HAMILTON, MAURICE. **GRAND PRIX CIRCUITS**, Collins, 2015.
HIGHAM, PETER. **WORLD ENCYCLOPEDIA OF RACING DRIVERS**. Haynes, 2013.
HODGES, DAVID. **A-Z OF FORMULA RACING CARS 1945-1990**. Bay View Books, 1990
HODGES, DAVID; BURGESS-WISE, DAVID; DAVENPORT, JOHN; HARDING, ANTHONY. **THE GUINESS BOOK OF CAR FACTS & FEATS**, Guinness Publishing, 1994
INDYCAR 1994 MEDIA GUIDE, Championship Auto Racing Teams, 1994
HONDA, JOE. **TYRREL P-34 1976**, MFH, 2011
JAMIESON, SUSAN; TUTTHILL, PETER. **WOMEN IN MOTORSPORT FROM 1945**, Jaker/BWRDC, 2003
JONES, BRUCE. **THE ENCYCLOPEDIA OF FORMULA 1**, Carlton, 1998
JONES, CHRIS. **ROAD RACE**. David McKay Company, 1977.

KETTLEWELL, MIKE. **25 YEARS OF BRANDS HATCH CAR RACING**. Brands Hatch Racing Circuit, 1975
L'ANNEE AUTOMOBILE, 1978/79, L'Edita Lausanne, 1979
L'ANNEE AUTOMOBILE, 1979/80, L'Edita Lausanne, 1980
LABAN, BRIAN. **LE MANS 24 HOURS. THE COMPLETE STORY OF THE WORLD'S MOST FAMOUS MOTOR RACE**, MBI, 2001
LANG, MIKE. **GRAND PRIX! RACE-BY-RACE ACCOUNT OF FORMULA 1 CHAMPIONSHIP MOTOR RACING** (Volumes 2, 3). Haynes.
LAWSON, DEREK. **FORMULA 5000**. Veloce Books, 2009
LAZZARI, MICHAEL JOHN. **TEODORO ZECCOLI, CUORE ALFA**, Maglio Editore, 2013
LECESNE, ENGUERRAND. **CIRCUIT DE ROUEN LES ESSARTS**, ETAI
LUDVIGSEN, KARL. **INDY CARS OF THE 1970s**. Iconografix, 2003.
LYONS, PETE. **CAN-AM**. Motorbooks International, 1995.
MARTIN, DIDIER. **LES MONOPLACES PYGMEE DE MARIUS ET PATRICK DAL BO**, editions du Palmier, 2002
MENEGAZ, GILBERTO; LAVA, PAULO; TORINO, PAULO. **TARUMA: UMA HISTORIA DE VELOCIDADE**. Imagens da Terra Editora, 2008.
MORELLI, MICHEL. **PEUGEOT ET LE SPORT AUTOMOBILE**, ETAI, 2005.
MULLER, WILFRIED. **24 HR NÜRBURGRING. DIE GESCHICHTE DER ERSTEN 40 RENNEN**. McKlein Publishing, 2013.
NASCAR OFFICIAL 1976 RECORD BOOK AND PRESS GUIDE, Nascar, 1976
NAVIAUX, CHRISTIAN. **CHAMPIONNAT D'EUROPE DES SPORT-PROTOS 2 LITRES 1970-1975**. Editions du Palmier, 2004
O`LEARY, MIKE. **MARIO ANDRETTI – THE COMPLETE RECORD**. MBI Publishing, 2002.
OVERED, RON. **THE 40TH ANNIVERSARY OF MALLORY PARK**. Mallory Park Motorsports, 1996.
PARFITT, PHILLIP. **RACING AT CRYSTAL PALACE**, MRP Books, 1991.
PRITCHARD, ANTHONY. **THE MOTOR RACING YEAR**, W. W. Norton, 1971, 1972, 1973
PRITCHARD, ANTHONY; DAVEY, KEITH **THE ENCYCLOPEDIA OF MOTOR RACING**, 2nd Edition. Robert Hale, 1973
REDMAN, BRIAN with MULLEN, JIM. **BRIAN REDMAN: DARING DRIVERS, DEADLY TRACKS**. Evro Publishing, 2016
RIBEIRO, ALEX DIAS. **MAIS QUE VENCEDOR**. Alex Publicacoes, 1981.
RUSZKIEWCZ, JOE. **PORSCHE SPORT 1976/77**, Ruszkiewcz Publishing, 1977
SCALI, PAULO. **INTERLAGOS 1940 A 1980**, Imagens Terra, 2004
SCHIMPF, ECKHARD. STUCK DI RENFAHRERDYNASTIE. Delius Klasing,
SCHMITT, ARNO. **HANDBUCH DER DEUTSCHEN RENNSPORT MEISTERCHAFT VON 1972 BIS 1980**, Copress. 1980.
SHELDON, PAUL; RABAGLIATI, DUNCAN. **FORMULA 1 REGISTER – FORMULA 5000 FACT BOOK – (1973-1977),** St. Leonard's Press
SHELDON, PAUL; RABAGLIATI, DUNCAN; DE LA GORCE, YVES. **FORMULA 1 REGISTER FACT BOOK – FORMULA 3 (1970-72, 1973-77, 1978-81)**, St. Leonard's Press, 1988.
STARKEY, JOHN; WELLS, KEN. **LOLA THE ILLUSTRATED HISTORY 1957 TO 1977**. Veloce Publishing, 1998
TEISSEDRE, JEAN MARC. **BOB WOLLEK EN MARGE DE LA GLOIRE**. Le Mans Racing, 2012.
THE NEW ILLUSTRATED ENCYCLOPEDIA OF AUTOMOBILES, The Wellfeet Press, 1992
VACARELLA, NINO. **IL PRESIDE VOLANTE: LA MIA STORIA AUTOMOBILISTICA**. Vacarella, 2013.
WIMPFEN, JANOS. **TIME AROUND SEATS**. Motorsport Research Group, 1999
YOUNG, EOIN S. **FORZA AMON**, Haynes Publishing, 2003.

Websites:
Alimosonline.gr
Archivesportauto.fr
Autoclassic.uy
Autocourse.ca
Autodiva.fr
Autoexplora.com
Automobilcub-muenchen.de
Automobilesport.com
Autopistapanama.com
Autoracingcommentary.blogspot.com
Auto-rennsport.de
Autosclasicoshistoricos.com
Autosport.pt
Autosportpalmares.fr
Aviagemdosargonautas.net
Barbadosrallyclub.com
Bbautomobiles.com
Blad.info
Brazilexporters.com/blog
Britishnewspapersarchive.co.uk
Campeonatohistoricodevelocidad.cl
Carlosdepaula.blogspot.com
Carplanet.mx
Classic cars.com
Classicarsinrhodesia.co.za
Cochosportcars.blogspot.com
Codeme.com.mx
Cronoscalate.it
Delagobay.wordpress.com
Elcomercio.com
Elsalvador.com
Equipebernoise.ch
Eresourcesnib.gov.sg
Euromontagna.com
F3history.co.uk
Ffsa.org
Forum.historisk.racing.no
Forum.motorlegend.com
Forum.motorlegend.com
Forum-auto.caradisiac.com
Forum-auto.com
Forums.autosport.com
Gdecarli.it
Gpgaucho.com.br
Hauenstein-archiv.ch
Hillclimbportal.com
Historiaat.com.ar
Historicrallybandama.overblog.com
Historictransam.com
Homburger-bergrennen.ed

Iamvenezuela.com
Ilchichingiolo.it
Infoauto-usa.com
Informulas.facundogallela.com
Jaf.or.jp
Jamaicamotorsports.com
Kirkistown.com
Lapatriaenliena.com
Mazungue.com
Modbase.infoonsports.gr
Motorpasion.com
Motorsport.ch
Motorsportinangola.blogspot.com
Motorsportmemorial.org
Motorsportwinners.com
Mundomotorizado.com
Newspapers.com
Nytimes.com
Oldracingcars.com
Overdrive.in
Passionalavelocidad.com
Primotipo.com
Puru.de
Racehistorie.nl
Racinghistory.lv
Racingcalendar.net
Racing-Reference.info
Racingsportscars.com
Racingyears.com
Rally.gr
Rallycross-photo.com
Rcbolivia.com
Revistamotortop.om
Rodrigofrancoseoane.blogspot.com
Scielo.br
Scotlandstockcars.com
Sergent.com.au
Silhouet.com
Speedqueens.blogspot.com
Speedwayandroadracehistory.com
Sportprototipo.argentino.blogspot.com
Sportsandhealth.com.pa
Svenskracing.se
Tellingstories.gr
Thebests2010.blogspot.com
The-fastlane.co.uk (formula2.net) (racingcircuits)
Thehindu.com
Todosautos.com.pe
Touringcar.net
Trinituner.com
Ultimateracinghistory.com

Ussr-autosport.ru
V8blog1971.files.wordpress.com
Vfsvideos.co.uk
Vidafundo.blogspot.com
Virhistory.com
Wegcircuits.nl
Wikipedia.org
Wsrp.cz

MAGAZINES
The following magazines and newspapers have been consulted and quoted at one point or another. Clippings of a large number of unidentified newspapers and magazines were also consulted.
Auto Esporte
Auto Motor Und Sport
Auto Racing Digest
Grand Prix
Auto Week
Auto Zeitung
Automobilsport
Autosport
Autosprint
Car and Driver
Formula
Motor Sport
Motor Trend
Motoring News
On Track
Parabrisas Corsa
Quatro Rodas
Road & Track
Sport Auto

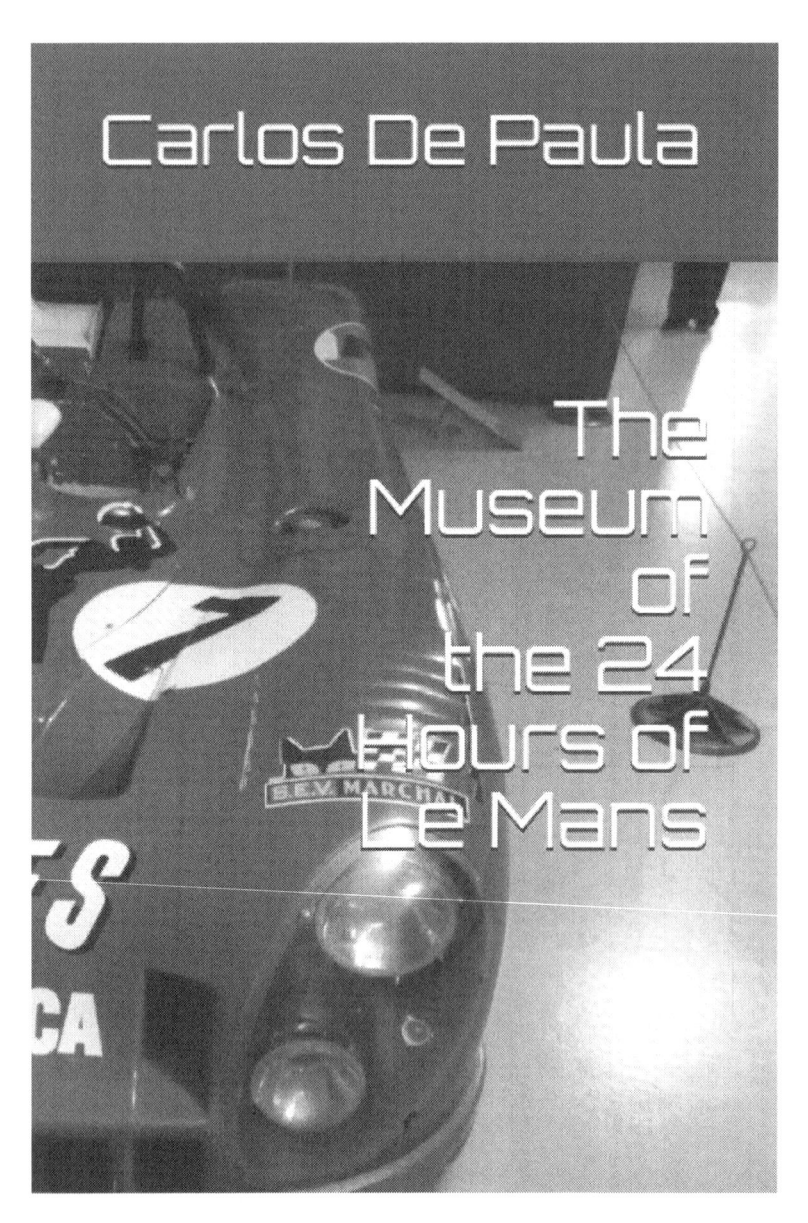

Available at

motorracingbooks.com

Carlos De Paula

Racing Car Constructors of the 1970s

Paperback and hard cover available at

motorracingbooks.com

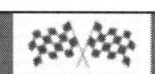

Carlos De Paula

Formula 1 Curiosities

Volume 1

Paperback available at
motorracingbooks.com

24 HOURS OF LE MANS CURIOSITIES

From 1923 to the Present
Carlos de Paula

Paperback available at
motorracingbooks.com

Carlos de Paula's other works

NEXUS EXPLICITUS (Fiction, in Portuguese), available at Amazon.com

MEMÓRIAS HIPERBÓLICAS DE RODOLPHO CHIMENTÃO (Fiction, in Portuguese), available at Amazon.com

PEACEFUL FACEBOOK, (Social commentary/humor, in English) available at Amazon.com

Printed in Great Britain
by Amazon